MADE IN HONG KONG

Studies of the Weatherhead East Asian Institute

STUDIES OF THE WEATHERHEAD EAST ASIAN INSTITUTE,
COLUMBIA UNIVERSITY

The Studies of the Weatherhead East Asian Institute of Columbia University were
inaugurated in 1962 to bring to a wider public the results of significant
new research on modern and contemporary East Asia.

For a complete list of books in the series, see page 421.

Made in Hong Kong

TRANSPACIFIC NETWORKS AND
A NEW HISTORY OF GLOBALIZATION

Peter E. Hamilton

Columbia University Press
New York

Columbia University Press
Publishers Since 1893
New York   Chichester, West Sussex
cup.columbia.edu
Copyright © 2021 Columbia University Press
All rights reserved

Library of Congress Cataloging-in-Publication Data
Names: Hamilton, Peter E., author.
Title: Made in Hong Kong : transpacific networks and a new history of
globalization / Peter E. Hamilton.
Description: New York : Columbia University Press, [2020] | Includes
bibliographical references and index.
Identifiers: LCCN 2020021222 (print) | LCCN 2020021223 (ebook) |
ISBN 9780231184847 (hardback) | ISBN 9780231184854 (trade paperback) |
ISBN 9780231545709 (ebook)
Subjects: LCSH: Economic development—China—Hong Kong. |
Globalization—China—Hong Kong. | Hong Kong (China)—Economic
conditions. | Hong Kong (China)—Commerce—United States. |
United States—Commerce—China—Hong Kong. | Hong Kong (China)—
Foreign economic relations—United States. | United States—Foreign economic
relations—China—Hong Kong.
Classification: LCC HC470.3 .A544 2020 (print) | LCC HC470.3 (ebook) |
DDC 337.5125—dc23
LC record available at https://lccn.loc.gov/2020021222
LC ebook record available at https://lccn.loc.gov/2020021223

Columbia University Press books are printed on permanent and durable acid-free paper.
Printed in the United States of America

Cover design: Julia Kushnirsky
Cover photograph: Alex Ogle

Contents

[v]

Acknowledgments

This book has been eight years in the making. Like all scholarship, it was made possible only by an astonishing generosity of financial, intellectual, and moral support from people and institutions around the world. My own network of mentors, colleagues, friends, and family has guided and enabled this project at every step.

I owe a huge debt to my first Hong Kong history mentors: May Holdsworth, Christopher Munn, Elizabeth Sinn, and John Carroll. They were the teachers who first intrigued me in this startling place and who generously invited a recent college graduate to collaborate on their research. It changed my life. In turn, I would never have had my first chance to live and work in Hong Kong without the opportunities provided by the Yale-China Association and New Asia College at the Chinese University of Hong Kong (CUHK).

My deepest thanks go to Madeline Hsu, my mentor at the University of Texas at Austin, who has guided, encouraged, and challenged me from our first conversation through today. She helped to refine my initial interests, patiently read and commented on evolving drafts, and has been my champion across all the challenges of an academic career. One such challenge is funding and academic affiliations. I was extremely fortunate to receive a year of research support in Hong Kong from CUHK's Hong Kong–America Center. UT's Department of History was also an immensely supportive, stimulating, and even fun place for me to write and develop as both a scholar and person. Invaluable mentors included Robert Abzug, H.W. Brands, Erika Bsumek, Indrani Chatterjee, Julie Hardwick, Jacqueline Jones, Mark Atwood Lawrence, Philippa Levine, Huaiyin Li, Mark Metzler, and Jeremi Suri. I also express my sincere thanks to Marilyn Lehman, an advisor-at-large to all history students, and both Seth Garfield and Courtney Meador at the Institute for Historical Studies, which provided an essential professional launching pad.

Two invaluable years as a postdoctoral fellow at Columbia's Weatherhead East Asian Institute engaged me in an exciting new community of scholars, who greatly enriched this project's evolution. I was particularly lucky to be guided by Eugenia Lean, Matti Zelin, Andy Nathan, Mae Ngai, and Kim Brandt. The monthly Modern China Seminar organized by Robbie Barnett and Chuck Woolridge also provided key ideas and feedback, including from David Weiman, Carl Riskin, Christian Murck, and Laurence Coderre. My time at Columbia would not have been complete without the knowledge and friendship of Katherine de Rosset Forshay, Jamie Tan, Ross Yelsey, Simon Toner, Victor Louzon, Miki Kaneda, Jack Neubauer, and Yanjie Huang.

I further revised and submitted this manuscript for review while a postdoctoral fellow at Tsinghua's Schwarzman College in Beijing. Schwarzman was an immersive hub of activity, and this manuscript benefited immensely from conversations there with a broad range of China scholars, including Xue Lan, David Pan, June Qian, Arne Westad, Paul Pickowicz, Bill Kirby, Daniel Bell, Wang Hui, Susan Shirk, Judy Shapiro, Michael Puett, Roger Ames, Joan Kaufman, and Daniel Armanios. In turn, living at Schwarzman was a joy because of the incredible students and the community fostered by Melanie Koenderman, Arn and Maryalice Howitt, my fellow postdocs Sam Galler, Ariel Shangguan, and Jonghyuk Lee, and the tireless staff who made it all work, especially Doug Hughes, Sisi Sung, Tingyu Li, Irma Jing, Arthur Yu, Yuyang Zhang, Zhang Xi, Lindsey Cohen Bavaro, and Helen Santalone. Outside the college, I gained new affection for Beijing through the friendship of Fil Lekkas, Yi-Ling Liu, Ahlaam Al-Khabori, Nicholas Ray, Amy Qin, Brett Gerson, Amy Du, Ernst-Jan Van Woerden, Santana Wulsin, Andy Chen, Niall McNulty, Michael Kowen, and Shazeda Ahmed.

I finalized this book at Trinity College Dublin, where I have received the warmest Irish welcome. I am indebted to Micheál Ó Siochrú, Lorna Carson, Christine Morris, Isabella Jackson, Joanne Lynch, Eilís Dunne,

Seán Hughes, Ning Jiang, Robert Armstrong, Anne Dolan, Molly Pucci, Katja Bruisch, Patrick Houlihan, Ciaran O'Neill, and Carole Holohan for making me feel so welcome and offering steadfast encouragement and support. I am also deeply grateful for the immediate friendship of Rob McGarrigle, Conor Mulvagh, Thea Tilley, Anna Della Subin, Hussein Omar, Carly Giltrap, Elizabeth Hamlett, Amanda Zinman, Jenny McClain, and Vinny Lawlor, who have kept me grounded as I have brought this project to a close.

Over my nomadic academic life, I have been privileged to benefit from the knowledge and feedback of an exceptional range of China scholars. Through numerous grants, I have been able to attend conferences where I received invaluable comments and suggestions, including two workshops at the University of Hong Kong, Madeline Hsu's "Transpacific China in the Cold War" conference at UT Austin, Mae Ngai's "Labor Migrations in the Pacific World" workshop at Columbia University, the "New Directions in Hong Kong History" workshop at the University of Bristol, and the "Elites, Knowledge, and Power" workshop hosted by the ENP-China Project at Aix-Marseille University. In turn, I am deeply grateful to the broader network of scholars who have generously read and commented on sections or chapters, including two anonymous reviewers, as well as Eugenia Lean, Matti Zelin, Andy Nathan, Kim Brandt, Robert Bickers, Christian Henriot, Ho-fung Hung, Arne Westad, and Julian Gewirtz. Many irreplaceable insights and corrections came through these collaborations, but any errors are of course mine.

One thrilling aspect of working on more recent histories is the opportunity to speak with people who lived your topic or knew your subjects. I remain deeply grateful for the generous hours of conversation with Yvonne Blackmore de Jong, Ewing "Bud" Carroll, S. J. Chan, Raymond Ch'ien, John Dolfin, Tom Gorman, John Kamm, Rick Kroos, Tunney Lee, Ambassador Burton Levin, Frank Martin, Mark Sheldon, Victoria Sperry Merchant, Jean Li Rogers, Sterling Whitener, Franklin Woo, and others. Their knowledge, perspectives, and memories deeply enriched this project.

In turn, publishing with Columbia University Press has been a smooth and low-stress experience. I am very grateful to Caelyn Cobb, Monique Briones, and Anita O'Brien, who have been so patient, kind, and helpful. The photographs in this book also represent the hard work and generosity of many people. Victoria Sperry Merchant went above and beyond to comb through family photographs and rescan and share them. I am also grateful to the Tang family for permission to use their private photographs, and to Carolyn Wakeman, Nicole Ching, and Tammy Ching for facilitating that connection. For other images, I express my sincere thanks to Ben Richardson and the team at AmCham Hong Kong; Amy Li at the CUHK Information Services Office; Laura Schieb and Morgan Swan at Dartmouth's Rauner Special Collections; Jenny Yu at the HSBC Archive; and Martha Smalley, Christopher Anderson, and Sara Azam at Yale Divinity School Library. Numerous efforts were made to contact *Ta Kung Pao* for permission to use the photograph in chapter 8.

Researching Hong Kong in a global context has entailed years of living in Hong Kong, research in many other expensive cities, and gaining new knowledge and perspectives from people in and outside of academia. In all these things, I have depended on family and the friends who are like family. I am particularly grateful to Alexander Cho, who has been a vital sounding board and source of critical inspiration, and to Dayo Olopade, who cut to the heart of the matter. In turn, I was often only able to pursue my research through generous housing, food, conversation, and introductions provided by friends. In this regard, I am particularly grateful to Simon and Janice Cheung Abbott, Oliver Blanch Merino, Brian and Jacko Chan, Shane Combest and Jennifer Shen, the entire Bristol family, Jan Foo and Matt Eisenson, Lynn Fung and Matt Barter, Henry Harding and Dan Feder, Nadia Harilela, Rina Hiranand, Walter Lamberson, Brian Lee, Rebecca Livengood and Nate Wenstrup, Wilson Lo, Laura McEgan, Matt Mendelsohn and Lauren Martini, Laura Myron, Maxine Riley and Yan Zhang, Elise and Arthur Van Stolk, Rachel Winston and Ali Jarvis, and Carl Zhang and Arwen Liu. No matter where I am, I am thankful for the daily love and companionship of my siblings, Andrew and Elizabeth, and my covens, Janice Wang, Abby Hafler, Brianna Jewell, Kit Krugman, Bryan Golden, Matt Leslie, and Tom Lindsay.

Above all, I thank my endlessly supportive and loving parents. Like some in this book, my parents have devoted their lives to the cause of education, most especially to that of their children. They made it possible, and this book is for them.

Note on Language

I
t is impossible to standardize the Chinese language in either characters or Roman letters without flattening important dialectical, historical, and political differences. This book includes Chinese-language names, terms, and sources originating in Mandarin, Cantonese, and Shanghainese. In turn, while the People's Republic of China (PRC) uses simplified characters, Hong Kong and Taiwan use traditional characters. As a result, I have sought to balance historical accuracy and recognition for a plurality of Chinese traditions against undue disruption to the reader.

For Hong Kong publications, organizations, and businesses, I transliterate their names through standard Cantonese and preserve traditional characters, such as the Wah On Association (華安商會) rather than the Hua An Association, or *kamshanchong* (金山莊) rather than *jinshanzhuang*. For the names of Hong Kong people, I preserve the romanization that they or contemporary sources used, which may reflect previous systems of romanization and/or a Cantonese or Shanghainese pronunciation. Thus chapter 4's subject is Li Choh-ming (李卓敏), not Li Zhuomin.

When introducing Qing- and Republican-era mainland Chinese, I utilize pinyin and traditional characters but often include alternative names, particularly if the person was Cantonese. The exceptions are individuals well known in English by alternative names, such as Yung Wing and Chiang Kai-shek, and individuals who in my research demonstrated a preferred English name or initials. Thus it is "K. P." Chen Guangfu (陳光甫)

on first instance and K. P. Chen thereafter. I also use pinyin and traditional characters for pan-Chinese terms or concepts, such as *guanxi* (關係). I reserve simplified characters exclusively for PRC actors and terms, concentrated in chapters 7 and 8.

In turn, this study never uses the term "Western." As many previous scholars have articulated, this term is vague and ideological, inevitably reifying Orientalist paradigms and imperialist epistemologies. Although many China scholars still refer to "Western education," "Western influence," or the "Western powers," the term muddles who or what is meant. The nations of Europe and North America are not the same and represent a diverse range of ethnic, educational, linguistic, legal, medical, and philosophical traditions and histories. For a place as sophisticated as Hong Kong, we cannot use this imprecise term.

Abbreviations

ACCA	Asia Christian Colleges Association
AmCham	American Chamber of Commerce
APL	American President Lines
ARCI	Aid Refugee Chinese Intellectuals
BNO	British National Overseas
C-100	Committee of 100
CARE	Cooperative for American Relief Everywhere
CAT	Civil Air Transport
CCC	Church of Christ in China
CCP	Chinese Communist Party
CCPIT	China Council for the Promotion of International Trade
CCRC	China Commercial Relations Committee
CEM	Chinese Educational Mission
CFA	Committee for a Free Asia
CHINATEX	China National Textiles Import and Export Corporation
CITIC	China International Trust and Investment Corporation
CLP	China Light and Power
CMSN	China Merchants Steam Navigation Company
CNAC	China National Aviation Corporation
CNRRA	China National Relief and Rehabilitation Administration
CPPCC	Chinese People's Political Consultative Conference
CUHK	The Chinese University of Hong Kong

CWS	Church World Service
ECA	Economic Cooperation Administration
ECAFE	United Nations Economic Commission for Asia and the Far East
FDI	foreign direct investment
GATT	General Agreement on Tariffs and Trade
GDP	gross domestic product
GSP	Generalized Scheme of Preferences
HAECO	Hong Kong Aircraft Engineering Company
HBS	Harvard Business School
HKBA	Hong Kong Baptist Association
HKBC	Hong Kong Baptist College
HKSAR	Hong Kong Special Administrative Region
HKTDC	Hong Kong Trade Development Council
HKU	University of Hong Kong
ICI	Imperial Chemical Industries
IIE	Institute of International Education
IPO	initial public offering
IRC	International Rescue Committee
LegCo	Legislative Council
LIBA	Lingnan Institute of Business Administration
LWF	Lutheran World Federation
MBA	master of business administration
MFA	Multi-Fibre Arrangement
MFN	most-favored-nation
NAEC	National Agricultural Engineering Corporation
NCUSCT	National Council on U.S.-China Trade
NCWC	National Catholic Welfare Conference
OOCL	Orient Overseas Container Line
PRC	People's Republic of China
RMU	Refugee and Migration Unit
SBBFM	Southern Baptist Board of Foreign Missions
SBC	Southern Baptist Convention
SCSB	Shanghai Commercial and Savings Bank
SEZ	Special Economic Zone
SOE	state-owned enterprise
TSEM	Tsinghua School of Economics and Management
TVEs	Township and Village Enterprises

UC	University of California
UMELCO	Unofficial Members of Executive and Legislative Council
UNRRA	United Nations Relief and Rehabilitation Administration
USLO	U.S. Liaison Office
WCC	World Council of Churches
WRF	World Rehabilitation Fund
WTS	Wong Tai Sin

MADE IN HONG KONG

INTRODUCTION

Made in Hong Kong

Transpacific Networks and a New History of Globalization

I had to tell myself I must follow my father's teaching, as his motto is, "Money and power isn't everything. What's important in life is your credit, your reputation, and your education. You can lose money and power any day, any time, but your reputation, your credit, and your education, nobody can take away from you."

—JACK CHI-CHIEN TANG (唐驥千), "1254 TANG, JACK CHI CHIEN,"
HONG KONG HERITAGE PROJECT

O nly a handful of societies journeyed from the so-called Third World to the First over the Cold War. Beyond a few Caribbean tax havens, just one did so without exploiting petroleum or achieving independence from colonial rule. That was Hong Kong. In the 1950s this British Crown colony was struggling with a humanitarian crisis of migrants from the new People's Republic of China (PRC). Yet by the 1990s Hong Kong had transformed into a glittering forest of skyscrapers with a gross domestic product (GDP) per capita higher than that of its erstwhile colonial overlord. It was a startling and singular metamorphosis that, to borrow a phrase from the final colonial governor, felt like "a grand slam for the human spirit."[1]

Despite this proverbial rags-to-riches story, scholars have paid surprisingly little attention to Hong Kong's economic transformation. For years the economist Milton Friedman trumpeted the territory as a "controlled experiment" in laissez-faire principles in order to promote his ideological agenda.[2] As we will see, narratives of Hong Kong as an archetype of free competition ignore a crucial other half of the story—an entrenched but mobile hierarchy. In the 1980s and 1990s other scholars forced Hong Kong into racialized East Asian "tiger" and "little dragon" models, which touted an imaginary connection between Confucian values and exceptional discipline and hard work. In contrast, this study begins with the simple premise that we must examine Hong Kong on its own terms. By remaining a

British colony until 1997, Hong Kong bucked the Cold War's global trend toward the nation-state. This extension of colonial rule disempowered its residents politically yet spared them from the traumas of Mao Zedong's rule over the PRC (1949–1976). It also enabled them to pursue some very unusual strategies within the man-made competition of U.S.-led global capitalism. This book centers Hong Kong as a key node in post-1945 capitalist globalization by foregrounding its residents' transpacific networks and strategies. We will see that although Hong Kong remained under a British colonial flag, its residents increasingly pivoted away from British imperial systems and instead engaged with U.S. international power structures through transpacific circulations. These circulations provided certain Hong Kong people with reliable access to and inside knowledge of the world's largest economy, as well as enormous in-flows of other talent, information, capital, and technology.

By putting Hong Kong at the center, we recover both its unique historical experience and an overlapping set of global histories that radiate outward from this node. In particular, foregrounding Hong Kong people's historical agency revises not only how we understand their economic evolution or experience of continued colonialism but also the origins of the enormous commercial and educational circulations that now bind together China and the United States. The United States first surpassed Japan as China's largest trading partner in 2004, while China surpassed Canada to become the largest trading partner of the United States in 2015.[3] This mutual reliance lasted until mid-2019 and President Donald Trump's trade war. Alongside commercial entanglement, the two giants are interlinked by enormous educational circulations. Before the COVID-19 pandemic, Chinese students had been the largest international student group in the United States for a decade, with 369,548 enrolled by fall 2019, while 10,000–15,000 American students have been studying annually in China.[4] Although asymmetric, U.S. donors and institutions have plowed enormous resources into name-brand projects in China, from Tsinghua University's Schwarzman College to the Yenching Academy at Peking University, the Hopkins-Nanjing Center, Duke Kunshan University, NYU Shanghai, the Harvard Center Shanghai, and countless exchange programs.

Yet both scholars and policy makers have misunderstood the origins of these Sino-U.S. entanglements by framing them almost exclusively through bilateral diplomatic lenses. Such state-centered perspectives focus on presidents and treaties but overlook the essential nonstate actor that has facilitated and molded the Sino-U.S. relationship at every step of the Reform era (1978–), an intermediary whose private-sector elites had their own agendas when brokering and sponsoring these transnational flows. Since 1978 Hong Kong has always been China's largest outside investor. By the mid-1990s it handled 40–45 percent of China's foreign trade, including two-thirds of China's exports to the United States.[5] In turn, long before mainland students enrolled en masse in U.S. higher education, it was Hong Kong that ranked as the world's largest sender of foreign students to U.S. colleges and universities in the mid-1970s. As a result, it became a nexus of U.S.-educated alumni who bankrolled commercial and educational bridges between China and the United States. In this book I examine how this former British colony developed such outsized transpacific circulations and argue that the networks and agency of private Hong Kong–based actors laid essential foundations for both aspects of today's Sino-U.S. relationship. In short, I reframe Hong Kong as the linchpin in a process that has enveloped and remade both China and the United States.

By reexamining key pieces of Hong Kong's social and economic history between 1945 and the 1997 handover, I offer radically new narratives of its economic development, of U.S.-led capitalist globalization, and of China's reintegration into that system. I contend that Hong Kong played a critical role in postwar globalization, such that we cannot understand either the consolidation of the U.S.-led capitalist system in the Pacific or China's subsequent path to export-driven development without it. In particular, I home in on a cohort of mobile, pragmatic, and adaptive Hong Kong elites whom I term kuàshāng (跨商) or "straddling merchants." The first kuashang were primarily Chinese bankers, industrialists, executives, academics, and Nationalist technocrats who fled from the mainland to Hong Kong during what I call the "communist transition" (1946–1952), alongside about 700,000 other people.[6] These elite émigrés lost most of their physical property in flight, but they did not "lose everything," as is often claimed. Due to their families, careers, and educations, they retained inside knowledge of the new U.S.-led capitalist system and the privileged social capital needed to access it. As a result, to survive transplantation, they implemented new strategies. Using their bicultural networks and skills, they built new careers and businesses focused on circulations within the transpacific order and pursued export-driven codevelopment with primarily the U.S. market from the mid-1950s on. These kuashang strategies to straddle the Pacific accumulated not just wealth but also new forms of economic power and privilege that operated on different planes than the nation-states that were coalescing elsewhere in the postcolonial world. In turn, the first kuashang transmitted these intangible assets across generations by dispatching their children to U.S. higher education and sponsoring other Hong Kong residents to do the same by collaborating with U.S. Cold War projects and renovating local educational systems along American models. These activities enabled Hong Kong's transpacific educational and commercial circulations to balloon in scale and positioned the colony to play a decisive role in midwifing China's reintegration into global capitalism after the restoration of Sino-U.S. trade in 1971.

For historians of modern China, the kuashang offer a new multigenerational history of Chinese capitalism that both spans the twentieth century and expands the boundaries of "China." Modern China narratives traditionally frame 1949 and 1978 as ruptures that divide the Republican, Mao, and Reform eras into separate conversations. In line with scholars such as Bill Kirby who have highlighted continuities across these divides, reincorporating Hong Kong and the kuashang offers a through-line across these periods.[7] They demonstrate not just that capitalism survived on the doorstep of Mao's revolution but, more specifically, that key continuities in families, companies, and systems of inherited privilege survived across these eras, intermingled with global actors and processes, and came back from the imagined "periphery" to help remake the "center." The kuashang thereby also reveal enduring legacies of the Republican era (1912–1949). Scholars have extensively examined the evolution of both educational patterns and native-place sentiments (*xiangyi*, 鄉誼, or *xiangqing*, 鄉情) and networks (*tongxiang guanxi*, 同鄉關係) in the late Qing (1644–1912) and Republican eras. Yet scholars have paid less attention to how these shifting educational patterns facilitated the formation of new, if overlapping, networks. I argue that, amid the Republican era's prolonged upheavals and the Nationalist (Guomindang) government's increasing cronyism, many elites pursued "modern" learning not just for the sake of knowledge but also an investment in instrumental networks and credentials that would complement their native-place ties and offer additional paths to security. The international social capital acquired through foreign-oriented educations efficiently advanced both elite families' commercial interests and their repeated relocations amid war and revolution. Through Chinese- and English-language sources gathered from Hong Kong, China, the

United States, and the United Kingdom, I track these mobile elites' accumulations, uses, and transfers of this social capital across continents, generations, and eras. I show their collective long-term reliance on these intangible assets in order to flee, resettle, and revive transplanted careers and businesses. And by analyzing these subjects in tandem, I demonstrate how privileged transnational networks became extraordinarily concentrated in Hong Kong from 1949, transforming a cohort of individuals' ties into a social ecosystem and this Cold War colony's unique methods of both economic development and what I term *informal decolonization*.

In turn, for scholars of capitalism and globalization, the kuashang offer a fine-grained tracing of the human actors behind processes that are routinely glossed over by terms such as *globalization, social capital*, and China's *reform and opening*. In particular, within the academy and public sphere, there has been much attention to China's and Asia's development, various "pivots" to Asia, and even a coming "Asian century." Yet there has been remarkably little attention to the actual people within this turn, especially the nonwhite and nonofficial actors. Through the kuashang, I do not celebrate such figures but rather offer a close examination of an interconnected elite network that reveals the persistence of inherited station and social class, the living contradictions of neocolonial power brokering, and at times the ruthless desire for wealth and status. Close attention to such historical networks provides a vital method to restore these embedded histories to our narratives of postwar globalization and China's export-driven development.

Finally, alongside new narratives in Chinese and global history, the kuashang also offer a very different lens into two of the twenty-first century's most pressing challenges: migration and inequality. The kuashang provide a rich historical dataset of an entrenched yet mobile hierarchy that repeatedly survived wars, revolutions, and migrations. They chose Hong Kong because it was open to migrants, and they revived their fortunes by embracing opportunities provided by transpacific circulations. Despite encountering racism and missteps, most succeeded over and over again because their social capital traveled with them, because upheavals discouraged complacency, and because shameless elitism often paid off. The kuashang thus show both how specific kinds of social capital shape individual economic outcomes and how assemblages of elite social capital can be transplanted and reshape larger socioeconomic possibilities, even at the national and transnational scales. Most scholars tend to look at elites through segmented labor roles (bankers, industrialists, scholars, and so on), but I frame the kuashang as a cross-professional spectrum of individuals in order to highlight their lived interconnections and provide a more realistic sense of how elite social capital operates and is reproduced across generations. In turn, scholars on the right have routinely misrepresented Hong Kong in order to celebrate the imaginary free market, but I underscore that these were not self-made people. Instead, Hong Kong's virtually singular success within U.S.-led globalization was inextricable from systemic inequality that predated the Second World War. Local public memory still celebrates rags-to-riches figures such as Li Ka-shing (李嘉誠), but these mythologized tycoons do not feature here. Instead, most Hong Kong elites came from long lines of inherited privilege, and yet we know little about them. I thus strive to offer a fresh historical perspective at the intersection of development, decolonization, migration, the Cold War, and globalization through interconnected individuals and families who reveal a great deal about today's starkly uneven geographies.

The Refuge of the *Huashang*

It cannot be overemphasized that Hong Kong became an increasingly exceptional space in the early Cold War. What I label as kuashang strategies depended on the opportunities that this unusual territory could provide. In particular, three external processes intersected to make Hong Kong unusual: the restoration of British colonial rule and its economic policies in August 1945, the transplantation of roughly 700,000 people during the communist transition, and U.S. imperial expansion in the western Pacific. This third factor has received the least attention in Hong Kong history, and thus I emphasize its intersections with the second. This emphasis does not imply that British officials or policies were unimportant. British law and financial systems were generally a source of stability and thus crucial to kuashang strategies. Yet it is worth stressing that colonial policies were also a root cause of repeated housing bubbles and banking crises, while officials were passive toward widespread corruption, smuggling, and organized crime into the 1970s.

Between its seizure by British forces in 1841 and its surrender to Japan on Christmas 1941, Hong Kong was one node in a network of European colonial entrepôts stretching all along the African and Asian coastlines.

Through the Great Depression, neighboring ports such as Manila, Shanghai, Bangkok, Singapore, Penang, and Rangoon shared similarly open trade and migration policies.[8] As a result, voluminous flows of capital, people, and goods developed between these interconnected emporia over the nineteenth and early twentieth centuries. This commerce was largely managed by overseas Chinese merchants or *huáshāng* (華商), and Hong Kong gradually became the nerve center of this mercantile diaspora. In historian Elizabeth Sinn's words, Hong Kong was the key "in-between space" linking China with the overseas Chinese communities across Southeast Asia and the Americas.[9] The commercial dominance of huashang in Southeast Asia stemmed primarily from their strategic collaborations with European colonial regimes through middlemen roles, allowing Chinese merchants to become the region's "essential outsiders."[10] Since the number of Europeans on the ground in Asia was miniscule, colonial regimes relied on huashang as tax farmers, labor contractors, and other go-betweens with indigenous populations. These roles allowed many huashang to become rich and cosmopolitan, such as the Peranakan communities of the Straits Settlements. Nonetheless, huashang generally remained socially separate from European and native communities through both exclusion and self-reliance.

The Second World War disrupted these patterns, but Hong Kong did reemerge as an "in-between space." Japan's rapid imperial expansion between 1937 and 1942 shattered the entwined European and huashang networks and signaled a reordering around Tokyo.[11] With the war's turn and Japan's surrender in August 1945, however, the possibility of a Japanese-led order collapsed. In its place, the U.S.- and Soviet-led orders began to compete for influence amid the ruins of Asia's European and Japanese empires. The Chinese civil war was among the first flashpoints. Following Mao Zedong's strategies, the People's Liberation Army enveloped the North China countryside, choked Chiang Kai-shek's Nationalists out of their urban strongholds, and pushed south by late 1948. As we will examine in chapters 1 and 2, this turn in the civil war triggered a prolonged exodus of several million people to primarily Hong Kong and Taiwan. The vast majority of these migrants were ordinary people with reasons to fear communism, but they included a substantial number of Republican China's elites. Nationalist government and military families tended to favor Taiwan, but elite capitalists preferred Hong Kong because of the comparative stability and openness associated with restored British rule.[12] As we will see, many of these migrants came from comprador families who had been working with foreigners, learning foreign languages, and converting to Christianity throughout the treaty-port era (1842–1943).[13] Many previous historians have studied these families' activities in Shanghai, Tianjin, and other cities before 1949, but this study extends this conversation to post-1949 Hong Kong.[14] As these displaced elites became huashang in Hong Kong, their capitalist outlook survived but adapted to a new international order.

Simultaneously, decolonization and economic interventionism were making Hong Kong unusual at a global level. Beginning with the Philippines in 1946, almost every Euro-American colony in Asia achieved self-determination as part of a nation-state. By 1965 the only spaces in Asia that remained colonies were Hong Kong, neighboring Portuguese Macau, and British Bahrain and Aden. As a result, the wider system of interconnected entrepôts and huashang did not revive as new nation-states absorbed these port-cities into state-led development plans. Socialist and capitalist states alike pursued land reform, currency controls, import-substitution tariffs, and the nationalization of key infrastructure and industries. These policies and their intersections with international development agencies had a varied record, as a vast scholarly literature has analyzed, but they circumscribed the huashang.[15] Many postcolonial states also fanned the flames of ethnic nationalism by targeting Chinese communities as outsiders. In Indonesia, Malaysia, and later Vietnam, the ensuing rhetoric, policies, and violence triggered outflows of Chinese capital and talent, again primarily to Hong Kong and Singapore.[16]

In stark contrast, Hong Kong further loosened its regulations on land, labor, and capital. Alongside modest political reforms, in the late 1940s the restored colonial regime removed restrictions on female and child labor, non-British investment, and industrial land acquisitions—greatly increasing the colony's attractions for capitalists in flight from postcolonial Southeast Asia and postrevolutionary China. In turn, as Catherine Schenk has underscored, the British government included Hong Kong in the Sterling Area (1945–1967) but granted it a key exemption. London imposed this empire-wide exchange control regime during the war in order to protect the value of sterling. After 1945 only Hong Kong and Kuwait were allowed to continue operating free markets in U.S. dollars due to their historic entrepôt and petroleum trades.[17] Amid the fixed rates of the Bretton Woods system and increasing global interventionism, these moves widened the opportunities that Hong Kong still offered to both huashang and outside actors. It was not alone in maintaining a light economic touch, however. As Vanessa Ogle has analyzed, a whole "offshore world" emerged from the ruins of European empires, "precisely at the moment when these state-based projects began to assume their greatest importance."[18] This archipelago of tax havens, offshore markets, and special economic zones blossomed between the 1940s and 1970s, allowing "free-market capitalism to flourish on the sidelines of a world increasingly dominated by larger and more interventionist nation-states." Hong Kong was thus one star in a constellation of places that favored low taxes and light regulation, or "positive noninterventionism" in local parlance. Yet the colonial government did remain active in the economy through key monopolies, mass public housing, and informal coordination with trade and industrial bodies. Hong Kong also stood apart from this "offshore world" because it attracted huge quantities of labor as well as capital. While most offshore sites still rely on tourism or shadow banking, Hong Kong's migration crisis delivered the low-cost labor to fuel a manufacturing boom. Previous scholars have explored the diplomatic, legal, and humanitarian aspects of this crisis, but I emphasize how elite migrants used their expertise, capital, and networks both to exploit fellow "refugees" as laborers and to steer their educational futures, transforming Hong Kong by the 1970s into both the world's largest exporter of textiles and apparel to the U.S. market and the largest sender of foreign students to U.S. colleges and universities.[19]

Only some of these émigré huashang evolved into what I term *kuashang*, however. This evolution occurred primarily among those with preexisting connections to the United States and those who were willing to collaborate directly with U.S. imperial expansion. Before the Second World War, American interests in British Hong Kong were small, but the formation of the PRC transformed the colony's value in Washington's eyes. Hong Kong first became the U.S. government's primary listening and espionage post on China, as Nancy Bernkopf Tucker analyzed.[20] As I emphasize in chapter 1, the outbreak of the Korean War and the imposition of U.S. and UN embargoes on the PRC in 1950–1951 reshaped Hong Kong into a key enforcement point for U.S. economic agendas. In turn, as we will see in chapters 2–4, Washington also began funneling extensive resources into Hong Kong through its "state-private network," particularly into educational projects.[21] These activities and the overlapping agendas of Beijing, Taipei, and the colonial government made Hong Kong an exceptional Cold War locale on par with Berlin.[22] The entanglement between so many contending agendas further enabled Hong Kong to function as a node of unique networks.[23]

Washington's efforts to win "hearts and minds" in Hong Kong most importantly opened unprecedented opportunities for Chinese residents to circulate within the new U.S.-led transpacific order. While projecting influence into Hong Kong through its state-private network, Washington also began reforming its race-based immigration systems. These reforms sanctioned rights and opportunities long denied to Chinese throughout the Exclusion era (1882–1943). As Madeline Hsu and others have analyzed, the repeal of Chinese Exclusion in 1943 only marginally widened possibilities for increased Chinese migration. Postwar quotas for Chinese refugees were miniscule in comparison with European refugees, but special acts of Congress allowed limited numbers of Chinese students and elites to enter or remain, while organizations such as Aid Refugee Chinese Intellectuals (ARCI) recruited "refugee" intellectuals to settle in Taiwan and the United States. The overall system was then transformed with the Immigration and Nationality Act of 1965, known as Hart-Celler. By abandoning white supremacy in favor of prioritizing education and family reunions, these reforms significantly increased Hong Kong residents' chances to migrate to the United States while also privileging the educated and those with American connections. Simultaneously, the United Kingdom was stripping citizenship rights from colonial subjects through the Commonwealth Immigrants Acts of 1962 and 1968 and the Immigration Act of 1971. As a result, between 1943 and 1965 the former huashang strategies of collaboration and circulation within the British imperial system had to adapt to the new U.S.-led order. Decolonization, postcolonial nationalism, economic interventionism, China's revolution, and U.S. imperial expansion all intersected to incentivize many Hong Kong–based huashang to reorient their ambitions and develop kuashang strategies.

Kuashang Strategies and Informal Decolonization

By the early 1950s Hong Kong–based industrialists, bankers, academics, and other professionals began to explore export-driven codevelopment with the U.S. market and to seed educational institutions oriented toward

American models. These entwined commercial and educational choices were particularly visible among the textile industrialists who had fled from the lower Yangzi region known as Jiangnan, composed primarily of southern Jiangsu, northern Zhejiang, and Shanghai. In his study *Emigrant Entrepreneurs* (1988), sociologist Wong Siu-lun sought to explain why this émigré group had dominated Hong Kong's spinning and weaving industry. Based on anonymized interviews from the late 1970s, Wong dissected the industrialists' experiences and business practices. Among many insights, he discerned a collective educational orientation toward the United States. Of thirty-two university-educated industrialists he interviewed, 90 percent spoke English fluently. In turn, 60 percent had studied either in the United States or in American missionary colleges in China, 12 percent had studied in the United Kingdom, and 6 percent in Canada. This pattern dovetailed with the educational and professional trajectories of the spinners' children, of whom ten were in the United States and only one each was in the United Kingdom and Taiwan. Wong identified that these educational choices were multigenerational business strategies: "The educational background of the spinners appeared to have provided them with a valuable social network for making business contacts as well as for gathering marketing information. . . . Those who had attended American or British universities were able to form direct social links with these countries." As a result, "the children of spinning families were usually sent to the United States and Britain which were principal markets for Hong Kong textiles."[24]

Although Wong rhetorically balanced Britain and the United States, his research demonstrates that these strategies were overwhelmingly American centered. I reframe these entwined business and educational strategies as core pieces of kuashang strategies and group the intangible assets that they produced as *American social capital*, a term I will unpack here and in the next section. Yet Wong's methodology of anonymized interviews rendered it difficult to view these networks and strategies in practice. Through historical methodologies, I am able to be more specific and look beyond the cotton spinners, demonstrating that interconnected clusters of émigré bankers, lawyers, executives, academics, and former Nationalist technocrats all developed similar strategies and played similar roles in reorienting Hong Kong's commercial and educational systems toward the United States. In turn, I document how Hong Kong's British-oriented Cantonese, Chaozhou (Teochew, 潮州), Jewish, and other elites also began to reorient toward the United States. This process thus blended Shanghainese-centered histories with those of overseas huashang, creating a creolized intensification of overlapping practices of collaboration in this disjointed Cold War colony. And as figures such as Li Choh-ming implemented increasingly substantial changes to local education (see chapter 4), I argue that these elite kuashang strategies became artificially naturalized over the 1960s as "good sense" among the upwardly mobile: go to college in the United States, acquire knowledge and social capital, and potentially return to profit from those assets.

I define kuashang strategies as a pragmatic style of thinking in which private-sector Hong Kong elites continuously read the shifting international terrain of power and moved to exploit both British imperial decline and the colony's interstitial position in the Cold War by building integrative business and educational relationships with the United States, and later by incorporating China into this ecosystem. These integrative relationships took diverse forms in pursuit of diverse goals, but some examples include studying in the United States as a business strategy; naturalizing as a U.S. citizen to gain proximity to American power; importing U.S. investment and/or expertise into local companies or institutions in order to circumvent or mold colonial policies; regularly touring the United States or joining the local American Chamber of Commerce to advance marketing and/or antiprotectionist agendas; and borrowing or adapting U.S. models for competitive advantage. What united these actions was the aim to accelerate transpacific circulations of people, capital, goods, and ideas and thereby, to borrow a Marxist phrase, annihilate the space and time separating Hong Kong and the United States—and later, separating China and the United States. More than a pun on huashang, the term *kuashang* underscores these actors' blending of older strategies of imperial collaboration from both overseas huashang and treaty-port merchants in the new context of a U.S.-led international order, while reinscribing power, strategy, and privilege into overly celebratory narratives of the transnational (*kuàguó*, 跨國) after 1945. In turn, some might wish to label these strategies as "pro-American," but such a term would oversimplify and impute a political or emotional identification with the United States that was often absent from or secondary to these actors' pragmatic considerations. Instead, kuashang strategies enabled a small but expanding set of nominally subaltern colonial subjects to invert the marginalized political, geographic, and racialized positions that both contemporaries and scholars today might assume constrained them. Through investments into and accumulations of American social capital, these mobile "Third World" actors inserted themselves into transnational flows of U.S. imperial state power and pulled Hong Kong toward the center of the global economy.[25]

The initial logic is easy to see. In the 1950s the United States was the center of global finance, the world's largest consumer market, and increasingly the essential sales destination for Hong Kong's manufacturing boom. The United States was also a potential source of "refugee" aid and the focus of exit strategies in the event of PRC invasion. Based on their experiences over the Republican era, these émigrés knew that an American education was a versatile method for advancing these goals. More than just prestigious, U.S. higher education offered an efficient path to modern knowledge, English fluency, bicultural behaviors, market insights, useful connections, and legal steps toward migration. Kuashang strategies then evolved alongside Hong Kong's codevelopment with the U.S. market, enabling particular local industrialists to access global capital flows and keep pace with U.S. consumer trends (chapter 5), while facilitating Hong Kong's broader upmarket transition in the 1970s (chapter 6). Thus while scholars AnnaLee Saxenian and Aihwa Ong have highlighted similar "Argonauts" and "astronauts" in the 1980s and 1990s, my kuashang analytic recovers continuities stretching back to semicolonial China and the colonial port–cities of Southeast Asia.[26] Since the late Qing, both overseas huashang and treaty-port capitalists had been crossing oceans, collaborating with foreign imperial powers, and pursuing instrumental transnational connections through education and business. When contingent political events reconfigured these imperial systems and reconcentrated many such families into Hong Kong, a potent assemblage of bridging social capital coalesced in the western Pacific.

It cannot be overemphasized that *kuashang* is not a term these figures used to describe themselves and is not intended to connote an identity. Instead, the term aims to draw out a spectrum of individualized strategies toward international power that evolved from former strategies of collaboration with European imperialism in China and Southeast Asia. As such, I seek to render visible a form of collaboration that was rarely made explicit after 1945 and instead kept private and diffuse across many elite professions. These strategies were inherently unstable and flexible, fostered by Republican China's instability, Hong Kong's own uncertain future after 1949, and the routinely masked nature of U.S. imperial expansion. We can discern this private orientation, however, by analyzing educational and naturalization choices, transnational movements, and social networks across generations. For these reasons, my analysis of social capital is qualitative and paired with an emphasis on individual strategies. Network diagrams and quantitative metrics can reveal patterns, but we need more particularized context and often affect to understand how unique individuals acquired, used, and maintained such interpersonal assets.

In turn, the displaced elites that pursued kuashang strategies not only built integrative transpacific relationships but also carved out new forms of power and privilege from under British colonial rule, what I term *informal decolonization*. Since Ronald Robinson's landmark article in 1972, scholars of empire have emphasized the key role played by local collaborators throughout the onset, operation, and end of empire.[27] Formal decolonization in particular occurred when anticolonial movements "succeeded in detaching mediators from the colonial regimes" and the colonial state "[ran] out of collaborators."[28] Yet this transition never occurred in Hong Kong. Scholars of empire might assume this absence stemmed from local elites continuing to collaborate with British colonialism. My kuashang analytic complicates that assumption. The elites examined here were rarely invested in the British colonial project and did not preserve it for the sake of British-sponsored opportunities. Instead, they did not directly undermine it in order to preserve other international opportunities that a PRC takeover would have prohibited. In this sense, continued British rule was a convenient placeholder beneath which kuashang strategies of collaboration with U.S. imperial systems could thrive. Hong Kong residents interested in careers in the civil service, the law, architecture, or medicine continued following colonial pathways because British credentials and networks still governed these professions. Elite business and academia were different realms, however. From 1949 on, as kuashang strategies accumulated new forms of social and economic power, such actors did challenge the colonial state and were able to use their American social capital to arrogate decisions and seize positions from colonial hands. As we will see through Ansie Lee Sperry (chapter 1), David W. K. Au (chapter 3), Li Choh-ming (chapter 4), H. J. Shen (chapter 5), and Jack Tang and Paul Cheng (chapter 8), kuashang who broke into or rose to lead colonial institutions and companies were not collaborating with Britain. They were instead using their American social capital to exploit British decline in service of personal agendas that often contravened colonial ambitions. Aware of their own receding power, British officials and executives generally bowed to this informal decolonization. From the 1950s on, informal decolonization ceded substantial power over Hong Kong from British to Chinese actors, but also from public- to private-sector elites.

The concept of kuashang strategies also highlights the multiplicity of experiences, priorities, and systems of inherited privilege among "overseas Chinese." Pioneered by Wang Gungwu, studies of overseas Chinese have long focused on questions of identity and these communities' relationships to China through debates over terms such as "diaspora" and new paradigms of "flexible citizenship" or "collaborative nationalism."[29] Yet this focus on the relationship with China can serve to overlook both other international connections and other motivations besides political identity. Through kuashang strategies, I seek to highlight and differentiate an elite cohort whose ambitions, mobility, and proximity to power diverged from both Exclusion-era huashang and less privileged contemporaries. The actors whom I label as kuashang generally viewed citizenships as commodities and rarely perceived their actions as claiming an American identity or serving Chinese nationalism. Although it was nothing new for overseas Chinese elites to pursue belonging in multiple imperial systems, it was new to do so legally with the United States. This shift in possibilities from the Exclusion era enabled Hong Kong's kuashang to naturalize as U.S. citizens and use that asset instrumentally to parry British colonialism and play greatly enhanced roles in transpacific integration. In turn, analyzing these individuals enables us to challenge a discourse that lumps together "overseas Chinese" investment in China after 1978. My framework restores the inherited privilege that shaped which individuals were best positioned to exploit China's reforms and complicates the patriotic motivations that hagiographic sources have ascribed to these investments.

In turn, amid vociferous debates over the purpose of higher education, kuashang strategies highlight the key role that U.S. higher education played in accelerating capitalist globalization. Scholars have shown increasing interest in Asian students' experiences of American education and the ensuing impact on various political, religious, literary, and racial projects.[30] This study, however, focuses on individuals whose motivations were more pragmatic. Republican-era Chinese elites and governments consistently steered most Chinese students in the United States toward subjects deemed "modern" and "useful," such as science, management, and engineering.[31] Hong Kong elites continued this preference, both for their own children in the United States and by recruiting such forms of U.S. expertise and money into Hong Kong institutions. As such, U.S. higher education functioned as a consistent access point for not only knowledge but also elite social connections, cultural behaviors, and market insights. I thus highlight how U.S. colleges and universities willingly facilitated the global expansion of American business models, professional ideologies, and class systems through transpacific educational circulations, including both Hong Kong students in the United States and expanding U.S. influence within Hong Kong higher education.[32] In turn, in chapter 6 I note how these transpacific circulations created feedback loops through alumni donations that helped fuel today's revenue-hungry "global" universities. Rather than framing U.S. higher education as somehow "better" or even as a force for democracy, my analysis frames it as a portal through which a spectrum of both U.S. and international actors largely advanced capitalist agendas.

The materialism and pragmatism of kuashang strategies do help explain why this phenomenon has escaped public and scholarly attention. Most Hong Kong people would be surprised by this book's arguments. I see four main reasons why this transpacific history has remained unknown. First, colonialism warps knowledge-making by laying claim to our initial assumptions and then culling both the archive and memory in support. In turn, Hong Kong schools do not teach local history, while most scholars of modern China pay little attention to Hong Kong, reflecting what Poshek Fu called the "Central Plains syndrome" (大中原心態).[33] Second, these strategies originated among a small elite and expanded primarily through education. As a result, kuashang strategies became artificially naturalized as "common sense," and Hong Kong people came to see studying in the United States as an obvious aspiration, often reflected in New Wave films.[34] Third, transpacific networks and strategies routinely led to emigration, and many of this study's descendants no longer live in Hong Kong, further dispersing this history. Fourth, rapid economic change, the Tiananmen Square Massacre, and the 1997 handover all led to seismic changes in Hong Kong culture and identity that diversified these strategies in complex ways.[35] Most simply, in the 1980s and 1990s the previous focus on American social capital bled into an urgent pursuit of Canadian, Australian, New Zealand, and other passports. I would posit that Hong Kong public memory has conflated these histories and led today's residents to see themselves as simply "international." The kuashang analytic begins to detangle and denaturalize these threads by recovering an earlier and largely forgotten strategic vision.

Finally, reading against the assumed British colonial edifice and tracing mobile Chinese elites has required me to adopt both global and multigenerational research methodologies. There has been a tendency when studying Hong Kong during the Cold War to rely on sources stored at Kew and College Park. In contrast, I rely on sources from the Public Records Office in Kwun Tong, the Hong Kong Heritage Project in Hung Hom, the text-searchable newspapers hosted online by the Hong Kong Central Library, and the special collections at the University of Hong Kong (HKU), Hong Kong Baptist, and the Chinese University of Hong Kong (CUHK). I supplement this research with Chinese- and English-language sources gathered from libraries and archives across the United States, the United Kingdom, and China in order to track the accumulation, use, and transfer of these intangible resources across shifting contexts and individual personalities. These sources are in Mandarin, Cantonese, and English, but I take seriously these subjects' English-language fluency and do not rank the authenticity of these figures' Chinese- and English-language sources. In turn, I believe it ahistorical and problematic to impose either pinyin or simplified characters on actors who left the PRC. I thus preserve traditional characters and only use simplified characters for PRC actors and terms. The term *kuashang* is rendered through Mandarin, however. Using Jyutping, it would be *kwaa-soeng* in Cantonese, while there is no standard romanization of Shanghainese. It is a thorny intellectual problem. Many figures here were not proficient in Cantonese or Mandarin, preferring Shanghainese and English. Only a few, such as Li Choh-ming, were equally comfortable in many of these. For the ease of most readers today, I think it best to acknowledge these issues but maintain a Mandarin rendering of 跨商. Finally, while the character *shang* (商) means "merchant," I apply *kuashang* to bankers, industrialists, and even academics. As we will see, all were quite commercial.

Social Capital, *Guanxi*, and Globalization

Social capital has become an endemic term in public and scholarly discourses. In its connections with globalization and economic change, scholars have largely focused on low social capital contexts, using quantitative metrics to analyze the impact of fraying communities.[36] Few, however, have foregrounded high social capital contexts, let alone that of Asian elites. In contrast, I argue that you cannot understand globalization without paying close historical attention to such concentrations of social capital. I would further argue that you cannot understand social capital's key role in globalization without Hong Kong—and not just as a template but also as a formative player. While scholars might assume that it was Euro-American elites in London or New York whose connections and strategies shaped the international economy, such assumptions impoverish our understanding of globalization and manage to marginalize a top-three global financial center. Eurocentrism and imperialized knowledge-making have reified North Atlantic–centered paradigms and extended an overly broad subaltern lens across the developing and postcolonial worlds. By focusing on Hong Kong elites' cultivations and uses of American social capital, we unearth more complex geographies and terrains of power. Through the kuashang, we see mobile Chinese elites anticipating the power shifts of the post-1945 world and quickly adapting by turning from British-led to U.S.-led institutions and worldviews in pursuit of safety and material gain. In so doing, they confronted numerous challenges—American ignorance about Asia, overt racism, and protectionism, to name a few—but their networks and strategies nonetheless fueled Hong Kong's manufacturing boom, accelerated globalization and its inequities, and adeptly positioned them to broker China's reemergence. By chapter 8, we will see them rebalancing between U.S.-led and PRC-led systems.

Many scholars instinctively trace "social capital" back to the French sociologist Pierre Bourdieu. He did not coin the term, however, and his most widely read works, such as *Distinction* (1979), focus on cultural capital.[37] I share Bourdieu's attention to education, however. In *The State Nobility* (1989), he analyzed the key role played by French educational institutions in distributing and reproducing cultural capital, including "institutionalized" forms such as credentials and "embodied" forms such as speech and dress.[38] Throughout his work, though, Bourdieu consistently viewed education as primarily reflective of and contributing to cultural capital, arguing that "the scholastic yield" of education is determined by a family's cultural capital and labeling degrees as "certificates of cultural competence." He did note, however, that the "economic yield" of an education "depends on the social capital, again inherited, which can be used to back it up."[39]

I also place great analytic weight on education but regroup both its "institutionalized" and "embodied" legacies as social capital. While Confucian educations aimed to reproduce cultural capital, my subjects' pragmatic pursuit of American educations was quite different. As explored further in chapter 1, late Qing and Republican business elites prioritized missionary and foreign educations for instrumental reasons. Studying overseas became prestigious, but a status-based "American cultural capital" did not coalesce into a bedrock goal. Amid foreign imperialism, domestic instability, commercial competition, Japanese invasion, civil war, and Hong Kong's own uncertainty, these mobile elites largely remained focused on how foreign education would secure access to new technologies, business practices and partners, and later citizenship. I thus argue that their approach to education is better understood as a method of acquiring a multigenerational, cross-cultural social capital that could be reliably converted into economic capital.

For the specific actors analyzed here, I make the same argument about the knowledge so acquired. Most scholars classify knowledge under the disquieting term *human capital*, which Bourdieu also disdained.[40] The logic of this term is the questionable assumption that the most significant outcome of education is some inherently valuable body of knowledge— whether a technical skill set or the liberal arts' emphasis on critical thinking. Economists have also long debated this assumption. In the 1970s Kenneth Arrow, Michael Spence, Joseph Stiglitz, and others interested in "human capital" debated the "screening" or "signaling" role of educational institutions in the market.[41] This debate centered on whether schooling's most important economic contribution was the assumed acquisition of new skills or ascertaining and signaling individuals' preexisting abilities in a world of imperfect information. Again, both Republican-era and post-1949 Hong Kong business elites focused on the acquisition of both practical skills and other assets, regularly instructing their children to acquire instrumental knowledge, professional experiences, and contacts while overseas. Their children generally complied, although they of course changed majors, dropped out, and rebelled. Yet overall my subjects primarily acquired knowledge that was for commercial and professional use vis-à-vis others. This knowledge was thus not categorically different from the contacts, credentials, and behaviors that their families also envisioned as coming from American educations. I thus neither separate nor rank knowledge among the diverse attractions of U.S. higher education. Instead, I group it alongside contacts, credentials, speech, dress, and sheer confidence as entwined pieces of a mobile, utilitarian American social capital.

We can observe these ideas in this introduction's opening quotation. Referencing the motto of his father "P. Y." Tang Pingyuan (唐炳源), Jack Tang groups education, reputation, and credit together as life's three most essential assets. Tang's argument is that no one can take these assets away from you. Similar attitudes are common among many diasporic and mercantile cultures. Yet there is more here than meets the eye. By "credit," Tang does not mean credibility. He literally means what banks will loan you. In turn, your reputation and credit *can* be taken away, whether by financial institutions or by shifts in others' opinions. Both assets are portable but not inherent. Only with Tang's third asset—education—do we understand his real meaning. By linking education with reputation and credit, he is referring to social capital and its convertibility into economic capital: "money and power." Tang is indirectly explaining his family's multigenerational approach to elite U.S. higher education as a reliable and socially sanctioned method of acquiring and transferring social capital across generations in the form of cross-cultural networks, credentials, behaviors, and knowledge. It was prestigious for Jack to attend MIT and Harvard Business School, but these degrees were most important because they cemented his access to and even financial credit among the "right" people, whether they be elite Americans, fellow U.S.-educated Chinese, or other international actors. This durable and mobile social capital survived war and revolution and facilitated the recovery of "money and power."

Many previous scholars have investigated this connection between social capital and economic outcomes but again have focused on low social capital and face-to-face contexts. For example, in the 1980s sociologists Mark Granovetter and James Coleman challenged core neoclassical assumptions such as the anonymous market and rational decision making by highlighting the role of "embedded" social relations and intergenerational norms in economic decision making.[42] By the 1990s and 2000s scholars demonstrated that individual social capitals do indeed shape communal economic outcomes. Robert Putnam's best seller *Bowling Alone* in particular amassed the evidence to demonstrate how individual relationships have a public "spillover" effect through the lens of declining American participation in civic and social organizations.[43] Drawing on these insights, I shift focus to the other end of the spectrum, a context of high and transnational social capital. I argue that this American social capital was not just enriching for kuashang families but also had an important spillover effect across Hong Kong society by setting productive educational norms, opening transpacific opportunities, and reshaping supposedly rational markets, as we will see in chapter 5 through banking and investment, chapter 6 through post-Fordist transitions, and chapters 7 and 8 through China's early reforms. Lest this argument be misinterpreted, however, let me underscore that this spillover effect was by no means automatic, natural, or even. As we will see, it entailed collaboration with multiple states and delivered wildly divergent returns.

China scholars, however, have long had a separate conversation surrounding networks, focused on culturally specific ideas of native-place ties, or *tongxiang guanxi*. Translated too simply as "relations" or "relationships," *guanxi* is a complex social construct that has evolved across time and space. As famed sociologist Fei Xiaotong (费孝通) established in his publication *Xiangtu Zhongguo* (鄉土中國, 1947), rural Chinese society was organized around "egocentric" notions of the self embedded into concentric circles (社會圈子) of guanxi, rather than "ascriptive ties to abstract collectives" as in Euro-American societies.[44] Guanxi practice was thus a particular way that one interacted with kin and native-place associates through an elastic web of mutual obligation radiating outward. As rural migrants moved from their home villages to cities or went overseas during the Republican era, these native-place guanxi remained vital. Traditionally, native-place sojourners formalized their ties through hierarchical *huiguan* organizations. As Bryna Goodman has analyzed, the Republican era saw the emergence of more democratic native-place associations called *tongxianghui*.[45] Native-place guanxi also shaped the membership of labor unions, charities, political organizations, commercial associations, company boards, and even criminal syndicates.[46] Yet native-place ties were not the only networks available to Chinese elites. Educational ties among fellow elites and foreigners provided a parallel network of equally valuable connections, which transferred to post-1949 Hong Kong in substantial quantities. In turn, guanxi continued evolving in distinct ways within the PRC, as Mayfair Mei-hui Yang has analyzed.[47]

By thus focusing on bicultural and transpacific relationships developed through education and business, my concepts of kuashang strategies and American social capital can be seen as branches of the guanxi tree that coalesced in Hong Kong after 1949. While most mainland migrants still relied on native-place guanxi to secure work and accommodation in the colony, such networks were insufficient to secure things like multinational corporate investment, access to the U.S. market, or exit strategies. These goals required access to international power structures through elite trans-national social connections. As such, while still honoring their native-place ties by joining organizations such as Hong Kong's Jiangsu and Zhejiang Residents' Association (蘇浙同鄉會), these actors came to rely less on native-place guanxi. Instead, they not only joined American alumni associations and the Lions or Rotary Clubs (as they had before 1949) but also now privately worked with proxies of the U.S. government, took U.S. citizenship, testified on Capitol Hill, and later served as intermediaries in the Sino-U.S. relationship. There is a key overlap, however, between native-place guanxi and American social capital that is worth stressing. As we will see from chapter 1 on, particular locales in Republican China became particularly oriented toward American educations, and thus native-place and educational networks did often overlap. Depending on the moment and perspective, such ties can be understood as *tongxiang guanxi*, American social capital, or simply lifelong friendships.

Historicizing Global Economic Change

Diverse scholars of the human past have continuously challenged the deductive logics and ahistorical assumptions of neoclassical economics—from Karl Marx and Friedrich Engels's historical materialism and the historical school of economics as represented by Max Weber, Joseph Schumpeter, and Karl Polanyi, to the Chinese philosopher Wang Yanan.[48] As noted previously, network sociologists too have challenged neoclassical precepts by presenting empirical evidence that markets exist only through state action and that exchange is routinely irrational and unequal due to human relationships. Even economists occasionally embrace these insights. In his text *Behind the Veil of Economics* (1988), Robert Heilbroner argued that "economics" as a discipline had come to function as an ideological veil due to its emphasis on rational self-interest and free competition, willfully ignoring and obscuring the man-made systems and relationships that underlie markets.[49]

Historians, too, have long championed more holistic views of political economy, but our picture of the twentieth century has remained Euro-American-centric. Historians of the early modern world have decentered Europe in the origins and expansion of global capitalism, instead foregrounding processes such as transatlantic African slavery and the production of sugar and silver in the Caribbean and Latin America. Historians of China such as R. Bin Wong, Sucheta Mazumdar, Ken Pomeranz, and Madeleine Zelin have amply demonstrated that China was the world's largest economy through 1800, the world's silver sink, and a center of robust industrial innovation.[50] In turn, historians of women and gender have led in revising androcentric narratives of capitalism—not only restoring women as overlooked laborers, managers, investors, and owners but also redefining the economic itself by recovering the marginalization of their labor and the household broadly from the imagined market.[51] Yet scholarship of twentieth-century "development" has moved more slowly, largely focusing on the political and intellectual *discourse* of development as conducted among governments and international organizations of the Global North.[52] Until recently, if the Global South figured at all, its governments were cast as passive recipients and its economic actors were invisible.[53]

Despite living in a small British colony through 1997, Hong Kong people have long been leading actors in the development and evolution of both Chinese and global capitalism. As I have argued elsewhere, Hong Kong became the first identifiably capitalist Chinese society in the 1840s, and it thereafter facilitated the transpacific integration of the expanding British and U.S. imperial economic systems.[54] In this study I seek not only to further highlight Hong Kong's place on the world stage but also to demonstrate more holistic views of political economy by focusing on social capital, transnational connections, educational institutions, and behind-the-scenes government efforts alongside more traditional business history subjects. In turn, by foregrounding "Third World" economic actors, I seek to complicate the prevailing discourse, highlighting the active and yet multifarious roles played by colonized and postcolonial elites in capitalist globalization. As the 2020 pandemic disrupts hyperglobalization, Hong Kong enters a new political era, Sino-U.S. relations sour, and the tolls of late-stage capitalism become ever more stark, it is imperative that we better understand such interstitial brokers.

Yet because the capitalist transformation of East Asia occurred during the Cold War, much of the previous literature on Hong Kong's development suffered from problematic "area studies" paradigms. Witnessing the phenomenal growth of Hong Kong, Taiwan, Singapore, and South Korea in the 1970s and 1980s, social scientists assumed there must be a common cause. They thus applied regional frameworks that grouped these societies together as "little dragons" or "tigers." These frameworks were built on assumptions of shared Confucian values, including supposedly heightened levels of paternalism, discipline, and respect for education.[55] The problems with this approach range from racialized generalizations to implicitly blaming the values of societies that did not achieve such success. Most acutely, this literature routinely sidestepped the basic reality that Hong Kong's economy was radically different from the state-led models of South Korea, Taiwan, and Singapore. For example, in an Edwin Reischauer lecture in 1990 on East Asia's industrialization, historian Ezra Vogel sought to bring greater nuance to the "little dragons" model and discussed numerous policies and actors in South Korea, Taiwan, and Singapore. Yet he did not mention one person or policy for Hong Kong.[56] As stated, Hong Kong merits examination on its own terms, not least because it led this imagined grouping. According to the World Bank, by 1990 its GDP per capita was US$13,485, followed by Singapore at $12,766, Taiwan at $10,048, and South Korea at $6,642.

Scholars have since developed more tailored analyses of transnational Chinese merchants and firms, but the framing has remained stubbornly one of type. Sociologists such as Gary Hamilton (no relation), Danny Kin-kong Lam, and Ian Lee have explored "overseas Chinese" firms' lean business models, reliance on social networks, and adaptive practices, labeling their business models as "network capitalism" or "guerilla capitalism."[57] David Meyer too has underscored that Hong Kong's success stemmed from its longtime operation "as the pivotal meeting-place of the Chinese and foreign social networks of capital in Asia."[58] Yet these scholars have generally relied on anonymized interviews and often exclusively on English-language sources. As a result, most of these studies also lack for named Chinese individuals or companies. Instead, they speak of "Chinese firms," "Chinese merchants," and "Chinese social networks" in opposition to "Japanese" or "Western" counterparts.[59] For Hamilton, this approach reflected a Weberian aim to "develop ideal-typical concepts that have particular relevance for Asian societies and to draw conclusions about

Asian development from an analysis using those concepts."[60] I believe such aims are destined to essentialize and are particularly problematic when still conferring individualized analysis on Euro-American people and firms. Through bilingual, archival research, I examine Chinese individuals, families, and firms as unique historical actors.

This scholarship, however, did guide me toward the understudied role of market demand and market access. Marxist legacies have led scholars to focus on questions of production, overlooking the challenges of selling. Gary Hamilton grasped this oversight and noted regarding Hong Kong's postwar development: "Using their commercial know-how and a lot of hard work, Hong Kong entrepreneurs began to link up with . . . the 'big buyers,' purchase agents who represented these large retail and wholesale firms in the West, such as Sears, Montgomery Ward, J.C. Penney, Marks and Spencer, and the Bon Marché."[61] This insight, however, skirts the real issue by making this process sound easy or fair. If all it took was "hard work," we might imagine that entrepreneurs the world over would have "linked up" with Euro-American retailers and exported their way to First World wealth. As demonstrated throughout this study, such know-how and links were complex, requiring precise networks and knowledge of intricate regulations and consumer tastes. As such, accumulations of American social capital were a decisive advantage.

Finally, I would stress that I do not view Hong Kong's growth as reproducible or scalable. By analyzing how Hong Kong–based elites tacked between British-, U.S.-, and Chinese-led power structures over the Cold War, I seek to highlight the ever-in-process making and remaking of "the global" as a terrain of power navigated by state and nonstate actors alike. Here I take inspiration from anthropologist Anna Lowenhaupt Tsing's study of precarity in the global economy through the lens of the matsutake mushroom. Tsing notes that for too long we have viewed economic change through "the misapprehension of progress blinders."[62] To minimize such normative assumptions, I want to underscore that I seek to frame Hong Kong's growth as in large measure the product of a historically specific set of "transformative relations" among enormous numbers of displaced Chinese people, a relatively stable colonial context, and the steroid of elite transpacific circulations and U.S. Cold War agendas. These factors intersected and helped engender Hong Kong to bloom like a field of mushrooms sprouting from wet soil. In short, we cannot separate economic change from detailed historical context and Hong Kong's transformation—while startling—was not inevitable, rational, or just. It was contingent, unsustainable, and grossly unfair.

Organization of the Book

This study begins and ends with trade conflict between China and the United States, from the U.S. and UN embargoes of 1950–1951 to the debates over China's most-favored-nation (MFN) status of the early 1990s. These signposts demarcate the roughly forty-five years in which Hong Kong functioned as the linchpin in a rapidly evolving set of trans-pacific relationships. Amid the fraught and/or nonexistent relations among Washington, Beijing, and Taipei during the 1950s and 1960s, it was Hong Kong's commercial and educational circulations that moved to the center and later drove the revival of Sino-U.S. trade between 1971 and 1997.

Chapter 1 reviews the history of colonial Hong Kong and reexamines the origins and relocation of mainland Chinese elites during the communist transition. The elites of the lower Yangzi region known as Jiangnan developed a noted affinity for U.S.-oriented education, and "American-returned students" came to dominate key professional areas in the Republican era. As the Nationalist regime disintegrated, many such U.S.-oriented elites fled to Hong Kong and fell back on their mobile social capital to survive and revive transplanted businesses. While the 1950 U.S. trade embargo disrupted Hong Kong's traditional entrepôt economy, the Korean War's trade boom saved many transplants and helped fuel the colony's first reorientations toward the U.S. market. These intersecting crises of the early Cold War set the conditions for kuashang strategies.

In chapter 2 I examine an overlapping émigré group that worked with U.S. imperial expansion in the western Pacific. Chinese Christians and American missionaries also came to Hong Kong in droves and sought to revive their shattered communities. Amid Hong Kong's broader "refugee" crisis, Washington funneled funds through American missionary organizations in the hope of fostering migrants' settlement while demonstrating the superiority of the so-called Free World. This covert U.S. aid helped Chinese-led church groups to establish a huge infrastructure of schools, community centers, and job-training programs across Hong Kong. Many such groups were led by kuashang elites for whom Christian agendas fit into their larger strategies. These groups' provisions of educational opportunity also offered limited chances for nonelite residents to pursue transpacific circulations and thus first expanded kuashang strategies beyond a privileged few.

Chapters 3 and 4 examine how similar processes transformed Hong Kong higher education in the 1950s. In chapter 3 I document how transplanted Chinese intellectuals and a handful of kuashang boosters partnered with U.S. missionaries and foundations to build four Chinese-language colleges in Hong Kong: Chung Chi (1951), New Asia (1953), United (1956), and Hong Kong Baptist (1956). Colonial officials felt threatened by these colleges' U.S. orientation and sought to reform them into Commonwealth institutions. This reform effort and the colleges' own demands for recognition eventually forced the government to concede to a second degree-granting university. From 1959 to 1963 the colonial government flooded Chung Chi, New Asia, and United Colleges with grants in an effort to reorient them into a federated Commonwealth institution: the Chinese University of Hong Kong.

Chapter 4 analyzes the frustration of these plans through CUHK's first vice-chancellor, Li Choh-ming. I argue that Li was the decisive kuashang who forcefully executed his own vision of a transpacific Chinese institution bound principally to U.S. educational and business systems. Drawing on his own extensive American social capital, he fostered enormous transpacific circulations that embodied the artificial naturalization of kuashang strategies and the acceleration of informal decolonization. By the end of Li's fifteen-year tenure in 1978, CUHK provided neither British colonial nor Confucian education but capitalist education tied to U.S. international leadership.

In Chapters 5 and 6 I combine the analysis of elite kuashang strategies with the previous three chapters' focus on education to offer a new narrative of the colony's rapid upmarket transition over the 1960s and 1970s. In chapter 5 I first argue that kuashang networks and strategies molded the colony's industrial lending in the 1950s and 1960s. After fleeing to Hong Kong, the industrialists discussed in chapter 1 urgently needed to reestablish bank credit and primarily did so through social capital, as evidenced by the Hongkong Bank's first ethnically Chinese manager, H. J. Shen. In turn, as Anglo-American protectionism mounted, many textile industrialists recruited direct outside investment in order to diversify production into nonquota textiles and apparel. The chapter concludes by examining kuashang-facilitated investments in Hong Kong in the mid-1960s by Esso and Mobil that heralded the global post-Fordist transition.

In chapter 6 I reinterpret the colony's startling development over the 1970s by arguing that its transpacific circulations enabled its adaptation to volatile shifts in the global economy. In 1973–1974 and again in 1975–1976, Hong Kong became the world's largest sender of foreign students to the United States. These outsized circulations delivered the knowledge, networks, and capital for Hong Kong firms with second-generation kuashang leaders to adapt to the end of the Bretton Woods system and the shift toward flexible production. Second-generation kuashang tapped into outflows of U.S. capital and piloted family companies through this storm into rapid upmarket transitions into commercial real estate development, container shipping, high finance, supply chain management, and other fields. Put simply, the colony's entwined educational and commercial circulations plugged kuashang companies into the U.S. economy at a far more sophisticated level than indicated by Hong Kong's GDP per capita.

In the final two chapters I demonstrate why we need this detailed understanding of Hong Kong's economic and educational evolution in order to understand China's reengagement with global capitalism. In chapter 7 I reconsider the timeline of China's Reform era by focusing on economics instead of high-level politics. We will see that China pursued limited reengagement with U.S.-led capitalist systems through Hong Kong from the reopening of Sino-U.S. trade in 1971. Through compensation trading and other channels, the colony's business elites began extending their networks into the mainland. In turn, as commercial engagement expanded and relations warmed, the international executives centered around the American Chamber of Commerce anticipated further reforms and built an infrastructure of committees, publications, and seminars through which to amass contacts and knowledge. Once Deng Xiaoping sanctioned reforms, however, these executives were first cautious, having already acquired access to China's low-cost mainland labor.

In the final chapter I offer an alternative narrative of China's 1980s through the tacit bargain struck between Beijing and Hong Kong elites. I first analyze how a few kuashang and PRC reformers partnered to lay key groundwork for China's later export-driven development through Gordon Wu's effort to build an expressway across the Pearl River delta. I then examine how Hong Kong elites' kuashang strategies evolved after the Sino-British Joint Declaration of 1984. With newfound trust in Deng and his allies, between 1984 and 1989 Hong Kong elites shifted from subcontracting to direct investment in Guangdong. Through the Esquel Group, we will see that this investment remained focused on connecting PRC labor with the U.S. market through Hong Kong. In the final section I examine the aftermath of the Tiananmen Square Massacre of June 1989. Kuashang actors moved to protect the transpacific ecosystem that they had helped build and collectively leveraged their American social capital to help ensure the renewal of China's MFN status until it was made permanent in 1995.

Together these chapters reframe Hong Kong as the metaphorical center of global history and capitalist globalization after 1945. By thinking through Hong Kong, we "reorient" and disrupt both assumed geographies and hegemonic relationships of power.[63] We instead place Asia—two-thirds of humanity—and elite colonial subjects at the center, displacing Eurocentric paradigms. We gain new insight into how foreign imperialism and domestic instability shaped many Republican-era Chinese elites' interest in international educations, as well as how prolonged crisis induced such elites to hedge against the nation-state with exit strategies. Through American social capital, we see how displaced migrants exploited both British imperial decline and U.S. imperial expansion, often by pragmatically collaborating with proxies of the U.S. government. In so doing, we complicate narratives of decolonization that lead inexorably toward the nation-state through interstitial elites and third-party flows of state power. We also gain a new perspective on U.S. colleges and universities as integral platforms in capitalist globalization and its inequalities. Finally, we see how these complex historical processes all set conditions for the Sino-U.S. commercial and educational entanglements we see today.

Several caveats are also in order. I have found Americans eager to hear this book's arguments as a credit to U.S. foreign policies. While Washington's Cold War agendas did provide invaluable educational opportunities to tens of thousands of Hong Kong people, it is worth stressing that U.S. educational outreach was not charity but rather an imperial project that aimed to reorient the world's best and brightest toward U.S. influence and leadership. Second, some have urged this study to make ethical judgments of the kuashang. Some see them as savvy entrepreneurs, while for others they are predatory tycoons. I caution against this instinct toward binary and underscore that this cohort was not a monolith in terms of wealth, profession, or politics, let alone character. In turn, while important and influential, kuashang actors are in no way demographically representative of Hong Kong people, overseas Chinese students, or Chinese Americans. These are unusual and often polarizing individuals. Finally, this analysis is also implicitly about patriarchy. While I highlight Ansie Lee Sperry as perhaps the first kuashang strategist, she was exceptional. My sources are generally filled with men because fathers prioritized the educations of sons and chose them over daughters to go overseas and/or lead the family company. Yet women were routinely decisive bearers and users of American social capital, as we will see. I hope new sources will enable future scholars to center them.

CHAPTER I

Capitalist Transplants

Elite Refugees and the First Reorientations of Hong Kong

Disruption realigns possibilities for transformative encounter.

—ANNA LOWENHAUPT TSING, *THE MUSHROOM AT
THE END OF THE WORLD: ON THE POSSIBILITY
OF LIFE IN CAPITALIST RUINS*

I n the spring of 1937 the Tang family fled Wuxi. Beside Lake Tai in
southern Jiangsu, Wuxi had been the Tangs' home for eighteen generations. Such ancestral seats held tremendous significance in Chinese
tradition due to shared dialects, guanxi networks, and ancestral obligations.[1] As a result, whole families rarely abandoned their native place. The
exceptions were "fleeing disaster" or *taonan* (逃難) and moments of
extreme opportunity.[2] This moment was both for the elite Tangs. After
monitoring events, they were certain that Japan would soon launch a full-
scale invasion of China. They did not flee westward into the interior,
however, as would the Nationalist government and tens of millions of
refugees. Instead, they seized a privileged opportunity and headed east,
directly into the oncoming crisis. While patriarch "P. Y." Tang Pingyuan
(唐炳源) rushed to England to arrange business interests, his wife "Kinmay" Wen Jinmei (温金美) moved their six children ninety miles to
Shanghai's French Concession, a leafy foreign enclave. She rented an
apartment just vacated by White Russians and took charge of the family's
affairs.[3]

Fleeing toward an invasion was counterintuitive yet shrewdly opportunistic. Japanese forces had already attacked Shanghai in 1932 and still
occupied swaths of the city. This time, Shanghai would face a full Japanese onslaught. Yet, like many Chinese elites, the Tangs calculated that
Japan would not risk war with France, Britain, and the United States. If

so, these powers' concessions within Shanghai would remain "solitary islands" (孤島) in the pending hurricane. While her husband purchased looms and spindles in Manchester, Kinmay returned to Wuxi, grabbed all the cash at their mills, and carried it to Shanghai in the backseat of a taxi.[4] She had secured the working capital for a new mill within the French Concession. It would be their life raft. When Japan did attack in August, the Tangs' Wuxi mills were bombed and seized, while the majority of factories in both Wuxi and Shanghai were destroyed.[5] Factories in the "solitary islands" flourished, however, amid the war's ensuing shortages. As over a million refugees poured into the concessions, prices skyrocketed and the Tangs' new mill proved "very profitable." They lived without "any real hardships," even continuing their children's riding lessons (figure 1.1).[6] When Japan did declare war on the Allies in December 1941 and seized the concessions, P. Y. Tang pragmatically pivoted to collaboration, paying 6.2 million yuan to regain his properties and joining the new regime's Cotton Control Commission.[7]

Chinese industrialists responded to the Second World War in myriad ways. Like the Tangs, most ended up "drawn into a web of collaboration" with Japan, as Parks Coble has argued.[8] The Tangs, however, proved particularly adept at negotiating this bloody terrain to their advantage due to constant pragmatism, mobility, and adaptation. While the Tangs' son Jack may have exaggerated his parents' prescience when recalling these events, his account succinctly distills his family's worldview. As cataclysms continued to strike in this war, the Chinese civil war, and the Cold War beyond, the Tangs consistently chose to keep relocating, shedding first their native place and then the nation-state in order to prioritize their own accumulation of economic and social capital.

The Tangs embody a subset of Nationalist China's industrialists and bankers who fled to Hong Kong during the communist transition. They emerged in the late Qing and Republican eras as part of a larger class of Chinese elites who thrived by working with foreign interests in China, pursuing overseas education, and returning to launch China's most modern business enterprises. The tumult of the Second Sino-Japanese War (1937–1945) and the Chinese civil war (1946–1949) pushed these capitalists to relocate repeatedly to try and safeguard their lives and property. For some, such as the Tangs, these relocations continued on to British Hong Kong when communism prevailed. This self-selecting group winnowed from China's elites would play a decisive role in spearheading Hong

Figure 1.1 P. Y. Tang and four children, Shanghai, 1937. Courtesy of the Tang family.

Kong's economic transformations over the Cold War. By 1970 the Tangs' new textile mill would be the largest manufacturer in the colony's largest industry.[9] These transplanted elites proved decisive for Hong Kong precisely because of their longstanding prioritization of both overseas education and strategic collaboration with foreign powers.[10] During the Cold War, however, it would no longer be the British or Japanese Empires with which they collaborated but instead the U.S. transpacific empire. Pursuing what I term *kuashang* (跨商) strategies, these elites would cultivate and use multifaceted American ties to reposition their transplanted businesses and Hong Kong itself for success as the United States redesigned global capitalism with itself at the center. This pivot toward American influence embodied a larger turn in world history, one that reveals both the original making of the U.S.-led order and alternative antecedents of what we now too broadly term as neoliberalism.

To understand the kuashang and their impact on Hong Kong, we must first survey this British colony's history prior to the Second World War. As a Crown colony between 1841 and its surrender to Japan on Christmas Day 1941, Hong Kong transformed from an island of fishing villages into South China's chief port. In addition to the opium trade, Hong Kong anchored enormous flows of goods and people back and forth with both Southeast Asia and North America, a legacy of the California Gold Rush.[11] It subsequently developed a highly commercial culture in which merchants predominated through collaboration with the colonial regime—in contrast to the Qing Empire's social order, yet similar to Southeast Asian colonial port-cities.[12] In turn, Hong Kong's Cantonese, Chaozhou, Eurasian, and South Asian elites became increasingly British-oriented in their educational and business strategies.

The commercial elites of the lower Yangzi region known as Jiangnan adopted similar but less exclusively British-centered practices. Instead, families such as the Tangs sought to demonstrate their Chinese nationalism while carving opportunities from the multiple empires laying stakes in China. They did so by cultivating mixed portfolios of international social capitals spanning the British, French, Japanese, and American imperial systems. Education was a key method in this process, and Jiangnan's commercial elites gradually came to prioritize missionary and foreign educations in order to access both "modern" knowledge and cross-cultural skills and connections. The early Republican era's instability and later the Nationalist government's cronyism heightened the urgency of this pursuit, while these elites used their international social capitals to collaborate with Japan, the Nationalists, and the United States alike during the Second Sino-Japanese War and Chinese civil war. The outcome of these conflagrations pushed them toward reliance on American social capital, but only a subset ultimately fled to Hong Kong during the communist transition.

The final section examines how the Second World War and early Cold War cracked British dominance in Hong Kong and initiated the first reorientations toward U.S.-led systems. Postwar U.S. international leadership engendered new social possibilities, while many old Shanghai business relationships were successfully transplanted to the Crown colony, processes we can glimpse through the mixed-race union of the American banker Henry Sperry and the Cantonese heiress Ansie Lee (利舜英). Yet more shifts were in store. The outbreak of the Korean War first created a trade boom that rescued many émigré industrialists, but the ensuing U.S. and UN embargoes on the new People's Republic truncated Hong Kong's entrepôt trades. By disrupting Hong Kong's place in China's orbit, the embargoes served to foster the colony's prolonged dependence on the U.S. market as the essential sales destination for its new manufactures. As I analyze further in chapter 5, émigré bankers and industrialists with prior U.S. connections found they had a competitive edge in this transpacific challenge. As a result, expanding U.S. imperial influence in the western Pacific dovetailed with the rooting of a transplanted class of Chinese elites into this British colony.

The Anglo-Cantonese Entrepôt

During its first century as a British colony, Hong Kong emerged as the chief port in South China and the hub of numerous entrepôt trades. After British troops raised the Union Jack in January 1841, officials proclaimed the territory's raison d'être to be the free movement of goods, people, and capital. In reality, just one commodity defined early Hong Kong: opium. Euro-American merchants had been smuggling ever-larger quantities of South Asian opium into China since the mid-eighteenth century in order to finance huge purchases of Chinese tea and silk. Qing officials debated how to respond, but by March 1839 one faction gained the upper hand at court and pushed to quash this drug trafficking. The British traders at

Canton were incensed by the ensuing crackdown, but their larger grievance was the Qing's mercantilist trade policies, known as the Canton System. This system had channeled Euro-American trade into Canton since the early 1700s in order to police its impact, exact customs, and maximize a steady stream of silver to Beijing.[13] In thrall to free trade theories, British merchants and their allies in London lambasted this system as an example of supposed "Asiatic despotism." They championed the superiority of free trade, even if they had to massacre Chinese to prove it. By August 1842 British forces had cut the vital Grand Canal and the Qing dynasty had sued for peace. The ensuing Treaty of Nanjing entwined free trade and imperial expansion. It abolished the Canton System, opened five Chinese ports to British trade, and ceded Hong Kong Island to Britain. It also granted British subjects extraterritoriality in China and exacted a huge indemnity. As the Qing faced a new era of foreign imperialism, the colony of Hong Kong began as the primary depot for a devastating narcotic and a symbolic free port.

In reality, early Hong Kong was very unstable and saved only by migration and the rise of a local Chinese merchant elite. As Christopher Munn has shown, during the 1840s the colony attracted little legitimate business beyond opium. Ironically, the regime fell back on anti–free trade policies, including auctioning numerous monopolies. The colony mostly proved a magnet for Chinese criminals, pirates, and marginalized minorities such as the Hakka and maritime Tanka. Tropical diseases and violent crime ran rampant, which triggered heavy-handed segregation, mass incarceration, and summary military justice. Many observers despaired for Hong Kong's prospects. Some urged London to abandon it.[14]

Elizabeth Sinn has demonstrated that it was the California Gold Rush and the globalization of the Pacific that rescued Hong Kong and accelerated its capitalist development. The news of gold in California electrified Hong Kong in 1849. The lure of "Gold Mountain" triggered excitement throughout South China and an ambition to migrate that only Hong Kong could facilitate. The Qing forbade overseas migration until 1860, so no mainland port could openly organize a mass transpacific migration. Chinese and European merchants alike repurposed Hong Kong's opium infrastructure to move people, while increasing collaboration between officials and merchants ensured that this migration was predominantly voluntary. The *kamshanchong* (金山莊) or "gold mountain firms" also pioneered new transpacific trade and moved into insurance and banking. The gold rush thus "transformed the Pacific into a highway linking North America and Asia," anchored primarily between Hong Kong and San Francisco. Simultaneously, Hong Kong and Singapore gradually developed a corridor of even greater scale to funnel Chinese laborers to the mines and plantations of colonial Southeast Asia.[15] By 1939 over 6.3 million Chinese had embarked at Hong Kong for foreign destinations and more than 7.7 million had returned, a volume of migrants comparable to New York's Ellis Island between 1892 and 1924.[16]

As Hong Kong stabilized through trade and migration and as a refuge from the Taiping Rebellion (1851–1864), collaboration increased between Chinese merchants and the colonial regime. Singapore integrated Chinese elites into government almost immediately, but it took nearly three decades for such collaboration to develop in Hong Kong. The earliest Chinese to prosper in Hong Kong had aided the British during the First Opium War, such as the Tanka mob boss Lo Acqui (盧亞貴) and the contractor Tam Achoy (譚亞才). Yet it was through charitable institutions that these parvenu merchants secured their position. As John Carroll states: "Colonial ignorance, indifference, and incompetence created a demand for services that these merchants were in a special position to offer."[17] In 1847 Lo and Tam built the first center of the Chinese community at Man Mo Temple, while in 1856 Tam sponsored the colony's first fire brigade.[18] In 1866 elite merchants formed the District Watch Committee, which privately organized a Chinese police force that finally secured order across the island and Kowloon peninsula, ceded after the Second Opium War (1856–1860). It was the formation of the Tung Wah Hospital in 1869, however, that cemented the power of Hong Kong's bourgeoisie.[19] As also studied by Elizabeth Sinn, the Tung Wah was never just a hospital. The first Chinese institution formally sanctioned by the colonial regime, the Tung Wah combined free medical services with wide-ranging social services for the diaspora. As such, the Tung Wah Board of Directors became a nexus of political influence and crowned Hong Kong's wealthiest Chinese merchants as semiofficial interlocutors between the colonial regime and ordinary Chinese. Another such nexus emerged with the formation of the Po Leung Kuk in 1878, which provided a mixture of Chinese charity and colonial reform to female sex workers, *mui tsai* bond servants, and other abused or abandoned women and children.[20]

These forms of collaboration continued to incentivize Chinese elites to participate in British systems of education and business. Under the Canton

System, Euro-American traders had relied on bilingual Chinese compradors. This position endured, and compradors often became the richest men in nineteenth-century Hong Kong. Yet only a cluster of families possessed the requisite skills. The regime invested in expanding this class in 1862 by establishing the Central School under Frederick Stewart to train Chinese interpreters, teachers, and clerks. This bilingual school and its successors became prized pathways into British companies and higher education. The compradors Ho Asek (何亞錫), Wei Akwong (韋亞光), and Wong Shing (黃勝) became the first local merchants to dispatch sons directly to British schools in 1867, while Hong Kong's first Chinese barrister, Ng Choy (伍才), studied law at Lincoln's Inn from 1874 to 1877.[21] Better known by his Mandarin name Wu Tingfang (伍廷芳), Ng later served as a Chinese diplomat and helped to draft both China's first commercial legal code and the Qing dynasty's abdication documents.[22] These elites reinforced these collaborative practices by extensively intermarrying, creating a British-oriented class. By 1911 this class was sufficiently invested in British higher education to bankroll a local replica, the University of Hong Kong (HKU). Later known for his strategies of "indirect rule" in Nigeria, Governor Sir Frederick Lugard envisioned HKU as a way to propagate British "civilization" in China via medical and engineering training. The Parsee merchant Sir Hormusjee Mody pledged $200,000 for the Main Building, while a campaign raised over $1.2 million among the Chinese community and foreign firms. As Alfred Lin has analyzed, this enthusiastic support was pragmatic: "Education was the key to wealth and power, and English education was then considered a special boon."[23]

This cycle of collaboration through education and business gradually made the colonial government and Cantonese elites into uneasy allies in defense of the status quo. Numerous observers, such as American journalist Emily Hahn, contrasted Hong Kong's stodgy atmosphere with freewheeling Shanghai and blamed both snobbish colonials and the "old-fashioned Cantonese" who "have stubbornly resisted change."[24] Hong Kong elites gave to local charities and even mainland revolutionaries but resisted local political reform and adamantly maintained their separation from ordinary Chinese. For example, in 1893 Sun Yat-sen's mentor Ho Kai (何啟) and Wei Yuk (韋玉) opposed the government's proposed expansion of the overcrowded Victoria Gaol. They argued its free food and individual cells would encourage poor Chinese to commit crimes. In 1901 the same two petitioned for a class-segregated Chinese school.[25] Such elites also wielded their influence to suppress labor strikes, root out communists, and oppose anti-imperialist boycotts, instead favoring pragmatic expressions of Chinese nationalism.[26]

Anglo-Cantonese collaboration nonetheless remained strained by colonial racial hierarchies. Into the early 1900s Chinese could not enter the Peak District except as servants or by written invitation. On the Star Ferry, Chinese could not buy first-class seats, while colonial policy barred Chinese from senior civil service positions.[27] In turn, interracial marriage was forbidden, although interracial sex was common and Hong Kong developed a prominent Eurasian community. As Emma Teng has analyzed, Eurasians exemplified the colony's prewar cleavages between racial hierarchies and cosmopolitan collaboration.[28] On one hand, interracial families were perceived as living threats to white prestige and Chinese patriarchy. On the other, Eurasians routinely possessed the bicultural and bilingual skills to serve as compradors. Eurasians thrived in these positions and often accumulated dazzling wealth, such as the famous Sir Robert Ho Tung (何東) and his brothers.[29] By cultivating influence across both the Qing and British Empires, interstitial elites such as the Ho Tung family encapsulate the material benefits that Chinese, Eurasian, and South Asian merchants accrued by collaborating with British imperialism, while carefully maintaining their belonging within multiple states.

Finally, Americans and American interests were a constant but minor presence in prewar Hong Kong. The New York–born merchant Charles Gillespie arrived weeks behind Queen Victoria's troops, while Boston-based firms Russell & Co. and Augustine Heard & Co. became major players in the opium and Gold Rush trades.[30] President Franklin Roosevelt's grandfather Warren Delano, Jr., pursued his fortune in Hong Kong as an employee of Russell & Co. throughout the U.S. Civil War. Like their European counterparts, American merchants also fathered children in Hong Kong. Russell & Co. partner George Tyson was the father of opium merchant Chan Kai-ming (陳啟明), a chairman of Tung Wah and a founding member of the Bank of East Asia.[31] By the First World War, though, only a handful of U.S. corporations maintained offices in the colony, such as American President Lines (APL), First National City Bank (later Citibank), Chase Bank, Standard-Vacuum Oil, and American Express. The most public action yet pursued by this American community was forming the American Club in 1925. It was primarily a social escape from stuffy colonial life, a place "to get together and make the 'eagle scream.'"[32] Unlike British clubs though, the American Club was always open to Chinese members.

In turn, transpacific migration positioned Chinese elites to develop their own connections to the United States. Because most Chinese migrants to California came from the nearby "Four Counties," it was common for Hong Kong merchants to have kin or native-place associates across the Pacific, and those *tongxiang guanxi* undergirded this transpacific highway. In turn, as managers of the *kamshanchong*, Hong Kong merchants dealt regularly with Americans and U.S. immigration policies. For example, the local Chinese Passengers Act (1855) and the U.S. Page Act (1875) both outsourced key oversight responsibilities to Tung Wah's directors.[33] In addition, while British higher education remained dominant, some local elites did choose U.S. schools, as evident in Woo Sing-lim's bilingual text *The Prominent Chinese in Hong Kong* (香港華人名人史略, 1937).[34] After graduating from the Central School, the future tycoon Sir Chow Shouson (周壽臣) went to Phillips Academy, Andover, in 1873 as a student of Yung Wing's Chinese Educational Mission, discussed in the next section.[35] The first members of the Li family of the Bank of East Asia who studied abroad also chose the United States.[36] Transpacific circulations were also formative among the pioneers of Hong Kong's Cantonese opera and cinema industries in the interwar years.[37] In sum, the transpacific migrations that had been vital to Hong Kong's nineteenth-century development made American connections a routine subtext in its British colonial world.

Jiangnan and the American-Returned Students

While Hong Kong elites pursued British-oriented strategies, the new commercial elites of the lower Yangzi began pursuing similar but more diversified strategies. British influence also predominated in Jiangnan, but this region was not a full-blown colony, and there were competing imperial systems jockeying for influence. The Jiangnan bourgeoisie is crucial for this study because at least one hundred thousand would flee to Hong Kong during the communist transition.[38] Later labeled "Shanghainese émigrés," this group came from many counties around Shanghai and included some who identified as Cantonese. The group comprised not only industrial and financial capitalists but also managers, lawyers, accountants, academics, and other professionals who played key roles in the colony's subsequent manufacturing boom. These émigrés would bring enormous investment and different knowledge and social capital to Hong Kong, and, most important, far more robust American experiences and connections.

Jiangnan's rich agriculture had supported flourishing urban centers for centuries, but the late nineteenth century's disruptions of foreign imperialism, internal rebellion, and state reform reshaped regional economies across the Qing Empire.[39] These disruptions heightened Jiangnan's overall commercial advantages but reordered its leading centers. While the Treaty of Nanjing opened Ningbo and Shanghai as treaty ports, it was the Taiping Rebellion that decisively reshaped the region's political economy. The Taiping devastated older trading cities such as Hangzhou, Suzhou, and Yangzhou (technically in Subei) and their established Huizhou merchants.[40] In tandem with the decline of the Grand Canal, commercial opportunities shifted toward the foreign-protected coastal treaty ports, especially Shanghai. Scores of Cantonese merchants such as Xu Run (Tsui Yuen, 徐潤) and Tang Jingxing (Tong King-sing, 唐景星) migrated north to replace the Huizhou merchants and became Shanghai's new leading "comprador-merchants" from the 1860s.[41] The Cantonese compradors' bilingualism and networks brought new connections to global markets, while the treaty ports continued to amass concentrated opportunities, such as privileged access to steamship traffic.[42]

The treaty-port compradors were leaders in gradually divesting from the Confucian examination culture and instead prioritizing self-consciously "modern" educations. This evolution first led compradors toward an early preference for missionary schools. Inextricable from foreign imperialism, Euro-American missionaries of every denomination established a huge educational infrastructure in China after the Treaty of Tianjin (1858). By 1890 there were purportedly some two thousand missionary schools in China, with forty thousand students, including thousands of female students.[43] British and American missionary schools were particularly widespread. Alongside quality English-language instruction, these schools offered access to foreigners and foreign-connected Chinese, while increasing students' chances for the rare opportunity of higher education, as I will discuss.[44] As such, this path held clear attractions for comprador families. Others established their own modern schools, such as Standard Oil's Ningbo-born comprador Ye Chengzhong (葉澄衷), who opened the Chengzhong Middle School in Shanghai in 1889.

As compradors leaned toward missionary schools, the Qing state was beginning to sponsor overseas studies. As part of the Self-Strengthening Movement, the dynasty first established schools of foreign language and military technology in the 1860s. By 1872 the Yale-educated Yung Wing (容閎) convinced the Qing to sponsor the famous Chinese Educational Mission (CEM). Its 120 largely Cantonese students were sent to schools across New England in order to study English, American technology, and military science. The young men were also charged with continuing classical studies and forbidden to adopt American ways, but their and Yung Wing's increasing defiance led to the mission's early recall in 1881.[45] During the 1870s smaller groups were also sent to Germany, England, and France to study military technology and tactics.[46] Yet only after the disastrous First Sino-Japanese War (1894–1895) did the conversation at court turn to "wealth and power" and more extensive educational reforms ensue.[47] In 1901 the Qing began to reform the civil service examinations and plan a new multitier educational system. Yet many men continued to pin their life ambitions on the examinations, and the exams' abolition in 1905 left many devastated and scrambling for alternatives, seeding rippling political consequences.[48]

The abolition of the exams triggered a seismic shift toward foreign models of education that privileged both Jiangnan and the bourgeoisie, particularly in accessing higher education. New data mining by the Lee-Campbell Group at the Hong Kong University of Science and Technology has confirmed a decisive shift in the regional origins of Republican-era tertiary students. In the late Qing, Jiangsu and Zhejiang provinces accounted for 17.8 percent of successful examination candidates. Under the Republic, they accounted for 39 percent of all tertiary students. When combined with Guangdong, this percentage reaches 58 percent.[49] In turn, there was a substantial shift in the class background of students reaching the highest levels of education. The Lee-Campbell Group found that 70 percent of successful late Qing examination candidates came from official or degree-holding families, but 60 percent of Republican-era university students came from merchant or professional families. Together, these radical shifts reflected who had geographic and social access to China's new colleges and universities. Not only were Jiangsu, Zhejiang, and Guangdong the richest provinces in China, but they also held a disproportionate share of its new and best colleges and universities.

At the forefront of Republican-era Chinese higher education were U.S.-linked institutions. American missionaries were particularly active, establishing at least thirteen Christian colleges or universities between the 1860s and the 1920s.[50] Most of these institutions taught in English and six were in Jiangnan, including Shanghai's prestigious St. John's University. In addition, both Tsinghua University in Beijing and Jiaotong University in Shanghai developed through secular American connections. Established in 1911 as a preparatory school for potential Boxer Indemnity scholarship recipients, Tsinghua remained a heavily U.S.-oriented institution even after becoming a university in 1929.[51] Similarly, from its foundation as Nanyang College, Jiaotong University received substantial U.S. aid and developed a heavily U.S.-educated faculty.[52] These institutions' steep tuition and the decline in government scholarships after the fall of the Qing put Jiangnan and Guangdong's new commercial elites in the best position to embrace these new educational pathways.[53]

These pathways led Jiangnan and Guangdong students over the 1910s and 1920s toward increasing connections with the United States. As many as 150,000 Chinese studied abroad before 1949. Around 40,000 graduated, according to the Lee-Campbell Group. Of these, at least 15,000 graduated from Japanese universities, 13,000 from U.S. institutions, and another 13,000 from all European institutions.[54] Japan was the early destination of choice, with as many as 10,000 Chinese students there by 1905, compared with just 200 in the United States.[55] Japanese-educated returnees figured prominently among this era's leading intellectuals, revolutionaries, and educational reformers. Yet as Y. C. Wang first emphasized, Japan's proximity and lower expenses encouraged a high rate of part-time and casual students, such that the vast majority did not graduate, and Chinese public opinion of studying in Japan gradually deteriorated.[56] In contrast, despite being farther and more expensive, the United States became increasingly popular over the 1910s due to the number of U.S.-linked colleges and universities in China, perceptions of U.S. institutions as more open and modern, the rising importance of the English language, Japanese aggression, and active U.S. government recruitment. U.S. Exclusion policies always exempted Chinese students, and both nations collaborated to open educational bridges, from the Boxer Indemnity scholarships (1908) to the China Institute in America (1926). With their comparative wealth and concentration of U.S.-backed institutions, Jiangsu, Zhejiang, and Guangdong provinces sent most of these students. Between 1909 and 1945, in any given year 57 to 82 percent of Chinese students in the United States came from just these three provinces. When we include where students attended secondary school, over half of Chinese students in the United States identified Jiangsu as their native province or where they attended secondary school.[57] Even more surprising, the Lee-Campbell Group found that roughly 40 percent of Republican-era students in the United States previously attended just fourteen schools in China.[58] Tsinghua and Jiaotong were the first and fourth largest senders, while another eight were American missionary institutions.

These patterns intersected to produce a growing concentration of U.S.-educated elites in the lower Yangzi who gradually achieved substantial influence in at least three key professional areas. The phrase "American-returned students" appears with increasing frequency in the English-language press from the late 1910s, while the Chinese press used terms such as *liumei xuesheng* (留美學生). American Returned Students' Clubs and American University Clubs appeared in many major cities, and one survey in 1920 counted 1,700 returnees with U.S. degrees, compared to 400 from Britain.[59] Some in the reading public even demanded that American-returned students use these connections to defend China.[60] Initial surveys found that most returnees from the United States became teachers, engineers, or civil servants, but this cohort eventually came to dominate senior Chinese academia and the senior ranks of the Nationalist government.[61] The Lee-Campbell Group has found that a foreign degree was virtually required to reach senior academia before 1949, with 80 percent of full professors reporting their highest degree coming from overseas, and 40 percent of all full professors receiving that degree in the United States.[62] Under the Nationalists, a similar situation developed for senior government positions. Alongside relocating the capital to the Jiangnan city of Nanjing in 1927, the new regime also gradually became dependent on U.S. aid in the Great Depression. It subsequently showed a marked preference for filling top positions with American-returned students. One study found that by 1939 an "astonishing" 71 percent of Nationalist officials had studied abroad, of whom 36 percent had gone to the United States.[63] The longtime director of the China Institute in America testified that the government actively sought "American-trained men" to "put in positions of importance, but there were not enough American-returned students to meet the demand."[64]

A third concentration developed at the juncture of the modern banking and textile industries in greater Shanghai and Tianjin. By 1937 more than half of China's factories were in greater Shanghai, followed by Tianjin and the Wuhan tri-cities.[65] While exaggerated by the Japanese seizure of Manchuria in 1931, this hyperconcentration reflected these two cities' layered advantages: plentiful labor, rail and steam networks, foreign legal protections, and concentrations of the modern Chinese-capitalized banks that rose after the Qing's abdication. There was a financial symbiosis between the textile and modern banking sectors in the 1910s and 1920s. In what Marie-Claire Bergère termed the first "golden age" of Chinese capitalism, both sectors were expanding rapidly amid the First World War's elimination of European competitors and patriotic boycotts against Japanese and British imperialism.[66] In turn, as Tomoko Shiroyama has emphasized, cotton spinning is a highly competitive global industry that incentivizes economies of scale. As a result, the Jiangnan textile mills rapidly became dependent on banks for unsecured credit to purchase cotton, low-cost loans borrowed against fixed assets to fund further expansion, and reliable foreign exchange.[67] This deep interlinkage was often undergirded by native-place guanxi between industrialists and bankers. For example, scholars have long noted that these modern banks were predominantly led by men from Jiangsu and Zhejiang who used native-place ties to secure investment and compose their boards.[68] The same held true for the textile industrialists. Yet Brett Sheehan has cautioned against overstressing native place, pointing out that different "blocs" of bankers routinely cooperated across supralocal networks as self-conscious professionals and cosmopolitans.[69] Educational networks were one such path to supralocal cooperation. The bond among classmates or *tongxue* (同學) is important across Sinophone cultures, and American missionary and/or U.S. higher educational backgrounds feature prominently among the era's leading bankers.

"K. P." Chen Guangfu (陳光甫) exemplifies the American-returned students who spearheaded the entwined development of Jiangnan's banking and textile industries. The future founder of the Shanghai Commercial and Savings Bank (SCSB), Chen was born into a Jiangsu merchant family, but his father moved the family to Hankou when he found work in a customs brokerage firm. Chen had his own apprenticeship at the firm while studying English at night. He then worked for Hankou's British-run postal service and later claimed to model the SCSB's management practices after the disciplined and efficient British.[70] He learned banking in the United States, however. According to a biography penned by his longtime friend, native-place associate, and banking colleague Zhang Jia'ao (張嘉璈), Chen also studied bookkeeping at a local commercial college and began working for the Chinese Maritime Customs Service in Hankou but resigned because of British mistreatment. He then moved to the Hanyang Iron Works, where comprador Jing Weixing (景維行) recognized his talents. Jing both arranged Chen's marriage to his daughter and lobbied Huguang governor-general Duanfang (端方) to add Chen to Hubei's delegation to the St. Louis World's Fair in 1904.[71] The subsequent journey was transformative for Chen. In St. Louis he introduced himself to the revolutionary Sun Yat-sen (孫中山) and became "bosom friends" with future finance minister Kong Xiangxi (孔祥熙). Chen decided to stay and study, first taking bookkeeping, typing, and correspondence classes in St. Louis. He wrote to the Chinese Embassy in Washington for financial aid and was granted US$100 a month by Ambassador Liang Cheng (梁誠), a CEM alumnus who was then negotiating the return of the Boxer Indemnity. After trying out Simpson College and Wesleyan, Chen settled on the University of Pennsylvania's Wharton School, where he spent three years studying economics, commerce, and the U.S. banking system.[72] After graduation in 1909 he worked in an American bank for a year before returning to China, where he first served as secretary to the governor of Jiangsu, then worked in a traditional bank, and finally revolutionized operations at the Jiangsu Provincial Bank. He also became a consultant to the new Bank of China, where he befriended Zhang Jia'ao, himself a graduate of Japan's Keio University.[73]

Together, these experiences and networks enabled Chen to found the SCSB and make it a success. In 1915 he secured the necessary backing for the bank through Zhang and the Zhejiang Industrial Bank's Li Ming (李銘), a graduate of an American missionary school in Hangzhou and the Yamaguchi Commercial College. He then implemented British management and American banking practices, while hiring German banker Gustav Baerwald to guide foreign exchange activity and the older Tang Yuanzhan ("Y. C." Tong Yuen-cham, 唐元湛) as his managing director. Tang was a Guangdong native and another CEM alumnus who had spent thirty years in the Telegraph Administration, as well as serving as a Rotary Club officer and board member at Fudan College.[74] Chen chose yet another American-returned student as his submanager, hiring St. John's and Yale graduate Zhu Chengzhang ("S. C." Chu, 朱成章) in 1917.[75] Chen thus drew on many networks and resources to launch the SCSB but demonstrated the value he set on his American college and banking experiences by developing a US$2 million fund to sponsor SCSB staff for advanced training in the United States. In turn, this U.S.-trained senior staff helped the SCSB to expand its international branches so that by the mid-1920s it was both China's leading conduit of foreign exchange and the favored lender to Shanghai's industrialists.[76]

As we will see repeatedly throughout this study, Chen became a key early node at the heart of the expanding network of U.S.-educated bankers, industrialists, and academics centered in Shanghai. A high proportion of the textile industrialists were also graduates of American missionary schools and/or U.S. higher education, such as P. Y. Tang, Mu Xiangyue (穆湘玥), Xue Shouxuan (薛寿萱), and Song Feiqing (宋棐卿). Many first met in the United States through organizations such as the YMCA-backed Chinese Students' Christian Association in North America (1909), while after return they used their American educations to build useful business relationships through shared contacts, their ability to speak English, and their knowledge of foreign business practices such as the limited liability company.[77] By 1919 Shanghai's press noted these interconnections, with multiple papers attributing the "sensational development" of the cotton industry to returned students and their access to capital: "Most of the growth is in the hands of American returned students who are trying their best to persuade the wealthy men to take interest in the industry."[78] In turn, some industrialists such as the Kwoks (Guo) of Wing On tapped into these networks by selecting U.S.-educated managers, not native-place associates.[79] Returnees from the United States were also social outside business, Chen, Mu, and Bian Baimei (卞白眉) all serving as officers in American Returned Students' clubs. In 1924 Shanghai's American Returned Students' Club even moved its meetings into the Cotton Goods Exchange, as Mu Xiangyue was leading both organizations.[80] Transpacific educational networks thus seem to have mirrored native-place guanxi in creating clusters of interlinked associates and overlapping organizations, albeit on a much smaller scale.[81]

Thus by the Nanjing Decade (1927–1937) an elite network of interconnected American-returned students was becoming concentrated in both Jiangnan and key professional clusters. As we will see throughout this study, this cohort suffered from the Nationalist government's increasing cronyism but benefited from its dependence on U.S. aid over the Great

Depression and Second World War, positioning these American-returned students to use their transpacific networks to profit from this diplomatic relationship. Such activities and connections would also increase their incentives to flee when China's civil war turned.

The Painful Choice

Despite prevailing over Japan in August 1945, China saw prolonged tremendous human suffering across the nation with the resumption of the civil war in June 1946 and the gradual collapse of the Nationalist regime. Together these wars killed more than thirty million people and dislocated unfathomable numbers, with as many as fifty million refugees by 1948.[82] Thus the flight of roughly 700,000 people to Hong Kong during the communist transition was a small part of a vast human uprooting. Yet this relocation forever changed Hong Kong, and thus capitalism itself. While ordinary migrants' motivations have remained difficult to characterize, previous scholars have analyzed the considerations that informed elite capitalists' decisions to stay or flee, from each figure's age and familial obligations to their relationship to Chinese nationalism and the nature of their business.[83] Magnates of heavy industry such as the Tianjin chemicals industrialist Li Zhuchen (李燭塵) were unlikely to leave, while bankers and light industrialists were much more inclined to do so.[84] Others have noted that many rehearsed escape during the war, with around seven hundred Shanghai factories relocating to neutral Hong Kong between 1937 and 1940.[85] Two less noted factors include industrialists' religion and education. For deducible reasons, Christians and those with British or American educations were more likely to flee, while fewer Japanese-returned students seem to have fled to Hong Kong, perhaps because of their higher rates of military and government service.[86] For capitalists, Hong Kong was the preferred destination over Taiwan because it was a free port of entry with minimal trade or financial controls. By mid-1946 the colony's newspapers were already chattering about "refugee businessmen from Shanghai" and documenting the transfer of companies, capital, and children.[87] K. P. Chen grumbled in his diary in April 1948 that the textile industrialists were the highest flight risks. Instead of supporting the government, "they would rather spend [their capital] in purchasing spindles and factory sites in Hongkong. . . . Mentally, they prefer to have nothing to do with the Government; they want to go ahead and build their own empire."[88]

The Tang family that opened this chapter epitomizes the U.S.-oriented textile industrialists who fled. Previous scholars have analyzed Wuxi's industrial boom of the 1910s and 1920s, in which the Tangs were leaders.[89] Born in 1898, P. Y. Tang grew up in Wuxi as the son of cloth merchant Tang Baoqian (唐保謙), who had little formal education but studied in a traditional Chinese bank and then strategically invested in industrial operations that catered to life's basic needs: food, clothing, housing, and transport.[90] These included the Qingfeng textile mill, the Jiufeng flour mill, the Jinfeng silk filature, the Runfeng vegetable oil plant, the Yiyuan rice mill, and the Linong brick factory.[91] P. Y. first studied at St. John's in Shanghai and then proceeded to the U.S.-endowed Tsinghua in Beijing (figure 1.2). He received a Boxer Indemnity scholarship in 1920 and studied at the Lowell Textile School before transferring to MIT. He graduated in 1923 with a degree in management and returned to Wuxi after the death of his older brother. Despite the intermittent Jiangsu–Zhejiang wars, he participated in the "golden age" by expanding the Qingfeng and Jiufeng mills and profitably applying his American education. He reorganized the factories and implemented American management techniques, such as training professional textile engineers and shifting worker recruitment from guanxi networks to skills-based assessments. Tang also invested in new industries, including the Jiangnan cement plant in Shanghai and later the Chrysler car agency for China.[92] He was also a Wuxi booster, serving as president of its Rotary Club and penning pieces in Shanghai's press that touted the city as "the Pittsburg of China."[93]

Similarly to K. P. Chen, Tang demonstrated the value that he attached to his American education through his marriage and children's education. After he returned, his first wife tragically died in childbirth. Tang then remarried into a Cantonese Christian family that similarly prized international education. His second wife, Kinmay, had studied in England but returned to teach at Shanghai's prestigious McTyeire School, run by American Southern Methodists (figure 1.3). Her father, Wen Bingzhong (Wan Bing-tsung, 温秉忠), was another CEM alumnus and by 1924 was the superintendent of customs in Suzhou. Kinmay's mother hailed from the devoutly Methodist Ni family (倪), and Kinmay's famous Song first cousins also studied at the McTyeire School and then in the United States. Before achieving international fame, the three Song sisters attended

Figure 1.2 A young P. Y. Tang, likely as a Tsinghua student. Courtesy of the Tang family.

Figure 1.3 A young Kinmay Tang. Courtesy of the Tang family.

school in Georgia and at Wellesley, while their brother "T. V." Song Ziwen (宋子文) attended St. John's and Harvard. And for their own children, P. Y. and Kinmay Tang first selected an American missionary school in Wuxi affiliated with St. John's.[94] Tang thus married into the core of the U.S.-oriented Nationalist elite, and this extended family consistently combined American missionary schools, U.S. and British higher education, and capitalist industrial development over generations. They cemented these new generative patterns through marriages into similar families and invested in the children's bilingualism and biculturalism from infancy. After higher education in primarily the United States, each generation returned to exploit the knowledge, networks, and access that they gained.[95] In turn, while Jack Tang later testified that "we stayed away from" the Song family because his father was "too proud to want to make use of that connection," that assertion is suspect. For one, P. Y. Tang was the only industrialist invited onto the prestigious Academia Sinica's new Advisory Council in 1935.[96]

After weathering the war in the French Concession, the Tangs utilized their financial and social capital to negotiate the dislocations of the communist transition. While many industrialists fled to Hong Kong during this upheaval, their businesses often did not survive transplantation. Success favored those who abandoned ship in advance, did not return, and attached themselves firmly to the United States. For example, previous scholars have focused on the Rong family, another Wuxi clan and Republican China's largest textile industrialists.[97] The Rong group was a behemoth, but its size hindered relocation. One branch chose to remain in the PRC, while other family members scattered across the world in the 1940s. Two family members came to Hong Kong in 1947 and launched the Nanyang Cotton Mill but did not recover a similar preeminence. The family would play a revived role in the Reform era though, as will be discussed in chapter 7.[98] In another example, by 1947 the Northwestern graduate Song Feiqing was also rerouting cash and machinery to Hong Kong and his children to the United States, but he stayed in Tianjin and tried to manage his mills under communist rule. When this proved untenable, he and his remaining family fled to the colony in 1950. His brief time in the PRC tainted him politically though, forcing him to retire and preventing U.S. immigration. They migrated instead to Argentina, where Song died in 1955 a broken man.[99]

In contrast, the Tang family's methodical evacuation strategy reflected a clear-eyed reading of shifting state power and capitalized heavily on their accumulated transpacific ties. When peace came in August 1945, P. Y. Tang recognized China's instability and began preparing exit strategies. He bought real estate in Taiwan in 1946 and the next year began rerouting machinery and staff to Hong Kong.[100] Simultaneously, his brother Tang Yeh-chu and nephew "H. C." Tang Xiangqian (唐翔千)—a graduate of Manchester University and the University of Illinois—also began relocating to Hong Kong.[101] P. Y. and Kinmay also positioned their children as they did their business interests. Jack had entered Jiaotong University in 1944, where he met his future wife Madeleine Huang Yue-mei, a St. John's student. Jack's attendance at Jiaotong was simply "transitional" though. His father demanded his degree be American, too. In May 1946 the nineteen-year-old went to the United States, beginning at Brown and transferring to his father's alma mater, MIT. The intrepid Kinmay then took all the other children two-by-two to the United States over 1947 and 1948. Jack graduated from MIT in 1949 and proceeded to Harvard Business School (HBS). As his father restarted operations in Hong Kong, Jack and Madeleine married and had three children in Boston (figure 1.4).[102] After a bout with tuberculosis, Jack graduated from HBS in 1953 and spent two years working for Mobil in New York, specifically because it was their energy supplier in Hong Kong. Both Jack and Madeleine received permanent residence as "displaced persons" in 1953, while Jack naturalized as a U.S. citizen in 1955.[103] And while all his siblings finished college and settled in the United States, Jack returned to Hong Kong in May 1955 as the junior partner in his father's reborn business, South Sea Textiles (南海紡織有限公司).[104] As I will explore in chapter 5, these intangible assets were crucial to South Sea's emergence by 1970 as the colony's largest manufacturer.[105]

The family of industrialist Liu Hongsheng (劉鴻生) offers a contrastive example of Jiangnan elites who pursued similar strategies but ultimately remained in the PRC. As analyzed by Sherman Cochran and Andrew Hsieh, between 1929 and 1937 Liu cultivated a mixed portfolio of international social capitals by sending his children to a layered set of British, Japanese, and American educational institutions. Liu had been born in Ningbo and came to Shanghai to attend St. John's Middle School and St. John's University. This American missionary education left him "in awe of U.S. power."[106] His subsequent bilingualism led to his first job in 1906 as an interpreter for the British police in Shanghai's International Settlement. In 1907 he married Ye Chengzhong's daughter, and in 1909

Figure 1.4 Jack and Madeleine Tang with children Martin and Nadine, Arlington, Massachusetts, 1951. Courtesy of the Tang family.

the head of Shanghai's Association of Ningbo Sojourners placed him into a job with the British-owned Kailuan Mining Administration, illustrating native-place guanxi at work.[107] As with P. Y. Tang, the First World War brought a breakthrough by enabling him to become Kailuan's chief comprador, and he then invested in a spate of industrial ventures, such as match and briquette factories, a cement plant, and a woolen mill.[108] While relying on native-place guanxi to staff his factories and market their production, Liu pursued similar educational strategies to the Tangs for his children, sending all eleven to the St. John's schools followed by foreign colleges and universities that would position each child to acquire useful knowledge, contact networks, and future markets.[109] Liu first pushed his three most promising sons to study at Cambridge, but over the 1930s his empire evolved and he now favored the industrial powerhouses of Japan and the United States. The first, fifth, and eighth sons studied at prestigious U.S. schools such as HBS, Penn's Wharton School, and MIT, as well as interning in the American coal industry and at Westinghouse. The sixth and sevenths sons studied in Japan, and the sixth son interned at the Mitsui Trading Company, Japan's biggest international corporation. The three Liu daughters studied in succession in Japan, England, and the United States. The Liu children often rebelled and confronted grave challenges overseas, but their parents continued to dispatch them and made each promise to return to Shanghai, to work in the family business, and not to marry foreigners. These guidelines governed the family's fate.

After the Japanese invasion the Lius at first cultivated both Japanese and American social capital, but after 1945 they became firmly U.S.-oriented. In 1937 Liu first went to Hong Kong and then Chongqing at the invitation of Chiang Kai-shek. There he and his younger sons worked with the Nationalists to launch a spate of mills and factories, but his elder sons remained in Shanghai and collaborated with the government of Wang Jingwei (汪精衛). As U.S. aid became crucial to China's war effort, Liu urged his fourth son "to socialize with young American intelligence officers in the U.S. Office of Strategic Services" and to join Chongqing's Masonic Lodge. With the Allied victory, however, the appeal of Japanese social capital collapsed, and those who bet on it paid dearly. The Liu family now tried to attach itself solely to the Nationalists and the United States. They wielded these connections to bury charges of wartime treason and secure lucrative positions in China's U.S.-backed reconstruction effort through the new United Nations Relief and Rehabilitation Administration (UNRRA) and the China National Relief and Rehabilitation Administration (CNRRA). They "set out to gain the confidence of their American supervisors" and then "took advantage of their positions . . . to rehabilitate their family's businesses."[110] Through the CNRRA and UNRRA—which spent more money in China than anywhere else—they directed mountains of aid to the family's wharves and warehouses, siphoning "handsome profits" and new machinery.[111] Such profiteering from U.S. aid even became political fodder, as K. P. Chen recorded in June 1948. In the Legislative Yuan, a representative "got up and attacked the American-returned students, citing the CNRRA as an example," and claimed they "brought into the organization extravagant habits."[112] Indeed, Liu reinvested in such manifestly profitable American connections by sending his sixth and eighth sons back to the United States.[113]

With the turn in the Chinese civil war, Liu considered multiple options. Like Song Feiqing and P. Y. Tang, he invested in Taiwan in 1947 and sent two sons to manage these assets. Also like Tang, his faith in the Nationalists soured as hyperinflation set in and their policies turned increasingly predatory.[114] Liu subsequently ruled out Taiwan and unsuccessfully urged his sons to return. When communist forces reached Shanghai in May 1949, he and several associates again fled to Hong Kong. He explored business opportunities for six months and evaluated reports from Shanghai. His sons were impressed by the new PRC and pleaded for him to return. Like shipping baron Lu Zuofu (卢作孚), Liu also received personal reassurances from Zhou Enlai.[115] After a new venture in Hong Kong failed, the sixty-one-year-old decided to return. Over the next few years, the former tycoon underwent a seemingly genuine socialist conversion. Yet in 1952 he and his sons were attacked during the Five Antis Campaign and reconsidered flight to Hong Kong. It was too late. In early 1956 the family's remaining assets were nationalized, and Liu passed away on October 1. With two sons in Taiwan, five other Liu children trickled out to Hong Kong and the United States during the 1960s and 1970s, while three remained and suffered in the Cultural Revolution. None of the children revived the family business.

The Tang and Liu families provide snapshots of the competing interests that governed the decisions of Jiangnan's elite capitalists, but by late 1948 hundreds of thousands were in flight. When the last Nationalist stronghold in the Northeast fell in October, British and U.S. authorities urged their citizens to evacuate.[116] Air passage out of Beijing and Shanghai then became jammed, while the U.S.-backed Civil Air Transport (CAT) evacuated thousands from Shenyang and Jinan.[117] Two Hong Kong papers blamed the departure of U.S. citizens for spreading rippling "dismay" among foreign-connected Chinese.[118] With air and rail passage booked, tens of thousands turned to ships. Throughout November and December 1948, the *SCMP* documented the diverse groups sailing aboard U.S. Navy and commercial vessels from Tianjin and Shanghai. By January 1949 the Associated Press reported Shanghai's international communities had dwindled "to less than 2,000 Americans, and probably slightly more British."[119] While one Hong Kong headline blared that Shanghai residents were "fleeing for refuge in droves" as the "fires of war" approached, another rightly emphasized: "The bulk of the population has no choice but to remain and face whatever the future holds in store."[120]

As hyperinflation erased lifetimes worth of savings and the urban social order disintegrated, aspiring travelers turned desperate, and their opportunities to extract durable assets shrank even further. Ticket prices were astronomical, and most people could only take what they could carry. Even then, it was illegal to remove assets such as gold from the country, and attempted smuggling led to many arrests. Nonetheless, there was wild press speculation about the capital in flight. Economist Edward Szczepanik later estimated that HK$7.1 billion reached Hong Kong from abroad between 1947 and 1955—today, at least US$12.6 billion.[121] Within this torrent of capital, however, many saw U.S. connections. Shanghai's U.S.-educated mayor, "K. C." Wu Guozhen (吳國楨), suddenly left for medical treatment in the United States, while the Song family was caught dispatching planes full of U.S. dollars.[122] A *Wen Wei Po* cartoon in November 1948 succinctly articulates such perceptions of American connections undergirding this wealth transfer. Entitled "Shanghai's Great Turmoil" (figure 1.5), the cartoon depicts windowless buildings shaking as chaos reigns. A hungry mob with rice bowls aloft tears through the streets. A shootout grips the lower right, while a figure on the left dives off a rooftop. A pipe-smoking bank surveys the scene with the sign "礼義廉恥" (*li yi lian chi*) falling off its façade. Meaning ritual, rightness, integrity, and a sense of shame, this *chengyu* had been the official slogan of the 1930s New Life Movement. Now, the fourth character, meaning "shame," has poignantly fallen off. Others hang from windows with bags outstretched, reaching for the exiting U.S. warplane, piloted by a Popeye lookalike. And behind the plane stream U.S. officers and Chinese elites clinging to each other, bags, and gleaming treasure.

Over the late Qing and Republican eras, the Jiangnan bourgeoisie built layered educational and business ties to the world's leading empires. These ties were a strategic response to foreign imperialism and domestic instability, while accelerating the industrial development of greater Shanghai and other treaty ports. U.S. ties had become increasingly useful, but only the destruction of the Japanese Empire, the decline of the British Empire, and the turn in the Chinese civil war cemented American social capital's preeminence. Some, such as the Tangs, put all their chips on it. Others, such as the Lius, divided their efforts or held back. These were painful choices in which families were wrenched apart. As K. P. Chen wrote when

Figure 1.5 "上海大騒動" or "Shanghai's Great Turmoil," *Wen Wei Po*, November 12, 1948, 1.

considering flight in January 1949: "In the event of a Communist victory and I follow my original plan to get out of here, I may be regarded as one of Chiang's [Kai-shek] men and may never be allowed to come back again. . . . I must consider this point very carefully before making a decision."[123] He and his wife evacuated to Hong Kong on April 25, 1949, as he informed his attorney on Wall Street.[124]

Hong Kong's First Reorientations

The Second World War cracked the racial and economic systems of Britain's Asian empire. Under a brutal Japanese occupation, Hong Kong's population declined by deaths and forced removals from 1.4 million to about 400,000 people. British troops liberated the colony in August 1945, but only with U.S. blessing and aid.[125] Throughout late 1945 and 1946 the colony was awash in British and American troops. Resident "Fan Kwai" (Foreign Devil) remarked facetiously in the *SCMP*: "Is this Colony at present British, Chinese or American?"[126] While the U.S. Navy had called at Hong Kong for decades, American GIs were a less familiar presence and elicited considerable press coverage throughout 1946. This U.S. military presence made tangible the war's shifts in state power, although some Britons hoped to revive "Britain in China."[127] Traffic in Shanghai even switched from the British left side to the American right side on January 1, 1946, while in Hong Kong the American Club's reopening in July 1948 featured unprecedented guests: both the new governor, Sir Alexander Grantham, and his American-born wife, Maureen.[128]

Hong Kong's trade networks revived quickly, buttressed by new links to the emergent U.S.-led order. APL renewed its service to California in spring 1946 through U.S. government assistance, cheaply acquiring two decommissioned U.S. Navy transports.[129] In August Pan-American Airways received authorization to launch regular service between Shanghai, Hong Kong, and Calcutta, making it "the first single airline to fly round the world."[130] In late 1947 Globe Wireless opened the first radio-cable service between Hong Kong and the United States via Manila, while in September 1948 the U.S. government initiated the first air parcel delivery service between the United States and the colony.[131] Simultaneously, discharged American servicemen were exploring prospects in the colony, including the Texan Roy Farrell, who in 1946 founded what would become Cathay Pacific.[132] While steam and telegraph networks had furnished game-changing connections to Europe and North America in the 1860s, this infrastructure positioned Hong Kong for Cold War opportunities.

Simultaneously, the restored colonial regime began lowering previous barriers to outside investment in 1948 and 1949. At the urging of the émigré industrialists, the regime first removed restrictions that prohibited women and children from working night shifts, allowing for their increased exploitation. K. P. Chen praised these shifts in his diary while lamenting Shanghai's disintegration: "It is now possible for factories to go on three shifts a day meaning a 24-working-hour basis, as it was not in the old days. It is also possible to use child labor in Hongkong . . . under the good name of apprenticeship."[133] Previous imperial policies had also stymied non-British investment in order to protect the Sterling Area and Imperial Preference. Those too now receded as Imperial Preference was subsumed within the General Agreement on Trade and Tariffs (GATT) from 1947. One cumbersome regulation had required all foreign companies to apply to the Governor-in-Council for consent to acquire any "immovable property," even for something as minor as renting an auto shop.[134] In early 1949 the regime amended these regulations and permitted foreign corporations to acquire immovable property without government consent, bringing Hong Kong law "into line with that now existing in the United Kingdom."[135] Soon after, the Imports and Exports Department was renamed the Department of Commerce and Industry, and officials began offering below market-rate leases to industrial ventures. These combined shifts made the colony much more attractive to global capital, particularly to Jiangnan industrialists in flight.[136]

Rising U.S. power and weakening British systems first enabled those with U.S. ties to carve new social opportunities on the ground. The mixed-race union of the Cantonese heiress Ansie Lee and the American banker Henry Sperry encapsulates these possibilities, as well as offering another lens into the transplantation of Jiangnan's U.S.-oriented bankers and industrialists. Ansie Lee was the youngest child of tycoon Lee Hysan (利希慎), an opium merchant and real estate developer who was famously assassinated in 1928.[137] Born in the Kingdom of Hawai'i in 1881, Lee Hysan had returned to Hong Kong and risen through the colony's traditional pathways: British schools, the opium trade, shipping, and real estate. He secured traditional summits of social power such as chairing the Tung Wah board and invested in the SCSB, which led to a close relationship between K. P. Chen and the Lee family.[138] He also prioritized British education for his children. Born in 1914, Ansie attended boarding schools in England and later studied Mandarin in Beijing, where she befriended the daughters of the U.S. military attaché, Joseph Stilwell. Yet in Hong Kong British-educated Chinese elites still confronted colonial hierarchies, such as in 1925 when Ansie's brother Richard was denied membership in the segregated Jockey Club.[139] White supremacy defined colonialism, and neither money nor education could surmount such discriminations until the war transformed this context and the renamed Ansie Lee Sperry leveraged American social capital to break through.

Ansie Lee met Henry Sperry when they were both Japanese prisoners in the Los Baños internment camp near Manila. Ansie had been sailing off the Philippines with Chiang Kai-shek's Australian aide W. H. Donald when the Pacific War broke out.[140] "Hank" had been working for First National City Bank in Asia since 1930, staffing its operations in Kobe, Osaka, Shanghai, Hankou, and Manila.[141] Since he was a U.S. citizen and she was a British subject, the Japanese imprisoned them both. Despite nearly starving, they fell in love. When U.S. forces liberated the camp in

February 1945, Hong Kong was still occupied, so Ansie was "repatriated" to the United States, "a country I had never set foot in before!" Her siblings wired her money through the Chinese consulate in San Francisco, and she spent the next year studying at Berkeley and Columbia, as well as visiting friends, such as the Stilwells and Song Ailing (宋靄齡) in New York.[142] Hank and Ansie also prepared to be married.

Unlike generations before them, Lee and Sperry's mixed-race union did not limit their prospects but instead demonstrated the transfer of international power from Britain to the United States and the ensuing U.S. renovation of transpacific racial codes. As noted, before the Second World War interracial marriages were forbidden in Hong Kong. Figures who violated this convention had faced social death into the 1930s.[143] While sexual relations between American GIs and Chinese women became a source of great tension in wartime Sino-U.S. relations, marriages gained increasing acceptance in the late 1940s if the husband was a white American.[144] Due to their mutual prominence, this particular match piqued the attention of U.S. and Nationalist authorities. In San Francisco, the couple socialized with one of First National's chief legal counsels. Ansie recalled that these meetings allowed the lawyer to "vouch for me when the bank officials were later determining whether I was 'suitable material' for one of their officers." This elitist investigation worked both ways. In New York, when Sperry informed bank chairman Gordon Rentschler of his engagement, Rentschler replied: "'Yes, I know.' Someone in Washington had asked who Henry Sperry was!" Ansie's brother Harold was working for the Chinese ambassador in London, Guo Taiqi (郭泰祺), a 1911 graduate of the University of Pennsylvania. When Guo came to the United States in 1946 for the founding of the United Nations, he directed the Chinese Embassy to enquire with First National about Sperry.[145] Both sides consented that it was, indeed, appropriate. The wartime alliance, the repeal of Chinese Exclusion in 1943, U.S. imperial expansion into Asia, and their mutual social capital all coalesced to sanction this union.

The couple's wedding was thus a private encapsulation of the Sino-American alliance and represented the vanguard in a broader reworking of class and racial hierarchies in the postwar U.S.-led Pacific. Henry Sperry returned to Shanghai in January 1946 to reestablish First National. While the bank's regional operations were now "largely determined by the demands of the American military," the Shanghai branch looked to expand its middle-class clientele by waiving its prewar requirements that clients be introduced by an account holder and sign in English.[146] Ansie returned in June, and they were married in July 1946 at an Anglican church (figure 1.6). K. P. Chen stood in for Ansie's father, while First National's manager Red Reed hosted the reception. And together the Sperrys helped integrate the two states' leading financiers and diplomats, as exemplified by one dinner party in 1948 hosted by a British–American Tobacco executive. The other guests included the Sperrys, several of Ansie's siblings, the U.S. consul, Song Qingling (宋慶齡), and L. K. Little, the American head of the Chinese Maritime Customs Service.[147] These integrative possibilities were open to nonelites, however. Amendments to the War Brides Act in 1946 and 1947 first permitted nonquota entry for Asian war brides and thereby sanctioned mixed-race marriages before U.S. courts struck down antimiscegenation laws.[148] In Hong Kong, weddings soared between Chinese women and U.S. servicemen of both European and Chinese descent, with flights even chartered to transport them.[149]

Figure 1.6 The wedding of Henry M. Sperry and Ansie Lee, Shanghai, July 1946. Courtesy of Victoria Sperry Merchant.

A record 3,600 Chinese nationals were admitted to the United States in 1948.[150] As Naoko Shibusawa has argued, Cold War tensions led mainstream Americans to rapidly reinterpret allied Asian peoples as feminine and childlike in order to naturalize U.S. leadership.[151] These imperial logics and the expanding U.S. military presence in Asia gradually endorsed interracial marriages between Euro-American males and Asian females.

Before fleeing Shanghai in 1949, Ansie used these shifts to successfully apply for naturalization as a U.S. citizen, and this passport positioned her to pioneer kuashang strategies. Once in Hong Kong, she wielded her new American social capital to shatter colonial glass ceilings. The Sperrys settled into a home on the Peak but found their union "was absolutely unheard of."[152] Yet the very same colonial clubs that previously denied her brothers no longer dared to deny her membership as an American. Ansie Lee Sperry thus became the first Chinese member of the Royal Hong Kong Yacht Club, the Hong Kong Club, and the Shek O Golf Club. "I was rather glad to be a wedge," Ansie said, "although the British really liked Hank's conservative ways."[153] It did not hurt that she spoke with a posh British accent, but the breakthrough depended on her new U.S. connection. While British hongs such as Jardine's and Swire's purportedly continued to forbid interracial marriage among their employees into the 1970s, the biracial Sperrys became the face of First National to major clients in Hong Kong and across the region (figure 1.7).[154]

First National tasked the Sperrys to remain in Hong Kong in 1949 because Hank's top Shanghai clients, the textile industrialists, had also relocated. In contrast to the SCSB or the Hongkong and Shanghai Bank, which had longstanding relationships with these clients, First National became a player in Shanghai's industrial lending only by serving as a conduit for postwar American aid. After the war the Shanghainese spinners urgently needed new spindles and a steady supply of raw cotton. Both goods came primarily through U.S. and UN aid and financing from First National.[155] A former bank staff member testified: "The Americans and Chinese had just signed an agreement to import cotton. We needed to import large amounts of cotton as there was strong demand for clothing among Chinese people after the war. . . . Business was excellent and in 1946 and 1947, we met a lot of the owners of Chinese spinning factories."[156] Amid hyperinflation, U.S. aid became so imperative that by March 1948 the Central Bank of China was still negotiating with First National to use its last gold reserves in New York as collateral to finance

Figure 1.7 Henry Sperry, Ansie Lee Sperry, and Jacqueline Kathe at the opening of Citibank's Taipei branch, 1965. Courtesy of Victoria Sperry Merchant.

US$10 million of American cotton imports.[157] By April 1949 K. P. Chen wrote bluntly in his diary: "Without American aid, the Shanghai business, including our own Bank, would have gone broke long time ago [*sic*]."[158] While postwar U.S. aid thus seeded a new financial relationship between Chinese industrialists and a multinational American bank, through Chen and the Sperrys we see how elite personal connections undergirded the transplantation of this relationship from Shanghai to Hong Kong. And the Lee family was actually embedded across several banks. With Sperry heading First National, Chen appointed Ansie's brothers Richard and Harold as the SCSB's Hong Kong branch managers, while their cousin "Q. W." Lee Quo-wei (利國偉) was then a rising executive at the Hang Seng Bank.[159] Chen viewed the Lee family's networks as so important that, even after discovering that the brothers had violated bank policies by availing themselves of a large loan, the normally earnest Chen let the incident go, explicitly due to their social standing.

After relocating, the émigré industrialists at first began to revive their operations within Hong Kong's traditional Southeast Asian and British imperial trading networks. In late March 1949 Chen reviewed the SCSB's Hong Kong branch and found it was financing imports of HK$4.59 million (US$1.1 million) of raw cotton, by far its largest overseas purchasing activity.[160] The bank was also issuing other short-term loans to many émigré industrialists, often with only the cotton itself as collateral. As a longstanding client from Shanghai, P. Y. Tang and South Sea already had an "overdraft" of HK$335,000.[161] Yet Chen also recorded that the vast majority of yarn and textile exports being financed by the Hong Kong branch were bound for regional or Commonwealth markets, such as Bangkok, Singapore, Chittagong, Dar-es-Salaam, and Mombasa.[162] In Chen's review, not one shipment was headed to the world's largest market, the United States.

Within ten years, however, the United States would transform into the dominant export market for Hong Kong textiles, and that reorientation began through the Korean War.[163] Britain had recognized the PRC in January 1950 in an effort to maintain existing commercial links, but a continued Nationalist naval blockade hurt Hong Kong's exports to the mainland. Simultaneously, the traditional Southeast Asian and Commonwealth markets were going through their own political and economic upheavals. As Jack Tang explained: "By 1950 a lot of [spinners] had inventory piled up. . . . If the Korean War hadn't come, maybe a lot of them would have gone bankrupt." The war's outbreak in June 1950 triggered a key shift. While some, such as Tang's uncle Tang Yeh-chu, panicked and fled to São Paulo, a temporary trade boom ensued that "saved the situation" owing to regional stockpiling and U.S. military orders.[164] Hong Kong's trade soared through late 1950 and early 1951, allowing many textile industrialists to repay their initial overdrafts, as we will see in chapter 5. Yet after the PRC entered the war in October 1950, Washington responded in December by issuing a total trade embargo and freezing all PRC-owned U.S. dollar accounts. Beijing retaliated by seizing all U.S. assets in China.[165] Once the United Nations imposed its own embargo on the PRC in May 1951 with British support, the colonial government was legally obligated to enforce these measures. The embargo's enforcement procedures took time to coalesce, but the long-term legal implications were clear to some. As soon as December 29, 1950, K. P. Chen instructed his staff to sever all ties with their mainland offices and reincorporate the SCSB as a Hong Kong company, now just the Shanghai Commercial Bank.[166] He understood that both the bank and the colony's future opportunities lay within the U.S.-led transpacific order.

The U.S. and UN embargoes on China rank alongside the California Gold Rush as a rupture in the economic history of Hong Kong. As seen, the colony's *kamshanchong* had thrived as a conduit for transpacific trade, migration, and remittances from the 1850s through the Great Depression and now the embargo.[167] Over 1951 and throughout 1952 and 1953, Hong Kong newspapers such as *Sing Tao Yat Po* (星島日報), *Wah Kiu Yat Po* (華僑日報), and *Ta Kung Pao* (大公報) devoted considerable attention to the *kamshanchong*'s plight and the response of their trade group, the Wah On Association (華安商會). Its representatives organized meetings of local manufacturers, lobbied the colonial government to take action, exhorted U.S. consulate officials, and worked with U.S. Treasury officials when they visited Hong Kong.[168] Yet these articles underscored that U.S. policies were gradually asphyxiating longstanding trade and remittance pathways, although some traders limped on by smuggling via Macau.[169] By February 1953 even pro-Nationalist newspaper *Kong Sheung Yat Po* (工商日報) complained that U.S. actions had been "a big blow to Hong Kong's specialized handlers of mainland remittances, trading firms, and private banks."[170] Local firms could neither accept Chinese-American remittances nor export goods with any PRC materials to any U.S.-affiliated market without risking serious secondary U.S. sanctions. U.S. imperial expansion thus began rerouting the trade systems in the western Pacific and pulling Hong Kong out of China's economic orbit.

Scholars have long framed the embargoes as a turning point for Hong Kong's manufacturing boom but have not sufficiently underscored how they fostered the colony's engagement and soon dependence on the U.S. market. The embargoes brought Washington's might directly into the boardrooms of almost all Hong Kong industrialists and financiers. By 1954 the official value of the colony's total trade had plummeted to 60 percent of 1948's total, devastating both Cantonese *kamshanchong* and Jiangnan transplants. Without the China market, the surviving textile industrialists desperately needed new export markets. Europe remained in postwar recovery, and most regional trading partners were becoming increasingly protectionist in order to nurture their own industries. Even worse, as noted, cotton spinning is a highly competitive global industry that incentivizes constant expansion to achieve economies of scale. Thus by the mid-1950s the vast U.S. market was Hong Kong industrialists' only practical option. Yet that market had stringent regulations. In 1953 the U.S. consulate and the Department of Commerce and Industry had instituted the Comprehensive Certificate of Origin system, through which officials inspected local factories and certified their goods as legally fit to enter the U.S. market. As a result, from 1953 to 1971 Hong Kong producers of any goods bound for the United States—from duck eggs to cotton yarn—needed to work closely with colonial and U.S. consulate officials.[171] Only goods thus certified as containing no PRC elements would be allowed entry. Yet somehow Hong Kong's surviving textile industrialists did successfully reorient toward the U.S. market. In 1955 Hong Kong's exports to the United States amounted to just HK$15 million, lower than its exports to British East Africa.[172] By 1959 the United States had already morphed into the colony's overwhelmingly dominant market, taking exports valued at HK$343.5 million in the first half of 1960 alone.[173] It was not just what Hong Kong was selling that changed, but to whom.

This reorientation depended on both the exploitation of the colony's plentiful low-cost labor and the U.S.-oriented transplants' social capital. Among its many strictures, the U.S. embargo prohibited any company owned by PRC nationals from trading with the United States. U.S. officials suspected all Hong Kong Chinese businesspeople of being PRC nationals, a classification that would have ruined transplants such as émigré "T. Y." Wong (王統元) and his father "C. Y." Wong Chi-yue (王啓宇). Originally from Ningbo, the Wong family had been pioneers of Shanghai's textile industry before relocating. Their new spinning mills had purchased a half million U.S. dollars of American cotton through the SCSB in early 1949 alone.[174] The Wongs spent two years negotiating with U.S. Treasury officials to be reclassified, which included severing any remaining links with their mainland businesses.[175] The U.S. embargo thus further increased the value of foreign passports among the émigrés, particularly the U.S. passport.[176] Through the Tangs and South Sea Textiles, we can succinctly see how American social capital immediately delivered tangible competitive advantages. While Jack's U.S. citizenship ensured legal access to the U.S. market, his time at HBS gave him crucial sales networks. There he had befriended U.S. Army officers who were now involved in procurement, while one of his brothers was even serving with U.S. forces in Korea.[177] These connections helped South Sea to secure lucrative Pentagon contracts, and former workers recalled that the U.S. Army remained a primary long-term client through the Vietnam War.[178] In turn, Tang used his broader HBS network for marketing. He wrote in to its alumni magazine in late 1957: "Jack Tang . . . wants to know if anyone can give him some help in selling a line of shirts his company is producing at the rate of 200 dozen per day. Any classmates who are department store buyers, please note."[179] China's communist transition and the transplantation of the U.S.-oriented Jiangnan émigrés thus intersected with Cold War U.S. imperial expansion to lay the foundations for kuashang strategies. These transplants' elite American social capital had followed them to Hong Kong and positioned them for revival within both the constraints and opportunities of the new U.S.-led order.

During China's communist transition, Hong Kong received an enormous influx of people. The vast majority were from Guangdong, but at least 100,000 people came from the lower Yangzi, including many of China's leading industrialists, bankers, and other professionals. Since the 1910s this Jiangnan bourgeoisie had developed increasingly noticeable ties to the United States through education and business. Many had studied in American missionary schools or U.S. colleges, worked with American businesses in China, or profited from U.S. government aid to the Nationalist regime. For those who fled, this mobile social capital accompanied them to Hong Kong. Largely regarding the colony as indefensible and Britain as an empire in decline, they considered how to survive and extract themselves. Alongside migration, both the size of the U.S. market and the U.S. embargo incentivized further investment into American social capital as a business strategy. While exceptional figures such as Jack Tang or Ansie Lee Sperry were able to naturalize as U.S. citizens, 117,000 other people applied for visas at the U.S. consulate in Hong Kong in 1950 alone and the vast majority were unsuccessful.[180] Yet over the 1950s and 1960s Hong Kong Chinese with American social capital would find increased chances as Washington reformed its previously race-based immigration policies. The intersection of these personal and business interests drove the first crystallizations of kuashang strategies. Export-driven codevelopment with the U.S. market and potential exit strategies strongly encouraged the acquisition of American social capital, as did goals such as defeating racist club policies. While British firms such as Jardine Matheson remained the largest economic players, the émigré bankers and industrialists were watching and adapting to the new U.S.-led transpacific order.

Incentives to connect with the United States soon expanded beyond these elites, however. Alongside the embargo, Washington's Cold War efforts to win "hearts and minds" began to affect ordinary Hong Kong residents directly from the mid-1950s. U.S. ambitions to steer Asia's future required new imperial technologies to conform with democratic claims of moral leadership. European empires had relied on formal hierarchies, permanent bureaucracies, and military occupations, but the United States sought to use less overt methods of control: cultivated influence that invited mass Asian participation. While maintaining the constant threat of military force, Washington's programs and policies encouraged the mass Asian pursuit of American opportunities under the banner of the "Free World." Both communist propaganda and the U.S. civil rights movement exposed the hypocrisy of these ideals, but internationally, American institutions moved quickly in the 1950s to minimize overt racism and promote mass buy-in into U.S. leadership.[181] As we will see over the next three chapters, Christian and educational outreach projects were foundational to those aims, and Hong Kong was a critical site. U.S. outreach through Christian and educational projects would help hundreds of thousands of Hong Kong residents to attend school over the next two decades and set terms for the expansion of kuashang strategies.

CHAPTER II

Christian Transplants

Nonelite Refugees and American Educational Outreach

孟母三遷

Mencius's mother moved three times.

—*THREE CHARACTER CLASSIC* (三字經)

L ight blanketed the horizon as the *Marine Lynx* sailed through the
Golden Gate and out into the Pacific. Hundreds of paper stream-
ers, voices raised in hymn, and the ship's horn intoned its departure from San Francisco on September 29, 1946. "What fun to sail under
the Golden Gate Bridge toward the sunset with the long slow Pacific
swells reminding us that this 12,000-ton troopship was no large cruise
liner," missionary Sterling Whitener reflected.[1] Recently decommissioned
from the U.S. Navy, the *Marine Lynx* had been repurposed to rush two
critical groups back to China: two hundred Chinese students and four
hundred American missionaries, the largest contingent ever to leave the
United States. Amid rationed postwar shipping, these two groups were
top priorities for the U.S. government. The missionaries were to renew
Christianity's crusade in China, while the repatriated students were
expected to lead China's continued modernization and future Sino-U.S.
relations.[2] All the students and most of the missionaries were bound for
Shanghai, but missionaries with assignments in South China continued
on to Hong Kong.

By 1946 the transpacific circulations of American missionaries to China
and Chinese students to the United States had been interrelated for a century. The two groups experienced very different levels of privilege overseas, but their contrapuntal movements represented the intersection
between U.S. imperialism in China and China's modernization efforts. As

seen in chapter 1, American missionary schools in China had been key launching pads for studying overseas before the Second World War. Many of the two hundred students onboard the *Marine Lynx* had passed through missionary schools. The war had transformed Sino-U.S. relations, however, through the wartime alliance, the repeal of Chinese Exclusion, and the heightened U.S. government interest in Chinese students as future leaders. The U.S. State Department had even supported many of these bright young minds during the war, while the renewal of the Chinese civil war pushed Washington to expedite the return of both groups in the hope of aiding China's reconstruction.[3] In fact, this unprecedented missionary contingent represented just "the vanguard" of eight thousand American missionaries who would disperse across eastern Asia and the Pacific during the late 1940s.[4]

All these flows shifted, however, with the establishment of the People's Republic (PRC) in 1949. The communist transition pushed thousands of foreign missionaries and Chinese Christians to flee the mainland as "refugees," a term just gaining legal meaning that would remain contested in Hong Kong.[5] In turn, Washington then pivoted to block Chinese students from returning to the PRC, and American mission boards rerouted their representatives to other parts of U.S.-allied Asia.[6] Yet the "loss" of China as a missionary field did not diminish missionaries' activities. Instead, missionaries' grassroots cultural knowledge, networks, and language skills made them valuable potential actors in U.S. efforts to contain communism. For example, Sterling Whitener had been born and raised in Yueyang, Hunan. He was fluent in multiple Chinese dialects and often went by his Chinese name, Hui Mian-lin (惠冕霖). The Church of Christ in China (CCC) had restationed him, his wife, and his parents in Yueyang in 1946.[7] Among Whitener's fellow passengers on the *Marine Lynx*, missionaries Merrill and Lucille Ady, John and Harriet Bechtel, Richard and Johanna Hofstra, and Henry and Sarah Refo had all worked in South China for decades.[8] If willing, such missionaries possessed rare capacities to promote anticommunism and U.S. international leadership alongside Christianity. Both the U.S. government and American mission boards grasped this potential and collaborated to redistribute missionaries from the PRC into overseas Chinese communities. With migrants still pouring into Hong Kong in the early 1950s despite the imposition of entry quotas in May 1950 and PRC exit controls in February 1951, the British colony became a linchpin in these redirected efforts.[9] The CCC reassigned the Whiteners to Hong Kong in 1952, while the Adys and the Bechtels shortly followed.[10]

For the missionaries in Hong Kong, the Cold War injected a powerful steroid into their activities in the form of U.S. government resources. Missionaries had been building schools and clinics across China since the early nineteenth century to lure potential converts.[11] This experience as institution builders was ideal preparation to assist Washington's public diplomacy efforts. The next section documents how the U.S. government began funneling resources through "state-private networks" into U.S. and international missionary organizations in Hong Kong, such as the CCC and the Church World Service (CWS).[12] Washington helped fund missionaries' activities in order to demonstrate the moral superiority of the so-called Free World and promote "refugee" settlement in Hong Kong, forestalling migrants' return to the PRC or their potential migration overseas. Partnering with elite U.S.-educated Chinese Christian émigrés, American missionaries brought these Cold War resources into new churches, clinics, and schools across the colony during the 1950s and 1960s (figure 2.1). By studiously deferring to Chinese leadership over these institutions, these partners effectively masked the U.S. resources and agendas behind them. As one mission emphasized, "Careful attention should be given to the development of the indigenous church" so as to "minimize the American mission aspect."[13] Thus while previous scholars have documented Washington's use of Hong Kong to spy on Beijing, screen visa applicants, and enforce its embargo, I show that the U.S. government also co-opted American missionaries and elite Chinese Christians in Hong Kong into serving as skilled agents of grassroots cultural diplomacy.

The second section analyzes how these U.S.-backed schools mapped onto British ambitions to shore up colonial rule amid Hong Kong's refugee crisis. While the British Empire had a long history of imprisoning undesired migrants in camps, the Hong Kong government pursued such policies only for former Nationalist soldiers and other loyalists.[14] Instead, the overwhelmed regime first assumed that most migrants were temporary and would return to the mainland once conditions stabilized. Thus the regime at first provided the absolute minimum in terms of humanitarian services. Only after realizing that the migrants were permanent did the government commit to the provision of mass public housing in 1953–1954 and the eventual goal of universal public education in 1956.[15] As a result, U.S.-backed missionary schools offered a crutch at a critical juncture, and

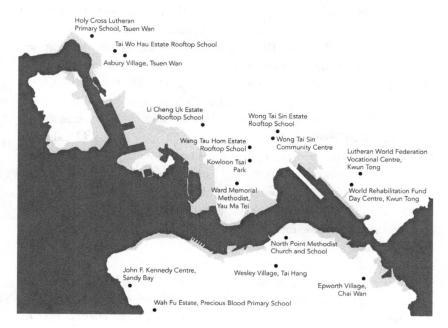

Holy Cross Lutheran
Primary School, Tsuen Wan
•
Tai Wo Hau Estate Rooftop School
•
•
Asbury Village, Tsuen Wan

Li Cheng Uk Estate
Rooftop School
•
Wong Tai Sin Estate
Rooftop School
•
Wang Tau Hom Estate
Rooftop School •
• Wong Tai Sin
Community Centre
Kowloon Tsai •
Park
Lutheran World Federation
Vocational Centre,
Kwun Tong

Ward Memorial
Methodist,
Yau Ma Tei
•
World Rehabilitation Fund
Day Centre, Kwun Tong

North Point Methodist
Church and School

John F. Kennedy Centre,
Sandy Bay
•
Wesley Village, Tai Hang
•
Epworth Village,
Chai Wan
•
Wah Fu Estate, Precious Blood Primary School
•

Figure 2.1 A map of the approximate locations of the U.S.-sponsored projects and institutions discussed in this chapter. The shaded areas represent land reclaimed since the late 1960s. Map by Andrew James Hamilton with information from oldhkphoto .com/coast/Map/html.

the colonial regime began heavily subsidizing them in the mid-1950s. While colonial officials restricted U.S. efforts to use these schools for anti-PRC propaganda, they did provide them with guidance and taxpayer support. This guidance and support helped these Chinese-led, U.S.-backed Christian groups to build a huge number of "grant schools" across Hong Kong. This infrastructure was critical to Hong Kong finally achieving universal primary education in 1971 and universal secondary education in 1978. Yet, as officials feared, U.S.-backed Christian schools did not just provide literacy, numeracy, or instruction in English and Christianity. They also advanced informal decolonization by extending American social capital into ordinary communities, particularly as missionaries and U.S.-educated Chinese guided low-income families toward U.S.-sponsored educational and labor opportunities.

The final section focuses on American missionaries' expansion into vocational training and college recruitment in the early 1960s. From the beginning, missionaries and Chinese Christians used their churches and schools to offer vocational classes. Following World Refugee Year (1959–1960), an influx of U.S. and British government cash allowed these groups to establish freestanding centers to train residents in industrial skills. While these training centers were framed as charity, both colonial and U.S. consulate officials designed them as tools to promote political stability and economic development by channeling low-income residents into industrial labor roles. Simultaneously, by the early 1960s U.S.-backed Christian schools were steering increasing numbers of local students toward U.S. higher education, as they had before 1949. The result was that Cold War American educational outreach began to create a layered system of opportunities that promoted capitalist development and transpacific integration under U.S. international leadership. Most important for our analysis, while chapter 1's elite émigrés had been developing American social capital since the late Qing, nonelite Hong Kong residents now gained their own limited opportunities through the combination of U.S. imperial expansion and colonial retrenchment efforts. This grassroots expansion laid the groundwork for the normalization of kuashang strategies in this disjointed Cold War colony.

Transplanted Communities

European and American missionaries acquired a century of experience in offering education to Chinese people before the Second World War. Jesuit missionaries first entered China in the 1500s, but evangelization remained illegal until 1858, when Britain and France forced the Qing to sign the Treaty of Tianjin, ending the first phase of the Second Opium War. Thousands of European and American missionaries then entered China during the late Qing and the Republican eras. Low conversion rates pushed them into educational and medical work to try to lure reluctant converts.[16] American missionaries made similar tactical shifts in other contexts, such as Korea and Hawai'i.[17] In China, missionaries also gradually questioned their complicity with the catastrophes striking the empire, particularly those in which Christianity played a key role, such as the Taiping Rebellion or Boxer Rising. As a result, by the early twentieth century most American missionaries in China were transitioning toward liberal theologies that emphasized institution building over proselytization as a way of demonstrating Christian service.

Hong Kong was a sideshow to this missionary campaign. The British colonial regime installed its own network of Anglican institutions in the colony, and the Anglicans ran prestigious schools for European, Chinese, and Eurasian students, such as the Diocesan and St. Paul's schools. The Vatican too relocated its regional headquarters from Macau, while several Catholic orders such as the Italian Canossians and the American Maryknoll Fathers and Sisters also worked in the territory.[18] In 1925 the Maryknoll Sisters' Convent School became the first American missionary school to educate Hong Kong children, well predating the Cold War.[19]

Many missionaries and Chinese Christians relocated to Hong Kong after the Japanese invasion of 1937, but the real exodus occurred during the communist transition. The U.S. consul-general began enquiring with the colonial government about issuing visas to relocated American missionaries in April 1949, which triggered subsequent internal conversations.[20] Most missionaries stayed in the mainland as long as possible, though.[21] PRC policies then gradually pushed them out, from worship controls to the surveillance of group gatherings. Simultaneously, Chinese arrivals in Hong Kong—about 700,000 by 1955—began pulling mission boards' attention to the colony.[22] In the ensuing crisis, missionaries rushed to provide food, shelter, and clothing and began to reconsider Hong Kong as a replacement mission field. By the early 1960s the number of American missionary groups operating in Hong Kong had surged to include the Chinese Christian and Missionary Alliance, the Church of Jesus Christ of Latter Day Saints, the Lutheran Church-Missouri Synod, the Sisters of the Precious Blood, the Southern Baptist Convention, and the American Methodists known as the Wei Li Kung Hui (衛理公會). Americans were also major constituencies within international missionary alliances operating in the colony, such as the CCC and CWS.

During the 1950s American missionaries were the single most important frontline of direct material relief to mainland migrants, becoming so critical that they were termed "'a third force' in Hong Kong society."[23] The success of this outreach required close attention to dialect and politics. For example, British and American Methodists divided the Chinese population between them. British Methodists continued working with Cantonese-speakers under the name "The Chinese Methodist Church,

Hong Kong District" or "Tsun To Kung Wooi" (循道公會). American Methodists focused instead on Mandarin- and Shanghainese-speakers under the aforementioned Wei Li Kung Hui. They remained formally separate institutions in Hong Kong until 1975. In another example, the CCC reassigned the Whiteners to the colony in 1952. A local pastor named Rev. John Ma had requested an American missionary owing to the youth demand to learn English, while the CCC wanted him to work with both Hunan migrants in Grampian Village and Cantonese-speakers in the Rennie's Mill camp, a bastion of Nationalist supporters. Whitener began to study Cantonese and already spoke the Xiang dialect due to growing up in Hunan.[24] By tailoring their work by dialect, American missionaries reached displaced communities that otherwise would have been ignored. Governor Alexander Grantham himself wrote in 1957 of American missionaries' contribution: "In this sphere of direct charitable relief (food and clothing) . . . the contribution of these organisations is greater than that of either the Government or of other charitable organisations, local or overseas."[25] Backed by the bounty of postwar America, these missionaries were the chief face of early refugee relief in Hong Kong.

This charity evolved, however, into assisting displaced Chinese Christians organize new communities. Sid and Olive Anderson were both over sixty years old in 1951 when the Methodist East China Service reassigned them to Hong Kong. A native Texan, Sid (安迪生) first came to China in 1914 after graduating from Vanderbilt Divinity School. The former Olive Lipscomb joined him after they wed in 1920. They became leaders at the Moore Memorial Church in Shanghai, still a landmark on People's Square.[26] After the Andersons were driven out in late 1950 by the Three-Self Patriotic Movement, their mission board sent them to Hong Kong to work with "non-Cantonese-speaking Christian refugees."[27] As they wrote later, "We met old friends on the crowded streets and everywhere we went; and their first question was, 'Where is our Church?'"[28] Such personal connections between missionaries and Chinese Christians could run very deep. Patsy Lee Queen's parents fled to Hong Kong in the early 1950s, where they raised her until she migrated to Dallas for high school in the mid-1960s. Upon both Sid and Olive Anderson's deaths in 1978, she wrote to their son and recounted how Rev. Anderson had officiated her parents' wedding in Shanghai. He remained their minister throughout their new lives in Hong Kong. Not only did the Andersons "speak such perfect Shanghainese and Mandarin," she declared, but also "Olive and Sid were the only grandmother and grandfather that I know of."[29]

By embedding themselves in Hong Kong among largely Shanghainese whom they had known for decades, the Andersons developed networks that made them a signpost around which a new Methodist community could coalesce. North Point was often called "Little Shanghai" for its concentration of Jiangnan migrants. The Andersons deliberately settled there. Along with their colleague Bishop Ralph Ward, they began to assemble Christian transplants and consider the formation of a new community: "Should this group try to locate a permanent church or only a place where a larger group might begin to 'coagulate'?"[30] Through teas and dinners, this group pooled information on Christians in the colony and those still in the PRC. The Andersons carefully compiled and annotated bilingual lists of "charter members" for a new church.[31] By early 1953 they were ready to send to the United States for an old colleague from Nanjing and Shanghai whom they handpicked to serve as this church's first minister, Rev. Timothy Y. H. Chow (周郁晞). He had earned his Ph.D. degree in theology at Boston University and was then serving as pastor to a congregation in the Florida panhandle.[32] He had never been to Hong Kong but arrived a few months later in mid-1953 after his Florida congregation sponsored part of his fare.[33] Another question the Andersons debated but left unanswered was, "Should we explain to this group how Dr. Chow is paid, and how he happened to come?"[34] In summer 1953 this North Point Methodist group rented ten adjoining garages beneath the Andersons' apartment. These garages became a makeshift church for about fifty members.

North Point Methodist's "Garage Church" grew rapidly while its leaders began organizing numerous other activities and institutions. Within five years North Point Methodist had grown to more than five hundred members, with services provided by both Revs. Anderson and Chow. The Andersons estimated that half of their congregants were "mature Christians" of assorted Methodist, Episcopalian, Baptist, and Presbyterian backgrounds, while about half were recent converts.[35] The group's youth programs had evolved into a formal school, which received a grant of free land from the colonial government in 1958.[36] With construction paid for by American congregations, in 1960 North Point Methodist broke ground on its permanent church and school (figure 2.2).

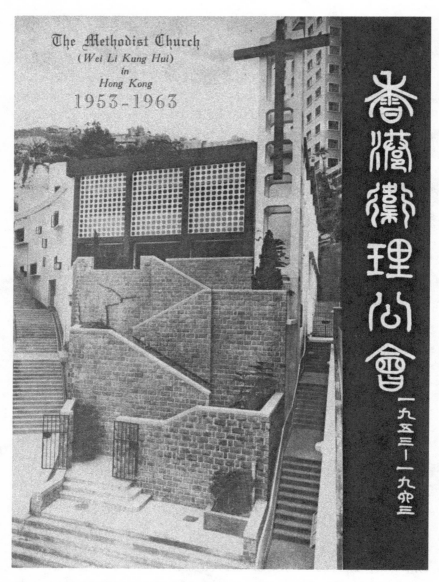

Figure 2.2 North Point Methodist pamphlet, PSRA, Box 2, Folder 23, YUDSL. Courtesy of Special Collections, Yale Divinity School Library.

At the summit of this new church and school were early kuashang, Chinese American attorney Jack Y. H. Yuen (阮潤桓) and his wife Maida Kuo.[37] Yuen had been born in Honolulu in 1908. Hawai'i was then a U.S. territory, and thus he had birthright U.S. citizenship. He attended the University of Michigan for college and law school. He and Maida met in Ann Arbor, where she was an overseas Chinese graduate student.[38] After law school, Yuen practiced law in the U.S. District Court for Hawaii until 1933, when the couple moved to Shanghai. There he was first a law clerk to George Richardson before being admitted to practice in the U.S. Court for China, where he largely practiced commercial law.[39] Maida was a graduate of the University of Shanghai, founded by American Baptists. Upon her return, she became the dean of women at Fudan University and then dean at the Besant School for Girls, named for the theosophist and anticolonial activist Annie Besant.[40] In 1937 Maida helped found and became principal at the Tseng Sui Primary School, a girls school with Fudan president and Yale graduate "T. H." Li Denghui (李登輝) as board chair and famed educator and College of Wooster graduate Guo Bingwen (郭秉文) as a trustee.[41] The Yuens stayed on in Japanese-occupied Shanghai, and in 1939 Richardson arranged for Jack to replace him as the lawyer for C. V. Starr, the founder of American Asiatic Underwriters.[42] During the Pacific War the Yuens were repatriated to Honolulu and then returned to Shanghai by 1947 but evacuated to Hong Kong in 1952.[43] The colony's different legal systems, however, meant that Jack could no longer practice law. Testifying to the power of connections, Starr then invited him to become a director of American Asiatic in Hong Kong. In this position, Yuen befriended another Christian transplant from Shanghai, former Bank of China executive and father of architect I. M. Pei, Pei Tsuyee (貝祖詒). Yuen would finish his career as AIA's general counsel for Asia.

The Yuens were devout Methodists, and together they became the public face of North Point Methodist. Jack served as the first chairman of the church's board from 1956 to 1961, while Maida was the first chairwoman and later principal of its affiliated school.[44] As such, they oversaw the crucial phase of this community's permanent establishment. Simultaneously, the couple was very social and joined numerous elite social clubs. With their son Allan off to boarding school and then their alma mater, Jack was elected president of the Y Men's Club in 1956 and president of the Lions Club of Hong Kong in 1958.[45] As a result, Jack and Maida Yuen were cross-pollinating figures. While legally and culturally American in many ways, they put Chinese faces on numerous American imports.[46] The available evidence suggests that their agenda focused on promoting ecumenicism, Christian brotherhood, and women's education, yet their varied activities and bicultural networks also illustrate how American ties quickly became embedded across an interlocking set of churches, schools, clubs, and companies. As such, Jack Yuen and Maida Kuo provide key insight into the successful integration of previously elite U.S.-oriented networks and opportunities at the grassroots of this British colony.

Under the Yuens' leadership, the North Point Methodist group continued branching outward. In 1960 the group established a second congregation in Kowloon called Ward Memorial, built with funds from the Methodist Church USA after Bishop Ward passed away in 1958.[47] They also began opening several rooftop schools in the colony's new resettlement estates, discussed in the next section. And this group found time to build two small, private resettlement estates, the Wesley Village (1955) in Tai Hang and Asbury Village (1959) in Tsuen Wan. Each village had eighty to one hundred cottages, a chapel, a community center, a primary school, and production brigades to help families earn money. CWS supplied both villages with food.[48] The villages hired their own ministers, such as Rev. Leo Hsu and Rev. Moses T. Y. Lee, one of whom studied in the United States while the other studied locally under U.S. missionary sponsorship.[49] The Andersons also taught at Chung Chi College, discussed in the next chapter.[50] This bonanza of activities reflects both the successful transplantation of the Andersons' and Yuens' overlapping social networks from Shanghai and the public and private U.S. financial resources imbuing these projects from behind the scenes.

While scholars have examined U.S. intelligence activities and immigration screenings in Hong Kong, they have overlooked the active U.S. government role in these missionary activities.[51] In part, this oversight stems from the masking of such outreach. While the British government recognized the PRC in 1950 for the sake of Hong Kong, Washington continued to support the Nationalists on Taiwan and eagerly sought to use Hong Kong to hurt and embarrass the PRC. Thus U.S. refugee outreach risked angering Beijing and jeopardizing Hong Kong's security. Colonial officials worried even when Americans used the term *refugee*. As Governor Grantham explained, the term led to arbitrary distinctions, and thus they preferred aid be distributed by "need rather than status."[52] The colonial government's ensuing "diplomacy of restraint" toward U.S. actions in

Hong Kong effectively prohibited overt U.S. propaganda or provocations, as Chi-kwan Mark has shown.[53] Yet these considerations did not prohibit educational and medical work, and the U.S. government channeled substantial aid in this direction through private groups, most especially missionary councils. The U.S. consulate formed a Refugee and Migration Unit (RMU) in 1954 to manage this outreach, and its major beneficiaries were umbrella organizations such as CWS, CCC, the National Lutheran Council, the Lutheran World Federation (LWF), the National Catholic Welfare Conference (NCWC), and the World Council of Churches (WCC), and secular bodies such as the Cooperative for American Relief Everywhere (CARE). Hong Kong officials, however, were not fooled as to why these missionaries were flush with cash. As Grantham reported to London: "It is consequently clear that these ostensibly non-Government agencies are to a considerable extent financed by the American Government and in fact the disguise is sometimes pretty thin."[54] Between July 1, 1954, and June 30, 1955, alone, he estimated that such organizations spent US$600,000 on food and clothing for forty-five thousand people. Noting that the NCWC had also built 527 cottages over the previous two years at a cost of US$105,000, he stated flatly: "The money was provided by I.C.A.," the State Department's International Co-operation Administration. Nominally international agencies were also tied to Washington, as Grantham reported about the WCC. Although headquartered in Geneva, it "obtains most of its funds from America." In early 1961 the RMU reported to colonial officials that it had channeled a total of US$7 million to local organizations between 1954 and 1959.[55] Roughly half of the funds were spent on resettlement overseas and half on local aid.[56] In total, as much as 25 percent of the colony's population was estimated to have received some help.[57]

These U.S.-funded missionary organizations often hosted complex leadership dynamics between Chinese Christians and American missionaries. In a trend known as "devolution," Chinese clergy and elite community members such as the Yuens were usually formally in charge.[58] Yet the American missionaries often represented the bulk of the funds. At the CCC, this power dynamic led to conflict between the Rev. Peter Wong and Sterling Whitener. Wong had been the executive secretary of the CCC's Guangdong Synod before 1949 and was allowed to leave the PRC only in 1955.[59] Whitener later praised Wong as "a strong, brilliant, and charismatic leader" but confessed that he was also "no shrinking violet."

The two worked together for eleven years until their differences became insurmountable over the CCC's long-term priorities. Wong believed in focusing on education and wanted Whitener to serve as an American face for the group's schools. Whitener wished to focus on social work and, in the end, "simply could not reconcile my own call to social services with the tasks in education administration which Peter Wong was adamant I undertake." He thus resigned in 1966.[60]

Education did become the predominant way that U.S.-backed church groups spent resources, built communities, and attracted converts in Hong Kong. All the American Methodists' schools offered Bible study alongside regular classes, reminding parents of the source of their children's educations. Church and school activities also offered venues to underscore these communities' material benefits. Between Pentecost and Christmas 1957, the Andersons recorded 160 new church members, including "whole families from Wesley Village" and "Christians just out of China." Alongside faith, these families' general poverty was key to these free schools' appeal and created asymmetrical power dynamics between parents and missionaries. For example, in 1958 the Andersons recorded meeting a "bright-eyed, smiling, irresistible 6-year-old who begged on our corner" and whose family lived in a nearby cave "from which we had seen smoke rising." They invited him to attend "our Free School" and hoped as a result "he may be one of the children baptized." While the boy's parents could have refused, free school spots were precious commodities. At another Wesley Village school event, the Andersons gave blue nametags to children who had been baptized and pink nametags to those who had not.[61] Non-Christian children were thus marked as different, while their families were reminded on whom their children's educations depended and what other opportunities this community might offer. As we will see, the ultimate such opportunity was no secret: assistance in accessing transpacific migration and U.S. higher education.

Colonial Reinforcement

The British colonial government had a direct stake in aiding U.S.-backed Christian schools. The colony's influx of humanity was a grave threat to social stability and thus the regime's survival. This influx also created vast shortfalls in social services. Officials sought to close those gaps quickly but cheaply. Toward this aim, in 1954 they launched a seven-year program of primary school expansion that aimed to provide 215,000 school places by 1961. With "the active co-operation of the numerous bodies interested in education in the Colony," they achieved 363,500 places with another 154,000 on the way.[62] In large measure this achievement stemmed from an official policy to provide taxpayer funds and guidance to all qualified faith-based organizations interested in building schools. Indeed, while colonial officials could be sensitive about U.S. intelligence and espionage activities in Hong Kong, they largely embraced American involvement in elementary and secondary education and extended these organizations many favors. When one official sought to penalize the Chinese Christian and Missionary Alliance for falling behind on a new school, the colonial secretary admonished the director of public works: "Government relies on such organisations as this to run schools on its behalf and provided there are no unreasonable delays it would be reasonable to grant free extensions."[63] Just as Washington's outreach was not benevolent, though, colonial officials were using U.S.-backed Christian groups to mask their own strained resources and preserve the façade of colonial power. In the long term, however, this outsourcing of public responsibility to private and largely American actors represented an early step in Hong Kong's informal decolonization.

Partnership between American missionaries and colonial officials first flowered in rooftop "schools" in the colony's new resettlement estates. In 1953–1954, the colonial regime committed to erecting mass public housing for Hong Kong's needy and displaced in the form of crammed concrete H-blocks.[64] Each block accommodated about 2,500 people, with each family allotted one 120-square-foot room on a floor with communal kitchens and bathrooms. By the end of 1959 the government had erected 103 such resettlement blocks over nine estates, housing roughly 230,000 people (figure 2.3).[65] These warrens included virtually no social services. As a result, the American Methodists first applied in July 1956 to open a "boys' and girls' club" at the Li Cheng Uk Resettlement Estate. Led by Rev. Chow and Jack Yuen, this club explicitly targeted Hong Kong's poorest families to maximize the chances of conversion, while strategically selecting that estate because "we understand that many people there speak Shanghai or Mandarin."[66] They also presented the idea to officials as a club rather than a formal school in order to exploit looser regulations. They received approval for "an experimental period of six months" in

Figure 2.3 Hong Kong Government pamphlet, "Homes for a million . . . And more to come!," c. 1968, PSRA, Box 2, Folder 22, YUDSL. Courtesy of Special Collections, Yale Divinity School Library.

October 1956, just as riots between Nationalist and communist supporters made social stability even more pressing.[67] In early 1957 it was among four clubs to receive permanent registration.[68] Utilizing the block's flat rooftop, the Methodists set up chairs, desks, and blackboards and taught Chinese literacy and numeracy to sixty younger children in the morning and sixty older children in the afternoon. The club's supervisor was an early graduate of Chung Chi College (see chapter 3), but officials noted that Americans were the legal and financial sponsors.[69] They also hosted literacy classes for estate parents, sewing classes for estate mothers, as well as Bible study and formal services. Critically, the government charged the Methodists no rent for the rooftop and only nominal rent to occupy several rooms for storage. The minister at the Methodists' second congregation in Kowloon, Rev. Chester Yang (楊震), followed up with education officers to thank them for providing staff training and to invite them to social events.[70] Originally from Tianjin, Yang had received a scholarship to study at the University of New Mexico from 1948 to 1952. Like Rev. Hsu, he then attended the Perkins Theological Seminary in Dallas, graduating in 1954 and coming to Hong Kong under Bishop Ward's sponsorship. Upon arrival he was reunited with his wife and children after eight years (figure 2.4).[71]

Estate residents, other missionary groups, and local Chinese organizations all rapidly embraced the rooftop "school" model. By September 1958 the colony's Executive Council was reviewing applications for similar

Methodist in Hong. kong welcomed Rev-Chester Yang at the wharf, February, 1955

一九五五年二月，香港衛理公會同工迎接楊震牧師來港主理九龍教會。

Figure 2.4 Rev. Chester Yang's arrival in Hong Kong, February 1955. *Ward Memorial Methodist Church 1967*, PSRA, Box 2, Folder 24, YUDSL. Courtesy of Special Collections, Yale Divinity School Library.

clubs from four other American and international missions.[72] And due to high demand from estate residents, the American Methodists were approved to establish a second club at Wong Tai Sin estate in 1960, a third at Tai Wo Hau in 1961, an expansion of their club at Wong Tai Sin in 1962, and a fourth club at Wang Tau Hom estate in 1964.[73] At Wong Tai Sin alone they soon had 200–220 students in the club and 350–400 children in its recreation program.[74] Demonstrating that working-class residents retailored these schools to their needs, Rev. Robert Turnipseed noted that they had launched "an afternoon 'preparation class'" due to the "pressure of parents of small children in the building."[75] Officials further aided these clubs' localization by mandating that all maintenance "servants" be hired from among the estate's residents. Aimed at creating jobs, this policy reinforced the schools' outward indigenization. As kaifong associations, Buddhist temples, and other Chinese groups launched their own rooftop schools, the total number in Hong Kong surpassed two hundred by the end of the 1960s. Rooftop schools remained a stopgap until the mid-1970s, when the government finally achieved sufficient school places and began to demolish the estates.[76]

The gradual shift toward freestanding schools did not diminish educational collaboration between colonial officials and U.S.-backed Christian groups, however. Rather, their collaboration was a primary reason for that achievement. In 1958 the regime passed the "Charities (Land Acquisition) Bill," which set out a standard formula to assist private charities build primary and secondary schools. Under this formula, if the private charity paid 20 percent of a school's building costs, then the government would provide the site for free, a 50 percent construction subsidy, and an eleven-year interest-free loan for the remaining 30 percent of construction costs. In effect, in exchange for some initial investment and running the school, the colonial government paid private organizations to assume much of its public educational responsibilities. American and international missionaries were the chief beneficiaries of this policy because of their reliable funding and because officials instinctively trusted projects that they deemed to be "sponsored by long established, well-regulated churches."[77] This collaboration was enormously effective for both sides. By 1967 the CCC alone had built three primary and eight secondary schools across Hong Kong, representing school places for twenty thousand children. By investing just HK$5 million of its own funds, the CCC had received government grants worth HK$15 million and loans for another HK$4 million.[78] By early 1968 the Lutheran Church-Missouri Synod, too, would be operating or constructing eight schools that represented its own investment of US$1 million.[79] For example, when it applied in 1966 to establish Holy Cross Lutheran Primary School in Tsuen Wan, the director of education was immediately sympathetic: "This body has been found very reliable and efficient in running both secondary and primary schools." With a good track record and a continued shortfall of school places in Tsuen Wan, the group was swiftly approved for a capital subsidy of HK$440,000, an interest-free loan of HK$264,000, a recurrent annual subsidy for staff salaries and tuition subsidies of HK$623,000, and a land grant to construct a twenty-four-classroom nonprofit primary school for 2,160 pupils. The American missionaries had to contribute only HK$176,000.[80] When the Lutherans became overextended and the project's costs rose, the government increased its support.[81]

Alongside funneling taxpayer dollars into American missionary activities, colonial officials also provided guidance to these projects. In 1963 the American Methodists were still expanding rapidly and applied to build yet another church, library, and community facility in Kowloon.[82] Official Rose Young decided to undertake a comprehensive review of their activities. Although the Methodists had "plenty of money," Young wanted "to see if the Methodists are doing all that they said they are doing." Without "great care and guidance from us," she feared their institutions would be "nothing more than a church and a parish hall in fact."[83] What she found at their new Epworth Village in Chai Wan impressed her. The village housed 350 families in 170-square-foot cottages for which the Methodists charged just HK$10 in monthly rent. The village's three-story community center housed a clinic, a kindergarten for 250 children, a playground, public showers, a chapel, and evening classes. Young spoke with a Rev. Wong, who told her that Epworth villagers were "much better off than many urban dwellers" since "they pay very cheap rents, cheap school fees and free or very cheap clinic al [sic] expenses." Because Chai Wan had two more community centers in the pipeline, Young concurred, concluding "no doubt, Chai Wan will be better served by welfare agencies than any other Resettlement Estate."[84] Colonial supervision did not always yield such ringing endorsements, however. When the Methodists applied to expand their club at Li Cheng Uk, one official commented: "Although its programme of activities is not very ideal, it does provide a needed service to pre-school children who would otherwise have nothing better to do."[85]

Over the 1960s the colonial regime developed a complex codependence with these U.S.-backed Christian schools. For example, officials could feel obligated to aid problematic projects for the sake of the larger relationship. In summer 1966 the CCC applied to expand one secondary school into a postsecondary college. Officials resisted for multiple reasons, but one conceded: "I am afraid that we might have to relax somewhat with this application. We rely on bodies such as the [CCC] fairly heavily in the educational field so that we may have to give them a grant of land." They decided to at first refuse and, if the CCC persisted, relent "for educational 'political' reasons."[86] Simultaneously, officials also co-opted rich American missionaries to fix their own mistakes and oversights, such as tapping the American Sisters of the Precious Blood to fill an unexpected gap in the Wah Fu resettlement estate.[87] This codependence also lent U.S.-backed groups great privileges. For example, in late 1960 the Southern Baptist Convention (SBC) purchased several properties for tax-exempt churches and charities without prior approval, a legal infraction that technically invalidated the sale and required "re-entry." How to punish this transgression perplexed officials. One wrote that the government should be eager "to rap the S.B.'s knuckles without forfeiting the land and buildings." Another was less forgiving and recommended forfeiture. The first official replied: "The Mission operates in H.K. on an annual budget of about HK$1 million exclusive of salaries, and is financed direct from the U.S.A. The missionaries are U.S. citizens. The Mission provides churches, schools, and a hospital. . . . I feel that [re-entry] involves a weighty decision and I am not at all sure that it is desirable."[88] This question reached the governor himself, to whom re-entry was presented as "a tremendous slap in the face to this worthy American charitable organization."[89] The governor forgave the mistake, so long as "this mission is made aware of what has been done."

These collaborations among Chinese Christians, American missionaries, and colonial officials continued to swell between 1958 and the mid-1970s. In January 1957 Governor Grantham could still state of local education: "With the exception of aid to post-secondary education it cannot be said that American aid reaches significant proportions in comparison with what comes from local sources, private and official."[90] The Charities (Land Acquisition) Bill of 1958 had opened a gate, however. By July 1959 the director of education informed Sterling Whitener that Hong Kong had 789 private primary schools, of which 218 were run by Protestant organizations and 91 by Catholic groups. Of 71 secondary schools, 56 were Christian.[91] Many of these 365 Christian schools predated the Second World War, but nonetheless 40 percent of primary schools and 79 percent of secondary schools were Christian in a predominantly non-Christian society. This expansion continued throughout the 1960s and testifies to a synergy among social need, U.S. resources, elite Chinese Christians, and the colonial regime's agendas. As the Andersons wrote wearily in 1961 of their own ever-increasing educational work: "And refugees still come, wanting schools. We Methodists have been pushed into more school work than we were prepared to do."[92]

Training for U.S.-Approved Capitalist Futures

Alongside elementary and secondary education, U.S.-backed Christian schools provided a narrow access-point into American higher education. As such, these schools played a key role in the expansion of kuashang strategies beyond the émigré elites. For example, in September 1960 Sid and Olive Anderson celebrated the departure of twenty students from North Point Methodist who were "going to America to enter colleges." The couple had even written to friends living near each student's college so that they might "find the same fellowship there that they have known here."[93] The next year the Andersons again recorded that their North Point congregation had recently lost eighty-four people "who have gone abroad for study or life in America."[94] In early 1961 Baptist missionaries Carter and Agnes Morgan described their own trips to Kai Tak Airport "on different occasions to watch a plane-load of young people leave by special flight for college in the U.S." While they doubted "how many of these young people might be introduced to the Lord Jesus during their study in America," the Morgans were confident that "they won't be able to miss the attractions of materialism . . . these will be the years that shape their lives."[95] U.S.-backed Christian schools and U.S. policies granting quota-free entry to foreign students led to "plane-loads" of Hong Kong students streaming into American higher education in the 1960s.[96] Using their knowledge and networks, missionaries such as the Andersons and elite émigrés such as the Yuens were offering much less privileged migrants access to these opportunities through guidance, recommendations, introductions, and scholarships.

These expanding educational circulations represented this British colony's gradual reorientation toward the United States and were inextricable from the overlapping expansion of its transpacific commercial circulations. In 1950–1951 New York's Institute of International Education (IIE) found only seventy-two students from Hong Kong in the United States.[97] By 1959–1960, however, that number had jumped to 1,060 students, and it reached 1,597 in 1961–1962.[98] As we will see extensively in chapters 3, 4, and 6, a combination of local and international processes coalesced in the 1960s to exponentially accelerate Hong Kong students' attendance in U.S. higher education, such that by 1973–1974 Hong Kong emerged as the world's largest sender of foreign students to the United States. This extraordinary transpacific pipeline began in U.S.-backed Christian schools like North Point Methodist. Yet, as the Andersons and Morgans made clear, U.S.-backed schools were also promoting American lifestyles, opportunities, and international leadership. Such strategic objectives behind ostensible charity were even made explicit regarding the provision of food. After director of Food for Peace and future presidential nominee George McGovern toured American projects in Hong Kong in 1962, he testified that such charity was a tool of market development: "It is clear that the children who develop a liking for bread, milk, cornmeal, and other U.S. foods may be commercial customers tomorrow. Food for Peace is definitely a useful instrument of market development."[99]

Such strategic objectives behind American educational outreach took years to materialize, however, and only a tiny portion of Hong Kong youth had any hope of entering higher education before the mid-1960s. As a result, both the U.S. government and American missionaries looked beyond traditional schooling to providing vocational education to Hong Kong teenagers and adults through Christian training centers that aimed to transform refugees into laborers and good citizens. As chapter 1's capitalist transplants led Hong Kong's accelerating manufacturing boom, their mills and factories needed workers with new skills. Missionaries, U.S. government representatives, and colonial officials worked together to provide these skills and even consulted with the industrialists themselves to tailor such training to their preferences. U.S.-backed Christian vocational training thus not only aided Hong Kong industry by supplying semiskilled labor but also helped foster the illusion that the colony's capitalist success was a free-market miracle. Instead, while presented as Christian charity and U.S. foreign aid, such vocational training helped push Hong Kong residents into U.S.-approved labor roles and informally subsidized the colony's development.

From the outset, American missionaries used their schools to offer vocational training to students' parents. On nights and weekends, both North Point Methodist and the rooftop schools offered such classes. Vocational training was another incentive for low-income residents to embrace the schools and Christianity. Within a few years, however, missionaries began to offer vocational training at bespoke centers. For example, attached to the Ward Memorial church and school in Yau Ma Tei, the American Methodists built a social welfare center with classes in electronics, sewing, carpentry, office work, and plumbing.[100] Social welfare officials met and corresponded regularly with Rev. Yang and Rev. Robert Turnipseed to plan this facility, down to the flooring in the training rooms.[101] In November 1961 Dorothy Lee gave her seal of approval: "I have had long discussions with Rev. Turnipseed and Rev. Yang and I am satisfied that they are quite clear of what they are after. The activities proposed are practical and would serve a very crowded and poor district, Yau Ma Tei."[102] Such consultations provided valuable feedback and continued as these centers evolved.[103]

Non-American missionaries also took U.S. government funds to expand into vocational training. For example, in October 1961 the LWF under German director Rev. Ludwig Stumpf applied for a land grant for a nonprofit vocational training center in Kwun Tong. The LWF proposed that the center offer classes to a thousand teenage and adult refugees per year in everything from English, typing, and accounting to porcelain painting, spinning, weaving, and air conditioner repair. The colonial government granted the land and then noted that the U.S. government immediately pledged US$100,000 for this project, more than half its estimated cost.[104] The center was finished in early 1964 and was fully operational by 1965.[105] More than three thousand people applied for its first four hundred spaces.[106]

In reality, the U.S. consulate's RMU planned much of this vocational training. Starting in July 1960 RMU officers met regularly with officials to consult on such proposals, while the colonial regime formed its own internal Central Coordinating Committee specifically to manage U.S. aid.[107] For example, in mid-1960 RMU officers Robert Aylward and Herman Washington announced that they had been allocated US$1 million for the coming year for refugee aid in Hong Kong, with $350,000 earmarked for "assisting migration" and $650,000 for projects within the colony. Their top priority was aiding "new arrivals," which unnerved colonial officials since "there may well be other reasons for which RMU wishes to get into touch with them."[108] Aylward and Washington had various ideas of how to spend the money but were keenly interested in vocational training. In addition to backing the LWF's Kwun Tong center, they also gave money to two CWS and NCWC training and rehabilitation centers and US$47,000 to the local branch of the International Rescue Committee (IRC) for refugee job training and placement assistance.[109] At colonial officials' suggestion, Aylward and Washington also pledged donations to vocational programs at secondary schools.[110] Simultaneously, when delays arose on these projects, the Americans sent assertive letters and colonial officials complained that "persons concerned with such projects" did not appreciate the work involved and should realize "that a year or two (even 3!) . . . is not unreasonable."[111] Others found these delays "peculiarly embarrassing for Government," while some counseled that Americans rarely want detailed explanations and instead "what they want is the removal of the delay," which was subsequently achieved.[112] One official even complained that they needed a new operating procedure to regularize this process: "I strongly recommend that all those concerned with welfare spending, both in Government and the American Consulate and in the agencies concerned, should have the problems brought to their attention in writing."[113] As this official implicitly recognized, both the U.S. consulate and the missionaries it funded had become key parties to "welfare spending" in Hong Kong by 1960.

While framed as charity, such vocational funding was driven by U.S. capitalist ideologies and specifically American ideals of self-reliance. Although local charities such as the Po Leung Kuk and even the Nationalist government had long sought to control the urban poor and remake them as "useful" citizens, U.S. aid was not focused on moral reform or national strength.[114] Instead, by retraining low-income residents for industrial labor roles, U.S. officials were fostering the illusion that Hong Kong's labor market was organically absorbing hundreds of thousands of migrants and thus presumably superior to the PRC's state-directed economy. In reality, the U.S. government was more subtly sponsoring development and scaffolding individuals' career options through imperial projections of power. While genuine altruism could complement these aims, it was Cold War politics that dictated Hong Kong's position of high international priority. In 1961 the RMU spent at least US$670,000 on local refugee aid and distributed 49.5 million pounds of U.S. agricultural surplus.[115] In 1962 it spent another US$600,000 on such training, from US$15,000 for a CWS program to teach young women with disabilities to knit to US$50,000 for the LWF's campaign against tuberculosis, framed as restoring patients' ability to work.[116] In 1963 the RMU's appropriation increased to almost US$1.8 million, fell to US$750,000 in 1964, and returned to US$1 million in 1965.[117] After IRC and CARE jointly sponsored the colony's first hotel management program, Herman Washington handed out the diplomas in October 1964.[118] The U.S. government was thus spending millions of dollars throughout the early 1960s to state-sponsor 'self-reliance' among Hong Kong workers.

Entwined with these economic aims were political ambitions that one American missionary described as "character and citizen training."[119] The U.S. government's donation of Wong Tai Sin Community Centre for World Refugee Year exemplifies this combination. Owing to the lack of social services in the resettlement estates, in 1959 colonial officials announced a plan to erect six major community centers. Privately, officials had recognized that "these people have come to live at Wong Tai Sin not for any positive reason but merely because they were offered resettlement there where [sic] the land on which they originally built their squatter huts was cleared for development. Thus they are unlikely to feel that they are part of a community."[120] Worried about unrest, officials hoped these centers would "give these unrelated family units a sense of belonging to the Hong Kong community, if they are not to fall under political or lawless influences."[121] The first "experiment" was to be in the northern Kowloon area of Wong Tai Sin (WTS).[122] The U.S. government immediately pledged the full US$200,000 required. The English-language press cheered, with a *China Mail* editorial declaring that "from the American viewpoint" it was "a practical expression of concern for the plight of victims of communism." Yet "from the local viewpoint," the paper ventured that the center would "contribute to making these people feel less like undigested, unwanted and useless parasites, than active, integrated, useful and even necessary members of a community which is both industrial-minded and labour-hungry."[123] Alongside the paper's presumption to adjudicate belonging, it makes explicit a proto-neoliberal linkage between political belonging and economic usefulness.

As with U.S.-backed Christian schools and training centers, the WTS Community Centre offered vocational training but nested that economic agenda in a rhetoric of care.[124] While colonial and U.S. officials framed this project as fostering "community," the *China Mail* confessed the real aim was "digesting parasites" into law–abiding laborers. Thus, alongside a casework center, youth activities, a Maryknoll nursery, a YWCA children's center, YMCA exercise classes, a library, and a mother's club, WTS offered vocational classes in everything from motor and electrical repair to spray painting and English. The daytime classes accommodated 240 students aged fifteen to twenty-one, while there were night classes for one hundred students aged eighteen and up.[125] The classes were free, air-conditioned (a luxury that officials found extravagant), and run by the Hong Kong Christian Welfare and Relief Council.[126] The council itself received HK$800,000 from the WCC to run the classes. After bilingual newspaper advertising, by 1962 the Social Welfare Department estimated that twenty thousand of the area's sixty thousand residents were using the facility.[127]

The WTS Community Centre exemplifies why substantial American outreach has largely been forgotten in Hong Kong. The U.S. government's role in this donation was no secret. The building displayed a plaque from the U.S. government, while the U.S. consul dedicated the center in July 1960, with the bilingual text of his speech distributed to every newspaper by USIS.[128] Then, however, the rhetoric of care and self-reliance took over. The *China Mail* falsely claimed this building was "not an impersonal handout from the US Treasury" but rather came "spontaneously from the people's pockets."[129] One *SCMP* headline blared triumphantly: "NEW CENTRE WILL MAKE SELF–RELIANT CITIZENS."[130] In its coverage of the dedication, the *SCMP* focused on the speech of resident Mrs. Au Kit-fong, a member of the WTS Mother's Club. The paper quoted her in translation from Cantonese: "I can never forget the opportunities it has given us to learn, to study, and to help each other to think and to find purposes in life. The fact that I am learning to use my leisure wisely and not to fritter it away as before, has made a great difference to my life. It helps us to appreciate that if we work by ourselves behind closed doors, we cannot make any progress."[131] With bilingual texts of her speech distributed (but not extant in the archive), Au's rhetoric of self-help dovetailed with American ideals of constant productivity and served the U.S. consul's challenge to "those who would be critical to discover one single string attached to this gift and leading back to government in London or Washington."[132] By presenting the WTS Community Centre as a grassroots gift, the stakeholders all began burying its ties to U.S. public diplomacy. The center was thus akin to a trellis, designed to guide residents' growth toward U.S.- and colonial-approved futures as industrial workers and apolitical citizens. Pro-Nationalist papers such as *Sing Tao Yat Po* did not even mention the U.S. role.[133] Planted in fertile ground, the WTS Community Centre did not need strings and instead artificially naturalized things such as "Christmas Fun Fairs" and the Boy Scouts. Residents such as Mrs. Au saw the facility as useful and quickly looked past the flows of U.S. state power behind it.

Many other training centers across Hong Kong continued to receive U.S. funding over the 1960s, run by both missionary and secular organizations. On March 10, 1967, Dhun Jehangir Ruttonjee spoke at the laying of the foundation stone for the World Rehabilitation Fund (WRF) Day Centre in Kwun Tong. Ruttonjee came from a wealthy Parsee family and was a member of Legislative Council. Speaking before a crowd of two hundred that included WRF founder Dr. Howard Rusk, Ruttonjee acknowledged a persistent American role in recent charities:

> Scarcely a week has gone by since many of us attended the dedication of the John F. Kennedy Centre for the education of Spastic Children and the turning over of that Centre to the Hong Kong Red Cross Society. Now we have come together for the laying of the Foundation Stone of the World Rehabilitation Fund Day Centre where our less fortunate fellow citizens suffering from all types of severe disabilities will receive vocational training and guidance to enable them to lead useful lives to their own benefit and that of the Hong Kong community in general. As was the case with the John F. Kennedy Centre, the Day Centre will be built and equipped by the World Rehabilitation Fund through a generous grant from the people of the United States of America.[134]

Both the Kennedy Centre in Sandy Bay and the WRF Day Centre were built from a U.S. State Department grant of US$1.2 million. Dedicated to the slain president, the JFK Centre provided schooling for children with special needs.[135] The WRF Day Centre also offered occupational therapy and vocational training for 340 adults with disabilities. Yet while Ruttonjee spoke of "fellow citizens," there has legally never been such a thing as a Hong Kong citizen. Nor was this center solely providing care. In a city that would be rocked over the next few months by Cultural Revolution–inspired riots and bombings, U.S. and colonial officials had tailored this center to match the "manpower needs of Hong Kong's major industries," even consulting closely with industrial associations and textile barons.[136] As a result, the WRF Centre's primary classes were tailoring and sewing, industrial machine-sewing, and machine-knitting.[137] And while Ruttonjee spoke of "guidance" for 'less fortunate fellow citizens,' the director of social welfare was franker in private: "The disabled are an additional source of potential labour which can be tapped to develop [Hong Kong's] economy." These training centers were thus intended "to enable them to take their place in a modern industrial society."[138] While channeling children and adults with "severe disabilities" onto low-wage assembly lines might seem Dickensian, the U.S. State Department sought pro-American press coverage for these donations. The ensuing coverage—carefully encouraged, collated, and analyzed by officials—reinforced positive attitudes about both U.S. international leadership and "our success story," in the governor's words.[139] In line with this laissez-faire bootstraps rhetoric, by the center's third anniversary all mention of the U.S. government had disappeared. In reality, though, the WRF's local director Halleck Rose was a "retired American diplomat" and most likely a CIA agent.[140]

During China's communist transition, both elite Chinese Christians and international missionary organizations were transplanted to Hong Kong. Drawn to the colony's humanitarian crisis, American missionaries quickly partnered with elite Chinese Christians to establish new communities. These transplants' joint projects were gradually co-opted by U.S. Cold War agendas with millions of dollars flowing through Washington's state-private networks. U.S.-backed Christian projects carefully maintained public Chinese leadership while guiding Hong Kong youth and adults toward jointly approved Christian, capitalist futures. Such projects exposed ordinary residents to Christianity and English, inculcated American values and U.S. international leadership, and trained most migrants to settle in Hong Kong and embrace new lives as laborers and "citizens." Both the colonial regime and Chinese elites supported these projects to stabilize the colony and advance their own interests. As a result, a century of Christian evangelism in China exacted a new imprint in Cold War Hong Kong.

This chapter's Sino-Anglo-American educational partnerships established a substantial infrastructure of Christian schools and training centers across Hong Kong. This process helped to root tens of thousands of displaced families into new communities, provided educational opportunity to hundreds of thousands of children, won converts for local congregations, and shored up British colonial rule. For Washington, though, these resources subtly advanced an overlapping set of Cold War agendas, most especially buttressing capitalism by fostering illusions of entrepreneurial self-reliance. While the free market had nothing to do with these institutions, the masked nature of American assistance clouded contemporary observers' understanding of Hong Kong's relationship to U.S. imperial expansion. For example, in 1963 Washington donated HK$760,320 for the new Kowloon Tsai Park's playground and youth center. During construction in 1967, one official suggested "finding a name for this new park which will remind future generations of its close association with the people of the United States."[141] Again, during a summer in which thousands of local youth rioted against Anglo-American imperialism, this suggestion fell flat. Officials minimized overt links, and the U.S. consul-general dedicated another small plaque.

The U.S.-backed Christian schools and training centers both aided Hong Kong's development and extended American social capital at the local grassroots. First, these institutions—whatever their quality—provided basic social services where otherwise there would have been none. Although Hong Kong lacked the ethnic or religious divisions that tore apart many postcolonial societies, its density and poverty could easily have sparked more prolonged unrest. Colonial officials understood this contribution toward stability and so must our analysis. Second, these schools and training centers were planting seeds of informal decolonization by leading ordinary residents to look toward American lifestyles, educational models, and migration opportunities—mirroring elites' kuashang strategies. Through these institutions, ordinary residents could reach for life-changing opportunities, from vocational training to admission to U.S. higher education. In short, each such institution offered narrows windows into a matrix of U.S.-sponsored opportunities and networks on both sides of the Pacific. U.S.-backed schools and training centers thus remolded strategies of upward mobility and valorized such American credentials as worthy and desirable.

The highest aim of U.S.-backed Christian projects, however, was the training of future leaders through higher education. In February 1966 the CCC's Rev. Peter Wong and Sterling Whitener wrote to the director of education. Despite the establishment of the new Chinese University of Hong Kong—discussed over the next two chapters—they noted that still only one in twenty secondary school graduates could enter CUHK or HKU. As a result, in the previous year more than ten thousand students had applied to continue their studies abroad, primarily in the United States.[142] They thus suggested that the government establish a junior college explicitly to prepare students to enter "Colleges in the U.S.A. and Canada which are associated with the Churches related to the Hong Kong Council Church of Christ in China." They hoped this clear "relationship of affiliation" would prevent culture shock and encourage students to "pursue their study to the completion of an AB degree in North America."[143] This proposal was unsuccessful, but it testifies to the ambition to build a transpacific educational circuit. Missionaries were re-creating in Hong Kong the educational infrastructure they had lost in China—the institutions that had once filled the *Marine Lynx* with both American missionaries and U.S.-educated Chinese students. As we will see next, by the mid-1960s Hong Kong students were indeed enmeshed in a graduated hierarchy of U.S.-sponsored educational opportunities. Each school, training center, and college was part of an interlocking system that was expanding the colony's transpacific circulations and accelerating its economic transformation into a key node in U.S.-led global capitalism.

CHAPTER III

CHAPTER III

Cold War Partners

Hong Kong's "Refugee Colleges" and American Aid

I n July 1951 the American Universities Club submitted a "scheme" to
the colonial government to provide "post-secondary classes for Chinese (vernacular) students."[1] This club was only one year old, and its
proposal seemed vague.[2] Yet it triggered real concern among senior officials because they suspected it was a front for the U.S. and Nationalist
governments. Paul Frillman of the United States Information Service
(USIS) had submitted the proposal, while the club's principal leaders were
American-returned students with close ties to Taipei and Washington.[3]
Service committee chairman Ernest Moy was a Chinese American
Nationalist operative, while the club's president, C. T. Wang Zhengting
(王正廷), was a 1908 Yale graduate who had served as both foreign minister and ambassador in Washington.[4] The son of a Ningbo Methodist pastor, Wang had been a founder of the Chinese Students' Christian Association and remained a prolific networker after returning to China. When he
fled to Hong Kong in 1950, he reconnected with his fellow Yalie and
native-place associate Tsufa Lee (李祖法). The Lee family's hometown was
near Ningbo, but the family fortune had been built in junk shipping and
real estate in Shanghai. Lee first attended St. John's but graduated from
Yale in 1919. He then became both a successful insurance executive and
the first husband of movie star Tang Ying (唐瑛).[5] Together, Moy, Wang,
and Lee launched this club with U.S. government support. Its mission was
to promote attendance in American colleges and universities, but as

officials suspected, its proposed classes were indeed a covert front for U.S. cultural diplomacy.

Colonial officials had another reason to be nervous, though. In fact, no postsecondary degree courses had *ever* been offered in the modern Chinese language in Hong Kong—as the parenthetical "vernacular" indicated. The Government Vernacular Middle School had been established in 1926, but the University of Hong Kong (HKU) only debated establishing Chinese-language degree courses throughout the 1920s and 1930s. The idea consistently floundered over prejudice and financing.[6] After the war, HKU was reestablished as an English-only institution committed to its original vision of serving as an "instrument for the manifestation of British prestige and the extension of British influence." As late as 1948 it employed only three ethnically Chinese professors.[7] Thus the American Universities Club's proposal threatened to inject new competition into local Chinese-language higher education. On August 2 Governor Grantham summoned the colonial secretary, the director of education, and the Anglican bishop of Hong Kong to discuss the scheme. Grantham instructed the director of education to inform Frillman "that it is not possible for Government to accord him unofficial status in *any* [emphasis added] representations he might make on behalf of the American Universities Club." He also instructed that the club be informed: "Government has under consideration other plans." It did not actually, but Grantham had decided to get some. The meeting concluded by charging Bishop Hall to quickly "submit a concrete and detailed scheme" for the colony's first ever postsecondary classes in Chinese.[8]

This charged intersection between elite U.S.-educated Chinese émigrés, British colonials, and U.S. Cold War agendas defined the transformation of Hong Kong higher education during the 1950s and 1960s. In the previous chapter we saw a similar dynamic fuel the rapid expansion of Christian schools and vocational training centers in Hong Kong. Higher education was a very different realm, however, in which colonial officials welcomed American money but not influence. Colonial officials considered English-language higher education a proud legacy of the British Empire—and one of vital significance to cement Commonwealth ties in the face of decolonization. Yet colonial higher education had always been exclusively for Chinese elites for whom English-language instruction was possible and even preferable. Now the colony's refugee crisis and the arrival of both U.S.-oriented elites and well-funded American organizations was disrupting this terrain. The result was a multivalent, jockeying melee among an intellectually diverse range of new Chinese colleges, their American backers, and an evolving colonial regime.

Scholars are just beginning to wrestle with how pervasive this Sino-Anglo-American dynamic was in the postwar expansion of Hong Kong higher education. Previous scholars once cast this development as apolitical or even natural.[9] In reality, the Cold War's global battle for "hearts and minds" was a driving factor. Émigré Chinese intellectuals and boosters such as C. T. Wang and Tsufa Lee recruited financial support from American organizations with which they had longstanding ties, such as the New York–based Trustees of Lingnan University, the United Board for Christian Colleges in China, the Harvard-Yenching Institute, the Yale-in-China Association, and the Ford and Asia Foundations.[10] Cut off from projects in the new PRC, these American organizations screened potential partners and selected those deemed to be ideologically "singing from the same hymn sheet."[11] This American funding then quickly became so important that no "refugee college" in Hong Kong survived without it. Four U.S.-backed colleges did survive, expand, and demand public support by the late 1950s: the interdenominational Chung Chi College (崇基書院), the Neo-Confucian New Asia College (新亞書院), the amalgamated United College (聯合書院), and the evangelical Hong Kong Baptist College (香港浸信會書院). In 1957 the first three banded together and formed the Chinese Colleges Joint Council to petition for the authority to grant full degrees rather than diplomas.[12] Gradually cornered by these demands, officials tried to regain control in 1959 by offering to fund these three schools to form a whole new second university: The Chinese University of Hong Kong (CUHK). As the colony's director of education stated unequivocally to the governor: "I do not <u>want</u> a second university, but feel that . . . a second degree-granting body may be the only practical solution."[13] By excluding Baptist and bankrolling these three schools, officials hoped to supplant three U.S.-oriented colleges with one Commonwealth university. As we will see in chapter 4, CUHK took on a life of its own under its first vice-chancellor, kuashang Li Choh-ming.

This rapid expansion of bilingual higher education was fundamental to Hong Kong's economic takeoff in the 1970s, analyzed in chapter 6. In the 1950s the colony had a tiny middle class and a very low rate of higher education. By 1967 only 13 percent of teenagers even finished secondary school.[14] Yet by the early 1970s Hong Kong's economy was soaring as the colony became the world's largest sender of foreign students to the United States. This jarring disconnect between mass undereducation and an economic takeoff depended on the particular way in which Hong Kong higher education expanded as both a by-product and a tool of elite transpacific circulations of knowledge and social capital. This chapter examines the first half of this story as the refugee colleges began working with American partners: Chung Chi in 1951, New Asia in 1953, and both Baptist and United in 1956. The chapter concentrates on Chung Chi and Baptist and shows Chinese Christian elites reorienting toward U.S. influence and working with Cold War American projects. Both Chung Chi and Baptist were led by capitalist boosters who adopted kuashang strategies in order to recruit U.S. resources for their personal and institutional benefit. Chung Chi's first chairman of the board, David "W. K." Au Wei-kuo (歐偉國), and Baptist's first president, Lam Chi-fung (林子豐), were both prominent bankers and industrialists before 1949. Yet unlike U.S.-oriented Jiangnan émigrés such as Wang and Lee, Au was Cantonese and Lam was Chaozhou, and neither had studied in the United States. In the shifting context of 1950s Hong Kong, however, they began cultivating American support for Chung Chi and Baptist and simultaneously opened transpacific pathways for themselves and their families. As such, they embody how new Hong Kong–based figures joined the Jiangnan émigrés over the 1950s in using elite social capital to adapt to the postwar U.S.-led order, from recovering their elite social status or replacing former businesses to planning exit strategies. In turn, together Au and Lam make manifest the colonial power structures that still constrained kuashang strategies. While Au and Lam successfully accelerated their colleges' development and improved their families' fortunes, there were also costs to themselves and their institutions.

Chung Chi

Bishop Hall delivered on Governor Grantham's request in only three weeks. In mid-August 1951 he applied to the Executive Council for permission to establish a Christian night school named Chung Chi, or "Honor Christ."[15] Foreign and Chinese Christians had been planning this school, and Hall co-opted their project in order to satisfy the governor's directive. In turn, the Executive Council approved Hall's application for one year as a statement of support for religious freedom against the PRC's repressions.[16] The council also noted the current void of Chinese-language higher education in Hong Kong and Southeast Asia. Since HKU offered only English-language degree courses, the regime suddenly grasped that the region's Chinese youth had no choice but to attend PRC institutions, "a convenient method whereby effortlessly the Canton educators can indoctrinate the youth of Hongkong if they wish."[17] Chung Chi's establishment thus seemed to offer a quick solution. After its approval, Bishop Hall orchestrated the loaning of additional premises in Anglican churches and schools and donated the college's first books. Chung Chi opened in fall 1951 with just 63 students but began the fall 1952 term with 232.[18]

Although the Oxford-educated Bishop Hall was Chung Chi's public sponsor, the college's Chinese leaders were largely U.S.-oriented and the school was reliant on American funding (figure 3.1). The college's board reflected a coalition of British and Cantonese Anglicans, diverse Chinese Protestants from the mainland, and both British and American missionaries.[19] Most of the faculty were émigrés from Guangzhou's Lingnan University, one of the former U.S.-backed Christian colleges. Chung Chi thus quickly came to see itself as the "heir of the 13 former Christian Universities and Colleges of China."[20] Its first president was even Lingnan's last president, "Y. L." Lee Ying-lam (李應林). Lee had attended Oberlin on a YMCA scholarship, worked for the YMCA in China, and rose to be its general secretary before becoming president of Lingnan in 1937. After the war he had also served as deputy director of the Guangzhou office of the China National Relief and Rehabilitation Administration (CNRRA), a position of considerable clout, as discussed in chapter 1.[21] He first fled to Macau in 1949, where he resumed work for the YMCA and started a bookstore, before relocating to Hong Kong in 1951 to join Chung Chi. He became one of the CIA-backed Committee for a Free Asia's "earliest project contacts" in Hong Kong, working on textbooks and serving as the first chairman of the Mencius Foundation, established in 1952.[22] Lee thus had strong American connections and used them to secure Chung Chi's initial grant of US$20,000 from the United Board through the Lingnan Trustees.[23] By comparison, Britain's China Christian Universities Association donated just £750.[24] Rounding out Chung Chi's senior leaders was its first chairman of the board, David Au. An old

Founders of the College

Bishop R. O. Hall, the late Dr. Y. L. Lee,
Mr. David W. K. Au.

Figure 3.1 "Founders of the College," *Chung Chi College, Special Bulletin* (March 1955), 1, in PSRA, Box 2, Folder 21, YUDSL. Courtesy of Special Collections, Yale Divinity School Library.

friend of both Lee and Bishop Hall, Au was a prominent banker and the former chairman of the board of St. John's. Thus he too was well connected among both American missionaries and the Jiangnan émigrés.

This college's coalition was fractious, however, and both Au and colonial officials complained of its "disunity."[25] Some conflicts stemmed from sectarian differences, national rivalries, or just clashing personalities. Conflict also stemmed from divergent visions of the college's mission.

Officials viewed Hong Kong as a small, dependent territory experiencing a temporary humanitarian crisis. Both they and the bishop thus sought to situate Chung Chi within the existing educational system as a diploma-issuing junior college. They aimed to steer the curriculum toward "British rather than American courses of study and methods of examination" and its graduates toward becoming a "useful source of teacher supply."[26] The college's Sino-American partners had a radically different vision of the school and Hong Kong. Rather than a small colony, they saw Hong Kong as the last bastion of Chinese tradition, free enterprise, and Christianity. Instead of training clerks and schoolteachers, they aspired to educate the Christian leaders of an alternative future China. To that end, they planned to develop a degree-granting institution independent of HKU. From the beginning, Y. L. Lee was writing to the United Board and Lingnan Trustees about circumventing "fixed colonial policy" and "the problem of conferring degrees."[27]

These divergent visions would lead to prolonged conflict between colonial officials and the "refugee colleges." Racism slowed both officials' and HKU's leaders' realization that Chung Chi's ambition to grant Chinese-language degrees reflected powerful grassroots aspirations. After the college opened, Governor Grantham appointed a committee to study "the general question of local provision for higher education in the medium of Chinese."[28] Led by Jardine Matheson chairman John Keswick, the Keswick Committee took nearly a year to report. Yet even Keswick realized the answer was obvious. He wrote to Grantham in April 1952, months before submitting the report: "My Committee is very strongly of the opinion that this need is so urgent that an attempt to meet it, even if only in part, should be made in September this year." He went further: "The need for it is almost self evident."[29] Grantham thereafter prioritized the issue and offered firm support to launch HKU's Chinese-language degree programs.[30] Yet the university's faculty and administrators delayed, largely on the grounds of finance.[31] In January 1953 Vice-Chancellor Lindsey Ride proposed admitting just thirty "vernacular" students and then cramming English into them through a special high school.[32] In February Director of Education Douglas Crozier, exasperated, wrote that "the scheme now put forward by the University Working Committee is so far removed from the spirit and intention of the recommendations of the Keswick Committee" as to be "part of the problem."[33] Keswick bluntly reminded officials that there were "a great many Chinese in Hongkong who earnestly desire to study in the Chinese language" and that "any attempt to ignore this very legitimate aspiration and to insist on 'English for the Chinese' is wrong."[34] Yet in March 1953 HKU proposed to admit just thirty to sixty Chinese-language students. Ride fancied that together Chung Chi and this program could "cater for practically the whole of the vernacular demand."[35] Since these opportunities were obviously insufficient, the refugee colleges continued to gain applicants and petition for degree-granting powers. As late as 1957 HKU education professor Kenneth Priestley was arguing that Chinese-language degrees were impossible because of an imagined lack of college-level Chinese textbooks.[36]

As a result, Chung Chi's development depended on its Chinese leaders' ability to recruit money through their American networks. It is critical to stress that these U.S. organizations had no desire to become Chung Chi's dominant backers, in part because many assumed that Hong Kong was doomed to a PRC invasion.[37] As a result, while Y. L. Lee's network secured the United Board's first check, he and Au lobbied continually to maintain their support, even using guilt.[38] In turn, the Americans constantly tried to recruit greater British contributions. The United Board's executive secretary William Fenn wrote in 1954: "We are reluctant to make Chung Chi too completely an American institution. Perhaps we have set too high a goal for the British in suggesting that one-quarter of the cost for plant and current support should come from British sources."[39] Indeed, through 1959 Chung Chi still received 40 percent of its operating funds from the United Board and Lingnan Trustees.[40] Its construction fund was also U.S.-dependent. By 1959 it had received HK$3.14 million from overseas: HK$2.725 million (86.8 percent) from American sources, and $418,000 (13 percent) from Canadian and British supporters.[41]

American support was not the inevitable byproduct of postwar U.S. power but rather depended on college leaders' American social capital. McCarthy-era politics made sending large amounts of money to the doorstep of "Red China" a questionable proposition. In May 1953 Olin Wanna-maker of the Lingnan Trustees wrote to Fenn to express concern about "Communist infiltration" of Chung Chi's board. Fenn's response is succinct evidence of the role played by visible American social capital in facilitating Hong Kong's transformative transpacific relations. Fenn replied that he did "not happen to know everyone personally," but "it is hard for me to think of a 'safer' group of people." He stated that because of the Chinese leaders' positions as "wardens, principals, and headmistresses of Church schools in Hong Kong," he was without "any reason to question their loyalty." They struck him as "eminently respectable and safe members of Hong Kong society." Fenn did not actually know them but was willing to stake his own credibility on their resumes and reputations. He concluded by reiterating that the half dozen Chinese members of the board would "be quite acceptable on Formosa," most especially the chairman, David Au.[42]

David Au encapsulates how the kuashang orientation expanded beyond Jiangnan émigrés and fused with older huashang practices of network building and foreign collaboration. Au was born in Sydney in 1889 to the manager of the local Sincere Department Store, Au Bin (歐彬). He first came to Hong Kong to complete his early education in Anglican schools, before moving to Shanghai and graduating from St. John's in 1918.[43] He then began working for Sincere in Shanghai and in 1921 married Frances Louie (Lei Yurong, 雷玉蓉), a graduate of St. Mary's Hall.[44] Sincere dispatched Au and Louie to London for four years to oversee its British operations. They returned to Shanghai in 1925, and in 1929 he joined the Shanghai Commercial and Savings Bank (SCSB) as an assistant manager under K. P. Chen (see chapter 1). By the early 1930s Au was also elected chairman of the board of St. John's, a position just vacated by Liu Hongsheng. In twelve years Au had soared from a graduate of this college to its ultimate authority. He also briefly led the SCSB's offices in Hong Kong from 1934, before former finance minister Song Ziwen poached him to reopen the Bank of Canton in November 1936.[45] K. P. Chen later described Au as one of his two "great disappointments" and complained that he left for "better pay . . . without giving us a chance to find a successor."[46] In 1939, with Shanghai and Guangzhou under Japanese occupation, Au returned to Hong Kong as Far East deputy manager of the British *hong* Butterfield & Swire. He became an active member of St. John's Cathedral and friends with Bishop Hall. As a result, by the outbreak of the Pacific War, Au had lived on three continents and built cross-pollinating networks that spanned domestic and overseas Chinese capitalists, senior Nationalist officials, U.S.-backed Christian institutions in China, the Anglican Church, and a leading British firm in Hong Kong. These accumulated experiences show a highly mobile and adaptive influence trader responding to crisis. After the war Au also served as president of the Grand Lodge of China Freemasons, providing entrée among Hong Kong's elite

Cantonese.[47] Richard Lee Ming-chak (李銘澤), brother of Ansie Lee Sperry (chapter 1), was a "dedicated" Freemason and an educational booster himself, serving on the Keswick Committee.[48]

As decolonization and China's communist transition changed the game, Au pragmatically reoriented toward the United States. He began covert collaboration with a bevy of U.S.-backed projects in Hong Kong. It was his lifeline. After fleeing Shanghai, he was re-elected president of the reconstituted St. John's alumni association in Hong Kong. In 1953 he became chairman of a new joint alumni association of all the former thirteen Christian colleges.[49] Upon hearing of this new association, the United Board rushed to offer him assistance. Au replied that 385 alumni had attended their first banquet, and that the association was managing thorny political issues and considering how to place alumni in jobs in Hong Kong.[50] Employing a classic immigrant strategy, Au was brokering labor opportunities for fellow immigrants of shared background—in this case, not on behalf of native-place guanxi but for his educational networks. These particular networks marked him as a valuable potential asset to U.S. government officers. As such, in 1952 Au was handpicked as the first Hong Kong director of Aid Refugee Chinese Intellectuals (ARCI). As scholars such as Madeline Hsu, Glen Peterson, and Meredith Oyen have examined, this nominally private organization aimed to recruit educated refugees deemed valuable and resettle them in Taiwan or the United States.[51] Like the American Universities Club, it was founded by Ernest Moy and sponsored by a virulently anticommunist congressman, Walter Judd. Its funding came primarily from the U.S. State Department and Central Intelligence Agency, and thus ARCI was a mask for U.S. government agendas. Au's simultaneous leadership over ARCI, Chung Chi, and the alumni associations is revealing. Through ARCI, he was directly in the pay of the U.S. government, while he was also in debt to the United Board, which loaned him US$2,000 in 1951 to cover his daughter's U.S. education because his assets were "locked up in Shanghai."[52] His new overlapping positions thus demonstrate how elite émigrés could repurpose and monetize existing social capital in order to build American social capital in post-1949 Hong Kong. In turn, the United Board came to rely on him.

Simultaneously, as an active Anglican and Swire executive, Au maintained visible British social capital that masked his new American associations. The United Board explicitly valued this layered dynamic, as Fenn related to Wannamaker when assuring him of Au's anticommunism: "Certainly the chairman, David Au, through long years of association with the firm of Butterfield and Swire, has established himself as both 'capitalistic and imperialistic.'"[53] Privately, Au described his faith in shades of gray: "Although I am classified as an Episcopalian, the Anglican tradition is not deep-rooted enough in me not to appreciate other points of view."[54] He was thus able to work between British and American interests in ways that proved transformative for Chung Chi. A succinct example is the appointment of Rev. James Pott. In October 1953 Au reported to Fenn that the American Episcopal Church had offered to transfer Pott to Hong Kong after "completion of his Army duties in Tokyo." Au intended to make him vice president to relieve Y. L. Lee, who was seriously ill.[55] When Fenn replied unenthusiastically, Au explained his real logic: "It is not so much enthusiasm on our part over his qualifications either as a teacher or as an administrator as the fact that he was offered to us." In particular, he elaborated on Pott's purchase in colonial eyes:

> Another factor which will put him in a favorable light in Hongkong is that he comes from the Episcopal Church and it happens that Mr. Crozier, the Director of Education, is head of the vestry of St. John's Cathedral. The Anglican Church still has a large influence in this Colony and short of an English celrgyman [sic], an American Episcopal layman comes a close second. I say this not because I am episcopalian [sic] nor because I think it is a healthy situation but facts are facts.[56]

Au valued Pott for his social capital and access to British trust and networks. Pott was duly elected vice president, while Au continued installing missionaries in other positions, including Sidney Anderson and Sterling Whitener (chapter 2), J. Theron Illick, Loren Noren, Andrew Roy, and his favorite E. E. Walline ("the sanest and soundest of the lot").[57] Some were simply free staff in his eyes, while others' bicultural skills granted them unique capacities. Roy for one served as vice president throughout the 1950s and routinely stepped in as acting president. His son J. Stapleton Roy later became U.S. ambassador to Singapore, China, and Indonesia.

Most important, David Au's layered social capitals allowed him to maneuver between American and British interests to procure the college's permanent campus and first buildings. Au and Fenn maintained a constant correspondence to discuss the college's needs and budget, as well as consult on appointments and the "impression their names will make on the educational authorities."[58] This dialogue was predicated on a sense of trust and common purpose derived from shared religion and memories of the thirteen Christian colleges. In the same November 1953 letter in which he discussed Pott, Au also suggested that the United Board act as guarantor for a HK$1 million loan from the government so that Chung Chi could construct a permanent campus.[59] Fenn dismissed this idea, stating that the board's answer was "almost certain to be a simple no. Such long term commitments are simply not part of United Board policy."[60] This refusal stemmed from their institutions' lack of a legal relationship, as well as doubts over Hong Kong's long-term security. Au anticipated this response but plunged ahead anyway. On December 11 he replied, "I rather expected that." He then revealed that Chung Chi had already applied for this loan, a land grant in the New Territories district of Shatin, and the government's erection of a railway station there.[61]

Colonial officials, the United Board, and Au all knew that Chung Chi could not afford library books. If this loan were approved, someone would have to help the college repay it. Au bluffed to officials that the loan would definitely be repaid "from its supporters, mainly in America."[62] Fenn, though, had refused repayment. Au was gambling that since the United Board and Lingnan Trustees had made "considerable annual appropriations," they likely would continue doing so "unless Hong Kong should get involved in actual fighting."[63] Au was exploiting the American backers' trust to reach into their pockets. Simultaneously, he flattered colonial officials. He wrote to Crozier about revamping particular syllabi along British lines and grooming students to be schoolteachers and social workers, precisely what officials wished to hear. Crozier singled out these remarks out for comment when forwarding the loan's application.[64] Yet he also concluded letters to Au with statements such as his "personal expression of goodwill for the Chung Chi College, and to assure you and the members of your Council of my support and sympathy at all times."[65] These are warm words from a senior colonial official. Such trust in Au made the loan seem like a win-win to the government. By fronting this loan, it would gain leverage to help "its man" and future British administrators turn this institution toward Commonwealth systems. And if American support faltered, Chung Chi would default and be directly reshaped with only a small loss. That expenditure was acceptable, as one official pointed out: "The assistance requested from Government is very small relative to the value of the type of College into which Chung Chi might develop."[66] Either way, the loan seemed to herald the remodeling of this young U.S.-oriented college.

Upon receiving the application, Governor Grantham appointed another commission, known as the Ad Hoc Committee, under HKU's Kenneth Priestley, the man arguing that Chinese-language degrees were inconceivable. Au also joined this committee and wrote assuring the government "of our every cooperation."[67] The next day he wrote to Fenn with a blunt analysis of the committee's power dynamics. He thought Crozier was "obviously pushing our case as far as his official duties permitted," while he and the Bishop considered the other members "sympathetic" and "cooperative." Yet Au warned that the loan posed "of course one danger": an increase in control of the college "at the expense of our independence and freedom as a Christian College." Public funding would impose oversight and curb proselytization. Au phrased this warning casually but knew this risk was unacceptable to the United Board. It violated their entire vision for the college. Au assured Fenn that since he was a committee member, "I shall be able to report from time to time the trend of their thoughts and if I sense there is a danger that our principles might be sacrificed, I shall take appropriate action to defend them."[68] Au was performing a situational identity. To colonial officials, he gave deference and conformity; to the Americans, he gave earnest confessions and friendly statements of common purpose. His life of mobility and adaptation had trained him to tack between competing centers of power by understanding their goals and locking them in to what network sociologists call "goal-oriented sequences of strategic play."[69] Sunzi might term it *shi* (勢).

The loan application worried Fenn, but not enough to grasp Au's real agenda. Fenn wrote promptly that he was "somewhat troubled" because the loan "seems to involve an indebtedness which only additional grants from the United Board (or possibly mission boards) can repay." Indeed, it did. Au had effectively committed both parties without New York's consent. Yet Fenn was determined to trust: "It therefore tends to involve the United Board, although of course not legally or even intentionally on your part, in a type of arrangement into which it is not its practice to go." Au and Y. L. Lee's American networks had led the United Board to put itself in a vague position as the school's primary backer yet without any control. Even within this letter, Fenn continued to refuse "any right to question your actions in this case," while implicitly doing that.[70] Two months later he sent Au a meditation on their organizations' relationship, "one which I find it a little difficult to define or describe." While the United Board had deliberately "avoided any long-term commitment," it now felt "a certain moral responsibility for seeing that [Chung Chi] continues to exist." He mused over options without resolution.[71] It was a fraught and codependent partnership produced by the intersection of U.S. imperial ambitions and Au's kuashang strategies.

The Ad Hoc Report debuted in March 1954 and predictably mandated the college's reorientation toward British academic models in exchange for the loan. The report found the college's ambitions pretentious and lamented both "the American-Chinese character of the curricular arrangements" and "the lack of connection between the entry standards of the College and the matriculation standards of a British University." It lectured that the college's "curriculum must beyond doubt spring from the functions appropriate to an institute of higher learning in a British Colony." It whined that "the needs of higher education in Hong Kong differ quite seriously from the needs of higher education in the United States, and from the needs of higher education upon the mainland of China."[72] The report's effort to reinscribe the imperial relationship is plain. American systems were viewed as illogical, even unnatural. Yet this distaste for the college's character was exactly what Au needed. He already knew what Priestley thought and let him write it. As Au had related to officials, he also knew the United Board had all the necessary funds and might just give it to them. To achieve that, he needed the United Board to see this threat in writing. He personally mailed Fenn his own advanced copy of the report, which inadvertently "peeved" the head of the Asia Christian Colleges Association (ACCA) in London.[73] Fenn reacted so strongly upon reading it that Au replied innocently "regarding your reaction." He explained: "We only approached the Government for a loan when there were indications that the [United Board] would not be able to help us." He continued wryly, "We thought that application to Government would have the advantage of knowing Government's attitude toward us." More precisely, he wanted New York to be confronted with "government's attitude." Au's only editorial assessment was that the report contained "valuable suggestions . . . some of them relevant and some not." He separated the kicker into its own bulleted paragraph, though: "The free grant of the land is not conditional upon the acceptance of the loan. If we have the money ~~available~~ to build, the land is available to us just the same."[74]

The loan application was a gamble that paid off handsomely. Fenn immediately replied with dramatic news: the United Board would approve "the full amount needed for the new campus of Chung Chi." This grant—not a loan—amounted to US$200,000 spread over three years, if the ACCA would contribute a matching one-third grant. The trustees were "unanimous" that Chung Chi should develop "without depending upon a loan from the Hong Kong government," since a loan would "increase the consideration Chung Chi would have to give to requests from that government." The Ad Hoc Report had ensured that New York could not stomach increased colonial control. Fenn also confessed that the ACCA stipulation was meaningless: "Therefore, the United Board gift is contingent upon action which ACCA appears to be in no position to take."[75] Indeed, the ACCA subsequently informed officials that it had "no intention of contributing on a large scale financially" until they were "confident that the organization and curriculum of the College are planned to fit adequately into the educational set-up of the Colony."[76] Eventually the United Board just made the whole grant.

David Au used kuashang strategies to invert Chung Chi's dependence by using network centrality to stage an influence bidding war. His layered British and American social capital allowed him to destabilize colonial control and position Chung Chi to receive a free campus and rail link from the government and free buildings from their American partners. Together, those contributions allowed a makeshift institution to transform into a permanent college within three years—an incredible achievement in any context. Au's success did not stem from just audacity or mendacity, though; it depended on elite networks, knowledge, and strategies. Neither colonial officials nor the United Board wanted this outcome. He had to understand both sides' priorities, tailor his language accordingly, and structurally isolate them from each other in order to maintain trust and hide his agenda. Colonial officials could easily have refused the loan or invested the money in another college. If Au had not correctly anticipated that the United Board would pony up, the college could have been stuck with the loan and been both secularized and Anglicized. Of all the parties, it was Au who had the broadest knowledge and networks.

The loan's evaporation left officials scrambling, and suddenly Au's own support at the college also evaporated. After he officially withdrew the loan application, officials still insisted on appointing two nominees to the college's board, a recommendation of the Ad Hoc Report.[77] Bishop Hall protested, but officials insisted to try to ensure that the college's development be "in line with our own British standards of education."[78] Yet officials debated how else to exert leverage without the loan. One reasoned: "We can still exercise control . . . through the requirements we shall impose when the Chung Chi graduates seek employment in the teaching and other public services."[79] Most thought that this influence was too indirect. They decided to insist on remaining the trustee of the new campus since it now "seemed fairly certain that the Board would get all their funds from America. Our sole remaining control lay, therefore, in the matter of the land."[80] As this situation played out, the dying Y. L. Lee resigned in August 1954 and Au became acting president amid a succession crisis.[81] Au told Fenn that he had "been in a rather difficult position as Chairman for the past two or three years" and was struggling "to maintain a sensible equilibrium" between the board members.[82] Others recalled it differently. According to Sterling Whitener, Au's succession as acting president triggered grave concern among his fellow Christians due to his worldly lifestyle and extramarital relationships. YMCA secretary S. H. Pang purportedly convinced Whitener to intervene and prevent Au from becoming the permanent second president.[83] At Pang's request, in January 1955 Whitener instead nominated Dr. Lin Dao-yang (凌道揚), a Christian Hakka forestry expert with a Ph.D. degree from Yale who had served with Y. L. Lee at the CNRRA.[84] Lin was duly elected and officially became president of Chung Chi in February 1955. Au resigned soon thereafter and passed away in March 1959, with college leaders surprised, the United Board realizing that he had not repaid their loan, and two of his three children settled in the United States.[85]

American social capital remained a hallmark of Chung Chi's development for the remainder of its independent existence. Lin Dao-yang maintained Andrew Roy as his second-in-command, while regularly traveling to the United States, where his son Jimmy was studying to be an electrical engineer.[86] As seen in chapter 2, the college's largely U.S.-educated faculty also increasingly channeled students toward transpacific futures. A survey in 1961 found that 31.8 percent of Chung Chi graduates had become local teachers, while 29 percent were now pursuing further studies abroad, largely in the United States.[87] After Bishop Hall torpedoed the renewal of Lin's contract in 1960, Lin moved over to United College as its second president and later retired to California.[88] Chung Chi's third president, Dr. "C. T." Yung Chi-tung (容啟東), was also a product of transpacific circulations. Yung's father had also been among Yung Wing's CEM students in the 1870s (see chapter 1), while C. T. Yung himself received his Ph.D. degree in botany from the University of Chicago in 1937 and taught at U.S. universities during the war.[89] As we will see next chapter, he would be the first to conceive what later became the first MBA program in East or Southeast Asia.

New Asia College

While officials labored to steer Chung Chi toward Commonwealth systems, a second and very different U.S.-backed college was taking shape. Grace Ai-ling Chou's excellent study of New Asia renders it necessary only to summarize its early history. It began in a high school in October 1949, days after Mao's proclamation of the new PRC. Rather than Chinese Christians, New Asia's founders were Neo-Confucian scholars devoted to preserving the essence of traditional Chinese culture, which they believed was "in every danger of being extinguished on its home ground by its own people." They viewed the communist victory as "the takeover of the homeland of Chinese culture by a force unmistakably hostile to it" and communism itself as "fundamentally antithetical to the basic premises and values of Chinese culture." The core essence they sought to preserve was the literature and philosophy of Confucianism. Leaders such as the historian Qian Mu (錢穆) and philosopher Tang Junyi (唐君毅) were both Neo-Confucian humanists, meaning that they still advocated for the continued relevance of post–Song Confucian thought with curated aspects of "Western" learning. New Asia quickly distinguished itself through its emphasis on the humanities and general education. Simultaneously, most of its leaders had low opinions of Hong Kong, believing "they had arrived in a cultural and intellectual wasteland." They thus did not encourage the study of Cantonese. All courses were taught in Mandarin, except English.[90]

While culturally proud and intellectually rigorous, New Asia struggled to survive. Although founded in 1949, it was not granted official registration until September 1950 and incorporated as a nonprofit only in July 1953.[91] In contrast, Chung Chi's registration in fall 1951 provoked discussion at the highest levels. Nowhere in these discussions of Chung Chi was

New Asia's existence even mentioned. Chung Chi's combination of Anglican and American support was essential to its rapid development, while the arrival of U.S. support and improved colonial relations would give New Asia a second wind. In the words of longtime Yale-in-China representative B. Preston Schoyer, in 1953 New Asia remained "a struggling, slum-housed little college of six teachers and 100 students."[92] Yet the college's intellectual rigor, anticommunism, and nonprofit status attracted Yale-in-China's game-changing support.[93]

Since New Asia's founders did not have kuashang strategies and lacked substantial British or American networks, it was Yale-in-China that provided the necessary funds and connections. After its representatives were expelled from the PRC in May 1951, Yale-in-China dispatched Yale history professor Harry Rudin to Hong Kong in June 1953 to investigate possible partners in this unfamiliar British colony.[94] Rudin had an old Yale classmate living in Hong Kong, the same Tsufa Lee who helped found the American Universities Club.[95] Rudin also connected with another Yale graduate working in Hong Kong as a journalist, Schoyer, who helped guide Rudin to New Asia.[96] Rudin was particularly impressed with Qian Mu but recalled that Qian was wary of Yale-in-China's missionary past and potential Christian strings. Rudin also examined Chung Chi but decided it had sufficient sponsors and too much "sectarian infighting."[97] Crucially, Rudin also reached out to the government to ensure that "the further development of this institution was both desirable and welcome to the Hong Kong Government."[98] He and Director Crozier met for a "long talk" that successfully secured "the 'green light.'"[99] As a result, Rudin concluded his visit by proposing that Yale-in-China award New Asia US$25,000 per year for five years, along with helping to secure a US$200,000 grant from the Ford Foundation. Yale-in-China then mined its donor networks to recruit support from the Asia Foundation, the Rockefeller Foundation, and Harvard-Yenching. As Chou highlights, this funding was "such significant support that New Asia may not have survived without it."[100] Simultaneously, Yale-in-China continued building relationships with officials and its representatives continued "mediating communications between the college's Mandarin-speaking refugee scholars and Hong Kong's often inscrutable British administrators."[101] As a result, in 1956 Yale-in-China secured a free land grant from the government for the college's first permanent location. It then donated the full construction funds.[102]

In no uncertain terms, American social capital was as transformative for New Asia as it was for Chung Chi. As with the United Board and Lingnan Trustees at Chung Chi, Yale-in-China's fundraising not only flowed into buildings, equipment, scholarships, and salaries but also built relationships.[103] In short, American aid enabled both schools to transform within a few years from virtual book clubs into permanent institutions. And because American aid also entrenched U.S. academic models, New Asia joined Chung Chi in beginning to channel students toward transpacific circulations. By 1959 a total of twenty-five New Asia graduates had entered graduate school—twelve at New Asia's own Research Institute, ten in the United States, and none in Britain.[104]

The key difference separating New Asia's American aid from that of Chung Chi was the absence of kuashang leaders. As late as 1959 New Asia's board of governors had just nine members: five Chinese scholars, two Yale-in-China representatives, one British academic, and one Chinese business-man, a contractor who had attended the University of Pennsylvania.[105] A year later the arrival of colonial funding mandated the board's expansion to seventeen members. Numerous businessmen now joined, including MIT graduate and manager of South East Textile Co. "H. T." Liu Hang-tung (劉漢棟).[106] Yet the college remained under the control of Neo-Confucian scholars. As a result, the institution was still run philosophically, as demonstrated by the crisis over the college's intention to fly the Nationalist flag in 1959 despite government prohibitions.[107] Without wading into this incident, it is hard to imagine the pragmatic David Au steering Chung Chi into an existential crisis over a flag. In turn, neither personal gain nor transpacific circulations were primary goals for New Asia's leaders when accepting American aid. As such, New Asia underscores the intellectual gulfs that still existed between the colleges and prepares us to understand the impact of kuashang Li Choh-ming in the next chapter.

Hong Kong Baptist

By 1956 there were nine 'refugee colleges' in Hong Kong, but two additional institutions now appeared through American backing: Hong Kong Baptist College (HKBC) and United College. United formed from a combination of five struggling institutions. Before CUHK's formation, United remained by far the least developed college and can thus also be briefly summarized. As Zhang Yang has analyzed, the Asia Foundation was the primary agent behind United's formation. The Committee for Free Asia (later the Asia Foundation) had established the Mencius Educational Foundation in 1952 as a covert arm for cultural diplomacy activities, with Y. L. Lee as chairman.[108] Through Mencius, the Asia Foundation had begun funding eight different colleges, including Chung Chi and New Asia. By 1956, however, Columbia University president and Asia Foundation director Grayson Kirk recommended consolidation to advance the institutions' development and the foundation's political aims.[109] Pingzheng, Huaqiao, Canton Overseas, Wenhua, and Guangxia Colleges agreed to form United College under Dr. Tseung Fat-im (蔣法賢), an HKU-trained physician. The Asia Foundation also strong-armed Mencius to cut off funding to the colleges that did not join. Tseung, however, was perceived as an ally of the colonial government and clashed with Chung Chi, New Asia, and his own board. He was forced to resign in 1959, which triggered waves of student and staff departures and left United "in a state of crisis" under Lin Dao-yang, who moved over from Chung Chi in 1960. Thus while United became part of CUHK, by fall 1962 it had just 107 students compared with 533 at Chung Chi and 432 at New Asia.[110]

Hong Kong Baptist was very different. It grew rapidly, pursued a clear ideological agenda, and had an esteemed founder and first president, Lam Chi-fung. Like United, though, Baptist grew primarily from the support of a single American backer, the Southern Baptist Board of Foreign Missions (SBBFM) of Richmond, Virginia. The Southern Baptists were the college's principal source of funding and nonlocal personnel, while Lam cultivated extensive connections to U.S. and global Baptist institutions, including serving as the vice president of the Baptist World Alliance from 1955 to 1965. Yet there was a virtual absence of British influence at Baptist that impaired its development. Lam's overreliance on kuashang strategies and the college's commitment to proselytization resulted in its exclusion from CUHK. As a result, Baptist underscores the balancing that was still necessary for kuashang strategies.

Lam was an influential Chaozhou coal merchant, banker, industrialist, and devout Baptist. Before the Second World War he lacked any discernible connection to the United States. Instead, like David Au, he had risen at the intersection of huashang strategies and European imperial networks. He grew up in the northeastern corner of Guangdong as the eldest son of a Shantou (Swatow) Baptist pastor. He first attended the Tung Man

College in Xiamen, where he learned English. He then began at the Rockefeller Foundation–funded Peking Union Medical College at his father's urging but decided to give up medicine and moved to Hong Kong in 1916.[111] There he worked as an English-language clerk for an importing firm before launching his own Sze Wai Co., which imported anthracite coal from French Indochina through the Charbonnages du Tonkin and distributed it across the southern China coastline.[112] Like Liu Hongsheng (chapter 1), coal remained the foundation of Lam's fortune, but in 1922 he also helped found the Ka Wah Bank (嘉華銀行), with branches in Guangzhou, Hong Kong, and later Shanghai.

Lam translated business success into traditional forms of social power through native-place and charity institutions, such as leading the Hong Kong Chaozhou Chamber of Commerce (潮州商會).[113] As its chairman, he cultivated relationships with Nationalist figures and lobbied them on Chaozhou people's behalf. In March 1939 he hosted a seaside dinner party for a striking set: the aforementioned C. T. Wang, just returned from Washington; Yan Huiqing (顏惠慶), another American-returned student and former ambassador to Washington who was now the chairman of China's Red Cross; and Xu Shiying (許世英), former Chinese ambassador to Japan and wartime head of the Central Relief Commission.[114] Months later the press recorded how Lam secured special aid for Chaozhou refugees from Xu.[115] This kind of successful networking led to Lam's election in 1939 as chairman of the Hong Kong YMCA. In this position he was socially active and often welcoming distinguished visitors to Hong Kong, such as Thai officials and leading Chinese Filipino merchants.[116] In 1941 Lam was also elected chairman of the Hong Kong Baptist Association (HKBA), which had formed in 1938 as the colony's congregations absorbed refugees from the Japanese invasion.[117] After Hong Kong's surrender to Japan, Lam and his family evacuated to neutral Portuguese Macau, except for eldest son Daniel Lam See-hin (林思顯), who had entered the University of the Philippines and was imprisoned by the Japanese, likely in the same camp as Henry and Ansie Sperry (chapter 1).[118] Thus Lam Chi-fung's prewar rise followed standard patterns for Hong Kong. A Guangdong native, he had thrived in the huashang trading networks that spanned Europe's Southeast Asian empires, led traditional Chinese and Christian social organizations, and cultivated ties to Nationalist officials.

With the Allies' victory, Lam began connecting his business and social activities to the United States. In January 1947 his son Daniel married the daughter of the newly independent Philippines' former wealthiest Chinese merchant, the late so-called Lumber King Dee Ching Chuan (李清泉). Before his death in California in 1940, Dee had developed his fortune primarily through privileged logging concessions granted to his Negros Philippine Lumber Company by the U.S. Insular Government.[119] It is thus striking that shortly after the wedding, Lam sent Daniel to Baylor Law School and launched his own first business aimed at the U.S. market.[120] Highlighting overlap between guanxi practice and kuashang strategies, he partnered with four native-place associates to found the Chiap Hua Manufactory Company (捷和), which brought the Pacific War's vast detritus of scrap metal to Hong Kong and melted it down to make consumer goods such as flashlights, lighters, and clocks, primarily for export to the United States—a remarkable example of salvage and repurposing from the ruins of industrialized warfare.[121] As cheap kerosene and war in French Indochina reshaped market conditions, Chiap Hua's salvage business even replaced coal as the foundation of Lam's fortune. This new transpacific circuit was so profitable that in 1954 Chiap Hua formalized a production partnership with the U.S. flashlight corporation Ray-O-Vac.[122] In the late 1950s they expanded this partnership with a joint venture in Bangkok.[123] Simultaneously, after second son David Lam See-chai (林思齊) graduated from Lingnan in spring 1947, he entered Temple University for his MBA degree, graduating in a year and beginning a Ph.D. degree in economics at NYU. After David decided against this path and returned to Hong Kong, his father put him in charge of the Ka Wah Bank.[124] Much like K. P. Chen (chapter 1), he applied his American studies in management and economics to update its operations.[125]

Lam also began engaging his Christian and social activities with expanding U.S. systems. Reelected as YMCA chairman in December 1947, he immediately invited its American representatives to Hong Kong and welcomed them with a speech described as "warmly praising in every possible way" (讚揚備至).[126] More unusually, he then directed the YMCA in August 1948 to host the Hong Kong Industry and Commerce Exhibition, arguing to a puzzled press that a trade goods fair did reflect "our organization's Christian spirit" through a liberal interpretation of the meaning of humanitarian service.[127] More likely, with the turn in the Chinese civil war, he was advertising his interlinked Christianity, anticommunism, and internationalism. In turn, as American missionaries began arriving to Hong Kong in 1949, Lam was "especially hospitable."[128]

He rented apartments on their behalf and had coal delivered during the colony's brief winter.[129] He wrote to U.S. mission boards requesting that they reassign "as many of these missionaries as possible to Hong Kong."[130] After these reassigned missionaries founded the Hong Kong-Macau Baptist Mission, they began funneling massive U.S. resources into collaborative institution building with the Hong Kong Baptist Association under Lam. In 1951 the HKBA launched a theological seminary to train ministers for congregations across Hong Kong and Southeast Asia, while the SBBFM and colonial government gave the Baptist Association HK$1.7 million in grants to reconstruct the Pui Ching Middle School.[131] Pui Ching reopened in fall 1953, and Lam remained its president until 1965. The HKBA also used Richmond's money to open houses of worship across the colony—by 1958, four churches, fifteen chapels, and numerous resettlement houses and clinics.[132] As in chapter 2, this rapid expansion demonstrates how Chinese Christians with kuashang strategies could tap into U.S. resources despite small numbers. The number of Baptist congregants rose from just 1,778 in 1938 to 11,348 by 1958 and 15,000 by the mid-1960s.[133] Although the total community thus remained small, Richmond encouraged the Baptist Association to launch a college and hospital.[134]

Hong Kong Baptist College opened in September 1956 with Lam as president, and the institution developed primarily through his networks. It held its first classes in Pui Ching Middle School, and Lam personally recruited all the initial staff from among Baptist congregants. He chose individuals who he knew were neither "Communist sympathizers" nor "militant Nationalists."[135] American missionaries also claimed that the student body was "carefully screened."[136] The money primarily came from the United States. Like Yale-in-China, the SBBFM provided roughly US$25,000 annually for the college's operating budget, and by 1965 a total of US$375,000 for buildings and equipment.[137] Richmond also provided access to networks of wealthy American Baptists, including flying out donors and facilitating U.S. trips for college leaders.[138] Lam himself began to go annually.[139] The college even set up a foundation in San Francisco in 1963 "to enable U.S.A. contributors to receive tax concessions."[140] Within Hong Kong, long-time vice president and missionary Maurice Anderson testified that Lam served as the institution's public "prestige-giver, fund-raiser, and chief agent for replenishment of energy." According to Anderson, Lam "had a large circle of governmental, church, business and other acquaintances and friends in the Colony. He was constantly in attendance at dinner parties and other functions. Not infrequently he attended three such occasions in one evening."[141] Lam also used his wealth to project Christian munificence and attract supporters. He and his wife Chan Chik-ting (陳植亭) celebrated their fiftieth wedding anniversary with a thanksgiving religious service and dinner for a thousand guests at which they personally donated HK$550,000 to the college.[142]

Dominant U.S. financial support ensured that Baptist College remained heavily staffed by American missionaries and U.S.-educated Chinese Baptists. According to Anderson, Lam left most day-to-day decisions "to his western counterparts." He "never presided over faculty and staff meetings and had little contact with faculty and staff members. The meetings were conducted in English and presided over by the Vice President."[143] In addition to serving as vice president, Anderson was also the first dean of studies and head of the Sociology Department.[144] The founding chairman of the board, Dr. David "Y. K." Wong Yue-kwong (黃汝光), had also graduated from Lingnan and studied architecture at the University of Redlands and Caltech.[145] He too began traveling regularly to the United States to receive honorary degrees, visit Baptist donors, speak at conferences, and attend his son's wedding.[146] He and his wife eventually retired to California.[147] Under Wong, six of the board's eighteen seats were reserved for American missionaries, while all its Chinese members as of 1958 possessed a college degree from a former American missionary college and/or a U.S. institution. The same held true for the college council. Throughout the early 1960s roughly 20 percent of the faculty and staff remained U.S. citizens, from retired professors to exchange fellows.[148] In turn, Baptist was much more evangelical than Chung Chi. It required students to take courses in Christianity, "urged" them to attend church and Sunday School, and sponsored campus revivals culminating in conversion services in chapels or Lam's home.[149]

Transpacific circulations were one of the college's top goals for students. Lam routinely touted the college's many "international" affiliations, exchanges, and postgraduate opportunities, but he largely meant the United States, as primarily only U.S. institutions accepted its diploma. By the mid-1960s the SBBFM had organized regular exchange programs on the college's behalf with Baylor and Oklahoma Baptist, while Lam had negotiated similar arrangements with Stetson and San Francisco State.[150] The college's recruitment materials also explicitly brandished such transpacific possibilities. Anderson explained that they used "possible affiliations with Baptist universities in the United States" as a lure because local youth were eager to seize "the possibility of transfer to American colleges." The college also expected its "faculty to help those who graduated with good records to pursue further studies in the United States."[151] As a result, Baptist graduates tended heavily toward U.S. graduate schools. The winter 1964 issue of its *College News* recorded that twenty-seven alumni had pursued further studies overseas since 1960. Twenty had entered U.S. institutions, five went to Canadian institutions, and two had combined studies.[152] In 1969 the publication celebrated that seventeen graduates now possessed doctorates in math and science—three from Canadian institutions, one from a British institution, and thirteen from U.S. institutions.[153] Thus, under Lam, Baptist coalesced as a kuashang institution that "heavily screened" students and staff before funneling as many as possible across the Pacific to pursue Christian, capitalist futures.

In turn, Lam's kuashang strategies brought substantial personal gain. His annual trips to the United States enabled him also to undergo medical treatment, receive honorary degrees, and give invited sermons and speeches at Baptist institutions with titles such as "What I See in America."[154] President Lyndon Johnson even addressed the same Baylor commencement in 1965, and the two men's ensuing photograph together received a place of honor on Lam's desk.[155] During these trips he met with Southern Baptist leaders to strategize the college's development and "made many contacts for the College in the States."[156] All the while, Lam was sending his children to the United States. After his eldest two sons attended U.S. graduate schools in the late 1940s, two more sons graduated from Oklahoma Baptist in the 1950s, while one daughter married a Chinese American professor. When Lam addressed the Wake Forest commencement in 1960, his sons Samuel and Timothy (林思耀) were both in the audience.[157] Daniel, David, and Timothy all returned to Hong Kong for a time and assumed management positions at Ka Wah, Chiap Hua, and Baptist College. Daniel Lam was particularly active in recruiting U.S. executives and investors to Hong Kong and traveled to the United States to attend conventions and meet potential clients and partners.[158] While Lam Chi-fung also accepted colonial honorifics such as an OBE, it was American social capital that had become his family's primary method to develop their fortunes and Baptist College.[159] In time, his children gradually left Hong Kong and forged new lives in the United States and Canada.

Baptist's reliance on kuashang strategies ultimately slowed its rooting in this Crown colony, however. After receiving its land grant in March 1958, the college received no further government assistance until 1970.[160] In contrast to Chung Chi, its application for an interest-free construction loan of HK$1 million in 1959 was rejected. In addition, Baptist's ambitions to join CUHK were denied. From that project's announcement, Lam made explicit the college's desire "to qualify in every respect with Government requirements in order that it may earn consideration in the proposed new Chinese University scheme."[161] The college publicly advertised these aspirations as well. Officials blocked its entry though, due both to Baptist's evangelism and worries at sponsoring another U.S.-oriented Christian college in a predominantly non-Christian society.[162] As a result, when Baptist applied for admission to the Joint Council in 1959, its application was rejected on the pretense that it "was only in its third year," a lame excuse since United was also only in its third year.[163] Baptist would remain in limbo for two decades, most especially because both the college and the SBBFM refused to forfeit evangelism.[164] Baptist was finally offered one government loan in 1970 but only accepted the second in 1975—with 4 percent interest.[165] After Lam passed away in 1971, the college soldiered on through private fundraising and steep tuition hikes under its second president, Baylor and University of Pittsburgh graduate Dr. Daniel Tse Chi-wai (謝志偉). Only in 1983 did the college and government reach an agreement to fund Baptist on similar terms to those with HKU and CUHK. That outcome set Baptist on the path to receive university status alongside City University and Polytechnic in November 1994.

Over the 1950s Hong Kong witnessed a flowering of poor but diverse "refugee colleges." Many of these institutions recruited or attracted support from U.S. and international organizations severed from former mainland projects. Yet because the colonial government did not grant taxpayer support until 1959, American support became essential to these schools' survival and helped four to take root. Chung Chi, New Asia, United, and Baptist survived and not only challenged colonial assumptions about higher education but also gradually cornered officials into accepting the formation of a second university. As the new governor, Robert Black, wrote in February 1959, it was simply that "two or three" of the colleges had achieved such success that it was "impossible not to accord them some degree of official recognition without risk of a serious outcry."[166]

While Christian and Cold War agendas motivated these American organizations, it was kuashang strategies that recruited and managed this support at Chung Chi and Baptist. David Au first attracted U.S. interest because of his elite educational networks, and he monetized them as a personal lifeline. He then used his dual British and American social capital to tack between the government and United Board on Chung Chi's behalf, securing its permanent campus and an American construction grant. Lam Chi-fung too first reoriented toward the United States out of commercial and Christian interests. In the early 1950s he rebuilt his business and social activities around U.S. markets and resources, while collaborating with U.S. missionaries to expand the colony's Baptist community. In turn, however, Baptist College adopted the most explicit kuashang strategies of any college, and its staff and students heavily pursued transpacific circulations. Yet because SBBFM's support encouraged Baptist's evangelism and minimized British input, the college managed to lock itself out of instrumental government support.

By threatening Commonwealth academic systems and redirecting Hong Kong students toward the United States, these colleges advanced informal decolonization and precipitated a virtually unprecedented decision within the British Empire. Before the Second World War, the empire's degree-issuing universities were limited to a handful of places beyond the metropole and dominions: Hong Kong, Malta, Jerusalem, Ceylon, and the crown jewel system in India.[167] Each taught exclusively in English. After South Asian independence, the expansion of access to English-language higher education became a key strategy to splice continued British influence into decolonizing and postcolonial societies. Multiple commissions began channeling funds into new universities across the empire, such as the University of Ghana (1948), the University of Malaya (1949), and the University College of Rhodesia and Nyasaland (1952). Yet all such institutions offered degree courses in English only and remained dependent on the University of London to grant degrees. In the mid-1960s former colonies such as British Guiana and Kenya were still establishing their first independent universities.[168] Thus Hong Kong officials' decision in 1959 to launch a second degree-granting university was very unusual. There were no plans for Hong Kong independence, and the colonial regime was still paying to rebuild HKU from wartime damage. As late as 1956 the Colonial Office had pronounced that Chung Chi's future depended on "how far the College proves willing to serve as a bridge between the high schools and the Hong Kong University rather than to follow an independent line and pass out 'finished' students with awkward or unrecognized qualifications."[169] Three years later this thinking had transformed. CUHK became only the second university in the empire or Commonwealth not to use English as its sole language of instruction. The other was in French Québec.[170]

The foundation of CUHK represented a government campaign to reassert colonial influence and reorient these colleges toward British academic systems. By pouring resources into Chung Chi, New Asia, and United, the government assumed that it could mandate their conversion. Governor Black noted that the colleges "bear a strong American imprint," but he was optimistic that this situation could be rectified. By committing to a chips-all-in approach, the government declared its intention "to induce the colleges to raise their standards and to orient themselves toward Hong Kong and the Commonwealth rather than Formosa and America."[171] It was a campaign of wholesale renovation, so much so that some New Asia and Chung Chi leaders advocated withdrawing.[172] Simultaneously, echoing the rhetoric of decolonization, Governor Black urged speed to combat the colleges' "growing belief . . . that they ought to be allowed considerable self-determination."[173]

This counteroffensive against the informal decolonization of Hong Kong higher education reached a key juncture in August 1962 with the decision to appoint a vice-chancellor. As Governor Black made clear, "I consider that the requirement is undoubtedly for a Vice-Chancellor of Chinese race, and, in the long term, that no other candidate will be acceptable." This logical condition for the Chinese University proved to be a fatal crack in their hopes. Old hierarchies and prejudices came back to haunt them, as there were no British-educated, ethnically Chinese academics in senior positions in the entire empire or Commonwealth. Black realized "that a suitable Chinese candidate is not likely to be found outside America." He also grasped the implications of this situation: "American influence is already predominant in the colleges, and the appointment of an American Vice-Chancellor, unless he is a person of the very highest quality, must tend to increase this influence and so to distort still further the relationship of the new institution with the community of Commonwealth Universities, within which framework we hope that its future will lie."[174] Li Choh-ming would bring his own ambitions to this project.

CHAPTER IV

The Turning Point

Li Choh-ming and Kuashang Strategies at Chinese University

ong Kong today has achieved an international status unrivalled anywhere in the world," Li Choh-ming (李卓敏) boldly asserted at his inauguration as the first vice-chancellor of the Chinese University of Hong Kong. "It has become the place of family reunions for the Overseas Chinese, the headquarters of their business enterprises and the reservoir of their capital. The Chinese University, established in this city, at this juncture, has a special role to play."[1]

This statement was unconventional for 1964. Li ignored what seemed like obvious constraints on the territory's future: British colonial rule, Cold War divisions, and an ongoing migration crisis. Instead, he focused on what others overlooked—the colony's vibrant transnational networks. In a draft of this speech, he had toyed with proclaiming Hong Kong "the Capital of the Overseas Chinese."[2] He refrained, but he committed the university to a "special role" in the diaspora. Pausing to acknowledge that CUHK had been "established as a public institution by the Government of Hong Kong," Li raced onward to discuss the "wide international interest in the University," and most especially "in its students and their potential leadership roles." Li was obsessed with the word *international*. He used it fourteen times in this speech alone, and he was still repeating the word fourteen years later at his retirement in October 1978.[3] In reality, it largely meant the United States and its intersections with the elite of the Chinese diaspora. These sources constituted the vast majority of the "international

Figure 4.1 Li Choh-ming above CUHK's completed campus, 1975, "Farewell Dr. & Mrs. Choh-Ming Li" (Hong Kong: CUHK, 1978). Photo courtesy of Information Services Office, Chinese University of Hong Kong.

interest," particularly money, talent, and recognition funneled through Washington's "state-private network."[4] The term allowed Li to pursue these resources on CUHK's behalf without embarrassing London or provoking Beijing.

Yet Li's agenda was bigger than this university. He was neither a virulent anticommunist nor a devout Christian like the kuashang discussed in chapter 3. He was an economist and development technocrat for whom Hong Kong's international status was primarily an economic condition. Trained as a scholar of international trade and monetary policy, he had worked in development for both the Nationalist government and the United Nations. After 1949 he had become a professor of business administration at the University of California, Berkeley, a naturalized U.S. citizen, and a collaborator with U.S. Cold War agendas. He was thus well positioned to grasp that two huge pools of capital and talent were overlapping in Hong Kong: that of the Chinese diaspora and that of U.S. Cold

War ambitions in Asia. Li set out to cross-pollinate these resources in order to build a global Chinese institution that could accelerate the transpacific circulations of knowledge and social capital that would carry Hong Kong from the Third World to the First. Sharing a stage with British and colonial officials, he declared that CUHK "inevitably" had to be "conceived not just as a Chinese institution with British affiliation but as a Chinese institution of international character."[5]

Over fifteen years as vice-chancellor (1963–1978), Li Choh-ming became the decisive kuashang by translating this study's previously elite émigré strategies into mass educational opportunities. Under cover of "international," Li used primarily U.S. resources to recruit Chinese scholars from around the world and funnel students, staff, and faculty across the Pacific to work and study in the United States. As a result, he expanded the existing networks linking Chung Chi, United, and New Asia with the United States and began to artificially naturalize these connections by installing American academic systems at CUHK. Because the University of Hong Kong's opportunities for Chinese-language degrees remained limited, the opportunities that CUHK represented for ordinary Hong Kong youth cannot be overemphasized. By using this institution to reorient the colony's expanding middle class toward transpacific educational and professional trajectories, Li's international agenda exemplified this society's transition from British to American hegemony and helped establish a new local educational culture—one that led directly to Hong Kong's emergence in the 1970s as the world's largest sender of foreign students to the United States. Li thus significantly accelerated Hong Kong's ongoing informal decolonization and used higher education to cement its economic reorientation.

The first section examines Li Choh-ming's early life, which was defined by transpacific migrations and the accumulation of elite social capital spanning Nationalist China and the United States. Between entering UC Berkeley as an undergraduate in 1930 and returning to the United States as a refugee professor in 1951, he amassed wide-ranging academic, governmental, and social networks that allowed him repeatedly to change hats. These evolutions granted him an unusually interstitial perspective on the postwar world. As an expert in international trade and a delegate for China to the Bretton Woods Conference (1944), Li understood the new operating structures of global capitalism as the United States redesigned them with itself at the center. Simultaneously, his academic career had solidified a pragmatic economic philosophy that favored rational markets and entrepreneurialism but accepted state-led land reform and planning for poor countries such as China. Thus Li's personal views resisted the Cold War's simplistic binaries. To boot, Li had experienced firsthand the Nationalists' own corruption and cronyism. Once at Berkeley, he threw himself into the study of the PRC's socialist development while observing in California a public research university's potential to power capitalist development.

When Li took up his duties as CUHK's vice-chancellor in 1964, he applied these accumulated experiences throughout the building of Hong Kong's second university. Holding one of the most distinguished positions yet granted to a Chinese person by this colonial regime, Li arrogated to himself a certain pretension to serve as its unofficial state planner by establishing what I term a *transpacific university*. The second section documents how he fostered transpacific circulations by importing U.S.-based scholars and American academic systems, while providing CUHK staff and students with reliable opportunities to work and study in the United States. Within a few years CUHK had an American library system, American academic honors, and even American degree programs. While not unique among his peers in turning toward the United States, Li was exceptional because he did not use American aid to forge a national elite, as Hong Kong was not a nation-state.[6] Instead, he viewed transpacific networks as the aim itself. As he stated in April 1967 amid the raging debate over so-called brain drains, "In my view the only way to look at the brain drain is positively . . . this drain, particularly of our graduates into post-graduate studies overseas, is a good thing . . . It is evidence that our universities are academically accepted by their sister universities abroad."[7] In contrast with most postcolonial academics and planners, Li did not seek to instill a national identity, jump-start certain industries, or train civil servants. Instead, he sought to accelerate middle-class access to the integrative transpacific systems that he and his family had used throughout the Republican era.

The capstone of this process was Li's pet project: the establishment of the first master of business administration (MBA) program in East or Southeast Asia. In the third section we will see how Li seized an inchoate project at Chung Chi and railroaded into place this American management program. Li recognized that the MBA would train local students in American methods of corporate organization, accounting, and finance. In so doing, this highly standardized import would cement Hong Kong's transition from British- to American-led systems while promoting market-driven views of higher education. Yet Li's use of higher education as a tool of economic development alarmed many CUHK scholars, most evidently New Asia's Neo-Confucians. Their ensuing clash embodies a larger collision over Chinese identity and education among overseas Chinese.

Finally, Li also supervised Chinese University's physical development. As the final section analyzes, Li proved a master fundraiser by cultivating a donor network spanning across Hong Kong elites. As a U.S.-educated Cantonese economist who had worked in Tianjin, Chongqing, and Shanghai, Li was well situated to reach across constituencies. With the aid of fellow kuashang, Li siphoned capital from the colony's elites into his transpacific university and garnered the influence to centralize power over CUHK. By the time he retired to California in 1978, Li had implemented radical alterations to the university's organization that circumscribed the colleges' autonomy and variegated intellectual cultures. Centralized power allowed his proto-neoliberal kuashang vision of higher education to occupy center stage and lay claim to mainstream common sense. By the mid-1970s kuashang strategies were transitioning into simply what Hong Kong's aspiring executives do: sojourn over the Pacific for higher education, accumulate instrumental knowledge and networks, and return to exploit those assets for profit.

Making the Decisive Kuashang

Li was born in Guangzhou in 1912 at the dawn of Republican era. He was the third child and first son of the wealthy industrialist Li Kan-chi (李鏡池) and his wife Tsin Mew-ching. His father was friends with Sun Yat-sen, and both parents were avid about education.[8] They hired private tutors for their children before sending them to an American Presbyterian school, Pui Ying (培英). As with Jiangnan émigrés (chapter 1), Li's parents used missionary schools to prepare their children for higher education: "Although they had not gone to college, they wanted each of their children to do so. Eventually, all 11 graduated."[9] This prioritization of higher education was prescient, privileged, and seen as advancing China's modernization, particularly in light of Guangzhou's revolutionary fervor. As if following the Northern Expedition, in 1927 Li left Guangzhou at the age of fifteen to enter the American missionary-run Nanking University. In 1930 he transferred to Berkeley and sailed from Shanghai to Vancouver that July.[10] He rapidly received his bachelor's degree in commerce in 1932, his master's in 1933, and his Ph.D. in economics in 1936, with a dissertation entitled "International Trade Under Silver Exchange: China, 1888–1935." His adviser Henry Grady was dean of the College of Commerce and later vice-chairman of the U.S. Tariff Commission and U.S. ambassador to India, Greece, and Iran.

Li was thus funneled through a layered set of American missionary schools in China into higher education in California. Yet his relationship to the United States remained pragmatic, and multiple factors pulled him home. First, his missionary education had left him with deep misgivings.[11] In turn, not only did Chinese Exclusion circumscribe U.S. immigration possibilities, but also a central aim of the China Institute in America (1926) under Director Paul Chih Meng (孟治) was to promote students' return to China.[12] Finally, the Great Depression substantially accelerated Chinese economists' and officials' embrace of state planning, and thus there were many opportunities awaiting such a promising young economist.[13] As a result, doctorate in hand and just twenty-five years old, Li returned in early 1937 as a professor at China's leading center of economic research, Nankai University's Institute of Economics in Tianjin. There he joined a community of distinguished U.S.-educated Chinese economists led by Professors Franklin Ho (何廉) and H. D. Fong (方顯廷). Both Ho and Fong were well connected on either side of the Pacific, maintaining close ties to the Institute of Pacific Relations in Hawai'i and the Rockefeller Foundation. They brought Li into these networks and soon carried their protégé into the Nationalists' expanding wartime bureaucracy.[14] Thus, unlike his fellow Guangdong natives David Au and Lam Chi-fung (chapter 3), who would adapt traditional huashang strategies to the post-1945 world, Li's later kuashang strategies were seeded by Republican-era engagement with U.S. higher education, as they were for Jiangnan elites.

It is worth underscoring, however, that Li's transpacific circulations reflected larger familial strategies. His family pushed all five sons into American higher education. His next brother, Li Choh-hao (李卓皓), was born in 1913 and also attended Nanking University, where he studied chemistry and met his future wife. In 1935 Choh-hao came to the United States for graduate school at Michigan, but Choh-ming successfully helped him lobby for admission to Berkeley before Choh-hao left for Ann Arbor.

Choh-hao received his Ph.D. degree in Chemistry there in 1938 and later, at the University of California, San Francisco (UCSF), became the first biochemist to synthesize the human pituitary growth hormone.[15] Three younger brothers also migrated to the United States for graduate school and settlement. Li Choh-luh became a prominent neurosurgeon at the National Institute for Health in Bethesda, while Li Choh-hsien also attended Berkeley and rose to be research director for the Minneapolis-Honeywell Corporation. In the 1980s he became the director of Taiwan's Hsinchu Industrial Park, an incubator of the island's high-tech take-off and itself an engine of transpacific circulations of knowledge.[16] Youngest brother Li Check-lap also settled in Berkeley. Yet such opportunities were largely denied to Li's sisters. Only the eldest attended college overseas (also Berkeley), although several attended college in China and became professors and secondary school principals.[17] All the sisters except one remained in the PRC after 1949, but they did try to remain in touch.[18] Thus, rather than a story of individual achievement or model minority stereotypes, Li's family underscores how privilege and patriarchy governed who was positioned for such mobility.

Li's return to China in early 1937 was inauspiciously timed, but his expertise opened enviable wartime opportunities. Japan invaded in July, and its bombs leveled most of Nankai University. As the government retreated to Sichuan, Nankai's staff and students fled to Kunming and joined with refugees from other universities to form a temporary institution, National Southwestern Associated University. On his way there, Li stopped in still neutral Hong Kong and proposed to Sylvia Lu Chi-man (盧志文), a graduate of the American missionary True Light Schools, a Lingnan student, and friend of his sisters.[19] Her father was a cousin of Sun Yat-sen's first wife, Lu Muzhen (盧慕貞).[20] They were married in September 1938 at the colony's Gloucester Hotel (figure 4.2). In Kunming, Li continued his research on monetary policy and international trade.[21] This expertise was actually a wartime priority because the Nationalists' largest source of revenue had long been customs tariffs.[22] The subsequent loss of China's coastal trading cities in the invasion and ballooning military expenditures thus quickly brought the government's finances to the brink of collapse. Having analyzed China's struggles to modernize its decentralized, silver-based currency in his dissertation, Li was among the few Chinese academics whose career thus benefited from the war. As such, in 1939 the government helped Nankai to relaunch its Institute of Economics in

Figure 4.2 The wedding of Li Choh-ming and Sylvia Lu Chi-man, September 17, 1938. Courtesy of Jean Li Rogers.

Chongqing and the young couple moved there, where Sylvia also gave birth to their first son, Winston, on June 1, 1941, amid a Japanese air raid.[23] Later that summer, Li had the chance to reunite with his former adviser Henry Grady, who came to Chongqing as an assistant U.S. secretary of state.[24]

Expertise opened the door, but Li's networks among both Americans and American-returned students carried him into ascending government service. As head of China's Currency Stabilization Board, K. P. Chen (chapter 1) spotted Li in Chongqing and invited him to join the board of the Shanghai Commercial and Savings Bank.[25] This friendship dramatically advanced Li's profile among both officials and Jiangnan capitalists such as Liu Hongsheng (chapter 1) who had fled west. Simultaneously, Franklin Ho and H. D. Fong were now key managers of China's wartime economy, and Li rode their coattails. Ho served as head of the government's Central Planning Board and Chiang Kai-shek's most consistent economic adviser, while Fong was dispatched to Washington to represent China on the U.S. government's Board of Economic Warfare. Li joined him there in late April 1943 as part of a postwar planning delegation.[26] Li remained away from his family for two and a half years, but during this time he joined the Chinese National Salvation Association and met Paul Chih Meng, Ernest Moy, and Walter Judd (chapter 3).[27] In late 1943 Ho designated Li to stay in Washington to coordinate China's aid application to the new United Nations Relief and Rehabilitation Administration (UNRRA).[28] This assignment allowed Li to join China's delegation to the Bretton Woods conference in July 1944, where the Allies designed the U.S.-led capitalist order. Simultaneously, he was busy advocating for Choh-hao to secure permanent status in the United States.[29] Li was still not an advocate of American capitalist models, though, and supported the Nationalist consensus to continue pursuing a planned economy. At a talk in New York in February 1945, he declared that China should follow a development path "falling midway between the American and Russian economic structures."[30] This perspective attracted controversy at home, particularly when he also advocated that international aid be allowed into communist-held areas.[31]

After Japan's surrender, Li could have returned to Tianjin to help rebuild Nankai University. Instead, he embraced his new path in government and development. He was appointed deputy director general of the China National Relief and Rehabilitation Administration (CNRRA), counterpart to the UNRRA. Its director general was Jiang Tingfu (T. F. Tsiang, 蔣廷黻), an Oberlin and Columbia graduate who taught history at Nankai and Tsinghua before serving as China's ambassador to the Soviet Union. The Li family moved to Shanghai, where the CNRRA opened its headquarters on the Bund. As discussed in chapters 1 and 3, the CNRRA was a funnel for massive U.S. and UN aid flowing into China and a nexus of corruption. Big capitalists such as Liu Hongsheng took full advantage, and Li was caught up in this gold rush. Both Jiang's and Li's families moved into the forty-room Shanghai mansion previously occupied by Wang Jingwei, former head of the Nanjing collaborationist government. The Lis' daughter, Jean, was born there in October 1946, followed by their second son, Tony, in June 1948.[32] Corruption rumors swirled, but a bombshell came in August 1947 when Li and a dozen other CNRRA officials were formally accused of corruption.[33] An informer had reported that Li and his colleagues were channeling millions of dollars in aid to friends and the black market, everything from crates of fans to raw cotton and cloth. The informer singled out Li for charges of "wanton extravagance," such as paying for the mansion from CNRRA accounts.[34] He was suspended and arraigned in Shanghai District Court in late September but released on bail under house arrest.

The evidence is scant of Li's guilt or innocence, but it does suggest that social capital again saved the day—this time from the U.S. government itself. On one hand, the CNRRA was notoriously corrupt, and this incident was not the last time that Li was accused of extravagance. On the other, Nationalist officials regularly manipulated the judicial system for political ends, and Sylvia argued that it was Choh-ming's support for distributing aid to communist areas that "incurred the wrath and jealousy" of senior officials.[35] Hong Kong newspapers insisted, however, that a decisive character witness was Major General Lowell Rooks, the American head of the UNRRA. The press reported that Rooks sent a letter to Nanjing vouching for Li, while Sylvia remembered Rooks as going there personally to meet with Chiang Kai-shek.[36] Either way, the intervention of a close colleague of General Eisenhower's was powerful. The CNRRA formally disbanded in November 1947, and in December the prosecutor ruled that there was "insufficient evidence" to bring formal charges against Li. He sent all the others accused but one to trial, however.[37] Two were found guilty and imprisoned for accepting bribes while distributing wool to mills.[38] Guilty or innocent, Li had had a crash course in cutthroat politics that likely underscored the power of connections and instilled a certain resilience to academic conflicts.[39] After a lecture tour of the United States in spring 1948, Li replaced Jiang Tingfu as China's representative to the United Nations Economic Commission for Asia and the Far East (ECAFE) when Jiang became China's UN ambassador.[40]

As the civil war progressed, Li saw the writing on the wall but remained at his post. In November 1948 he attended the fourth ECAFE conference in Australia, after which he met his family in Hong Kong.[41] He directed Sylvia and the children to remain there while he returned to Shanghai. As Sylvia remembered, "Rumors abounded that Shanghai would soon be lost. . . . Choh Ming wanted us to remain in Hong Kong, and told us that he would probably join us in a few days."[42] He did not pass through the colony again until March 1949, on his way to the fifth ECAFE conference in Bangkok. He and K. P. Chen flew back together to Shanghai in early April.[43] The city fell to communist forces a few weeks later. Li flew to Guangzhou on "official business" and crossed into the colony. The Nationalists offered him a position on Taiwan, but Sylvia stated, "Choh Ming did not consider it worthwhile."[44] Instead, they stayed with her family and he practiced calligraphy for a year, emulating fourth-century master Wang Xizhi (王羲之) and flirting with retirement.

That wasn't Li's personality, though. He became "edgy and unhappy" and decided to return to work.[45] Prospects for refugee Chinese intellectuals were limited, as colleges were forming but lacked financing (see chapter 3). Most scholars who managed to migrate overseas encountered greatly reduced circumstances. Franklin Ho came to Columbia's new East Asian Institute in 1949, but Hu Shih only found work as a librarian at Princeton. Li demonstrated his capacity for leveraging familial and academic networks by returning to Berkeley in 1951 as a lecturer in economics. Choh-hao was still on faculty there, while Choh-ming's former mentors and colleagues eagerly "welcomed him back to his alma mater." One friend was Clark Kerr, a fellow graduate of Berkeley's economics program who had become a professor of industrial relations. Kerr would become the California system's first chancellor in 1952, at which point Li was put on tenure track. By 1958 he was promoted to full professor of business administration and chairman of the Center for Chinese Studies. He was also naturalized as a U.S. citizen.[46] Li's family, however, once more paid a heavy price. Until he became a permanent resident in 1955, Li could neither leave the United States nor sponsor his family, creating another painful separation. Sylvia recalled fainting at the U.S. consulate when she learned of this prospect, but "for his own future and that of his family, I had to trust our lives to the luck of the draw again, completely surrendering my family to the unknown, and just let it be."[47] They finally sailed in June 1955, and the *Berkeley Daily Gazette* featured their reunion, while also misspelling the children's names.[48]

Most refugees suffer profound dislocation, but a shift in research and a talent for networking proved transformative for Li. He enmeshed himself among prominent Cold Warriors and reinvented himself as a U.S. national expert on the PRC's economic development. A few months after arrival, in December 1951 he attended the Institute of World Affairs conference in Riverside, California. There he spoke alongside State Department officials, leading historians, the vice president of NBC, and Paul Hoffman, formerly director of the Marshall Plan and now president of the Ford Foundation.[49] Entitled "The Economic Problems of the Peasant in the Far East," Li's speech advocated urgent land redistribution and state-led development across Asia as the only solution "in our quest for peace."[50] He also began covert work with the Asia Foundation on propaganda to mold overseas Chinese public opinion. Alongside Berkeley colleague Chen Shih-hsiang (陳世驤), he helped tailor the organization's Chinese-language periodicals.[51] In turn, he pragmatically realigned his research with U.S. national security agendas. Abandoning international trade, he began reviewing Walt Rostow's work on the PRC's development, while his own subsequent monographs were seminal works in this field.[52] The first, *Economic Development of Communist China* (1959), accomplished the feat of a macroeconomic empirical study based on fragmentary data.[53] One review labeled it "the most thorough and authoritative economic study of Communist China that has yet appeared."[54] This work received mainstream attention as well, such as from columnist Joseph Alsop.[55] Amid anticommunist hysteria, Li offered sober analysis—an achievement all the more impressive due to his personal relationship with this topic. He was critical of the PRC's engineered statistics, inattention to consumer goods, and "excessive control" of investment and large-scale enterprise. Yet he emphasized that the First Five-Year Plan achieved tremendous strides in both agriculture and capital formation, particularly with Soviet assistance in heavy industry. While his second book, *The Statistical System of Communist China* (1962), sounds dry, Li delivered a fascinating history of the development of the PRC's state statistics bureau under Xue Muqiao (薛暮橋), an economist he knew and admired.[56] In this book and other research, Li also wrestled with the origins and impact of the catastrophic Great Leap Forward.[57]

Despite his research excellence, it was Li's networks in Washington's state-private network that elevated him as a candidate to become CUHK's first vice-chancellor. Colonial officials first considered this question in June 1961 and feared that the best candidates would be U.S.-based.[58] By December the Asia Foundation was indeed secretly pushing Li's candidacy on colonial officials, as well as lobbying an unenthusiastic Clark Kerr to grant him leave.[59] When the vice-chancellor of the University of Leeds began the official search in 1962, he contacted Harvard president Nathan Pusey, who sent out his own enquiries.[60] Pusey received suggestions of Chinese scholars across the United States and Taiwan, but President Elvis Stahr of Indiana University suggested Li and Dartmouth's Chan Wing-tsit (陳榮捷).[61] Chan was both a former dean of Lingnan and a world-leading expert on Neo-Confucianism, New Asia's prevailing philosophy. He was thus a good candidate to work across the colleges and topped Pusey's recommendations. Li did not make Pusey's list.[62] By December 1962, however, the Hong Kong government had narrowed its list to Li, the University of Malaya physicist Thong Saw-pak, and HKU mathematician Y. C. Wong.[63] Governor Black purportedly dismissed Wong as lacking "presence and personality" and wanted an investigation as to whether

Thong "has it in him." In contrast, he considered Li to have "lots of personality" and to have "done useful work on previous visits." Lord Fulton, however, strongly objected to Li as "definitely unsuitable."[64]

No documentation makes clear why Li was chosen—a curious absence in a meticulously documented project. His administrative experience, relative youth, trilingualism, and relevant expertise were clear advantages. Both Sylvia and Choh-ming claimed that he declined a first offer but was won over by the university's excellent land grant, Berkeley's approval of three years' leave, and the possibility that his refusal might lead to the selection of a non-Chinese scholar.[65] In reality, Li was primarily negotiating the terms of his appointment, compensation, and benefits throughout fall 1963. The position of vice-chancellor paid less than his Berkeley appointments, such that he refused to accept the position until the Asia Foundation intervened and offered to secretly supplement his salary by US$7,000 annually (about US$58,000 today).[66] As with David Au (chapter 3), Li was thus in the pay of a U.S. government proxy. The colonial government consented to this arrangement so long as it remained secret and issued a formal offer on October 24. Li arrived in Hong Kong one week later, on November 1, 1963.[67]

Establishing a Transpacific University

Governor Black announced Li's appointment on November 2, and Li plunged into rounds of interviews. He proclaimed that CUHK "would serve as one of the effective avenues for exchange between Chinese and Western cultures."[68] Such rhetoric can be meaningless cliché, but for Li it provided useful cover for orienting this institution toward the United States in the quest for resources, talent, and recognition. Li even commandeered his own introduction to brandish the news "that a grant of $1,450,000 had been contributed by the American people to the University through the Church World Services for a student centre." As seen in chapter 2, "the American people" meant the U.S. State Department, and such funds were already flowing through Washington's state-private network into projects all over Hong Kong. This close connection between Li's appointment, his salary supplement, and another large U.S. government check begs further questions about his relationship with Washington. A few months later, though, Li made explicit that his "international" agenda was instrumental in nature. In a speech at the Rotary Club he stated: "Now you might be a little surprised why I should place so much emphasis on the international side of the Chinese University," but

> the reason is simple. To develop a new university is not an easy matter. It requires a tremendous amount of resources, human as well as material. How are we going to get them? Well, the Chinese University, it happens, has attracted a tremendous amount of goodwill at this point. There was a tremendous amount of interest around the world in the establishment and development of the Chinese University. This gave us the opportunity of tapping the resources for our purpose.[69]

Li plainly states his kuashang strategies here. Yet such frank statements rarely remain center stage in institutional narratives. As such, while CUHK leaders have echoed Li's rhetoric ever since, his agency and ambition have gradually been sidelined.[70]

Li proved himself an energetic but willful vice-chancellor whose administration encapsulates a turning point in Hong Kong elites' embrace of American social capital as a method of both economic development and informal decolonization. The activities of early kuashang such as Ansie Lee Sperry (chapter 1) and Jack Yuen (chapter 2) had posed little threat to the regime, while David Au was always polite to officials, even if circumventing them. In contrast, Li's speaking style was "familiar" and often polarizing.[71] Some colleagues nicknamed him "Mr. Energy" and "Mr. Cool" for his "unflappable composure and aplomb," but others used euphemisms such as "daring" or even "vigorous and pushing."[72] As vice-chancellor, he had a chauffeur, always flew first class, played weekly tennis, and made sure his lodgings were finely appointed. Many colonial officials were discomfited by him. He routinely announced projects without consultation, made proposals they found gauche, or dismissed their budgetary objections through private fundraising. For example, when a budget-conscious official requested a reduction in the guest list for his inauguration, Li simply lowered his estimate of the number of invitees who would attend—not the number of invitations he sent. Another official quipped, "I must say it's a most un-business like approach."[73] Li would have disagreed. His assertiveness reflected his reading of the local and international terrains of power. As decolonization and Britain's balance of payments troubles attenuated London's authority, this Chinese American economist was taking charge of the biggest and most expensive project in Hong Kong history. Put bluntly, the government and colleges needed him, and he knew it. As such, Li represented two key shifts in power. He not only cemented the shift from British to American hegemony, but he also heralded the rise of elite nonstate actors and their increasing power to reshape transpacific integration according to their own agendas.

Li's ambition was to build a transpacific university. Indeed, his first priority was expanding this institution's network. While presenting CUHK as passively "attracting" all this international "goodwill," in reality he began a ceaseless campaign to nurture global interest. Regarding his inauguration, one official noted: "Dr. Li is convinced that there is much support to be had in other countries for the Chinese University and that it would be well to be generous with the guest list so as to maintain and stimulate that interest."[74] His kuashang strategies are visible here too as he intently expands both his and the university's international relationships in order to cull recognition and funds. This campaign required constant international travel. Before his Rotary Club speech, he spent two weeks in the United States for the inauguration of Yale's new president, Kingman Brewster.[75] In July he led a delegation to tour Japanese universities before flying to Manila to meet with the president of the University of the Philippines.[76] That December he went to Bangkok for a higher education conference, while squeezing in a visit to Britain.[77] His family escaped Hong Kong's summer humidity in the United States, and Li also used these monthslong sojourns to recruit staff and meet with heads of universities and foundations.[78] In reality, though, he was always recruiting staff via his correspondence with U.S.-based Chinese scholars such as the esteemed linguist Yuen-ren Chao (趙元任).[79] In turn, he and Sylvia labored to bring high-level guests to Hong Kong and roll out the red carpet. They hosted Brewster, Cornell president James Perkins, and their wives in Hong Kong in August 1965, including a reception at Hang Seng Bank attended by the governor and two hundred guests.[80]

Beyond such social visits, Li continually infused CUHK's academics with American models and expertise. Soon after arrival, Li appointed three advisory boards to supervise CUHK's academic development.[81] Each was dominated by U.S.-based academics, particularly old friends and leading lights of the diaspora such as Li Choh-hao, Franklin Ho, and Nobel laureates Lee Tsung-dao and Yang Chen-ning. Li defended this choice, declaring that CUHK sought "the help of experts and specialists from all available sources. . . . Whether they are British, American or Chinese does not matter, as long as they are right for the special assignment."[82] Yet for the university's external examiners—a hallmark of British-descended academic models—Li again ensured that U.S.-based scholars predominated. Of sixty-one examiners by 1969, twenty-five came from U.S. institutions, sixteen from Taiwanese institutions, and just six from British institutions.[83] In the classroom, too, visiting American professors constituted a core part of this new institution's staff. Between 1965 and 1969, seventy-one visiting scholars taught at CUHK. Forty-six, or 65 percent, came from U.S. institutions, with their salary generally paid by their home institutions or the U.S. government. Japanese universities represented the second largest contingent, with six scholars, and British institutions accounted for just four.[84]

These intellectual choices reflected Li's strategy to cross-pollinate overseas Chinese networks with U.S. Cold War resources. By recruiting so many U.S.-based scholars of both Chinese and European descent, Li fostered new relationships that would encourage CUHK undergraduates to look to the United States for graduate study, while positioning CUHK staff and graduate students to secure introductions, grants, conference invitations, recommendation letters, and so on. The "Comings and Goings" section of the *University Bulletin* is riddled with professors sojourning back and forth from the United States, from senior scholars enjoying research sabbaticals to junior faculty pursuing advanced training at U.S. institutions under State Department sponsorship.[85] While also reflecting the three college's established relationships, Li's connections expanded these opportunities for junior faculty through Washington's state-private network. Before 1969 the Ford Foundation made two grants to the CUHK Staff Development Programme totaling HK$4.7 million, and these grants allowed eighty-nine junior faculty to go abroad for postgraduate study. Li led the "somewhat lengthy negotiation" for the grants, including "intensive talks . . . about the University's plans for future development."[86] By 1969 forty-eight staff had gone to U.S. institutions, twenty to British institutions, and eight combined the two. Thus by securing American expertise and money, Li was embedding transpacific networks within the university and fostering future circulations.

Li also ensured that such mobility enveloped students. As he declared at his inauguration, he was keenly aware of the "international" interest in these students' "potential leadership roles." In spring 1965 he first established an exchange program with his alma mater, the University of California. Li had put his old friend Clark Kerr on CUHK's University Council, and they negotiated an agreement under which admitted CUHK faculty and students could attend any UC campus under a full tuition waiver.[87] In return, California agreed to send both students and faculty to CUHK to conduct research and teach in areas chosen by Li. By the fall 1968 term, each university had sent twelve students and teachers to the other.[88] At the program's inauguration, the chancellor of UC, Santa Barbara, Vernon Cheadle, credited Li's "imaginative and forceful will" for the program's rapid development.[89] And while the program was presented as just "international" goodwill, Cheadle confessed that the exchanges were financed by the U.S. State Department through Fulbright-Hayes. In turn, Li used this program as the template for exchange negotiations with other British, Canadian, and American universities.[90]

These deals opened reliable pathways for CUHK staff and students, but a skeptical reader might query: Were such relationships just good sense? Li's strategies crystallize, however, with his efforts to weld American academic systems onto this Commonwealth institution. CUHK's library is a deceptively simple case-in-point. Before his arrival, the government had invited the chief librarian at London's School of Oriental and African Studies to advise on the integration of the three colleges' libraries. In March 1964 Li tossed out that study. He recruited the dean of California's School of Librarianship and the curator of Stanford's Hoover Institute "to advise the Vice-Chancellor on the establishment of the University Library." They recommended that CUHK instead adopt the U.S. Library of Congress system in order to build "a close relationship . . . between the University's Libraries and the Library of Congress as well as the large number of libraries around the world which make use of this system." Li promptly did so. Easily overlooked, this reorientation required all future CUHK librarians to receive U.S. library science training. It thus structured a rippling set of future hiring and academic decisions. Indeed, the university's first chief librarian was the distinguished Alfred Kaiming Chiu (裘開明), Harvard-Yenching's founding librarian.

Even more boldly, Li grafted American academic honors onto this Commonwealth institution. Li had privately consulted with members of the Honours Degree Committee about this choice, but he then misrepresented their views when recommending in May 1966 that the University

Council adopt Chinese terms that would translate through the American honors system—*chengji youliang* (成績優良) for cum laude and *chengji youyi* (成績優異) for magna cum laude.[91] In reality, Lord Fulton had expressed skepticism with polite English indirection. He said that "if for good reason this is not a practicable way of dealing with the situation," then this proposal was "a good alternative."[92] University of Malaya professor (and later HKU vice-chancellor) Rayson Huang (黃麗松) had questioned this decision more bluntly. Since the American terms were "of common usage mainly in the United States, and not in the Commonwealth," and the point of these terms was for top graduates "to be recognised as of the same standing as an Honours graduate," he argued that "we should use a title which will convey exactly that meaning to prospective employers."[93] Huang reiterated something obvious: the Commonwealth had an established precedent. Why diverge? In addition to circumventing them, Li also did not consult officials. Only after CUHK's Senate voted to adopt the American-style system in June 1966 did Li inform them and demand that they recognize cum laude and magna cum laude as equivalent to British honors for employment and salary with the colonial government. As if it needed saying, one official wrote, "From Government's point of view it would be preferable for Chinese University to follow the British system of Honours rather than the United States' *cum laude* system."[94] Yet officials recognized that they could not force him. The director of education eventually signed off but complained that the American terms were "inconvenient and possibly misleading."[95]

Li was seeding a new educational culture in Hong Kong. He did not oppose postgraduate studies in the United Kingdom or other international exchanges, but he was using American resources and systems to encourage transpacific trajectories. He was making CUHK's degrees recognizable to U.S. graduate schools and corporations in order to promote future circulations and the trade and investment that would ensue. A few weeks later he noted the new use of this honors system and praised it as part of an "international course that is to keep our Chinese University in the closest touch with universities overseas."[96] Yet this "international course" represented larger shifts. Not only did CUHK herald a new era of social mobility in Hong Kong, but also its vice-chancellor was one of the most visible Chinese figures in the 1960s colony. As such, Li ensured that the colony's rising middle class began to experience the word "international" in connection with transpacific opportunities to an extent not seen since the California Gold Rush.

The MBA: Capitalist Education and Chinese Identity

The formation of *the* Chinese University occurred amid profound flux for Chinese identity outside of the PRC. What did it mean to be Chinese when the mainland now subscribed to a foreign ideology that many saw as antithetical to traditional Chinese culture? What was a "modern" Chinese education if not rooted in Confucianism, nationalism, or communism? As scholars such as Grace Ai-ling Chou, Andy Chih-ming Wang, and Huang Jianli have analyzed, higher education across Hong Kong, Taiwan, and Singapore became a battleground over such questions during the Cold War.[97] As vice-chancellor, Li was immersed in these debates, and his international agenda was his core response.

Yet by the late 1960s Hong Kong was seething with far more violent unrest. The Star Ferry Riots of 1966 lit up Kowloon with demands for improved social services, while the Cultural Revolution–inspired riots of 1967 gravely shook society with anti-imperialist protests and bombings.[98] All the while, Hong Kong was receiving refugees from the mainland and thousands of American service members on R&R from the nearby Vietnam War.[99] Li interpreted these crises as underscoring an urgent need for CUHK to provide a rapid return on taxpayers' investment. He repeatedly acknowledged that locals viewed the liberal arts as "a luxury" and affirmed their "clamour for more technical rather than liberal education." He promised that CUHK would never "flounder in the residue of Western élitism" and committed it to what he viewed as a "proper balance" between liberal arts and professionally oriented majors.[100] To this effect, Li set out two separate academic missions for CUHK: "conventional educational objectives" and a "distinctive educational mission."[101] The conventional objectives were CUHK's "first and basic educational goal" and aimed to funnel the majority of students through vocationally oriented programs in order to "meet Hong Kong's need for young men and women with highly specialized or professional competence to play important roles in its advanced social and economic structure." In Li's mind, CUHK's primary purpose was thus supplying the capitalist labor market. He carved a reservation for China's ancient traditions though, through the 'distinctive' mission. He insisted that CUHK bore an "institutional responsibility for preserving and enriching the Chinese intellectual and cultural tradition." "Preserving" and "enriching" meant conservation and scholarship, however, not structuring students' studies around Chinese philosophy. In contrast, New Asia's Neo-Confucian leaders remained committed to an ancient principle that education's primary mission was moral edification and the development of character. As a result, Li's economic agenda and his increasing centralization of power alarmed them.

These gulfs came to a head over Li's pet project: the establishment of the first MBA program in East or Southeast Asia. Today the MBA has become a status symbol and even a rite of passage in the minds of global executives, academic leaders, and upwardly mobile youth—including in China. This trend was just beginning in the mid-1960s, however. A late nineteenth-century American invention, the MBA remained exclusively U.S.-based through the Second World War. Numerous sources cite the University of Western Ontario as the first non–U.S. institution to award the MBA, in 1950, while the first MBA program in Asia began in Karachi in 1955 through USAID assistance. The Asia Foundation had begun sponsoring management conferences and lectures in Hong Kong in the late 1950s, but the degree itself spread more slowly.[102] British institutions had long offered courses in commerce and economics, but not until 1965 did Manchester Business School offer the UK's first American-style management course. Glasgow's University of Strathclyde became the first to offer a twelve-month MBA in 1966. As a result, the establishment of CUHK's own MBA program in 1966 was quite new to colonial officials and Chinese scholars alike.

The idea of business education first intrigued Chung Chi's third president, C. T. Yung. In 1962 he started investigating the idea of a school of economics or commerce. He asked the Lingnan Trustees in New York to send Skidmore professor Yu-kuang Chu to study the idea. Chu enthusiastically endorsed the establishment of a "Lingnan School of Economics and Commerce" at Chung Chi, but Chu's and Yung's rationales focused primarily on strategic incentives, not any particular intellectual or pedagogical goal. In his final report, Chu underscored: "President Yung felt that this is probably the one field of professional training that Chung Chi may well emphasize, since under conditions in Hong Kong Medicine, Engineering and Teacher Training are more or less the prerogatives of government institutions."[103] This sentence again makes kuashang strategies visible. Colonial systems dominated medicine, education, and engineering, rendering them impractical for U.S.-oriented initiatives. Commerce was different, though. American business education—whatever that meant—seemed likely to produce dividends by attracting donations from "leading alumni in Hong Kong" and creating "wealthy alumni in business and international trade." As such, Yung and Chu used transpacific networks to recruit resources and expertise, circumvent British colonial systems, and promote profitable transpacific integration. Chu recommended that Yung be invited to New York and that "an American with a doctor's degree in Economics" come "to teach at Chung Chi."[104] Yung then elaborated on these requests to the United Board.[105] While scholars might wish to see it as "empire by invitation," this request did not come from a government seeking military or economic aid. It came from private-sector elites tapping into U.S. resources to advance informal decolonization and economic development in tandem.[106]

In their initial planning, Chu and Yung consistently framed this school through the discipline of economics, not business administration. That mutation occurred when Yung traveled to New York for six weeks in spring 1963 to meet with the Lingnan Trustees and the United Board.[107] HBS professor Franklin Folts was invited to join.[108] An expert in industrial management and a pioneer of Harvard's case-study methodology, Folts had grown up in Hong Kong when his father was Standard-Vacuum's local manager.[109] Their meetings concluded that the trustees would back "a strengthened School of Commerce," help form an advisory committee of businessmen, and fund Chung Chi Ph.D. students to attend "Harvard for one year to learn at first-hand the case history method of teaching business administration."[110] A key intellectual permutation was in progress, from an economics program to an American management program. The remaining caveat was the imminent founding of CUHK and the opinion of the then unknown vice-chancellor. Li Choh-ming, however, had been a professor at Berkeley's business school and leapt at the idea. Two weeks after he took up his duties, the vice-chancellor's office took over direct supervision of "the proposed Institute" in the hope of receiving "much more support from Lingnan Alumni and the Chinese University."[111] In short, Li immediately co-opted this project and then sent for Folts.[112]

As planning accelerated, Li again did not consult officials and relied on his own transpacific networks. In reality, the government likely would have supported a business program and only objected to an MBA program specifically, as the degree did not yet exist in Britain. Li did not ask. He spent a year recruiting faculty and in October 1965 made the surprise announcement that CUHK would soon establish a full graduate school with an institute of business administration. He declared: "This is a critical part of the University's development and the University cannot exist without it."[113] As officials scribbled question marks and fretted over the budgetary implications, Li's former Berkeley colleague Maurice Moonitz arrived for final consultations. In April 1966 Li signed an accord with the Lingnan Trustees for the requisite funds: a first-year grant of US$63,000 and US$50,000 for each of the next two years.[114] A professor of accounting, Moonitz agreed to serve as the first director of the Lingnan Institute of Business Administration (LIBA) with rotating Berkeley professors to assist. LIBA's nine-member Advisory Board was also heavily U.S.-oriented, including P. Y. Tang (chapter 1). The institute accepted six candidates for the 1966–1967 school year.[115]

We again see how American social capital allowed Li to circumvent colonial oversight and establish an educational institution aimed at accelerating Hong Kong students' entry into U.S.-led corporate systems. At LIBA's inaugural ceremony in September 1966, the president of the Lingnan Trustees, Yorke Allen, Jr., framed the institute's purpose around leaping ahead within the intense competition of global capitalism: "In this race for business the victory is not necessarily being won by those who work the longest or the hardest. It is being won by those who most skillfully utilize all the latest techniques employed in the production, marketing and financing of consumer and capital goods."[116] This statement frankly acknowledges that capitalism rewards capital over labor and thus produces unjustified inequalities. Allen stated that it was not hard work but access to capital and know-how that determined success—and that was what this credential was really selling. He even wondered aloud "how the great majority of the nations in the world will ever be able to catch up with the leaders of this race." Li evidently agreed, as he lifted pieces of Allen's speech (unacknowledged) to put in his six-year report.[117] "Catching up" was why he prioritized this expensive degree in a colony that still lacked universal primary education. The aim was to endow a select number of young people with the "latest techniques" of U.S.-led capitalism. While most of his fellow academic economists were investigating Marxist dependency theories and import-substitution policies, Li was approaching and planning economic development through the radical vector of trans-national circulations of knowledge. He would train an executive corps with the knowledge and social capital to cross oceans and pull Hong Kong from the low-cost manufacturing "semiperiphery" into the financialized "core." LIBA awarded just four degrees in 1968, but today CUHK's Business School has thirty-five thousand living alumni.[118]

As this MBA program began, it also provided a crucible for the raging debates over overseas Chinese education and identity. As discussed in chapter 3, Qian Mu had been the president of New Asia since 1949. He resigned in July 1964 primarily because of his violent disagreements with Li. The *Kong Sheung Evening News* got wind of this "unstable situation" (風雲) and reported his resignation was due to "personnel issues" (人事問題) (figure 4.3).[119] Qian's lengthy resignation letter to New Asia's board details more intense grievances. He described Li as a high-handed and duplici-tous administrator whose methods of recruiting faculty had already "led to external criticism in the academic world and internal complaints among the faculty." While personality clashes are endemic to academia, Qian contended that such tensions were not the end of "my long disputes with Vice-Chancellor Li." In particular, he focused on their battle over LIBA, about which Qian noted derisively: "This project has been foremost in the planning of the Vice-Chancellor ever since his arrival in Hong Kong."[120] Qian had accepted the idea but wanted to reward its directorship to a long-serving New Asia professor who would soon reach the mandatory retirement age. Unsurprisingly, Li intended to select this director himself and by corporatist parameters, not Neo-Confucian ethical obligations.

Figure 4.3 News report on the resignation of Qian Mu as president of New Asia in *Kung Sheung Evening News*, July 1, 1964.

In the conclusion of his resignation, Qian articulated their philosophical clash. He complained: "I was told that the Vice-Chancellor has said that I should retire rather than resign. But my resignation is an expression of general protest and not just against the procedure of appointing professors." Qian had found Li's moral character wanting. He thus could neither cooperate with him nor simply retire. Duty demanded protest: "The Vice-Chancellor has never discussed with me the ideals and purposes for the establishment of a university, nor any necessary steps for progress in the establishment of a university." He declared that he had expressed his views "as an outspoken faithful friend" and "both privately and openly at meetings." As his views "were not accepted" by Li, "I thought the next best course of action would be not to differ with the Vice-Chancellor" and forge, in classic Confucian terms, "common consent on everything so as to achieve personal harmony and the avoidance of unnecessary dispute."[121] Yet Li did not seem to operate according to ethical obligations and Qian refused to pretend. Put simply, Qian had realized that CUHK's daily operations would have little to do with Confucianism, and a few weeks later he departed permanently for Taiwan.

Li and Qian's clash was both a tropic academic squabble and a revealing philosophical debate. Even degree candidates in the late Qing had debated whether education was primarily for social mobility or moral edification. Yet these men's conflict provides a glimpse into paths that Chinese education could still have taken in 1960s Hong Kong. In founding New Asia, Qian had seen himself as an exile in a cultural wasteland, a humanist devoted to preserving the essence of Chinese civilization, and a defender of moral integrity.[122] This agenda was principled and yet essentialist in its definition of Chinese culture. It was also hypocritical, as Yale-in-China had been helping to conceal Qian's extramarital affair since 1954.[123] Yet, in keeping with modern Neo-Confucianism's selective engagement with foreign learning, he had accepted the idea of a business school.[124] Administering a university by corporatist logics was a step too far, however. In contrast, Li was seventeen years younger, a data-oriented economist, and now an American. He had a much more fluid understanding of what was "Chinese" versus "foreign" and "modern." In a speech in 1971 he defined "culture as a living process" and insisted: "When we speak of Chinese culture, we must think of the saying, 'Inherit the past and pioneer the future' [繼往開來]."[125] He did not see Hong Kong as a cultural wasteland or repository but as a key node in global networks. In the end, his CUHK would offer neither Confucian nor colonial education but capitalist education and a Chinese identity tied to material success in the U.S.-led international order. And while officials resented Li's modus operandi, they were also unsympathetic to Qian. Governor Trench terminated officials' discussion of Qian's resignation: "Thank you. Dr. Li did not mention this morning + I did not feel it necessary to do so merely on the point of the undesirability of publicity—of which Dr. Li will be fully aware."[126] Indeed, he was, and while Qian clearly pondered this conflict, Li likely gave it little thought at all. He interpreted Hong Kong's development potential as an educational imperative. The colony's ensuing transformation over the next decade reinforced his choice and marginalized lingering contention from memory.

University Development and Intellectual Uniformity

Li Choh-ming oversaw not only the academic integration of CUHK's colleges but also its literal construction. Hong Kong's human density and mountainous terrain rendered the university's physical establishment a pressing challenge. Before Li's appointment, the government had decided to relocate New Asia and United to join Chung Chi in Shatin. It proposed to carve the mountain rising above Chung Chi and form a unified campus of tiered terraces. Chung Chi would remain at its base, while a midlevel plaza would be leveled for the university's main buildings. At the summit, another plaza would be leveled for New Asia and United Colleges. In 1966 Li invited rising star I. M. Pei, the son of his old friend Pei Tsuyee, to Hong Kong to consult on the final design. Site formation work began in 1967, and the first completed building was the U.S. government's donation, the subtly named Benjamin Franklin Student Centre. By New Asia's relocation to the campus in 1975, a total of sixty-one buildings occupied this transformed mountain.[127]

The colonial regime bankrolled this project with taxpayer funds, but Li and officials both sought private funds to accelerate the process and ease the strain. Fundraising was not yet the chief preoccupation of university administrators, but CUHK's ground-up construction pushed Li to pioneer this trend. He proved a natural. The longtime head of CUHK's Universities Service Centre, John Dolfin, stated: "He was a genius at money raising. . . . The most important thing for him was raising money, having good relations with the Hong Kong government, and knowing wealthy people in Hong Kong for money. He was a builder and a very good one."[128] Li indeed began fundraising from the outset, flying to London in early 1964 to secure a British government grant of £250,000 for the University Science Center.[129] As with LIBA, Li was also adept at redirecting the three colleges' existing American networks to his ends, while his own longstanding ties to the Ford and Asia Foundations allowed him to regularly pivot to those organizations.[130] By 1967, when CUHK's chief architect estimated the total campus would cost nearly HK$127 million, Li could report that the university had pledges and expectations reaching over HK$19 million.[131]

Although a deliberately concealed process, fundraising positioned Li to expand his network among the colony's elite Cantonese establishment. Many such figures were already involved with CUHK before he arrived and volunteered to help, including solicitor Sir Kwan Cho-yiu (關祖堯), Bank of East Asia scion Sir Kenneth Fung Ping-fan (馮秉芬), and cofounder of the Hang Seng Bank "S. H." Ho Sin-hang (何善衡). Each brought professional expertise and elite financial and social capital to this institution, and each received an honorary doctorate during Li's tenure. He also used his academic networks to provide advantageous introductions for big donors' children, including to Choh-hao.[132] Among the old Cantonese though, no family was more involved than the Lee family of Ansie Lee Sperry. Her eldest brother, Richard Lee, their fourth brother, "J. S." Lee Jung-sen (利榮森), and their cousin Q. W. Lee all served on the University Council. Richard Lee and the vice-chancellor had known each other for two decades, sharing a mentor in K. P. Chen and serving together on ECAFE. They were also social outside of business hours, such as when Choh-hao came to town.[133] In turn, J. S. Lee helped the vice-chancellor to establish CUHK's Institute of Chinese Studies, another pet project. Li first used another Asia Foundation grant to launch this institute in 1967 and appointed himself its director.[134] The next year he persuaded the Lee family to donate the full HK$2 million for its permanent home.[135] To this day, the institute features a dedication stele engraved with Li's calligraphy and his posthumous memorial statue.

Li's most consistent and reliable partner, however was a fellow kuashang: P. Y. Tang (chapter 1). As South Sea Textiles blossomed into the colony's largest manufacturer, Tang assumed a spate of civic positions, becoming the first Shanghainese on the colony's Legislative Council in 1964, for which the Jiangsu and Zhejiang Residents' Association feted him.[136] After joining Executive Council in 1969, he helped found the Hong Kong Trade Development Council in 1971 and the Hong Kong Polytechnic in 1972. Tang had been an active sponsor of vocational schools for training industrial engineers and managers since the 1920s, and he shared Li's view of CUHK's role in supplying the capitalist labor market. As a result, Tang not only joined CUHK's University Council in 1963 but also—according to Li—immediately reached out after the vice-chancellor's appointment about making a major donation. Tang ended up donating half the funds for the university library, HK$3 million, in honor of his late father (figure 4.4).[137]

Despite coming from Cantonese and Shanghainese backgrounds, Li and Tang made natural allies as kuashang of similar class origins, American educations, and pragmatic politics. Over Tang's final years, they worked together on numerous projects for CUHK. In addition to joining LIBA's board, in 1969 Tang donated two full scholarships to the institute on behalf of South Sea Textiles.[138] The next year the pair traveled together to Manila and Tokyo to study other management programs.[139] Perhaps

Figure 4.4 Tang Pao-Che Library, Chinese University of Hong Kong, 1971. Courtesy of the Tang family.

most significantly, in 1964 Tang succeeded Qian Mu as chairman of New Asia's Board of Governors. As chairman, Tang ended the philosophical running of the college and initiated its realignment with the rest of the university. He also became the primary intermediary between New Asia's faculty, the vice-chancellor, and Yale-in-China. As such, he traveled regularly back and forth to the United States on New Asia's behalf, and he and Li coordinated their transpacific flights so that they could have "long conversations" in transit about the university. The self-consciously patrician Tang may have even mentored Li, confessing that on one flight he counselled the vice-chancellor to adopt greater tact.[140]

In turn, P. Y. Tang made a valuable fundraising ally and put his networks among the Jiangnan industrialists to work for New Asia and the university. For example, by spring 1973 the college's Development Fund reported surpassing HK\$1 million in pledges, including a HK\$250,000 pledge from the Tang family and HK\$49,755 already paid by Tang himself. The vast majority of the remaining funds also came from émigré industrialists, including six-figure donations from MIT graduate H. T. Liu (劉漢棟), Y. C. Ho (何英傑), and John Tung (董之英). C. L. Hsu (徐季良) and Godfrey K. N. Yeh (葉庚年) each gave HK\$50,000, while T. Y. Wong of Hong Kong Cotton Mills and Hong Kong Spinners (chapter 1) gave HK\$20,000. Cha Cha-ming (查濟民) of China Dyeing Works gave HK\$10,000.[141] These industrialists were hardly Neo-Confucianists, and most were U.S.-educated or sending their children to receive higher education in the United States. Instead, they were perennial supporters of education and longtime colleagues of Tang. He did not live to see the completion of these endeavors, though. He passed away suddenly in June 1971—without a will—and Li served as one of his eight pallbearers.[142] At the dedication of the Tang Library in December, Li officiated, while Jack Tang gave the keynote address and Kinmay cut the ribbon. The press provided little background on the family, instead repeating Jack's claim that the "true interest" of his father had "always been with people."[143]

Perhaps most important, Li's fundraising contributed to his ongoing centralization of power over CUHK. The university had been established with a federal structure that left "great powers in terms of organization" to the colleges and made the University Headquarters responsible for only the Central Office, the University Library and Laboratory, advanced research programs, and projects specifically designated by the University

Council.[144] This decentralized authority had been key to convincing the colleges to join. Li steadily expanded his mandate, however, through both logical efficiencies and his ambitions, including securing donations for priorities such as LIBA.[145] His office not only centralized all student admissions in 1971 but then pushed for instruction to be "quietly centralized in the headquarters of the University."[146] Li saw these and other centralizing moves as an effort "to institutionalize the whole system I have been developing so that when I retire the whole university will go on as it should be," joking that the university without him was "CUHK − CM = 0."[147] Predictably, New Asia did not agree. One college leader asserted that his strategy was the gradual "breaking down of the autonomy" of the colleges via "indirection."[148] By August 1974 even Tsufa Lee (chapter 3) was protesting to Li against this "vast concentration of power" and the "stripping of the Colleges the role they should rightly play in a federal university." Lee declared that centralization would "lead to a sterile uniformity within the university as against the mutually enriching diversities of the Colleges under a genuine federal system."[149] In March 1976, however, a government commission sanctioned Li's annexation of all academic policy, development, finances, student matriculation, staff appointments, curriculum, examinations, and the awarding of degrees. The college presidents were demoted to college heads, while the colleges themselves continued only as "trustees" for their assets, student welfare, and general education.[150] As Li implemented these changes, most of New Asia's remaining leaders severed their final connections with the college in summer 1977. While Yale-in-China's B. Preston Schoyer wrote letters to each with hopes that the college could "still exert a strong humanistic influence," several replies were quite tart.[151] By Li's retirement in 1978 he had consolidated the former medley of intellectually diverse colleges into a single university bound to his kuashang orientation.

Li Choh-ming was a pivotal figure at the nexus of British imperial decline, U.S. imperial expansion, the globalization of higher education, and the economic transformation of Hong Kong. His leadership at CUHK reveals perceptive insight into the world's momentum and economic operating systems. Atop an existing decade of American partnership with Hong Kong's missionary schools and "refugee colleges," he used public and private funding to build a transpacific university that capped a new hierarchy of U.S.-oriented institutions. Shielded by the word "international," he tapped into the resources of Washington's state-private network in order to gather support for CUHK and funnel its staff and students into transpacific opportunities. This kuashang strategy was an instrumentalist response to the global shift from British to American hegemony that advanced Hong Kong's informal decolonization and reflected his belief in expert-led economic planning. Simultaneously, he enacted a vision of Chinese modernity that eluded many previous intellectuals, neither reinventing nor demonizing tradition but instead consigning it to archival preservation.

Examining Li's life before 1963 allows us to map his repeated migrations, evolving relationship with the United States, economic philosophy, and knack for leveraging networks. Born to parents who already favored American missionary schools and U.S. higher education, he was put onto a privileged path shared by many Republican-era elites. As a Berkeley graduate student, he came to believe in state economic management and expert-led development. He returned from California to advance his career, but the Pacific War shunted him onto a new path. The young economist's expertise and connections elevated him into government positions in wartime Chongqing, Washington, and postwar Shanghai. He observed firsthand both the American renovations of the global capitalist system and the failure of Nationalist development efforts. Profoundly disoriented by the communist transition, he fell back onto American social capital and secured his return to California, if not yet his family's. Once more at Berkeley, Li pragmatically shifted his research to suit U.S. national security interests and collaborated with Cold War programs to steer overseas Chinese toward U.S. international leadership.

As vice-chancellor, Li modeled CUHK on his own example. From junior faculty's graduate degrees to the library's organizational system, he steadily spliced American content into this nascent institution, indigenized its expansion, and incentivized both staff and students to look toward the United States for future opportunities. These strategies expanded his power, made CUHK into a hub of transpacific networks, and directly enabled Hong Kong to emerge as the world's largest sender of foreign students to the United States during the 1970s. We see his agenda most succinctly in the establishment of LIBA, which reverse-engineered American business systems into this British colony. As we will see over the next two chapters, CUHK's transpacific circulations helped fuel the expansion of a second generation of kuashang who would renovate Hong

Kong companies along American models and provide the executives to staff U.S. multinationals' expansion across Asia over the 1970s.

There were casualties of Li's education-as-development agenda, however. He routinely gestured toward Chinese tradition, from citing Confucius and practicing calligraphy to later authoring a new Chinese character lexicon.[152] These were curated selections of Chinese tradition, though—ones palatable to international audiences and severable from the political conflict of the Republican era. He never publicly discussed the civil war, let alone democracy or self-determination. In contrast, Qian Mu was still advocating for a Neo-Confucian Chinese modernity and objected strenuously to Li's path, but Li prevailed. He framed the "Chinese intellectual heritage" as a foundation that could not survive without imported additions such as "Western empirical methods," "scientific knowledge," and the "indispensable" asset of "bilingualism." He commanded CUHK's graduates "to move between these two great cultures and to interact effectively with each."[153]

To twenty-first-century observers, Li's strategies might appear deceptively obvious. Does it matter which library system CUHK adopted or where its faculty received advanced degrees? Yet, as Li's conflicts with colonial officials and New Asia demonstrate, it was not obvious that a Chinese institution in a British colony should have an MBA program or adopt the U.S. Library of Congress system. These were Li's kuashang strategies—choices that another vice-chancellor such as philosopher Chan Wing-tsit were unlikely to have made. The world was ablaze with war and protest in the late 1960s, but a subtle turning point had been reached that held enormous implications for both Hong Kong's development and future Sino-U.S. relations. Aided by CUHK and its transpacific networks, Hong Kong's second generation of kuashang would be well positioned to respond to the 1970s crisis in global capitalism and the first signs of China's reforms.

CHAPTER V

Decolonization by Investment

American Social and Financial Capital in Hong Kong

Very little of the "hard" data in business is as hard as it's made out to be.
—MATTHEW STEWART, *THE MANAGEMENT MYTH:*
DEBUNKING MODERN BUSINESS PHILOSOPHY

Hong Kong's transpacific reorientation crossed a threshold in 1963. As Li Choh-ming was appointed CUHK's first vice-chancellor, the United States surpassed Britain and Japan as the colony's lead outside investor. As noted in chapter 1, before the Second World War the British Empire restricted outside investment into its colonies in order to protect Imperial Preference and the Sterling Area. Postwar economic realities pushed the Hong Kong government to lower these barriers, particularly to receive capital in flight from China and Southeast Asia. As I analyze here in greater detail, the colony's bankers and industrialists first worked in tandem to channel this flight capital into labor-intensive manufacturing. The ensuing manufacturing boom then created new opportunities for foreign direct investment, led by U.S. companies purchasing equity in their suppliers or investing in joint ventures. Yet the U.S. embargo and the ensuing Comprehensive Certificate of Origin system tempered such opportunities by raising legal and logistical barriers to U.S.-Hong Kong trade. As late as 1955 the colony's trade with British East Africa remained larger than its trade with the United States. Yet by 1959 the United States had morphed into the colony's leading export market, and just four years later direct U.S. investment became the colony's dominant source of outside capital.[1]

On a global scale, Hong Kong's post-1945 reorientation toward U.S. trade and investment should be unsurprising. U.S. economic output surpassed that of the entire British Empire in 1916.² The continued dominance of British investment in Hong Kong was largely a function of established British banks, imperial trading networks, and active state intervention. As the colonial government lifted the restrictions discussed in chapter 1, Imperial Preference dissolved, and decolonization accelerated, Hong Kong became much more exposed to U.S.-led capitalist systems. Simultaneously, U.S. overseas investment was soaring, from US$7 billion in 1946 to US$32 billion in 1960 and US$160 billion by 1978.³ In this stable context where the government no longer restricted outside investors, never pursued import-substitution policies, did not legally distinguish between foreign and local companies, and did not enforce a minimum wage until 2013, increasing engagement with U.S. capital and corporations is not surprising.

Yet a mythos of postwar British dominance over Hong Kong's economy has held remarkable staying power. As early as 1983, scholar Y. C. Jao concluded that "the widely held belief" that the Hongkong and Shanghai Bank (hereafter, the Hongkong Bank) had held on to "a monopolistic stranglehold on Hong Kong's banking business" had been, in short, "a myth."⁴ Officials themselves did not suffer from these illusions. In the same year, Secretary for Home Affairs Denis Bray stated at an American Chamber of Commerce luncheon: "Constitutionally it is Britain which is responsible for administration here. Economically it is America which is the more significant."⁵ Yet popular narratives of Hong Kong's development have continued to foreground the Hongkong Bank, Jardine Matheson, and so on. This misconception testifies to the way that imperialism can warp knowledge making by valorizing and inflating everything associated with the formal overlord. The kuashang methodology helps correct this mythos by examining individuals' and families' evolving orientations toward international power through their educational and business relationships. We will see that elite networks of U.S.-oriented Chinese bankers and industrialists were leading even the Hongkong Bank toward transpacific markets and capital flows from beneath the British colonial flag.

This chapter explores how social capital facilitates access to and the accumulation of financial capital. In the next section we will see that personal relationships molded local industrial lending throughout the 1950s and 1960s. Business historians have built a broad picture of the capital formation that undergirded Hong Kong's manufacturing boom but have paid less attention to the human relationships that determined who accessed bank capital and on what terms. Upon arrival, the Jiangnan textile industrialists urgently needed to re-establish banking relationships in order to jumpstart operations and maintain working capital. While I discussed the Shanghai Commercial and Savings Bank and First National City Bank in chapter 1, here I focus on the Hongkong Bank and argue that it gradually became the dominant lender to the émigrés by hiring its first ethnically Chinese manager: the U.S.-educated émigré "H. J." Shen Hsi-jui (沈熙瑞). Shen made himself indispensable to the bank, and its reliance on him exemplifies informal decolonization. This colonial institution maintained its public image of power by quietly ceding day-to-day decisions to this well-connected kuashang. Yet Shen's networks and strategies were themselves inextricable from his lifelong friendship with Dr. Francis K. Pan (潘光迥). From conjoined educations and careers across the United States, China, and Hong Kong, their relationship reveals how Shen acquired his capacious networks and some of his agenda as a lending broker.

In the second section, I turn to an examination of direct outside investment in Hong Kong industry during the 1960s and early 1970s. As the émigré spinners expanded operations, first the United Kingdom and then the United States imposed restrictions on Hong Kong's yarns and fabrics. This protectionism incentivized diversification into new kinds of textiles and apparel. Relying on previously overlooked government surveys, I examine how direct outside investment helped the cotton spinners to diversify production. Here the assumption has been that Japanese capital was dominant in Hong Kong, but these surveys demolish this theory and further challenge frameworks that imagine Hong Kong within East Asian "tiger" geographies. Instead, aided by their American social capital, the émigrés primarily secured U.S. investment to produce nonquota products and circumvent Anglo-American protectionism. I will note a stark contrast with the electronics industry, however, where direct investment stemmed primarily from U.S. corporations' calculations to exploit local low-cost labor.

In the final section I examine two huge U.S. multinational investments in the late 1960s that developed in part from personal relationships and kuashang strategies. The first was a partnership between Esso and China Light and Power (CLP) to expand the colony's power generation capacity, while the second was Mobil's redevelopment of its local storage depot into the world's largest private housing project, Mei Foo Sun Chuen (美孚新邨). Both projects were extremely capital-intensive and helped Hong Kong to escape looming development traps. Both were also far outside Esso's and Mobil's established business activities. Kuashang actors used their contacts and credibility to convince these multinationals to venture into this unprecedented territory. Exploiting Hong Kong's interstitial context, these kuashang executives molded public policy to offer artificially attractive investment terms. The ensuing profits altered Esso's and Mobil's global business strategies and represented key steps toward post-Fordist global capitalism.

Industry and the Decolonization of the Hongkong Bank

The history of Hong Kong banking has received substantial scholarly attention, most especially the Hongkong Bank.[6] As a result, despite incomplete data, scholars have built a broad picture of the capital formation that financed Hong Kong's manufacturing boom through the early 1960s. Most initial capital came in flight as cash and machinery: first, billions of Hong Kong dollars from China and then an additional HK$4–6 billion from overseas Chinese in Southeast Asia as they faced instability in the 1950s and 1960s.[7] Yet large capital inflows can easily be squandered through maladministration. Hong Kong's historic role as a trade and migration hub meant it possessed experienced banks that were prepared to turn these inflows into credit and other financial products. The leading British institutions were the Hongkong Bank and the Standard Chartered Bank, while the modern Chinese banks included the Bank of East Asia, the Hang Seng Bank, the SCSB, the Bank of Canton, the Liu Chong Hing, and Ka Wah Bank (chapter 3). The British banks catered to the colonial government and hongs such as Jardine Matheson, while the modern Chinese banks served most residents and overseas communities, as did a host of traditional banks. The Bank of China was a leading player in handling overseas remittances after 1949, while American outfits such as First National largely financed U.S. dollar trades. As a result, there was diverse financial expertise in Hong Kong, and both the number of banks and total deposits expanded rapidly during the 1950s and early 1960s. It should be stressed, however, that the banking sector was "notoriously unregulated." The Banking Ordinance in place between 1948 and 1965 did not mandate any reserve requirements, liquidity ratios, or even the need to prepare complete balance sheets.[8]

Y. C. Jao and Catherine Schenk have demonstrated that these banking and manufacturing booms were intertwined, as was the case in Republican-era Jiangnan. In particular, a key factor linking the banking and manufacturing booms was that Hong Kong was just one of two places in the Sterling Area allowed to maintain a free market in U.S. dollars. This sanction enabled Hong Kong to straddle the sterling and dollar areas and made foreign exchange comparatively plentiful in the colony.[9] As both Jao and Schenk emphasized, the colony's ensuing high supply of U.S. dollars offered a critical advantage for both the colony and the émigré industrialists. Since Hong Kong lacked a local supply of cotton and possessed a tiny local market, the transplanted spinning industry was reliant on imported cotton and the overseas export of its products. Cheap and reliable access to U.S. dollars was thus crucial, and the entire textile industry would have struggled without it. This dependency also underscores the imperative for local industrialists to abide by the U.S. embargo. Moreover, since U.S. dollars were a lucrative asset for local banks to resell internationally, Jao found that the Hongkong Bank was particularly willing to extend low-interest loans to manufacturers with high foreign exchange turnovers if they would reciprocate by assigning a major portion of their turnover to the bank. It was a mutually beneficial quid pro quo because "the spread between the buying and selling rates of foreign exchange is one of the most lucrative sources of bank profit in Hong Kong."[10] As a result, contingent factors aligned to finance the transplanted textile industry: flight capital, an established banking sector, a free market in U.S. dollars, and experienced émigré industrialists. By importing large amounts of American cotton and increasingly selling their yarn and textiles to the U.S. market, the industrialists gradually became conduits for U.S. dollars and thus attractive clients.

Yet it remains unclear how particular industrialists and banks established their relationships. Upon arrival to Hong Kong, most émigrés lacked collateral beyond limited cash and rerouted machinery. As a result, obtaining initial credit depended more on networks and social capital than on mathematics, particularly in such a laxly regulated context. Yet the requisite social capital was not necessarily British. Again, many industrialists had active relationships with the SCSB, First National, and others. Jao and Schenk have asserted that the Hongkong Bank was always the dominant lender to local manufacturers but admit that the evidence for this claim is thin: "Although quantitative evidence for the earlier period [1950–1965] is scanty, it can be inferred with confidence that the Bank accounted for more than half of all bank loans and advances to the manu-facturing industries."[11] This "more than half" figure is based on records from 1966 that show the Hongkong Bank accounting for 48.3 percent of total bank finance to the manufacturing sector and 54 percent of textile financing in particular. It is problematic to assume that 1966 accurately reflects the previous twenty years. In reality, both the Hongkong and Hang Seng Banks established specialized industrial lending offices in 1959 in order to build long-term relationships with the industrialists.[12] Both these specialized sections and the banking relationships described in chap-ter 1 instead signal a wider competition in which personal connections were key. In examining these networks, I argue that the Hongkong Bank's dominant share of industrial lending as of July 1966 was more likely a highpoint (it declined thereafter) that resulted from its growing reliance on kuashang networks and the broker H. J. Shen.

I should first emphasize that the vast majority of Hong Kong manufac-turers were small-scale enterprises with small capital needs. In 1955 there were 2,437 factories in the colony employing 110,574 people, yielding an average of about 43 workers per factory. By 1965 the number of total fac-tories and workers had roughly tripled, but the average number of workers fell to 40.[13] By 1977 over 90 percent of the colony's manufacturers still employed fewer than 50 people.[14] As a result, most Hong Kong factories were small partnerships that relied on kinship networks and local Chinese banks for financing. Such factories comprised a few dozen people working in rented office floors and repurposed spaces to make consumer goods such as plastic flowers or wigs. Scholars Danny Kin-kong Lam and Ian Lee have labeled this model as "guerilla capitalism."[15] Prevalent in both Hong Kong and Taiwan, "guerilla" firms were lean enterprises focused on short-term, small-scale production opportunities that required low investment. Such firms constantly shifted their production and relied on subcontract-ing networks to deliver large orders. For example, a firm with metal stamping equipment might move from stamping belt buckles to making automobile parts. Their low capital needs and racial discrimination meant that few such guerilla firms would have gone to the Hongkong Bank in the 1950s and 1960s. Thus if most local manufacturers borrowed little to nothing from the Hongkong Bank, a few manufacturers had to borrow a lot for it to account for 48.3 percent of industrial lending by 1966.

The émigré cotton spinners fit this bill. Cotton spinning is a capital-intensive business ineligible for guerilla models. During Hong Kong's first manufacturing wave in the 1920s and 1930s, several hundred firms opened weaving and knitting plants in the colony, but only a handful tried to enter cotton spinning.[16] This absence stemmed from local disadvantages of climate and topography, as well as stiff competition from Jiangnan's spinning industry. Before the Japanese invasion it was more profitable to import yarn from Shanghai or Japan than to start a mill in humid and hilly Hong Kong. In addition, as Wong Siu-lun and Tomoko Shiroyama have discussed, cotton spinning is a highly competitive global industry that incentivizes economies of scale. As a result, profitability requires high fixed-capital investments for substantial sites and specialized equipment, alongside steady working capital for a stream of raw cotton purchased locally or on the international market.[17] In pre-1937 Jiangnan, these requirements led cotton spinning to rely heavily on bank loans borrowed against fixed assets.[18] This structure proved precarious. These long-term loans were "in effect a mortgage" on the mills' property, while the short-term loans used to purchase cotton were often unsecured credit extended in a manner "so precarious that their Japanese counterparts called it 'circular financing.'"[19] This perilous situation became evident during the Great Depression, when deflation and a credit crunch caused numerous Jiangnan spinners to default and trigger a banking crisis in 1934–1935. Put simply, the Jiangnan cotton-spinning industry had been profitable in boom years but leveraged to the hilt and vulnerable to inevitable busts.

These Shanghainese experiences were well known to Hong Kong banks, and thus due diligence by the Hongkong Bank would have discouraged unsecured lending to the émigrés. Their lucrative U.S. dollar accounts did not yet exist, while it is not true that the Shanghainese simply had "stronger" financial abilities than their Cantonese counterparts.[20] Indeed, even émigrés themselves marveled that the banks were lending to them. After returning from New York in 1955, Jack Tang (chapter 1) recalled saying to his father, P. Y. Tang: "I'm surprised that the banks lend you money." He made this comment "because the balance sheet was not very strong. We didn't have much running capital, operating capital, as I say. You only had the fixed assets, the land and the buildings."[21] When looking at the numbers, he concluded that Hong Kong banks were gambling by lending to cash-poor refugees in an industry with a shaky record.

Jack Tang soon learned that industrialists like his father were relying on personal networks to secure privileged access to low-cost capital. As Naomi Lamoreaux has analyzed, this situation was not unusual historically. What is now called insider lending was the norm in both Europe and North America through the mid-nineteenth century, with banks primarily dol- ing out loans to the bank's founders.[22] Traditional Chinese native banks also primarily issued loans based on personal reputation, while the Hong Kong Monetary Authority did not regulate the exposure of connected parties until the 1990s. For his part, P. Y. Tang took unsecured loans from a number of banks with which he had established relationships in order to launch South Sea in October 1948: First National under Henry Sperry, the Hongkong Bank, and K. P. Chen's SCSB. As seen in chapter 1, as of March 1949 the SCSB had extended South Sea a euphemistic "overdraft" of HK$335,000 to buy cotton. Jao concluded that many such initial loans to the émigré spinners were "granted practically on an unsecured basis."[23] This lending was structured by interpersonal assumptions of who was creditworthy. It enabled high social capital individuals such as the Tangs to secure initial credit and restart operations.

Reputation and favors, however, will not last forever. Tang took a risk with this borrowing, and only the Korean War allowed him to repay it. The war stimulated stockpiling and a trade boom that "saved the situa- tion" for many transplanted spinners. P. Y. Tang then used this influx to move rapidly into new production lines.[24] South Sea entered into weaving during the Korean War by purchasing spindles and looms from Toyota, a deal that would have required permission from U.S. Occupation authori- ties and financing by American banks. Then, in 1953, South Sea was among the first to begin working with the U.S. consulate to receive the certificates of origin for its products to clear U.S. customs. Yet Tang con- tinued diversifying. He also bought Mayfair Industries, a small zipper plant that he deputized to Jack's management after he returned as a U.S. citizen in 1955.[25] And, as noted, by 1957 South Sea was also producing dress shirts that Jack marketed to U.S. department stores through his HBS contacts. In short, South Sea took root by first converting the Tangs' elite social capital into working capital. They then used the U.S.-financed Korean War boom to expand into new products aimed at the U.S. market. U.S.–Hong Kong trade was growing by as much 40 percent annually, and by 1962 P. Y. Tang would declare that the U.S. market was "life and death" for Hong Kong.[26]

Social capital was thus not just useful initially. It remained a core busi- ness strategy for the Tangs, as Jack explained in one oral history interview. Discussing the 1950s, he stated: "The industry people, the refugees, didn't have much of a position in the eyes of the government." The Jiangnan transplants were new to Hong Kong's Anglo-Cantonese world and had to integrate. The Tangs' American social capital was a crucial advantage. Jack continued: "I was fortunate enough to have had American connections and Manchester connections, and I was fortunate enough to be in the position of meeting a lot of visitors: people from New York, and London, *but mostly from the States* [italics added]." With prized international contacts, the Tangs had entrée to trade. He and his father consciously put this social capital to work: "So every Sunday, as I told you, we would go on the boat, and I invited anybody who just happened to be in town and called me up. We would have a boat picnic, go swimming and all that stuff, every Sunday. So I met a lot of people that way." By cultivating a milieu of coveted international contacts, the Tangs were advancing their social and business interests in tandem. It is easy to imagine how they parlayed these biracial and bicultural networks into loans, deferred payments, sales and marketing relationships, foreign exchange arrangements, and government favors. Jack concluded this discussion: "Within Hong Kong, as I say, I know a lot of government people—bankers, friendly competitors, and the successful retailers, and other real estate people. . . . I don't want to use the word 'class'—but you don't really associate with [anyone] other than these people."[27] Through unapologetic elitism, the Tangs used their international connections to reclaim social status and integrate local and international power structures.

Few émigrés had the Tangs' social capital, however. Instead, most turned to another kuashang as their broker: H. J. Shen. Wong Siu-lun originally pointed out: "It is customary, when dealing with strangers, for Chinese businessmen to enlist the assistance of intermediaries with whom they have some common particularistic bonds. When the Shanghainese spinners arrived in Hong Kong, they also followed this practice in seeking bank loans."[28] Wong identified one "Eurasian of Anglo-Chinese parentage" as the first intermediary, but Wong, Jao, and Schenk all agree that this role gradually passed to Shen, who became the first ethnically Chinese managing director of the Hongkong Bank in 1964.[29] According to Jao, Shen's decisive advantage was his "intimate ties with the Shanghai-born industrialists." In turn, Andrew Smith has argued that Shen's success was "likely a function of the networks he had from his U.S. education."[30] Through the kuashang analytic, it becomes evident that these networks were heavily overlapping and allowed Shen to achieve network centrality between the Hongkong Bank and the U.S.-oriented émigré industrialists.

To understand Shen, we must also understand Francis Pan. They were born a few months apart in 1904–1905 around Shanghai and may have been kin through Pan's mother, Shen En-pei.[31] Pan's older brother was Quentin Pan Guangdan (潘光旦), Republican China's premier anthropologist and eugenicist.[32] Their brother-in-law Ho Lin-yi (何林一) had graduated from St. John's in 1908 and Dartmouth in 1911, but Quentin first attended Tsinghua and then Dartmouth on a Boxer Indemnity scholarship.[33] Francis followed his older brother, graduating from Dartmouth in 1926 and proceeding to its Tuck School of Business. He then entered New York University in fall 1927 for doctoral work and defended a dissertation on financial interventions in 1929. H. J. Shen precisely imitated Francis: graduating from Dartmouth followed by Tuck and then NYU.[34] In New York they lived together at Columbia's International House, while Pan also worked for the new China Institute in America. The two friends jointly returned to Shanghai in 1930, where both undertook commercial and educational work. Pan joined Shanghai's famous Commercial Press, while teaching at the Shanghai College of Commerce. Shen became an accountant for General Electric's Shanghai subsidiary while teaching at the American missionary-sponsored University of Shanghai and the National Shanghai Business School.[35] They even married around the same time. In November 1930 Pan married Cecilia Chang Nyoh-tsung, a graduate of Oberlin and Juilliard, while Shen seems to have married Ida Chu (朱懿大) a few months later, but information on Ida is unfortunately scant.

Shen made his own first steps into banking, but the two men's shared networks facilitated a joint transition into railway finance. In 1933 Shen left General Electric and joined the Bank of China in Qingdao. In 1935, however, he took a huge step up by suddenly becoming the chief accountant of the key Jinpu rail line, as well as secretary-general of the Sinking Fund Committee for Chinese Railway Bonds.[36] At the same moment, Pan left the Commercial Press and became chief secretary to the new minister of railways, Zhang Jia'ao (chapter 1), whom the Nationalists had ousted from the Bank of China.[37] As chief secretary to the minister, Pan was directly involved in the "negotiations for the rehabilitation of all railway loans then outstanding," which "brought him into direct contact with top bankers and diplomats."[38] In short, Pan and Shen were suddenly both in key interlocking positions at the heart of China's rail infrastructure. In 1936, when corresponding with Tuck, Pan made their conjoined personal and professional trajectories explicit: "Am writing separately to Dean Gray. Mr. Shen Hsi Jui is now connected with my Ministry. You may reach him through me."[39] In Nanjing, Pan also involved himself in a flurry of other U.S.-linked diplomatic and educational activities, while he and Cecilia were social-page fixtures.[40] The press rarely mentioned Shen, however, suggesting which friend was more active socially.

Following the Japanese invasion, both couples fled inland to Chongqing, which from late 1938 became the wartime capital and a hub of frenetic socializing among Nationalist officials, displaced Jiangnan capitalists, and U.S. government representatives. It was a highly factionalized and corrupt atmosphere in which inside information traded hands at nightly dinner parties. American-returned students were well positioned in this environment. Cecilia Pan was in the Oberlin alumni club with Minister of Finance Kong Xiangxi, and Francis used such connections to bounce from position to position, from becoming director-general of the Ministry of Communications in November 1940 and leading an Executive Yuan aid mission to the United States to later becoming a China National Aviation Corporation (CNAC) director and general manager of the National Agricultural Engineering Corporation (NAEC), a CNRRA subentity.[41] In contrast, Shen continued to focus on railway finance. He first became deputy governor of the Bank of Guangxi with supervision over the Xianggui line.[42] When the line fell to Japanese forces in 1942, Shen became deputy director-general of the Chinese Postal Remittance and Savings Bank, which managed overseas remittances and bond sales.[43] Through these positions, the Pans and Shens rose high in Chongqing's macabre social whirl, as observed by L. K. Little, the American head of the Chinese Maritime Customs Service (chapter 1). Underscoring how U.S. educational networks facilitated contacts in ways parallel to native-place guanxi, Little was also a Dartmouth alum. He used this link to reach out to the Pans upon arrival in 1943. Little was captivated by Cecilia, whom he would describe as "the loveliest and most charming woman in the room," even remarking, "Pretty lousy dinner, but, as I was next to Cecilia Pan, it didn't matter."[44] Little and the Pans became close and their circle included familiar figures such as K. P. Chen, Pei Tsuyee, and the Lee brothers; the British, Dutch, and American ambassadors; Nationalist officials and advisers such as Sun Fo (孫科) and Arthur Young; and of course the Shens. In November 1944 Little noted meeting Shen at a "most delightful" dinner party at the Pans' home. He recorded: "Mr. Shen (Dartmouth) . . . said they [the Guangxi railway] had to leave some 25,000 workmen to shift for themselves. No money, no food. Many have sold their children; some have killed them."[45] While not "most delightful" dinner conversation, it is a lens into how Shen's networks grew through the Pans.[46]

After Japan's surrender, Shen reached the summit of the Nationalists' increasingly U.S.-dependent financial bureaucracy, positioning him for his later role in Hong Kong. While Francis joined the private sector in Shanghai, the Shens returned to Nanjing, and by 1949 he was both the deputy director-general of the Central Bank of China and the assistant general manager of the Central Trust of China, the government's primary purchasing agent.[47] In these roles Shen worked directly with Zhang Jia'ao, Song Ziwen, and Kong Xiangxi, as well as Little and Young. Shen also became vice-chairman of the Foreign Exchange Stabilization Fund, where he worked under K. P. Chen in the failing effort to shore up the spiraling currency.[48] He also briefly took on the role of secretary-general of the Council for U.S. Aid to China, which worked with Washington's Economic Cooperation Administration (ECA) to distribute American aid.[49] He soon resigned over the endemic corruption, but not before appointing Pan its deputy chairman.[50] By April 1949 Shen had decided to flee, flying to Hong Kong alongside Zhang Jia'ao.[51] The Pans vacillated but relocated to Hong Kong in early 1950.[52]

Derailed at the height of their careers, Shen and Pan fell back in Hong Kong on their entwined American social capitals and moved jointly to embrace kuashang strategies. Once again, Pan first established an investment firm that he advertised as "specializing on American securities," but he confessed to Little that it lost money.[53] Little then helped Pan to reach out to the CIA-backed Committee for a Free Asia (CFA, later the Asia Foundation) in late 1951. He proposed that they establish an anticommunist publication with him as its head. He and staffer Alan Valentine discussed this idea over lunch, but Valentine subsequently rejected involvement with Pan. Although Pan was "a very old friend" and "dapper and charming," Valentine declared his "categorical belief" that Pan was "unsuitable for work or identification with our Committee" because he was "hopelessly muddled in his thinking." Valentine meant that Pan was insufficiently ideological because he had urged CFA propaganda to not "make enemies of the Chinese people" and even declared that the communists had "good intentions," just "unreasonable methods of execution." Valentine concluded that Pan's motivation was opportunistic because he "raised the question of asylum," while the U.S. naval attaché in Taipei affirmed his affection for the Pans but agreed he "simply had nothing to offer."[54] Other CFA staffers echoed that Pan was "interested in lining up with the Committee for personal gain."[55]

Pan analyzed the failure of this proposal and subsequently moved to embrace the United States more explicitly. He re-established active communications with Dartmouth in early 1952 and began lecturing in economics at Chung Chi (chapter 3).[56] He also gave public speeches promoting America in Hong Kong and Hong Kong in America. In May 1955 he gave a speech at the colony's Y Men's Club entitled "America's New Economy," in which he urged Hong Kong businessmen to learn from U.S. economic strength.[57] In December 1957 he gave a paid speech to the Hanover Bank in New York that emphasized Hong Kong's geostrategic position and inflows of flight capital, while identifying potential opportunities for American banks.[58] After their daughter Shirley graduated from Wellesley in 1961 and proceeded to Columbia's medical school, Pan finally secured a stable U.S.-backed position as head of the Mencius Foundation.[59] As noted in chapter 3, the CFA had established Mencius as a covert front for U.S. cultural diplomacy with Y. L. Lee as its first head. Thus, like David Au at ARCI or Li Choh-ming at CUHK, Pan was collaborating with a proxy of the U.S. government. Through Mencius, he often traveled to San Francisco for Asia Foundation meetings and to visit old friends, such as both he and Shen's old boss Zhang Jia'ao.[60] He also befriended CIA agents embedded with the Asia Foundation in Hong Kong.[61] Over the 1960s Pan would also head the Lion's Club alongside Jack Yuen (chapter 2) and help organize the Dartmouth alumni group, while Li Choh-ming later appointed him as the first head of CUHK's Publications Office.[62]

Pan's path toward kuashang strategies once again dovetailed with Shen's. After taking Ida and their children to San Francisco in late 1950, Shen returned to Hong Kong and resigned his government positions. Like Pan, he too started a trading and investment firm that lost money. Pan then helped Shen to search for work by putting him in touch with fellow Dartmouth alumni, such as the local head of Standard-Vacuum Oil, George Bell (figure 5.1). By 1954 Pan reported to Dartmouth that Shen was working with Anker Henningsen & Co., an American family firm transplanted from Shanghai that had acquired the colony's Coca-Cola bottling rights.[63] The Henningsens were also friends with L. K. Little, so that shared connection was likely key. Shen shifted into the textile industry in 1958, when the Jiangnan émigré Samuel Yen (嚴欣淇) hired him as managing director of the East Sun Textile Mill (怡生紗廠) and its fifteen hundred workers, who worked around the clock to produce for the U.S. and UK markets. In this role, Shen was able to combine trips to California to see his family with attending American trade fairs, touring U.S. colleges and universities, and building relationships with New England textile merchants and industrialists (figure 5.2). As if living in parallel with Pan, Li Choh-ming also recruited Shen to share his expertise at CUHK as well.[64]

This examination of Shen's and Pan's interwoven networks and shift toward kuashang strategies enables us to understand Shen's emergence as the colony's leading broker of industrial lending. Rather than just expertise, his former government positions and extensive networks among both Americans and fellow American-returned students were essential to carving out this lucrative role and to clinching an unprecedented title from the

CLASSMATES IN HONG KONG: '28ers Hsi Jui Shen, managing director of the Maysun Trading and Investment Co. and George Bell, China Area Manager, Standard-Vacuum Oil Co., both of Hong Kong, posed for this picture in October, at the request of the Class Secretary.

Figure 5.1 H. J. Shen and George Bell in the Dartmouth alumni magazine, 1954. "Shen, Hsi-Jui 1928," RSCLDC. Courtesy of Dartmouth College Library.

Ivy League Hong Kong Industrialist
Visits Firm Here, Makes Tour Of Yale

H. J. Shen, globe-circling industrialist from Hong Kong, is briefed on New Haven history during one-day visit here as Shen, center, with h's hosts, Murray Feinberg, left, president of the Federal Textile Corp., and S. E. Goldstein, vice president, toured the Federal plant and Yale.

H. J. Shen, Graduate of Dartmouth, Is Textile Corp. Guest

where his wife, three children, and grandchildren are, before returning to Hong Kong.

Educational Growth

Shen evidenced interest in the

to over 3.5 million people now living in an area of about 100 square miles.

"It is an interesting city," he said, "but not a very pleasant

Figure 5.2 H. J. Shen visits Yale and New Haven textile plants, reported in *New Haven Register*, June 12, 1960. "Shen, Hsi-Jui 1928," RSCLDC. Courtesy of Dartmouth College Library.

Hongkong Bank. He did it by inserting himself between the industrialists and the bank, as he related to Wong Siu-lun in an interview in the late 1970s:

> When I arrived, I told [the cotton spinners] that they did not have to do this [go through the China Engineers Ltd]. I knew these spinners personally, so I approached the Hongkong and Shanghai Bank on

their behalf. We had to persuade the colonial officials and the Bank that textiles were good for Hong Kong. It was not too difficult when they saw the financial side of it. This was the period just after the war, and there was a big demand for textiles. Because of the demand, textiles were very profitable. The factories could recoup their capital investment within three years. When the Bank saw the profit, they said, "Here's the money. Lend it to them." So I functioned as an informal adviser for the Bank. I held a dinner on its behalf every week. Later I became very busy. But the Bank said, "We need you." So I stayed, first for three years, then six years, until now. There has never been any contract.[65]

Shen tells us a great deal here. By "the period just after the war," he means the Korean War. Its trade boom allowed this former Nationalist official and American-returned student to up-sell the spinners' recent performance to the British bank and secure loans on their behalf. Korea thus both rescued the industrialists and gave Shen a taste of how to become an intermediary. As an informal adviser and pass-through lender, he monetized his social capital and achieved a temporary network centrality between the bank and the industrialists. Yet his own failed firm and stints at Anker Henningsen and East Sun testify that he did not immediately corner this lucrative role. Instead, over the 1950s he learned more about the textile industry, deepened his relationships in Hong Kong and the United States, recommended investments, and explored the industry's essential sales market. He needed additional expertise and networks to understand and assemble these deals. By the 1960s, his success led the bank to recruit his continued services, recalled as "We need you." However, his pride in the absence of "any contract" boasts of his agency and autonomy. In effect, his networks and dinner parties were a shadow court of lending, which helps explain why the HSBC archive lacks records on Shen beyond a few photographs (figure 5.3). Neither he nor the bank would have wished to document his activities.

It should be stressed, however, that Shen's networks were not just about the Hongkong Bank from the industrialists' perspectives. They had other challenges beyond bank loans. Through Shen as well as Pan, they could also access officials in Washington and Taipei; Anglo-American textile buyers; Ivy League administrators; and probably almost any prominent American-returned student. Shen could thus offer manifold kinds of

Figure 5.3 H. J. Shen (*second from right*) with textile industrialists (*from left*) Y. C. Chen, Eric Chen, S. T. King, H. C. Yung (Rong Hongqing), and Y. C. Wang, March 1977. Reproduced with the permission of HSBC Holdings plc.

insider access, likely what motivated his colleagues at the Cotton Textile Association to choose him as their representative in 1962 to help negotiate in Washington against proposed U.S. cotton fabric tariffs.[66]

Indeed, in line with parrying U.S. protectionism, Shen's activities illustrate how elite social capital can mold supposedly rational markets. After the Hongkong Bank appointed Shen, the Chinese Manufacturers' Association hosted a banquet in his honor.[67] According to *Wah Kiu Yat Po*'s transcript of his speech, Shen urged local bankers and manufacturers to collaborate.[68] More specifically, he argued that the colony's lack of a central bank was the reason that local banks were engaged in a destructive competition in pursuit of the highest interest rates. He praised local banks for their role in local development after 1949 but asserted that banks were now driving up real estate prices by issuing high-interest loans to speculators: "Therefore, real estate developers have had better ability than manufacturers to borrow at higher interest rates." In effect, high-risk real estate speculation was crowding out industrial lending. Yet, viewing manufacturers as essential to taking "care of its ever-increasing population," Shen urged the banks to adopt a Rotary-inspired "spirit of service" by curbing this speculation and instead channeling capital to manufacturers. He declared: "This is an existential struggle of an issue and where the public interest lies."[69]

While this proposal was framed in a rhetoric of public service, Shen was lobbying for his friends and colleagues to arrogate the power of economic planning and coordinate among themselves to mold local financial markets. He was right that many banks were speculating in a real estate bubble that soon burst, but his proposal to effectively subsidize manufacturers was not in the Hongkong Bank's financial interests. It was in his and his friends' personal financial interests. Thus we see the flipside of informal decolonization. While Shen's appointment heralded another transfer of power from British- to U.S.-oriented Chinese actors, this shift also empowered unaccountable private-sector elites. Through Shen and Pan we get a new picture of how interconnected émigrés reestablished themselves, unlocked this colonial bank, and gradually reshaped its lending. Indeed, through Shen's implicit suggestion that industrial lending was not particularly profitable, we might question whether the Hongkong Bank's eventual dominance of industrial lending was even rational or wise. As such, Shen and Pan drive home that neither financial lending nor economic change broadly is ever exclusively a question of "objective" numbers. Instead, such historical relationships remind us that the unearned, the irrational, and the fabricated must remain front and center in our economic narratives.

Diversification by Direct Investment

From no cotton spinning industry in 1945, Hong Kong had thirteen mills by 1953 and forty by 1965, when the total plateaued.[70] These mills were much larger than "guerilla" manufacturers. Instead of 40 workers, each spinning mill employed on average 500 workers by the 1970s.[71] At the apex, by 1970 the Tangs' South Sea Textiles employed nearly 2,500 people working twenty-four hours a day in three shifts to run 57,000 spindles and 915 power looms.[72] Substantially brokered by H. J. Shen, the Hongkong Bank had surpassed rivals such as the SCSB and First National to become the dominant lender to these mills. Yet were these mills also taking direct outside investment? With their extensive overseas connections, did the industrialists supplement bank loans with foreign capital?

These questions interested the colonial government. Despite a general reluctance to collect economic statistics, the Department of Commerce and Industry conducted surveys of direct outside investment that remain in the Hong Kong Public Records Office, files I have not seen previous scholars utilize. In 1960 officials found just 26 Hong Kong factories with nonlocal direct investment, including from Britain. These 26 factories employed 10,264 people. By 1970 there were 162 factories with nonlocal direct investment employing 54,562 people.[73] And within three years, 71,000 people were working at 257 foreign-invested factories—about 12 percent of the total manufacturing labor force.[74] Officials consistently found that U.S. investment was dominant in both capital and employment. For example, by May 1970 total U.S. investment into fully owned industrial firms in Hong Kong amounted to HK$271.5 million, or 61 percent of the total. British investment followed at 17.5 percent, and Japanese investment constituted just 11.7 percent.[75] Among joint ventures, Japanese-invested partnerships led at 35.5 percent, but British and American investment followed at 29.4 and 25.7 percent, respectively.[76] By March 1973 total U.S. investment in local manufacturing amounted to HK$465.7 million, while Japanese and British investment trailed at HK$279.7 million and HK$107.7 million, respectively.[77] Investment from all three countries pooled into the same few industries though, with electronics and textiles always the leaders, followed at a distance by shipbreaking, food manufactures, and plastics. All foreign-invested plants were geared toward exports, with foreign-invested electronics and apparel plants exporting over 90 percent of production. By 1972, 50 percent of all production from foreign-invested plants was flowing across the Pacific to the United States, while just 6.6 percent went to West Germany, 4.9 percent to the United Kingdom, and 3.7 percent to Japan.[78] Thus we can say that between 1960 and 1973 Hong Kong industry absorbed significant outside investment from first the United States, followed by Japan and Britain. This foreign capital concentrated in the electronics and textiles sectors and primarily facilitated Hong Kong's exports to the U.S. market.

Direct U.S. investment first increased in the 1950s as U.S. corporations purchased stakes in small- and medium-sized manufacturers. For example, in 1955 Mattel purchased the majority stake in Precision Moulds Limited, which by the 1970s would have 120 workers producing plastic molds and tools at a Kennedy Town plant.[79] In 1956 the Eveready Flashlight Co. purchased the Hung Hom flashlight plant of Shanghainese émigré V. K.

Song (宋文魁) in order to produce for export to the U.S. and regional markets.[80] This Eveready subsidiary became Sonca Industries (崇佳實業) in the 1960s.[81] The Corn Products Refining Co., known as CPC International, first invested in Hong Kong in 1957 to produce jellies, cornstarch, iodized salt, chicken cubes, and the sweetener dextrose.[82] Alongside corporate investments were investments by Chinese American families. In 1958 the Chiu family opened the Hong Kong Industrial (Woodwork) Company with over a hundred employees in Wong Chuk Hang. John Chiu was the resident partner, while five Chiu relations were equal investors from the United States.[83]

A few textile émigrés began to recruit outside investment around 1960 in order to diversify production and circumvent Anglo-American protectionism. As noted, Hong Kong's low-cost yarns and textiles aroused a backlash in its two largest export markets, the United Kingdom and the United States. Agreements such as the Lancashire Pact (1959–1965) and the Cotton Textile Arrangement (1962–1973) created nominally voluntary quotas that served to freeze the relative output of each Hong Kong mill. Washington also enacted such "voluntary" restrictions on Japanese cotton textiles and apparel in 1957.[84] Much like the U.S. embargo on China, these quota systems elicited considerable local press backlash.[85] They also "greatly handicapped" new competitors from entering into cotton spinning or weaving, while conferring "enormous advantages to textile mills which were in operation before 1960."[86] Anglo-American quotas thus ironically cemented the established mills' market access—quotas H. J. Shen helped negotiate. By the early 1960s the established spinners thus recognized that "new investment in the industry will prove detrimental rather than profitable" and that "in future, our emphasis should be laid on making better use of the existing production resources." With new local competitors effectively barred from entry, the spinners instead devoted resources to developing nonquota goods such as synthetic blends and ready-made apparel. We can succinctly observe this evolution through the declining exports of local yarn and fabric production. In the 1950s the vast majority was exported, while by 1969 as much as 98 percent was consumed locally.[87] Local yarn and fabric thus ceased to be a finished export and became a raw material undergirding new weaving and apparel production. The textile and apparel industries nonetheless remained the core of Hong Kong manufacturing, accounting in 1965 for 52 percent of exports and 41 percent of industrial laborers.[88]

There was a stereotype that the Shanghainese émigrés jealously guarded their financial autonomy, preferring to borrow heavily from banks rather than go public.[89] It is true that by 1967 just nine industrial companies had gone public in Hong Kong.[90] Yet at least a third of Hong Kong's spinning mills eventually did sell equity to overseas investors, and many more formed joint ventures and other production relationships with overseas partners, particularly in apparel. In one 1969 survey, personnel at forty-one textile and apparel plants reported taking direct overseas investment. Of these, twelve were spinning and weaving mills and twenty-nine (71 percent) were apparel plants. Since the total number of spinning mills in Hong Kong peaked in 1965 at forty, we can estimate that at least 30 percent of spinning mills had foreign stakeholders. Among the twenty-nine apparel plants, thirteen reported being fully foreign-owned and sixteen reported being joint ventures between foreign and local investors.[91] By March 1973 the number of apparel plants self-reporting direct overseas investment rose to forty-three, while the number of such spinning and weaving plants climbed to nineteen.[92] Since these surveys were voluntary, however, we can surmise that the real totals were higher. Thus while generally avoiding the stock market as a source of investment capital, Hong Kong's textile industry did take substantial direct overseas investment to finance diversification, particularly from Japan and the United States.

These surveys cannot answer the most interesting questions about this investment, however. For example, who initiated such deals and how? It is helpful here to examine one family that pursued kuashang strategies and one that did not. The family and business of industrialist "C. C." Lee Chen-che (李震之) remained noticeably not American-oriented. Like the Rongs or Tangs, the Lees had been among Jiangnan's early textile industrialists. In the 1920s and 1930s Lee's father, Lee Chung-bun, had primarily exported textiles from Shanghai to Southeast Asia via Hong Kong. C. C. Lee attended a small Shanghai university but dropped out in the war and helped run the Datong Cotton Mill (大同紗廠) from the concessions.[93] By 1947, as the Nationalists refused import licenses owing to dwindling foreign exchange reserves, C. C. Lee diverted their new American machinery and sixty skilled workers to Hong Kong.[94] He first started a cotton spinning mill in Sheung Wan named Great Southern Spinning and Weaving (大南紡織), but over the 1950s he launched five other textile and garment plants in Kowloon: Great Eastern Spinning and Weaving (大東紡織), Gold Star Spinning and Weaving (金星紡織), Nanxin Printing and Dyeing

Factory (南新印染廠), Asian Jianye Garment Factory (亞洲建業製衣廠), and Xingzhou Malaya Spinning and Weaving (星洲馬來亞紡織).[95] To finance this rapid expansion, Lee built professional and social relationships with two colonial financial institutions, the Hongkong and Standard Chartered Banks.[96] H. J. Shen likely assisted Lee in this through their native-place guanxi, as both were officers in the Jiangsu and Zhejiang Residents' Association.[97] Yet, although the United States was his firms' largest market, Lee's overseas trips focused on Western Europe, particularly Britain and West Germany, where he attended trade fairs, toured competitors, and built marketing relationships.[98] In 1960 he was appointed a Justice of the Peace and sent his eldest son Richard Lee Yun-shee (李雍熙) to Imperial College London.[99]

This British social capital paid off in 1962 with a game-changing investment that midwifed the formation of the TAL group (聯業製衣有限公司). In May Jardine Matheson chairman Hugh Barton announced that he would partner with C. C. Lee to consolidate his dispersed factories into one corporate joint venture in order to achieve economies of scale and better compete for market share amid tightening international regulations.[100] When the group formed in July with Barton as chairman and Lee as managing director, it was temporarily the colony's largest spinning and weaving operation.[101] The next year TAL launched its own women's clothing brand, "Daili" (黛麗), while in September 1964 the Lees followed the Rongs and Tangs as the third family to take their mills public.[102] The IPO was jointly managed by the Hongkong Bank and Standard Chartered.[103] TAL expanded rapidly over the late 1960s, with annual profits increasing from HK$670,000 in 1967 to HK$15 million in 1969.[104] The Lees remained focused on European markets, however, and Lee only made his first U.S. business trip in 1966.[105] When TAL needed to upgrade apparel equipment in 1968, it took HK$15 million of direct investment from the Japanese textile trading conglomerates Toray and C. Itoh & Co.[106] These further infusions helped it to move into nonquota goods and outsource low-margin operations across Taiwan, Malaysia, Thailand, Mauritius, and Nigeria.[107] At the peak of TAL's profitability in 1973, its total assets had increased 270 percent in five years to HK$480 million.[108] Now over sixty years old, C. C. Lee began grooming Richard to take over, while his nephew Henry Lee Nai-shee (李乃熙) joined the firm in 1973 after also graduating from Imperial and earning a Ph.D. degree in electrical science at Brown. In short, the Lee family and TAL Group conform to what we might expect of Hong Kong industrialists: reliance on British and Japanese capital, regional production relationships, and a focus on European sales.

In contrast, the Tangs' kuashang strategies led South Sea Textiles to complement local and British investment with U.S. production relationships and pay close attention to American consumer trends. As noted, P. Y. Tang had been diversifying production aimed at the U.S. market throughout the 1950s. As Anglo-American protectionism escalated, though, South Sea's spinning and weaving operations plateaued around 1964 and Tang hunted for new export markets, such as heading a 1965 trade delegation to the newly independent countries of Kenya, Tanzania, Uganda, and Zambia.[109] Seeking cash to expand spinning and weaving, Tang announced his intention to take South Sea public in 1964. This announcement seems to have prompted Britain's Imperial Chemical Industries (ICI) to reach out about a partnership. ICI had invented a polyester fiber that it wanted to manufacture in Hong Kong. In the subsequent deal, ICI bought 5 percent of South Sea in 1963, followed by 10 percent in the 1964 public listing. This injection of British capital allowed South Sea to buy new polyester-cotton spindles, set up a subsidiary factory within South Sea, and retrain workers to produce these blends.[110] Simultaneously, however, the Tangs' U.S. orientation pushed them to hunt for American partners for an apparel joint venture. The big New York garment importer Charles Meltzer of Marlene Industries first came to Hong Kong in the early 1960s to meet with potential suppliers. Recognizing the potential value of this relationship, the Tangs sought him out, but his racist disrespect nixed any deal. In 1964, however, Levi Strauss also "came to us" with an offer for a joint venture to treat denim with permanent press creases. Attuned to the "denim craze" in America and to Levi's brand name, the Tangs accepted.[111] The ensuing joint venture was their single most profitable diversification. In 1969 Levi's went public and the Tangs had to sell their stake, but that capital allowed South Sea "to go into the garment industry on our own after 1969."[112]

After P. Y. Tang's passing in 1971, Jack also began to outsource low-margin operations but relied on American networks to manage this expansion. He first went to Taiwan to meet with Finance Minister Li Kwoh-ting (李國鼎), who offered attractive terms for their subsidiary Tristate to start a weaving mill in the Kaohsiung Export Processing Zone. Jack Tang agreed, and he then deliberately chose an American general manager who he knew had good connections in the U.S. garment industry: "I thought that was pretty ideal. This man had bought textiles, cloth, from me for many years, from South Sea—and he was actually vice president in charge of sales, of fabrics, to the garment factories in the States. Levi was one, for instance. I thought that was perfect. Because of his connection with the U.S. garment factories, he would be able to sell our garments to the U.S. garment factories who would be sourcing from abroad." Privileged transpacific relationships were thus at the heart of Tang's marketing strategies, but such faith can be misplaced. This American manager extended credit to a buyer who ran off. After three years of legal action in U.S. courts, the Kaohsiung venture finally became profitable and grew into South Sea's main weaving operation. In the mid-1970s Tang also entered into joint ventures with Japan's Kuraray and Mitsui & Co., but both proved disastrous. By the late 1970s Hong Kong manufacturing had peaked, and Jack Tang began to sell some of South Sea's real estate to developers, including a joint venture with rising property tycoon Li Ka-shing. That deal "ended up making more money than in all the years of textile spinning and weaving—by far more money than all the profits added up together from 1949."[113]

The stories of TAL and South Sea flush out the government surveys and provide a window into the impact of personal networks and social capital on long-term business evolutions. The Lees chose to cultivate British social capital through business and education and relied on British banks and investors. The Tangs' American social capital positioned them to seek out American buyers, embrace a joint venture with Levi's, and hire American managers. Their overall kuashang strategies were not an exclusively American orientation, however. They took British investment when offered, pursued Japanese joint ventures, and explored African markets. Yet most of their non-American relationships largely served South Sea's continued codevelopment with the U.S. market. In turn, while generally presenting the initiative as coming from British and U.S. corporations, the Tangs' degrees, bilingualism, and biculturalism were key components in securing these deals. In the next chapter we will revisit the South Sea/TAL comparison and see how their strategies played out in the post–Fordist crises of the 1970s.

Finally, the electronics industry provides another data point to underscore the role of social capital in recruiting and controlling foreign investment. Outside investment in Hong Kong's electronics sector was even larger but yielded foreign-owned subsidiaries that were cogs in global multinationals' commodity chains. According to the American Chamber of Commerce's monthly publication, local entrepreneurs set up the first small electronics factories in 1959 to assemble transistor radios from Japanese components. By 1962 there were fourteen factories in the colony with exports valued at US$7.3 million and employing 881 people. Yet it was 1962 when "American and Japanese firms began to realise the potential available in Hong Kong," particularly its stability "coupled with the favorable tax and labor situation." U.S. and Japanese capital then poured in, and the ensuing production purportedly diversified "away from consumer products and into components."[114] As with textiles, foreign-invested electronics plants quickly became much larger than their "guerilla" counterparts, but this shift toward components steered Hong Kong toward lower value-added pieces of the production chain. In early 1974, 78 percent of computer parts, 55 percent of transistors, and 89 percent of integrated circuits were shipped to the United States, primarily to parent companies for redistribution, final assembly, and/or transshipment around the world. The toy industry similarly sent 50–60 percent of its local production to the United States.[115]

This overseas investment produced only temporary diversification and no parallel upmarket transition for two reasons: minimal government assistance and the lack of high social capital electronics industrialists who could negotiate and control such flows. As a result, electronics became a transitory industry that exploited Hong Kong's low-cost labor and left when costs rose. The Hong Kong government's "positive noninterventionism" courted initial investment but did not incentivize local research and development or recruit strategic industries.[116] As a result, the local electronics industry largely evaporated to China in the late 1980s and 1990s, leaving no notable Hong Kong electronics brands or high-tech jobs, in contrast to Taiwan. As such, though, the wave of U.S. and Japanese electronics investment primarily stemmed from corporate agency, not social networks or local kuashang strategies.

Esso's and Mobil's Game-Changing Investments

Hong Kong's economy boomed throughout the early 1960s, achieving 14 and 15 percent annual GDP growth in 1962 and 1963. Yet serious cracks were appearing. International competition and soaring labor and real estate costs were intensifying the pressure on the manufacturing sector to move upstream into higher value-added products. As H. J. Shen had articulated, Hong Kong's rapid population growth, limited land, and loose regulations encouraged rampant financial and real estate speculation that was likely to gradually crowd out industry. Such speculation was intensifying the boom-bust cycle and triggered a banking crisis at the Liu Chong Hing Bank in 1961, followed by a run on the Hang Sang Bank in late 1964 that resulted in its takeover by the Hongkong Bank in April 1965.[117] Put simply, Hong Kong's labor-intensive, export-oriented industrial model was unstable and unsustainable.

Simultaneously, this overheating economy was bringing social tensions to the brink of implosion. In April 1966 the colony's lack of affordable housing, worker protections, and social services triggered the Star Ferry Riots. Half of the colony's population was under twenty-one, but only 13 percent of teenagers attended secondary school.[118] This youth rose up across Kowloon to denounce their unaccountable government, and police and Gurkha troops used bayonets and tear gas to contain the crowds. In spring and summer 1967 another labor dispute exploded into further riots and violence inspired by the Cultural Revolution. Protestors blanketed public buildings with posters denouncing Anglo-American imperialism and planted real and fake bombs in buildings and transport. Mainstream opinion coalesced against these disturbances in August 1967 and set the stage for the reforms of the MacLehose era (1971–1981), but Hong Kong remained a simmering colonial sweatshop throughout the late 1960s.[119]

Beneath these social and economic crises there were potential time bombs in two core sectors: energy and housing. The manufacturing boom had led to a gargantuan increase in electrical demand, while speculation was crowding out investment in affordable housing. Both sectors needed drastic, market-shifting investments to affect a sudden increase in supply. Neither was likely to get it without government intervention. In both cases, however, game-changing investments suddenly arrived in 1964 and 1965 from two of the world's largest corporations: Esso and Mobil. Separate descendants of John D. Rockefeller's Standard Oil, these giants had operated jointly in Asia as Standard-Vacuum between 1933 and 1962, when corporate disagreements dissolved their union into Jersey Standard (later Esso) and Mobil. It cannot be overemphasized that it was bizarre for both corporations to decide virtually simultaneously to invest hundreds of millions of U.S. dollars into unprecedented projects in an indefensible, petroleum-free British colony on the doorstep of an assertive communist state. Neither company had ever made large-scale fixed investments in Asia beyond the infrastructure to store and distribute energy products. With no suggestion that either investment would produce oil or gas, why did Esso and Mobil suddenly embrace these projects?

Both corporations were coaxed into these investments by Hong Kong executives pursuing kuashang strategies. These executives grasped that these energy and housing time bombs could also lead to lucrative opportunities with sufficient outside investment. They used personal networks and inside knowledge to mold the relevant colonial policies and guide Esso and Mobil to these opportunities. In essence, kuashang actors filled a trough and then led these corporate horses to it. Simultaneously, by triangulating between the government and the multinationals, these kuashang executives further advanced informal decolonization by reshaping housing and energy policy to their interests.

Esso was recruited by the Kadoorie family. The Kadoories encapsulate how previously British-oriented elites followed the Jiangnan émigrés in pivoting toward U.S. systems. They also illustrate that kuashang strategies were not limited to Chinese actors. Descended from Mizrahi Jews who migrated from Baghdad to Bombay in the eighteenth century, the brothers Eleazar "Elly" and Ellis Kadoorie first came to Hong Kong in the 1880s to work for the Sassoons. After becoming independent traders, Elly and his wife Laura moved to Shanghai in 1911, where he made a fortune trading in Malayan rubber. Ellis remained in Hong Kong and bought major stakes in the Hong Kong & Shanghai Hotel Company, owner of the Peninsula Hotel, and in China Light and Power (CLP), which generated the electricity for Kowloon and the New Territories. The opportunity to make the latter investment likely stemmed from British actors seeking liquidity amid the First World War. Laura and Elly sent their sons Lawrence and Horace to the elite Clifton School in Bristol, after which Lawrence read law at Lincoln's Inn. The family was imprisoned by the Japanese during the war, and after 1945 it fell to Lawrence and Horace to restore the family businesses, as the British blew up the CLP power station in 1941 and the Peninsula Hotel had served as a wartime barracks.[120]

A byproduct of the family's history in Shanghai was that Lawrence and Horace already knew many of the émigré industrialists. They joined them in the 1950s in developing new businesses aimed at the U.S. market. In the wake of the U.S. and UN embargoes, Lawrence spotted a lucrative new niche: the international market for Chinese knotted carpets could now be supplied from Hong Kong.[121] In 1956 Kadoorie founded Hong Kong Carpet Manufacturers Ltd. with two members of the Rong family (chapter 1). Other partners included Tse Koong-kai (朱孔嘉), a former SCSB banker and chief accountant of AIA in Shanghai, and two Americans: Los Angeles–based trader Allen Rabin and the Hong Kong–based industrialist Linden Johnson. The latter owned Mandarin Textiles, whose 1,300 employees produced high-end women's silk and cotton apparel for the U.S. market.[122] With these experienced and interconnected founders, Hong Kong Carpets began producing knotted carpets at a plant in Tuen Mun in order "to cater to the booming U.S. consumer market." Their "Tai Ping" brand opened a showroom in the Peninsula Hotel, where Lawrence Kadoorie showed the carpets to John D. Rockefeller, Jr., during his visit to Hong Kong in 1959. Rockefeller's company Products of Asia then signed on as the carpets' sole U.S. distributor, and Rockefeller used his own networks to secure lucrative orders, including for Grauman's Chinese Theatre in Hollywood and the boardrooms of Ford and Chase Manhattan. By 1960 the company had grown to five hundred employees and relocated to a new plant on Tolo Harbour.[123]

This experience guided Kadoorie toward kuashang strategies when crisis loomed at CLP. The monumental growth in electrical demand had led to blackouts, rate hikes, and public demands for a government take-over. CLP wanted to expand, but how to pay for it? Lawrence felt that further rate hikes were politically impossible, while even the Hongkong Bank could not loan the necessary capital for a new plant—despite Lawrence joining its board in 1957. According to his son Michael, Lawrence was "really grappling with what to do" and "how to inject money into China Light in terms of having a partner rather than borrowing from a bank."[124] One day he invited an American friend from Caltex to Sunday lunch. Michael recalled that the friend noted: " 'Well, you know, the oil companies are always willing to look at equity for a long-term purchase of oil.' And this had never *dawned* on dad at all." Lawrence first went to CLP's longstanding petroleum supplier Royal Dutch Shell, but its chief officer rejected the proposal, reminding Kadoorie that they were "in the business of selling oil . . . not in the business of generating electricity." He then decided to try the Americans. He spoke with another old American friend from Shanghai, the former head of Standard-Vacuum and Dartmouth alum shown in figure 5.1, George Bell. Through Bell, Kadoorie arranged a meeting in New York with Esso chairman Michael Haider. The dissolution of Standard-Vacuum in 1962 had cut Esso out of the Hong Kong market, and Kadoorie presented a joint venture with CLP as Esso's chance to get back in. Haider expressed interest, and they began negotiations "in strictest secrecy."[125]

Kadoorie's ace was his positioning between Esso and the colonial government, much as it had been for David Au between the United Board and the government (chapter 3). To pull off this deal, Kadoorie needed to convince a fiercely anticommunist corporation to make an unprecedented investment into a shaky colony on the doorstep of "Red China."[126] To do so, Kadoorie worked with colonial officials to mold new energy regulations. The result was the "Scheme of Control," which debuted in November 1964. Virtually coauthored by officials and CLP executives, the scheme aimed to contain electrical prices and avoid a government takeover, but not by fixing prices or taxing profits. Instead, it capped CLP's maximum rate of return at 13.5 percent of the value of its fixed assets. By capping profits based on fixed assets, the scheme incentivized the under-negotiation CLP-Esso joint venture to continually expand its physical plant in order to continually increase profits. Yet the scheme did not return excess profits to customers. It instead recycled them into a tax-free "Special Development Fund" to finance further expansion.[127] In short, in his negotiations with Haider, Kadoorie could promise that one large initial investment would give Esso a highly profitable, largely tax free, and self-expanding business in Hong Kong. It was a very unusual public-private opportunity enabled by Hong Kong's unaccountable government and the informal decolonization that was ceding de facto authority to executives. Unsurprisingly, the scheme also received loud support from CLP's largest customer—more old friends from Shanghai—the Tangs of South Sea Textiles.[128]

As a result, a landmark joint venture was struck that provides a clear example of the intangible development advantages that this "Third World" colony acquired through kuashang strategies and American social capital. On December 31, 1964, CLP and Esso incorporated their first joint venture: the Peninsula Electric Power Company. Esso owned a 60 percent controlling stake, and CLP took a 40 percent share. Esso agreed to provide the capital to build Hong Kong's new power plants, while CLP would construct the plants and distribute the electricity.[129] Yet while Kadoorie bucks the standard kuashang model by not attending U.S. higher education or collaborating with U.S. Cold War projects, he did not need those pathways to American social capital. He already had existing relationships with elite American executives such as Rockefeller, Bell, Rabin, and Johnson and émigrés such as the Rongs and Tangs. The CLP-Esso relationship was tremendously profitable and built several of the largest power plants in Asia over the 1970s and 1980s. Esso's initial investment into the Tsing Yi A and B plants was HK$700 million. Within twenty-six years Exxon Energy's assets in Hong Kong were estimated to have grown 1,428 percent to HK$10 billion.[130]

The Esso–CLP joint venture was already unusual, but only a few weeks later Mobil announced its own unprecedented investment into Hong Kong: the redevelopment of its petroleum storage depot at Lai Chi Kok into the colony's first private mass housing estate. Just as Esso had never entered the power business before, this deal represented Mobil's first foray into real estate development. And as with the Esso–CLP deal, this opportunity arose through kuashang strategies that advanced and exploited Hong Kong's unusual context and informal decolonization. At the helm was Mobil's new local managing director, John L. Soong (宋啓郎).

Like many kuashang, John Soong developed his U.S. ties through American missionary institutions and the wartime Sino-American alliance. Born in Hankou in July 1918, he was the son of a railway engineer whose work moved the family to Beijing and Qingdao. John and his brother attended the Railway Middle School in Qingdao before studying Japanese at the Senshu Daigaku in Tokyo from 1936 to 1937.[131] John returned to Qingdao in April 1937 and studied English at a Catholic girls' school until the invasion in July. The school's American nuns helped him secure admission to Notre Dame, including a scholarship. He and his brother crossed the Pacific that summer. John graduated from Notre Dame in spring 1941 and completed an accelerated MBA degree at the University of Chicago. Although deemed ineligible for citizenship, like many Chinese immigrants Soong was still drafted into the U.S. Armed Forces in January 1943 under threat of deportation.[132] After training in Mississippi and Maryland, he was granted an exception and naturalized as a U.S. citizen in early April 1943—eight months ahead of the repeal of Chinese Exclusion.[133] He was posted to air force intelligence in Karachi and worked in censorship in Assam, Kunming, and Chongqing, where he married Rebecca Hu. Soong rose to become General George Marshall's personal aide and interpreter, earning a Bronze Star. He completed his service in 1947 with the U.S. State Department's Foreign Liquidation Commission in Shanghai, where he likely met familiar figures such as K. P. Chen, H. J. Shen, and Li Choh-ming. He then entered the private sector as an accountant with Standard-Vacuum and remained in Shanghai until July 1952, relocating to Hong Kong in June 1953.[134] Following Bell's retirement and Standard-Vacuum's dissolution in 1962, Soong became Mobil Hong Kong's managing director in 1963. Simultaneously, his son John, Jr. (宋賢慶), was graduating from Andover and entering Princeton.[135]

The opportunity to redevelop Mobil's storage depot arrived in 1964. The company's forty-five-acre depot was blocking the construction of the Kwai Chung expressway, and the government needed a thin 9.3-acre stretch of land through the site. Rather than pursue eminent domain, officials worked with Soong to craft a land-exchange agreement that was highly advantageous to Mobil. In exchange for the 9 acres, the government offered not only equal lands on Tsing Yi where Mobil could relocate the depot, but also the right to redevelop the remaining 36 acres.[136] That provision was very unusual. All land in Hong Kong was technically under lease from the colonial government, and officials were under no obligation to effectively double Mobil's holdings. With the local real estate market soaring in 1964, Mobil thus received an extraordinary opportunity. Soong then requested that Mobil New York dispatch a real estate consultant. Mobil chose the developer John W. Galbreath, who owned and operated the skyscraper that housed Mobil's New York offices.[137] Galbreath claimed that he advised Soong's team that the whole project should be redeveloped as a middle-class housing estate.[138] Evidently Soong's team agreed, and they hired Galbreath-Ruffin to conceive and manage the whole project, along with the architects Wong & Tung Associates of Hong Kong and Dallas and New York's Turner Construction to supervise. With extraordinary speed, by summer 1965 Mobil was submitting formal plans to the Hong Kong Housing Authority for approval. As the project gained international attention, Soong touted its size and speed to the *New York Times*.[139]

This project was not just any housing estate. The plans called for constructing "the world's largest privately financed residential condominium," to be named Mei Foo Sun Chuen or "Mobil Oil New Village" (figure 5.4).[140] The phrase "Mei Foo," or "beautiful and trustworthy," had served as the Chinese name for Standard Oil since the 1880s, and the company's Mei Foo kerosene lamp had gradually become a standard household item in China. It was thus a valuable brand name.[141] In total, Mei Foo Sun

Figure 5.4 Feature on Mobil's investment in Mei Foo Sun Chuen, reported in *AmCham* in 1976. Courtesy of American Chamber of Commerce, Hong Kong.

Chuen would have ninety-nine twenty-story cruciform towers built over eight stages. Upon completion of the final stage in 1976, there would be thirteen thousand units housing upward of eighty thousand people— around 2 percent of Hong Kong's population. And Mei Foo was not just big but also set a new middle-class standard, much like the Tokiwadaira complex outside Tokyo.[142] Each set of towers was designed to operate like a middle-class American suburb. Beneath the towers would be elevated podiums containing parking, shops, restaurants, markets, banks, schools, playgrounds, and a bus terminal. Kentucky Fried Chicken quickly opened a location, while planners added several Mobil service stations.[143]

Crisis hit just as this project got moving, however, and it took Mobil's deep pockets to plow ahead. Mobil Hong Kong formed the subsidiary Mei Foo Investments Ltd. in mid-1965 to manage construction and postleasing maintenance, but soon the bank crises and riots of 1965 and 1966 sent the real estate market tumbling. Constructing the world's largest housing estate suddenly seemed more arrogant than ambitious. Mobil called in the big guns, however. Mobil president Rawleigh Warner visited in October 1966, and Soong hosted a star-studded banquet at the Hongkong

Hilton in his honor.[144] Several weeks later Governor Trench attended the foundation-stone ceremony.[145] Soong also relied on networks of fellow U.S.-oriented transplants in the construction process. For example, stage 1's construction contract went to Hsin Chong Construction, the firm of Jiangnan émigré Godfrey K. N. Yeh (葉庚年) and his younger brother Geoffrey M. T. Yeh (葉謀遵), a University of Illinois and Harvard graduate.[146] As seen in chapter 4, the Yehs were also New Asia donors. In another example, the contract for Mei Foo's windows went to Chiap Hua of the Lam family (chapter 3).[147] Construction on stage 1 began in 1968, and tenants moved in from July 1969.[148] In total, stage 1 alone represented an investment by Mobil of about HK$450 million and the construction process employed more than 3,500 workers.[149]

This enormous investment paid off, however, and altered Mobil's global rent-seeking strategies. By setting a new standard with round-the-clock staff, professional management, and cruciform design, Mei Foo was extremely desirable. In a colony where 25–30 percent of residents lived in cell-block resettlement estates with communal lavatories, Mei Foo embodied a middle-class dream. As such, it delivered a stark return on both Mobil and residents' investments: by 1976 its average flat price had jumped by 600 percent.[150] This explosive appreciation reflected a highly manipulated housing market built on artificial scarcity, but the subsequent impact was global. In the wake of Mei Foo's success, in 1970 Mobil took a key step in the financialization of its global revenue model by forming Mobil Land Development. Its task was to transform more of the conglomerate's real estate portfolio, starting with Redwood Shores south of San Francisco.[151] By generating new income from fixed assets rather than production, both Mobil and Esso began moving toward post-Fordist, late-stage capitalism in late 1960s Hong Kong through opportunities created by "Third World" kuashang strategists.

This chapter examined how elite social capital shaped transpacific flows of financial capital into Hong Kong industry and real estate during the late 1950s and 1960s, accelerating both local development and informal decolonization. Since the communist transition, dense networks of émigrés had preserved their old relationships while integrating into local society, succinctly encapsulated by Ansie Lee Sperry receiving a long line of guests at her husband's 1967 retirement party from Citibank (figure 5.5). Through figures such as Francis Pan and H. J. Shen, I showed how additional

Figure 5.5 Ansie Lee Sperry receiving guests at her husband's retirement party at the Mandarin Oriental, Hong Kong, in 1967. Courtesy of Victoria Sperry Merchant.

émigrés developed kuashang strategies to survive, eventually tapping into the Hongkong Bank's coffers and promoting collaboration between bankers and industrialists in pursuit of continued export-driven codevelopment with primarily the U.S. market. Ensuing Anglo-American protectionism incentivized many textile industrialists to diversify production in the 1960s by recruiting direct foreign investment and formalizing production partnerships with U.S., British, and Japanese partners. The early part of the chapter underscores the inadequacy of explaining Hong Kong's development as an archetype of free market competition. Through the kuashang, we see an essential other half of the story in the form of an entrenched mobile hierarchy prepared by education, experience, and contacts to revive their businesses, mold market conditions, and compete in U.S.-led capitalist systems. Shen and his favored industrialists colluded to mold the colony's financial markets to their interests, while elites such as the Tangs, the Lees, and the Kadoories had privileged access to multinational corporations. The stark contrast with ordinary "guerilla" capitalists and electronics entrepreneurs underscores these links between social capital and global financial capital. While the TAL Group testifies that transpacific networks were by no means the only source of opportunity, they were increasingly prevalent. In turn, Esso's and Mobil's investments reveal how Hong Kong's transpacific networks could deliver other unlikely benefits, while leading global trends toward financialization and flexible production. As the next chapter will explore, those shifts would indeed yield families such as the Tangs "by far more money than all the profits added up together from 1949."

Considering these kuashang actors in detail also allows us to avoid caricature or even conspiracy theory. It is worth repeating that these actors were mostly migrants who lost most of their tangible assets when fleeing to Hong Kong. Many, such as Shen and Pan, struggled to find new careers, while the Tangs took substantial risks that paid off only with the contingent Korean War. Their ability to read the international terrain of power and monetize their social capital was what consistently separated these elites from ordinary transplants. Yet, as the educational processes examined in chapters 2, 3, and 4 began to mature, such connections and opportunities became more widespread. Transpacific circulations engendered by the intersection between kuashang strategies and U.S. Cold War ambitions would allow Hong Kong to emerge as the world's largest sender of foreign students to the United States in 1973–1974. As a result, in the next chapter we will see that Hong Kong's stunning growth over the 1970s began to pivot from the exploitation of low-cost local labor toward knowledge- and access-based services on behalf of Asia's low-cost labor. While textile exports increased by 50 percent in 1973 alone, manufacturing's share of local GDP peaked in the early 1970s at just above 30 percent, as regional competitors offered cheaper wages, the "Nixon Shock" roiled global financial markets, and the European Economic Community ruled that Hong Kong was no longer entitled to preferential tariffs as a developing country.[152] Rather than be caught in a midlevel development trap, however, Hong Kong rocketed upward as second-generation kuashang tapped into global capital flows and renovated family companies into Hong Kong's own U.S.-style multinationals.

CHAPTER VI

The Kuashang Effect

American Social Capital and Hong Kong's 1970s Takeoff

> Historical experience suggests that the principal mechanism for conver-
> gence at the international level as well as the domestic level is the diffusion
> of knowledge. In other words, the poor catch up with the rich to the extent
> that they achieve the same level of technological know-how, skill, and edu-
> cation, not by becoming the property of the wealthy.
>
> —THOMAS PIKETTY, *CAPITAL IN THE TWENTY-FIRST CENTURY*

Hong Kong's economy took off in the 1970s. In 1960 the World
Bank put the colony's GDP per capita at just US$429, on par
with Jamaica and South Africa. Agriculture and fishing still
employed more Hong Kong workers than manufacturing—400,000 people compared with 230,000.[1] As discussed in chapter 5, over the 1960s the
colony continued rapid industrialization, and by 1970 industrial employment reached 600,000 out of 1.5 million workers.[2] As in many societies
after the Second World War, the benefits of Hong Kong's 1960s growth
were widespread, and the colony's GDP per capita more than doubled to
US$960, a bit ahead of Jamaica and South Africa. Yet by 1980 Hong
Kong's GDP per capita had shot to US$5,700. This startling 600 percent
increase in a decade left the developing world behind and put Hong Kong
in league with Israel and Ireland. Yet the decade's growth was highly
unequal. The rising tide lifted most boats, but the 600 percent increase
testifies to the creation of a new class of powerful global economic actors,
including many kuashang. A nondemocratic colony with low taxes and
lax financial regulations, Hong Kong was at the center of pioneering the
neoliberal financialized global economy.

Scholars long cast this transformation as part of a broader East Asian
"miracle" and largely assumed that Hong Kong's development was related
to the region's other so-called tigers or dragons—South Korea, Taiwan,
and Singapore. In particular, social scientists and economic historians

advanced three main frameworks to explain these four economies' phenomenal growth. The most fruitful explored the role of the region's robust developmental states and their relationship to Japan and Japanese capital.[3] Those who acknowledged Hong Kong's lack of a developmental state tended to credit its success to the opposite factor: the free-market policies of British colonialism, most famously Milton Friedman.[4] And the third framework emphasized shared Confucian heritages, trumpeting a supposedly exceptional respect for education, discipline, and authority.[5]

In reality, none of these three frameworks is particularly helpful in explaining Hong Kong's rapid growth in the 1970s. The cultural explanations often veer toward racialized stereotypes that cast implicit aspersion on societies that did not achieve similar success. The diverse cultures of East Asia were no more or less destined for capitalist success than those of Africa, Latin America, Oceania, or the rest of Asia. Moreover, Hong Kong's culture was not solely of Chinese origin but was influenced by the British and many other diverse communities. In turn, not only did Hong Kong lack a developmental state, but also the colony was never dominated by Japanese trade or capital, as the interrelated "flying geese" theory posited.[6] As analyzed in chapter 5, by the early 1960s the United States figured as Hong Kong's largest trade and investment partner. As a result, scholars' incorporation of Hong Kong into narratives of an "East Asian miracle" served to marginalize its most significant bilateral relationship. Finally, scholars such as Friedman who have celebrated Hong Kong as a laissez-faire laboratory have routinely ignored numerous interventions by the regime and reproduced rosy views of colonialism.[7] To top it off, Hong Kong was not only distinct from its regional peers but in fact generally ahead of them. In 1980, when Hong Kong's GDP per capita reached US$5,700, Singapore's was US$5,003, Taiwan's was US$4,056, and South Korea's was US$1,778.

Hong Kong's success in the 1970s thus begs for an explanation that foregrounds the agency of its Chinese residents. The previous five chapters have laid the groundwork for us to analyze here how Hong Kong encountered and thrived amid the decade's crucial shift in the global economy: the end of the Bretton Woods system. After two decades of struggling with balance of payment deficits, the Bank of England abruptly devalued the British pound in November 1967. This snap action unraveled the Sterling Area and came without warning to Hong Kong, which found its holdings of £400 million suddenly devalued.[8] The devaluation infuriated the colonial government and underscored the perils of Hong Kong's political status within a decaying empire. As a result, after the Nixon administration decided to resolve U.S. balance of payments problems by suspending the U.S. dollar's convertibility into gold in August 1971 (the "Nixon Shock") and London floated the pound in June 1972, the Hong Kong government detached the colony economically from the British Empire. It pegged the Hong Kong dollar directly to the U.S. dollar in July 1972 and then tried a floating exchange rate from 1974 through 1983, before repegging to the U.S. dollar.

This transition created volatile evolutions in global capital markets and coincided with the much-discussed 1970s transition from mass production to flexible production, or Fordism to post-Fordism.[9] In chapter 5 we observed a key first step toward that transition through Esso and Mobil's landmark investments. As previous scholars have identified, all of East Asia benefited from the shift toward flexible production through increased orders from the U.S. market.[10] This chapter argues that Hong Kong benefited disproportionately from the shift toward flexible production because of its elites' kuashang strategies and transpacific networks. By the 1970s there were numerous sources of cheaper labor in the region, including Taiwan, South Korea, the Philippines, and Malaysia. Yet Hong Kong had other advantages, including its emergence as the world's largest sender of foreign students to the United States in 1973. Many local manufacturers began to adapt to rising local costs and these volatile financial shifts by outsourcing, as seen in chapter 5 with TAL and South Sea. Yet the knowledge, access, and capital acquired through transpacific circulations made particular Hong Kong firms better prepared to channel outflows of U.S. capital to their own ends and adapt to the emergent flexible networks of transnational subcontracting. Put simply, the colony's entwined transpacific educational and commercial circulations plugged kuashang-led companies into the U.S. economy at a far more sophisticated level than the colony's GDP per capita would have suggested.

The next section examines the rapid expansion of Hong Kong's educational circulations in the 1960s and how they were structured by class and U.S. Cold War agendas. Nonelite students aspiring to study in the United States were screened and sponsored by Washington's "state-private network," privileging those with ties to American missionaries or U.S.-backed institutions.[11] In reality, though, Hong Kong students in the United States had one of the world's highest rates of self-support, indicating a high proportion of elite backgrounds. As we will see, this skewed ratio and Hong Kong's own political uncertainty created a feedback loop in which a minority of elite male students returned to Hong Kong to assume control over family companies, while the vast majority of students remained in the United States. As we will see in the final section, many of the roughly 15 percent of students who did return used social capital gained in the United States to renovate their family companies into U.S.-style corporations. These corporate overhauls allowed kuashang-led companies to negotiate the volatile shifts of the 1970s by tapping into outflows of U.S. investment and maximizing the benefit of multinational corporations' search for flexible production and investment opportunities in Asia.[12] Kuashang-led companies seized shifting subcontracting opportunities, tapped into integrated global capital markets, and branched into knowledge-based services—to the extremely disproportionate financial benefit of their owners and shareholders.

Divergent Patterns—Immigration and Circulation

We have seen that Hong Kong began reorienting from British toward U.S. higher education over the 1950s through the combination of elite kuashang strategies and resources from Washington's state-private network. Familiar figures such as Jack and Maida Yuen, David Au, Lam Chi-fung, Li Choh-ming, and the Tang family consistently used U.S. resources to provide opportunities for nonelite youth to study in the United States. They did so by embedding the colony's new churches, schools, colleges, and universities with staff, scholarships, and academic systems geared toward facilitating transpacific opportunities. As a result, while youth all over the world would have leapt at the chance to study in the United States, many more Hong Kong students got that chance because of these post-1949 activities and institutions. In so doing, the original strategies of the Jiangnan émigrés continued to cross-pollinate with older Cantonese practices of splitting families through migration for economic advantage, expanding the kuashang orientation. While New York's Institute of International Education found just seventy-two students from Hong Kong in the United States in 1950–1951, by 1959 the number of Hong Kong students in the United States was already triple the number in Britain.[13] In 1961–1962 the number of Hong Kong students studying in the United States reached 1,597, and by

1963–1964 it reached 3,000 students.[14] Ten years later, in 1973–1974 and again in 1975–1976, Hong Kong students were the largest group of international students in the United States, numbering 10,764 and 11,930, respectively.[15] This startling development cannot be overemphasized: tiny Hong Kong had outpaced far more populous countries such as Canada, India, Iran, and Taiwan. Throughout the early 1970s, Hong Kong's attendance was so high that the total number of Hong Kong students in the United States routinely exceeded the *combined* student bodies of every college and university within the colony.[16]

This soaring attendance, however, was bifurcated by class. Hong Kong students also had one of the highest rates of self-support of any international student group in the United States. In short, the IIE found that between 37 and 57 percent of Hong Kong students' families paid their full tuition in any given year. Thus 37 to 57 percent of students came from families with significant resources. The other 43 to 63 percent were nonelite youth who relied on aid to access these opportunities. Such aid could come from anywhere but primarily came from U.S.-linked sources, particularly the U.S. government and its extended state-private network of missionary and educational foundations. It must be emphasized, however, that neither Washington nor these organizations sought to create a "brain drain." Rather, they sought to extend educational opportunity within noncommunist societies in order to steer Asia's future leaders toward American values and U.S. international leadership, as they had in late Qing and Republican China. As noted in chapter 2, American missionaries had made explicit the values that they hoped these future American-returned students would bring back to Hong Kong.[17]

Most Hong Kong students had different aims, however: to study in the United States in order to remain permanently by securing employment and gradually sponsoring family members' migrations. Recall that in 1950 alone 117,000 local residents applied at the U.S. consulate in Hong Kong for passports as derivative citizens.[18] Most were unsuccessful after enduring rigorous yearslong screenings. Admission to an American college or university was thus a chance to sidestep this process and accelerate the entire family's migration. Often called the "student side door," these options were possible because the United States did not put quota restrictions on foreign students admitted to higher education. Moreover, after years of stopgap measures and private bills, the landmark Hart–Celler Act of 1965 had removed racial quotas in order to privilege "the migration of economically useful, value-added elites."[19] Hong Kong graduates of U.S. colleges and universities were precisely the kind of "useful" immigrants to be given preference. Moreover, Hart-Celler also prioritized family reunifications, enabling what scholars have long called chain migration.

The most common exceptions to this pattern were male students from well-off backgrounds, particularly elder sons. Because they had privileged opportunities awaiting their return, they were far more likely to conform to the U.S. government's aspirations and eventually return to Hong Kong. An early example of such elite circulations is the future tycoon Sir Gordon Wu Ying-sheung (胡應湘). In the fall of 1953 the seventeen-year-old Wu sailed to San Francisco on his way to study at the University of Manitoba. This journey was not solely his initiative. As with many previous examples, his entire family was pursuing transpacific circulations. His father Wu Chung (胡忠) had grown up on a pig farm in Pokfulam before building prewar Hong Kong's biggest taxi company. He lost his vehicles during the Japanese occupation, but business rebounded after 1945 and the family again became wealthy. Several Wu relatives had migrated to the United States before the war, while Wu Chung used Dodges for his taxis, leaving him with a positive impression of America. Gordon's mother, Kong Sum, was determined that all nine of her children would receive the educational opportunity that she had not. Thus, after missionary schools, "all nine children were encouraged to further their studies after their high school graduations, and most chose the United States as the place to be."[20] Eldest son James pursued engineering at the University of Hong Kong, but Gordon's siblings Linda, Phyllis, Cynthia, Clyde, Sophie, Benoni, and John all pursued studies in the United States. By the time Gordon arrived in 1953, most were settled from California to Michigan.

Guided by his family's U.S. orientation, Gordon was able to acquire transformative knowledge, relationships, and credentials. He was overwhelmed by "the size of the shopping malls, the unbelievable amount of choice in the supermarkets, the length of the highways and the number of traffic lights." Driving over the Bay Bridge, he was "speechless" and determined that he would build something like it himself. Although Gordon began his studies at Manitoba, his brother Clyde urged him to switch to an Ivy League institution. He transferred to Princeton. There he saw a sign for a nearby town called Hopewell and "mused on how uplifting it would be to live in a place with such a positive, feel-good name." Yet he was one of just five Asian students in his Princeton class, and he struggled academically with poor English. He persevered under the mentorship of engineering professor Norman Sollenburger, while gaining experience in New York's construction industry during the summers. He graduated in 1958 with a degree in engineering and a deep attachment to Princeton. Unlike most graduates, however, he returned to Hong Kong. After two mandatory engineering apprenticeships, Gordon and his father first started an experimental family-owned property investment venture and then launched a family-owned construction firm in 1963.[21] Recalling that uplifting New Jersey town, he named it Hopewell Construction. It did well, although Hong Kong's frenetic real estate market brought multiple financial crises. We will see in the next section that Wu's Ivy League education helped prepare him to survive and transition from an ordinary investor and engineer into a large-scale commercial developer during the 1970s.

For now, Wu illustrates three key aspects of Hong Kong's educational reorientation. First, his wealthy parents were exceptional in their ability to prioritize higher educations for all their children. Even cash-strapped émigrés such as David Au (chapter 2) depended on the financial assistance and agendas of U.S. organizations. Second, although Jiangnan émigrés led this trend, Cantonese such as the Wu family had their own histories of transpacific migration, and those histories were now overlapping and intersecting. Third, even in this elite family, U.S. higher education still led primarily to permanent immigration. Wu's siblings were among over 310,000 Hong Kong people who achieved permanent legal status in the United States between 1950 and 1989, the vast majority after 1965.[22] Hong Kong's total was thus significantly more than the 268,000 immigrants from Taiwan.[23] In turn, Hong Kong migration to the United States between 1950 and 1989 exceeded its combined migration to Canada (188,541), Australia (58,087), and Britain (50,000–60,000).[24]

Less privileged students did return, but often when sponsored to do so. The partnership between the United Board and Chung Chi College (chapter 3) embodies this circulatory dynamic. The United Board annually sponsored junior members of college faculty for graduate study in the United States. In the mid-1960s officer Abigail Hoffsommer helped identify these candidates, supervised their applications, and monitored their progress once enrolled. Each candidate was obligated to correspond with Hoffsommer while in the United States and return to Chung Chi upon graduation. In 1963–1964 she oversaw eight Chung Chi lecturers who were studying in the United States as United Board fellows.[25] One case was the physics lecturer Li Seung-ping (李尚平), whom Chung Chi identified as "one of our most valuable science teachers." The college lobbied for the United Board to support his U.S. doctoral studies.[26] Although Li was not Christian, the United Board funded him anyway.[27] Hoffsommer guided his applications, consulted with schools about their decisions, and advised Li on his final choice. Once at the University of Colorado, Boulder, Li had to check in every term with Hoffsommer and provide updates on his grades and expenses. His adviser also sent reports.[28] In turn, she pressured Li's adviser that they were "anxious that he be able to return to Hong Kong to resume his teaching duties at the earliest possible time."[29] He finished his dissertation in two years and promptly became chairman of Chung Chi's physics department. Thus while elite scions completed transpacific circulations at familial expense in order to return to familial businesses, students of modest financial means primarily immigrated but did circulate when structured to do so.

As with Li Seung-ping, one of the best ways for a student to stand out was by studying the Cold War priorities of math and science. The Hong Kong government's Postsecondary Scholarship and Bursary Files offer valuable insight in this regard. Throughout the 1950s and early 1960s, the colonial regime annually offered just ten to fifteen scholarships and twenty-five to forty bursaries to the most promising students at the "refugee colleges."[30] This colonial support came with strings, including a one-year postgraduate course in teacher training followed by two years' service as an elementary school teacher. Over and over, though, these files document scholarship and bursary recipients deferring or abandoning these obligations due to admission to U.S. institutions, usually to study math and science. For example, in late 1962 Chung Chi's vice president notified officials that third-year chemistry student Fung Shun Chong (馮順創) "will discontinue his study in this College . . . for the purpose of pursuing further studies in the U.S.A."[31] Without a new source of funding, Fung pursued chemical engineering at Berkeley and went on to a distinguished career with ExxonMobil, including election to the National Academy of Engineering in 2007.[32] When these students deferred in order to pursue graduate studies, they routinely went on to pursue Ph.D. degrees and stayed in the United States or Canada.[33] In these situations, American missionaries could prove valuable allies by helping to subsidize students' travel expenses or acting as guarantors for the repayment of their colonial scholarships.[34]

It must be reiterated, however, that U.S. educational outreach was not charity and often exacted serious sacrifices. For example, in December 1962 Baptist College student Nieh Chung-yit was forced to withdraw from his bursary after his family successfully applied for U.S. resettlement through the Aid Refugee Chinese Intellectuals (ARCI) program.[35] Nieh wanted to finish his degree in Hong Kong, however, and appealed to the U.S. State Department for permission to remain behind. It denied his request. Since remaining might prevent his entire family's immigration, he conceded. A week later his brother also withdrew from his studies at Chung Chi.[36] The Nieh family had "run into debt in order to make the trip," while the State Department's insistence that the two brothers accompany their parents meant that they had to reimburse the colonial government for the whole of their education.[37] Nieh gradually reimbursed his bursary under the new name Edward Nieh while studying at Southern Methodist University and earning his doctorate in chemistry at Rice.[38] To accelerate these student flows, in 1967 the IIE chose Hong Kong as one of four world cities to host an overseas IIE office and library. The IIE offered resources and counseling to encourage Hong Kong students to study in the United States, including administering the local Fulbright Program and other scholarships.[39] The IIE's Hong Kong office soon became its largest overseas site. By 1972 it annually welcomed 42,000 separate visitors—1 percent of the entire population. Its annual report featured a tailored welcome by Li Choh-ming (chapter 4).[40]

This educational reorientation is startling in its dominance before the late 1970s. Within the Scholarship and Bursary files, only a few students left Hong Kong for studies in Canada or Australia. Critically, not one ever withdrew or deferred in order to pursue higher education in Britain. This absence testifies to a lack of funding opportunities at UK institutions before the 1970s, not a lack of desire. Throughout the 1950s and 1960s, sponsored provisions of opportunity led Hong Kong students to shift radically toward U.S. higher education. Hong Kong students' admission to Canadian and British institutions began to reach parity with American institutions only in 1972 and 1978, respectively, and then did surpass them in the 1980s.[41] U.S. institutions such as the Ivy League, Stanford, MIT, and Caltech remained the most prestigious options, however, rivaled only by Oxbridge and the London School of Economics. As a result, American degrees continued to predominate among the largely elite male students who returned.

Golden Tickets Home

It is difficult to determine the percentage of Hong Kong students who immigrated to the United States and the percentage who returned. Reinforcing that U.S. degree-holders acquired increased mobility, many sojourned back and forth. Eric Fong calculated Hong Kong's rate of return from Canada during the 1970s at 6.42 percent, while during the 1980s the Hong Kong government estimated that 10 percent returned from all overseas studies.[42] Scholars have suggested similar or lower percentages for Taiwanese students in these decades, but Taiwan was under martial law until 1987, disincentivizing return.[43] In 1990, however, the U.S. consul-general stated that 55,000 Hong Kong residents—or 2.5 percent of the workforce—were U.S. college graduates.[44] If we accept that figure and recall that 310,000 Hong Kong residents achieved permanent legal status in the United States between 1950 and 1989, we calculate a total of 365,000 people who either immigrated or returned and a return rate of 15 percent (55,000 out of 365,000 people). This number is high for the developing world and is inflated by ignoring the undocumented, yet also deflated by including those who immigrated without connection to education.

U.S. degrees did exceed Commonwealth degrees among Hong Kong's business leaders by the mid-1960s, however. The *Hongkong Album* publications offer valuable snapshots in this regard. Like a *Who's Who*, the album provides names, photographs, and biographic data such as the citizenship, education, and profession of the colony's supposed movers and shakers. It is unclear how these volumes' editors chose the individuals, but it is a broad dataset. For example, the 1967 volume has 1,176 entries.[45] By my count, 481, or about 40 percent, of the entries did not pursue formal higher education, did not list their higher education, or attended institutions outside of China, the Commonwealth, or the United States. Yet among the Chinese entries, U.S. degrees exceeded those from the combined Commonwealth. Among 700 entries with Chinese surnames, only 50 attended higher education anywhere in the Commonwealth. More had attended U.S. institutions for their undergraduate (53) and graduate (82) degrees. In turn, among those who studied domestically, 74 individuals had attended HKU, but 172 had attended the thirteen former American missionary colleges or Tsinghua. There was a particularly strong correlation between attending an American missionary college and subsequent attendance at a U.S. graduate school. Of the 53 who attended missionary colleges and went on to any graduate school, 42 (nearly 80 percent) enrolled at American institutions. Among the U.S.-educated entries in the 1967 *Hongkong Album*, the vast majority were business professionals, followed by academics and journalists.

By the 1960s we also see other émigré industrialists besides the cotton spinners realigning their companies' futures with U.S.-led capitalist systems through their children's higher educations. For most, this interest developed primarily because the United States had become the family company's primary market, source of investment, or source of competition. The émigré plastics manufacturer H. C. Ting (Ding Xiongzhao, 丁熊照) is one example. He gained prominence in prewar Shanghai for establishing the Wei Ming Flashlight and Battery Works (滙明電筒電池廠) and the Pao Chiu Light Bulb Factory (保久小燈泡廠), whose batteries and flashlights competed successfully with U.S. and Japanese imports. He relocated Wei Ming to the French Concession's "solitary island" amid the Japanese invasion and snapped up Shanghai real estate at rock-bottom prices during the war. During the civil war, he first established a plastics plant in Hong Kong in 1947 called Kader Industries (開達實業) and then relocated himself in April 1949. By 1954 Ting decided that Kader should diversify into plastic toys aimed at the U.S. market. He was thrilled when American manufacturers began to write, "asking that we enter into cooperative arrangements with them."[46] This engagement altered his worldview. In the press he trumpeted Kader's profits from its contracts with big U.S. toy companies and hailed the U.S. market as the future of Hong Kong industry.[47] A key such partner was Louis Marx and Company, then the largest toy manufacturer in the United States. In July 1957 Marx himself came to Hong Kong to negotiate a joint venture with Ting, as well as to meet other industrialists through him.[48] As with the Tangs, such transpacific relationships were not only prestigious but a tangible competitive asset. Ting explained succinctly that such licensing and joint venture relationships with U.S. companies "increased our sales volume" and "spared us some of the trouble in dealing with a large number of scattered and small retailers."[49] In short, social capital facilitated market access, sales networks, and outside investment. And as with the Tangs, such strategies were not exclusively U.S.-focused. By 1959 Ting was exploring relationships with Japanese manufacturers, leading to a joint venture in the early 1960s with Sanyo to produce transistor radios.[50] The family also took a round-the-world tour in 1962 to inspect international factories and explore European relationships.[51] Yet once again it was primarily U.S. relationships and the U.S. market that undergirded Kader's growth into Asia's largest plastic toy manufacturer by the early 1960s.

As with the spinners, this reliance on the U.S. market combined with familial exit strategies to lead Ting to view U.S. higher education as a crucial pathway to a versatile American social capital. Viewing the government in Beijing as "harsh and tyrannical" and Hong Kong as vulnerable, he could not "help thinking that I have no home to return to" and so explored migrating to the United States. He first invested in San Francisco real estate in 1951 and used ensuing trips to visit friends in California, including the familiar Zhang Jia'ao, who wrote a preface for Ting's memoir.[52] Then in 1959 Ting sent his second son, Dennis Ting Hok-shou (丁鶴壽), to Maine's Colby College. Upon graduation, Dennis immediately returned and became a director of Kader.[53] Ting sent his fourth son, Kenneth Ting Woo-shou (丁午壽), to the University of Illinois at Urbana-Champaign in 1964.[54] After graduation in 1968, he too returned as a vice-director of Kader Industries. The next year Kenneth married Nancy Wang Wan-sun (王雲心), herself a student in the United States, which the press deemed a "perfect match."[55] The whole family toured the United States for several months in 1969 to visit business interests and meet with "many top American businessmen in various cities as well as leaders of the local overseas Chinese communities." Ting disapproved of the "excesses and intemperance of freedom and democracy in America," but he concluded that the country's "role as the leader of the Free World was not likely to be enfeebled."[56] As their father aged, Dennis and Kenneth gradually took over in the 1970s and led the transformation of Kader and its subsidiaries into a multibillion-dollar conglomerate, particularly after its 1985 public listing.[57] Both Kenneth and Dennis later sent their own sons to U.S. colleges and universities as preparation to succeed them.

The Ting family's kuashang strategies thus developed in the interstitial context of Hong Kong from a combination of business interests and exit strategies. For two generations American higher education helped cement Kader's production relationships with the world's largest toy companies and the family's understanding of the world's largest toy market. The famous shipping magnate C. Y. Tung (董兆榮 or 董浩雲) made similar calculations at almost exactly the same time. From a Ningbo family, he first entered the shipping industry as an apprentice in Tianjin at seventeen, relocated to Shanghai in 1938 to found his own company, and then relocated to Hong Kong and Taiwan during the communist transition. His Orient Overseas Line grew rapidly during the 1950s by transporting the production from Hong Kong's manufacturing boom, and by the early 1960s Tung was one of the world's largest ship owners. His first substantial attention from the local Chinese-language press came in 1962, when his shipping line opened a high-speed passenger service from Hong Kong to the U.S. West and East Coasts via Japan. To mark the occasion, New York City mayor Robert Wagner had presented him with a key to the city.[58] Such international recognition is what led the papers to dub Tung an "East Asian Giant" and the "East Asian Shipping King."[59]

The press, however, did not mention that Tung's eldest son, Tung Chee-hwa (董建華), was already living in New York City. Having not attended higher education himself, C. Y. Tung was famously passionate about it. He is often remembered for buying the RMS *Queen Elizabeth* in 1970 in order to establish a floating university, but unfortunately it burned in Hong Kong harbor in 1972. He was also involved in establishing the United Nations University in Tokyo and lobbied for Li Choh-ming to head this project.[60] Unsurprisingly, Tung was thus also deliberate in guiding his five children's educations. Worried that Chee-hwa was "not smart enough" to enter HKU, he sent him to English boarding schools in the early 1950s. The young heir then worked to secure a place at the University of Liverpool to study marine engineering. After Tung Chee-hwa graduated in 1960, however, his father abruptly pivoted toward the United States. As Chee-hwa explained, "My late father had his very special views. He said, 'CH, the United States is about the future, so go and learn as much as you can about what the future is going to be like.' "[61] Tung Chee-hwa stayed in America for ten years, first working for GE in Boston and then representing Orient Overseas in New York and San Francisco. He became a passionate fan of American sports and purportedly felt "as much at home in the United States as in Hong Kong." He and Betty Chiu Hung-ping (董趙洪娉) even married in New York in 1961. All three of their children were born in the United States and claimed birthright U.S. citizenship.[62] As preparation to take over Orient Overseas, Chee-hwa spent most of his time in the United States as an "avid networker," and he amassed extensive political and business connections that would later facilitate his selection as Hong Kong's first chief executive in 1997, discussed in the conclusion.[63] Simultaneously, C. Y. Tung sent all his other children to the United States. Second son Tung Chee-chen (董建成) also first attended Liverpool and then MIT for his master's degree, while all three daughters—Shirley Peng Tung Shiao-ping (彭董小萍), Alice King Tung Chee-ping (金董建平), and Mary Liu Tung Yih-ping (劉董亦萍)—attended boarding school and college in the United States. Two settled in New York, and one returned to Hong Kong.[64] Likewise, all four daughters of rival shipping tycoon Y. K. Pao (包玉剛) also studied in the United States at this time.

With his sons now British- and American-trained engineers with extensive relationships in the U.S. corporate world, C. Y. Tung recalled Chee-hwa and Chee-chen to Hong Kong in 1969 specifically to aid him in tackling containerization. The U.S. shipping firm Sea-Land Service had introduced container shipping on transatlantic routes in the early 1960s and then launched the first regular container shipping service to Hong Kong in July 1969 as part of its contracts with the Pentagon to supply U.S. troops in Vietnam.[65] The reduced costs and accelerated handling of container shipping signaled to many owners that this was the shipping industry's future despite the predictable devastation it would bring to dock workers around the world. With his sons' knowledge and networks, C. Y. Tung was quickly able to follow Sea-Land's lead in late 1969, and Orient Overseas became the first Asian-based shipping line to offer transpacific container shipping. The company even renamed itself Orient Overseas Container Line (OOCL) in response. In 1970 the colonial government began construction on a container terminal at Kwai Chung, and its completion by 1972 allowed Hong Kong to emerge as one of the world's top three container ports alongside New York and Rotterdam.[66]

Tycoons such as H. C. Ting and C. Y. Tung did not need American educations for their own success, as evident in that neither attended higher education. Yet by the early 1960s both of their businesses had become enmeshed with the U.S. market, American clients, and American competitors. As a result, both did come to see U.S. degrees, networks, and even citizenship as essential components in their children's futures and their companies' evolutions. They grasped that U.S. higher education and work experience could provide their children with knowledge and relationships to help surmount key transitions in a highly competitive global economy, from branching into toys to tackling containerization. Privately, the student side door doubled as insurance for the family's exit in the event of crisis. American social capital thus became an instrumental piece in Ting's and Tung's worldviews in the 1960s in line with Li Choh-ming's implementation of American academic systems at CUHK. These mobile, adaptive, and pragmatic strategies brought a second generation of kuashang into being in the late 1960s and 1970s as elite scions returned to Hong Kong.

Hong Kong's transpacific circulations complicate debates over Cold War "brain drains" of technically trained graduates from developing to wealthy economies, most especially the United States.[67] As scholars such as AnnaLee Saxenian and Madeline Hsu have underscored, in the long run, so-called brain drains proved to be the first stage of a symbiotic "exchange of knowledge workers."[68] The kuashang analytic helps draw our attention to the overlooked role of inherited privilege within these decisions. Most Hong Kong students remained in the United States, but those from elite backgrounds returned at much higher rates in order to assume waiting opportunities.[69] The contrast with Taiwan's increasing transpacific circulations is particularly illuminating. Saxenian has highlighted the role of foreign-born U.S.-educated engineers in both Silicon Valley's success and the global diffusion of high-tech industries. Termed "New Argonauts" by Saxenian, such U.S.-educated migrants returned to their countries of origin during the 1980s and 1990s and jumpstarted tech sectors in Taiwan, India, Israel, and later China.[70] Yet the "Argonauts" were rarely from elite backgrounds. Instead, they returned as entrepreneurs to found new businesses. In Taiwan, the government enacted deliberate policies to recruit and keep them, such as setting up technology parks and incubators. Their new ventures became engines of technology transfer, innovation, and class mobility for young professionals, particularly in the island's semiconductor industry. In Hong Kong, however, the social and economic impact of U.S.-educated returnees was very different. Due to the colony's uncertain future, return appeared risky. The colonial government's "positive noninterventionism" also offered minimal assistance to new businesses. It was thus safer for Hong Kong students from ordinary backgrounds to find employment in the United States and gradually sponsor family members for transpacific immigration. Only when the payoff was virtually guaranteed did return make sense. That calculation was clear for scions such as Jack Tang, Gordon Wu, and the

Ting and Tung brothers, or when taking up employment with the U.S. multinationals that were investing heavily in Hong Kong during the late 1960s and 1970s. As a result, rather than seeding new high-tech industries or generating social mobility as in Taiwan, Hong Kong's kuashang strategies created transpacific circulations that served to retailor existing family companies to the evolution in U.S.-led capitalist systems and thereby multiply existing accumulations of wealth.

Kuashang Transformations

Hong Kong's spectacular but highly unequal 600 percent growth in GDP per capita over the 1970s stemmed in large measure from its residents' ability to exploit both the end of the Bretton Woods system and the overlapping transition from Fordist to post-Fordist production. From a hub of low-cost, export-driven manufacturing aimed at the U.S. market, Hong Kong began to transition into Asia's leading coordination center for multinational commodity chains. We can trace this process through family companies that shifted from low-end manufacturing or services into higher value-added products and services. For example, in the previous chapter we saw TAL and South Sea Textiles begin to outsource spinning in order to focus local operations on apparel. Simultaneously, Orient Overseas was moving into container shipping, and Hopewell Construction entered commercial real estate development.

Such transitions required both advanced knowledge and outside investment, which, as I showed in chapter 5, is often linked with social capital. There was no shortage of banks in Hong Kong, and by 1965 the colony was already the world's third-ranked city by number of foreign banks, surpassing Paris.[71] In the early 1970s, however, local companies began to fund such transitions in a new way: by tapping into a stock market fever that had gripped the colony. As noted, very few industrial companies went public in Hong Kong before 1970. Between 1957 and 1967 there were just 50 to 70 companies listed at any one time on the British-dominated Hong Kong Stock Exchange. Between 1969 and 1973, however, 251 new companies rushed to go public and cash in on this speculative fever.[72] This boom was part of a global bubble produced by floods of U.S. capital escaping domestic bounds. Three new Chinese-led exchanges opened to take advantage, particularly the Far East Exchange founded in 1969 by Wharton

MBA graduate Ronald Li Fook-shiu (李福兆).[73] Dreams of easy wealth fueled many locals to throw their hard-earned capital into trading. Like all bubbles, however, it eventually peaked in March 1973, and then the market plunged over the next few months in a global sell-off stemming from the Nixon Shock and compounded by the global oil crisis.[74] Yet numerous Hong Kong companies were able to exploit this wave and transform from family-based operations into remodeled corporate conglomerates. They did so in large part because they possessed a key advantage: returned second-generation kuashang.

In July 1972 Gordon Wu's Hopewell Holdings went public in the biggest initial public offering (IPO) to date in Hong Kong, cosponsored by Jardine Fleming and Wardley's, the investment arm of the Hongkong Bank. The company raised HK$125 million.[75] Rival real estate developer Hang Lung then surpassed it in September 1972 by raising HK$240 million. And in April 1973 trading firm Li & Fung blew past them both with an IPO that raised HK$2.3 billion.[76] At each of these family-run companies, the decision to go public stemmed from a new generation of returning heirs: Gordon Wu at Hopewell, Ronnie Chan Chi-chung (陳啟宗) at Hang Lung, and Victor (馮國經) and William Fung (馮國綸) at Li & Fung. When Hong Kong's U.S.-infused stock bubble finally burst, swaths of ordinary locals lost their investments and Hopewell, Hang Lung, and Li & Fung all suffered. Yet these kuashang-led companies weathered this downturn and rebounded in the late 1970s. In so doing, they had used this global tide of U.S. capital to achieve risky transitions into higher value-added, knowledge-based services.

In Gordon Wu's case, American social capital gave him several advantages to ride this financial wave to become a world-class developer. Princeton not only trained him as a civil engineer but also gave him English fluency, American mannerisms, and exposure to both New York City construction practices and models of U.S. affluence that fed his ambition and appetite for financial risk. By 1968 the family-owned Hopewell Construction owned twelve properties, but Gordon wanted to strike out on his own. He convinced his father to sell off the family's holdings and distribute the proceeds to the family. Gordon used his share to launch Hopewell Holdings in 1969, but he needed more financing. He applied to the Hongkong Bank for a HK$15 million loan. There were two reasons that William Purves, later first group chairman of HSBC, approved this "vast amount of cash." First, Wu's father agreed to act as guarantor. Second,

Wu himself had become "a powerful conveyor of ideas." Princeton had given him both the credentials and skills to sell British bankers on a young Chinese man's bold ideas, at least so long as he was backed by a wealthy father. Over the next four years, Hopewell Holdings incorporated fifteen new subsidiaries and invested in real estate across Central and the Mid-levels. Yet it remained strapped for cash. In 1971 the British investment bank Jardine Fleming contacted Wu and suggested going public. Although he himself did not understand all the details, he knew this path was necessary, and he no longer needed to convince his entire family. Simultaneously, Purves "gently reminded Wu of the bank's support," and the two firms negotiated to cosponsor Hopewell's 1972 IPO.[77] Infused with the resources of a public company, Hopewell continued to do well by investing heavily in the redevelopment of Wan Chai as an upmarket district, including in 1980 completing then Hong Kong's tallest building, the circular Hopewell Centre. Thus, developing first from his family's larger U.S. orientation, Wu's credentials, fluent English, and American-inspired ambitions were key to unlocking the respect and backing of elitist colonial financial institutions at just the right moment. Indeed, we need only look at his children to understand the value that Wu set on his American education. He and his wife Ivy not only named their first son Thomas Jefferson Wu (胡文新) but eventually sent all their children to Connecticut's Taft School. As heir, Thomas followed his father in studying engineering at Princeton and received an MBA degree from Stanford.

Ka Wah Bank (chapter 3) provides another example of a local company whose transformation over the 1970s was undergirded by previous transpacific circulations. Lam Chi-fung founded the bank in 1922, but his sons Daniel and David took over during the 1960s after returning from studying law at Baylor and management at Temple, respectively. They applied American management and banking practices to modernize and grow Ka Wah's operations. With their father's death in 1971 and the family's continued migration overseas, in 1974 they sold a controlling stake to the Singaporean investor and former Exxon executive C. S. Low (刘灿松). The combination of his Southeast Asian networks and the bank's established local and U.S. networks was powerful. *Euromoney* noted that the bank continued to rely on U.S.-educated returnees to staff senior and middle management, while Low dispatched more than sixty Ka Wah staff for training programs at the First National Bank of Chicago, Citibank, Chase, Bank of America, Midland, and the Swiss Banking Corporation in

Zurich. As a result of these circulations of knowledge and social capital, Ka Wah acquired a reputation as one of the most modern local banks. Over the late 1970s its assets doubled every other year, and net earnings rose by 2,200 percent between 1975 and 1983. The bank's 1980 IPO was underwritten by Chase Manhattan, while Bank of America served as the agent of its 1981 sale of floating rate certificates of deposit.[78]

The transformation of trading firm Li & Fung into the world's premier global supply chain management firm most dramatically encapsulates the transpacific networks undergirding Hong Kong's 1970s ascent and key role in the global shift toward post-Fordist production. Throughout the 1990s and early 2000s, American retailers such as Wal-Mart, Target, Kohl's, and Gymboree relied on Li & Fung as their primary intermediary to search, order, and deliver stock from around the world at the lowest possible prices, from clothing to toys. Yet this firm has never owned a single factory or ship. Instead, its model relied on building and leveraging a global network of contracted suppliers to build a custom supply chain for each and every order. This ability primarily came through the extensive renovations implemented during the 1970s by the second-generation kuashang brothers Victor and William Fung. Fortunately, the Fung brothers are fond of documenting the company's history.[79] Most recently, in 2007 they invited economic historian Feng Bang-yan to produce a high-quality study of Li & Fung's history, giving us much greater detail.

Li & Fung mirrors key aspects of Hong Kong's economic history and embodies the U.S. connections that the first generation of kuashang brought from the mainland. In 1906 merchants Fung Pak-liu (馮柏燎) and Li To-ming (李道明) founded an export company in Canton to try and break the Euro-American dominance of China's export trades.[80] Li To-ming had prior experience in the porcelain business and was the paternal uncle of Li Choh-ming, underscoring the dense interconnections among many of these families.[81] Fung Pak-liu too was prepared to compete through his education at Queen's College in Hong Kong, giving him English fluency and helping to precipitate the family's conversion to Catholicism. With headquarters in Canton, shipping offices in Hong Kong, and sourcing networks throughout South China, Li & Fung began exporting porcelain, fireworks, jade, silk, rattan, and bamboo wares, primarily to the United States. Indeed, from 1906 through the 1980s, the United States was always the firm's all-important market.[82] The company's export trades did well even during the Great Depression due to *chinoiserie* fads and cultivated American connections. Yuan Shikai's government had invited Fung Pak-liu to join China's delegation to the Panama-Pacific International Exposition in San Francisco in 1915, and during this trip Fung befriended Joseph Sipser of New York's Ignaz Strauss & Co., a major sourcing company for U.S. department stores and mail-order companies. Sipser was keen to import "exotic" products from China, and Ignaz Strauss and Li & Fung began a long-term mutually beneficial association. Despite Exclusion-era policies, Fung bravely commenced annual trips to the United States in the 1920s order to forge personal relationships with American merchants and bankers.[83] He bequeathed these hard-earned American connections by ensuring that his children first obtained prestigious English educations in Hong Kong and then introducing them to his American partners.

Like many future kuashang, the Fung family's Anglo-American social capital helped them to weather both war and generational shifts. As with many Jiangnan elites, Fung Pak-liu anticipated the threat from Japan and ordered his second son, Fung Hon-chu (馮漢柱), to Hong Kong in 1937 in order to reincorporate Li & Fung as a limited liability company. This timely relocation was directly enabled by the company's preexisting relationship and credit with the Hong Kong branch of First National.[84] Access to short-term loans and U.S. dollars enabled Li & Fung to continue trading until the outbreak of the Pacific War in 1941. Then, like many in this study, Fung Pak-liu used the wartime alliance to send most of his eleven children to the United States via Chongqing.[85] He passed away of a stroke in 1943, and after the war a dispute led the Li family to sell their shares to Fung's heirs. Fung Hon-chu and his brother Fung Mo-ying (馮幕英) were now the primary leaders. Rapidly adapting to the new U.S.-led order, their first major postwar initiative was to import the latest American ball-point pens—on chartered PanAm flights, no less. The firm claimed to have coined their Chinese translation as *yuanzibi* (原子筆) or "atomic pens."[86] Li & Fung then responded to the U.S. embargo on China by shifting from exporting traditional goods to exporting Hong Kong's new manufactures such as textiles, wigs, and plastics.

Keenly aware of Li & Fung's deep connections to the U.S. market, Fung Hon-chu also prioritized U.S. higher educations for his two sons. The elder Victor graduated from MIT in 1966, earned a master's degree there in electrical engineering, and received his doctorate in business economics from nearby Harvard Business School in 1971. He and Julia Shen

Nai-kee (沈乃琪) were also married in Boston in 1969.[87] They then moved to New York where Victor worked for Li & Fung's longtime banker Citibank, before joining the faculty at HBS in 1973. Younger brother William chose Princeton, earning his bachelor's degree there in electrical engineering in 1970 before he too went to HBS for an MBA, graduating in 1972. As William told a 2014 gathering of the Princeton-Fung Global Forum in Paris, the first time he ever boarded a plane was to go to Princeton. That experience exerted a profound impact, as the first sight of America had on Gordon Wu.[88] But the brothers did not just have interesting experiences in the United States. They both accumulated elite social capital, including the knowledge and mannerisms picked up at university, the credibility conferred by prestigious degrees, networks throughout finance and academia, and Victor's naturalization as a U.S. citizen, which conferred regulatory advantages.[89]

Most important, Victor and William Fung returned to Hong Kong and proceeded to overhaul Li & Fung based on American models. Both Honchu and Mo-ying were ageing and wished to pass the mantle of leadership, as their father had to them. William returned first in 1972 and joined Li & Fung's leadership. While still teaching at HBS, Victor also joined as a manager in 1974 before returning to Hong Kong in 1976.[90] Unafraid of change, Fong Hon-chu told his sons: "Now that you possess the latest business administration knowledge from the U.S., go and take a look at Li & Fung and figure out what its problems are and what improvement should be made." It was precisely such moments that positioned companies with returning second-generation kuashang to thrive in this decade's global economic shifts. Together the brothers conducted a prolonged HBS–style case study of Li & Fung in order to apply the latest U.S. management theories. They found that the management structure had remained largely unchanged since its 1906 founding, and they set out to systematically reorganize the company, introducing American accounting methods and staff training, requiring strategic planning from each department, and forcing out family members in favor of professional, university-educated managers. In 1973, none of the company's employees had a university education; by 1978, 20 out of 120 did. Victor and William also convinced the older generation that to grow properly, Li & Fung needed the capital and accountability of going public. As Feng Bang-yan recorded, the brothers "regarded public listing as a catalyst that would enable the company to dispense with its old management style, to distinguish between the company's ownership and management, and to embark on a professional and modern management." As noted, the company's IPO in April 1973 was so successful that its shares were oversubscribed 113 times. Reinvented as a public corporation, Li & Fung then weathered the global economic turmoil of the mid-1970s by "very methodically" cultivating new U.S. clients. Victor was making multiple annual trips in order to forge new relationships and shift the firm from "mere interpreters" to a diversified investor, production manager, consultant, and retailer. One such ensuing relationship was a 1977 joint venture with Leslie Fay International, then the second or third largest U.S. women's apparel group, in which Li & Fung took over all their sourcing from across East and Southeast Asia. Over the late 1970s it established similar partnerships with the Gap, Lewis Galoob, Dutch chain Peek & Cloppenburg, and the Combined English Stores Group.[91] Through these corporate relationships, built in part by personal social capital, Li & Fung pioneered many of the now standard practices of supply chain management, such as assortment packing and dispersed manufacturing.[92]

Li & Fung's transformation from a patriarchal Chinese family company into a multibillion-dollar conglomerate encapsulates why we cannot understand U.S.-led capitalist globalization without Hong Kong. In no uncertain terms, this firm's transformation stemmed from multigenerational kuashang strategies, accumulations of American social capital, and their interplay with the seismic economic shifts of the 1970s. The fusion of the Fung brothers' native cultural knowledge with their American business school techniques and transpacific network building allowed Li & Fung to exploit the end of Bretton Woods and accelerate the global trend toward flexible production, while positioning the firm to begin incorporating mainland China into Hong Kong's networks after the reopening of Sino-U.S. trade in 1971, as analyzed over the next two chapters. By 1997 Li & Fung would have operations across twenty-six countries, generating an operating profit of HK$399 million from annual revenue of HK$13.3 billion (US$1.7 billion).[93]

Finally, it is important to note a local company that was devastated by the shifts of the 1970s, the TAL Group (chapter 5). Since relocating from Shanghai, the Lees had primarily pursued British-oriented collaborative strategies. TAL had formed in 1962 through investment from Jardine Matheson and gone public in 1964 in an IPO managed by the Hongkong and Standard Chartered banks. TAL achieved spectacular growth over the late 1960s and early 1970s, with operations scattered across Southeast Asia and Africa. Yet the Nixon Shock of 1971 and the collapse of Bretton Woods, the plunge in the Hong Kong stock market, and the oil crisis in 1973 inflicted body blows on TAL. Again, these events also hurt kuashang-led companies, but TAL was insufficiently plugged in to U.S. financial markets, consumer trends, and management theories to adapt. The local press first noted concern for the firm in August 1971 during the Nixon Shock, but in May 1973 *Kong Sheung Wan Pao* sounded the alarm.[94] Amid stock market panic, it reported that TAL had only just begun to frantically research and produce synthetic blends, which had been the rage for years. Recall that South Sea went into both synthetics and denim in the mid-1960s. The same article also reported that the company's "dispersed investment policy" (分散投資政策) to exploit cheaper overseas labor had been prompted not by foresight and planning but instead by desperate cost-cutting in response to substantial losses in international trade. And rather than investing in a better understanding of TAL's largest market—always the United States—the firm reportedly was betting on new Japanese joint ventures to secure new technology and boost exports to Japan.[95]

TAL's choices consistently misread global economic shifts. Not only was its regional outsourcing prompted by losses, but it was financed by a huge amount of debt aimed simplistically at expanding the scale of production, rather than innovating. Despite year-on-year growth in profits suddenly falling to just 3 percent in 1973 as a glut of cheap textiles flooded the market, in September 1973 TAL took on HK$70 million in loans in multiple currencies to fund further overseas expansion. To carry this debt, the company then issued 5 million new shares in an effort to raise HK$50 million. Yet, as *Kong Sheung Wan Po* warned, TAL's stock price had already sunk from HK$30 to HK$24 a share amid the global sell-off. To now issue millions of new shares would drive down the price further. Put simply, only a company desperate for cash would undertake this maneuver.[96] This substantial debt was badly timed and mistargeted at scale, while the Japanese market was also a bad bet, a mistake that Jack Tang would repeat in the 1980s.[97] By September 1974 TAL's board of directors issued a report warning of trouble, and by 1975 the company reported "the largest loss ever by a listed Hong Kong company."[98] The family tried to liquidate the substantial U.S. inventories that had built up during TAL's overexpansion, but the company went into public receivership.[99] After two years of restructuring, in December 1978 the shareholders repurchased the publicly owned shares at HK$10 a share, but Jardine sold its stake and TAL delisted from the stock exchange.[100] In 1983 it sold off its remaining textile business to Toray and C. C. Lee retired.

Many factors contributed to TAL's crisis, but the kuashang analytic helps us to place the Lee family's strategies and lack of American social capital into the mix. Although the U.S. market was consistently TAL's dominant market, the family minimally pursued U.S. higher education or work experiences and proceeded to misstep on U.S. consumer and financial trends. In stark contrast to South Sea, Hopewell, Li & Fung, Hang Lung, Orient Overseas, Ka Wah, and other companies with returning second-generation kuashang, C. C. Lee had not finished higher education, while his sons studied chemical engineering in the United Kingdom. Those educations were geared toward an old regime of textile production, but the shifts toward flexible production and financialization were rapidly increasing the importance of American-style business educations and work experiences. Such training might have altered the Lee family's inattention to textile trends or their decisions to take on huge loans and issue new shares, if only because American experiences would likely have instilled the dogma of shareholder wealth maximization that Milton Friedman was then aggressively promoting.[101]

Kuashang strategies and transpacific circulations undergirded Hong Kong's rapid economic transition over the 1970s from a low-wage manufacturing hub toward a knowledge- and service-based economy. The educational endeavors examined in chapters 2, 3, and 4 enabled Hong Kong by 1973 to surpass far more populous countries such as India, Iran, and Canada as the world's largest sender of foreign students to U.S. colleges and universities. Most students stayed permanently, but I argue that a comparatively high rate of 15 percent returned—disproportionately elite males. Returning scions such as Gordon Wu, Ronnie Chan, and the Ting, Tung, Lam, and Fung brothers represented a second generation of kuashang who began replacing their parents at family companies and using familial wealth to found new companies. As stock market fever boomed and bust, Bretton Woods collapsed, and multinational corporations embraced flexible production, these returnees were well prepared to understand these shifts and exploit new opportunities within them. With degrees concentrated in fields such as engineering, management, finance, and law, as well as professional contacts and work experiences, second-generation kuashang renovated family companies or built new companies into homegrown shipping, real estate, banking, and sourcing conglomerates. These reborn firms positioned Hong Kong to rely less on the exploitation of its own residents' low-cost labor and instead emerge as the key broker between the U.S. consumer market and low-cost labor spread across Asia. As we will see in the remaining two chapters, from the restoration of Sino-U.S. trade in 1971, that process included mainland China.

My analysis necessarily negotiates around still limited archival sources but testifies to the key role played by U.S. higher education in both facilitating transnational student mobility and accelerating capitalist globalization based on preexisting inequalities. Very few second-generation kuashang were self-made. Instead, from the late 1940s Hong Kong–based elites such as Wu Chung, P. Y. Tang, H. C. Ting, C. Y. Tung, Lam Chi-fung, and Fung Hon-chu had analyzed the consolidating U.S.-led order and prioritized U.S. higher education for their children, especially older sons, as a form of both advanced training and transpacific integration. They then empowered their returning sons to remodel the family business and/or backed them as they entered new businesses. In short, the economic transformation that Friedman and others extolled as testament to the so-called free market was actually deeply structured by inherited wealth and its owners' global strategies for self-preservation.

It should be stressed, however, that there were returnees from nonelite backgrounds who forged careers outside of family firms, such as Lydia Dunn (鄧蓮如). Born in Hong Kong to ordinary Cantonese refugees, she graduated from the University of California, Berkeley, in 1964 with a degree in business administration and returned to Hong Kong as an executive trainee with the Swire Group. In 1970 she became the first Chinese person, the first woman, and the youngest person to rise to be export manager of this colonial *hong*, and later she embarked on a political career.[102] We might consider another contemporary, the actor Bruce Lee. Born in 1940 in San Francisco to traveling Cantonese opera stars, Lee Jun-fan (李振藩) was a U.S. citizen by birth but returned and grew up in 1950s Hong Kong. When his partial European heritage provoked conflict with his classmates, Lee's family sent him to live with his sister in San Francisco in 1959. He completed high school in Seattle and graduated from the University of Washington before marrying his college sweetheart, Linda. Throughout the 1960s he taught martial arts and landed supporting roles in Hollywood films and television, but racial discrimination provoked

Lee to return to Hong Kong in 1971. His burst of wildly successful films before his tragic death in 1973 popularized kung fu around the world, critiqued U.S. and Japanese imperialism, and transformed popular images of Chinese masculinity. Yet, as historian Penny Von Eschen has noted, Lee's global superstardom was not just about athletic prowess, acting talent, or good looks. It also depended on the superior education that he earned through his family's backing, the professional experience garnered while suffering Hollywood's discrimination, and eventually the networks of Hollywood itself in order to market his Hong Kong–made films.[103] Once again, the combination of American social capital and Hong Kong's interstitial position undergirded this path-breaking career.

In the end, the kuashang themselves continue to demonstrate their own estimation of the value of American social capital by reinvesting heavily in U.S. colleges and universities. Since the 1970s, second-generation kuashang have repeatedly shattered records for donations to American institutions. Following P. Y. Tang's donation for CUHK's university library in 1967, the Tang family has given tens of millions of U.S. dollars to MIT, UC Berkeley, Princeton, Columbia, and Skidmore, as well as Andover and the Metropolitan Museum of Art.[104] After giving US$1 million to Princeton in 1981 to endow a professorship in Chinese studies, Wu donated Wu Hall in 1983, put US$7.5 million toward Bowen Hall, and in 1995 announced a US$100 million pledge to the university, the single largest donation ever by a "foreigner" to a U.S. college or university.[105] In 2014 Ronnie and Gerald Chan surpassed Wu's record with a US$350 million pledge to Harvard's School of Public Health, leading to its renaming for their father, T. C. Chan. The Victor and William Fung Foundation, too, has plowed tens of millions into Harvard's Asia Center, scholarships at Princeton and Oxford, and a Fung Family Chair in Chinese at St. Paul's School. In addition to naming buildings, this Hong Kong money has fueled knowledge-making about China through endowed chairs and centers, such as Columbia's Tang Center for Early China, the Oscar L. Tang Family Professorship at Duke, and the Gordon Wu '58 Professor of Chinese Studies at Princeton. Yet just as U.S. educational outreach in Hong Kong was not charity, these donations stemmed from strategic self-interest. Studies of alumni donations emphasize that donors tend "to seek maximization of utilities for self, others, or both," including the admission of descendants, sociocultural acceptance among international elites, and simple egotism.[106] As Aihwa Ong first pointed out, though, such donations could have better benefited any number of other educational institutions or charities.[107] Instead, Hong Kong's kuashang focused their philanthropic investments on the prestigious U.S. institutions that fueled their own success. In so doing, the Cold War agendas and inequalities that first structured Hong Kong's transpacific circulations ricocheted back to help widen the financial inequalities between U.S. colleges and universities.[108] As such, Hong Kong's 1970s economic transformation further underscores how prewar China's social hierarchies have continued to mold even late-stage capitalist globalization.

CHAPTER VII

Leading the Way

Kuashang Brokers in China, 1971–1982

In early 1980 Li & Fung escorted its largest client, the Gap, to Shanghai.[1] They aimed to convince the Gap to start purchasing fabrics from the Shanghai Textile Import/Export Company, a state-owned enterprise (SOE) trying to vend its yarns and fabrics on the highly competitive international market.[2] The American retailer "harbored reservations about doing business with China," but Li & Fung assured its executives that PRC politics had stabilized and that fabrics produced by low-cost mainland labor would be highly profitable. The two companies found the Shanghai fabrics to be of "reasonable" quality but concluded that the SOE lacked the technology or expertise to produce orders to exacting international standards. As a result, as precondition to a deal, the Gap insisted that Li & Fung deliver new looms to Shanghai and that all the ensuing apparel be assembled in Hong Kong and exported to the United States as a Hong Kong product. Because Hong Kong had secured large exports quotas under the Multi-Fibre Arrangement (MFA) and China had almost none, this rerouting was essential. This deal proved tremendously successful for the Gap and crucial to the low-cost, high-turnover fashion model that made it an international retail phenomenon in the 1980s. Soon other major U.S. retailers such as The Limited, Express, Lerner, and Petrie all came to Li & Fung for help ordering fabrics from the PRC. By 1985, Li & Fung recalled a U.S.-based employee to set up an entire PRC sourcing group to cater to the Limited.[3] In turn, Li & Fung reinvested its "conspicuously outstanding" profits, buying part of Toys "R" Us, opening Circle K convenience stores across Hong Kong, and branching into U.S. venture capital and global insurance.

Li & Fung succinctly demonstrates how Hong Kong's established transpacific networks expanded into mainland China and began to structure the PRC's trade in the early Reform era. As analyzed in chapter 6, Hong Kong had transformed over the 1970s. The colony's GDP per capita had surged 600 percent in ten years. This leap reflected an accelerating transition from low-wage manufacturing—particularly textiles and apparel—toward a knowledge-based economy of finance and services, particularly for transpacific commodity chains. Yet while the colony's middle class expanded over the 1970s, this surging income disproportionately accrued to the colony's elites and created a new class of powerful global actors. As we will see in this chapter, Hong Kong elites and companies were simultaneously extending their trading networks into mainland China after 1971, when Sino-U.S. trade legally reopened, and engaging with both PRC officials and SOEs. In turn, as commercial engagement expanded and Sino-U.S. negotiations proceeded toward the reestablishment of full diplomatic relations in 1979, Hong Kong's corporate executives anticipated further mainland reforms and built an extensive infrastructure of committees, publications, and seminars through which to amass contacts and share knowledge. By October 1978 Hong Kong executives were already discussing their anticipation of "pragmatic policies," such as the "liberalization of wage and incentive schemes" and the "restructuring of trade and production units."[4] And once Deng Xiaoping solidified power and sanctioned reforms, Hong Kong companies such as Li & Fung simply expanded this engagement.

Careful attention to Hong Kong thus historicizes today's enormous Sino-U.S. trading relationship and helps to rewrite the standard narratives of both China's Reform era and the rise of neoliberalism. Scholars of modern China routinely reference the Third Plenum of the Eleventh Central Committee of December 1978 as the turning point when China abandoned self-reliance and began to embrace "reform and opening."[5] Scholars of globalization, too, cast this same moment as a "revolutionary turning-point" in the global ascent of neoliberal thought.[6] This characterization in part reflects Deng's own self-mythologizing through the "Resolution on Party History" (1981), which enshrined December 1978 as a "crucial turning point of far-reaching significance," while trying to bring "ideological closure" to the Mao Zedong era.[7] This periodization is misleading though because it conflates elite Chinese politics with economic activity and falsely casts Deng as the wise "architect of reforms."[8] In reality, as both Chinese- and English-language scholarship has shown, economic changes were in motion long before Deng cemented power in December 1978. Recent Chinese-language studies have underscored that the PRC first imported industrial technologies and equipment from Western Europe and Japan in the wake of the 1960 Sino-Soviet split and the withdrawal of Soviet aid. This 1960s pivot toward engagement with U.S. allies was significant but remained limited because Mao opposed foreign debt and direct foreign investment—and later the Cultural Revolution suspended these projects.[9] Historian Mark Selden has argued that market reforms then began in the early 1970s due to China's expanding trade with Japan and the United States, but he noted Hong Kong as a factor only in the 1980s.[10] Political scientist Dali Yang, too, has argued that agricultural reforms began in the early 1970s when peasants hard hit by the Great Leap Forward's famine (1958–1961) returned to unsanctioned methods of household farming.[11] More commonly, scholars have noted Zhou Enlai's issuance of the "Four Modernizations" in January 1975 and future general secretary Zhao Ziyang's (趙紫陽) light market reforms as party secretary of Sichuan.[12] Yet, as Kazushi Minami has argued, Mao's own views of China's national interest were also vacillating between development and revolution.[13] Upon succeeding Mao, Hua Guofeng took an important step in his brief reign by prioritizing stability and modernization through foreign technology.[14] In sum, Deng's address in 1978 was seizing on numerous trends and liberalizations.[15]

This chapter offers a different sort of revision. It steps back from intensive analysis of elite politics and senior leaders' psyches and instead draws attention to international forces and nonstate actors at work in and around China before 1978, especially in the Pearl River delta. Despite previous discussions of economic liberalization and outside engagement before 1978, scholars have largely ignored Hong Kong. When we incorporate Hong Kong into our field of vision, however, the picture changes substantially. By examining Hong Kong's transpacific trade flows and multinational corporate activities in the 1970s, it becomes clear that many PRC actors were abandoning self-reliance long before Deng's address. In particular, with the restoration of Sino-U.S. trade in June 1971, Hong Kong's global business networks began extending into the mainland and setting conditions for full-fledged reform after Mao died. Despite the Cultural Revolution's ongoing foment against capitalism and imperialism—and despite all the political back-and-forth in Beijing—concerns over the PRC's stagnant economy still prompted a range of SOE administrators and nonsenior officials to explore engagement with Hong Kong and through it the United States.

In the next section I examine the economic activities that developed between Hong Kong and the PRC between 1971 and 1978. President Richard Nixon first eased the U.S. embargo on China in 1969 and opened Sino-U.S. trade in 1971, before famously visiting the PRC in February 1972. For both Beijing and Washington, this diplomatic thaw was primarily anti-Soviet in calculation, but Sino-U.S. trade once again began moving through the colony. In 1972 China's SOEs also began to ink deals with major Hong Kong companies to garner badly needed foreign exchange and to invite Hong Kong executives to visit the PRC to discuss deals. By 1974 the PRC had begun to procure substantial amounts of international technology through the colony. In turn, the roughly ten thousand U.S. citizens in Hong Kong conversed with PRC officials as soon as it was legal and first established business operations in Bao'an in 1973, years before it became the Shenzhen Special Economic Zone. By early 1975 numerous U.S. corporations were engaged in major projects in the PRC, while more than forty American trading firms in Hong Kong were pursuing trade ventures with China.[16] These pre-1978 commercial activities push back the standard timeline of the Reform era and foreground Hong Kong as a critical but overlooked channel of China's reengagement with the capitalist world.

These pre-1978 initiatives and thawing Sino-U.S. relations etched unmistakable writing on the wall for Hong Kong's savvy entrepreneurs, most evidently its corporate executives and elite kuashang. As the second section analyzes, these Hong Kong elites also spent the 1972–1978 period predicting and preparing for PRC reforms. Perhaps arrogantly, after Nixon's visit, most assumed that reforms would inevitably follow. They built contacts, explored compensation trading, and anticipated substantial revisions to Mao's economic policies well before Deng's speech.[17] Steadily expanding Chinese membership and U.S.-educated Chinese leaders enabled the American Chamber of Commerce (AmCham) in Hong Kong to serve as a preeminent nexus for this corporate planning. By the mid-1970s, AmCham rivaled and even surpassed the less integrative, British-dominated General Chamber of Commerce as the epicenter of elite business life. AmCham's rising prominence allowed its leaders to become increasingly influential in U.S. policy making toward China and confident in opening private communications with PRC officials, such as at the Canton Trade Fairs.[18] As a result, by the time Deng Xiaoping cemented power, elite Hong Kong capitalists already possessed ongoing production ventures, contact networks, and know-how about pursuing business in the PRC.

Finally, in the third section I explore how these pre-1978 activities molded the first few years of China's post-1978 reengagement with global capitalism. The vast majority of China's growth in the 1980s was due to rural decollectivization and the sanctioning of Township and Village Enterprises (TVEs).[19] Simultaneously, even though Deng lacked any "comprehensive theories on how the Chinese economy should be transformed," export-driven production was nonetheless a long-term state priority in order to garner foreign exchange and avoid the common problem of developing-world debt.[20] As a result, Deng and his allies sought to expand engagement with U.S.-led global capitalism through the new Special Economic Zones (SEZs) and China's first joint venture scheme. The formation of the Shenzhen SEZ on Hong Kong's doorstep consciously sought to tap the colony's investment and know-how. Yet these initiatives were not wildly successful. Having established low-risk access to China's low-cost labor in the 1970s, most Hong Kong companies continued to pursue compensation trade ventures and avoid fixed investments. In contrast to ardent patriots such as Henry Fok Ying-tung (霍英東), most Hong Kong executives focused on networking with PRC officials and pushing for further SEZ and joint venture reforms. As such, while much attention has been paid to "overseas Chinese" investors, in reality it was not the whole diaspora. It was primarily an elite stratum of Hong Kong executives who began to broker engagement in the 1970s and helped set policies in the 1980s that enabled Zhao Ziyang's endorsement of the "coastal development strategy" in 1988.[21]

Reengaging with Global Capitalism Through Hong Kong, 1971–1978

Mao's China was not isolationist and maintained significant trade with the socialist world from 1949 to 1971, alongside limited forms of exchange with U.S. allies. As Bill Kirby has emphasized, the new regime was "a leading actor in a global revolutionary movement" and member of "a military-political-economic alliance that stretched from Berlin to Canton."[22] Chen Jian, too, has underscored the PRC's fundamentally universalist outlook.[23]

The PRC's disengagement from global capitalism was not isolationism but rather a pivot toward the socialist world economy. Under the Bureau and then Ministry of Foreign Trade, the PRC "leaned" toward the Soviet Union and Eastern Europe for tremendous material and technical aid. Mao's regime also set up the China Council for the Promotion of International Trade (CCPIT) and more than a dozen state-owned foreign trade corporations to supervise communist bloc exchanges and "Third World" aid. It also organized the biannual Canton Chinese Export Commodities Fair starting in spring 1957. European merchants visited the Canton fairs from the beginning, while many Japanese joined in the early 1960s.[24] Yet with the withdrawal of Soviet aid after the Sino–Soviet split, Zhou Enlai's disappointing 1963–1964 Africa tour, and the Cultural Revolution, the PRC's international aid and trade declined severely by the late 1960s.[25] The fall 1967 Canton fair was postponed by a month and rescued only by Zhou's personal intervention.[26] Thus direct trade with the capitalist states was indeed circumscribed by the height of the Cultural Revolution.

Trade between Hong Kong and mainland China was an entirely separate matter, however. It had never stopped since 1949, underscoring how Hong Kong became an exceptional interstitial space amid the Cold War's increasing bifurcations.[27] While Washington sought to enforce its embargo through Hong Kong, the colony's Chinese residents continued to enter the mainland to visit family and even work, particularly on shipping crews. The colony continued to receive most of its fresh water and large portions of its foodstuffs from the PRC, while Hong Kong residents continued purchasing basic Chinese consumer products. These imports from China hovered around 20 percent of Hong Kong's total imports, and the resulting foreign exchange earnings grew into an "indispensable resource" for Beijing.[28] As the case of restaurateur "Pop" Gingle illustrates, even ex-GI Americans with good Cantonese contacts could participate in these networks of exchange and information across the porous "Bamboo Curtain."[29]

As a result, the first easing of the U.S. embargo after 1969 laid groundwork for the Reform era by permitting China's trade through Hong Kong to grow. The Nixon administration began easing the embargo by first allowing overseas American tourists to buy PRC-made goods and then permitting commerce in nonstrategic goods.[30] In March and April 1971 it further eased restrictions on U.S. visitors and remittances to China, followed by the exchange of U.S. and PRC national table tennis teams. The administration officially ended the trade embargo in June, and in October allowed the PRC to assume the UN seat occupied by Taiwan. Then in February 1972 Nixon undertook his surprise visit to China. While scholars still debate what Nixon and Henry Kissinger intended regarding U.S. commitments to Taiwan, there was no doubt that a major geopolitical rebalancing had occurred vis-à-vis the Soviet Union.[31] David Bruce opened the U.S. Liaison Office (USLO) in Beijing in 1973, after which George H. W. Bush succeeded him. Negotiations to normalize relations continued throughout the 1970s due to political complications on both sides.

This high-level Sino-U.S. thaw actually accelerated Hong Kong's strategic significance as a channel of previously overlooked flows of contact and exchange. From just US$5 million of Sino-U.S. bilateral trade in 1971, the commerce reached an initial peak of US$933.8 million in 1974, primarily exchanging American agricultural products and technology for traditional Chinese products such as fireworks, silk, antiques, and teas.[32] Not only was this trade largely coordinated, ordered, and shipped through Hong Kong, but it also signaled the changing terrain to Hong Kong firms. In 1972 Li & Fung shifted sourcing its U.S.-bound "Black Cat" and "Giraffe" fireworks from Macau to Guangdong.[33] The colony was also the essential entry and exit point for a wave of American academic, cultural, and business tours.[34] While the Cultural Revolution still raged in the early 1970s, an overlapping flurry of ideologically incompatible, Cantonese-dominated dabbles with capitalism were underway.

In addition to Sino-U.S. trade moving through Hong Kong, the colony helped make visible SOE efforts to purchase foreign technologies and engage with multinational corporations. For symbolic state occasions, Beijing bypassed Hong Kong, such as before Nixon's visit when the Chinese Telecommunications Administration contracted with RCA Globcom to install a US$3 million satellite communications station near Shanghai.[35] Later that year, however, China's pressing need for foreign exchange prompted Sinopec to quietly begin kerosene and diesel exports to Hong Kong via special oil trains on the Kowloon-Canton Railway. By the end of 1975 this commerce surpassed HK$200 million in annual sales and accounted for nearly 13 percent of the colony's liquid fuel market.[36] In return, Mobil Hong Kong under John Soong (chapter 5) signed a contract in April 1972 with the Hoi Tung Machinery Company to sell as many as three thousand barrels of lubricant per month to China's merchant navy, while in September 1973 Mobil Chemical contracted to sell fifteen thousand tons of diammonium phosphate fertilizer to the China National Chemicals Import and

Export Corporation.[37] The colony's British *hongs* too began inking lucrative contracts with SOEs. Jardine Matheson immediately entered Sino-U.S. trade in 1971, while in 1973 the Swire Group's Hong Kong Aircraft Engineering Company (HAECO) began servicing the PRC's state-owned Viscount and DART engines. In December 1975 its executives traveled to Beijing and negotiated with the China National Machinery Import and Export Corporation the "first long-term aircraft and engine maintenance contract" between China and a noncommunist country.[38] U.S. corporations in Hong Kong such as Caterpillar also secured early contracts for PRC offshore drilling, prompting drilling firms such as Dresser Industries of Dallas to open offices in Hong Kong "in anticipation of an exploration boom" in the South China Sea.[39] In 1974 Kellogg signed a US$200 million deal with the China National Technical Import Corporation to build eight 1000-metric-ton-a-day ammonia fertilizer plants across China. The four-year project entailed more than 140 U.S. employees living in the PRC across multiple sites.[40]

SOEs inked these deals with Hong Kong–based multinationals, but the end of the U.S. embargo also legalized smaller possibilities for Hong Kong–based entrepreneurs to pursue "compensation trading." An elaborate form of barter that became common between capitalist and communist nations during détente, compensation trade allowed entrepreneurs to establish operations in the PRC by contributing the necessary capital, technology, or equipment in exchange for payment in the form of goods. The investor gained access to low-wage workers, while the host gained technology and some limited foreign exchange.[41] Vice Premier Li Lanqing noted that this trend, rather than a top-down initiative, began at the local level in the Pearl River delta, gained the State Council's attention, and then the "trade pattern was quick to catch on." Dongguan County near Hong Kong even set up a special office on its own initiative to expedite such projects.[42] Li was incorrect that this trend only began in 1978, however. U.S. citizen and longtime Hong Kong executive Alex Blum first launched textile and apparel operations in China under the compensation scheme in 1973. The California native found the quality to be terrible and supply problems endemic, but he and his Hong Kong Chinese staff slowly trained PRC workers to produce everything from flannel shirts to corduroy jeans at U.S. buyers' standards.[43] Blum then circumvented both PRC and U.S. trade regulations by transshipping silk from Shanghai to Long Beach, rerouting it back to Hong Kong without clearing U.S. customs, and finally reexporting the finished goods with "Made in Hong Kong" labels.[44] By

1979 the so-called Silk King already employed seven hundred PRC workers in nine silk factories.[45] Alan Lau of Millie's Holdings also established three mainland factories in late 1978 under the compensation system for shoes, shirts, and gloves, employing over six hundred people. He declared that his HK$3 million investment was "not prompted by profit" but rather by the feeling that "Hong Kong businessmen have a role to play in introducing modern industrial management techniques."[46] In turn, his fellow AmCham members toured Lau's operations in Bao'an, and Lau explained why he had been "a little disappointed" owing to workers' absenteeism and officials' interference but urged a long-term perspective.[47]

Such pre-1978 forms of exchange and knowledge building occurred most dramatically at the biannual Canton Trade Fairs in Guangzhou, the essential forum for international trade and networking. At these multi-week sessions, traders and representatives from across the capitalist and communist worlds were invited to view and order PRC products. All invitations to non-PRC citizens came from the Hong Kong arms of the Ministry of Foreign Trade or China Resources and were essential yet difficult to procure. Depending on China's current political situation, international traders found varying success in vending their products to SOE representatives.[48] These fairs and any ensuing deals were routinely mutually frustrating lessons in cultural differences. Americans were commonly baffled by the Chinese products offered for export, disappointed in their quality, or simply enraged by their counterparts' indirect style of negotiations. In turn, Chinese traders found the Americans to be brash and demanding, U.S. consumers' tastes to be volatile, and the U.S. market exceedingly regulated and expensive.[49] Nonetheless, the Canton fairs remained essential to China's trade—primarily due to the proximity and access of Hong Kong. Scholars estimate that as much as half of the PRC's annual international trade was arranged at these fairs before 1979.[50]

Hong Kong–based U.S. citizens immediately joined their European and Japanese passport-holding colleagues at the fairs in spring 1972, and both they and PRC officials tested what was politically possible. Immediately after Nixon's visit, AmCham set up a China Commercial Relations Committee (CCRC) to study PRC trade opportunities and liaise with state trading bodies, while individual businessmen such as Al Florea began attending each fair.[51] For many Chinese members of AmCham, these shifts were distressing. Jack Tang saw Nixon's visit as "a disappointing about-turn for America," while Gordon Wu was "appalled" by his first visit to

Guangzhou for the fall 1972 Canton fair.[52] Nonetheless, their bicultural leadership would become key. After his April 1972 deal, John Soong personally led a Mobil delegation to the fall 1973 Canton fair.[53] By 1975 the U.S. presence had become the second largest after Japan's, with 350–420 businesspeople attending each fair. AmCham commenced regular meetings at the fairs with CCPIT, Bank of China, and other SOE representatives, emphasizing how Hong Kong could provide international market access and help PRC production to circumvent tariffs, particularly in textiles and electronics.[54] From the first, AmCham's representatives also stressed to the SOEs that "Amcham was the ideal catalyst to develop this type of trade opportunity between Hong Kong and China and between China and American corporations."[55] AmCham representatives then reported back on these meetings both at luncheons and in articles.[56] By fall 1977 the CCRC was holding off-the-record luncheons for members to share information after the Canton fairs. This group was "unanimous" that officials had become "much more relaxed and eager to do business" in the past year.[57] By spring 1978 numerous international visitors concurred that the goods and communications at the fairs had improved substantially.[58]

Scholars often overlook provincial and local officials' agency in favor of senior leaders, but we can see that Guangdong officials were key. It was Guangzhou officials who invited AmCham to start sending official delegations in 1974 to facilitate Sino-U.S. trade. Meanwhile, as longtime Hong Kong executive John Kamm pointed out, as early as 1973 the Ministry of Foreign Trade had granted Guangdong's Foshan Prefecture special privileges to explore export-oriented production and even utilize foreign capital in limited ways. Foshan's success led two more Guangdong prefectures to successfully request this designation.[59] Local officials also deployed selective enforcement and disobedience. As Kamm wrote while an executive with Diamond Shamrock: "As is so often the case, however, the central regulations were not enforced in Guangdong," and local officials and SOE managers routinely "professed total ignorance of their responsibilities" so as to ignore those deemed inconvenient.[60] These ordinary acts underscore that Beijing's perspective and actions were not the whole story. In an even more mundane example, in early 1978 local officials allowed the infamous Dong Fang Hotel to contract through the Canton fair to purchase U.S. industrial pesticides to kill its cockroaches.[61] Well before Deng's December 1978 address, many Guangdong officials' and even ordinary workers' attitudes toward capitalist engagement were shifting.

It should be noted that U.S. officials also pivoted to advise, encourage, and guide Hong Kong executives once importing foreign technology became PRC state policy. Between 1973 and 1977 Deng and Zhou Enlai would authorize 250 projects to import foreign technology at a cost of US$4 billion.[62] Washington blessed this sharing of U.S. technology as a pathway to claim future market share. In 1974 Herbert Horowitz of the USLO urged AmCham members to tap into this "'tremendous thirst' for technical information in China." He intoned: "The initiative . . . rests on the foreigner to open contacts" and advised "interested businessmen" to correspond with appropriate PRC officials and "provide brochures and literature."[63] This 'thirst' contributed to the flurry of Sino-U.S. academic exchanges during the 1970s, with Hong Kong again functioning as the point of entry and exit.[64]

Together, a range of PRC representatives, Hong Kong executives and entrepreneurs, and U.S. policy shifts engendered a medley of economic initiatives between China and U.S.-led capitalist systems between 1971 and 1978. In January 1976 the China National Native Produce and Animal By-Products Import and Export Corporation invited John Kamm, then of the National Council on U.S.-China Trade, to visit Shanghai for the China Feather and Down Garments Minifair.[65] While he recalled a bumpy trip filled with inhospitable officials, Kamm nonetheless independently explored Shanghai, met with the fair's top official, and flew to Beijing to attend a fur minifair—all amid Zhou Enlai's funeral and before Mao's death. In 1975 Kamm's fellow Hong Kong executive Tom Gorman launched his own China-focused company, CCI Asia-Pacific. Its purpose was to cultivate the grassroots thirst in China for information and technology from the capitalist world. At the Canton fair, he contacted the large SOEs responsible for industrial machinery. He freely distributed to them the digests *American Industrial Report* and *European Industrial Report*, featuring the latest industrial products. His strategy was wildly successful. In 1977 the CCPIT permitted Gorman to survey his readers in order to learn their interests—a breakthrough in communications. The following year he was allowed to include a response card.[66] By 1980 the *American Industrial Report* alone had thirty-five thousand PRC subscribers with an estimated pass-along readership of fifty readers per copy—reaching more than one million readers.[67] By the mid-1980s CCI was distributing more than thirty industrial digests that funneled international know-how through Hong Kong into the hands of PRC officials, traders, engineers, and budding industrialists. And it began long before December 1978.

Anticipating PRC Reforms in Hong Kong, 1972–1978

Between 1971 and 1978 a range of PRC- and Hong Kong–based actors tested new forms of engagement following the resumption in Sino-U.S. trade. Japan and China had resumed controlled trade in 1964 after the Liao-Takasaki agreement, but the resumption of Sino-U.S. trade was a more critical gateway, both because the United States was Hong Kong's dominant trading partner and because it opened access to U.S.-dominated global systems. For example, the resumption in trade helped shift the international climate to allow Beijing to claim China's seat at the United Nations in fall 1971 and normalize relations with Japan, Britain, West Germany, Australia, and New Zealand in 1972. In turn, PRC officials began an international charm offensive. Deng Xiaoping led study tours to France in 1975 and Singapore in November 1978, while in 1978 alone twenty-one other delegations of senior officials traveled abroad. Suddenly new foreign leaders were also welcome in Beijing, such as Yugoslavia's Josip Broz Tito. Mao had long criticized Tito as a "revisionist," but Hua Guofeng warmly welcomed him in September.[68]

These economic and political signals elicited a conscious effort among Hong Kong's multinational corporate community to organize for future PRC opportunities. Such preparations were particularly significant because corporate forums such as AmCham were increasingly "local." The chamber had been founded in 1969 as an expatriate organization and liaised regularly with the U.S. consulate.[69] Yet AmCham possessed crucial links to Chinese elites from the beginning. Mobil's John Soong was a founding member, while Henry and Ansie Lee Sperry (chapter 1) left retirement so that Hank could help organize and lead the chamber.[70] As the organization grew from 212 members in 1969 to 687 by 1973, familiar kuashang such as Jack Tang, Victor Fung, and Gordon Wu all joined.[71] By the end of 1976 AmCham had 1,100 individual members, but only 55 percent were U.S. citizens.[72] Underscoring that the other 45 percent were not principally Europeans, the chamber began publishing its member directory in English and Chinese to "assist our Chinese-reading members."[73] The "Meet Our New Members" section of its monthly publication throughout the 1970s underscores that Chinese traders, manufacturers, bankers, and executives of all stripes were flocking to the chamber (figure 7.1). Crucially, Chinese members also rose into leadership positions. A protégé of Soong's at Mobil, Helen Kar Chan, chaired the Labor Relations Committee in 1979 and

Meet our new members

(photographed)

1. George K. T. Ma
   Plutus International Tdg. Co.
2. D. J. Savarese
   Singer Sewing Machine Company
3. Richard S. Zee
   Collins Radio Co. (F.E.) Ltd.
4. Davie K. C. Ma
   Int'l Assoc. of Students in
   Economics & Commercial
   Sciences—HK
5. Wilbur F. Hoehing
   Fisher Radio
6. Simon S. M. Lai
   Int'l Assoc. of Students in
   Economics & Commercial
   Sciences—HK
7. I.M. Angus
   The National Cash Register Co.
   (HK) Ltd.
8. Harry Bhalla
   Nordson Pacific Inc.
9. Michael G. Hartley
   Jardine Matheson & Co. Ltd.
10. Suzanne F. Green
    Business Int'l Asia/Pacific Ltd.
11. S. F. Heffner III
    First National City Bank
12. Timothy J. Williams
    Bank of America NT & SA
13. K. K. Wong
    Eveready Hong Kong Co.

14. Robert Mettler
    Affiliated Machinery Agencies
15. James E. Hood
    Intrusion-Prepakt (F.E.) Ltd.
16. Stanley W. Hong
    Jardine Matheson & Co. Ltd.
17. Michael J. Heasman
    Dredge Masters International
18. Abe Chitayat
    Amerex International (HK) Ltd.
19. Rainer Franz
    The Chase Manhattan Bank NA
20. Raymond J. Stone
    Dow Chemical Pacific Ltd.
21. Graeme C. Woodbrook
    First National City Bank
22. Anthony P. Golamco
    Sun Hung Kai-SGV Management
    Consultants Ltd.
23. A. J. Noble
    Trans World Airlines, Inc.
24. R. Diehl
    Singer Sewing Machine Company
25. Theodore C. Yang
    Merrill Lynch, Pierce, Fenner &
    Smith Hong Kong
26. David C. L. Tsang
    Hang Seng Bank Ltd.
27. Kurt R. Marschall
    Goodyear International Corp.

28. Thomas M. T. Tso
    Int'l Assoc. of Students in
    Economics & Commercial
    Sciences—HK
29. Martin H. W. Wong
    Kidder, Peabody & Co. Ltd.
30. Maurice Chung
    Merck Sharp & Dohme (Asia) Ltd.

(not photographed)

31. David Cohen
    W. T. Grant Company
32. James K. O. Lee
    Int'l Assoc. of Students in
    Economics & Commercial
    Sciences—HK
33. Charles K. H. Tang
    Microfilms (Far East) Ltd.
34. Martin Spurrier
    The HK Convention Centre Ltd.

26

Figure 7.1 The American Chamber of Commerce's expanding membership in the 1970s, reported in *AmCham* in February 1975, reflected growing ethnic (if not gender) diversity and the influence of the U.S. multinational corporate community. Courtesy of American Chamber of Commerce, Hong Kong.

27

Figure 7.1 (continued)

became the first ethnically Chinese person and the first woman elected to the Board of Governors, in January 1980.[74] Spencer Stuart executive Paul M. F. Cheng (鄭明訓) joined in 1977 and was elected chairman of the Commercial and Industrial Development committee in 1980, while Victor Fung joined the Board of Governors in 1983.[75]

This trend was not just a prestigious fad but reflected AmCham's utility as a key forum for manufacturers and retailers to gain insights into their all-important market. It is worth stressing that 30–40 percent of the colony's exports still flowed to the U.S. market at this time, and more than half of all outside investment in Hong Kong industry remained U.S. capital.[76] As a result, American consumer tastes and the nuances of U.S. trade and tax laws remained essential knowledge for the colony's executives, as TAL (chapter 6) learned too late. AmCham sessions helped filled that need. For example, in April 1980 the editor-in-chief of *Textile Asia* and member Kayser Sung led packed sessions of the chamber's Textile Committee in detailed forecasting of the third-round of the MFA agreements that regulated the global textile trade.[77] Through the Textile Committee, even small- and medium-sized manufacturers could monitor trends, consult with the U.S. consulate, and strategize complex U.S. regulations.[78] The founding chairman of the Hong Kong Stock Exchange, too, partnered with AmCham to build the Woo Hon Fai Prevocational School in Tsuen Wan.[79] For similar reasons that Hong Kong students were streaming into U.S. colleges and universities in the 1970s, ambitious Hong Kong executives were joining AmCham to capitalize on its networks of information and social capital.[80] Indeed, even the colonial old guard came calling. In 1977 the Hongkong Bank chairman pronounced: "The courtship was at times stormy, but today I believe that the American businessman and his Hong Kong counterpart are married together in a durable and mutually beneficial relationship."[81] Asked why his conglomerate participated so actively in AmCham, Hutchison Whampoa's chief executive reacted: "How could any major Hong Kong trading company afford not to be a member?"[82]

AmCham's localization encapsulates the transpacific circulations that had bound Hong Kong elites to the United States since the 1950s and accelerated both the colony's economic takeoff and informal decolonization in the 1970s. In essence, local Chinese executives' embrace of AmCham reflected the indigenization of the kuashang strategies that the émigrés had brought to Hong Kong and artificially naturalized through educational endeavors. For example, in 1976 one U.S. executive asserted in the chamber's monthly that the PRC lacked genuine trade laws. A leading solicitor of the colony's Supreme Court, Dorothy Liu Yiu-chu (廖瑤珠), responded in China's defense. Liu was a graduate of HKU, Oxford, and

Harvard Law School who in the 1980s became a local pro-Beijing politician, including serving as a Hong Kong delegate to the National People's Congress and helping to draft Hong Kong's Basic Law. She pointed out that the PRC had "an execellent [sic] record for honoring her contracts," while in contrast the United States "professes" to follow a system of free enterprise, but really "governmental control of foreign trade is extremely subtle and, therefore, complex." In the end, however, she declared that she was "proud" that "our Committee" had "made this place into a forum for the discussion of these matters" and suggested future ways that "our" chamber could prevent such misunderstandings.[83] In turn, AIA attorney T. C. Chan wrote to critique her editorial.[84] As AmCham's membership extended throughout the ranks of Hong Kong's upwardly mobile, we can see the overlapping sets of educational and professional experiences that had shifted Hong Kong professionals such as Liu and Chan away from Britain and toward the United States since 1949. Increasing numbers of such local decision makers—even someone with pro-Beijing politics such as Liu—claimed AmCham as "ours." To explain the revival of Sino-U.S. trade, these interstitial Hong Kong elites are fundamental. Indeed, three years later Beijing tapped Liu to help draft China's first regulations of export-driven joint ventures, discussed in the next section.[85]

AmCham's diverse members prepared for future business opportunities on the mainland by pooling knowledge and contacts. The SOE deals and Canton fairs of the early 1970s made obvious that know-how and experience were critical to cutting through PRC red tape. In 1975 AmCham published a lengthy guide to trading in the PRC, while Union Carbide executive John Goudey became the first member to meet with senior officials in Beijing to discuss business possibilities—again, while Mao was living.[86] The CCRC, too, was hosting regular briefings for members, featuring trade fair veterans, journalists, academics, as well as representatives from the U.S. consulate and the U.S. State and Commerce Departments.[87] As political developments unfolded, this committee's membership soared from 120 to 200, and it put increasing energy into fostering contacts and "an *esprit de corps*" with local Chinese associations.[88] AmCham also published features on PRC economic and legal systems, while jointly with HKU's law department offering seminars on PRC trade regulations, negotiating techniques, payment and credit, and dispute resolution.[89] Despite finding China's trading machinery frustrating, surveyed executives felt increasingly confident because PRC partners quickly proved themselves zealous to "adhere closely" to contracts—as Dorothy Liu Yiu-chu had insisted.[90]

Alongside know-how, AmCham's bicultural leaders cultivated personal relationships with PRC officials before December 1978 in order to be well connected for future opportunities. The importance of guanxi in any Chinese culture was obvious, while simple corruption remained common in Hong Kong at this time. Robert Woodwin of Alcoa had first laid out this agenda to cultivate officials in 1974: "The Chinese are not yet fully aware of the role and importance of the Hong Kong regional offices of American corporations in China trade." The chamber's key aim was to advance officials' "growing realization that the China experts based here are the appropriate people to contact."[91] By spring 1976 the AmCham community enshrined its collective commitment to cultivating PRC officials under the slogan "friendship, patience, and trade."[92] They curried favor in ways politically unthinkable just a few years before, including sending a delegation to the local memorial services for Zhou Enlai.[93] Members such as W. K. Szeto, H. C. Chow, and Herbert Minich labored to establish "a pattern of continuity with officials of the PRC" through meetings in Hong Kong, Guangzhou, and Beijing.[94] More than just talk, these interactions built social capital and directly guided SOEs through trade hurdles. AmCham members instructed SOEs on U.S. customs requirements, holding seminars for the China National Textiles Import and Export Corporation (CHINATEX) on U.S. textile quotas and then translating and distributing free instructions for the preparation of U.S. customs invoice form 5515. CHINATEX promptly requested forty additional copies.[95] They organized tours of Hong Kong factories for PRC delegations and labored to ensure that officials understood "AmCham's role and influence in Hong Kong."[96]

Alongside signing deals and organizing for the future, this community also eagerly enmeshed itself in the formulation of U.S. China policy before official relations resumed on January 1, 1979. Since the late 1960s the U.S. government had relied on multiple nongovernmental organizations to foster relations with the PRC. In particular, the National Council on U.S.-China Trade (NCUSCT) coalesced in 1973 in order to supervise Sino–U.S. trade as a quasi-official counterpart to the CCPIT.[97] The NCUSCT and AmCham immediately cross-pollinated leaderships. Esso executive Mel Searls first came to Hong Kong in 1971 and promptly joined AmCham and its new CCRC.[98] As recorded by George H. W. Bush during a 1974 trip to Beijing, Searls met secretly with senior officials in Beijing to discuss "the possible purchase of PRC crude" and the "supply of fuel to Chinese civil aircraft."[99] The next year Searls became vice president of NCUSCT and relocated to Washington. He continued routine travel between Washington and Beijing, always stopping in Hong Kong to brief his friends at AmCham.[100] AmCham and NCUSCT had "a very close relationship," and Searls even characterized the chamber as "a 'training ground'" for the National Council. Indeed, AmCham's next executive director succeeded him as vice president of the National Council.[101] John Kamm became the new NCUSCT representative in 1976. A revolving door would later open between AmCham and the new U.S. Embassy in Beijing.[102] Not only did chamber members such as Searls and future U.S. ambassador to China Clark "Sandy" Randt, Jr., lead the embassy's commercial sections after 1979, but for a time AmCham even took over Hong Kong representation of NCUSCT.[103] In turn, this rising profile in Sino-U.S. relations augmented AmCham's sway within domestic U.S. business circles. Within five years of its founding, AmCham had become the largest of the eighteen U.S. chambers in Asia and an obligatory stop on any U.S. business leader's regional travels. Between late 1976 and early 1978 alone, it hosted talks by the presidents of Dow Jones and Security National Pacific Bank, Alan Greenspan, fresh from chairing the U.S. Council of Economic Advisers, Merrill Lynch CEO and President Reagan's future treasury secretary Donald Regan, and David Rockefeller, chairman of Chase Manhattan.[104]

As a result, by the time Deng solidified power, Hong Kong's multinational corporate community had long anticipated wider reforms and conscientiously positioned itself across the Pacific to broker expanded Sino-U.S. trade. In 1979 this community's cultivated ties to PRC officials allowed its members to swing into action, from giving presentations in Mandarin to the Ministry of Foreign Trade's International Trade Research Institute and hosting dinner parties for the Peking Institute of Foreign Trade to inviting a delegation from the Hunan Province Chemical Bureau to Hong Kong.[105] Local Chinese and Euro-American executives had found a common forum in AmCham, while Chinese executives and PRC officials soon had other venues through which to pursue elite-to-elite "patterns of continuity." These connections increased as officials and AmCham members developed shared goals, such as normalizing relations and U.S. congressional approval of China's most-favored nation (MFN) status.[106] Indeed, these Hong Kong elites felt increasingly confident in their role at the center of Sino-U.S. trade. When Congressman Lester Wolff led a delegation to China to meet with Deng Xiaoping in July 1978, AmCham hosted a group breakfast before their return flight home—but only because members wanted to discuss "more domestic issues."[107]

Tentative First Steps, 1979–1982

Alongside the activities of AmCham and other Hong Kong organizations, Deng and his allies began privately cultivating the colony's tycoons in 1977. These senior leaders solicited not only investment but also these elites' counsel and networks. As a flurry of international academic exchanges and conferences helped Chinese economists to formulate Reform-era policy, as Julian Gewirtz has argued, Hong Kong elites provided a different sounding board for the highest ranks in government. In turn, the colony's business leaders could offer access to global systems that China could not gain by itself. Building on last chapter's analysis, by 1979 Hong Kong's transnational shipping, financial, and information networks were rivaled only by London, Tokyo, and New York. Chase Manhattan relocated its Asia-Pacific headquarters to Hong Kong in mid-1977, and in 1979 the Bank of China invited Hong Kong Chase to become its U.S. correspondent for remittances and letters of credit.[108] This kind of first-rank financing both expanded the liquidity of local companies and provided ideal compensation for cash-strapped SOEs. Simultaneously, in part through kuashang actors, Hong Kong had secured extensive trade access to the U.S. market. In 1974 the local textile industry won extensive quotas under the new MFA, discussed further in the next chapter, while local organizations such as the Hong Kong Trade Development Council successfully fought for admission to the U.S. Generalized Scheme of Preferences (GSP) in 1976.[109] By wedding first-rank financial capacities, manufacturing expertise, and preferential trade access, Hong Kong could offer vital resources to China.

Those resources sat center-stage in the conception and design of the SEZs. In April and May 1978 representatives of the State Planning Commission and the Ministry of Foreign Trade made an unprecedented visit to the colony to exchange ideas with the business community about economic experimentation in Bao'an County.[110] We have seen that compensation trading had been ongoing in Bao'an since 1973, so it was already understood that this area had special rules. Then in May and early June Vice Premier Gu Mu (谷牧) toured France, Germany, Switzerland, Denmark, and Belgium. It was his first trip outside China and Gu was astonished by Western Europe's economic prosperity. One innovation he noticed was the use of export processing zones in cities such as Hamburg and Copenhagen. Upon his return, he submitted a lengthy report to the Politburo that received hours of discussion at its June 30, 1978, meeting. Gu advocated establishing similar export-processing zones in Guangdong that would take advantage of Hong Kong's proximity. Other senior leaders seconded this proposal.[111] In follow-up conversations, senior leaders decided that such zones should first "concentrate on textiles" in order to ease ongoing textile shortages, build public support, and piggyback on the investment and know-how of the world-leading textile industries in Hong Kong and Japan.[112]

Beijing's representatives in Hong Kong were thinking similarly. Former intelligence officer Yuan Geng (袁庚) had moved to Hong Kong in early 1978 to take over the state-owned China Merchants Steam Navigation Company (CMSN), a historic company first launched during the Self-Strengthening Movement but torn apart during the communist transition.[113] In August 1978 Yuan submitted a report to the Ministry of Transport on how to develop CMSN and utilize Hong Kong's shipping industry for China's benefit. Shipping encapsulated the stark differences between Hong Kong and the mainland. The average turnaround time for a ship in Hong Kong was just 2.6 days, while the average in a PRC port was 7.7 days and the *record* in Tianjin in 1979 was a whopping 11.6 days.[114] As such, Yuan proposed that CMSN construct a new port in Guangdong to anchor an export-processing zone. Yuan's report was forwarded to the State Council.[115] A few weeks later, on the eve of the October 1 National Day celebrations, Deng and Vice Premier Li Xiannian (李先念) invited leading Hong Kong and Macau business leaders such as Gordon Wu and Henry Fok to Beijing's Great Hall of the People. Publicly the officials encouraged them to study China's situation and help the country conquer "the new Long March" of the Four Modernizations. Privately they likely discussed these export-processing zone proposals.[116] Two days after the normalization of Sino-U.S. relations on January 1, 1979, CMSN submitted a more detailed proposal to the State Council for a US$10 million wharf and export-processing zone at Shekou, a peninsula jutting out from Bao'an.[117] China Merchants would build and operate this Shekou Industrial Zone as a direct subsidiary. Li Xiannian and Gu Mu approved the proposal within the month and granted Yuan permission to independently recruit skilled workers, while the State Council sanctioned Guangdong governor Xi Zhongxun (习仲勋) to begin recruiting outside investment.[118] Construction began in April, and the wharf was completed in 1981.[119]

The first four SEZs also received preliminary approval in April 1979, but the details of business operations there were vague and evolving. Bao'an would be reincorporated as Shenzhen—technically including Shekou, but administratively separate. There would be two more SEZs in Guangdong at Zhuhai and Shantou, with a fourth in Fujian at Xiamen. The purpose of the SEZs was to garner technology and foreign exchange, primarily through international joint ventures. Yet the first joint ventures were primarily hotels intended as showpieces for the new China. By mid-1979 Henry Fok had been recruited to construct two hotels in Guangdong under compensation trade terms, while several SOEs launched equity joint ventures with U.S. and Hong Kong companies to build or renovate hotels around Beijing, including the Great Wall, the Jianguo, the Minzu, the Xiyuan, and the I. M. Pei–designed Fragrant Hills Hotel.[120] Intended as showpieces, these projects largely exposed the PRC's byzantine procedures and inexperience. In turn, the hotel contracts seem to have served as the primary legal template for the Law of the PRC on Chinese-Foreign Joint Ventures, passed by the Fifth National People's Congress on July 1, 1979.[121] In October AmCham published an article-by-article analysis of the law by numerous chamber members. They were generally excited by this initiative, but most found the fifteen-point scheme to be ambiguous.[122] Over the next two years AmCham continued to highlight the law's many unknowns, and the conclusion largely remained that the law was "brief and often cryptic."[123] Particular requirements also made investors wary, such as not defining equity and requiring every joint venture to maintain a PRC national as chair. Others were simply unrealistic, such as that every project import "state of the art technology from abroad."[124] Observers drew similar conclusions regarding another State Council decision in July 1979 to allow certain enterprises outside the SEZs to retain a portion of their profits.[125]

As a result, there was no flood of joint ventures, and many contemporary partnerships became well-known horror stories. One example is the late 1979 deal between the Hong Kong firm Harpers International, the China National Machinery and Equipment Export Corporation, and the Guangdong Motor Vehicle Industrial Corporation to produce Ford tourist coaches in Shenzhen. The deal was still arranged under compensation trade terms, and Harpers sank HK$10.5 million into equipment and construction, while the SOE put RMB2.5 million into the site, foundations, and roadwork. Yet when the plant opened in late 1980, the workers provided by the Labor Services Bureau "lacked all technical and mechanical skill."[126] Since PRC workers could still not legally be dismissed, additional skilled workers had to be brought in. The plant still eventually floundered, but Harpers won reimbursement.[127] Other early joint ventures were often organized out of national pride, such as Henry Fok's hotels or the April 1980 venture to revamp Air China's in-flight services undertaken by the U.S.-born restaurant tycoon James Tak Wu (伍沾德) and his U.S.-educated daughter, Annie Wu Suk-Ching (伍淑清).[128]

Although there was no stampede of deals, social networking did accelerate rapidly. Shortly after submitting his Shekou proposal, CMSN's Yuan Geng hosted a cocktail party for four hundred guests at the Furama Hotel to introduce himself to Hong Kong society, inviting colonial officials, diverse business leaders, and other local PRC representatives.[129] In turn, local PRC representatives with CMSN, Xinhua, and the Bank of China all joined AmCham.[130] By early 1980 two vice-governors of Guangdong and one of China's most influential economists, Xu Dixin (许涤新), all visited Hong Kong within days of one another and either gave a talk at AmCham or allowed it to arrange meetings on their behalf.[131] As ever, this socializing was strategic and instrumental to larger-scale economic possibilities, as perhaps best encapsulated by the China International Trust and Investment Corporation (CITIC).[132] Beijing established CITIC in July 1979 to recruit and supervise inflows of foreign capital and technology. To accomplish that mission, officials handpicked its chairman for his Hong Kong social capital: the recently rehabilitated Rong Yiren (荣毅仁). As seen in chapter 1, the Rong family had been Jiangnan's leading textile industrialists before 1949. Rong was a St. John's graduate, but his branch of the family had stayed in the mainland, and the PRC initially allowed them to continue managing their Shenxin mills under state ownership.[133] As with Liu Hongsheng, however, these privileges were stripped by 1956, and Rong was purged during the Cultural Revolution. After the fall of the Gang of Four, he was rehabilitated and sat for a lengthy interview with Hong Kong's pro-Beijing newspaper *Ta Kung Pao* in order to speak on behalf of the "national capitalists."[134] In March 1979 he made his first visit to Hong Kong in thirty years and gave multiple interviews expressing his eagerness to reconnect with his old friends and relatives, while underscoring that Hong Kong had a special role to play in promoting "economic cooperation" with the mainland.[135]

After his appointment, Rong Yiren focused on building ties to Hong Kong and the United States. Within days he grabbed front-page headlines by declaring that Hong Kong and Macau investors were eligible for the same privileges as international partners under the new joint venture law.[136] He returned to Hong Kong in late August, clarifying aspects of the joint venture law and announcing CITIC's intention to set up a Hong Kong branch.[137] After signing CITIC's first contract on October 5—a $150 million joint venture with the U.S. power company Eaton—on October 7 Rong commenced a monthlong tour of the United States at the invitation of the NCUSCT.[138] The trip's purpose was to "make contact" with as many U.S. officials and business leaders as possible in order to promote Sino-U.S. trade and investment.[139] In Washington, executives from a hundred U.S. corporations turned out to greet him, while in New York he laid out foreign investment principles at a reception organized by Ambassador Christopher Philipps.[140] After returning to Washington for lunch with Vice President Walter Mondale followed by an evening reception with Secretary of Defense Harold Brown and Secretary of State Cyrus Vance, Rong flew to Chicago to sign a joint venture with the First National Bank of Chicago.[141] He and Wu Zhichao (吴志超) then flew back to Hong Kong to address a packed AmCham luncheon at the Hilton.[142] Before prominent guests such as Henry Fok, John Soong, the U.S. consul general, and the local head of Banque National de Paris, Rong reviewed his U.S. tour and outlined China's new path in a speech entitled "The Role of Foreign Investment in China's Four Modernizations Program." Papers on both sides of the ideological spectrum covered the speech, while AmCham subsequently published a transcript of the question-and-answer session, which focused on joint ventures.[143] And by late May 1980 Rong was returning to New York at the head of a delegation of PRC vice-ministers and Bank of China representatives to attend a Chase Bank conference on China's reforms and Sino-U.S. economic engagement, hosted by David Rockefeller.[144] The language was all about mutual benefit, and it was a promising moment for such engagement. The U.S. Congress had conditionally conferred MFN status on February 1, while in April the Carter administration created a new category of "P" export licenses to expedite the export of sensitive technologies to China after the Soviet invasion of Afghanistan.[145]

In May Rong had deputized someone of a very similar background as CITIC's first permanent representative in Hong Kong: Wu Zhichao.[146] The son of prewar Shanghai's "MSG King" Wu Yunchu (吳蘊初), Wu had grown up in the same Jiangnan milieu and was himself an American-returned student.[147] He first gave a talk on joint venture regulations at the Chinese General Chamber of Commerce in December 1979, and in February 1980 he gave a talk on expanding Sino-U.S. trade at a crowded AmCham reception.[148] AmCham president Jim Sweitzer introduced Wu and began by noting their shared alma mater, the University of Michigan. Both Sweitzer and Wu praised the recent approval of China's MFN status, while Wu also offered both insights into the joint venture changes and praise for AmCham's role in Sino-U.S. trade.[149] Together Rong and Wu underscore how residual American social capital from before 1949 could be revived and used to plug CITIC into Hong Kong's transpacific networks. While Wu's and Rong's old degrees, contacts, and bicultural skills had been grave liabilities during the Cultural Revolution, now they repositioned them to court Hong Kong elites and encourage them to expand their kuashang strategies into China.

Without overdrawing a causal link, we can map this social engagement onto key evolutions in SEZ and joint venture policies. Throughout such speeches, Rong and Wu often noted that they were listening to Hong Kong executives' feedback, most especially regarding joint venture regulations. Changes such as the right to dismiss workers that Hong Kong executives had demanded were then incorporated into Guangdong's initial regulations for its SEZs, approved by the National People's Congress in August 1980. Yet the business community still had complaints. For one, the SEZ company tax was set at 15 percent, only 1.5 percent lower than Hong Kong's corporate rate. For another, the SEZ regulations promised additional "special preferential treatment" for certain enterprises but did not lay out procedures for receiving such preferences.[150] As a result, a few weeks later an AmCham delegation met in Beijing with the deputy director of the Ministry of Finance's Bureau of Taxation, Lin Rongsheng. He listened "politely" and took notes on their "litany" of complaints over the PRC's tax policies before "calmly" informing them that new regulations would satisfy all their requests. The same delegation also met and registered additional complaints about foreign exchange with the Bank of China and Hong Kong–born vice premier Yao Yilin (姚依林), who oversaw all PRC financial institutions.[151] One month later, in December 1980, the State Council's new regulations on foreign exchange opened the way for the SEZs to begin formulating their own foreign exchange policies.[152] In turn, in May and June 1981 senior officials gathered in Beijing to further overhaul SEZ policies in response to the zones' "general lack of success."[153] The State Council's subsequent ten supplementary regulations of November 1981 closely mirrored Hong Kong executives' tax complaints and further empowered the SEZs to experiment.[154] By December Shenzhen was issuing new land regulations that took effect almost immediately on January 1, 1982.[155]

We can say that Hong Kong executives were leveraging their high-level PRC networks to lobby for specific reforms and were an important part of the conversation molding the young SEZs. This role both encouraged practical reforms such as firing unqualified or undisciplined workers and yet also opened the door for elite social capital to exert substantial influence over policy making and its enforcement. As future CCP general secretary Jiang Zemin politely put it, without "definite legislation and procedural regulations to go by," the increasingly autonomous SEZ officials were routinely caught "in an awkward position" and their decisions were "often inconsistent or mutually conflicting."[156] Less generously, we can surmise how Hong Kong elites used their networks to secure favors and engage in corruption. When the Lo's Mee Kwong Group opened a wholly foreign-owned printing and dyeing factory outside Shenzhen, it still successfully demanded all the SEZ's privileges.[157] Chicago's Beatrice Foods, too, received special privileges in its November 1981 joint venture with CITIC and the Guangzhou Foodstuffs Corporation to open a canning and packaging plant operated by La Choy and Tropicana. Although such joint ventures were supposed to produce for export, this plant was mysteriously allowed to produce for both domestic consumption and export.[158]

Finally, the inchoate SEZs and evolving joint venture regulations also reflected political conflict in Beijing. Rural decollectivization quickly increased ordinary incomes but spiked inflation as spending increased.

Simultaneously, state schemes to import foreign technology and a war with Vietnam had triggered a soaring deficit in 1979. Combined with price control reforms, more moderate and conservative leaders led by elder Chen Yun (陈云) feared a loss of control. As a result, by the end of 1980 they were forcing economic retrenchment. From late 1980 throughout 1981, Beijing abruptly reduced spending, halted planned reforms, and canceled numerous foreign-invested heavy industrial projects in order to shift toward lighter industry. Barry Naughton has termed this shift "the great write-off."[159] As a result, however, the economy entered a sharp recession, and by late 1981 there remained no more than forty signed and approved joint equity ventures in all China.[160] That total rose to just forty-eight by the end of 1982, with twenty-two coming from Hong Kong and eleven from the United States.[161] And of the six hundred outside-invested industrial projects underway in Shenzhen by mid-1981, 70 percent came from Hong Kong. The vast majority remained compensation trade and other subcontracting operations of the kind that had been ongoing since the early 1970s.[162]

This chapter has reconsidered the standard periodization of Chinese's economic reforms in the 1970s and early 1980s. By focusing on Hong Kong and economic rather than political activity, we gain a more gradualist view of the Reform era. Rather than a dramatic break with the accession of Deng Xiaoping, international economic engagement ticked unevenly upward after the restoration of Sino-U.S. trade in 1971. Compensation trade ventures in Bao'an laid the groundwork for the future Shenzhen SEZ, while Hong Kong's elite business community explicitly anticipated and prepared for further reforms. After Deng's address and the restoration of Sino-U.S. relations on January 1, 1979, new possibilities opened, but the first SEZ and joint venture regulations were perceived as vague, especially as Hong Kong actors already had access to low-cost mainland labor. While pro-Beijing loyalists such as Henry Fok and banker Chuang Shih-ping (莊世平) engaged out of patriotism, Chuang himself stressed to Beijing that overseas Chinese would not invest out of patriotism alone. In the words of Vice Premier Li Lanqing, "only if people could 'smell' and see money would they come in droves."[163] Combined with an inherited distrust of the CCP, most Hong Kong business leaders continued to focus on compensation trade ventures, building relations with PRC officials, and lobbying for specific reforms.

Thus, as of 1982 it was difficult to imagine China becoming an export powerhouse or Sino-U.S. trade mushrooming into either country's largest bilateral relationship. In 1982 total Sino-U.S. trade stood around US$5.3 billion, or about 12.8 percent of China's total foreign trade, while Sino-Japanese trade amounted to US$8.9 billion, down from US$10.4 billion the previous year.[164] Yet figures such as Rong Yiren and Wu Zhichao had grasped the scale of Hong Kong's transpacific networks and begun positioning CITIC to capitalize on them. In turn, Beijing was launching other ventures in Hong Kong in order to recruit overseas finance and technology, especially from the United States. One was CCIC Finance Ltd., a merchant bank sponsored jointly by the Bank of China's Hong Kong branch, the First National Bank of Chicago, the Industrial Bank of Japan, and China Resources and launched in July 1980 out of Gordon Wu's Hopewell Centre. CCIC's managing director was seconded from First National and assisted by PRC and Japanese deputies. CCIC thus brought U.S. banking expertise directly into PRC-funded export-oriented projects and helped cash-strapped SOEs to purchase everything from Japanese ships to a West German chemical plant. CCIC also offered itself as both a direct coinvestor with U.S. companies in China and as an established affiliate of the Bank of China, meaning that it could establish letters of credit, handle remittances, and negotiate technological investment directly with provincial branches.[165] Another was the China Everbright Group, which Beijing established in order to purchase international equipment and technology. Its first head was Wang Guangying (王光英), the brother of Wang Guangmei (王光美) and brother-in-law of Mao's former heir apparent, Liu Shaoqi (刘少奇). Wang moved to Hong Kong in 1982 and even into the same apartment building as Jack Tang. He joined both the General Chamber and AmCham.[166] As recorded by the General Chamber's monthly magazine in an issue devoted to U.S.–Hong Kong trade, Wang addressed the largest AmCham luncheon ever in April 1984. He purportedly stated that "China has 400,000 factories and all of them need technological updating." AmCham's executive director John Goudey replied giddily: "I think the place is going to blow its stack."[167]

Such exuberant hopes for China's export-driven development would await the mass transfer of Hong Kong industry into Guangdong after 1984. That transfer was by no means inevitable. Large areas of Guangdong still lacked electricity or reliable transportation to carry manufactures to a serviceable port. Without such groundwork, the mainland's low-cost labor was of minimal attraction to international capital. Moreover, a seismic issue remained unresolved that could either derail or cement Hong Kong's role in China's development. Britain's ninety-nine-year lease on Hong Kong's New Territories was set to expire on June 30, 1997, yet there was no understanding of what that meant. Beijing had maintained a determined silence on Hong Kong's future throughout the Mao era. Deng and Governor MacLehose first discussed the issue in 1979, but nothing substantial ensued. Only as uncertainty over 1997 began to effect local real estate investment did the issue gain momentum. Prime Minister Margaret Thatcher first proposed exchanging legal sovereignty over Hong Kong Island and Kowloon for a new lease to extend British administration over the whole colony beyond 1997. This suggestion evoked painful memories of imperialism and riled Chinese nationalism, particularly after Thatcher made several ill-advised statements during her state visit in 1982.[168]

As the 1997 event-horizon dawned, instability ensued. Deng's allies such as Gu Mu made pledges to preserve Hong Kong's autonomy, but few residents trusted promises from communist officials. When Beijing made clear in August 1983 that it intended to regain both sovereignty and administration over Hong Kong in 1997, panic began to grip this territory of migrants and their children. By late September 1983 the local property market was near collapse and the stock market had shed 35 percent of its value. The Hong Kong dollar lost so much that it had to be repegged to the U.S. dollar in October 1983, a peg that remains in place as of 2020. Tens of thousands of Hong Kong families rushed to migrate overseas, and even Jardine Matheson abandoned ship. If ebbing British power in Hong Kong were not already evident through the informal decolonization advanced by kuashang strategies, it became very plain when the quintessential *hong* announced in March 1984 that it would redomicile its headquarters to Bermuda. Both its shares and the stock index tumbled further.[169] Yet this crisis did not just threaten Hong Kong but all China's reforms. Hong Kong was by far the largest source of investment in the SEZs and joint ventures. Its troubles could sink these initiatives. As we will see in the final chapter, this realization prompted a world-shaping negotiation between Beijing and Hong Kong elites, and their ensuing bargain would reshape kuashang strategies.

CHAPTER VIII

The Gatekeepers

Kuashang Strategies and a New Global Order, 1982–1992

> The recurrent expansions and restructurings of the capitalist world-economy have occurred under the leadership of particular communities and blocs of governmental and business agencies that were uniquely well placed to turn to their own advantage the unintended consequences of the actions of other agencies.
>
> —GIOVANNI ARRIGHI, *THE LONG TWENTIETH CENTURY: MONEY, POWER AND THE ORIGINS OF OUR TIMES*

In June 1984 Jack Tang led the first delegation of Hong Kong executives to meet with Deng Xiaoping in Beijing in order to discuss the 1997 handover.[1] The stakes for their summit were incredibly high. Over the previous two years, Sino-British negotiations over the handover had thrown Hong Kong's entire future into question. The colony's currency, stock, and property markets had all tumbled, and many feared that the territory's days were numbered.

At this juncture, Tang had come to speak for the colony's most important power brokers: its business leaders. After 123 years, the once stolidly British General Chamber of Commerce had just elected him as its first Chinese chairman.[2] This breakthrough in informal decolonization pushed Beijing to request him specifically to meet with Deng. At his side were his cousin H. C. Tang (唐翔千) as chairman of the Federation of Hong Kong Industries and Ngai Shiu-kit (倪少傑) as chairman of the Chinese Manufacturers Association (figure 8.1). Together, these three capitalists represented the core of the colony's business establishment. The same could not be said for their representation of the general public, however. While Deng showered these executives with warmth, in "marked contrast" he scorned the political representatives of Hong Kong people. In 1983 Deng had blocked the Unofficial Members of Executive and Legislative Council (UMELCO) from participating in the handover's formal negotiations, insisting that Beijing already spoke for Hong Kong people. The day after

Figure 8.1 Deng Xiaoping meeting with H. C. Tang, Jack Tang, and Ngai Shiu-kit in Beijing, June 22, 1984. Courtesy of *Ta Kung Pao*.

Tang's visit, he finally met with UMELCO's representatives but only in an unofficial capacity, and the press labeled his cold demeanor a "public humiliation."[3] Deng was succinctly demonstrating not only an ideological hostility toward figures associated with British colonial rule but also his reading of where power rested in Hong Kong.

Indeed, the power dynamic between these Hong Kong executives and Beijing was not as asymmetric as one might assume today. As seen in the previous chapter, Deng and fellow reformers such as Gu Mu had been cultivating Hong Kong elites since 1977 because they needed their help.[4] Some, such as H. C. Tang, had warmed toward Beijing, but Jack held back because of engrained anticommunism and his business interests in Taiwan. Such withholding had only added to Beijing's eagerness for him to come, but Tang then predicated his acceptance on first conferring with officials in Taipei. Predictably, this action infuriated Beijing. Xu Jiatun (许家屯), the new director of the Xinhua News Agency in Hong Kong, convinced the leadership to concede, though.[5] Tang then again upped the ante, now insisting on bringing his second-in-command at the General Chamber—a British national—despite instructions to the contrary: "I wanted to see what happened. I didn't care whether I got to Beijing or not. I was actually personally quite reluctant! It was because of duty that I had to go. I certainly didn't go for the glory. So I wanted to make things quite difficult for them." And once in Beijing, Tang further emphasized his lack of deference. When Deng lit a cigarette and offered him one, Tang claimed to pull out a cigar and light it as a provocative "sign of capitalism."[6] Thus, rather than coming cap in hand before the great leader, Tang was testing Deng. His message was that Hong Kong elites' demands were nonnegotiable if they were to remain after 1997.

In his "quiet New England accent" and assisted by a translator, Tang emphasized to Deng that any Sino-British treaty must preserve Hong Kong's social freedoms, independent judicial system, separate currency, autonomous international memberships, and right to free mobility.[7] Without such continuities and genuine autonomy, he indicated, business leaders like him would evacuate before the handover. If that occurred, not only would Hong Kong's economy sink, but full-blown social panic might ensue. In essence, the children of the émigrés who had fled collapsing Shanghai in advance of the communists implicitly threatened to do it again. Yet Tang's demands for the status quo underscored whose interests he represented. The UMELCO leader Sze-yuen Chung (鍾士元) queried Tang as to why he had focused on things such as free mobility but not even raised universal suffrage. Tang claimed to retort: " 'You don't have the right psychology. In Shanghai, the Shanghai expression is like a crab in a cage.' I said, 'The first thing to do is get out of the cage. Then you can think of where to go. . . . The Shanghai refugees have a better feel for this than the old Cantonese in Hong Kong. They've never had the experience of a refugee: can I get out?' "[8] As seen throughout this study, the Jiangnan émigrés and those who adopted kuashang strategies had indeed never prioritized political reform within Hong Kong. Instead, they had pragmatically focused for thirty-five years on building instrumental transpacific relationships as a strategy of economic advancement, informal decolonization, and potential escape. Tang's priority was to ensure that their privileged last resort remained.

Deng, however, had long since accepted Tang's terms. The PRC's first handover proposal in 1982 stated that Hong Kong could maintain its legal and capitalist systems after 1997. This policy came to be known as "One Country, Two Systems" (一国两制) and is usually attributed to the Sino-British negotiations. In reality, it was negotiations between Beijing and Hong Kong business leaders such as Tang that defined this policy in practice. Most Hong Kong people would have to trust in Deng's catchy pledge to safeguard their lifestyle: *Ma zhao pao, wu zhao tiao* (馬照跑, 舞照跳) or "the horses will continue to run, and the people will continue to dance."[9] Footloose capitalists such as Tang, however, wanted more detailed and direct reassurances. In their meeting, Tang "asked again and again for assurance," and eventually Deng "got a little impatient with me, and he said, 'Well, if you don't believe me, it's very difficult. You wouldn't believe me even if I went to the temple and swore in front of the Buddha. You still wouldn't believe.' "[10] In Tang's account, what finally changed his mind was his assessment of Deng's character. After two days in Beijing, he flew home. Once there, he realized that "all the fear of 1997 evaporated [after] that one visit. He was such a powerful person, human and modest. As far as I'm concerned, he will go down in history as one of the greatest— *the* greatest person perhaps for this century. That's how impressed I was." Speaking to social capital at its most basic and visceral, Tang at least claimed to decide to trust Deng after one face-to-face meeting, particularly after Deng reiterated that China needed "our help" for its development.[11] In another oral history interview, Tang declared: "I would say that meeting changed my life and my view of things."[12]

Deng and Tang's meeting encapsulates a bargain between Hong Kong elites and Beijing that defined "One Country, Two Systems," secured Hong Kong's assistance for China's development, and precipitated a rapid evolution in kuashang strategies over the late 1980s and early 1990s. This gentleman's agreement was a transformative event in both Chinese and world histories. Scholars consistently excise the handover process from the main narrative of China's "reform and opening" (改革开放), but you cannot understand one without the other. As Deng himself pointed out in June 1988 in order to buttress Premier Zhao Ziyang's new "coastal development strategy" (沿海地区外向型发展战略), Hong Kong's autonomy was foundational to China's entire development: "Not only do we need to reassure the people of Hong Kong, but we also have to take into consideration the close relationship between the prosperity and stability of Hong Kong and the strategy for the development of China. . . . Now there is only one Hong Kong, but we plan to build several more Hong Kongs in the interior."[13] This was not empty rhetoric. By 1988 Hong Kong was by far China's largest outside investor, and by 1996 it accounted for 59 percent of China's cumulative foreign direction investment (FDI).[14] In turn, that investment primarily flowed into export-driven enterprises. As a result, from just 4 percent in 1979, by 1996 Hong Kong handled 41.3 percent of

China's foreign trade and 70 percent of its exports to the United States.[15] In no uncertain terms, this bargain was foundational to China's path to export-driven development and today's Sino-U.S. trading relationship. Yet for all its import, this bargain was nothing new in practice. It was textbook imperial collaboration of the kind that Hong Kong and treaty-port elites had practiced since the mid-nineteenth century. The dominant outside power was just shifting again—first from Britain to the United States and now to China. In this bargain, Hong Kong's business elites agreed to remain, help maintain their territory's stability, and use it to accelerate China's development. In exchange, Hong Kong would receive genuine autonomy after 1997, but elites such as Tang accepted that full democracy would remain unfulfilled. As such, a rapid evolution in their kuashang strategies ensued over the late 1980s and early 1990s: from building transpacific networks to repositioning Hong Kong as the linchpin between U.S. and PRC systems.

In the next section we see that a few familiar kuashang, such as the Fung brothers and Gordon Wu, began clearing the way for the coastal development strategy as early as 1980 and 1981. As discussed in chapter 7, most Hong Kong investors were initially ambivalent about engaging with China. Yet several kuashang not only saw the potential of China's low-cost labor but also recognized that they possessed the transpacific access and post-Fordist expertise necessary to profitably connect this labor with the U.S. consumer market. All they lacked was help from senior PRC leaders. By focusing on Wu's herculean pet project—the "Guangshen" expressway that today links Hong Kong, Shenzhen, Guangzhou, Zhuhai, and Macau—we will see that the intersection between kuashang strategies and reformers such as Zhao Ziyang was crucial to enabling the possibility of export-driven development. Through Zhao's personal intervention, by 1987 Wu's expressway began to integrate the Pearl River delta into the world market.

In the second section I examine the evolution in kuashang strategies after the Sino–British Joint Declaration of December 1984. As late as 1984, only 8.9 percent of Hong Kong's FDI went to China.[16] By 1988, however, a Hong Kong Trade Development Council (HKTDC) survey found that 36 percent of its members were manufacturing exports in the mainland and by 1993 China's take of Hong Kong's FDI reached 61 percent, representing over US$200 billion in investment and five million jobs in the Pearl River delta alone.[17] This shift occurred as a result of both widespread decisions to trust Deng and increasing assistance from allies such as Zhao. As such, between 1984 and 1989 second-generation kuashang such as Marjorie Yang Mun-tak (楊敏德) began to shift from subcontracting to direct investment in Guangdong. The ensuing production, however, remained enmeshed in Hong Kong's transpacific sales networks. As such, while scholars such as Yasheng Huang have framed China's globalization as "the story of the 1990s, not of the 1980s," through Hong Kong we see that momentum built from 1984.[18]

In the final section I examine how the Tiananmen Square Massacre of June 1989 threatened to upend these developments. Although shocked by the violence and Zhao's downfall, most kuashang quickly suppressed their emotions. The pragmatism, mobility, and adaptation that had become engrained in these families since the treaty-port era had instilled frank attitudes about power and self-preservation. Rather than the CCP's brutality, it was the U.S. political backlash that Hong Kong elites feared. As such, they rebalanced their strategies and collectively leveraged their American social capital to safeguard the entwined futures of Hong Kong and Sino-U.S. trade amid the U.S. congressional debates over China's most-favored-nation (MFN) status.

The First Stones of Coastal Development, 1981–1984

Scholars have long underscored that China lacked a comprehensive development plan and instead set out, in Deng's phraseology, to "cross the river by feeling for stones" (摸着石头过河). As a result, what crystallized in 1988 as Zhao Ziyang's coastal development strategy was enabled by many prior steps, from securing PRC access to international trade systems and launching the SEZs to planning infrastructure capable of bringing production to the world market. In each of these realms, Hong Kong provided key stones in the early 1980s.

Hong Kong's ability to provide China with access to international trade systems, to jumpstart the SEZs, and to build infrastructure derived not just from capital accumulation but more precisely from the processes examined over this study. The kuashang strategies and transpacific circulations that helped lift Hong Kong from the so-called Third World to the First had endowed the colony with tens of thousands of U.S.-educated returnees who continually updated the local economy with new technologies, management techniques, and social connections. As the chairman of the Hongkong Bank stated in 1977: "Advanced management and organizational disciplines are becoming increasingly apparent in many companies in Hong Kong. Typically these changes have taken place when American educated sons and daughters of the local businessman return to Hong Kong bringing new ideas and new management techniques."[19] We can observe these flows at work through the careers of Philip Kwok (郭志權) and Karl Kwok (郭志樑) of Wing On, or the future chairman of the MTR and Hang Seng, Raymond K. F. Ch'ien (錢果豐). We can also see them through Li Choh-ming's MBA program at CUHK. By 1977 not only were kuashang such as Victor Fung lecturing there, but each of its 129 graduates was certified as bilingual.[20] These intangible assets of social capital were as important as financial capital in terms of what Hong Kong could offer China. Jack Tang even recalled Deng making this explicit, telling him: "He said, 'Money is one thing, but it's your management, your know-how, your knowledge of the Western markets.'"[21]

These transpacific networks were crucial to China's reform and opening because, as emphasized, global capitalism is a highly regulated and man-made system in which countries have unequal levels of access. Just as social capital shapes lending and investment, as seen in chapter 5, so too does it impact international regulatory structures. Between 1950 and 1971 the U.S. embargo had almost entirely excluded the PRC from global capitalist systems. While reintegration had begun, it took decades to erase China's ensuing deficits of know-how and access. Hong Kong became the primary lender of these intangible assets. For example, as noted in chapter 7, the State Council decided in 1979 that the SEZs would focus on textiles and apparel, yet textiles and apparel were among the most tightly regulated sectors in global trade. After normalizing relations and rounds of tough negotiations, Washington and Beijing signed a bilateral agreement that allowed for the unlimited export of PRC textiles to the U.S. market between 1980 and 1982 but denied China quotas for the major apparel categories.[22] In contrast, in 1979 Hong Kong was the world's largest exporter of textiles and apparel to the United States.[23] As a result, as encapsulated by the example of Li & Fung and the Gap, it remained essential to export most mainland-made apparel to Hong Kong for finishing and re-export until the 1995 Agreement on Textiles and Clothing.[24] In turn, it cannot be overemphasized that Hong Kong's quotas were divvied up among individual manufacturers and traders according to previous years' trade figures. More than half were in the hands of thirty senior firms, such as South Sea, Li & Fung, and later Mast Industries, owned by the Limited.[25] As a result, the decision as to whether Hong Kong would lend regulatory access to China's apparel aspirations largely rested with a few dozen kuashang. Their decisions were not preordained. For example, as the negotiations over the second renewal of the Multi-Fibre Arrangement accelerated over 1980 and 1981, Jack Tang was using all his American social capital to wine, dine, and lobby U.S. industrial groups such as the American Textile Manufacturers Institute in order to preserve Hong Kong's own access.[26]

If Hong Kong's textile barons could lend regulatory access, its real estate developers provided the investment and vision to jumpstart the SEZs, especially Shenzhen. At first the SEZs failed to help with the interrelated bottlenecks of low foreign exchange reserves and the specter of foreign debt.[27] The Third World debt crisis of the early 1980s had acutely impressed Beijing with the imperative of expanding its foreign exchange reserves.[28] Yet while Shenzhen attracted HK$9.2 billion in pledged investment between 1979 and 1982, 90 percent of those funds came from Hong Kong and 70 percent went into real estate development, which does not produce foreign exchange. And as noted in chapter 7, industrial investment largely remained in the same flexible processing and compensation trade ventures that Bao'an had hosted since the early 1970s.[29]

To attract more substantial investment, rural Shenzhen needed competitive infrastructure. It was not the provincial or central governments that built this infrastructure, though, but big Hong Kong developers in coordination with Shenzhen's first mayor, Liang Xiang (梁湘).[30] As Liang came up with the necessary ideological justifications, these developers began in 1981 to plow millions of dollars into leveling the terrain and installing infrastructure such as roads and electrical, water, sewer, and telecommunication systems.[31] Known as the "seven linkages and one levelling" (七通一平), this process provided Shenzhen with systems superior in quality to any other city in mainland China. And the single largest actor in this process was Gordon Wu's Hopewell Holdings. Hopewell's ability to undertake this gargantuan project depended fundamentally on its own transformation over the 1970s, as analyzed in chapter 6. Hopewell was able to undertake work on such a colossal scale only because it had evolved into a publicly traded, multibillion-dollar corporation with experience in assembling complex international financing. As such, Hopewell encapsulates why we must understand Hong Kong's development before 1978 in order to understand China's development under Deng.

While later portrayed as an act of patriotism, Hopewell's investments in Shenzhen occurred primarily because Wu sensed big profits and the path to something even greater: a U.S.-modeled expressway linking the whole Pearl River delta. Wu was among the Hong Kong and Macau executives invited to meet with Deng and Li Xiannian at the Great Hall of the People before 1978's National Day (see chapter 7). He later claimed that this meeting inspired him to help improve China's abysmal transport and electrical systems. He recalled his first impression of the New Jersey Turnpike in 1954 and envisioned similarly transformative infrastructure. He took this idea to the head of the Guangdong Travel and Transport Bureau, Li Wu (李牧). Li had never driven a car or left China, however, so he and his subordinates were skeptical of Wu's proposal. One official reasonably pointed out that "Chinese people can hardly afford bicycles. So why would they need a highway for cars?"[32]

Naïve as to the difficulties he would face, Wu pushed ahead and used Hopewell's Shenzhen investments to advance this vision. In November 1981 he signed a partnership between Hopewell and the Shenzhen SEZ Development Corporation to form a joint venture that would develop thirty square kilometers in the Futian district.[33] The ensuing HK$2 billion investment was Shenzhen's largest to date. As Hopewell leveled the site and installed infrastructure, Futian became the new center of Shenzhen. Yet Wu strategically wove his expressway into this project. Alongside rail, the plans for Futian incorporated the first 18.1-km segment of a Shenzhen-to-Guangzhou Expressway from the boundary with Hong Kong. A few days after signing this contract, in early December 1981 Wu flew back to Beijing to meet and discuss the project directly with Gu Mu, now supervising all foreign economic cooperation.[34] Gu Mu was so impressed by Wu's expressway that he arranged a meeting that afternoon with Zhao Ziyang at Zhongnanhai's Purple Light Pavilion. Zhao too praised the proposal as "foresighted" (有遠見), "daring" (有膽略), and expressing confidence in China's reforms.[35] Privately, however, he warned Wu that this project would face enormous obstacles.[36] Nonetheless, with such senior support, Wu charged ahead. He began to detail his plans to the press and boldly predicted that the expressway would partially open to traffic by 1984 and repay its investors within ten years.[37] On December 14, 1981, Hopewell and Guangdong officials signed a preliminary letter of intent to construct the Shenzhen-to-Guangzhou Expressway and operate it under joint ownership for thirty years. Wu said that he expected the formal contract to be signed in four to five months.[38]

That prediction proved absurd. Although record-setting infrastructure is now a hallmark of China's development and foreign policy, it took three years to sign the expressway's formal contract and six years to begin construction outside Shenzhen. In the meantime, Wu pursued other projects, such as Guangzhou's first five-star hotel, the China Hotel. He used these projects to continue ingratiating himself with officials and lobbying for the expressway. For example, in March 1981 Wu led Guangdong and Guangzhou's first party secretaries Ren Zhongyi (任仲夷) and Liang Lingguang (梁靈光) through the China Hotel site plans.[39] He also used his international networks to stimulate attention and investment. When Chase Manhattan's David Rockefeller visited Hong Kong in April 1982, Wu and fellow developer Fung King-hey (馮景禧) escorted him to Shenzhen. They toured Shekou, met with Yuan Geng (chapter 7) and Mayor Liang Xiang, and inspected both Futian and the expressway site.[40] Ten days later Wu squired another delegation of "Japanese friends" around his Shenzhen projects, including Kanematsu's chairman and the Bank of Tokyo's international manager. They also met with Liang Lingguang and the governor of Guangdong, Liu Tianfu (劉田夫).[41]

Yet the expressway project continued to stall owing to Beijing politics and global economics. As noted in the previous chapter, a conservative backlash led to economic retrenchment in 1981 and the "Combat Spiritual Pollution" campaign of 1983. As a result, only on June 29, 1982, was a commission even established to study Wu's scheme.[42] In August Guangdong's collective leadership felt compelled to personally reassure Wu that they had not lost interest. Simultaneously, underscoring that PRC officials routinely linked reforms with the handover, the officials also stressed their commitment to Hong Kong's post-1997 prosperity.[43] Yet the U.S. economy remained in recession, while the colony's own real estate market was sliding in response to the Sino-British negotiations. Despite vowing to press on at Hopewell's mid-November shareholder meeting, two weeks later the normally dogged Wu admitted that grave challenges faced the expressway, particularly as the dissolution of the People's Communes began to parcel out land, making its acquisition infinitely more difficult.[44]

Gradually concluding that "the villains . . . tended to be at the middle levels of government," Wu decided to focus his energies on building networks at the highest level.[45] Through him, we can thus see the first pieces of the bargain that would be cemented after 1984. One year after first meeting Zhao and Gu, Wu and fellow developer Cheng Yu-tung (鄭裕彤) returned to Beijing in December 1982 to discuss increased "economic cooperation."[46] This visit extended into the evening. That night, Wu and Cheng cohosted a lavish banquet at the Diaoyutai State Guesthouse for distinguished guests, including Gu Mu, Liao Chengzhi (廖承志) as head of the Hong Kong and Macau Affairs Office, and other leading economic officials. Diaoyutai is where Mao lived during the Cultural Revolution and still where PRC leaders host visiting heads of state. It was thus a striking mark of favor for Hong Kong capitalists to host a private event there. They toasted to "economic cooperation," and Wu's speech expressed unyielding determination to overcome any obstacles.[47] A week later Wu was granted an unusually rapid second meeting with Zhao Ziyang to discuss the biggest obstacle to such "cooperation": the handover. Afterward, he relayed to the press Zhao's pledge that Hong Kong would maintain its capitalist system after 1997.[48] Wu then returned to Hong Kong to preside over Hopewell's topping out ceremony for the new China Resources building in Wan Chai.[49]

The expressway finally moved forward in 1983 through Wu's high-level relationships and a fateful trip to the United States. In 1983 Wu accepted an invitation to join the Chinese People's Political Consultative Conference (CPPCC, 政协), a symbolic body that has served since 1949 as a forum for the CCP to incorporate businesspeople and members of other parties. The previous year local politicians such as Sze-yuen Chung, Ann Tse-kai (安子介), and Yuet-keung Kan (簡悅強) had been invited, but most declined the offer as a conflict of interest.[50] Wu accepted and attended its March 1983 meeting in Beijing. There Deng purportedly instructed him to "expedite construction on the superhighway.'"[51] Wu made the bold decision to re-create his own life experience from thirty years earlier. He flew six Guangdong officials to California in June 1983 so that they could experience U.S. highways. He bought a van and drove them on this tour himself. Officials were bowled over, and "Wu knew exactly what they were feeling." The vice-mayor of Guangzhou marveled at being able to write in his diary while in the car, impossible on PRC roads.[52] Upon their return, the expressway accelerated. At the end of June 1983 Wu announced that many challenges were being resolved over land acquisitions, border-crossing procedures, license plates, insurance, and choke points. He believed that construction would begin in spring 1984.[53] In October Wu returned to Beijing to brief Gu Mu and brought along Japanese bankers to discuss financing.[54] Evidently successful, a month later he announced that initial financing for the expressway was secure, while delaying groundbreaking until October 1984.[55]

Standard narratives of the Reform era have long framed 1984 as a "turning point" due to Zhao Ziyang's increasing primacy and the start of urban reforms, but few connect these shifts with Hong Kong.[56] Wu's expressway demonstrates the problem with that absence by showing that officials closely considered reform in tandem with both Hong Kong's resources and its future. For example, after the State Council opened fourteen coastal cities to outside investment in April, Beijing sponsored a symposium in Hong Kong to advertise these cities' opportunities, and it contracted US$2.2 billion in investment.[57] In turn, in May Zhao Ziyang invited Wu back to Zhongnanhai to update him on the expressway and advise on this recruitment of foreign investment, suggesting a deepening relationship and Zhao's recognition that most investment would come from Hong Kong.[58] After their meeting, Wu had his first private meeting with Deng. As Jack Tang would do just two weeks later, Wu pushed Deng for direct reassurances about 1997. According to Wu, Deng told him that if Hong Kong's leaders were uneasy about the handover, they should visit Beijing and meet directly with PRC officials until all their questions were answered.[59] Deng was not just signaling transparency but literally instructing officials to make themselves available to the colony's elites in order to build trust and relationships.

When London and Beijing initialed the Sino-British Joint Declaration in late September 1984, it promised Hong Kong autonomy in everything except defense and foreign affairs for fifty years after 1997. With the reacquisition of China's largest outside investor and trading partner now assured, in October two breakthroughs ensued. The Central Committee approved the first comprehensive outline of economic reform, while Hopewell and Guangdong officials finally signed the expressway's formal contract.[60] In exchange for state approval and access to the land, Hopewell would build and operate the expressway as a for-profit toll road for thirty years, receiving 40 percent of the profits for ten years and 30 percent thereafter. After thirty years, ownership would revert to the state. These concomitant breakthroughs on the expressway, the handover, and national reform encouraged Wu to immediately branch into new projects. A week before the formal signing of the Joint Declaration in Beijing on December 19 (where Wu and Tang were two of Hong Kong's 101 guests), Wu announced his long-term plans to invest US$100 million into tourism infrastructure in Guilin.[61] Although rural China remained the center of national economic growth, by late 1984 a decisive bargain was coalescing between PRC officials and Hong Kong's gatekeepers that would steer China's export-driven integration into the world market over the next two decades.

Delivering on the Bargain, 1984–1989

Kuashang strategies evolved rapidly between 1984 and 1989, from building transpacific networks with the United States to repositioning Hong Kong as the linchpin between the two giants. This evolving role was largely blessed by all three national governments. Sino-U.S. relations were at a high, and Washington joined London and Beijing in promoting the Joint Declaration, despite its lack of democratic legitimacy.[62] This campaign to promote the Joint Declaration and the repegging of the Hong Kong dollar to the U.S. dollar helped stabilize the colony, although thousands continued to emigrate. From its nadir in July 1984, the Hang Seng Index almost quadrupled in value before the "Black Monday" jolt of October 1987. Simultaneously, the nature of Hong Kong investment in the mainland began to change. In 1984, 82 percent of all outside investment in China remained compensation trade, joint oil ventures, or nonequity joint ventures in which firms simply subcontracted orders to mainland labor.[63] At that point, Guangdong produced just 11 percent of China's exports. By 1994 the province was producing a "staggering" 44 percent of China's exports.[64] While a range of overseas Chinese investors contributed to this growth, as scholars such as Min Ye have emphasized, the core factor behind Guangdong's rise was the deindustrialization of Hong Kong. The Rong family's Nanyang Cotton Mills invested in their first Shenzhen mill in early 1984, while even skeptics such as Jack Tang were professing faith in Deng by June.[65]

Along with Hong Kong's future, senior leaders also made clear that China as a whole would continue to integrate into the world market. There was increasingly close dialogue among Chinese economists, the World Bank, and other international colleagues, while in April 1986 Zhao

Ziyang personally intervened to accelerate Wu's expressway by appointing a special national committee to take over the project. Zhao personally threatened "severe repercussions" if provincial authorities created further delays, while the new governor of Guangdong Ye Xuanping (叶选平) greased local wheels by consenting that all adjoining counties and townships could share in the construction and profits—a pragmatic acceptance of mass graft and an interesting parallel with the construction of the Jinpu railroad in the 1900s.[66] Zhao subsequently announced in June 1986 that China would work to join the General Agreement on Tariffs and Trade (GATT). China could not yet meet its requirements, but the announcement signaled reformers' clout and long-term intentions.[67] And in September Zhao endorsed a request from Rong Yiren (chapter 7) that CITIC be reorganized and given greater autonomy. After the State Council approved this reorganization in 1987, CITIC Hong Kong began a streak of aggressive acquisitions under Rong's son, known locally as Larry Yung Chi-kin (榮智健).[68] While just a few examples, these interventions and moves exemplify Zhao and his allies' increasingly clear commitment to reform and integration with the world market. This message was reiterated in person to Hong Kong business elites, such as in February 1987 when Gu Mu toured Shenzhen with Wu, Henry Fok, H. C. Tang, the Bank of East Asia's David Li (李國寶), and others. Gu not only praised the expressway but emphasized that such "cooperation" with Hong Kong and Macau was essential to China's development plans.[69] A few weeks later, in April, Wu formally broke ground on the HK$8 billion expressway.[70]

With Hong Kong's post-1997 autonomy assured and China's reforms accelerating, we can trace the ensuing evolution of kuashang strategies through the Yang family of the Esquel Group (溢達集團). Founder Yang Yuanlong (楊元龍) had launched this firm in 1978 explicitly to pair mainland labor with the major U.S. apparel retailers. Yet Yang's strategy was again part of a multigenerational familial enmeshment with the United States. By the late 1970s four generations of Yang's and his wife Dora Cai Yungfong's (楊蔡詠芳) families had been U.S.-educated or U.S.-oriented. Dora's grandfather Mo Shangqing (莫觴清) had hailed from Wuxing County before migrating to Shanghai, where he eventually became comprador to the American silk importer Robert Lang & Co. (兰乐壁洋行).[71] In 1917 Mo used the First World War's removal of European competition to partner with Lang and found a silk weaving mill in Shanghai, the Mayar Silk Mills (美亞織綢廠). In 1919 Mo's daughter Mo Huaizhu (莫怀珠)

had married a young American-returned student and fellow Wuxing native named Cai Shengbai (蔡聲白).

Cai was yet another of the well-known American-returned students who pioneered Jiangnan's textile industry (chapter 1). Hailing from an elite scholar-official family, Cai began his studies at Tsinghua in 1911 and proceeded on a Boxer Indemnity scholarship to Andover. He then entered Lehigh University to study mining and metallurgy, graduating in 1919 and returning to China. Mo Shangqing then hired his new son-in-law as Mayar's general manager and imported the latest American power looms, introducing American management practices to cut production costs and compete against Japanese imports. His efforts were extremely profitable, as the firm set up numerous silk filatures and other plants across Shanghai in the 1920s. Hagiographic sources insist that Cai treated his workers well, but the silk industry was notorious for its inferno-like conditions of boiling water and exploited female and child labor.[72] Through Cai's friend, the familiar Zhang Jia'ao, Mayar also purportedly secured both favorable loans and import tax waivers from the Bank of China as a "bonded" or duty-free factory (保稅工廠).[73] Cai even borrowed Euro-American marketing strategies such as fashion shows, and Mayar's products won prizes at the 1926 Philadelphia World Exposition. By 1934, when Mayar reincorporated as a limited liability company, it had three thousand employees operating more than twelve hundred looms, as well as offices in Bangkok and New York.[74] Like many émigrés, Cai relocated Mayar's operations to Shanghai's "solitary islands" during the Japanese invasion and then rerouted new American machinery to Hong Kong during the communist transition. He did not attempt to revive operations, however. Instead, depressed and in reduced circumstances, he left the textile business and eventually emigrated to Australia.

Although war and revolution destroyed Mayar, the family's continued transpacific circulations undergirded their revival. Dora Cai was herself studying in the United States, and she married Y. L. Yang in New York in the late 1940s.[75] Yang was a graduate of St. John's University in Shanghai who proceeded to the Lowell Textile Institute in Massachusetts for a second master's degree in textiles and chemical engineering. The newlyweds then joined her parents in Hong Kong in 1951, where Marjorie was born in 1952. With his father-in-law's reduced circumstances, Yang did not have the means to found his own company. Instead, with his American education and his in-laws' social capital, he eventually became TAL's manager (chapters 5 and 6). While today often remembered for his 1986 conviction for gambling and race-fixing at the Jockey Club, as TAL's manager Yang regularly featured in the press as a respected industry leader. He served as an officer of the Jiangsu and Zhejiang Residents' Association alongside H. J. Shen and his boss C. C. Lee, as well as with the Chinese Manufacturers Association, the Garment Manufacturers Association, and the Cotton Advisory Board.[76] In these roles, Yang helped represent Hong Kong and negotiate against Euro-American protectionism throughout the early 1960s.[77] Yang's participation in these negotiations further underscores the trade know-how and regulatory access that Hong Kong elites accumulated over the Mao era. In turn, he positioned Marjorie to succeed in these systems after him. He sent her to boarding school in Pennsylvania in the mid-1960s, and she graduated from MIT in 1974 with majors in mathematics and philosophy. She proceeded to Harvard Business School. Finishing in 1976, she then worked in investment banking in New York under First Boston's Joseph Perella before returning to Hong Kong in 1978.[78] As with many previous kuashang—and in contrast to TAL's Lee family—these experiences gave her inside knowledge of American management and finance, along with high-powered connections. It also likely enabled her to secure U.S. permanent residency or citizenship.

Transpacific circulations were thus constants that undergirded this clan's evolution over four generations from late Qing compradors to U.S.-oriented Hong Kong capitalists. As TAL faltered and mainland opportunities increased, Y. L. Yang jumped ship in 1978 and took many of its managers and production processes with him. His new venture focused on exploiting compensation trade opportunities, as Marjorie explained to HBS's alumni magazine: "Although joint ventures, not to mention private ownership, were not possible at that time, through a kind of barter system we could send machinery to the Chinese factories we managed. In return, we received shipments of apparel that we then sold to discount retailers in the United States."[79] Her father quickly established a representative office in New York, while also cultivating PRC officials. By November 1978 the press covered him feasting with both Liao Chengzhi—whom Wu would fête at Diaoyutai—and the head of the Overseas Chinese Affairs Office, Lin Xiude (林修德).[80] Yang was in poor health, however, and recalled Marjorie to Hong Kong. Despite lacking experience in textiles, she was prepared to help her father establish efficient corporate structures and navigate rapidly evolving U.S. consumer tastes and financial systems.

Like most Hong Kong firms, Esquel waited to invest in China due to both U.S. protectionism and poor infrastructure. In particular, while China had secured unlimited textile exports to the United States for 1980–1982, in 1983 the Reagan administration negotiated a new agreement with Beijing to restrict half of China's textile export categories over the next four years. That December, China also joined the MFA, and its admission brought mixed effects because U.S. officials quickly exploited its "consultation calls" to further raise restrictions on Chinese textile exports from 50 percent of categories to 75 percent.[81] And in May 1984 President Reagan bowed to swing-state interests during a presidential election and signed Executive Order 12475, empowering the secretary of the treasury to further tighten import restrictions on all global textiles. Don Regan's Treasury Department subsequently issued new stipulations requiring that "substantial transformation" occur in a product's final country of origin in order to receive recognition as that country's product. These shifts brought substantial worry to Hong Kong firms by threatening to reassign many PRC-made, Hong Kong-finished products.[82] As a result, as Thomas Moore has analyzed, these restrictions slowed the relocation of Hong Kong industry to the mainland.[83] Esquel actually relocated production to Mauritius before it invested directly into China.

Yet, with Hong Kong's accession to GATT in 1986, the groundbreaking on Wu's expressway in 1987, and Zhao Ziyang's announcement of the coastal development strategy in early 1988, Esquel pulled the trigger. Partnering with the local government, it invested millions into an enormous spinning and weaving joint venture in Gaoming, west of Foshan. The new Guangdong Esquel Spinning and Weaving Company (廣東溢達紡織有限公司) thus did not develop from "overseas Chinese" familial or native-place ties, as scholars often imply. It developed from Jiangnan émigrés' kuashang strategies to exploit low-cost mainland labor, state subsidies, and new infrastructure in order to maximize longstanding U.S. marketing relationships.[84] Marjorie recruited the Gaoming plant's top managers from U.S. business schools, while in the 1990s she ensured that middle managers were retrained at company expense at Tsinghua and Fudan's new MBA programs. With efficient management and lower labor costs, the Gaoming plant increased Esquel's profit margins and allowed it to reinvest in the higher-quality design, packaging, and merchandising demanded by upmarket Euro-American brands. By the mid-1990s Esquel employed more than fifty thousand workers in Guangdong who produced tens of millions of shirts per year for Nike, Polo, Hugo Boss, Tommy Hilfiger, Ralph Lauren, and Banana Republic. In 1998, 85 percent of Esquel's Guangdong production flowed to the U.S. market. At that point, attentive to American consumers' shifting tastes, Yang began prioritizing sustainable production methods, such as upgrading Gaoming's water treatment systems and launching more sustainable cotton farms in Xinjiang.[85] And while receiving far less press than her male peers, Yang has continued pursuing her family's multigenerational kuashang strategies, from serving as chairwoman of the Hong Kong-U.S. Business Council to joining MIT's board and aiding the university's outreach in Asia.[86]

Esquel and the Yang family testify that the origins of today's gargantuan Sino-U.S. trading relationship lie in older pre-1949 histories of transpacific circulation that survived transplantation to Hong Kong and then expanded over the Cold War. The experiences of Cai Shengbai and Mayar provide the context to understand why Y. L. and Marjorie Yang were exceptionally positioned to explore opportunities in China from the late 1970s onward. They quickly grasped how to combine access to low-cost mainland labor with the U.S. market due to engrained familial strategies and intangible assets that had been passed down across the twentieth century. Once the Sino-British Joint Declaration sealed the bargain between Beijing and Hong Kong elites and regulatory hurdles such as Hong Kong's GATT membership fell into place, the Yangs directly invested in Guangdong in the late 1980s but kept this production enmeshed in their established transpacific networks. Again, 85 percent of the ensuing production went to the United States by 1998. In short, while overall Sino-U.S. trade remained statistically small at US$14 billion in 1988, the Yangs and other kuashang were already assembling a transpacific pipeline running through Hong Kong.[87] In turn, only in 1988 were Taiwanese companies legally allowed to begin openly investing in China.

Yet clouds were gathering in the mainland. The introduction of urban reforms in 1984 had unleashed a national spending spree. SOEs were investing in new plants and equipment while offering wage increases, bonuses, and amenities to workers. PRC banks had expanded lending to match, and in 1984 alone wages rose on average 20 percent and the money supply increased by 50 percent. Unsurprisingly, inflation jumped from 2 percent in 1981 to 9 percent in 1985 and 27 percent by 1987. In short, the urban economy began to overheat. As runaway inflation was a critical factor in the downfall of the Nationalists, this issue was politically sensitive.

Simultaneously, rising urban wages were luring rural residents to defy the *hukou* system, abandon their fields, and seek higher wages in the cities at a volume of eight million people per year. This migration became so extensive that, despite the productivity gains of decollectivization, agricultural production fell in 1987 and rationing had to be reintroduced. This embarrassment was compounded by increasing labor unrest as entrepreneurial managers sought to turn greater profits and corruption grew, especially in and around the SEZs. While it seemed to many ordinary people that only elites were getting ahead in the "New China," conservative forces in the State Council gained momentum and began pushing austerity policies in 1988.

Hong Kong executives noticed these troubles, but their exuberance over the momentum toward reform and the colony's own soaring economy tempered their normally sensitive alarm bells. Indeed, with Zhao Ziyang installed as CCP general-secretary at the Thirteenth Party Congress in fall 1987 alongside the retirement of many conservatives, it seemed that a younger, more liberal generation was coming to the fore. As such, despite warnings, by early 1988 Zhao pushed ahead with the coastal development strategy. Its main thrust was that each province would be freed from maintaining self-sufficiency in grain production. Provinces such as Guangdong would thus be able to embrace fuller participation in the global economy according to comparative advantage. Driven by foreign investment and the labor power of millions of migrants to the SEZs, Zhao's strategy was the jumping-off point for the trading powerhouse of China today. Yet we cannot understand that strategy solely through senior officials. From trade access and the Guangshen expressway to huge industrial investments, Hong Kong's evolving kuashang strategies helped steer this course.

Tiananmen and the Transpacific Ecosystem

The year 1989 marked the fortieth anniversary of the PRC. Instead of a celebration, it became a year of tragedy. Numerous studies have analyzed the Tiananmen Square Massacre, and we need not revisit its main narrative here.[88] Less remembered is how this crisis shaped the future of Hong Kong and Sino-U.S. trade. Like people around the world, Hong Kong residents watched the escalating events of May and early June 1989 on television. A week before the massacre, almost a quarter of the population had marched in the streets in solidarity. The massacre of June 3–4 then provoked a cultural crisis that has never fully dissipated. After the violence, another million came out as the tentative optimism that had built since 1984 suddenly collapsed. The carnage renewed fears that Britain was returning the colony to a brutal regime. Many residents rushed to leave, with about forty thousand fleeing for Canada in the next year alone. These local anxieties molded the drafting of Hong Kong's post-1997 constitution, the Basic Law, and encouraged the final governor, Chris Patten, to accelerate democratic reforms, viewed by many as violating the Joint Declaration. Through 2020 at least, Hong Kong remains the only society in the Chinese world that annually commemorates June 4 with a mass vigil, a dedicated museum in Tsim Sha Tsui, and replicas of the Goddess of Democracy across several universities.

Tiananmen was not only a political crisis but also triggered an economic one. China's worldwide credit dried up almost instantly, as the Bush administration directed the World Bank to freeze seven loans worth US$780.2 million, and both the Asian Development Bank and major Japanese banks followed suit. Major SOEs had to halt planned projects, such as the China National Metal and Mineral Import-Export Corporation shelving its efforts to raise US$200 million in new capital.[89] As a result, Beijing had to deepen the austerity policies initiated in 1988. The central government dramatically tightened credit and reduced the number of bodies authorized to borrow internationally from a hundred to just ten. Beijing also devalued the RMB in December 1989. The combination of these measures jolted China's economy, and overall growth slumped to an anemic 4 percent, down from 12 percent the year before.[90] China's international arrivals, too, fell by 70 to 90 percent in the second half of 1989.[91] Until Deng Xiaoping's "Southern Tour" (南巡) of January 1992, many observers believed that economic liberalization was over.

For the kuashang, Tiananmen imperiled both their access in Beijing and the transpacific ecosystem that they had been remodeling since the 1970s. Suddenly, key allies were gone, including Zhao Ziyang, local Xinhua representative Xu Jiatun, and the former Shenzhen mayor Liang Xiang, who had since become the governor of Hainan and was purged after allowing protestors to flee through the island.[92] After an emergency session on June 6, AmCham's Board of Governors issued an unusual condemnation and put the Statue of Liberty on the July cover of its monthly magazine.[93] Yet after the initial shock material interests reasserted themselves. By fall, AmCham was highlighting that U.S. banks were taking the "long view strategy."[94] Jack Tang experienced an even more rapid evolution. Having professed faith in Deng after their June 1984 meeting, he initially found the massacre distressing. On June 7 the pro-Beijing *Ta Kung Pao* quoted him as saying that the "Beijing situation" (北京局勢) would "definitely" have an impact on Hong Kong's economy. More radically, he contended that if Zhao Ziyang could "regain power" (能重新執權), the impact on Hong Kong would be less severe. If "the army continued to oppose the people" (若軍隊繼續與人民對抗), however, Tang predicted a far-reaching impact.[95] These words were dangerous, and by late June he changed tunes. After a board meeting of the subsidiary Tristate Holdings, Tang referred to the massacre more euphemistically as the "Beijing matter" (北京事件) and said he was not worried about the impact on the company or implicitly Hong Kong.[96] And in October 1989 Tristate made its first direct investment in China, buying a factory in the Pearl River delta. In an oral history interview, Tang stated plainly, "That says a lot." He elaborated: "Most of the business community, I don't think has felt that this was the end of China. . . . Sometimes emotions can be whipped up. . . . And the Democrats organizing big meetings and all that. Emotional people get more emotional."[97] Regarding Deng personally, Tang contended he was still "a world hero" who "made China into a responsible citizen of the world" and ensured its stability.

The kuashang analytic offers emic insight into Tang's opportunistic evolution. We should again recall that at no point did kuashang strategies ever include a democratic agenda. That was not the goal of these families' multigenerational transpacific circulations. In turn, while Tang later claimed that Tristate's investment reflected Chinese patriotism, the kuashang framework throws cold water on that claim, too. Chapter 1 examined the Tang family's decisions in early 1937, as narrated by Jack in the same oral history interview. Confronting a Japanese invasion, his parents had exploited a privileged opportunity to cull a windfall from a national crisis. Jack evidently knew this story well. Now, in a far less dangerous crisis, he acted similarly by investing in Guangdong. As international investment dried up, Tristate likely snapped up this asset at a significant discount, while boosting Tang's political cachet. The "Beijing matter" was regrettable, but investing made sense for his own family's accumulations of financial and social capital. Or, as a classic *chengyu* warns when considering sticking one's neck out, "A wise man looks after his own hide" (明哲保身).

Gordon Wu too quickly made his peace with Beijing. Even before June 4, the protests had threatened his interests as Hopewell's stock price tumbled 25 percent over the preceding few weeks, forcing him to cancel a US$500 million share offering. He then went into the PRC to inspect his projects, missing his daughter's high school graduation in Connecticut. Once back in Hong Kong, he watched "stunned" as tanks rolled into Tiananmen, while his wife Ivy helped Princeton evacuate its staff and students to Hong Kong. Because international banks were pulling out, Wu had to put the expressway on hold for nearly three years. Reflecting later, Wu felt that his years in the United States "had given him a feeling for how democracy and freedom worked," even naming his first-born son for Thomas Jefferson. Yet he also decided that "China was not ready for an instant introduction of democracy" since he believed "that history attested that the introduction of democracy needed a long, gradual process." More fundamentally, his kuashang strategies too had never included political reform in either Hong Kong or China. His American higher education had left a patina of liberal values, but his subsequent career had focused on using those experiences to import primarily American models of development, technology, and finance in pursuit of material gain. Despite his friendship with Zhao, Wu pragmatically shifted to working with his replacements, Jiang Zemin and Li Peng.[98]

By fall 1989 Hong Kong elites were far more concerned by U.S. politics. The White House and Congress had virtually opposite reactions to Tiananmen, unsurprising since different parties controlled the two branches. Although the American public expressed outrage, the first Bush administration took a pragmatic approach similar to that of the kuashang. President Bush was eager to contain the damage and preserve the larger U.S. relationship with Beijing. Like all presidents since Nixon, he still saw China as a valuable partner against the Soviet Union. Washington also had a long history of tolerating brutal but useful dictators. As a result, while the U.S. Embassy harbored the astrophysicist-turned-activist Fang Lizhi (方勵之), President Bush imposed only light sanctions and confided in his diary that he hoped to "cool the rhetoric."[99] The president also reached out to his "friend" Deng to explain that if further sanctions happened, it was solely a concession to public pressure. He underscored his own commitment to preserving this strategic relationship. In tandem, on

July 1 the administration secretly dispatched National Security Advisor Brent Scowcroft and Deputy Secretary of State Lawrence Eagleburger to Beijing on a U.S. Air Force plane. They met at Zhongnanhai with Deng, Li Peng, the foreign minister, and others. Deng accused the United States of fostering the crisis and predictably demanded respect for China's internal affairs, while Scowcroft and Eagleburger urged care for international opinion.[100]

In contrast, Congress made bipartisan calls for harsher punishments on China, from tariffs to severing relations. Senator Jesse Helms (R–North Carolina) bluntly urged the nation not "to pussyfoot on a bunch of murderers over there."[101] Bipartisan support built for action, and in July Congress imposed the "Tiananmen Sanctions" through amendments to that year's foreign aid bill, HR 1487. The amendments banned U.S. arms sales to China, scuttled high-level military talks, and restricted both the U.S. Trade and Development Agency's and the Overseas Private Investment Corporation's dealings with China. Congresswoman Nancy Pelosi (D–California) also introduced HR 2712 to allow as many as forty thousand Chinese students in the United States to extend their visas and potentially claim asylum. Bush vetoed this bill, however, in response to Beijing's objections and his own belief that U.S. influence was best served by expediting the return of U.S.-educated students.[102] Many Chinese students, however, would later be granted permanent residency through the Chinese Student Protection Act of 1992. Most important for Hong Kong, there was an unsuccessful proposal to remove China's MFN status.

This failed proposal to revoke MFN status triggered grave concern among Hong Kong business elites. If successful, it would have instantly hiked duties on PRC goods and stunted Sino-U.S. trade, Hong Kong's economy, and thus the direction of the kuashang's evolving strategies. One AmCham member described the Bush administration's sanctions as "a controlled hemorrhage with a scalpel" in comparison to Congress "charging in with a battle axe."[103] In August the chamber hosted a press conference in support of the Bush administration's "measured response," while its monthly magazine reprinted speeches from the Heritage Foundation that labeled harsher sanctions as "naïve" and only facilitating Japanese commercial dominance.[104] The proposal to revoke MFN was not a one-off question, however, because China's status was reviewed annually. Under the Jackson-Vanik amendment to the Trade Act of 1974, communist countries that restricted citizens' free emigration could receive an annual grant of MFN status only through a presidential waiver and agreement by Congress. Presidents Reagan and Bush had been issuing these waivers since 1980 with congressional consent. Tiananmen had not changed that calculation for the Bush administration, but it had for many members of Congress. As a result, while the Heritage Foundation characterized the president's decision to issue the waiver in 1990 as "agonizing," in reality the White House was focused on ensuring that Congress did not override the president's waiver.[105] President Bush even began lifting some post-Tiananmen sanctions in January 1990, while the World Bank's American president recommended resuming loans. In contrast, more members of Congress were heading in the opposite direction. They looked to the renewal of China's MFN status in June 1990 as a way to challenge the White House and signal U.S. concern for human rights in China.

Hong Kong executives' collective campaign to defend China's MFN status provides a fitting conclusion to this study. We have seen that Hong Kong industrialists had been working with U.S. trade restrictions ever since 1950 and actively parrying U.S. protectionism since the early 1960s, but this case provoked a qualitatively different reaction. Leveraging every network at their disposal, Hong Kong elites warned American friends and colleagues, the local and international press, and both the White House and Congress of catastrophic consequences were China's MFN status to be revoked, especially for Hong Kong. Their arguments did not remain solely economic. In a new tack, some claimed that the territory was likely to encourage and facilitate China's continued liberalization and even democratization after 1997. A range of figures led this campaign, including AmCham's 1990 president and the future founder of Duihua, John Kamm; lawyer and future U.S. ambassador to China Clark T. Randt, Jr; and AmCham's first Chinese president, Paul M. F. Cheng (鄭明訓). Kamm and Randt likely had a bigger impact in Washington, while we see, through Cheng, the encapsulation of this study's key threads: the intersection between émigrés and U.S. interests in the Cold War colony; transformative transpacific circulations of knowledge and social capital; the gradual localization of AmCham; and the evolution and expansion of kuashang strategies to incorporate China.

Born in Xiamen in 1936, Cheng came to Hong Kong in 1938 when his parents fled the Japanese invasion. Dovetailing with the analysis in chapters 2, 3, and 4, he attended a Catholic missionary school and then crossed the Pacific on a scholarship in 1954 at the age of seventeen to enter Lake

Forest College, north of Chicago. He was the only Chinese student. As emphasized in chapter 6, structural provisions of opportunity encouraged Hong Kong youth to study math and science, and Cheng duly received his degree in biology. He gave up medicine, however, and proceeded to Penn's Wharton School, graduating with an MBA in 1961. Cheng then bounced from position to position. He worked for IBM in New York for a year, then became a salesman for Vicks Chemical, and rose to be its marketing manager across Singapore, Malaysia, and Bangkok.[106] He was naturalized as a U.S. citizen in 1965 at the age of twenty-nine and returned to Hong Kong in 1969 to work for another U.S. pharmaceutical giant, Warner-Lambert. As Hong Kong's economy took off in the 1970s, Cheng headed Warner-Lambert's Asia division before joining executive search firm Spencer Stuart & Associates in 1977 as managing director. As such, much like H. J. Shen (chapter 5), he literally became a professional network broker and helped source many of the executives behind Hong Kong's upmarket transition.[107] As Cheng's version goes, he remained at Spencer Stuart until a "chance meeting" in 1986 "with the head of Inchcape [Charles Mackay] at a London cocktail party, and again on the subsequent flight home to Hong Kong," which "led to Mr. Cheng joining the company and eventually becoming chairman of Inchcape Pacific."[108] Others contend that Cheng ran Spencer Stuart's search for this position and decided to take it himself.[109] Either way, again like Shen with the Hongkong Bank, Cheng's appointment to lead and modernize this old British *hong* further advanced informal decolonization.

Cheng's involvement with AmCham substantially raised his profile and opened the way to other public roles. He was elected as the first Chinese vice-president of AmCham in 1986, followed by the presidency in 1987. In this role, his agenda centered on fighting U.S. protectionism and promoting Sino-U.S. trade.[110] Another responsibility of this role was networking with PRC officials, as his predecessors had done for ten years. Cheng quickly built a working relationship with Xu Jiatun, who was himself seeking to "cultivate a group of 'pro-China' capitalists in Hong Kong."[111] One of Cheng's first actions as AmCham president was to host a January 1987 luncheon at which Xinhua and AmCham agreed to regularly scheduled meetings, today an unimaginable pairing but then cause to publish a proud photograph of Xu and Cheng together.[112] That summer Cheng was also appointed to the Trade Advisory Board and joined a delegation of sixteen executives to Beijing to meet with the Hong Kong and

Macau Affairs Office, the Ministry of Foreign Affairs, and State Council.[113] In October 1988 Cheng also became the first (open) U.S. citizen to be appointed to a Legislative Council (LegCo) seat.[114] Across these roles, Cheng manifested a fluid identity straddling Hong Kong, China, and the United States. Asked whether he saw himself as American or Chinese, "he leaned back in his chair, pondered for minute [sic], and said 'It's a good question.' His answer came down to expediency, he confided with a grin. He saw himself as either, depending on what suited him best at the time."[115] While Chinese immigrants to the United States had fought for generations to be deemed "assimilable," Cheng came from a very different background. His interstitial life had engendered a situational identity and kuashang strategies. Through all these positions, Cheng consistently hailed Hong Kong's future as the linchpin of China's integration into U.S.-led economic systems.[116]

As the protests in Beijing expanded in April and May 1989, Cheng first interpreted this political crisis as an economic opportunity. Both the mainland and Hong Kong press extensively documented the protests, and on May 26 *Wah Kiu Yat Po* featured statements from three leading businessmen: Cheng, tycoon Li Ka-shing, and fellow LegCo member Stephen Cheong (張鑑泉). Li stated that the student movement was patriotic and that he would not change his investment plans. Cheong was more cautious, calling on the demonstrations not to turn into a "blind tide" (盲潮).[117] Cheng struck a totally different note. Speaking at an executives' breakfast in New York sponsored by the Asia Society, he focused on the protests' "potential benefit for Hong Kong," particularly if liberalization widened international access to China's market. He intoned that many observers only saw "One Country, Two Systems" through the lens of politics, overlooking "the geographic and economic realities of the situation." In his view, Hong Kong was "leading China's huge economic change plan in numerous aspects" and was likely to be the "financial and service center" of South China after 1997.[118] Although unaware of the violence that would ensue, Cheng nonetheless laid out a kuashang interpretation of this political crisis. After June 4 he laid low until the battle over China's MFN status began in spring 1990.

Unsurprisingly, AmCham led Hong Kong's collective forces in this battle. Its leaders began writing to members of Congress and working with the U.S.–China Business Council and the Asia Society. In February chamber president John Kamm wrote directly to President Bush and deployed the argument that would redefine U.S. policy toward China throughout the 1990s and early 2000s: that only "constructive engagement" would improve human rights.[119] Put simply, the solution was to trade and invest *more*, not less. Cheng then repeated these neoliberal arguments in the Chinese press. On April 20 two politically opposing newspapers published statements in which Cheng warned that two-thirds of China's exports to the United States flowed through Hong Kong and that the potential termination of China's MFN status would deal a "heavy blow" to both the colony and Sino-U.S. trade.[120] He also announced that AmCham would dispatch a delegation to Washington to lobby on Hong Kong's behalf. Kamm would lead this delegation, Randt would coordinate many meetings, and Cheng would join as a former president. Randt had been in the same DKE pledge class at Yale as George W. Bush, and he used that connection to "set up meetings with key administration leaders and members of Congress."[121] AmCham had thus become a structural fold through which its bicultural leaders recombined and deployed their collective American social capital.

The apex of AmCham's 1990 delegation was Kamm's sensational testimony on May 16 before the House Asian and Pacific Affairs Subcommittee. He brought with him petitions from the Hong Kong government and the colony's major commercial and industrial bodies. Echoing dire warnings about U.S. protectionism first made by P. Y. Tang in 1962, Kamm characterized the question of China's MFN status as one of "life or death for Hong Kong" and, crucially, "the reform movement in China." For those concerned about the 1997 handover, Kamm warned that "China's loss of MFN will devastate Hong Kong economically and psychologically. It will be a crippling blow to confidence, completing the job begun by Chinese troops that tragic night one year ago in Tiananmen Square." Rendering this congressional trade decision as almost morally equivalent with mass murder, Kamm laid out why punishing China in this way would "badly destabilize Hong Kong." In addition to threatening major economic losses—billions in trade and tens of thousands of jobs—he reframed this British colony as a bastion of U.S. influence in Asia. He emphasized that there were 900 U.S. firms employing 250,000 people in Hong Kong. He underscored that the colony was the fourteenth largest export market for U.S. goods and services and that each resident annually purchased more than US$1,000 of U.S. goods, far more per capita than either Europeans or Japanese. If Congress were to remove MFN, he argued it would be throwing all this onto a pyre: "Ruining Hong Kong—and make no doubt about it, ruining Hong Kong—will engender deep resentment and, yes, anti-Americanism in one of the most pro-American cities in the world." And if supposedly Hong Kong's entire future were not weighty enough, Kamm framed the colony as Washington's best chance to change China: "If we're on the side of the reformers, then we must renew MFN. We must seek them out and do more not less business with them." Urging Americans to do "business" with "reformers" conveniently conflated political and commercial actors, while Kamm asserted that "Hong Kong is a force for democracy and reform in China," even though the territory has never been a democracy. The conclusion was clear, though. MFN needed to be renewed both "for the sake of Hong Kong and the reform movement in China."[122] Despite questionable conflations, it was a brilliant rhetorical strategy that played into historically rooted American ambitions to change China. Kamm did it by pragmatically exploiting the right networks and Hong Kong's interstitial position, collapsing the distinction between its interests and U.S. interests. This kuashang strategy also dovetailed with Washington's increasingly bipartisan neoliberalism. In effect, he and AmCham argued that the path to improved Chinese human rights lay not in principles but in profit. For members of Congress, this counsel was welcome. Committee chairman Stephen Solarz (D-New York) expressed the deep impression that Kamm's testimony made on him.

A week later, on May 24, 1990, the Bush administration announced its intention to renew China's MFN status and, crucially, seized on Hong Kong as a reason. As Kamm pointed out to AmCham members, "not a single word" had previously been spoken about Hong Kong in this debate.[123] Now, Press Secretary Marlin Fitzwater picked up Kamm's language and argued that revoking MFN would harm U.S. interests, deprive millions of Chinese of their "stake in China's market-oriented reforms," and "deliver a terrible blow to Hong Kong."[124] Bush himself stated succinctly: "Hong Kong weighed on my mind. Hong Kong would be an innocent victim of our dispute with Beijing."[125] After Bush formally recommended the waiver to Congress on June 2, Congress had until fall to override. In October the Democratic-controlled House first passed a bill to repeal China's MFN status and then voted to maintain it but attach new human rights conditions. The Senate did not take it up. As a result, by fall 1990 the U.S.-oriented business community in Hong Kong was claiming a pivotal role in steering U.S. policy: "AmCham won a great victory for Hong Kong this past May. . . . Our mayday signals were acknowledged and heeded as is obvious in President Bush's having singled out the economic health of the territory as one of the bases upon which his MFN renewal decision was made."[126] Secretary of Commerce Robert Mosbacher also cited the delegation's influence over President Bush's decision when speaking at an AmCham luncheon in July.[127]

We know that Bush made his decision long before Kamm's testimony, but the perception that AmCham helped frame the argument and secure MFN renewal led the General Chamber and the HKTDC to join forces when the issue returned in spring 1991. As fate would have it, Paul Cheng had been elected vice-chairman of the General Chamber, and Victor Fung had been elected vice-chairman of the HKTDC.[128] Once again there was another steady drumbeat of warnings. Gordon Wu's old backer, HSBC chairman William Purves, predicted that the loss of China's MFN status would reduce Hong Kong's GDP by 2 percent and eliminate 35,000–45,000 jobs. University of Chicago–educated CUHK economist Richard Wong Yue-chim (王于漸) anticipated that it would divert investment to Singapore, Malaysia, and Thailand, undermining Hong Kong's long-term competitiveness.[129] With the rising temperature, AmCham, the General Chamber, and the HKTDC worked in tandem to form an even larger structural fold and maximize their American social capital. Cheng told the press that the three groups were carefully coordinating all their meetings in Washington in order to maximize their personal contacts and avoid scheduling conflicts. AmCham's delegation would lead, followed by the General Chamber and finally the HKTDC.[130] And once again underscoring the role of education in these transpacific networks, the General Chamber delegation featured only U.S.-educated leaders, from Cheng and the aforementioned Raymond Ch'ien to the Northeastern and Harvard graduate David Chu (朱幼麟). The General Chamber delegation left on May 17 and continued reiterating the same dire warnings that Kamm had made the year before.[131] Cheng declared the battle would "be fought to the bitter end."[132]

In reality, kuashang strategies had already succeeded in injecting Hong Kong's economic future and imagined liberalizing potential into the U.S. debate over China's human rights. As a result, on June 3, 1991, President Bush again cited Hong Kong when issuing his waiver. Upon returning from Washington a few days later, Cheng proclaimed that he was "content with this journey's results."[133] He also began toning down his rhetoric. Addressing the General Chamber on June 6, he reincorporated some nuances. He declared that local industrialists "need not worry or rush to withdraw funds" from the mainland and scaled back his predictions of Hong Kong's potential losses if MFN were revoked.[134] In the meantime, he urged the General Chamber's U.S. citizens to write to their members of Congress and announced his intention to hire Washington lobbyists. Underscoring the ongoing evolution of kuashang strategies, though, a few weeks later Cheng and the General Chamber's chairman also commenced annual missions to Beijing to network and lobby senior officials.[135] In July, once the U.S. Senate again failed to consider a House bill attaching human rights conditions to China's MFN status, Cheng announced that his sights were now set on China's admission to GATT, which would obviate this whole issue.[136] Congress continued renewing China's MFN status annually until making it permanent in 1995. Each year familiar figures such as Cheng and Fung returned at the head of a phalanx of Hong Kong organizations, wielding their collective American social capital.[137] Cheng even declared that Hong Kong was the one "honest broker" between the two giants.[138] In reality, its business leaders had long been implementing their own agenda.

Around 1984 senior PRC officials and Hong Kong elites made a bargain. Their accord shaped the future of the territory, China's development, and global capitalism itself. In exchange for autonomy after 1997, Hong Kong elites agreed not to execute the exit strategies that they had prepared since the communist transition. In return, they would midwife China's reintegration into global capitalism. As figures such as Jack Tang, Marjorie Yang, Gordon Wu, and Paul Cheng underscore, this "United Front" was mutually beneficial and enabled both opportunists and patriots to exploit China's reforms. As a result, between the signing of the Joint Declaration in December 1984 and the MFN debates of the early 1990s, the colony anchored massive inflows of investment into southern China and rising outflows of goods through Hong Kong to the U.S. and world markets. These flows fueled Shenzhen and the Pearl River delta's emergence into a manufacturing powerhouse and garnered crucial foreign exchange, know-how, and technology for China. The U.S. political reaction to the Tiananmen Square Massacre, however, was the most serious threat to this ecosystem since the U.S. embargo in 1950. Hong Kong's diverse U.S.-oriented elites exercised their collective kuashang strategies and American social capital to inject Hong Kong's economic interests into the center of Sino-U.S. relations. By framing the colony as an innocent bystander and the best hope for American fantasies to change China, they steered the rhetoric of the Bush administration and many hearts in Congress. Having thrice declined to revoke or attach conditions to China's MFN status, Congress became even less likely to do so after Deng's "Southern Tour" of 1992 signaled the revival of reform.

In this way, as the Soviet Union disintegrated and the first Gulf War solidified a new era of U.S. hegemony, Hong Kong elites' kuashang strategies played their own key role in setting conditions in the post–Cold War Pacific and advancing a truly global capitalism. Many scholars have cited China's admission to the World Trade Organization in 2001 as the key benchmark in the rapid expansion of Sino-U.S. trade, but that was the endpoint of a much longer process. Hong Kong business elites had been laying groundwork for China's reintegration into global capitalism since the 1970s. Their efforts to defend China's MFN status in the early 1990s helped overcome the last major challenge to that prospect. By 1992, under Jiang Zemin's leadership, construction resumed on Gordon Wu's expressway, and the Pudong Development Zone opened in Shanghai. In March 1993 the Fourteenth Party Congress amended China's constitution and declared the country to be a "socialist market economy," a major ideological leap toward reform.[139] By the mid-1990s it was estimated that fifty thousand companies in Hong Kong were managing supply chains that incorporated China.[140] That did not occur solely because of the decisions of China's senior leaders or even just because Hong Kong existed. It occurred because of Hong Kong people's own histories, networks, and strategies.

Conclusion

As June 30 turned to July 1, 1997, millions around the world watched on television as the United Kingdom ceded its last major colony to the People's Republic of China. It featured fireworks, royalty, and grave officials extoling proud legacies in the rain. The Hong Kong handover was the made-for-television finale of both the British Empire and China's "century of humiliations."

Although emotions ran high, the handover was carefully staged theater. Its treaties and ceremonies were negotiated solely by Beijing and London and gave each key prizes. For the United Kingdom, the handover offered a dignified exit and fueled its public's fantasies that empire had stood for development and the rule of law, not blood and plunder. For the PRC, the handover was an invaluable symbol of national unity amid seismic change. From a countdown clock in Tiananmen Square to hit pop songs and films, the handover received blanket coverage in China. Internationally, this smooth transition of power helped to rehabilitate the Chinese Communist Party's image after the carnage of June 4, 1989.[1]

No one ever asked ordinary Hong Kong people whether they wished to "return" to China. That was because British colonial rule was never democratic, and Beijing would not have allowed it. In probably a first for empire, if the territory's permanent residents had been allowed to vote, the outcome would almost certainly have been an extension of British administration.[2] Yet it was not solely the expiration of the New Territories'

[279]

ninety-nine-year lease nor Chinese nationalism that demanded the "recovery" of Hong Kong. Even a patriot as fervent as Mao Zedong had not thought Hong Kong terribly important, stating in the late 1940s: "I am not interested in Hong Kong; the Communist Party is not interested in Hong Kong, it has never been the subject of any discussion amongst us."[3] Yet two key things had changed since 1949: Hong Kong had emerged as a first-rank node in global capitalism, and the PRC had initiated market-oriented reforms. Over the 1970s and 1980s it became self-evident that Hong Kong could provide invaluable assistance to China's development. It was the goose that laid the golden eggs.

Underscoring that Hong Kong's development assistance was a chief concern, the CCP consulted seriously with only one local constituency before 1997: its oligarchs. Yet, as seen in this book, Hong Kong elites had been building transpacific networks and securing exit strategies since 1949. As Jack Tang's 1984 meeting with Deng encapsulated (chapter 8), that transnational mobility had functioned as leverage to ensure that Hong Kong retained genuine autonomy after 1997, at least for a time. As a result, while hundreds of thousands of middle-class families migrated to Canada, Australia, and elsewhere, the territory's business leaders largely welcomed the handover, confident that it would bring them exclusive opportunities to continue exploiting China's reforms from within their gated community. Fittingly, the newly rebranded Hong Kong Special Administrative Region (HKSAR) would not even have a governor or minister but a chief executive picked by a stacked nominating committee. The first was Tung Chee-hwa. His selection provides an apt coda.

In chapter 6 I noted how Tung's father, shipping baron C. Y. Tung, became U.S.-oriented around 1960. Suddenly the elder Tung had rehoned both his business strategies and his children's pathways toward the United States. While the Tung children all gradually went there, Orient Overseas opened a transpacific passenger service that earned C. Y. Tung a key to New York City. And when U.S. firm Sea-Land introduced container shipping to Hong Kong, he rushed to keep up by recalling his sons from the United States in 1969. He passed away in 1982, and Chee-hwa assumed the reins. Yet the early 1980s downturn in the global economy significantly hurt the shipping industry and put OOCL into serious financial trouble. Like the TAL Group in the 1970s, OOCL had funded rapid expansion by taking on colossal amounts of debt—later estimated at US$2.68 billion. The recession made this debt unserviceable. Tung warned

OOCL shareholders in June 1983 that the shipping industry had entered a downturn and recovery might take years.[4] By 1986, however, the company was hemorrhaging over US$100 million a year.[5] One Saturday that spring, Tung phoned upstairs to his neighbor and friend, Jack Tang. He asked if he could come up after dinner. Jack was an outside director on OOCL's board, and Tung informed him that he would soon announce the group's insolvency. He recommended that Tang retain a lawyer, as he might have exposure. By Tang's account, he replied that he knew what was involved from "my business school days" at Harvard Business School but did not need a lawyer, claiming Chinese culture prevented him from deserting his friend "at his darkest moment."[6] More cynically, we should question what Tung really advised Tang to do.

Once the news went public that OOCL might implode, Tung began dizzyingly complex negotiations with more than seventy international banks in an effort to restructure the group's debt and secure new capital. In Tang's recollection, those negotiations hinged on the Bank of Tokyo and the Industrial Bank of Japan. At first "those two banks said no. They could have pulled the rug." The latter eventually agreed to consider additional loans if Tung could muster support from Beijing. Once again underscoring how social capital molds global capital flows, Tung reached out to two familiar figures, Henry Fok and Xu Jiatun. While once Lawrence Kadoorie (chapter 5) had used old American friends from Shanghai to arrange a meeting in New York with the Esso chairman, now Tung used pro-Beijing locals to arrange his Hail Mary investment. A few weeks later, on May 16, Tung met with OOCL's creditors and proposed that the group split in two, forming the New Container Group (新貨櫃集團) and the Tung Tanker and Bulk Carrier Group (董氏油輪及散裝貨輪集團). A Tung family holding fund would own the latter and 90 percent of OOCL's ordinary shares. In turn, OOCL would be an investor in the New Container Group, alongside an investment of US$100 million from Fok.[7] As the creditors studied this proposal, Yuan Geng (chapter 7) announced that CMSN would buy one of OOCL's subsidiaries for HK$170 million.[8] Tung and Fok formally signed the restructuring deal for US$120 million in September 1986, with Fok claiming his investment was a "commercial action" to get the group back on its feet.[9] In reality, he was just a front—or "a Communist fat cat," in Tang's blunt description.[10] Fok did not invest anything. He was simply a passthrough for cash from the Bank of China and CMSN. This PRC infusion was hardly enough to resolve OOCL's debts but staved off collapse and allowed Tung to reorganize a reduced operation.[11] In turn, Beijing acquired not only a stake in a global shipping company but also a loyal client in Tung.

The Orient Overseas bailout both further exemplifies the bargain analyzed in chapter 8 and returns us to the Tang quote that opened this study. You might lose money or power, but specific and elite social capital could hold greater long-term value. After losing most of their material assets during the communist transition, the émigrés had repeatedly survived by falling back on their mobile American social capital. Maintained and expanded through kuashang strategies, these elites' transpacific networks had provided repeated opportunities to get back on their feet, revive or start new businesses, and secure their family members' educations and exit strategies. While the Tangs had received "overdrafts" from the SCSB and used U.S. military and HBS alumni networks for marketing, others had collaborated covertly with proxies of the U.S. government, called in favors from old American or American-returned-student friends, or even hired such brokers as H. J. Shen (chapter 5). Through their renovations of local educational systems, these kuashang had artificially naturalized these strategies among the upwardly mobile and guided Hong Kong society to straddle the giant "structural hole" of the Pacific.

Tung Chee-hwa's use of privileged connections to rescue OOCL in 1986 was thus nothing new. What was comparatively new was the source of the investment. By acting through its own "state-private network," Beijing had begun to buy influence in Hong Kong much as Washington had in the 1950s and 1960s through figures such as David Au (chapter 3), Li Choh-ming (chapter 4), and Francis Pan (chapter 5). Indeed, Tung was not alone. By 1986 Ka Wah Bank was also on the verge of bankruptcy, and together C. S. Low and the Lam family (chapters 3 and 6) sold a 74 percent equity stake to CITIC (chapter 7).[12] Hong Kong elites were ever-sensitive barometers of shifts in the international terrain of power. Thus they did not shun Tung for what might be seen as an embarrassing business failure but instead pragmatically extended him new honors. For example, in January 1987 the Yeh family (chapter 5) suddenly invited him onto the board of their Hsin Chong Construction Group, alongside Kenneth Ting (chapter 6) and yet another cousin of Ansie Lee Sperry (chapter 1).[13] By inviting him, the Yeh family was not just backing up Tung. Now U.S.-educated for three generations, the Yehs were rebalancing their strategies and currying favor with Beijing.

Although an extreme case, Tung Chee-hwa nonetheless illustrates how kuashang strategies continued evolving through the 1997 handover. What had originated in the 1950s among predominantly anticommunist émigrés as urgent strategies of transplantation and survival had morphed into a powerful network centrality between two giants: the world's largest source of labor power and the world's largest consumer market. Despite personal anticommunism, Hong Kong elites had begun experimenting with China's low-cost labor in the 1970s. Their kuashang strategies then evolved with Deng Xiaoping's reforms and the handover bargain. As these developments aligned, Hong Kong businesses enveloped more and more mainland labor into their transpacific ecosystem, and kuashang elites rebalanced their network strategies between China and the United States, bridging both the production and the sales ends of their commodity chains. As a result, after Tiananmen they collectively leveraged their American social capital to defend China's access to the U.S. market. In turn, Beijing rewarded this leverage, as Tung Chee-hwa's selection underscores. It was not just that he owed them or would be loyal. Many Hong Kong elites could meet that requirement, such as Henry Fok. As Sze-yuen Chung pointed out, there were also more relevant civil servants with actual experience in running a government, such as Anson Chan (陳方安生) or the future chief executive Donald Tsang (曾蔭權).[14] Instead, another reason that Beijing handpicked Tung was his wide-ranging connections both among Hong Kong elites and in the United States. Throughout the 1990s he had distinguished himself as a member of Chris Patten's cabinet and as head of the Hong Kong–U.S. Economic Cooperation Committee, for which he made numerous trips to Washington to lobby on behalf of Sino-U.S. trade. Through these trips the adopted San Franciscan repeatedly demonstrated the value of his "personal connections with representatives in both the Senate and Congress," such as California senator Dianne Feinstein.[15] In turn, after the handover Tung's first major overseas trip as chief executive was to Washington for meetings with the Clinton administration and on Capitol Hill.[16]

Simultaneously, the same elite clusters began ramping up their political networking in Beijing. Familiar kuashang such as Tung Chee-hwa, Victor Fung, Marjorie Yang, and Hong Kong Baptist president Daniel Tse followed Gordon Wu's lead in the 1990s by accepting invitations to join the Chinese People's Political Consultative Conference. Although a purely advisory body, CPPCC membership is prestigious and carries favored access in Beijing. Through informal dialogue and behind-the-scenes meetings, members can engage with senior officials, advise on policies, and lobby for state favors and contracts. Like U.S. degrees or collaboration with Washington's state-private network during the Cold War, CPPCC membership opens up new networks and advertises Hong Kong elites' collaborations with the new power center. Others, such as Tung, Paul Cheng, and William Fung, also served on the Preparatory Committee for the Hong Kong Special Administrative Region, established by the PRC to prepare for 1997. As such, they traveled monthly to Beijing between 1994 and 1997 "to discuss key transition issues with Chinese officials."[17] Many members of the Preparatory Committee rolled over onto the Selection Committee that confirmed Tung as chief executive.

Thus many kuashang strategists have long since evolved to straddle the PRC and U.S. political communities in ways that are not just cultural or social but also legal. This latter form of straddling is possible only because, just before 1997, Beijing opened an overlooked path for elite Hong Kong people to enjoy dual citizenship. Back in 1980 the Third Session of the Fifth National People's Congress had passed China's first new nationality law since 1929. This law redefined the right to PRC nationality by whether either of an individual's parents was a Chinese national and/or both parents were "settled in China." Any person of Chinese descent born in Hong Kong was also deemed a Chinese national. Yet this law forbade dual citizenship, including the automatic loss of PRC nationality if a citizen were naturalized overseas. The next year Parliament passed the British Nationality Act of 1981, which denied Hong Kong people full British nationality and instead offered the second-class British National Overseas (BNO) passport. Although the BNO did not entitle recipients to live or work in the United Kingdom, about half of Hong Kong people—about three million residents—still applied between its 1985 debut and 1997. In Beijing, the Politburo's Standing Committee rejected this passport and any naturalization of Hong Kong Chinese as British citizens. Just before the handover, however, the Standing Committee reclarified: those Hong Kong people who were "Chinese nationals . . . with right of abode in foreign countries" could continue to hold those "travel documents," although they would "not be entitled to consular protection" within China.[18] Through the euphemism of "travel documents," the Standing Committee quietly exempted Hong Kong residents with non-British foreign passports from the automatic loss of PRC nationality. As such, Beijing opened an exceptionally privileged loophole for Hong Kong elites to keep both PRC nationality and primarily U.S., Canadian, Australian, and New Zealand passports. This exemption has helped facilitate Hong Kong's continued role in China's development and yet privileges Hong Kong people over mainland people and Hong Kong elites over ordinary residents. Almost all decision makers in the HKSAR today hold international passports, with even Chief Executive Carrie Lam's family's British passports coming under recent scrutiny.

Yet by 1997 kuashang strategies were also increasingly indistinguishable from the broader neoliberal turn in Sino-U.S. relations. Continued economic and educational integration and the active use of elite networks were now routine aspects of this bilateral relationship. For example, we might look at the Committee of 100 (C-100). Purportedly, Henry Kissinger first suggested to I. M. Pei at a dinner party in 1987 that elite Chinese Americans form an organization to promote intercultural relations and understanding. After Tiananmen, Pei joined with Yo-Yo Ma, investment banker Henry S. Tang, executive Shirley Young, nuclear physicist Chien-Shiung Wu, and Jack Tang's brother Oscar Tang to found C-100. Its founders were shocked by June 4 but feared the U.S. political reaction would short-circuit China's reforms. As such, C-100 framed itself as a nonpartisan body with a dual mission: to promote constructive Sino-U.S. relations and represent the Chinese American community. These laudable goals, however, were inextricable from elite social capital trading. Pei, Ma, and Oscar Tang all came from elite émigré families, while membership in C-100 remains by-invitation only. Alongside the rich and famous of the Chinese American community, many members are U.S.-naturalized kuashang, from Victor Fung and Ronnie Chan to sixth CUHK vice-chancellor Lawrence Lau (劉遵義).[19] When C-100 hosted its first conference in Hong Kong in 2005, it was entitled "Bridging the Pacific" and Tung Chee-hwa wrote a dedication.[20] In short, while promoting a valuable agenda such as educational scholarships, C-100's membership and activities embody how Sino-U.S. business and educational relationships continued to flourish after Tiananmen: by relying on elite-to-elite relationships and consciously sidestepping politics, human rights, deindustrialization, and everything else contentious or unprofitable. In short, we might say that the older Hong Kong history of kuashang strategies became subsumed within a broader neoliberal turn in Sino-U.S. relations that these strategies helped make possible in the first place.

Higher education again played a key role in this neoliberal turn. Just as kuashang strategies had become artificially naturalized in Hong Kong through educational choices, Hong Kong's transpacific networks also molded China's new educational path. As the founding dean of Tsinghua's School of Economics and Management (TSEM) and later the premier of China, Zhu Rongji (朱镕基) began exploring potential partnerships with U.S. business schools in the late 1980s. His colleague and TSEM associate dean Zhao Chunjun (赵纯均) found the right partner in 1995 while studying at MIT's Sloan School of Management on a Fulbright. At Zhao's instigation, Sloan approached Tsinghua later that year about a formal exchange program. A potential sticking point emerged, however, over funding. C-100 leader Shirley Young cautioned against the strings that would accompany government funding, so MIT instead tapped into its wealthy alumni networks in Hong Kong. Associate Dean Alan White discussed the matter with Philip Kwok (chapter 8), who in turn roped in Marjorie Yang. Yang was extremely enthusiastic, and the principal funding for the MIT-China Management Education Project came from kuashang families, including the Yangs, Kwoks, Tangs, and Fungs. As a result, Tsinghua and MIT were able to sign a Memorandum of Understanding in fall 1995, and the MIT-China Project has remained instrumental in expanding and enriching the MBA programs now offered at Tsinghua, Fudan, Lingnan, and Yunnan Universities.[21] They offer U.S.-modeled, Hong Kong-financed business education for the future leaders of the twenty-first-century People's Republic.

As stated in the introduction, Hong Kong was practically the only society to move from the so-called Third World to the First over the Cold War without exploiting petroleum or achieving national independence. As such, I have argued that we need to understand Hong Kong's development on its own terms in order to gain a new perspective on the evolution of U.S.-led global capitalism and China's reintegration into that system. In so doing, I have homed in on the strategies of figures that I label as *kuashang* or "straddling merchants." Their pragmatic, multigenerational strategies to exploit British imperial decline, U.S. imperial expansion, and Hong Kong's interstitial position in the Cold War allowed them to build integrative business and educational relationships with first the United States and then China. They illustrate that Hong Kong's rapid but highly unequal development was inseparable from longer histories of inherited privilege, strategic imperial collaboration, transpacific educational circulations, and instrumental network building.

In contrast to laissez-faire orthodoxies, East Asian "tiger" models, or fantasies of sheer hard work, Hong Kong's success was neither preordained nor a "miracle." It was primarily the product of intersecting and contingent historical events such as the restoration of British colonial rule, the outcome of the Chinese civil war, the transplantation of both elite and ordinary "refugees," and the provisions of opportunity created by U.S. imperial expansion in the western Pacific. While not the only factors in Hong Kong's economic success, these elements created an increasingly unusual political and economic space from which the previously overlooked kuashang could utilize their accumulated social capital to circulate within the U.S.-led Pacific and plug themselves into the world's largest economy. They adapted to the U.S. embargo by working with the Certificate of Origins system and recruiting American partners, investors, and clients. They collaborated with U.S. Cold War agendas in order to seed new educational institutions and helped others access new transpacific opportunities. They closely monitored the U.S. consumer market by dispatching their children to U.S. higher education and continuously adapting their business models to new American trends. These U.S.-oriented economic and educational endeavors advanced an informal decolonization that left British rule in place but carved new forms of social and economic power out from under it. By the 1970s tiny Hong Kong was both the world's largest sender of foreign students to the United States and the largest exporter of textiles and apparel to the U.S. market. These enormous transpacific circulations enabled Hong Kong to pull itself toward the metaphorical center and enabled yet another transformation into the primary broker of China's reintegration into global capitalism before 1997.

I have thus framed higher education and its entwined mobilities and social capital as major factors in historical economic change. This approach is interwoven with the realization that widening inequality is not just an after-effect of capitalist globalization, as we often hear today. Examining the kuashang allows us to understand that current inequalities have been shaped, maintained, and widened by older and enduring hierarchies of power. Across the postcolonial and so-called Third worlds, particular elites experienced decolonization and globalization with vastly greater opportunities—not just because they held wealth or political power, but often because they had privileged educations and the ensuing networks.

The individuals whom I label as kuashang were overwhelmingly from such backgrounds. Their parents were Republican-era industrialists, bankers, merchants, and scholars who routinely prioritized their children's attendance in American missionary or U.S. institutions. Often it was their parents who first grasped that such education was important not only for "modern" knowledge but also for the acquisition of useful networks, credentials, behaviors, and later citizenships. As such, for generations these mobile Chinese elites pursued economic strategies in which U.S. colleges and universities functioned as key pieces.

I would conclude by offering an unexpected historical parallel to this book's arguments. The transpacific circulations and networks that linked Hong Kong with the United States during the Cold War evoke a comparison that nonetheless underscores how "small" places can capitalize on the power and markets of "large" imperial-states. In *The Long Twentieth Century*, world-systems sociologist Giovanni Arrighi argued that today's global capitalist system evolved from the late 1300s through a sequence of periods termed "long centuries." Building on the work of Joseph Schumpeter, Immanuel Wallerstein, Fernand Braudel, and Eric Hobsbawm, Arrighi defined each long century by its hegemonic center of capital accumulation: first the northern Italian city-states, then Holland, Britain, and, most recently, the United States. The transition period between each hegemonic center was marked first by a "signal" crisis and then by a "terminal" crisis, usually moments of political conflict and/or economic distress.

In the first long century, multiple Italian city-states such as Florence and Venice were centers of trade and capital, but Arrighi argued that Genoa in particular developed new tactics of capitalism that subordinated the state to mercantile interests. This subordination grew out of strategic necessity and gave birth to new forms of high finance that funded the rise of Spanish power. In particular, during the late fourteenth and early fifteenth centuries, there was dramatically intensified warfare and competition in Europe, from the Hundred Years' War (1337–1453) to what Braudel termed the "Italian" Hundred Years' War (1350–1454). In the wake of the apocalyptic Black Death (1346–1353), Europe's kingdoms now depended on liquid forms of capital to organize reduced human resources and sustain prolonged war making. This reliance intensified systems of long-distance capital movement and gave birth to new innovations in its use. For Genoa, these crises were particularly acute. After the collapse of the Eurasian

Mongolian Empire and its trade systems in the mid-1300s and Venice's seizure of its eastern Mediterranean trade routes after the Peace of Turin (1381), Genoa began devoting its surplus capital to securing new "'protection-producing' partners" and finding oceanic pathways to Asia. In pursuing both goals, Genoese merchants grasped that their interests were best achieved by enmeshing their capital and expertise with the western Mediterranean's rising power, the dual monarchy of Aragon and Castile. Genoa's Iberian enmeshment—including a Genoese mercantile diaspora into Spanish cities after Jewish expulsions—resolved the city-state's "serious and chronic disproportion between . . . its huge reserves of money, information, business know-how, and connections, and, on the other side, its meager capabilities to protect itself and its traffics in an increasingly competitive and hostile world." Instead, after the Spanish invasion of the Americas, Genoa organized and managed the ensuing silver flows into Seville. It was Genoese merchants who exchanged Spanish galleons' American silver for gold and made liquid capital available to Spanish forces in their costly conflicts in the Low Countries. This "Genoese 'gamble' on Castilian trade" was a key ingredient in the organization of the new Atlantic economy and the larger European financial expansion of the late sixteenth and early seventeenth centuries.[22]

The kuashang strategies of Hong Kong elites display key parallels with Genoa's experience. In the wake of the Second World War and the ensuing power struggle with the Soviet Union and the PRC, the United States promoted an unprecedented expansion in global trade and finance through the Marshall Plan (1948–1951), the Occupation of Japan (1945–1952), and the Bretton Woods system. For Hong Kong, these developments posed great uncertainty. Politically tied to the unraveling British Empire, it was not a client-state of Washington and not automatically protected or destined to benefit from U.S. aid. Moreover, the U.S. and UN embargoes on the PRC in 1950–1951 disrupted the colony's traditional entrepôt economy, much as Genoa was severed from its traditional trades during the mid-1300s. Yet, like Genoa, Hong Kong possessed tremendous other assets and advantages. In particular, before its traditional trades collapsed, the colony gained two well-paired resources: the knowledge, capital, and connections of elite émigrés and the low-cost labor of hundreds of thousands of ordinary migrants.

Hong Kong's rapid industrialization and codevelopment with the U.S. market was the result—its version of Genoa's pivot toward the power of

Spain. This profitable pivot generated enormous capital accumulation in Hong Kong that had few outlets. China's relative inaccessibility under Mao Zedong, violent turmoil in Southeast Asia, and protectionism across South Korea, Taiwan, and Japan all made scarce the regional opportunities for the profitable export of capital. Crucially, like the Genoese before them, Hong Kong elites were not interested in turning their capital into state or empire making. Instead, they sought to cross oceans and reach ever-higher levels of the global economy. Thus, to repurpose a quotation by Braudel that was also used by Arrighi, Hong Kong—like Genoa before it—had

> to live forever on the *qui-vive*, obliged to take risks and at the same time to exercise great prudence. . . . Time after time, Genoa [Hong Kong] changed course, accepting on each occasion the need for another metamorphosis. . . . Such was the destiny of Genoa [Hong Kong], a fragile creation and ultra-sensitive seismograph, whose needle quivered whenever there were stirrings in the rest of the world. A monster of intelligence—and of hard-heartedness if necessary—was Genoa [Hong Kong] not doomed to eat or be eaten?[23]

The kuashang invested in transpacific trade and production relationships, labored to ensure their children acquired the same skills and networks through U.S. higher education and work experiences, and, crucially, helped others to follow them through the renovation of Hong Kong higher education. Like Genoa's Iberian diaspora, these elites enmeshed themselves with the biggest "protection-producing partner" and became a linchpin in the enmeshment of Asia and North America.

For Hong Kong, the shifts in great-power relations that led to restored Sino-U.S. relations in 1979 and the Sino-British Joint Declaration of 1984 were as momentous an opportunity as the Spanish colonization of the Americas was for Genoa. With strong ties spanning the United States and China, kuashang such as the Fung brothers, Marjorie Yang, and Gordon Wu enabled and guided the development of Sino-U.S. trade, working to pair the world's largest labor supply with the world's largest consumer market. Multigenerational products of Hong Kong's interstitial Cold War history, they and thousands like them were leading architects of today's Sino-U.S. trade and educational relationships. Without them, we cannot understand the origins of the new "long century" in global capitalism: a dual-star system of Sino-U.S. codependence and rivalry.

Abbreviations in Notes

AFF	Asia Foundation Files
ATLU	Archives of the Trustees of Lingnan University
BCAH	Briscoe Center for American History
CHLP	Choh Hao Li Papers
CM	*China Mail*
CMP	Carter Morgan Papers
CTSP	Carl T. Smith Papers
CWR	*China Weekly Review*
DHKB	*Dictionary of Hong Kong Biography*
EMHC	ExxonMobil Historical Collection
HISU	Hoover Institution, Stanford University
HKBUL	Hong Kong Baptist University Library
HKCID	Hong Kong Commerce and Industry Department
HKHP	Hong Kong Heritage Project
HKMBM	Hong Kong-Macau 眾 Baptist Mission
HKRS	Hong Kong Record Series
HKS	*Hongkong Star*
HKTS	*Hongkong Tiger Standard*
HKUSC	University of Hong Kong Libraries, Special Collections
HKUST	Hong Kong University of Science and Technology
HYL	Harvard-Yenching Library
IIE	Institute of International Education
KPC	Kwang Pu Chen Papers
KSWP	*Kong Sheung Wan Bo*
KSYP	*Kong Sheung Yat Po*

MHDB	Modern History Databases, Academia Sinica
MRFE	*Millard's Review of the Far East*
NAUK	National Archives of the United Kingdom, Kew
NCHSCCG	*North-China Herald and Supreme Court & Consular Gazette*
PSRA	Papers of Sidney R. Anderson
RBLC	Rare Book and Library Collections, Columbia University
RSCLDC	Rauner Special Collections Library, Dartmouth College
SCMP	*South China Morning Post*
SCMPHKT	*South China Morning Post & Hongkong Telegraph*
SoSC	Secretary of State for the Colonies
STYP	*Sing Tao Yat Po*
TKP	*Ta Kung Pao*
WKYP	*Wah Kiu Yat Po*
WWP	*Wen Wei Po*
UB	*University Bulletin*
UBCHEA	United Board for Christian Higher Education in Asia
USITC	U.S. International Trade Commission
UT Austin	University of Texas at Austin
YCA	Yale-China Association
YUDSL	Yale University Divinity School Library
YUMA	Yale University Library Manuscripts & Archives

Notes

Introduction. Made in Hong Kong

1. Chris Patten, *East and West* (Basingstoke, UK: Macmillan, 1998), 21.
2. See, for example, Milton Friedman, "The Real Lesson of Hong Kong," speech at the University of Chicago, May 14, 1997; Milton Friedman and Rose D. Friedman, *Free to Choose: A Personal Statement* (1979; New York: Houghton Mifflin, 1990), 34, 37, 39, 40–41, 50, 57, 60.
3. For China's statistics, see World Bank, "World Integrated Trade Solution: "China Trade Statistics: Exports, Imports, Products, Tariffs, GDP, and Related Development Indicator," https://wits.worldbank.org/CountryProfile/en/CHN, accessed September 20, 2019. For U.S. statistics, see U.S. Census Bureau, "Foreign Trade: Top Trading Partners," https://www.census.gov/foreign-trade/statistics/highlights/top/index.html#2015, accessed September 20, 2019.
4. International Institute of Education (IIE), "Open Doors 2019: Places of Origin," https://www.iie.org/Research-and-Insights/Open-Doors/Data/International-Students/Places-of-Origin.
5. Yun-wing Sung, "The Hong Kong Economy Through the 1997 Barrier," *Asian Survey* 37, no. 9 (August 1997): 705–19.
6. I define the communist transition as beginning with the resumption of civil war in 1946 and ending with the Five Antis campaign of 1952.
7. William C. Kirby, "Continuity and Change in Modern China: Economic Planning on the Mainland and on Taiwan, 1943-1958," *Australian Journal of Chinese Affairs* 24 (1990): 121–41.
8. For a comparative study of Rangoon, Penang, and Bangkok in the interwar years, see Su Lin Lewis, *Cities in Motion: Urban Life and Cosmopolitanism in Southeast Asia, 1920–1940* (Cambridge: Cambridge University Press, 2016).

9. Elizabeth Sinn, *Pacific Crossing: California Gold, Chinese Migration, and the Making of Hong Kong* (Hong Kong: Hong Kong University Press, 2013).

10. Daniel Chirot and Anthony Reid, eds., *Essential Outsiders: Chinese and Jews in the Modern Transformation of Southeast Asia and Central Europe* (Seattle: University of Washington Press, 1997); Philip Kuhn, *Chinese Among Others: Emigration in Modern Times* (Lanham, Md.: Rowman & Littlefield, 2009).

11. On Hong Kong during the Second World War, see Philip Snow, *The Fall of Hong Kong: Britain, China, and the Japanese Occupation* (New Haven, Conn.: Yale University Press, 2003).

12. On the sequence of events leading to the restoration of British rule, see Wm. Roger Louis, "Hong Kong: The Critical Phase, 1945–1949," *American Historical Review* 102, no. 4 (October 1997): 1052–84.

13. On compradors, see Hao Yen-p'ing, *The Comprador in Nineteenth-Century China: Bridge Between East and West* (Cambridge, Mass.: Harvard University Press, 1970).

14. For late Qing and Republican-era financiers and industrialists, see Sherman Cochran, *Big Business in China: Sino-Foreign Rivalry in the Cigarette Industry, 1890–1930* (Cambridge, Mass..: Harvard Studies in Business History, 1980); Marie-Claire Bergère, *The Golden Age of the Chinese Bourgeoisie*, trans. Janet Lloyd (Cambridge: Cambridge University Press, 1989); Sherman Cochran, *Encountering Chinese Networks: Western, Japanese, and Chinese Corporations in China, 1880–1937* (Berkeley: University of California Press, 2000); Parks M. Coble, *Chinese Capitalists in Japan's New Order: The Occupied Lower Yangzi, 1937–1945* (Berkeley: University of California Press, 2003); Brett Sheehan, *Trust in Troubled Times: Money, Banks, and State-Society Relations in Republican Tianjin* (Cambridge, Mass.: Harvard University Press, 2003); Tomoko Shiroyama, *China During the Great Depression: Market, State, and the World Economy, 1929–1937* (Cambridge, Mass.: Harvard East Asian Monographs, 2008); Sherman Cochran and Andrew Hsieh, *The Lius of Shanghai* (Cambridge, Mass.: Harvard University Press, 2013); Sherman Cochran, ed., *The Capitalist Dilemma in China's Communist Revolution* (Ithaca, N.Y.: Cornell University East Asia Program, 2014); Brett Sheehan, *Industrial Eden: A Chinese Capitalist Vision* (Cambridge, Mass.: Harvard University Press, 2015).

15. To start, see Sara Lorenzini, *Global Development: A Cold War History* (Princeton, N.J.: Princeton University Press, 2019); Stephen Macekura, *Of Limits and Growth: The Rise of Global Sustainable Development in the Twentieth Century* (Cambridge: Cambridge University Press, 2015). Also see David C. Engerman, *The Price of Aid: The Economic Cold War in India* (Cambridge, Mass: Harvard University Press, 2018); Michael E. Latham, *The Right Kind of Revolution: Modernization, Development, and US Foreign Policy from the Cold War to the Present* (Ithaca, N.Y.: Cornell University Press, 2011); Nils Gilman, *Mandarins of the Future: Modernization Theory in Cold War America* (Baltimore: Johns Hopkins University Press, 2004); Michael E. Latham, *Modernization as Ideology: American Social Science and "Nation Building" in the Kennedy Era* (Chapel Hill: University of North Carolina Press, 2003).

16. Wong Siu-lun, *Emigrant Entrepreneurs: Shanghai Industrialists in Hong Kong* (Hong Kong: Oxford University Press, 1988), 42–46; Catherine R. Schenk, *Hong Kong as an*

International Financial Centre, Emergence and Development 1945–65 (London: Routledge Studies in the Growth Economies of Asia, 2001), 75, 142.

17. Schenk, *Hong Kong as an International Financial Centre*, 72–73.

18. Vanessa Ogle, "AHR Forum: Archipelago Capitalism: Tax Havens, Offshore Money, and the State, 1950s–1970s," *American Historical Review* 122, no. 5 (December 2017): 1433.

19. On Hong Kong's refugee crisis, see Laura Madokoro, *Elusive Refuge: Chinese Migrants in the Cold War* (Cambridge, Mass.: Harvard University Press, 2016); Madeline Y. Hsu, *The Good Immigrants: How the Yellow Peril Became the Model Minority* (Princeton, N.J.: Princeton University Press, 2015), 130–97; Meredith Oyen, *The Diplomacy of Migration: Transnational Lives and the Making of US-China Relations in the Cold War* (Ithaca, N.Y.: Cornell University Press, 2015), 154–84.

20. See Nancy Bernkopf Tucker, *Uncertain Friendships: Taiwan, Hong Kong, and the United States, 1945–1992* (New York: Twayne of Macmillan, 1994); Nancy Bernkopf Tucker, ed. *China Confidential: American Diplomats and Sino-American Relations, 1945–1996* (New York: Columbia University Press, 2001).

21. Helen Laville and Hugh Wilford, eds., *The US Government, Citizen Groups and the Cold War: The State-Private Network* (London: Routledge, 2006).

22. Chi-kwan Mark, *Hong Kong and the Cold War: Anglo-American Relations, 1949–1957* (Oxford: Oxford University Press, 2004).

23. Priscilla Roberts and John M. Carroll, eds., *Hong Kong in the Cold War* (Hong Kong: Hong Kong University Press, 2016).

24. Wong, *Emigrant Entrepreneurs*, 39–40, 42–56, 64–65, 74–75.

25. In thinking through "the imperial" as a method of analyzing long-distance asymmetries of power operating in nonterritorial and networked forms, I draw on Paul A. Kramer, "Power and Connection: Imperial Histories of the United States in the World," *American Historical Review* 116, no. 5 (December 2011): 1348–92.

26. See AnnaLee Saxenian, *The New Argonauts: Regional Advantage in a Global Economy* (Cambridge, Mass.: Harvard University Press, 2006); Aihwa Ong, *Flexible Citizenship: Cultural Logics of Transnationality* (Durham, N.C.: Duke University Press, 1999).

27. Ronald Robinson, "The Non-European Foundations of European Imperialism: Sketch for a Theory of Collaboration," in *Studies in the Theory of Imperialism*, ed. Roger Owen and Robert B. Sutcliffe (London: Longman, 1972), 117–42.

28. Ronald Robinson, "Imperial Theory and the Question of Imperialism after Empire," in *Perspectives on Imperialism and Decolonization: Essays in Honour of A. F. Madden*, ed. R. F. Holland and G. Rizvi (London: Routledge, 1984), 45.

29. For some key examples, see Wang Gungwu, *China and the Chinese Overseas* (Singapore: Times Academic Press, 2003); Huei-Ying Kuo, *Networks Beyond Empires: Chinese Business and Nationalism in the Hong Kong–Singapore Corridor, 1914–1941* (Leiden: Brill, 2014); John M. Carroll, *Edge of Empires: Chinese Elites and British Colonials in Hong Kong* (Cambridge, Mass.: Harvard University Press, 2005); Ong, *Flexible Citizenship*.

30. For several examples, see Liping Bu, *Making the World Like Us: Education, Cultural Expansion, and the American Century* (Westport, Conn.: Praeger, 2003); Andy Chih-ming Wang, *Transpacific Articulations: Student Migration and the Remaking of Asian America*

(Honolulu: University of Hawai'i Press, 2013); Sarah Steinbock-Pratt, *Educating the Empire: American Teachers and Contested Colonization in the Philippines* (Cambridge: Cambridge University Press, 2019).

31. For example, both Qing and Republican regulations directed Chinese scholarship students toward "practical" subjects. See Y. C. Wang, *Chinese Intellectuals and the West, 1872–1949* (Chapel Hill: University of North Carolina Press, 1966), 57–58.

32. For one study of expanding American systems in Europe, see Victoria de Grazia, *Irresistible Empire: America's Advance Through Twentieth-Century Europe* (Cambridge, Mass.: Harvard University Press, 2006).

33. Poshek Fu, "Between Nationalism and Colonialism: Mainland Émigrés, Marginal Culture, and Hong Kong Cinema, 1937–1941," in *The Cinema of Hong Kong: History, Arts, Identity*, ed. Poshek Fu and David Desser (Cambridge: Cambridge University Press, 2002), 199–201.

34. For more on this, see Jenny Kwok Wah Lau, "Besides Fist and Blood: Michael Hui and Cantonese Comedy," in *The Cinema of Hong Kong: History, Arts, Identity*, ed. Poshek Fu and David Desser (Cambridge: Cambridge University Press, 2002), 159, 166.

35. Ackbar Abbas, *Hong Kong: Culture and the Politics of Disappearance* (Minneapolis: University of Minnesota Press, 1997), 6.

36. For an introduction, see Ming Yu Cheng and Ron Mittelhammer, "Globalization and Economic Development: Impact of Social Capital and Institutional Building," *American Journal of Economics and Sociology* 67, no. 5 (November 2008): 859–88.

37. Pierre Bourdieu, *Distinction: A Social Critique of the Judgment of Taste*, trans. Richard Nice (1979; London: Routledge, 1984). His essay "The Forms of Capital" (1986) is more helpful to understand Bourdieu's distinctions between cultural, social, and economic capital. See Pierre Bourdieu, "The Forms of Capital," in *Handbook of Theory and Research for the Sociology of Education*, ed. John G. Richardson (New York: Greenwood, 1986), 241–58.

38. Pierre Bourdieu, *The State Nobility: Elite Schools in the Field of Power*, trans. Lauretta C. Clough (1989; New York: Polity Press, 1996).

39. Bourdieu, "The Forms of Capital," 244, 248.

40. Generally traced back to Theodore W. Schultz, "Investment in Human Capital," *American Economic Review* 51, no. 1 (March 1961): 1–17.

41. To begin, see Kenneth J. Arrow, "Higher Education as a Filter," *Journal of Public Economics* 2, no. 3 (July 1973): 193–216; Michael Spence, "Job Market Signaling," *Quarterly Journal of Economics* 87, no. 3 (August 1973): 355–74; Joseph E. Stiglitz, "The Theory of 'Screening,' Education, and the Distribution of Income," *American Economic Review* 65, no. 3 (June 1975): 283–300.

42. Mark Granovetter, "Economic Action and Social Structure: The Problem of Embeddedness," *American Journal of Sociology* 91, no. 3 (November 1985): 481–510; James S. Coleman, "Social Capital in the Creation of Human Capital," *American Journal of Sociology* 94 (1988): S95–S120.

43. Robert D. Putnam, *Bowling Alone: The Collapse and Revival of American Community* (New York: Simon & Schuster, 2000), 20.

44. Fei Xiaotong, *From the Soil: The Foundations of Chinese Society*, trans. Gary G. Hamilton and Wang Zheng (Berkeley: University of California Press, 1992).

45. Bryna Goodman, "New Culture, Old Habits: Native-Place Organization and the May Fourth Movement," in *Shanghai Sojourners*, ed. Frederic Wakeman, Jr., and Wen-hsin Yeh (Berkeley: Institute of East Asian Studies, University of California Press, 1992), 76–107.

46. On native-place and dialect-group ties in cities and overseas, also see Emily Honig, *Sisters and Strangers: Women in the Shanghai Cotton Mills, 1919–1949* (Stanford, Calif.: Stanford University Press, 1986); Bryna Goodman, *Native Place, City and Nation: Regional Networks and Identities* (Berkeley: University of California Press, 1995); Madeline Y. Hsu, *Dreaming of Gold, Dreaming of Home: Transnationalism and Migration Between the United States and South China* (Stanford, Calif.: Stanford University Press, 2000); Kuo, *Networks Beyond Empires*.

47. Mayfair Mei-hui Yang, *Gifts, Favors, and Banquets: The Art of Social Relationships in China* (Ithaca, N.Y.: Cornell University Press, 1994).

48. On Wang Yanan, see Rebecca E. Karl, *The Magic of Concepts: History and the Economic in Twentieth-Century China* (Durham, N.C.: Duke University Press, 2017).

49. Robert L. Heilbroner, *Behind the Veil of Economics: Essays in the Worldly Philosophy* (New York: Norton, 1988).

50. R. Bin Wong, *China Transformed: Historical Change and the Limits of European Experience* (Ithaca, N.Y.: Cornell University Press, 1997); Sucheta Mazumdar, *Sugar and Society in China: Peasants, Technology, and the World Market* (Cambridge, Mass.: Harvard University Asia Center, 1998); Li Bozhong, *Agricultural Development in Jiangnan, 1620–1850* (New York: St. Martin's Press, 1998); Andre Gunder Frank, *ReORIENT: Global Economy in the Asian Age* (Berkeley: University of California Press, 1998); Kenneth Pomeranz, *The Great Divergence: China, Europe, and the Making of the Modern World Economy* (Princeton, N.J.: Princeton University Press, 2000); Madeleine Zelin, *The Merchants of Zigong: Industrial Entrepreneurship in Early Modern China*, Studies of the Weatherhead East Asian Institute (New York: Columbia University Press, 2005).

51. For a few examples, see Ellen Hartigan-O'Connor, "The Personal Is Political Economy," *Journal of the Early Republic* 36, no. 2 (Summer 2016): 335–41; Amy Dru Stanley, "Histories of Capitalism and Sex Difference," *Journal of the Early Republic* 36, no. 2 (Summer 2016): 343–50; Stephanie E. Jones-Rogers, *They Were Her Property: White Women as Slave Owners in the American South* (New Haven, Conn.: Yale University Press, 2019).

52. For a lively discussion of the state of this field, see Sara Lorenzini, *Global Development: A Cold War History* (Princeton, N.J.: Princeton University Press, 2019), reviewed by Julia F. Irwin, Nathan J. Citino, Nils Gilman, Stephen Macekura, Christy Thornton, Corinna R. Unger, and Alden Young, *H-Diplo Roundtable Reviews* 21, no. 41 (2020), https://issforum.org/roundtables/PDF/Roundtable-XXI-41.pdf.

53. For an example of more global work, see Stephen Macekura and Erez Manela, eds., *The Development Century: A Global History* (Cambridge: Cambridge University Press, 2018).

54. Peter E. Hamilton, "The Imperial and Transpacific Origins of Chinese Capitalism," special issue of the *Journal of Historical Sociology* 33, no. 1 (March 2020): 134–48.

55. For an illustrative example, see S. Gordon Redding, *The Spirit of Chinese Capitalism* (Berlin: Walter de Gruyter, 1990).

56. Ezra F. Vogel, *The Four Little Dragons: The Spread of Industrialization in East Asia*, Edwin O. Reischauer Lectures (Cambridge, Mass.: Harvard University Press, 1991).

57. Gary G. Hamilton, ed., *Business Networks and Economic Development in East and Southeast Asia* (Hong Kong: Centre of Asian Studies, University of Hong Kong, 1991); Danny Kin-kong Lam and Ian Lee, "Guerilla Capitalism and the Limits of Statist Theory: Comparing the Chinese NICs," in *The Evolving Pacific Basin in the Global Political Economy: Domestic and International Linkages*, ed. Cal Clark and Steven Chan (Boulder, Colo.: Lynne Rienner, 1992), 107–24.

58. David R. Meyer, *Hong Kong as a Global Metropolis* (Cambridge: Cambridge University Press, 2000), 3.

59. Gary G. Hamilton, "Hong Kong and the Rise of Capitalism in Asia," in *Cosmopolitan Capitalists: Hong Kong and the Chinese Diaspora at the End of the Twentieth Century*, ed. Gary G. Hamilton (Seattle: University of Washington Press, 1999), 14–34; Gary G. Hamilton, *Commerce and Capitalism in Chinese Societies* (London: Routledge, 2006), 129–45.

60. Hamilton, *Commerce and Capitalism*, 5.

61. Hamilton, "Hong Kong and the Rise of Capitalism in Asia," 27; Hamilton, *Commerce and Capitalism*, 142.

62. Anna Lowenhaupt Tsing, *The Mushroom at the End of the World: On the Possibility of Life in Capitalist Ruins* (Princeton, N.J.: Princeton University Press, 2015), 40.

63. Gunder Frank, *ReORIENT*.

1. Capitalist Transplants

1. On native-place ties in Republican China and overseas, see Emily Honig, *Sisters and Strangers: Women in the Shanghai Cotton Mills, 1919–1949* (Stanford, Calif.: Stanford University Press, 1986); Frederic Wakeman, Jr., and Wen-hsin Yeh, eds., *Shanghai Sojourners* (Berkeley: Institute of East Asian Studies, University of California Press, 1992); Bryna Goodman, *Native Place, City and Nation: Regional Networks and Identities* (Berkeley: University of California Press, 1995); Madeline Y. Hsu, *Dreaming of Gold, Dreaming of Home: Transnationalism and Migration Between the United States and South China* (Stanford, Calif.: Stanford University Press, 2000); Huei-Ying Kuo, *Networks Beyond Empires: Chinese Business and Nationalism in the Hong Kong-Singapore Corridor, 1914–1941* (Leiden: Brill, 2014).

2. Philip Kuhn, *Chinese Among Others: Emigration in Modern Times* (Lanham, Md.: Rowman & Littlefield, 2009), 4, 25–28.

3. Tang Pingyuan was also known as Tang Xinghai (唐星海). For the family's move, see Jack Chi-Chien Tang, "The Textile Industry and the Development of Hong Kong, 1949–1999," oral history conducted by Carolyn Wakeman in 1999, Regional Oral History Office, Bancroft Library, University of California Berkeley, 2003.

4. Tang, "The Textile Industry," 15–17.

5. Parks M. Coble, *Chinese Capitalists in Japan's New Order: The Occupied Lower Yangzi, 1937–1945* (Berkeley: University of California Press, 2003), 13.

6. Tang, "The Textile Industry," 13, 17. For similar wartime profiteering, see Brett Sheehan, *Industrial Eden: A Chinese Capitalist Vision* (Cambridge, Mass.: Harvard University Press, 2015), 95–96.

7. Parks M. Coble, "Chinese Capitalists and the Japanese: Collaboration and Resistance in the Shanghai Area, 1937–45," in *Wartime Shanghai*, ed. Wen-hsin Yeh (London: Routledge, 1998), 66.

8. Coble, *Chinese Capitalists*, 16–17, 96. For collaboration among northeastern elites, see Rana Mitter, *The Manchurian Myth: Nationalism, Resistance, and Collaboration in Modern China* (Berkeley: University of California Press, 2000).

9. South Sea Textile Manufacturing Company, "Number of Spindles & Automatic Looms in Operation," June 1970, University of Hong Kong Libraries, Special Collections (HKUSC).

10. A parallel situation occurred in the migration of Baba families from Malacca to Singapore in the 1820s. See Kuhn, *Chinese Among Others*, 101–2.

11. Elizabeth Sinn, *Pacific Crossing: California Gold, Chinese Migration, and the Making of Hong Kong* (Hong Kong: Hong Kong University Press, 2013).

12. Kuhn, *Chinese Among Others*, 63–77.

13. On the Canton System, see Paul A. Van Dyke, *The Canton Trade: Life and Enterprise on the China Coast, 1700–1845* (Hong Kong: Hong Kong University Press, 2012).

14. Christopher Munn, *Anglo-China: Chinese People and British Rule in Hong Kong, 1841–1880* (Hong Kong: Hong Kong University Press, 2009).

15. Kuhn, *Chinese Among Others*, 107–14, 139.

16. Sinn, *Pacific Crossing*, 1–4. For Ellis Island, see "Ellis Island: the Portal to America for 12 Million Immigrants from 1892 to 1954," http://www.nyharborparks.org/visit/elis.html.

17. John M. Carroll, *Edge of Empires: Chinese Elites and British Colonials in Hong Kong* (Cambridge, Mass.: Harvard University Press, 2005), 60.

18. Munn, *Anglo-China*, 2, 75–76; Carroll, *Edge of Empires*, 21–36.

19. Elizabeth Sinn, *Power and Charity: A Chinese Merchant Elite in Colonial Hong Kong* (Hong Kong: Hong Kong University Press, 1989).

20. Angelina Y. Chin, "Colonial Charity in Hong Kong: A Case of the Po Leung Kuk in the 1930s," *Journal of Women's History* 25, no. 1 (Spring 2013): 135–57.

21. Peter E. Hamilton, "Ho Asek"; John M. Carroll, "Wei Akwong"; and Edward J. M. Rhoads, "Wong Shing," all in *The Dictionary of Hong Kong Biography* (*DHKB*), ed. May Holdsworth and Christopher Munn (Hong Kong: Hong Kong University Press, 2012), 186, 453–55, 462–63.

22. John M. Carroll, "Ng Choy," in Holdsworth and Munn, eds., *DHKB*, 337–338. On Ng's role in the Qing's abdication, see Edward J. M. Rhoads, *Manchus & Han: Ethnic Relations and Political Power in Late Qing and Early Republican China, 1861–1928* (Seattle: University of Washington Press, 2000), 210–28.

23. Alfred H. Y. Lin, "The Founding of the University of Hong Kong: British Imperial Ideals and Chinese Practical Common Sense," in *An Impossible Dream: Hong Kong*

University from Foundation to Re-establishment, 1910–1950, ed. Chan Lau Kit-ching and Peter Cunich (Hong Kong: Oxford University Press, 2002), 18.

24. Emily Hahn, *China to Me* (Garden City, N.Y.: Doubleday, Doran, 1944), 216–17.

25. Carroll, "Ho Kai" and "Wei Yuk," in Holdsworth and Munn, *DHKB,* 188–90 and 455–56.

26. Carroll, *Edge of Empires,* 63, 86–87, 126; Huei-Ying Kuo, *Networks Beyond Empires: Chinese Business and Nationalism in the Hong Kong-Singapore Corridor, 1914–1941* (Leiden: Brill, 2014), 82–129; Chan Lau Kit-ching, "Business and Radicalism: Hong Kong Chinese Merchants and the Chinese Communist Movement, 1921–1934," in *Colonial Hong Kong and Modern China,* ed. Pui-tak Lee (Hong Kong: Hong Kong University Press, 2005), 169–83.

27. Philip Snow, *The Fall of Hong Kong: Britain, China, and the Japanese Occupation* (New Haven, Conn.: Yale University Press, 2004), 3–4.

28. Emma Jinhua Teng, *Eurasian: Mixed Identities in the United States, China, and Hong Kong, 1842–1943* (Berkeley: University of California Press, 2013).

29. On Ho Tung's brothers, see Eric P. Ho, "Ho Fook"; May Holdsworth, "Ho Komtong," in *DHKB,* 187–88, 190–91.

30. Sinn, *Pacific Crossing,* 37.

31. Holdsworth and Munn, *DHKB,* 71.

32. "American Club, Elaborate Plans for Hongkong," *China Mail (CM),* January 10, 1925, 13.

33. Sinn, *Pacific Crossing,* 233–64.

34. Woo Sing-lim (吳醒濂), *The Prominent Chinese in Hong Kong* (香港華人名人史畧) (Hong Kong: Wuzhou shuju, 1937), 38.

35. Holdsworth and Munn, *DHKB,* 97–98.

36. Frank Ching, *The Li Dynasty: Hong Kong Aristocrats* (Oxford: Oxford University Press, 1999), 20, 91, 128, 173.

37. Law Kar, "The American Connection in Early Hong Kong Cinema," in *The Cinema of Hong Kong: History, Arts, Identity,* ed. Poshek Fu and David Desser (Cambridge: Cambridge University Press, 2002), 44–70.

38. In 1958 the president of the Jiangsu and Zhejiang Residents' Association estimated that 350,000 Shanghainese lived in Hong Kong. Wong Siu-lun placed the figure closer to 100,000 in his *Emigrant Entrepreneurs: Shanghai Industrialists in Hong Kong* (Hong Kong: Oxford University Press, 1988), 5–6.

39. For another example, see Kenneth Pomeranz, *The Making of a Hinterland: State, Society, and Economy in Inland North China, 1853–1937* (Berkeley: University of California Press, 1993).

40. On the Huizhou merchants, see Antonia Finnane, *Speaking of Yangzhou: A Chinese City, 1550–1850* (Cambridge, Mass.: Harvard University Press, 2004).

41. Hao Yen-p'ing, *The Comprador in Nineteenth-Century China: Bridge Between East and West* (Cambridge, Mass.: Harvard University Press, 1970). These merchants were also sometimes labeled "Xiangshan men." See Sherman Cochran, *Encountering Chinese Networks: Western, Japanese, and Chinese Corporations in China, 1880–1937* (Berkeley: University of California Press, 2000), 21.

42. Anne Reinhardt, *Navigating Semi-Colonialism: Shipping, Sovereignty, and Nation-Building in China, 1860–1937* (Cambridge, Mass.: Harvard University Asia Center, 2018), 32–37, 51–62, 65–71.

43. Marianne Bastid, "Servitude or Liberation: The Introduction of Foreign Educational Practices and Systems to China from 1840 to the Present," in *China's Education and the Industrialized World: Studies in Cultural Transfer,* ed. Ruth Hayhoe and Marianne Bastid (Armonk, N.Y.: M. E. Sharpe, 1987), 3–20.

44. Wen-hsin Yeh, *The Alienated Academy: Culture and Politics in Republican China, 1919–1937* (Cambridge, Mass.: Harvard University Asia Center, 1990), 12–15.

45. On Yung Wing's mission, see Xu Guoqi, *Chinese and Americans: A Shared History* (Cambridge, Mass.: Harvard University Press, 2014), 76–100; Teng, *Eurasian,* 27–51; Edward J. M. Rhoads, *Stepping Forth in the World: The Chinese Educational Mission to the United States, 1872–81* (Hong Kong: Hong Kong University Press, 2011).

46. Y. C. Wang, *Chinese Intellectuals and the West, 1872–1949* (Chapel Hill: University of North Carolina Press, 1966), 45–49.

47. On "wealth and power," see Benjamin Schwartz, *In Search of Wealth and Power: Yen Fu and the West* (Cambridge, Mass.: Belknap Press of Harvard University Press, 1964), 18–19, 25–26. On Zhang Zhidong's evolution as a lens, see William Ayers, *Chang Chih-tung and Educational Reform in China* (Cambridge, Mass.: Harvard University Press, 1971).

48. On the evolving examinations, see Benjamin A. Elman, *Civil Examinations and Meritocracy in Late Imperial China* (Cambridge, Mass.: Harvard University Press, 2013). For one left scrambling, see Henrietta Harrison, *The Man Awakened from Dreams: One Man's Life in a North China Village, 1857–1942* (Stanford, Calif.: Stanford University Press, 2005). For political implications, see Joseph W. Esherick, *Reform and Revolution in China: The 1911 Revolution in Hunan and Hubei,* Michigan Studies on China (Berkeley: University of California Press, 1976).

49. 李中清 (James Z. Lee), 任韵竹 (Yunzhu Ren), and 梁晨 (Chen Liang), 中国知识阶层的来源与形成, 1912–1952 (Beijing: Zhongguo shehui kexue wenxian chubanshe, 2020).

50. These included St. John's University (1879), the University of Nanking (1888), Canton Christian College (later Lingnan University, 1889), Hangchow Christian College (1897), Soochow University (1900), Cheeloo University (1902), Boone College (later Huachung University, 1905), Peking Union Medical College (1906), Fukian Christian University (1907), Shanghai Baptist College and Theological Seminary (1911) (University of Shanghai after 1929), West China Union University (1914), Ginling College (1915), Hwa Nan College (1917), and Yenching University (1919). See Daniel H. Bays and Ellen Widmer, eds., *China's Christian Colleges: Cross-Cultural Connections, 1900–1950* (Stanford, Calif.: Stanford University Press, 2009).

51. Joel Andreas, *Rise of the Red Engineers: The Cultural Revolution and the Origins of China's New Class* (Stanford, Calif.: Stanford University Press, 2009), 20. Also see "Who's Who of American Returned Students," *Millard's Review of the Far East (MRFE),* August 4, 1917, 4 (published by Tsinghua).

52. Yeh, *The Alienated Academy,* 94.

53. Wang, *Chinese Intellectuals and the West*, 150–56.

54. For the 150,000 estimate, see Liping Bu, *Making the World Like Us: Education, Cultural Expansion, and the American Century* (Westport, Conn.: Praeger, 2003). Y. C. Wang put the total a little higher in *Chinese Intellectuals and the West*, 119–20. For graduation rates, see 李中清, 任韵竹, and 梁晨, 中国知识阶层的来源与形成.

55. Wang, *Chinese Intellectuals and the West*, 82.

56. Wang, *Chinese Intellectuals and the West*, 116–20.

57. Wang, *Chinese Intellectuals and the West*, 156–61.

58. The biggest senders, in order, were Tsinghua, St. John's, Huachung/Central, Shanghai Jiaotong, Yenching, Lingnan, Peking, Shanghai, Ginling, Soochow, Zhejiang, and Sun Yat-sen. See 李中清, 任韵竹, 梁晨, 中国知识阶层的来源与形成.

59. M. T. Z. Tyau, "Chinese Returned Students: Are They Making Good?" *North-China Herald and Supreme Court & Consular Gazette* (*NCHSCCG*), April 3, 1920, 33.

60. For one example, see Ida Kahn (康愛德), "An Appeal to American Returned Students," in both *MRFE*, June 22, 1918, 131, and *Peking Leader*, June 28, 1918, 3.

61. For surveys of American-returned students' work, see Tyau, "Chinese Returned Students," 33; "Those Returned Students," *MRFE*, November 13, 1920, 573.

62. 李中清, 任韵竹, and 梁晨, 中国知识阶层的来源与形成.

63. Madeline Y. Hsu, "Befriending the Yellow Peril," in *Trans-Pacific Interactions: The United States and China, 1880–1950*, ed. Vanessa Künnemann and Ruth Mayer (New York: Palgrave Macmillan, 2009), 116.

64. Chih Meng, *Chinese American Understanding: A Sixty-Year Search* (New York: China Institute in America, 1981), 168.

65. Coble, *Chinese Capitalists*, 2.

66. Marie Claire Bergère, *The Golden Age of the Chinese Bourgeoisie*, trans. Janet Lloyd (Cambridge: Cambridge University Press, 1989).

67. Tomoko Shiroyama, *China During the Great Depression: Market, State, and the World Economy, 1929–1937* (Cambridge, Mass.: Harvard East Asian Monographs, 2008), 60–87.

68. Marie-Claire Bergère, "The Shanghai Bankers' Association, 1915–1927: Modernization and the Institutionalization of Local Solidarities," in *Shanghai Sojourners*, ed. Frederic Wakeman, Jr. and Wen-hsin Yeh (Berkeley: Institute of East Asian Studies, University of California Press, 1992), 15–34.

69. Brett Sheehan, "Urban Identities and Urban Networks in Cosmopolitan Cities: Banks and Bankers in Tianjin, 1900–1937," in *Remaking the Chinese City: Modernity and National Identity, 1900–1950*, ed. Joseph W. Esherick (Honolulu: University of Hawai'i Press, 2000), 47–64.

70. K. P. Chen, "Half Century Notes," January 16, 1950, 1, Kwang Pu Chen Papers, 1936–1958 (KPC), Box 9, Folder 10, Rare Book and Library Collections, Columbia University (RBLC).

71. Zhang Gongquan (張公權), 陳光甫興上海銀行, 36–37, KPC, Box 9, RBLC.

72. Zhang, 陳光甫興上海銀行, 38–43.

73. Zhaojin Ji, *A History of Modern Shanghai Banking: The Rise and Decline of China's Finance Capitalism* (New York: Routledge, 2016), 118–19.

74. On Baerwald see Ji, *A History of Modern Shanghai Banking*, 120. Also see Chen, "Half Century Notes," 1. On Tong, see "Who's Who in China," *MRFE*, October 4, 1919, 200; "Y. C. Tong Dies," *Weekly Review of the Far East*, November 12, 1921, 518.

75. "Obituary: Mr. S.C. Chu," *NCHSCCG*, January 6, 1931, 15.

76. Ji, *A History of Modern Shanghai Banking*, 120–21. See also "Ch'en Kuang-fu," in *Biographical Dictionary of Republican China*, ed. Howard L. Boorman (New York: Columbia University Press, 1967), 192–96.

77. On Song Feiqing's education and the LLC, see Sheehan, *Industrial Eden*, 5, 17–24, 55.

78. B. Y. Lee, "Foreign Competition and Chinese Cotton Mills," *China Weekly Review* (*CWR*), August 30, 1930, 492.

79. B. Y. Lee, "Cotton Manufacturing in China," *Shanghai Times*, December 15, 1919, A14. See also "Those Returned Students," *MRFE*, November 13, 1920, 573.

80. "Men and Events," *CWR*, May 24, 1924, 464.

81. Bryna Goodman, "New Culture, Old Habits: Native-Place Organization and the May Fourth Movement," in *Shanghai Sojourners*, ed. Frederic Wakeman, Jr., and Wen-hsin Yeh (Berkeley: Institute of East Asian Studies, University of California Press, 1992), 89–92.

82. Janet Y. Chen, *Guilty of Indigence: The Urban Poor in China, 1900–1953* (Princeton, N.J.: Princeton University Press, 2012), 174.

83. Sherman Cochran, ed., *The Capitalist Dilemma in China's Communist Revolution* (Ithaca, N.Y.: Cornell East Asia Program, 2014).

84. Man Bun Kwan, "Janus-Faced Capitalism: Li Zhuchen and the Jiuda Salt Refinery, 1949–1953," in Cochran, *The Capitalist Dilemma*, 89–118.

85. Kuo, *Networks Beyond Empires*, 223.

86. Wang, *Chinese Intellectuals and the West*, 85–87.

87. Quoted in Wong, *Emigrant Entrepreneurs*, 16; *Far Eastern Economic Review*, December 11, 1946, 8.

88. K. P. Chen, "Stabilization Notes," April 2, 1948, 2, KPC Papers, Box 9, Folder 7a, RBLC.

89. On Wuxi's development, see Toby Lincoln, *Urbanizing China in War and Peace: The Case of Wuxi County* (Honolulu: University of Hawai'i Press, 2015).

90. Tang, "The Textile Industry," 12.

91. Lincoln, *Urbanizing China*, 39; Tang, "The Textile Industry," 12.

92. "Jack Tang ('Mr Textiles')," *Bulletin* (Hong Kong General Chamber of Commerce), June 1984, 9, HKUSC; Tang, "The Textile Industry," 12–13.

93. "唐炳源字星海," in 環球中國名人傳略, ed. 李元信 (Shanghai: Huanqiu chubanshe, 1944), 189. Accessed through the Modern History Databases (MHDB), Academia Sinica; P. Y. Tang, "Wusih—The Pittsburg of China," *CWR*, November 1, 1925, 35–37.

94. Tang, "The Textile Industry," 2–3, 5.

95. Cochran, *Encountering Chinese Networks*, 140–43.

96. "中央研究院, 1935–36," 國民政府職官年表, 1925–49, 第一冊 (Taipei: Zhongyanyuan jin shi suo, 1987), 424. Accessed through MHDB.

97. Wong, *Emigrant Entrepreneurs*, 18–22, 28–31; Cochran, *Encountering Chinese Networks*, 117–46; Coble, *Chinese Capitalists*, 114–39.

98. Coble, *Chinese Capitalists*, 147.

99. Sheehan, *Industrial Eden*, 165–66, 192–93, 196–201.

100. Tang, "The Textile Industry," 18, 28, 45.

101. "Yeh Chu Tang Is Dead at 78; Ex-Manufacturer of Textiles," *New York Times*, November 14, 1986.

102. Tang, "The Textile Industry," 18–23, 27–31.

103. "Granting of Permanent Residence to Certain Aliens," May 11, 1953, in U.S. Department of State, *United States Statutes at Large* (Washington, D.C.: U.S. Government Printing Office, 1953), B8.

104. Tang, "The Textile Industry," 10–12.

105. South Sea Textile Manufacturing Company, June 1970, HKUSC; "1953," *Harvard Business School Bulletin* 36, no. 2 (April 1960): 58.

106. Sherman Cochran and Andrew Hsieh, *The Lius of Shanghai* (Cambridge, Mass.: Harvard University Press, 2013), 293.

107. Cochran, *Encountering Chinese Networks*, 152.

108. Cochran and Hsieh, *The Lius of Shanghai*, 14–15, 17, 69–70. Also see Cochran, *Encountering Chinese Networks*, 147–51.

109. Cochran and Hsieh, *The Lius of Shanghai*, 238.

110. Cochran and Hsieh, *The Lius of Shanghai*, 264–66.

111. The UNRRA spent US$518 million in postwar China. See Meredith Oyen, *The Diplomacy of Migration: Transnational Lives and the Making of U.S.-Chinese Relations in the Cold War* (Ithaca, N.Y.: Cornell University Press, 2015), 72.

112. K. P. Chen, "Legislative Diary: US Aid," June 22, 1948, 2, KPC, Box 9, Folder 7b, RBLC.

113. Cochran and Hsieh, *The Lius of Shanghai*, 267–71.

114. Cochran and Hsieh, *The Lius of Shanghai*, 281. For the Tangs, see Tang, "The Textile Industry," 21. Wong also discusses them in *Emigrant Entrepreneurs*, 19.

115. Reinhardt, *Navigating Semi-Colonialism*, 251.

116. "Quit Peiping, Consul's Advice," *South China Morning Post* (*SCMP*), October 30, 1948, 1.

117. "天津撤退忙, 北平航機已登記到明年, 天津中央機關正計畫撤退," *Wen Wei Po* (*WWP*), November 8, 1948, 1. On CAT, see William M. Leary, *Perilous Missions: Civil Air Transport and CIA Covert Operations in Asia* (Tuscaloosa: University of Alabama Press, 2006), 48–49.

118. "北平美僑百五十人, 即撤退返國, 京滬美僑尚無動靜," *WWP*, November 10, 1948, 1; "旅滬美僑撤退," *Kong Sheung Yat Po* (*KSYP*) 工商日報, November 21, 1948, 1.

119. "Evacuees Leave, Another IRO Vessel Departs From S'hai," *SCMP*, January 20, 1949, 12.

120. E"戰火迫近人心惶惶, 上海居民紛紛避難, 十里洋場一片混亂景色," *Sing Tao Jih Pao*, April 27, 1949, in KPC Papers, Box 9, Folder 8, RBLC; "S'hai Conditions, Big Slump In Land And Luxuries," *SCMP*, November 26, 1948, 1.

121. Edward Szczepanik, *The Economic Growth of Hong Kong* (Oxford: Oxford University Press, 1958), 183. For an example of the speculation, see "Chinese Capital, Over Sixty Billion Idle in H.K.," *SCMP*, June 26, 1948, 1.

122. Helen Zia, *Last Boat Out of Shanghai: The Epic Story of the Chinese Who Fled Mao's Revolution* (New York: Penguin Random House, 2019), 217–18, 260.

123. K. P. Chen, "Notes on Current Situation," January 21, 1949, 1, KPC Papers, Box 9, Folder 8, RBLC.

124. K. P. Chen to Lawrence Morris, Hawkins, Delafeild [sic] & Wood, May 3, 1949, 1, KPC Papers, Box 9, Folder 8, RBLC.

125. Wm. Roger Louis, "Hong Kong: The Critical Phase, 1945–1949," *American Historical Review* 102, no. 4 (October 1997): 1052–84.

126. "Correspondence: Some Questions," *South China Morning Post & Hongkong Telegraph* (*SCMPHKT*), January 30, 1946, 4.

127. Robert Bickers, *Britain in China: Community, Culture and Colonialism 1900–1949* (Manchester, UK: Manchester University Press, 1999). For a few such attempts, see "The Old Resident," *SCMPHKT*, March 9, 1946, 4; "The New Hongkong," *SCMPHKT*, March 18, 1946, 4; "Life on Subsidy," *SCMPHKT*, March 25, 1946, 4.

128. Zia, *Last Boat*, 170; "Glorious Fourth, American Community in Celebration," *SCMPHKT*, July 6, 1948, 8.

129. "American Shipping, President Line Plans for Pacific Service," *SCMPHKT*, March 27, 1946, 7.

130. "New HK Air Link, Pan-America Airways Service to Colony," *SCMPHKT*, August 3, 1946, 1.

131. "USA to Hongkong, Opening of Radio-Cable Service Announced," *SCMP*, September 7, 1947, 1; "Air Parcel Post, Gift to Governor to Mark Inauguration," *SCMP*, September 25, 1948, 5.

132. For U.S. veterans looking for work, see the *SCMP*'s "Positions Wanted" throughout 1947. For Farrell and Cathay, see "Air Shuttle Service, War Veterans Bringing in Supplies to Colony," *SCMPHKT*, June 19, 1946, 4. Also see Gavin Young, *Beyond Lion Rock: The Story of Cathay Pacific Airways* (London: Hutchinson, 1988).

133. K. P. Chen, "Hongkong," January 6, 1949, 2, KPC Papers, Box 9, Folder 8, RBLC.

134. Wallace Harper to Public Works Department, Hong Kong, July 26, 1929 (Hong Kong Public Records Office, Kwun Tong), Hong Kong Record Series (HKRS) 58-1-147.

135. "Foreign Firms, May Acquire Immovable Property in Colony," *SCMP*, January 13, 1949, 11.

136. Wong, *Emigrant Entrepreneurs*, 24–25.

137. "Assassination of Mr. Lee Hysan," *Hong Kong Telegraph*, April 30, 1928, 1.

138. York Lo, "Lee Hysan; Lee, Richard Charles Ming-chak; and Lee, Harold Hsiao-wo," in Holdsworth and Munn, *DHKB*, 249–50; Ansie Lee Sperry, *Running with the Tiger: A Memoir of an Extraordinary Young Woman's Life in Hong Kong, China, the South Pacific and POW Camp* (N.p.: Sperry Family Trust: 2009), 4–6.

139. Hahn, *China to Me*, 216–17; Poy, *Building Bridges*, 16–18.

140. Sperry, *Running with the Tiger*, 112–15, 172–75.

141. Peter Starr, *Citibank: A Century in Asia* (Singapore: Editions Didier Millet, 2007), 58, 66; Sperry, *Running with the Tiger*, 117.

142. Sperry, *Running with the Tiger*, 219–21, 238, 244.

143. Peter E. Hamilton, "Pop Gingle's Cold War," in *Pacific America: Histories of Transoceanic Crossings*, ed. Lon Kurashige (Honolulu: University of Hawai'i Press, 2017), 62–79.

144. Zach Fredman, "GIs and 'Jeep Girls': Sex and American Soldiers in Wartime China," *Journal of Modern Chinese History* 13, no. 1 (2019): 76–101.

145. Sperry, *Running with the Tiger*, 240, 244. Also see Starr, *Citibank*, 82.

146. Starr, *Citibank*, 81.

147. Chihyun Chang, ed., *The Chinese Journals of L. K. Little, 1943–54: An Eyewitness Account of War and Revolution*, vol. 2 (New York: Routledge, 2018), 103.

148. On U.S. scrutiny of Chinese war brides, see Oyen, *The Diplomacy of Migration*, 78–87.

149. See "Marriage Notices," *SCMP*, November 22, 1947, 2; "G.I. War Brides, Leave for America by Special Plane," *SCMP*, November 19, 1948, 4.

150. "Chinese for U.S.A.," *SCMP*, December 24, 1948, 13.

151. Naoko Shibusawa, *America's Geisha Ally: Reimagining the Japanese Enemy* (Cambridge, Mass.: Harvard University Press, 2010).

152. Sperry, *Running with the Tiger*, 254.

153. Starr, *Citibank*, 82.

154. Rick Kroos, *Kroos Control: American Roots, Chinese Traditions* (Hong Kong: Inkstone Books, 2012), 92.

155. For example, in 1947 the Rongs ordered 47,000 spindles from U.S. manufacturers. See Coble, *Chinese Capitalists*, 132.

156. Starr, *Citibank*, 83.

157. K. P. Chen, "Equalization Diary," March 8, 1948, KPC Papers, Box 9, Folder 7a, RBLC.

158. K. P. Chen, "Peace Mission to Peiping," Feb. 2, 1949, 3, KPC Papers, Box 9, Folder 8, RBLC.

159. K. P. Chen, "Cooperation," March 16, 1949, 1–4, KPC Papers, Box 9, Folder 8, RBLC.

160. K. P. Chen, "記購證大戶," March 23, 1949, 1, KPC Papers, Box 9, Folder 8, RBLC.

161. K. P. Chen, "押放款大戶表," March 22, 1949, 1; and "放款透支質押品分拆表" and "大戶透支表," March 23, 1949, 1, all in KPC Papers, Box 9, Folder 8, RBLC.

162. K. P. Chen, "出口押匯大戶," March 23, 1949, KPC Papers, Box 9, Folder 8, RBLC; Huei-ying Kuo, "Chinese Bourgeois Nationalism in Hong Kong and Singapore in the 1930s," *Journal of Contemporary Asia* 36, no. 3 (2006): 396–97.

163. "Economic Report on Hong Kong: Prepared by American Consulate General," July 18, 1960, 5, HKRS 269-1-6.

164. Tang, "The Textile Industry," 45, 49.

165. Catherine R. Schenk, *Hong Kong as an International Financial Centre: Emergence and Development 1945–65* (London: Routledge, 2001), 34–43.

166. K. P. Chen, December 29, 1950, KPC Papers, Box 9, Folder 10, RBLC.

167. On the firms' difficulties in the Great Depression, see Kuo, *Networks Beyond Empires*, 192–200.

168. For one meeting with local manufacturers, see "金山庄行華安商會, 昨召集各廠商開會, 應付禁運土產輸美," *Wah Kiu Yat Po* (*WKYP*), August 29, 1951, 6. For two interactions with the U.S. consulate, see "金山庄行函請美領事, 向華府呼, 籲以前定下貨品准予輸美," *WKYP*, September 7, 1951, 6; "港方如發給出口證明, 士產可准輸美, 華安商會將謁美領事條陳," *Sing Tao Yat Po* (*STYP*), June 28, 1952, 5. For a U.S. Treasury visit, see "美財部代表來港, 金山庄行華安商會, 提供港貨原料來源," *STYP*, October 17, 1952, 7.

169. For one who limped on, see Tomoko Shiroyama, "The Hong Kong–South China Financial Nexus: Ma Xuchao and His Remittance Agency," in *The Capitalist Dilemma in China's Communist Revolution*, ed. Sherman Cochran (Ithaca, N.Y.: Cornell East Asia Program, 2014), 203–24.

170. "美嚴禁僑匯, 經港轉共區," *KSYP*, February 4, 1953, 5.

171. Nancy Bernkopf Tucker, ed., *China Confidential: American Diplomats and Sino-American Relations, 1945–1996* (New York: Columbia University Press, 2001), 109–10.

172. Szczepanik, *The Economic Growth of Hong Kong*, 164.

173. "Economic Report on Hong Kong: Prepared by American Consulate General," July 18, 1960, 5 (Hong Kong Public Records Office, Kwun Tong), HKRS 269-1-6.

174. K. P. Chen, "記購證大戶," March 23, 1949, KPC Papers, Box 9, Folder 8, RBLC.

175. Eleanor Wong, "A History of the Wong Family Textile Business, Part Two: Life in Hong Kong," 3–4, http://industrialhistoryhk.org/wp-content/uploads/2014/11/A -History-of-the-Wong-Family-Textile-Business-Part-Two-Life-in-Hong-Kong .pdf.

176. Oyen, *The Diplomacy of Migration*, 106–15; Mae Ngai, *Impossible Subjects: Illegal Aliens and the Making of Modern America* (Princeton, N.J.: Princeton University Press, 2004), 206–12.

177. Tang, "The Textile Industry," 10, 29–30.

178. Hui Chor Tin, "Training Programme of Apprentices at South Sea Textiles," *Hong Kong Memory*, "Post-war Industry" Collection, http://www.hkmemory.hk/collections /postwar_industry/, accessed October 24, 2017.

179. "News: 1951," *Harvard Business School Bulletin* 33, no. 3 (Autumn 1957): 56, https:// www.library.hbs.edu/Find/Collections-Archives/Special-Collections/Collections /HBS-History/School-Publications.

180. Ngai, *Impossible Subjects*, 206–7.

181. See Christina Klein, *Cold War Orientalism: Asia in the Middlebrow Imagination, 1945–1961* (Berkeley: University of California Press, 2003).

2. Christian Transplants

1. Sterling H. Whitener, *In the Shadow of the Pagoda* (N.p.: CreateSpace, 2013), 116–17.

2. On Chinese students in the United States during the war and postwar, see Madeline Y. Hsu, *The Good Immigrants: How the Yellow Peril Became the Model Minority* (Princeton, N.J.: Princeton University Press, 2015), 104–29; Meredith Oyen, *The Diplomacy of Migration: Transnational Lives and the Making of US-China Relations in the Cold War* (Ithaca, N.Y.: Cornell University Press, 2015), 42–68, 189–95.

3. Hongshan Li, *US-China Educational Exchange: State, Society, and Intercultural Relations, 1905–1950* (New Brunswick, N.J.: Rutgers, 2007).

4. "Enthusiastic Advances in the Foreign Mission Enterprise," *Wachovia Moravian*, January 2, 1947, 2.

5. Laura Madokoro, *Elusive Refuge: Chinese Migrants in the Cold War* (Cambridge, Mass.: Harvard University Press, 2016).

6. On U.S. actions to keep Chinese students from returning, see Oyen, *The Diplomacy of Migration*, 189–91.

7. Whitener, *In the Shadow*, 124–29.

8. "Coming and Going: Many Missionaries Due on the Marine Lynx," *South China Morning Post (SCMP)*, October 6, 1946, 4. For the Refos, see Sarah Refo Mason Papers, RG 175, Yale University Divinity School Library (YUDSL). For the Hofstras, see Nancy Swinyard, "Hofstra, Johanna A., Oral History Interview: Old China Hands Oral History Project," July 19, 1976, "Digital Commons @ Hope College," vi. For the Bechtels, see Joseph Walker, ed., *Hong Kong Who's Who: An Almanac of Personalities and Their Comprehensive Histories, 1970–1973*, University of Hong Kong Libraries, Special Collections (HKUSC), 28–29.

9. On boundary controls, see Laura Madokoro, "Borders Transformed: Sovereign Concerns, Population Movements and the Making of Territorial Frontiers in Hong Kong, 1949–1967," *Journal of Refugee Studies* 25, no. 3 (2012): 407–27.

10. Whitener, *In the Shadow*, 195–99.

11. See Jane Hunter, *The Gospel of Gentility: American Women Missionaries in Turn-of-the-Century China* (New Haven, Conn.: Yale University Press, 1984); Lawrence D. Kessler, *The Jiangyin Mission Station: An American Missionary Community in China, 1895–1951* (Chapel Hill: University of North Carolina Press, 1996); Lian Xi, *The Conversion of Missionaries: Liberalism in American Protestant Missions in China, 1907–1932* (University Park: Pennsylvania State University Press, 1997); Daniel Bays, ed., *Christianity in China: From the Eighteenth Century to the Present* (Stanford, Calif.: Stanford University Press, 1999); Ryan Dunch, *Fuzhou Protestants and the Making of a Modern China, 1857–1927* (New Haven, Conn.: Yale University Press, 2001).

12. Helen Laville and Hugh Wilford, eds., *The US Government, Citizens Groups and the Cold War: The State-Private Network* (London: Routledge, 2006).

13. "Some Policies of Christian and Missionary Alliance," September 1975, Carl T. Smith Papers (CTSP), RG 12, Folder 2, Hong Kong Baptist University Library (HKBUL).

14. Aidan Forth, *Barbed-Wire Imperialism: Britain's Empire of Camps, 1876–1903* (Berkeley: University of California Press, 2017).

15. Chi-kwan Mark, "The 'Problem of People': British Colonials, Cold War Powers, and the Chinese Refugees in Hong Kong, 1949–62," *Modern Asian Studies* 41, no. 6 (November 2007): 1151–52.

16. On this shift, also see Peter E. Hamilton, "An American Family's Mission in East Asia, 1838 to 1936: A Commitment to God, Academia and Empire," *Journal of the Royal Asiatic Society Hong Kong Branch* 49 (August 2009): 229–65.

17. On Hawai'i, see Jennifer Thigpen, *Island Queens and Mission Wives: How Gender and Empire Remade Hawai'i's Pacific World* (Chapel Hill: University of North Carolina Press, 2014). On Korea, see Robert E. Buswell, Jr., and Timothy S. Lee, eds., *Christianity in Korea* (Honolulu: University of Hawaii Press, 2007).

18. Bernard Hung-kay Luk, "A Brief Outline of the History of the Catholic Church in Hong Kong," CTSP, Folder 1, "Catholic Papers, 1970–79," HKBUL.

19. Cindy Yik-yi Chu, *The Maryknoll Sisters in Hong Kong, 1921–1969: In Love with the Chinese* (Basingstoke, UK: Palgrave Macmillan, 2004).

20. Raymond P. Ludden to G. F. Tyrell, April 27, 1949, and G. F. Tyrrell to R. H. Wood-head, April 29, 1949, both in Hong Kong Public Records Office, Kwun Tong, HKRS 41-1-5050.

21. For example, "US Missionaries, Protestants to Stay in China Despite Reds," *SCMP*, January 1, 1949, 16.

22. Hsu, *The Good Immigrants*, 136.

23. Madokoro, *Elusive Refuge*, 57.

24. Whitener, *In the Shadow*, 195–96, 201–3.

25. Alexander Grantham to the Secretary of State for the Colonies (SoSC), "American Aid (Governmental and Private)," January 2, 1957, 2, FO371/127303 (1957), National Archives of the United Kingdom, Kew (NAUK).

26. F. P. Jones, "Bio Sketches," Papers of Sidney R. Anderson (PSRA), Box 10, Folder 51, YUDSL.

27. Olive Anderson, "A Few Notes on Former Influences Affecting the Methodist Church Work in Hong Kong," PSRA, Box 10, Folder 49, YUDSL.

28. "Thinking of the Beginning of the Work of the United Methodist Church (Wei Li Kung Hui) in Hong Kong," 1, PSRA, Box 10, Folder 50, YUDSL.

29. Patsy Queen to Sid Anderson, Jr., March 20, 1978, PSRA, Box 9, Folder 32, YUDSL.

30. "Questions," PSRA, Box 2, Folder 20, YUDSL.

31. "Group Attending Tea at 6 Humphreys Avenue, Nov. 22, 1952," "Invitations to Tea to," and "N. Point Charter Members," all in PSRA, Box 2, Folder 20, YUDSL.

32. "Chow, Dr. Timothy Yu Hsi," in *Hong Kong Who's Who: An Almanac of Personalities and Their Comprehensive Histories, 1970–1973*, 93, HKUSC.

33. Ralph A. Ward, "Another 'Upper Room' In Hongkong," *Louisiana Methodist*, July 2, 1953, 2, PSRA, Box 3, Folder 34, YUDSL.

34. "Questions," PSRA, Box 2, Folder 20, YUDSL.

35. Sid and Olive Anderson to Dr. Fink and Friends, November 7, 1962, PSRA, Box 9, Folder 28, YUDSL.

36. "Jet Plane View of Methodist Work in Hong Kong," PSRA, Box 10, Folder 50, YUDSL; "North Point Methodist Church, Cheung Hong Street, Hong Kong," PSRA, Box 2, Folder 25, YUDSL.

37. 循道衞理聯合教會北角衞理堂，金禧紀念特刊，1953–2003 (Hong Kong: Methodist Church, Hong Kong, 2003), 16, Chinese University of Hong Kong Library.

38. Fred Richardson, *Expatriate Adventures* (N.p.: Trafford, 2012), 82–83.

39. "Honolulu Chinese Admitted to US Bar," *China Press*, January 9, 1934, 9; "US Court for China: Raven Law Suits Stayed," *North-China Herald and Supreme Court & Consular Gazette* (*NCHSCCG*), November 6, 1935, 248; "US Court for China, Reliance Motors Summoned," *NCHSCCG*, April 15, 1936, 120.

40. "Besant School for Girls to Open Tomorrow," *China Press*, September 9, 1925, 16.

41. "Many Attend Dedication of Primary School," *China Press*, January 24, 1937, 9; "CWC Have Party at Park Hotel," *China Press*, October 15, 1935, 4.

42. Richardson, *Expatriate Adventures*, 150.

43. Richardson, *Expatriate Adventures*, 158; "News . . . from Alumni Centers," *Michigan Alumnus*, September 20, 1947, 513.

44. Sid and Olive Anderson to Friends, September 1961, PSRA, Box 9, Folder 28, YUDSL; "New School at North Point, N.Y. Methodist Women's Funds," *SCMP*, June 18, 1959, 4.

45. "Allan Yuen '59," *Michigan Alumnus* 64 (1957): 94; *25 Years of Lionism in Hong Kong, 1955–1980* (October 1980), 3, 25, HKUSC; "Mr Jack Yuen New President of Y's Men's Club," *SCMP*, March 30, 1956, 5; "Mr Jack Yuen Chosen President of Lions Club," *SCMP*, May 17, 1958, 7.

46. Richardson, *Expatriate Adventures*, 62.

47. "Death of Bishop Ralph Ward," *SCMP*, December 12, 1958, 1. For several service hymnals, see 中華基督教衛理公會，九龍安素堂, Ward Memorial Methodist Church, HKRS 306-1-134.

48. See 中華基督教衛理公會，衛斯理村十週年紀念特特刊 (Wesley Village, Hong Kong, 1955–1965) in PSRA, Box 2, Folder 27, YUDSL; 衛理公會亞斯里村 (Asbury Methodist Village), in PSRA, Box 3, Folder 30, YUDSL.

49. Leo L. Hsu, "The Stewardship of the Methodist Church in Hong Kong," M.A. thesis, Perkins School of Theology, Southern Methodist University, 1962, PSRA, Box 3, Folder 45, YUDSL.

50. See PSRA, Box 9, Folder 28, YUDSL.

51. On U.S. intelligence operations, see Nancy Bernkopf Tucker, *Taiwan, Hong Kong, and the United States, 1945–1992: Uncertain Friendships* (New York: Twayne of Macmillan, 1994); Chi-kwan Mark, *Hong Kong and the Cold War: Anglo-American Relations, 1949–1957* (Oxford: Oxford University Press, 2004). On immigration screenings, see Hsu, *The Good Immigrants,* 130–97; Oyen, *The Diplomacy of Migration,* 110–13, 154–84; Mae M. Ngai, *Impossible Subjects: Illegal Aliens and the Making of Modern America* (Princeton, N.J.: Princeton University Press, 2004), 206–12; Glen Peterson, "To Be or Not to Be a Refugee: The International Politics of the Hong Kong Refugee Crisis, 1949–55," *Journal of Imperial and Commonwealth History* 36, no. 2 (June 2008): 171–95.

52. Grantham to SoSC, "American Aid (Governmental and Private)," NAUK.

53. Mark, *Hong Kong in the Cold War.* Officials also vigorously policed politics in schools; see Grace Ai-ling Chou, *Confucianism, Colonialism, and the Cold War: Chinese Cultural Education at Hong Kong's New Asia College, 1949–63* (Leiden: Brill, 2011).

54. Grantham to SoSC, "American Aid (Governmental and Private)," NAUK.

55. "Far East Refugee Program, American Consulate General, Hong Kong, FERP Funds Expended or Obligated—May 1, 1954–December 31, 1960," HKRS 890-2-18.

56. "Breakdown by Agency and Type of Expense," HKRS 890-2-18.

57. Madokoro, *Elusive Refuge,* 61.

58. See Whitener's discussions of devolution in *In the Shadow,* 147–50.

59. Whitener, *In the Shadow,* 209.

60. Whitener, *In the Shadow,* 238–42.

61. "Sid and Olive Anderson to Friends-Around-the-World," December 15, 1958, PSRA, Box 9, Folders 28 and 9, YUDSL.

62. "Report for United Nations High Commissioner for Refugees: Chinese Refugees in Hong Kong—Summary of Recent Developments," September 9, 1960 (8-1), 5, HKRS 890-2-18.

63. J. T. Wakefield for Colonial Secretary [CS] to Director of Public Works [DPW], April 19, 1962 (13), HKRS 156-1-5473.

64. For the debate over the government's decision making, see Alan Smart, *The Shek Kip Mei Myth: Squatters, Fires and Colonial Rule in Hong Kong, 1950–1963* (Hong Kong: Hong Kong University Press, 2006).

65. "Report for UN High Commissioner for Refugees," 2–3, HKRS 890-2-18.

66. Timothy Y. H. Chow and J. C. Phillips, Jr. to the Urban Council, "Application to Carry on Roof-top Work on a Multi-Storey Block" (1), July 5, 1956, HKRS 306-1-134.

67. Mark, "The 'Problem of People,'" 1164–65.

68. Li Fook Kow to J. C. Phillips, Jr. (5), October 5, 1956, HKRS 306-1-134.

69. M. 117 (125), M. 126 (131), and J. C. Phillips, Jr., to Josephine Chau (3), September 6, 1956, all in HKRS 306-1-134.

70. 牧師楊震至雪晶小姐的一封信 (6), April 6, 1957; 牧師楊震至雪晶小姐的一封信 (13), August 7, 1957, HKRS 306-1-134.

71. "Dedicated to the Memory of Reverend Chester Yang," in Ward Memorial Methodist Church & Yang Memorial Social Service Centre (1967), PSRA, Box 2, Folder 24, YUDSL.

72. "Extracted from Minutes of the 4th Ex. Co. Meeting of BGCA held on 17.9.58" (18), HKRS 306-1-134.

73. S. E. Alleyne to Robert Turnipseed, June 5, 1959 (30); Chu Liang-man to Turnipseed, November 7, 1962 (135); Cheng Fook-yui to S. Ruth Hansen (158), July 22, 1964, all in HKRS 306-1-134.

74. Robert Turnipseed to H. M. A. Bristow (125), July 12, 1962, HKRS 306-1-134.

75. Robert Turnipseed to H. M. A. Bristow (130), August 29, 1962, HKRS 306-1-134.

76. "Rooftop Dilemma," *Hongkong Star* (*HKS*), September 25, 1975; "Prove You're Non-Profit Making or Else, 160 Rooftop Schools Face Closure Threat by Govt," *HKS*, December 22, 1975; "Statement on Roof Top Schools," *HKS*, September 25, 1975, all in HKRS 70-6-493.

77. Registrar General to the Deputy Colonial Secretary [DCS], "New Life Temple: Charities (Land Acquisition) Ordinance 1958" (15), May 2, 1960, HKRS 835-1-41.

78. "Development Loan Fund—Interest-Free Loans to the Church of Christ in China" (12), HKRS 229-1-682.

79. Roy Karner to the Director of Education [DE], Feb. 1, 1968, HKRS 156-2-2576.

80. DE to CS, "Proposed Holy Cross Lutheran Primary School," March 22, 1966, HKRS 229-1-675.

81. DE to CS, "Application for Additional Capital Subsidy and Interest-free Loan, Proposed Holy Cross Lutheran Primary School at T.W.T.L. 91, Tsuen Wan, New Territories," December 12, 1968, HKRS 229-1-675.

82. CS to DPW, "Memorandum for Executive Council: Application from Methodist Church for Site for Church and Welfare Centre in Waterloo Road" (138-1), January 29, 1963, HKRS 306-1-134.

83. M.144, Rose Young, November 1963, HKRS 306-1-304.

84. M.147, Rose Young, November 21, 1963, HKRS 306-1-304.

85. K. Lo for Director of Social Welfare (DSW), "Board of Missions of the Methodist Church" (143), September 4, 1963, HKRS 306-1-134.

86. M.9, July 14, 1966, HKRS 156-1-6158.

87. F. C. Gamble to Financial Secretary, "Proposed Opening of Precious Blood Primary School, Wah Fu Estate, in Temporary Premises" (4), November 17, 1967; and Commissioner for Housing to DE, "Wah Fu Estate—Primary Schools" (4-1), October 24, 1967, both in HKRS 229-1-630.

88. M.3, December 17, 1960; M.4, December 21, 1960; and M.5, December 22, 1960, all in HKRS 337-4-862.

89. M.7, January 10, 1961, HKRS 337-4-862.

90. Grantham to SoSC, "American Aid (Governmental and Private)," NAUK.

91. DE to Sterling Whitener (2, 3), July 11, 1959, HKRS 147-7-59.

92. Sid and Olive Anderson to Friends, September 1961, PSRA, Box 9, Folder 28, YUDSL.

93. Sid and Olive Anderson to Friends, September 1960, PSRA, Box 9, Folder 28, YUDSL.

94. Sid and Olive Anderson to Friends, March 15, 1961, PSRA, Box 9, Folder 28, YUDSL.

95. Carter and Agnes Morgan, February 1961, Carter Morgan Papers (CMP), RG 6, "Correspondence, 1955–1975," HKBUL.

96. Hsu, *The Good Immigrants*, 198–235.

97. Institute of International Education (IIE), "Part 1, Four Corners of the Earth, Where They Come From," in *Open Doors 1950–51*, 15.

98. IIE, "Foreign Students: Home Country, Sex, Year Studies in U.S. Began, Financial Support. Academic Status," in *Open Doors, 1961–62*, 21.

99. George McGovern, "Report on Food for Peace Mission, February 1–March 7, 1962: Hong Kong, India, United Arab Republic, Tunisia, and Western Europe" (43-1), 6, HKRS 890-2-18.

100. "Vocational Training, Ward Social Center" (161), undated, HKRS 306-1-134.

101. M.91, August 19, 1961, HKRS 306-1-134.

102. M.96, November 2, 1961, HKRS 306-1-304.

103. Kenneth McIntosh and Jesse Clements to Chan Joy Yin, November 11, 1964; McIntosh to S. W. Dang, November 30, 1964; McIntosh to Chan Joy Yin, Dec. 1, 1964, all in HKRS 306-1-134.

104. "Memorandum for Executive Council: Application from the Lutheran World Federation for a Vocational Training Centre Site at Kwun Tong" (25-1), in HKRS 306-1-116.

105. "New Vocational Centre, Governor to Open It on Thursday," *SCSP-H*, May 16, 1965, in HKRS 306-1-116.

106. W. D. F. Williams, "Vocational Training in Hong Kong—Some General Comments," March 10, 1967, 3, HKRS 306-1-116.

107. See "Activities of Refugee Migration Unit (American Aid)," HKRS 890-2-19.

108. "Minutes of a Meeting Held in the Office of the Deputy Colonial Secretary at 2.15 P.M. on Friday, 29th July, 1960" (2-1), HKRS 890-2-18; D. W. B. Baron to G. T. Rowe (5), September 17, 1960, HKRS 890-2-18.

109. "Minutes of a Meeting Held in the Office of the Deputy Colonial Secretary at 2.15 P.M. on Friday, 26th August" (6-1); "Contract No. S188-fa-420, Agreement Between

the Secretary of State of the United States of America and International Rescue Committee" (19), both in HKRS 890-2-18.

110. DE to CS, "American Aid," January 17, 1961, in HKRS 890-2-18.

111. M.1, October 5, 1961, HKRS 156-1-10405.

112. M.2, October 5, 1961; M.3, October 5, 1961; M.5, October 10, 1961; and G. T. Rowe to Robert Aylward, October 19, 1961, all in HKRS 156-1-10405.

113. A. M. J. Wright to CS (7), October 7, 1961, HKRS 156-1-10405.

114. On the Po Leung Kuk, see Angelina Y. Chin, "Colonial Charity in Hong Kong: A Case of the Po Leung Kuk in the 1930s," *Journal of Women's History* 25, no. 1 (Spring 2013): 135–57. On Nationalist approaches, see Janet Y. Chen, *Guilty of Indigence: The Urban Poor in China, 1900–1953* (Princeton, N.J.: Princeton University Press, 2012), 86–127.

115. DSW, "Note of Discussion with Mr. R. Aylward, Chief of RMU on 21st February, 1961" (20), 1–2; and DSW to CS, "Surplus American Foodstuffs" (51), July 30, 1962, both in HKRS 890-2-18.

116. "FERP Proposed Budget for 1962, Hong Kong"; "Project Summary Forms," both in HKRS 890-2-18.

117. "FERP Program in Hong Kong for CY 1963" (68-1); "List of CY 1964 Contracts" (80-1); "Summary of Recommended CY 1965 Budget for FERP Program in Hong Kong" (82-1), all in HKRS 890-2-18.

118. "H.K. Training School Graduates All Get Jobs," *SCMP*, October 31, 1964, in HKRS 306-1-116.

119. S. Ruth Hansen to Dorothy Lee (142), August 14, 1963, HKRS 306-1-134.

120. "Restricted: Not for Publication, Wong Tai Sin Community Centre" (50-2A), 5, HKRS 156-3-28.

121. "With the Compliments of the Director of Information Services: Visit of H.E. The Governor to Wong Tai Sin Community Centre," September 7, 1960, 1, HKRS 70-2-273.

122. "Restricted: Not for Publication, Wong Tai Sin Community Centre (50-2A)," 5, HKRS 156-3-28.

123. "Extract from China Mail, Wednesday, 13/7/60," in HKRS 70-2-273.

124. On the rhetoric of care in U.S. refugee policies, see Sam Vong, "'Compassion Gave Us a Special Superpower': Vietnamese Women Leaders, Reeducation Camps, and the Politics of Family Reunification, 1977–1991," *Journal of Women's History* 30, no. 3 (Fall 2018): 107–37.

125. "The First Community Centre in Hong Kong: At Wong Tai Sin Resettlement Estate" (71), 2, HKRS 156-3-28.

126. DSW to CS, "World Refugee Year Community Centre at Wong Tai Sin" (33), December 10, 1959, HKRS 156-3-28.

127. "介紹黃大仙社區服務中心" and "Translation: Introducing the Wong Tai Sin Community Centre," HKRS 156-3-28; Ernie Pereira, "Community Centre Helps Refugees," *HKS*, May 20, 1962, HKRS 70-2-273.

128. "黃大仙社區服務中心揭幕儀式中, 美國總領事賀諶士演辭全文, 12.7.60"; and "Text of Speech Delivered by The Honourable Julius C. Holmes, Consul General of the United

States at the Wong Tai Sin Community Center, Kowloon," July 12, 1960, both in HKRS 70-2-273.

129. "Vocational Training at Wong Tai Sin," *SCMP*, July 4, 1960; "Comment of the Day: Resettlement Alka Seltzer," *China Mail*, July 13, 1960, both in HKRS 70-2-273.

130. "New Centre Will Make Self-Reliant Citizens," *SCMP*, May 4, 1960, HKRS 70-2-273.

131. "Community Centre at Wong Tai Sin Opened, World Refugee Year Gift from the US Government, Housewife's Welcome Speech," *SCMP*, July 13, 1960, HKRS 156-3-28.

132. "Text of Speech Delivered by The Honourable Julius C. Holmes," July 12, 1960, HKRS 70-2-273.

133. "Vocational Training for Refugees," *Sing Tao Jih Pao* 23, no. 3, HKRS 70-2-273.

134. "The Hon. Dhun Ruttonjee's Speech on the Occasion of the Laying of the Foundation Stone for the World Rehabilitation Fund Day Centre in Kwun Tong, 10th March 1967" (123), HKRS 306-1-200.

135. See "An Institution for Spastic Children at Sandy Bay (John F. Kennedy Memorial Centre)," HKRS 156-2-2337; and "GIS Press: John F. Kennedy Centre (for Spastic Children in Sandy Bay)," HKRS 70-2-469.

136. Commissioner of Labour to DSW, "Proposed Day Centre for the Disabled" (42), April 23, 1966; T. Y. Tsau, "Notes for Record" (50), May 9, 1966; Commissioner of Labour to DSW, "World Rehabilitation Fund Day Centre for the Handicapped Tsui Ping Road, Kwun Tong" (87), October 4, 1966; all in HKRS 306-1-200.

137. "World Rehabilitation Fund Day Centre, Open Day on Friday, 1 Sep. 1970," HKRS 70-7-400.

138. DSW to CS, "World Rehabilitation Fund Day Centre for the Handicapped, Tsui Ping Road, Kwun Tong" (81), August 19, 1966, 2, HKRS 306-1-200.

139. "Governor Opens World Rehabilitation Fund Day Centre, Thursday, September 5, 1968," HKRS 70-1-331.

140. "World Rehabilitation Fund Day Centre, Celebration to Mark Third Anniversary, 30 Aug. 1971," HKRS 70-7-400. On Rose, see "ROSE, Halleck L.," in *Hongkong Album, Fifth Edition*, ed. P. C. Lee (Hong Kong: Sin Poh Amalgamated, 1967–1968), 277–78, HKUSC.

141. "Urban Council Meeting, 4 June 1963," 2; and "Rain Didn't Dampen the Spirits at the Kowloon Tsai Park Yesterday," *HKS*, June 10, 1967, 8, both in HKRS 70-3-361.

142. Peter Wong and Sterling Whitener to DE, February 11, 1966, HKRS 147-7-59.

143. "Hong Kong Council—Church of Christ in China, Proposed Junior College," February 11, 1966, HKRS 147-7-59.

3. Cold War Partners

1. Director of Education [DE] to Colonial Secretary [CS], "Confidential" (10-1), August 2, 1951 [Hong Kong Public Records Office, Kwun Tong], Hong Kong Record Series (HKRS) 163-1-1599.

2. "American Universities Club Proposed," *Hong Kong Sunday Herald*, April 23, 1950, 2; "Dr. C. T. Wang Elected President of American University Club," *China Mail*, May 18, 1950, 3.

3. "What Is AUC?" *AmCham* 9, no. 7 (July 1978): 77. For Frillman see Ellen D. Wu, *The Color of Success: Asian Americans and the Origins of the Model Minority* (Princeton, N.J.: Princeton University Press, 2013), 131. For Moy, see Madeline Y. Hsu, *The Good Immigrants: How the Yellow Peril Became the Model Minority* (Princeton, N.J.: Princeton University Press, 2015), 137–39.

4. For C. T. Wang, see Chinese Students' Christian Association in North America Archives, RG 13, Yale University Divinity School Library (YUDSL).

5. "上海交際花, 唐瑛結婚," *Dongnan Ribao* (東南日報), July 5, 1936, 6.

6. Anthony Sweeting, "The University by Report," in *An Impossible Dream: Hong Kong University from Foundation to Re-Establishment, 1910–1950*, ed. Chan Lau Kit-ching and Peter Cunich (Oxford: Oxford University Press, 2002), 220; Jun Fang, "Lai Jixi and the Development of Chinese Education at the University of Hong Kong," *Journal of the Royal Asiatic Society Hong Kong Branch* 52 (2012): 267–89.

7. Chan Lau Kit-ching, "The Post-War Re-establishment of the University of Hong Kong, 1945–1950," in *An Impossible Dream: Hong Kong University from Foundation to Re-Establishment, 1910–1950*, ed. Chan Lau Kit-ching and Peter Cunich (Oxford: Oxford University Press, 2002), 244, 258.

8. DE to CS, "Confidential (10-1)," August 2, 1951, HKRS 163-1-1599.

9. For example, see, Pui Wing Fung, "The Development of Higher Education in a Developing City: Hong Kong, 1900–1980," Ph.D. dissertation, University of Hull, September 1988.

10. The United Board soon changed its name to the United Board for Christian Higher Education in Asia.

11. Helen Laville, "The Importance of Being (In)Earnest: Voluntary Associations and the Irony of the State-Private Networks During the Early Cold War," in *The US Government, Citizen Groups and the Cold War*, ed. Helen Laville and Hugh Wilford (London: Routledge, 2006), 53.

12. Li Choh-ming, *The First Six Years, 1963–1969*, 3, Papers of the Yale-China Association (YCA), Yale University Library Manuscripts & Archives (YUMA).

13. Grace Ai-ling Chou, *Confucianism, Colonialism, and the Cold War: Chinese Cultural Education at Hong Kong's New Asia College, 1949–63* (Leiden: Brill, 2011), 119–20.

14. John Carroll, "A Historical Perspective: The 1967 Riots and the Strike Boycott of 1925–1926," in *May Days in Hong Kong: Riot and Emergency in 1967*, ed. Robert Bickers and Ray Yep (Hong Kong: Hong Kong University Press, 2009), 75.

15. Hall to DE (10-3A), August 14, 1951, HKRS 163-1-1599.

16. DE to CS, "Memo: Chung Chi College," May 18, 1953, 1, HKRS 163-1-1599.

17. Austin Coates to DE (10), August 28, 1951, HKRS 163-1-1599.

18. "The Annual Report of the President of Chung Chi College, 1952–1953" (14-1D), 1–2, HKRS 163-1-1599.

19. David Au, "Chung Chi College," July 28, 1952, United Board for Christian Higher Education in Asia (UBCHEA), RG 11A, Box 114A, Folder 1562, YUDSL.

20. "Minutes of the Annual Meeting of the Board of Governors, Chung Chi College, June 27, 1958," 2, UBCHEA, RG 11A, Box 110A, Folder 1508, YUDSL.

21. 李瑞明, 南國鳳凰: 中山大學嶺南（大學）學院 (Hong Kong: Commercial Press, 2005), 88–91, 98–103.

22. Thomas D. Scott to President, CFA San Francisco, September 9, 1953, Box P-55, "Hong Kong: Individuals—General (Overseas Chinese Contacts)," Hoover Institution, Stanford University.

23. William Fenn to Olin Wannamaker, "Memorandum: Chung Chi College in Hong Kong," November 10, 1952, Archives of the Trustees of Lingnan University (ATLU), Box 22, Folder 311, YUDSL.

24. "Report of the Ad Hoc Committee on the Establishment of Chung Chi College," 17, UBCHEA, RG 11A, Box 110A, Folder 1518, YUDSL.

25. Au to Fenn, November 16, 1954, UBCHEA, Box 114A, Folder 1564, YUDSL.

26. "Government House Conference, May 16th, 1953: Chung Chi College," 2; and DE to CS, "Memo: Chung Chi College," May 18, 1953, 1, both in HKRS 163-1-1599.

27. Lee to Wannamaker, June 8, 1953, ATLU, RG 14, Box 41, Folder 481, YUDSL.

28. DE to CS, "Memo: Chung Chi College," May 18, 1953, 1, HKRS 163-1-1599.

29. Keswick to Grantham (1), April 30, 1952, HKRS 41-1-7283.

30. Deputy Colonial Secretary (DCS) to Lindsey Ride (4), May 22, 1952, HKRS 41-1-7283.

31. See Ride to CS (6), June 4, 1952; Ride to CS (9), July 22, 1952; Ride to CS (11), August 15, 1952; Crozier to CS (12), October 25, 1952; all in HKRS 41-1-7283.

32. Ride to Grantham (14), January 19, 1953; "Memorandum on the Proposed Chinese Courses" (16), January 1953; CS, "Note of a Meeting Held in the Colonial Secretariat at 9.45 A.M. on Wednesday, 28th Jan., 1953" (17), all in HKRS 41-1-7283.

33. DE to CS (23), February 11, 1953, HKRS 41-1-7283.

34. Keswick to CS (25), February 24, 1953, HKRS 41-1-7283.

35. Ride to DE (3), May 5, 1953, HKRS 163-1-1599.

36. Chou, *Confucianism, Colonialism, and the Cold War*, 110–16.

37. Alfred Hayes to Wallace Donham, January 8, 1952, ATLU, RG 14, Box 12, Folder 157, YUDSL.

38. Lee to Wannamaker, June 8, 1953, ATLU, RG 14, Box 41, Folder 481, YUDSL.

39. Fenn to Andrew Roy, June 3, 1954, UBCHEA, RG 11A, Box 124A, Folder 1729, YUDSL.

40. "Exhibit 'A': Proposed Budget for Chung Chi College, Aug. 1, 1957 to July 31, 1958," UBCHEA, RG 11A, Box 59A, Folder 775, YUDSL; "Chung Chi College, Statement of Income & Expenditure as against the Budget, Oct. 31, 1959," UBCHEA, RG 11A, Box 110A, Folder 1513, YUDSL.

41. "Chung Chi College Building Fund, Financial Statement, as at May 31, 1959," UBCHEA, RG 11A, Box 110A, Folder 1513, YUDSL.

42. Fenn to Wannamaker, May 19, 1953, ATLU, RG 14, Box 22, Folder 311, YUDSL.

43. "歐偉國逝世," *Wah Kiu Yat Po* 華僑日報 (*WKYP*), March 5, 1959, 4; "歐偉國昨病逝，遺體今日舉殯," *Kong Sheung Yat Po* 工商日報 (*KSYP*), March 5, 1959, 4

44. "歐偉國," in 吳醒濂, 香港華人名人史畧 (Hong Kong: Wuzhou Shuju, 1937), 76.

45. "宋子文: 電告來港行期, 廣東銀行總行行長, 已内定歐偉國繼任," *KSYP*, November 16, 1936, 9; "今晨廣東銀行復業, 宋子文定今晚或明日晉省, 新經理歐偉國談廣東銀行復業後方針, 仍以粵人之資金發展粵人商業為前提," *KSYP*, November 23, 1936, 9.

46. K. P. Chen, "Cooperation," March 16, 1949, 2, Kwang Pu Chen Papers, 1936–1958, Group B, File 8, Rare Book and Library Collections, Columbia University.

47. "歐偉國逝世," *WKYP*, March 5, 1959, 4.

48. York Lo, "Lee Hysan; Lee, Richard Charles Ming-chak; and Lee, Harold Hsiao-wo," in *Dictionary of Hong Kong Biography* (*DHKB*), ed. May Holdsworth and Christopher Munn (Hong Kong: Hong Kong University Press, 2012), 250.

49. "聖約翰大學校友會, 新職員昨選出, 歐偉國當選本屆制度," *WKYP*, September 14, 1951, 6.

50. Mary Ferguson to Au, April 7, 1953, and Au to Ferguson, April 16, 1953, both in UBCHEA, RG 11A, Box 114A, Folder 1563, "David W. K. Au, 1953," YUDSL.

51. On ARCI, see Hsu, *The Good Immigrants*, 130–65; Glen Peterson, "Crisis and Opportunity: The Work of Aid Refugee Chinese Intellectuals (ARCI) in Hong Kong and Beyond," in *Hong Kong in the Cold War*, ed. Priscilla Roberts and John M. Carroll (Hong Kong: HKU Press, 2016), 141–59; Meredith Oyen, *The Diplomacy of Migration: Transnational Lives and the Making of US-Chinese Relations in the Cold War* (Ithaca, N.Y.: Cornell University Press, 2015), 154–84.

52. Au to Ferguson, August 12, 1952, and Ferguson to Au, August 13, 1952, both in UBCHEA, RG 11A, Box 114A, Folder 1562, YUDSL.

53. Fenn to Wannamaker, May 19, 1953, ATLU, RG 14, Box 22, Folder 311, YUDSL.

54. Au to Fenn, November 16, 1954, UBCHEA, RG 11A, Box 114A, Folder 1564, YUDSL.

55. Au to Fenn, October 15, 1953, UBCHEA, RG 11A, Box 114A, Folder 1563, YUDSL.

56. Au to Fenn, November 2, 1953, UBCHEA, RG 11A, Box 114A, Folder 1563, YUDSL.

57. Au to Fenn, November 16, 1954, UBCHEA, RG 11A, Box 114A, Folder 1564, YUDSL.

58. Fenn, October 16, 1952, UBCHEA, RG 11A, Box 114A, Folder 1562, YUDSL.

59. Au to Fenn, November 2, 1953, UBCHEA, RG 11A, Box 114A, Folder 1563, YUDSL.

60. Fenn to Au, December 2, 1953, UBCHEA, RG 11A, Box 114A, Folder 1563, YUDSL.

61. Au to Fenn, December 11, 1953, UBCHEA, RG 11A, Box 114A, Folder 1563, YUDSL.

62. "Report of the Ad Hoc Committee on the Establishment of Chung Chi College," 2, UBCHEA, RG 11A, Box 110A, Folder 1518, YUDSL.

63. Au to DE, "Re: Site at Ma Liu Shui (New Territories) (14-1)," November 26, 1953, 3, HKRS 163-1-1599.

64. DE to CS, "Memo: Chung Chi College" (14), November 30, 1953, HKRS 163-1-1599.

65. DE to Au (11-1), June 8, 1953, HKRS 163-1-1599.

66. M.33, Acting DE to CS, March 27, 1954, HKRS 163-1-1599.

67. Au to DE (16-1), December 16, 1953, HKRS 163-1-1599.

68. Au to Fenn, December 17, 1953, UBCHEA, RG 11A, Box 114A, Folder 1564, YUDSL.

69. John F. Padgett and Christopher Ansell, "Robust Action and the Rise of the Medici, 1400–1434," *American Journal of Sociology* 98, no. 6 (May 1993): 1264.

70. Fenn to Au, December 31, 1953, UBCHEA, RG 11A, Box 114A, Folder 1563, YUDSL.

71. Fenn to Au, February 1, 1954, UBCHEA, RG 11A, Box 114A, Folder 1564, YUDSL.

72. "Report of the Ad Hoc Committee," 3.

73. Postscript, Au to Fenn, August 18, 1954, UBCHEA, RG 11A, Box 114A, Folder 1564, YUDSL.

74. Au to Fenn, May 12, 1954, UBCHEA, RG 11A, Box 114A, Folder 1564, YUDSL.

75. Fenn to Au, 1–3, May 25, 1954, UBCHEA, RG 11A, Box 114A, Folder 1564, YUDSL.

76. Acting DE to CS, "Memo: Chung Chi College—Funds from America and British Sources" (74), October 21, 1954, HKRS 163-1-1599.

77. For the withdrawal, see Au to CS, November 13, 1954. For the board nominees, see DE to CS, "Chung Chi College" (80), December 20, 1954, both in HKRS 163-1-1599.

78. M.110, DCS to CS, October 15, 1954, 50, HKRS 163-1-1599.

79. M.116, DCS to CS, October 25, 1954, 53, HKRS 163-1-1599.

80. M.117, ACS to Grantham, October 26, 1954, 54, HKRS 163-1-1599.

81. Au to Fenn, August 16, 1954, 1, UBCHEA, RG 11A, Box 114A, Folder 1564, YUDSL.

82. Au to Fenn, November 16, 1954, UBCHEA, RG 11A, Box 114A, Folder 1564, YUDSL.

83. Sterling H. Whitener, *In the Shadow of the Pagoda* (N.p.: CreateSpace, 2013), 213–14.

84. Au to Fenn, January 26, 1955, UBCHEA, RG 11A, Box 114A, Folder 1564, YUDSL. Also see Chihyun Chang, ed., *The Chinese Journals of L. K. Little, 1943–1954: An Eyewitness Account of War and Revolution*, vol. 2 (Oxford: Routledge, 2018), 34.

85. "歐偉國昨病逝，遺體今日舉殯," *KSYP*, March 5, 1959, 4; "Chung Chi College, Minutes of the College Council Meeting, March 13, 1959," UBCHEA, RG 11A, Box 110A, Folder 1513, YUDSL. On the loan, see Henry Palmer to Au, December 19, 1955; James Cameron to Fenn, November 2, 1960, both in UBCHEA, RG 11A, Box 114A, Folder 1564, YUDSL.

86. For Lin's travels and relationship with Roy, see "Minutes of the Meeting of the Board of Governors, Chung Chi College" between 1956 and 1960 in UBCHEA, RG 11A, Box 110A, Folder 1508, YUDSL.

87. "本校歷屆畢業生就分配圖, Professional Distribution of Graduates," *Chung Chi College: Story in Pictures, 1951–1961*, 47, Papers of Sidney R. Anderson, Box 10, Folder 49, YUDSL.

88. For Hall working against Lin, see M.144, Sir Alexander Grantham, February 27, 1958, HKRS 163-1-1599.

89. "College Presidents," *University Bulletin* 1, no. 2, (July 1964): 7.

90. Chou, *Confucianism, Colonialism, and the Cold War*, 18–19, 38, 40.

91. C. L. Chien, "Report on New Asia College" (1), May 15, 1959, 1, HKRS 147-3-4.

92. B. Preston Schoyer, "A New Asian University: The Chinese University of Hong Kong," *Yale Alumni Magazine*, March 1966, 32.

93. Chou, *Confucianism, Colonialism, and the Cold War*, 23–24, 51.

94. Nancy E. Chapman with Jessica C. Plumb, *The Yale-China Association: A Centennial History* (Hong Kong: Chinese University of Hong Kong Press, 2001), 75.

95. Betsy Lee (Mrs. Ming Cho Lee) to Henry Baldwin, July 30, 1990, Yale College Records, Class of 1919, Box 1, Folder "Lee, Tsufa, 1987, 1990," YUMA.

96. Preston Schoyer, "Biographical Sketch of B. PRESTON SCHOYER (made up in 1962)," YCA, RU 233, Box 49, Folder 721, YUMA. Also see Joseph Walker, ed., *Hong Kong Who's Who: An Almanac of Personalities and Their Comprehensive Histories, 1970–1973* (Hong Kong; N.p., 1970), 415.

97. Chapman, *The Yale-China Association*, 81.

98. "A Note on the Chinese Post-Secondary Colleges," 2, BW90/556 (1958–1960), National Archives of the United Kingdom, Kew (NAUK).

99. "Speech of Prof. Harry Rudin at 22d Anniversary of Founders' Day, New Asia College, Kowloon, Hong Kong," September 28, 1971, 3, YCA, RG 37, Box 41, Folder 592, YUMA.

100. Chou, *Confucianism, Colonialism, and the Cold War*, 3–4.

101. Chapman, *The Yale-China Association*, 83.

102. C. L. Chien, "Report on New Asia College" (3), April 12, 1961, 2, HKRS 147-3-4.

103. Yale-in-China Association, "Statement on the Development of Higher Education for the Free Chinese of Hong Kong and Southeast Asia," n.d., 4–6, YCA, RU 233, Box 52, Folder 771, YUMA.

104. C. L. Chien, "Report on New Asia College" (1), May 15, 1959, 6, HKRS 147-3-4.

105. Chien, "Report on New Asia College" (1), May 15, 1959, 1.

106. C. L. Chien, "Note on New Asia College" (2), April 4, 1960, 2–3, HKRS 147-3-4.

107. Chou, *Confucianism, Colonialism, and the Cold War*, 138–42.

108. Zhang Yang, "Cultural Cold War: The American Role in Establishing the Chinese University of Hong Kong (CUHK)," in *The Power of Culture: Encounters Between China and the United States*, ed. Priscilla Roberts (Newcastle Upon Tyne: Cambridge Scholars, 2016), 150–61.

109. Alice N. H. Lun Ng, "The Founding," in *The Quest for Excellence: A History of The Chinese University of Hong Kong from 1963 to 1993*, ed. Alice N. H. Lun Ng (Hong Kong: Chinese University Press, 1994), 15–16.

110. "The Vice-Chancellors' Statement on the Supplementary Budget of 1964/1965 and the Annual Budget of 1965/66," 6, HKRS 229-1-564.

111. "Dr. LAM Chi Fung, 1892–1971," Carter Morgan Papers (CMP), RG 6, "Correspondence 1955–75," Hong Kong Baptist University Library (HKBUL).

112. Reginald H. Roy, *David Lam: A Biography* (Vancouver: Douglas & McIntyre, 1996), 6–9.

113. "潮州人邑商會主席, 林子豐談赴省請願經過," *KSYP*, March 11, 1938, 11.

114. "林子豐宴顏惠慶,"*KSYP*, March 2, 1939, 4.

115. "汕頭難民集中礐石, 林子豐今日謁許世英請示救濟," *KSYP*, June 27, 1939, 4; "林子豐等, 今日謁許世英," *KSYP*, June 27, 1939, 7; "中賑會撥款二萬, 賑濟潮汕難民, 林子豐昨往謁許世英, 將首先購運糧食接濟," *Ta Kung Pao* 大公報 (*TKP*), June 28, 1939, 6.

116. "王泉笙, 定期回菲," *TKP*, January 20, 1940, 6; "泰國宣傳部長, 威拉斯返泰港, 林子豐等昨日設宴款待," *TKP*, May 11, 1940, 6; "華南婦女節制會, 展賣會昨日舉行, 王立明主席林子豐揭幕, 出品精美遊藝極爲豐富," *TKP*, June 16, 1940, 6; "林子豐昨晚廣播演講, 青年會之歷史, 公開呼籲協助籌募, 今晚慶祝四十週年紀念," *TKP*, November 20, 1941, 6.

117. "Glory to God in the Highest: Twenty Years of History of the Hong Kong Baptist Association," 1–3, 1958, Papers of the Hong Kong-Macau Baptist Mission (HKMBM), RG 3, Folder 13, HKBUL.

118. Roy, *David Lam*, 43.

119. On Dee, see Maybelle Tan, "Dee Ching Quan," in *Southeast Asian Personalities of Chinese Descent: A Biographical Dictionary*, ed. Leo Suryadinata (Singapore: Institute of Southeast Asian Studies, 2002), 229–31. On his wartime activities, see Antonio S. Tan, "The Philippine Chinese Response to the Sino-Japanese Conflict, 1931–1941," *Journal of Southeast Asian Studies* 12, no. 1 (March 1981): 218. Also see "李清泉遺產, 損養難民," *WKYP*, October 31, 1940, 2.

120. "Ka Wah Bank: Standing Tall in Hong Kong," *Euromoney* (June 1984), S12.

121. Roy, *David Lam*, 59–61.

122. "Governor Pays Visit to Local Factories," *China Mail*, February 18, 1957, 10.

123. Roy, *David Lam*, 66–67.

124. "David See-Chai Lam," in *Online Encyclopedia of Canadian Christian Leaders*, http://www .canadianchristianleaders.org/leader/david-see-chai-lam/, accessed May 14, 2017.

125. Roy, *David Lam*, 63.

126. "青年會新董事, 林子豐等十五人當選," *WKYP*, December 24, 1947, 8; "青年會昨夕歡迎, 美籍幹事來華服務, 林子豐致詞讚揚備至," *WKYP*, January 20, 1948, 6.

127. "不錯, 青年會本身不是工商業團體, 但青年會是對社會任何方面都去服務衲團體, 我們本會基督精神向人類服務, 我們舉辦道次展覽, [smudged character] 就是向人類服務的一種措施." See "會長林子豐致詞, 申述舉辦展會目的," *KSYP*, August 16, 1948, 5. Also see "林子豐報告, 工商展覽意義," *TKP*, August 16, 1948, 4; "林子豐闡述, 展覽會意義," *WKYP*, August 16, 1948, 4.

128. Maurice Anderson, *The Survival Strategies of a Complex Organization* (Hong Kong: N.p., 1972), 47.

129. Carter Morgan, "Requiem for a Refuge—169 Boundary Street, Kowloon, Hong Kong," 1–2, April–May 1996, CMP, "Articles, 1996," HKBUL.

130. Roy, *David Lam*, 79.

131. Carter Morgan, "Hong-Kong Baptist Theological Seminary," June 1956, CMP, "Correspondence, 1955–75," HKBUL.

132. "Glory to God in the Highest," 4, HKBUL.

133. "Glory to God in the Highest," 1; Gertrude Tharpe, "The History of Hong Kong Baptist College," M.A. thesis, Furman University, 1965, 59, HKBUL.

134. C. L. Chien, "Note on Hong Kong Baptist College" (53), 1, HKRS 147-4-8.

135. Anderson, *Survival Strategies*, 59–60.

136. Carter and Agnes Morgan, "Post-Script #36," November 1957, CMP, "Correspondence, 1955–75," HKBUL.

137. Lowe, Bingham, and Matthews, "Hong Kong Baptist College, Statement of Accounts for the Year Ended July 31, 1964"; and "Hongkong Baptist College Building Fund," November 4, 1965, both in HKMBM, RG 3, Folder 54, HKBUL.

138. Anderson, *Survival Strategies*, 70, 90, 93. "Library Gift Received," *College News*, 2–3, March 1959 (41), HKRS 147-4-8; "Board Chairman Visited Dr. David Carter," *Our College* 1, no. 1 (April 1968): 14, HKBUL.

139. Roy, *David Lam*, 103.

140. Tharpe, "The History of Hong Kong Baptist College," 73–74.

141. Anderson, *Survival Strategies*, 59–60, 64–65, 56.

142. "林子豐博士, 陳楫亭女士, 金婚大慶, 捐獻五十五萬浸大教會," *KSYP*, December 31, 1970, 6.

143. Anderson, *Survival Strategies*, 65, 73.

144. "Newsmaker: Dr. M. J. Anderson, President of HKSS," *Our College* 1, no. 1 (April 1968): 18, HKBUL.

145. Carter Morgan, "Post Script #71, David Y. K. Wong," October 1975, CMP, "Correspondence 1955–75," HKBUL.

146. "Board Chairman Visited Dr. David Carter," and "Visitors from Redlands U.," both in *Our College* 1 no. 1 (April 1968), 14, HKBUL.

147. "Former BWA President David Wong Dies at 97," *Baptist News Global*, September 23, 2008, http://www.abpnews.com/archives/item/3534-former-bwa-president-david-wong-dies-at-97#.UwaJoijOa44.

148. C. L. Chien, "Note on Hong Kong Baptist College" (53), 1–3, HKRS 147-4-8.

149. Chien, "Note on Hong Kong Baptist College," 5. On revivals and conversions, see "Religious Emphasis Week," *College News* 2 (January 1, 1962) (115), HKRS 147-4-8. Also see Anderson, *Survival Strategies*, 86.

150. "Staff & Grads at Stetson," *Our College* 1, no. 1 (April 1968): 16; "Faculty & Staff: Mr. Bernard Liebes," *Our College* 1, no. 2 (July 1968): 21, HKBUL.

151. Anderson, *Survival Strategies*, 54, 81.

152. "Baptist College Graduate News," *College News* (Winter 1964), 6–7, HKMBM, Folder 54, HKBUL.

153. "Ph.D.'s from HKBC Alumni," *Our College* 1, no. 3 (April 1969): 12, HKBUL.

154. Lam Chi-fung, "What I See in America: Hong Kong Chinese Christian Church Retreat," in *A Collection of Speeches and Writings of Dr. Lam Chi-Fung*, ed. Lee King Sun (Hong Kong: Hong Kong Pui Ching Middle School, 1965), 312.

155. Morgan, "Dr. LAM Chi Fung, 1892–1971," HKBUL.

156. Lam Chi Fung, "A Message to All," *Our College* 1, no. 3 (April 1969): 4; "Faculty & Staff: Dr. Lam Chi Fung," *Our College* 1, no. 3 (April 1969): 19, both in HKBUL.

157. Kim McGrath, "A Gift of Chinese culture," *Wake Forest News*, January 20, 2012, http://news.wfu.edu/2012/01/20/a-gift-of-chinese-culture/. Also see "Legacy: About Tim," Timothy S. Y. Lam Foundation, http://timothysylam.org/legacy.aspx, accessed May 14, 2017.

158. "美電池廠經理來港視察業務," *WKYP*, May 21, 1953, 5; "林思顯飛美參加業務會議," *WKYP*, May 24, 1957, 10; "捷和電筒廠總經理林思顯反港," *WKYP*, July 27, 1957, 10.

159. "LAM Chi-fung, Dr., O.B.E., LL.D.," *Hongkong Album*, 1967–68, HKU Libraries, Special Collections (HKUSC).

160. Lam to DE (21), March 18, 1958, HKRS 147-4-8.

161. Lam to DE (52), September 25, 1959, HKRS 147-4-8.

162. Tharpe, *The History of Hong Kong Baptist College*, 54, 62.

163. *College News*, May 15, 1962, quoted in Tharpe, *The History of Hong Kong Baptist College*, 57.

164. Tharpe, *The History of Hong Kong Baptist College*, 55.

165. "Question 9: Reply by the Honourable J. Canning, JP, to Question by the Honourable Wilfred WONG Sien-bing, OBE, JP, in Legislative Council on 31.1.73"; and "Government Loan to Baptist College," January 28, 1975, both in HKRS 70-6-479-1.

166. Black to Secretary of State for the Colonies, "Post-Secondary Colleges," February 7, 1959, BW90/556 (1958–1960), NAUK.

167. Ramachandra Guha, "Pluralism in the Indian University," *Economic and Political Weekly* 42, no. 7 (February 2007): 564–70; A. J. Stockwell, " 'The Crucible of the Malayan Nation': The University and the Making of a New Malaya, 1938–62," *Modern Asian Studies* 43, no. 5 (September 2009): 1149–87.

168. Gatian F. Lungu, "Colonial Zambia: The Case of Higher Education for Africans from 1924 to 1964," *Journal of Negro History* 78, no. 4 (Autumn 1993): 207–32.

169. Far Eastern Department, Colonial Office, "Chung Chi College, Hong Kong," August 1956, 2, HKMS 158-1-11.

170. "Conference at the Education Department," May 20, 1959, 1, UBCHEA, RG 11A, Box 110A, Folder 1513, YUDSL.

171. "Confidential: Chinese Post Secondary Colleges in Hong Kong," 2, 4, BW90/556 (1958–1960), NAUK.

172. For New Asia, see Vermier Y. Chu to DE, July 15, 1959, HKRS 147-3-1. For Chung Chi, see "Minutes of the Meeting of the Board of Governors, Chung Chi College, July 14, 1959," 2, UBCHEA, RG 11A, Box 110A, Folder 1508, YUDSL.

173. Black to CS, February 7, 1959, HKRS 264-3-2.

174. Black to W. I. J. Wallace, Colonial Office, August 25, 1962, 2, CO1030/1099 (1960–62), NAUK.

4. The Turning Point

1. Li Choh-ming, "Inauguration Speech," September 9, 1964, 1, Papers of the Yale-China Association (YCA), RU232, Box 80, "CUHK Vice-Chancellor, 1963–65," Yale University, Manuscripts and Archives (YUMA).

2. Li Choh-ming, "Draft (Inauguration Speech)" (21-1), September 1, 1964, 1 [Kwun Tong, Hong Kong Public Records Office], Hong Kong Record Series (HKRS) 146-5-30.

3. "李卓敏校長在就職禮表示, 決心辦好中文大學, 成為世界知名學府," *Kong Sheung Yat Po* (*KSYP*), September 10, 1964, 5; "Red, Purple and Gold: Dr. Li Installed as Chinese Varsity [*sic*] V-C," *Hongkong Tiger Standard* (*HKTS*), September 10, 1964, 2; "決使大學成國際性, 但並非要完全西化," *Sing Tao Yat Po* (*STYP*), September 10, 1964, 20; "New University An International Institution," *South China Morning Post* (*SCMP*), September 10, 1964, 6. For his retirement speech, see "Address by Dr. Choh-Ming Li," *Chinese University Bulletin* (Winter 1978), 6–7.

4. Helen Laville and Hugh Wilford, eds., *The US Government, Citizens Groups and the Cold War: The State-Private Network* (London: Routledge, 2006).

5. Li Choh-ming, "Inauguration Speech," 1.

6. For example, see Ross Barrett, "Aligning India in the Cold War Era: Indian Technological Elites, the Indian Institute of Technology at Kanpur, and Computing in India and the United States," *Technology and Culture* 50, no. 4 (October 2009): 783–810.

7. Li Choh-ming, " 'Cultural Desert Is Now Meaningless!' " *University Bulletin (UB)* 3, no. 9 (April 1967), 2.

8. "Choh-Ming Li, Business Administration: Berkeley," in *University of California: In Memoriam, 1992*, ed. David Krogh, 102, http://texts.cdlib.org/view?docId=hb7c6007s j&query=&brand=calisphere.

9. "Man in the News: Hormone Synthesizer Choh Hao Li," *New York Times*, January 7. 1971, 23.

10. "Passengers," *China Press*, July 27, 1930, 14.

11. Li Choh-ming, *"Addendum:* A Message to the Colleges," October 28, 1977, in *A New Era Begins, 1975–1978: The Chinese University of Hong Kong* (Hong Kong: Chinese University of Hong Kong, 1978), 33, Harvard-Yenching Library.

12. Madeline Y. Hsu, *The Good Immigrants: How the Yellow Peril Became the Model Minority* (Princeton, N.J.: Princeton University Press, 2015), 71–74. Also see Chih Meng, *Chinese American Understanding: A Sixty-Year Search* [忠恕堂: 六十年之追求] (New York: China Institute in America, 1981).

13. Tomoko Shiroyama, *China During the Great Depression: Market, State, and the World Economy, 1929–1937* (Cambridge, Mass.: Harvard East Asian Monographs, 2009); William Kirby, "Continuity and Change in Modern China: Economic Planning on the Mainland and on Taiwan, 1943–1958," *Australian Journal of Chinese Affairs* 24 (July 1990): 125–27.

14. Paul B. Trescott, "H. D. Fong and the Study of Chinese Economic Development," *History of Political Economy* 34, no. 4 (2002): 789–809. Also see Xi Zhou, "The Institute of Pacific Relations and the Nankai Institute of Economics," M.A. thesis, University of Hawai'i at Manoa, 1999, 62–64.

15. See Choh Hao Li Papers (CHLP), UCSF Manuscript Collections MS88-9.

16. John F. Burns, "Taiwan Is Seeking High-Tech Growth," *New York Times*, May 12, 1986, D1. On Hsinchu, see AnnaLee Saxenian, *The New Argonauts: Regional Advantage in a Global Economy* (Cambridge, Mass.: Harvard University Press, 2006), 122–96.

17. Author's interview with Jean Li Rogers, March 27, 2018.

18. "Choh-Ming Li," *San Francisco Chronicle*, April 23, 1991, B6; Li Choh-ming to family, December 26, 1972, CHLP, UCSF, Box 6, Folder "Chinese University of Hong Kong, 1965, 1968–72."

19. Sylvia Zhi-Wen Lu Li with Xin Li, Emma Yee Li, and Winston Li, "Good Fortune Indeed: My Cup Runneth Over" (1997), 74–75, http://www.loassociates.com /FamilyTree/makeup/g3.%20CM,%20Sylvia.pdf.

20. Author's interview with Jean Li Rogers, March 27, 2018.

21. Li's early publications include "The Effect of Depreciated Exchange Upon Merchandise Movements," *Quarterly Journal of Economics* 49, no. 3 (May 1935): 495–502; "On Chinese Foreign Exchange Control," *Amerasia* (August 1939); "The Theory of International Trade Under Silver Exchange," *Quarterly Journal of Economics* 53, no. 4 (August 1939): 491–521; and "War and Trade in China," *China Forum* (December 1939).

22. Felix Boecking, *No Great Wall: Trade, Tariffs, and Nationalism in Republican China, 1927–1945* (Cambridge, Mass.: Harvard University Asia Center, 2017).

23. Sylvia Lu Li, "Good Fortune Indeed," 75–76.

24. Henry F. Grady with John T. McNay, *The Memoirs of Henry F. Grady* (Columbia: University of Missouri Press, 2009), 63–64.

25. Li Choh-ming, review of *China's Postwar Markets* by Chih Tsang, *Pacific Affairs* 18, no. 4 (December 1945): 381.

26. "Chinese Educators to Work in U.S.," *Austin Statesman*, April 28, 1943, 5; Kirby, "Continuity and Change," 130.

27. "Chinese Mission Refutes Rumor of Defeat," *Christian Science Monitor*, June 4, 1943, 8; "Anniversary Mass Meeting Planned for Wednesday," *Washington Post*, July 2, 1943, B4; "6th Anniversary of China's Stand to Be Celebrated," *Washington Post*, July 5, 1943, 9.

28. Trescott, "H. D. Fong," 802–3.

29. Li Choh-ming to Li Choh-hao and Annie Li, August 3, 1944; and T. L. Tsui, Chinese Embassy to Choh Ming Li, Chinese Supply Commission, August 15, 1944, both in CHLP, UCSF, Box 1, Folder "Department of State, 1944."

30. "Economic Policy of China Revised, New Official Program for the Nation's Reconstruction Told Here by Dr. Choh-Ming Li," *New York Times*, February 4, 1945, 19.

31. "李卓敏談: 救濟品分配無國共之分," *KSYP*, July 17, 1946, 4. Also see Li, "Good Fortune Indeed," 79.

32. Li, "Good Fortune Indeed," 78; author's interview with Jean Li Rogers, March 27, 2018.

33. "李卓敏談:救濟品分配無國共之分," *KSYP*, July 17, 1946, 4; "出席聯總會議，李卓敏昨過港," *KYSP*, July 16, 1946, 4.

34. "大貪污案, 行總高級官員, 密告檢舉, 李卓敏生活窮奢極侈, 寓所費用由行總付賬," *Wah Kiu Yat Po (WKYP)* 華僑日報, August 16, 1947, 1.

35. Li, "Good Fortune Indeed," 79. Also see Rong Zongjing's use of networks to blunt government extortion in 1927: Sherman Cochran, *Encountering Chinese Networks: Western, Japanese, and Chinese Corporations in China, 1880–1937* (Berkeley: University of California Press, 2000), 138–40.

36. "李卓敏被控案, 下不起訴處分, 魯克斯致函表彰工作, 李現應聘赴美講學," *KSYP*, January 15, 1948, 2; Li, "Good Fortune Indeed," 79.

37. "行總李卓敏貪污案成立," *KSYP*, September 16, 1947, 1; "李卓敏罪名任用私人," *KSYP*, September 17, 1947, 1; "李卓敏貪污, 受停職處分, 移送監察院依法審查," *KSYP*, September 19, 1947, 1; "李卓敏, 先行停職, 依法審查," *WKYP*, September 19, 1947, 1; "李卓敏等多人被滬法院控告," *KSYP*, September 30, 1947, 2; "Yuan Opens Attack on Soong's Post, Thirteen CNRRA Officials Indicted," *China Mail (CM)*, September 30, 1947, 1; "李卓敏等, 交保候訊," *KSYP*, October 1, 1947, 1; "行總舞弊案, 李卓敏等九名, 下不起訴處分," *WKYP*, December 20, 1947, 1.

38. "CNRRA Charges," *CM*, January 26, 1948, 1; "CNRRA Heads Sentenced," *CM*, April 3, 1948, 1.

39. Author's interview with Jean Li Rogers, March 27, 2018.

40. "李卓敏被控案, 下不起訴處分, 魯克斯致函表彰工作, 李現應聘赴美講學," *KSYP*, January 15, 1948, 2.

41. "任何培養日戰爭經濟建議, 我必堅決反對, 李卓敏在遠東經委會說明立場," *Ta Kung Pao (TKP)*, June 6, 1948, 2; "李卓敏周錫年，訪總督詳談，出席遠東經濟會議經過," *WKYP*, December 16, 1948, 7.

42. "李卓敏返滬," *WKYP*, December 24, 1948, 7; Li, "Good Fortune Indeed," 80.

43. "陳光甫李卓敏昨曼谷抵港," *TKP*, April 6, 1949, 4.

44. "李卓敏氏, 在穗辦公," *KSYP*, June 6, 1949, 1; "李卓敏在穗辦公," *WKYP*, June 6, 1949, 2; Li, "Good Fortune Indeed," 80.

45. Li, "Good Fortune Indeed," 82.

46. Naturalization Certificate No. 7739370, "LI, Choh-Ming," July 1, 1958, Ancestry.com.

47. Li, "Good Fortune Indeed," 82.

48. Fred Herman, "UC Man, Family Reunited After Ordeal in China," *Berkeley Daily Gazette*, July 7, 1955, 13.

49. "US Power Held Only Bar to War," *Los Angeles Times*, December 12, 1951, 4.

50. The conference's speeches were reprinted as a special volume. See Li Choh-ming, "Economic Problems of the Peasant in the Far East," *World Affairs Interpreter* 22, no. 4 (Winter 1952): 431–39.

51. Choh-ming Li and Shih-hsiang Chen to the Asia Foundation, April 8, 1957; and James L. Stewart to Woodbridge Bingham, April 10, 1957, both in Asia Foundation Files, Hoover Institution, Stanford University (HISU).

52. See Li Choh-ming, review of *The Prospects for Communist China* by W. W. Rostow et al., *American Economic Review* 45, no. 3 (June 1955): 407–9.

53. Choh-Ming Li, *Economic Development of Communist China: An Appraisal of the First Five Years of Industrialization* (Berkeley: University of California Press, 1959).

54. Audrey G. Donnithorne, review of *Economic Development of Communist China* by Choh-Ming Li (Berkeley: University of California Press, 1959), *Economica*, New Series, 27, no. 105 (February 1960): 95.

55. Alexander Eckstein, "Conditions and Prospects for Economic Growth in Communist China," *World Politics* 7, no. 1 (October 1954): 1–37; Joseph Alsop, "Mao as Stalin," *New York Herald Tribune*, November 25, 1959, 18.

56. I thank Carl Riskin for this insight. Li Choh-ming, *The Statistical System of Communist China* (Berkeley: University of California Press, 1962).

57. Li Choh-ming, "What Happened to the Great Leap Forward?," *Challenge* 11, no. 10 (July 1963): 4.

58. Robert Black to W. I. J. Wallace, August 25, 1962, 2, CO1030/1099, National Archives, Kew, Surrey (NAUK).

59. W. Mallory-Browne to Li Choh-ming, December 18, 1961; Robert Blum to Clark Kerr, January 30, 1962, both in Asia Foundation Files, Box P-266, "Education: School & Univ. Chinese Univ. Vice-Chancellor/Advisor on Chinese Studies," HISU.

60. Nathan M. Pusey to Sir Charles Morris, November 13, 1962, CO1030/1099, NAUK.

61. Elvis Stahr to Nathan M. Pusey, December 7, 1962, CO1030/1099, NAUK.

62. Untitled pages 15–18, CO1030/1099, NAUK.

63. W. S. Carter to Christopher Cox, December 7, 1962, CO1030/1099, NAUK.

64. Christopher Cox to W. S. Carter, December 10, 1962 (8), CO1030/1099, NAUK.

65. Li Choh-ming, "Addendum: An Interview with Dr. Choh-Ming Li," in *A New Era Begins*, 97; Li, "Good Fortune Indeed," 85.

66. See the correspondence beginning with Raymond V. Johnson, "Li Choh-ming— Telephone Conversation with Mallory Browne," August 30, 1963, Asia Foundation

Files, Box P-266, "Education: School & Univ. Chinese Univ. Vice-Chancellor/ Advisor on Chinese Studies," HISU.

67. E. B. Teesdale to Li Choh-ming, October 24, 1963, HKRS 229-1-514.

68. "The Chronicler: November 7, 1963," *UB* 1, no. 1 (June 1964): 11.

69. Li Choh-ming, "Basic Ideas of a University," *UB* 1, no. 1 (June 1964): 1–2.

70. See Quo-wei Lee, "Foreword," and Sze-kwang Lao, "Chinese Studies and Cultural Integration," both in *The Quest for Excellence: A History of The Chinese University of Hong Kong from 1963 to 1993*, ed. Alice N. H. Lun Ng (Hong Kong: Nam Fung, 1994), xii, 133.

71. "Vice-Chancellor's Reception to New Students," *UB* 3, no. 5 (December 1966), 3.

72. Yuet-keung Kan, "Tribute to Mr. Energy," September 29, 1978, in "Farewell, Dr. and Mrs. Choh-Ming Li," CUHK Library; Yuet-keung Kan, "Speech at the Foundation Stone Laying Ceremony for the Choh-Ming Li Building," *Chinese University Bulletin* (Autumn 1978): 11. For "daring," see 陈方正, "大刀阔斧的开创者：李卓敏校长侧影," in 李振军, 送你一座玫瑰园：香港中文大学 (Changsha: Hunan Renmin Chubanshe, 2006), 42. For "vigorous and pushing," see Francis Hutchins to Bill Kitchen, January 15, 1968, YCA RU232, Box 79, "Lee, Tsufa F," YUMA.

73. M.11 (13), AFSCC to Deputy Financial Secretary (DFS) via Principal Assistant Colonial Secretary (PACS), June 24, 1964, HKRS 146-5-30.

74. M.8, PACS to DFS, June 16, 1964, HKRS 146-5-30.

75. "Comings and Goings," *UB* 1, no. 1 (June 1964): 5.

76. "Delegation to Japan," *UB* 1, no. 2 (July 1964): 2–3; "Comings and Goings," *UB* 1, no. 2 (July 1964): 8.

77. "Comings and Goings," *UB* 1, no. 6 (December 1964): 5.

78. For example, see "Comings and Goings," *UB* 2, no. 12 (July 1966): 4.

79. See Yuen Ren Chao Papers, Carton 5, Folder 74, Bancroft Library, University of California, Berkeley.

80. "Comings and Goings," *UB* 2, no. 3 (October 1965): 7.

81. "The Chronicler: February 21, 1964," *UB* 1, no. 1 (June 1964): 11.

82. Li Choh-ming, "Advisory Bodies and Visiting Scholars," in *The First Six Years, 1963–1969* (Chinese University of Hong Kong, 1970), 19–20, YCA RU233, Box 12, Folder 174, YUMA.

83. Li, *The First Six Years*, appendix 6, "External Examiners," 90–93.

84. Li, *The First Six Years*, appendix 4, "Visiting Scholars," 86–88.

85. For a useful example, see "Comings and Goings," *UB* 1, no. 4 (October 1964): 7.

86. "Ford Foundation Grant," *UB* 3, no. 8 (March 1967): 1.

87. "Exchange Programme with California," *UB* 1, no. 12 (June 1965): 1.

88. "Orientation Programme for Californian Students," *UB* 5, no. 1 (September 1968): 1.

89. "Speech by Dr. Vernon I. Cheadle, Chancellor, University of California, Santa Barbara," *UB* 2, no. 3 (October 1965): 2.

90. "Speech by Dr. Choh-Ming Li, the Vice-Chancellor," *UB* 2, no. 3 (October 1965): 5; "Leverhulme Exchange Programme," *UB* 3, no. 10 (May 1967): 2–3; "Exchange Programme with Indiana University," *UB* 3, no. 12 (September 1967): 4.

91. "The Vice-Chancellor's Memorandum on the Report of the Undergraduate Examinations Board Regarding the Award of Degrees with Marks of Distinction" (14-1), HKRS 147-3-19.

92. John Fulton to Li, April 27, 1966, HKRS 147-3-19.

93. R. L. Huang to Li, May 2, 1966, HKRS 147-3-19.

94. CS to Secretary, Public Services Commission, "Chinese University—Honours Degree Standards," August 6, 1966 (14-1), HKRS 147-3-19.

95. DE to CS, "Chinese University—Honours Degree Standards," September 13, 1966 (15-1), HKRS 147-3-19. Also see "Government Recognition of University Honours Degrees," UB 3, no. 3 (October 1966): 3.

96. Li Choh-ming, "Signs of Maturity and Development," UB 3, no. 3 (October 1966): 1–3.

97. Grace Ai-ling Chou, Confucianism, Colonialism and the Cold War: Chinese Cultural Education at Hong Kong's New Asia College, 1949–63 (Leiden: Brill, 2011); Andy Chih-ming Wang, Transpacific Articulations: Student Migration and the Remaking of Asian America (Honolulu: University of Hawai'i Press, 2013); Huang Jianli and Hong Lysa, The Scripting of a National History: Singapore and Its Pasts (Hong Kong: HKU Press, 2008).

98. Gary Ka-wai Cheung, Hong Kong's Watershed: The 1967 Riots (Hong Kong: HKU Press, 2009).

99. Peter E. Hamilton, "'A Haven for Tortured Souls': Hong Kong in the Vietnam War," International History Review 37, no. 3 (June 2015): 565–81.

100. Li, The First Six Years, 5–6.

101. Li, "The Chinese University of Hong Kong, Its Character and Its Aspirations," November 3, 1977, 2–3, YCA RU233, Box 13, Folder 178, YUMA.

102. "Letters to AmCham: Business Leaders," AmCham 7, no. 9 (September 1976): 27–29.

103. Yu-kuang Chu, "Report to the Trustees of Lingnan University on Trip to Hong Kong, July 1962," 9–10, Archives of the Trustees of Lingnan University (ATLU), Box 42, Folder 495, YUDSL.

104. Chu, "Report to the Trustees of Lingnan University," 9–10, 20.

105. C. T. Yung to Yorke Allen, Jr., "Proposed Lingnan School of Economics," November 14, 1962, 1–3, United Board for Christian Higher Education in Asia (UBCHEA), RGIIA, Box 110A, Folder 1515, YUDSL.

106. Geir Lundestad, "Empire by Invitation? The United States and Western Europe, 1945–1952," Journal of Peace Research 23, no. 3 (1986): 263–77.

107. "Minutes of the College Council, April 19, 1963," 1, UBCHEA, RGIIA, Box 110A, Folder 1515, YUDSL.

108. Yorke Allen, Jr. to C. T. Yung, April 8, 1963, UBCHEA, RGIIA, Box 110A, Folder 1515, YUDSL.

109. Franklin Folts, Introduction to Industrial Management, 5th ed. (New York: McGraw-Hill, 1963); DeFold Folts, "Placement and Rising Salary Curve," Harvard Business School Bulletin 39, no. 6 (November–December 1963): 11.

110. "Appendix A: Acting President's Report, 14 June, 1963," 1, UBCHEA, RGIIA, Box 110A, Folder 1515, YUDSL.

111. C. T. Yung, "Presidents' Report to the Board of Governors, February 21, 1964," 1, UBCHEA, RG11A, Box 110A, Folder 1510, YUDSL.

112. "The Chronicler, April 1, 1964," *UB* 1, no. 1 (June 1964): 12.

113. See "Confidential: Extract from the Vice-Chancellor's Congregation Address to Be Delivered on the 15th October, 1965" (29), 1, HKRS 229-1-492; Li Choh-ming, "The Long and Arduous Road: The Vice-Chancellor's Speech at the Fourth Congregation," *UB* 2, no. 4 (November 1965): 2.

114. "Comings and Goings," *UB* 2, no. 7 (February 1966): 8; Yorke Allen, Jr., to Li Choh-ming, "Attention of the Vice-Chancellor," April 15, 1966, 1–2, ATLU, Box 1, Folder 5, YUDSL.

115. "The Lingnan Institute of Business Administration," *UB* 2, no. 10 (May 1966): 1–2.

116. Yorke Allen, Jr., "Speech by Mr. Yorke Allen, Jr.," *UB* 3, no. 2 (September 1966): 3–4.

117. Li, *The First Six Years*, 52.

118. CUHK Business School website, https://alumni.bschool.cuhk.edu.hk/, accessed December 25, 2018.

119. "中文大學忽其風雲，錢穆博士提出辭職，李卓敏校長說絕不錢氏引退," *Kong Sheung Wan Bo* 工商晚報, July 1, 1964, 1.

120. Ch'ien Mu to New Asia Board of Governors, July 20, 1964, 1–5, HKRS 457-3-21.

121. Ch'ien Mu to New Asia Board, 7.

122. Chou, *Confucianism, Colonialism, and the Cold War*, 34, 40.

123. George D. Vaill, "Report of the Executive Secretary to the Special New Asia Committee," October 27, 1955, 1–2, YCA, RU233, Box 48, Folder 707, YUMA.

124. On Qian's views, also see Rebecca Karl, *The Magic of Concepts: History and the Economic in Twentieth-Century China* (Durham, N.C.: Duke University Press, 2017), 104.

125. "Dr. Choh-Ming Li's Speech," *UB* 8, no. 3 (October 1971): 4; "李卓敏校長演講詞," 中文大學校刊 8, no. 3 (October 1971): 4.

126. David Trench to CS, August 29, 1964 (35-1), HKRS 457-3-21.

127. "Chinese University Gets a New Look: Works to Finish in 1975," *Hongkong Star*, July 10, 1972, HKRS 70-3-58-2.

128. Author's interview with John Dolfin, November 2, 2012.

129. "Opening of Science Extension to Chinese University," April 12, 1972, 1, HKRS 70-3-58-1.

130. For an example, see Mrs. E. J. Fehl to K. V. Arrowsmith, March 13, 1967, followed by M.125 and M.126, HKRS 229-1-583.

131. "Exhibit I: The Vice-Chancellor's Memorandum on the Basic Building Programme" (March 1966), 3–5, ATLU, RG14, Box 40, Folder 469, YUDSL.

132. Li Choh-ming to Li Choh-hao, December 16, 1965, CHLP, UCSF, Box 6, Folder "Chinese University of Hong Kong, 1965, 1968–72."

133. Li Choh-ming to Li Choh-hao, November 15, 1971, CHLP, UCSF, Box 6, Folder "Chinese University of Hong Kong, 1965, 1968–72."

134. "Institute of Chinese Studies Established," *UB* 4, no. 2 (November 1967): 3.

135. "Exhibition of Chinese Art at the Institute of Chinese Studies," *UB* 8, no. 3 (October 1971): 2–4.

136. "P. Y. Tang Honoured," *South China Sunday Post-Herald*, August 2, 1964, 7.

137. "The Chinese University of Hong Kong: Ceremony of the Laying of the Foundation Stone of the University Library, Dr. Choh-Ming Li's Remarks, 28th September, 1970," 1–2, HKRS 70-3-58-1.

138. "Gifts to the University," *UB* 6, no. 1 (September 1969): 7.

139. "Vice-Chancellor as Director of LIBA," *UB* 6, no. 4 (January–February 1970): 12.

140. Francis Hutchins, "Confidential: Conversation with P. Y. Tang and Tsu-fa Lee, July 1st, 1968," YCA RU232, Box 79, Folder "Lee, Tsufa F (Chairman of Board, New Asia College, 1967–72)," YUMA.

141. "New Asia College Development Fund," April 19, 1973, YCA RG37, Box 41, Folder 588, YUMA.

142. "Service at Cathedral for P. Y. Tang," *SCMP*, June 22, 1971, 6; "行政局非官守議員, 唐炳源舉殯哀榮," *WKYP*, June 22, 1971, 12.

143. "'He Practised What He Preached,' Mr. Jack C. Tang's Speech," *UB* 9, no. 4 (January 1973): 2–3; also see "中大新圖書館, 昨日落成啟用," *STYP*, December 16, 1972, 20; "中文大學圖書館紀念, 故唐炳源博士," *WKYP*, December 16, 1972, 4.3; "New Library for Students, Staff," *SCMP*, December 18, 1972, 15.

144. Tak Sing Cheung, "Institutional Changes," in Ng, *The Quest for Excellence*, 84.

145. "工商管理夜校課程中大今年九月開辦, 李卓敏昨接受馮景禧鄭裕彤捐款," *TKP*, March 25, 1977, 6.

146. Tak, "Institutional Changes," 86.

147. Li Choh-ming to Li Choh-hao and Annie Li, March 3, 1975, CHLP, UCSF, Box 11, Folder "Chinese University of Hong Kong, 1973–76."

148. Chuck Shepard to Bill Kitchen and Ed Worthy, "Re: Conversation with Prof. Yu Ying-shih in Cambridge, 10/21/72," 1, YCA RG37, Box 41, Folder 592, YUMA.

149. Tsufa Lee to Li, Aug. 30, 1974, YCA RG37, Box 41, Folder 593, YUMA.

150. Tak, "Institutional Changes," 91–92.

151. B. Preston Schoyer to T. C. Ou, Aug. 5, 1977, YCA RG37, Box 41, Folder 593, YUMA.

152. Li Choh-ming, *Li's Chinese Dictionary* (Hong Kong: Chinese University Press, 1980).

153. Wong, "Overseas Academic Links and International Exchanges," in Ng, *The Quest for Excellence*, 203. Also see Li Choh-ming, "The Chinese University of Hong Kong, Its Character and Its Aspirations," CUHK Eighteenth Congregation, November 3, 1977, 3, YCA, Box 13, Folder 178, YUMA.

5. Decolonization by Investment

1. "Economic Report on Hong Kong: Prepared by American Consulate General," July 18, 1960, 5 [Hong Kong Public Records Office, Kwun Tong,] Hong Kong Record Series (HKRS) 269-1-6.

2. Adam Tooze, *The Deluge: The Great War, America and the Remaking of the Global Order, 1916–1931* (New York: Viking Penguin, 2014).

3. Melville J. Ulmer, "Multinational Corporations and Third World Capitalism," *Journal of Economics Issues* 14, no. 2 (June 1980): 454.

4. Y. C. Jao, "Financing Hong Kong's Early Postwar Industrialization: The Role of the Hongkong and Shanghai Banking Corporation," in *Eastern Banking: Essays in the History of The Hongkong and Shanghai Banking Corporation*, ed. Frank H. H. King (London: Athlone Press, 1983), 560–62.

5. D. C. Bray, "America and Hong Kong," *AmCham* 15, no. 5 (May 1983): 16.

6. Y. C. Jao, *Banking and Currency in Hong Kong: A Study of Postwar Financial Development* (London: Palgrave Macmillan, 1974); King, *Eastern Banking*; Frank H. H. King and Catherine King, *The History of the Hongkong and Shanghai Banking Corporation*, vols. 1–4 (Cambridge: Cambridge University Press, 1988–1991).

7. Wong Siu-lun, *Emigrant Entrepreneurs: Shanghai Industrialists in Hong Kong* (Hong Kong: Oxford University Press, 1988), 42–46; Catherine R. Schenk, *Hong Kong as an International Financial Centre, Emergence and Development 1945–65* (London: Routledge Studies in the Growth Economies of Asia, 2001), 75, 141–42.

8. Schenk, *Hong Kong as an International Financial Centre*, 45, 44–71.

9. Schenk, *Hong Kong as an International Financial Centre*, 72–80.

10. Jao, "Financing," 552; Schenk, *Hong Kong as an International Financial Centre*, 141–52.

11. Jao, "Financing," 566.

12. Jao, "Financing," 554; Schenk, *Hong Kong as an International Financial Centre*, 147.

13. Schenk, *Hong Kong as an International Financial Centre*, 6.

14. Wong, *Emigrant Entrepreneurs*, 9.

15. Danny Kin-kong Lam and Ian Lee, "Guerilla Capitalism and the Limits of Statist Theory: Comparing the Chinese NICs," in *The Evolving Pacific Basin in the Global Political Economy: Domestic and International Linkages*, ed. Cal Clark and Steven Chan (Boulder, Colo.: Lynne Rienner, 1992), 107–24.

16. Frank Leeming, "The Earlier Industrialization of Hong Kong," *Modern Asian Studies* 9, no. 3 (1975): 337–42.

17. Wong, *Emigrant Entrepreneurs*, 50–53; Tomoko Shiroyama, *China During the Great Depression: Market, State, and the World Economy, 1929–1937* (Cambridge, Mass.: Harvard University Press, 2008), 60–87.

18. Jao, "Financing," 563.

19. Shiroyama, *China During the Great Depression*, 68–76.

20. Judith Mary Nishida, "Japanese Influence on the Shanghainese Textile Industry and Implications of Hong Kong," Master's thesis, University of Hong Kong, 1990, 118.

21. "I254 Tang, Jack Chi Chien," Hong Kong Heritage Project (HKHP), 13.

22. Naomi R. Lamoreaux, *Insider Lending: Banks, Personal Connections, and Economic Development in Industrial New England* (Cambridge: Cambridge University Press, 1996), 4–5.

23. Jao, *Banking and Currency in Hong Kong*, 210.

24. Jack Chi-Chien Tang, "The Textile Industry and the Development of Hong Kong," oral history conducted by Carolyn Wakeman in 1999, Regional Oral History Office, Bancroft Library, University of California Berkeley, 2003, 45.

25. Tang, "The Textile Industry," 35. Also "Number of Spindles and Automatic Looms in Operation," in *South Sea Textiles: Cotton, Polyester, Polynosic, Acrylic* (1970), HKU Libraries, Special Collections (HKUSC).

26. "Economic Report on Hong Kong," 5, HKRS 269-1-6; "Textileman's Plea: U.S. Market 'Life and Death' to H.K.," *South China Morning Post* (*SCMP*), April 14, 1962, 6.

27. Tang, "The Textile Industry," 48.

28. Wong, *Emigrant Entrepreneurs*, 117.

29. Jao, "Financing," 557; Schenk, *Hong Kong as an International Financial Centre*, 147; Wong, *Emigrant Entrepreneurs*, 118–19.

30. Andrew Smith, "The Winds of Change and the End of the Compradore System in the Hongkong and Shanghai Banking Corporation," *Business History* 58, no. 2 (January 2016): 195–96.

31. See "Pan, Quentin 1924" and "Pan, Francis 1926," Alumni Files, Rauner Special Collections Library, Dartmouth College (RSCLDC).

32. Lynn Pan, *When True Love Came to China* (Hong Kong: Hong Kong University Press, 2015), 20. Also see Ruth Rogaski, *Hygienic Modernity: Meanings of Health and Disease in Treaty Port China* (Berkeley: University of California Press, 2004), 240–44.

33. "P'an Kuang-tan," in *Biographical Dictionary of Republican China*, vol. 3, ed. Howard L. Boorman and Joseph K. H. Cheng (New York: Columbia University Press, 1967), 61–62.

34. "Dartmouth Grants Degrees to 396," *New York Times*, June 20, 1928, 21; "Amos Tuck School Holds Graduation," *Daily Boston Globe*, May 14, 1929, 5.

35. "沈熙瑞," in 上海時人誌, ed. 戚再玉 (Shanghai: Zhanwang Chubanshe, 1947), 62, accessed through the Modern History Databases (MHDB), Academia Sinica.

36. "H. J. Shen '28," November 1949, in "Shen, Hsi-Jui 1928," RSCLDC. On the finances of Chinese rail lines, see Elisabeth Köll, *Railroads and the Transformation of China* (Cambridge, Mass.: Harvard University Press, 2019), 60, 71–77.

37. "鐵道部, 1936–37," in 國民政府職官年表, 1925–49, 第一冊, ed. 張朋園, 沈懷玉 (Taipei: Zhongyanyuan jin shi suo, 1987), 213, accessed through MHDB.

38. "The 1926 Newsletter," March 27, 1952, 3, in "Pan, Francis 1926," RSCLDC.

39. "The Amos Tuck School of Administration, Dartmouth College, Report of Graduates, 1936," in "Pan, Francis K.," Tuck Alumni Records, RSCLDC.

40. For U.S.-linked activities, see "Trade Mission Party Leaves for Tsingtao," *China Press*, May 5, 1935, 9; "Chinese-U.S. Group Scores Cable Charges," *China Press*, October 31, 1935, 12; "New York U. Club Opened at Nanking," *China Press*, August 23, 1936, 3. For an example of social pages, see Wu Ai-lien, "Chinese Social Notes," *North-China Herald and Supreme Court & Consular Gazette* (*NCHSCCG*), June 2, 1937, 395.

41. "交通部, 1940–41," 國民政府職官年表, 204; "Foreign-Trained Men Holding China's Economic Rein," *China Critic*, May 18, 1939, 107.

42. "沈熙瑞," 上海時人誌, 62. Also see "政令: 人事: 任命狀," 广西省政府公報, 1938, 7.

43. On remittance banking and China's war effort, see Elisabeth Köll, "Professional Managers at Political Crossroads, Hsia Pin-fang at the Bank of China in New York and London, 1939–1951," in *The Capitalist Dilemma in China's Communist Revolution*, ed. Sherman Cochran (Ithaca, N.Y.: Cornell East Asia Program, 2014), 271–97.

44. Chihyun Chang, ed., *The Chinese Journals of L. K. Little, 1943–54: An Eyewitness Account of War and Revolution*, vol. 1 (New York: Routledge, 2018).

45. Chang, *The Chinese Journals of L. K. Little*, 90.

46. This topic was later spun by postwar publications. See "沈熙瑞," 上海時人誌, 62.
47. See Pan's resume, "Francis K. Pan," 1–2, in "Pan, Francis 1926," RSCLDC. For Shen, see "中央銀行, 1948–49," 國民政府職官年表, 381. Also see Shen's resume, "H. J. Shen '28," in "Shen, Hsi-Jui 1928," RSCLDC.
48. "沈熙瑞等堅決請辭," *Wah Kiu Yat Po* (*WKYP*), May 28, 1948, 1.
49. "美援會秘書, 沈熙瑞繼任," *Kong Sheung Yat Po* (*KSYP*), June 18, 1948, 1.
50. "美援不來委員求去, 廠家淪沈熙瑞等辭職," *Ta Kung Pao* (*TKP*), January 9, 1949, 2; "沈熙瑞接任, 中信局局長, 劉攻芸任理事會主席," *WKYP*, January 22, 1949, 2.
51. "利便港滬趕班客機降落, 啓德機場開放夜航, 自滬來港客機一日二十餘架; 張嘉璈, 劉攻芸, 沈熙瑞均已到港," *WKYP*, April 27, 1949, 5.
52. Chang, *The Chinese Journals of L. K. Little*, 2:200.
53. "Confidential: Graduate Survey Questionnaire, The Amos Tuck School" (1955), 1 in "Pan, Francis K.," Tuck Alumni Files, RSCLDC; Francis Pan to L. K. Little, January 17, 1952, Asia Foundation Files (AFF), Box P-55, "Hong Kong Individuals, General M-Z," Hoover Institution, Stanford University (HISU).
54. Alan Valentine to J. L. Stewart, "Proposals of Dr. Francis K. Pan in Hong Kong," January 21, 1952, 1–2, AFF, Box P-55, "Hong Kong Individuals, General M-Z," HISU.
55. James Ivy to Harold Noble, November 30, 1951, AFF, Box P-55, "Hong Kong Individuals, General M-Z," HISU.
56. Francis Pan to Holt McAloney, February 1, 1952, in "Pan, Francis 1926," RSCLDC.
57. "潘光迥講, 美國新經濟," *WKYP*, May 27, 1955, 14.
58. Francis Pan to Karl Hill, March 31, 1958. For the speech, see Francis K. Pan, "Whither Hongkong?" *Far Eastern Economic Review* 24, 9 (February 27, 1958). Both in "Pan, Francis K.," Tuck Alumni Files, RSCLDC.
59. "潘光迥正式接任, 孟氏基金會主席," *KSYP*, April 7, 1961, 7.
60. L.Z. Yuan to Fenton Babcock, May 19, 1961, AFF, Box P-169, "Hong Kong Individuals, General M-Z," HISU.
61. Fenton and Evelyn Babcock, *New Lives for Old* (Pittsburgh: RoseDog Books, 2011), 120–23.
62. "獅子會亞洲區大會, 今日揭幕, 昨夕三百餘人酒會," *WKYP*, September 23, 1961, 7; "獅子會友要使人與人之間, 增進友善, 發揮服務精神貢獻社會, 國際獅子會亞洲區第四屆會議昨日在港開幕," *WKYP*, September 24, 1961, 5; "Dr. Francis Pan on CUP," *Chinese University Bulletin* (Summer 1977): 12.
63. Francis Pan to Osmun Skinner, February 8, 1954, in "Shen, Hsi-Jui 1928," RSCLDC. On the Henningsens, see Hong Kong Bottlers, Fed. Inc. USA, 1949–66, HKRS 113-2-230.
64. Li Choh-ming, *The First Six Years, 1963–1969* (Hong Kong: Chinese University of Hong Kong, 1969), appendix 6: External Examiners, 90; "Economics Research Centre," *University Bulletin* 1, no. 10 (April 1965), 2. For a speech to students, see "英鎊的前途與香港, 港豐銀行經理沈熙瑞講, 昨在聯合書院學生會有詳盡闡釋," *WKYP*, April 23, 1965, 10.
65. Wong, *Emigrant Entrepreneurs*, 118.

66. "香港代表團赴美，參加美國關稅委員會，有關棉織品輸入調查," *WKYP*, Feb. 9, 1962, 5; "美欲加稅限制棉品輸入，港派代表赴美調查, 由巴璐朱誠信沈熙瑞充任代表," *TKP*, Feb. 9, 1962, 4.

67. "廠商會定今晚宴賀, 沈熙瑞任匯豐經理," *KSYP*, March 5, 1964, 6; "沈熙瑞任匯豐經理, 廠商會今設宴祝賀," *TKP*, March 5, 1964, 5; "廠商會宴賀沈熙瑞, 榮任匯豐銀行經理," *KSYP*, March 6, 1964, 5; "發展香港工業, 有賴銀行合作, 廠商會昨宴沈熙瑞, 尹致中在席上講話," *TKP*, March 6, 1964, 5.

68. "廠商會今宴賀, 沈熙瑞氏榮任," *WKYP*, March 5, 1964, 7; "廠商會宴賀, 沈熙瑞榮任," *WKYP*, March 6, 1964, 7.

69. Also see "匯豐銀行經理，沈熙瑞籲請港銀行界，割愛一部份優利貨歎，來支持生產事業之發展與生存," *WKYP*, May 21, 1964, 13.

70. Schenk, *Hong Kong as an International Financial Centre*, 6.

71. Wong, *Emigrant Entrepreneurs*, 9, 65.

72. "Number of Spindles and Automatic Looms in Operation," in *South Sea Textiles*.

73. Hong Kong Commerce and Industry Department (HKCID), "Table No. 22: Growth of Employment—Pre 1960 to 31st October 1973," February 1971, HKRS 1056-1-265.

74. HKCID, "Foreign Investment in Hong Kong Manufacturing Industry—by Industry," March 14, 1973, HKRS 1056-1-251.

75. HKCID, "Table No. 7: Investment—by Country of Origin (by Fully Foreign-Owned Companies) as at May 1970," HKRS 1056-1-265.

76. HKCID, "Table No. 8: Investment—by Country of Origin (Combining the Hong Kong & Foreign Interest in Joint Ventures) as at May 1970," HKRS 1056-1-265.

77. "Table 1: Foreign Investment in Hong Kong Manufacturing Industry—by Country—(Position as at 14th March, 1973)" (148B), HKRS 1056-1-251.

78. HKCID, "Table No. 12: Export to Major Markets in 1972," HKRS 1056-1-265.

79. "Particulars of Factory with Foreign Investment: Precision Moulds Limited" (53), HKRS 1056-1-270.

80. "美商重視本港工業, 斥巨資經營電筒廠，以三百餘萬元港幣承購一工廠," *Sing Tao Wan Po* 星島晚報, July 22, 1956, 4.

81. Sze-yuen Chung, *Hong Kong's Journey to Reunification: Memoirs of Sze-yuen Chung* (Hong Kong: Chinese University Press, 2001), 18–20.

82. "Particulars of Factory with Foreign Investment: Corn Products Co. (HK), Ltd." (81), HKRS 1056-1-270.

83. "Particulars of Factory with Overseas Interest: Hong Kong Industrial (Woodwork) Company" (105), HKRS 1056-1-271.

84. H. Richard Friman, "The Eisenhower Administration and the Demise of GATT: Dancing with Pandora," *American Journal of Economics and Sociology* 53, no. 3 (July 1994): 257–72.

85. See the collected press and commentary in AFF, Box P-169, "Federation of Hong Kong Industries," HISU.

86. Wong, *Emigrant Entrepreneurs*, 120.

87. HKCID, "Foreign Investment in Hong Kong Industry," (1970), 4, HKRS 1056-1-265.

88. Shou-eng Koo, "The Role of Export Expansion in Hong Kong's Economic Growth," *Asian Survey* 8, no. 6 (June 1968): 510.

89. Wong, *Emigrant Entrepreneurs*, 56.

90. Schenk, *Hong Kong as an International Financial Centre*, 108–9.

91. HKCID, "Foreign Investment in Hong Kong Industry," (1970), 2–3 and table 3, HKRS 1056-1-265.

92. HKCID, "Table 2: Foreign Investment in Hong Kong Manufacturing Industry—by Industry," (1973) (148B-2) HKRS 1056-1-251.

93. "李霈之," 上海人名錄 (Shanghai, 1941), 439, accessed through MHDB.

94. Toh Han Shih, "Fate Wove the Textile Industry Into the Fabric of Hong Kong," *SCMP*, October 28, 2004.

95. "港九僑領名流繼承三院善業," *WKYP*, April 5, 1957, 10.

96. "雞尾酒會慶祝," *WKYP*, August 2, 1960, 7; "吳文政李霈之孫麒方, 就會招待紀禮涵," *WKYP*, November 5, 1972, 8.

97. "蘇浙同鄉會, 宴賀李霈之晉紳, 八五壽星林康侯善頌善禧," *WKYP*, February 22, 1960, 9.

98. "大南董事長李霈之飛歐," *WKYP*, December 2, 1958, 7; "聯業公司總經理李霈之飛歐," *TKP*, September 14, 1963, 8; "李霈之飛西德參展," *WKYP*, Sept. 14, 1963, 12.

99. "任太平紳士," *KSYP*, January 9, 1960, 5.

100. "怡和巴頓與李霈之, 商組棉紡聯營機構, 雙方說願意達成協議應付局面," *TKP*, May 11, 1962, 4; "六大棉系工廠卽將合併聯營," *WKYP*, May 11, 1962, 5.

101. "怡和大南等七廠合併成功, 總資本五千萬元定名爲聯業紡織, 此乃本港棉業合併首次在產銷盈利各方面將有良好反映," *WKYP*, July 3, 1962, 17.

102. "職業紡織公司門市部, [黛麗]開始營業巴頓主持揭幕禮," *WKYP*, June 9, 1963, 17.

103. "繼南海紗廠公售之後, 聯業紡織亦將上市, 定九月發售一百萬股," *WKYP*, July 15, 1964, 17; "本港紡織漂染印花製衣整系列組合, 聯業紡織公司股票, 本月底公開發售," *WKYP*, August 11, 1964, 18; "聯業紡織股公開出售, 認股申請書業已發出, 該公司最近一個年度結算, 純利四五八萬元," *WKYP*, August 28, 1964, 17.

104. "聯業紡織派息每股七毫五仙," June 6, 1968, 7; "聯業紡織有限公司, 推行三年發展計劃, 動用資金千五百萬," *KSYP*, July 13, 1968, 4; "本港聯業紡織公司, 在英倫展出服裝, 做了千多萬生意," *KSYP*, September 19, 1968, 5; "聯業紡織公司宣佈盈利逾千五百萬元," *KSYP*, July 17, 1969, 5; "聯業紡織盈利," *WKYP*, July 18, 1969, 11; "聯業紡織發紅股, 中期股息為六角," *WKYP*, November 27, 1969, 8.

105. "李霈之飛歐美," *WKYP*, January 17, 1966, 5.

106. "聯業紡織有限公司, 推行三年發展計劃, 動用資金千五百萬," *KSYP*, July 13, 1968, 4.

107. "適應國際生產水準, 聯業紡織精益求精, 去年貿易投資金額六千萬," *KSWP*, May 28, 1973, 6. Also see Shu-Ching Jean Chen, "Staying Close to Roots, Lees of Hong Kong Restored a Garment Leader," *Forbes Asia*, November 2016, https://www.forbes.com /sites/shuchingjeanchen/2016/11/21/staying-close-to-roots-lees-of-hong-kong -restored-a-garment-leader/#7c4b21ae63e6.

108. "紡織業面臨困境盈益仍增3%, 垂直式綜合性企業聯業紡織保持平穩," *KSWP*, September 17, 1973, 6.

109. "Personalities: Trade Mission Off to East Africa," *SCMP*, June 12, 1965, 7.

110. Tang, "The Textile Industry," 39; "I254 Tang, Jack Chi Chien," HKHP, 13.

111. "I254 Tang, Jack Chi Chien," HKHP, 10, 14–15.

112. Tang, "The Textile Industry," 60.

113. Tang, "The Textile Industry," 61, 19, 61–70, 40, 106.

114. For the labor force, see "Hong Kong's Electronic Industry—What Does the Future Hold?" *AmCham* 5, no. 11 (November 1974): 6.

115. "The Hong Kong Toy Industry—Searching for a Santa Clause!" *AmCham* 5, no. 12 (December 1974): 5–9.

116. Chyau Tuan and Linda F. Y. Ng, "Evolution of Hong Kong's Electronics Industry Under a Passive Industrial Policy," *Managerial and Decision Economics* 16, no. 5 (1995): 509–23; Richard Cheung Lam and Hong-Kin Kwok, "Global Supplier Without a Global Brand Name: A Case Study of Hong Kong's Electronics Industry," *Asian Journal of Social Science* 32, no. 3 (2004): 476–500.

117. Schenk, *Hong Kong as an International Financial Centre*, 58–71.

118. John Carroll, "A Historical Perspective: The 1967 Riots and the Strike Boycott of 1925–1926," in *May Days in Hong Kong: Riot and Emergency in 1967*, ed. Robert Bickers and Ray Yep (Hong Kong: Hong Kong University Press, 2009), 75.

119. For the riots, also see Gary Ka-wai Cheung, *Hong Kong's Watershed, The 1967 Riots* (Hong Kong: Hong Kong University Press, 2009).

120. On the Kadoories, see Judith Green, "Kadoorie, Sir Elly," "Kadoorie, Sir Ellis," "Kadoorie, Lawrence," and "Kadoorie, Sir Horace," in *Dictionary of Hong Kong Biography* (Hong Kong: HKU Press, 2012), 216–18.

121. Elizabeth LaCouture, "Inventing the 'Foreignized' Chinese Carpets in Treaty-Port Tianjin, China," *Journal of Design History* 30, no. 3 (September 2017): 300–314.

122. On Tse, see "朱孔嘉," in 上海工商人名錄, ed. 中國徵信所 (Shanghai: Meihua Shuju 1936), 22, accessed through MHDB. On Johnson, see Gene Gleason, *Hong Kong* (New York: John Day, 1963), 140–41.

123. "Tai Ping Carpets—A Brief History," Hong Kong Heritage Project, https://www .hongkongheritage.org/pages/post.aspx?post=18, accessed December 22, 2017.

124. "I009 Westphal, Frederick," HKHP, 2.

125. York Lo, "Fred Westphal—the American Oil Taipan from New Orleans Who Helped to Power Hong Kong," in *The Industrial History of Hong Kong Group*, October 21, 2016, http://industrialhistoryhk.org/fred-westphal-the-american-oil-taipan-from-new -orleans-who-helped-to-power-hong-kong/.

126. "I009 Westphal, Frederick," HKHP, 3–4.

127. Changqi Wu and Leonard K. Cheng, "Hong Kong's Business Regulation in Transition," in *Deregulation and Interdependence in the Asia-Pacific Region*, ed. Takatoshi Ito and Anne O. Kreuger (Chicago: University of Chicago Press, 2000), 158; Pun-Lee Lam, *The Scheme of Control on Electricity Companies* (Hong Kong: Chinese University Press, 1996), 76, 84.

128. "I254 Tang, Jack Chi Chien," HKHP, 12–13.

129. "I009 Westphal, Frederick," HKHP, 4.

130. Exxon Energy, *Exxon Energy Ltd, Hong Kong: Power Generation for Hong Kong* (Hong Kong: Exxon Energy, 1991), 5, 12, 18, HKUSC.

131. "Soong, John Louis," in *Hong Kong Who's Who: An Almanac of Personalities and Their Comprehensive Histories, 1970–1973*, ed. Joseph Walker (Hong Kong: N.p., 1970),

434–35; "Witness to the Making of a New China: John Soong . . . the Man in the Middle," *SCMP*, July 31, 1983, 12.

132. Meredith Oyen, *The Diplomacy of Migration: Transnational Lives and the Making of US-Chinese Relations in the Cold War* (Ithaca, N.Y.: Cornell University Press, 2015), 50–60.

133. "Friendly Alien on War Duty in China, Recollections—a Series by Jane Ram," *SCMP*, June 30, 1974, 24.

134. "Pickering Gets Post In N.Y. Temporarily; Bardens at Shanghai," *Stanvac Meridian* 2, no. 4 (January 1951): 1, ExxonMobil Historical Collection (EMHC), Box 2.207/E172, Folder 8, Briscoe Center for American History (BCAH), University of Texas at Austin (UT Austin).

135. "宋啟鄖之公子宋賢慶昨返美," *WKYP*, September 3, 1963, 14; "June Wedding for Miss Mau," *New York Times*, January 10, 1971, 78; "Married in Honolulu," *SCMP*, June 22, 1971, 5.

136. Mei Foo Investments, *The Story of Mei Foo Sun Chuen* (Hong Kong: Mei Foo Investments, 1974), 2, HKRS 353.55 STO 1978.

137. "Mobil News Release," November 17, 1966, EMHC, Box 2.207/E173, Folder 1, BCAH, UT Austin.

138. "Housing Project for H.K.'s Middle Income Group," *SCMP*, September 17, 1966, in HKRS 70-3-297.

139. "Mobil Oil Plans Hong Kong Suites, Socony Unit to Build Middle-Income Housing," *New York Times*, July 18, 1965, R8.

140. *The Story of Mei Foo Sun Chuen*, 2; "美孚新邨私人建屋計劃, 世界最大, 今日奠基典禮由港督主持, 預計建屋萬五層容八萬人," *WKYP*, November 17, 1966, 7.

141. On Mei Foo kerosene lamps, see Frank Dikötter, *Things Modern: Material Culture and Everyday Life in China* (London: Hurst, 2007), 179–80.

142. Norimitsu Onishi, "A Lonely Death," *New York Times*, November 30, 2017, F1.

143. *The Story of Mei Foo Sun Chuen*, 5.

144. "無比石油總裁盛讚, 美孚新邨計劃," *WKYP*, October 15, 1966, 10.

145. Editorial: "Mobil Housing Project," *SCMP*, November 18, 1966; and "Foundation Stone of Estate Alaid, Governor Stressed Need for More Inexpensive Flats," *SCMP*, November 18 1966, both in HKRS 70-3-297.

146. "美孚新邨上蓋工程, 由新昌營造公司承建," *KSYP*, February 18, 1967, 10. Also see "Building Project," February 18, 1967, *Hongkong Tiger Standard*, in HKRS 70-3-297.

147. "Housing Project Helps Local Industries Broaden Know-How," *SCMP*, January 5, 1968, 12.

148. "Estate Stage 1 by July," *Hongkong Star*, May 19, 1969; "Flats for 80,000," *China Mail* (*CM*), May 21, 1969, both in HKRS 70-3-297.

149. Ronnie Poon, "$440m Housing Project for Kowloon," *CM*, July 13, 1966; "Multi-million $ Housing Plan at Laichikok," *Hongkong Standard*, July 14, 1966, both in HKRS 70-3-297. Also see "Mei Foo: The $700m Giant Takes Shape," *CM*, February 25, 1974, in HKRS 70-7-36-1.

150. Sherry Rosen, *Mei Foo Sun Chuen: Middle-Class Chinese Families in Transition* (Taipei: Chinese Association for Folklore, 1976), 2–4, 7, 9, 15–17.

151. "New Land, New Cities," *Mobile Overview* 1, no. 3 (Winter 1977–1978), in EHMC, Box 2.207/E173, Folder 2, BCAH, UT Austin.

152. David R. Meyer, "Hong Kong's Enduring Global Business Relations," in *Hong Kong in the Cold War*, ed. Priscilla Roberts and John M. Carroll (Hong Kong: HKU Press, 2016), 68. For all these challenges, see "Hong Kong's Textile Industry—When Will the Slump End?" *AmCham* 6, no. 1 (January 1975): 7–9.

6. The Kuashang Effect

1. *Hong Kong: Report for the Year 1960* (Hong Kong: Hong Kong Government Press, 1961), 42.

2. *Hong Kong: Report for the Year 1970* (Hong Kong: Hong Kong Government Press, 1971), 16.

3. See Alice H. Amsden, *The Rise of the "The Rest": Challenges to the West from Late-Industrializing Economies* (New York: Oxford University Press, 2001); Meredith Woo-Cummings, ed., *The Developmental State* (Ithaca, N.Y.: Cornell University Press, 1999); Peter Evans, *Embedded Autonomy: States and Industrial Transformation* (Princeton, N.J.: Princeton University Press, 1995); Chalmers Johnson, *MITI and the Japanese Miracle: The Growth of Industrial Policy, 1925–1975* (Stanford, Calif.: Stanford University Press, 1982).

4. For example, see Milton and Rose Friedman's ten-part television series *Free to Choose* (1980). Also see Milton Friedman, "The Real Lesson of Hong Kong," *National Review*, December 31, 1997.

5. See Gary G. Hamilton, *Commerce and Capitalism in Chinese Societies* (London: Routledge, 2006); Wei-ming Tu, ed., *Confucian Traditions in East Asian Modernity: Moral Education and Economic Culture in Japan and the Four Mini-Dragons* (Cambridge, Mass.: Harvard University Press, 1996); Kim Kyong-Dong, "Confucianism and Capitalism in East Asia," in *Capitalism and Development*, ed. Leslie Sklair (London: Routledge, 1994), 87–106; Gilbert Rozman, ed., *The East Asian Region: Confucian Heritage and Its Modern Adaptation* (Princeton, N.J.: Princeton University Press, 1991); Ezra Vogel, *The Four Little Dragons: The Spread of Industrialization in East Asia* (Cambridge, Mass.: Harvard University Press, 1991); S. Gordon Redding, *The Spirit of Chinese Capitalism* (New York: de Gruyter, 1990); Tai Hung-chao, ed., *Confucianism and Economic Development: An Oriental Alternative?* (Washington, D.C.: Washington Institute Press, 1989); Peter L. Berger and Hsin-Huang Michael Hsiao, eds., *In Search of an East Asian Development Model* (New Brunswick, N.J.: Transaction Books, 1988); Ronald Dore, *Taking Japan Seriously: A Confucian Perspective on Leading Economic Issues* (Stanford, Calif.: Stanford University Press, 1987).

6. Terutomo Ozawa, *Institutions, Industrial Upgrading, and Economic Performance in Japan—The "Flying-Geese" Paradigm of Catch-up Growth* (Northampton, Mass.: Edward Elgar, 2005); Terutomo Ozawa, *Multinationalism, Japanese Style: The Political Economy of Outward Dependency* (Princeton, N.J.: Princeton University Press, 1979).

7. For the interventions, see Fujio Mizuoka, "Contriving 'Laissez-Faire': Conceptualising the British colonial rule of Hong Kong," *City, Culture, and Society* 5, no. 1 (March 2014): 23–32.

8. Catherine R. Schenk, "The Empire Strikes Back: Hong Kong and the Decline of Sterling in the 1960s," *Economic History Review* 57, no. 3 (2004): 570.

9. For an introduction, see David Harvey, *The Condition of Postmodernity* (Oxford: Blackwell, 1990).

10. Robert C. Feenstra and Gary G. Hamilton, *Emergent Economies, Divergent Paths: Economic Organization and International Trade in South Korea and Taiwan* (Cambridge: Cambridge University Press, 2006); Giovanni Arrighi, *The Long Twentieth Century: Money, Power, and the Origins of Our Times* (London: Verso, 1994).

11. Helen Laville and Hugh Wilford, eds., *The US Government, Citizen Groups and the Cold War* (London: Routledge, 2006).

12. AnnaLee Saxenian first pointed to educational circulations in the success of Taiwan, Israel, and India since the 1980s. See her *The New Argonauts: Regional Advantage in a Global Economy* (Cambridge, Mass.: Harvard University Press, 2006).

13. Institute of International Education (IIE), "Part 1, Four Corners of the Earth, Where They Come From," in *Open Doors, 1950–51: Report on International Educational Exchange* (New York: IIE, 2005), 15. In the 1959–1960 academic year, 1,060 left for studies in the United States, 711 for Australia, 326 for the United Kingdom and Ireland, and 180 for Canada. See *Hong Kong: Report for the Year 1960*, 113–14.

14. IIE, "Foreign Students: Home Country, Sex, Year Studies in U.S. Began, Financial Support. Academic Status," in *Open Doors, 1961–62*, 21; IIE, "Table I: Foreign Students: Home Country, Sex, Year Studies in U.S. Began, Financial Support, Academic Status," in *Open Doors, 1963–64*, 16–21.

15. See IIE, *Open Doors, 1973–74* and *1975–76*.

16. For example, in 1970–1971 CUHK's enrollment was 2,437 and HKU's enrollment was 3,012. See Government Secretariat, "The Hong Kong Education System" (1981), 38, http://www.edb.gov.hk/attachment/en/about-edb/publications-stat/major-reports/edsys_e.pdf. Baptist's enrollment was 3,300; see Gordon W. Sweet, et al., *A Special Report on Hong Kong Baptist College: Prepared at the Request of the Foreign Mission Board of the Southern Baptist Convention* (1975), 13, Hong Kong Baptist University Library (HKBUL).

17. Carter Morgan, Post Script #41, Feb. 1961, Carter Morgan Papers (CMP), RG 6, Correspondence, 1955–75, HKBUL.

18. Mae M. Ngai, *Impossible Subjects: Illegal Aliens and the Making of Modern America* (Princeton, N.J.: Princeton University Press, 2004), 206.

19. Madeline Y. Hsu, *The Good Immigrants: How the Yellow Peril Became the Model Minority* (Princeton, N.J.: Princeton University Press, 2015), 198–203.

20. Rosemary Sayer, *The Man Who Turned the Lights On: Gordon Wu* (Hong Kong: Chameleon Press, 2006), 21–30.

21. Sayer, *The Man Who Turned the Lights On*, 25–26, 28, 32–33.

22. Between 1953 and 1962 about 10,000 Hong Kong residents migrated legally. Between 1970 and 1989, 209,814 migrated, two-thirds of the total. See Ronald Skeldon,

"Emigration and the Future of Hong Kong," *Pacific Affairs* 63, no. 4 (Winter 1990–91): 504.

23. Hsu, *The Good Immigrants*, 226.

24. Ronald Skeldon, "Hong Kong in an International Migration System," in *Reluctant Exiles?: Migration from Hong Kong and the New Overseas Chinese*, ed. Ronald Skeldon (Hong Kong: Hong Kong University Press, 1994), 25–26; Office of Immigration Statistics, *2011 Yearbook of Immigration Statistics*, "Table 2: Persons Obtaining Legal Permanent Resident Status by Region and Selected Country of Last Residence, Fiscal Years 1820 to 2011," 8,https://www.dhs.gov/sites/default/files/publications/immigration-statistics/yearbook/2011/ois_yb_2011.pdf.

25. Abigail Hoffsommer, "Notes on Fellows as of April 28, 1964," United Board for Christian Higher Education in Asia (UBCHEA), RGIIA, Box 19A, Folder 240, Yale University Divinity School Library (YUDSL).

26. C. T. Yung to Abigai Hoffsommer, "U.B. Fellowship, 1963–64," January 12, 1963, UBCHEA, RGIIA, Box 19A, Folder 240, YUDSL.

27. Abigail Hoffsommer to C. T. Yung, "Subject: Mr. Li Seung-ping," UBCHEA, RGIIA, Box 19A, Folder 240, YUDSL.

28. Li Seung-ping to Abigail Hoffsommer, January 25, 1965; Hoffsommer to Li, February 1, 1965; and Stanley C. Miller, Jr., to the United Board, "Report or Faculty Adviser," all in UBCHEA, RGIIA, Box 19A, Folder 240, YUDSL.

29. Abigail Hoffsommer to Stanley C. Miller, Jr., January 18, 1965, UBCHEA, RGIIA, Box 19A, Folder 240, YUDSL.

30. "Award of Government Bursaries at Chinese Post-Secondary Colleges, 1962" (43-1); and "Award of Government Scholarships at Chinese Post-Secondary Colleges, 1962," both in Hong Kong Record Series (HKRS) 147-1-14.

31. Leslie G. Kilborn to Director of Education, November 28, 1962, HKRS 147-1-14.

32. Fung Shun Chong to Education Dept., December 7, 1962, HKRS 147-1-14; also see News from the National Academy of Engineering, "National Academy of Engineering Elects 64 Members and Nine Foreign Associates," February 9, 2007, http://www.nationalacademies.org/onpinews/newsitem.aspx?RecordID=02092007.

33. For some examples, see Zee Yun-Cheng to Director of Education, March 17, 1964 (190); C. H. Mak to Zee Yun-cheng, March 24, 1964 (191); Zee Yun-Cheng to C. H. Mak, April 4, 1964 (202); Chan Ka-kong to C. H. Mak, April 14, 1964 (206); Lum Kin-kwong to Director of Education, April 29, 1964 (209); Ng Yiu-qwing to C. H. Mak, May 19, 1964 (222), all in HKRS 147-1-17.

34. See M.17, N. C. Fong, "Mr. MEI Wai-kwok," December 2, 1963, HKRS 147-1-17.

35. Nieh Chung-yit to C. H. Mak, December 9, 1962; Nieh Chung-yit to C. H. Mak, December 13, 1962 (78); C. H. Mak to Post-Secondary College Scholarships and Bursaries Selection Committee, December 28, 1962 (91), all in HKRS 147-1-14.

36. Nieh Tsung-kong to C. H. Mak, December 27, 1962 (82), HKRS 147-1-14.

37. Nieh to Mak, December 9, 1962, 2, HKRS 147-1-14.

38. Nieh Chung-yit to DE, "Repayment of Bursary," (226), HKRS 147-1-14. Also see "Rice University, Fifty-ninth Commencement Exercises: Candidates for Degrees,

Doctor of Philosophy," May 20, 1972, http://scholarship.rice.edu/bitstream/handle/1911/61712/wrc01146.pdf?sequence=1.

39. "Training Hong Kong's Future Leaders," *AmCham* 7, no. 7 (July 1976): 53–55.

40. "In Some Small Way," *AmCham* 9, no. 2 (February 1978), 27; IIE, *Annual Report, 1973*, 23.

41. Between 1971 and 1989, 65,342 Hong Kong students studied in Britain, 61,750 in Canada, and 53,709 in the United States. See Ronald Skeldon, "Emigration and the Future of Hong Kong," *Pacific Affairs* 63, no. 4 (Winter 1990–91): 511.

42. Eric Fong, "Return Migration from Canada to Hong Kong," *China Review* 12, no. 1 (Spring 2012): 33–35; Skeldon, "Emigration and the Future of Hong Kong," 522.

43. Andy Chih-ming Wang, *Transpacific Articulations: Student Migration and the Remaking of Asian America* (Honolulu: University of Hawai'i Press: 2013), 52.

44. "Chamber Events: Hong Kong, China and the United States," *AmCham* 21, no. 6 (June 1990): 83.

45. P. C. Lee, ed., *Hongkong Album*, 5th ed. (Hong Kong: Sin Poh Amalgamated, 1967), HKUSC.

46. H. C. Ting, *Truth and Facts: Recollections of a Hong Kong Industrialist* (Hong Kong: Kader Industrial, 1974), 46–66, 96.

47. "本港製品銷美前途樂觀,開達廠丁熊照透露玩具銷美數量猛增, 且以獲得代理權為榮," *Wah Kiu Yat Po (WKYP)*, January 25, 1956, 7.

48. "港美合作設廠先聲, 美國玩具大王洛易馬克斯訪港, 與開達實業公司洽商合作設廠," *WKYP*, July 15, 1957, 6.

49. Ting, *Truth and Facts*, 96.

50. "丁熊照等飛日考察," *WKYP*, May 16, 1959, 9.

51. "丁熊照伉儷環遊世界考察工業," *Kong Sheung Yat Po (KSYP)*, July 9, 1962, 7; "圖: 丁熊照夫婦環遊世界,與公子鶴壽夫婦及康樂攝於機場," *WKYP*, July 9, 1962, 8; "丁熊照返港談,歐美龐大工廠,有如一個城市," *Kong Sheung Wan Bo (KSWP)*, September 25, 1962, 4.

52. Ting, *Truth and Facts*, i–vii.

53. "丁熊照次公子由美學成返港, 獲工商管理優異獎," *KSWP*, February 2, 1960, 4.

54. Ting, *Truth and Facts*, ix, 16–17, 22, 33–35, 84–85.

55. "丁午壽王雲心結婚," *KSYP*, May 4, 1969, 6; "丁午壽王雲心大喜," *WKYP*, May 4, 1969, 7.

56. Ting, *Truth and Facts*, 119–20.

57. See Kader Holdings Company Limited, "開達集團有限公司: 更換主席, 辭任非執行董事, 更換董事總經理 及委任非執行董事," 1, http://www.kader.com/investor_relations/pdf/press_100630c.pdf, accessed June 18, 2018.

58. "如雲號抵紐約, 中美人士歡迎, 董浩雲獲贈紐約市金鑰," *WKYP*, February 24, 1962, 3.

59. "南來華僑印象記, 董浩雲 '東亞巨人,'" *WKYP*, April 27, 1962, 8.

60. See Yuen Ren Chao Papers, Carton 5, Folder 74, and Carton 8, Folder 102, Bancroft Library, University of California, Berkeley.

61. Cliff Buddle, "Hong Kong's First Chief Executive Tung Chee-hwa Takes a Trip Down Memory Lane," *SCMP Magazine*, July 2, 2017, http://www.scmp.com/magazines/post-magazine/long-reads/article/2100528/hong-kongs-first-chief-executive-tung-chee-hwa.

62. "Shipping Tycoon, at Ease in U.S., to Govern Hong Kong for China," *New York Times*, December 12, 1996, A1; "New Hong Kong Leader Says His Kids Hold US Passports," *Chicago Tribune*, July 2, 1997, http://articles.chicagotribune.com/1997-07-02/news /9707030210_1_hong-kong-tung-passports.

63. Stephen Vines, "Profile: Tung Chee-hwa; China's secret weapon," *Independent*, November 24, 1996, https://www.independent.co.uk/voices/profile-tung-chee-hwa -chinas-secret-weapon-1354010.html.

64. "3 Are Attendants of Shirley Tung at Her Marriage; Senior at NYU, Bride of John Y. K. Peng at Notre Dame Church," *New York Times*, July 19, 1964, 63; "Spring Nuptials for Miss Tung," *New York Times*, November 8, 1970, 96; "Proud Sibling Plays to Gallery," *South China Morning Post (SCMP)*, December 13, 1996, 2.

65. William Armbruster, "Gala Marks 50th Anniversary of Containerization," *Canadian Sailings*, May 29, 2006, 7; J. R. Wachtel, "American Merchant Marine in Hong Kong," *AmCham* 8, no. 8 (August 1977): 17–18.

66. Howard Winn, "How Containers Made the World Smaller and Its Economy Bigger," *SCMP*, November 25, 2014, http://www.scmp.com/business/article/1647905/how -containers-made-world-smaller-and-its-economy-bigger.

67. For one of the first major studies of the issue, see Walter Adams, ed., *The Brain Drain* (New York: Macmillan, 1968).

68. Hsu, *The Good Immigrants*, 202.

69. *Open Doors, 1958*, 11. For one example, see "美國銀行陳旭權升主任," *WKYP*, May 5, 1971, 4.

70. AnnaLee Saxenian, *The New Argonauts*; see also her *Regional Advantage: Culture and Competition in Silicon Valley and Route 128* (Cambridge, Mass.: Harvard University Press, 1996).

71. Schenk, *Hong Kong as an International Financial Centre*, 125–26.

72. Stephen Chiu and Tai-lok Lui, *Hong Kong: Becoming a Chinese Global City* (New York: Routledge, 2009), 67–69.

73. Frank Ching, *The Li Dynasty: Hong Kong Aristocrats* (Hong Kong: Oxford University Press, 1999), 190–94.

74. Y. C. Jao, *The Asian Financial Crisis and the Ordeal of Hong Kong* (Westport, Conn.: Greenwood, 2001), 47–48.

75. Sayer, *The Man Who Turned the Lights On*, 48–49.

76. "董事會主席報告" (Chairman's Statement), in 恆隆有限公司, 一九七二／七三年年報, *Hang Lung Development Company, Limited, Annual Report 1972–73* (August 1973), 8, HKUSC; "Li & Fung Limited, Announcement," April 18, 1973, in 利豐 *Li & Fung Ltd.* (1974), HKUSC.

77. Sayer, *The Man Who Turned the Lights On*, 41–45, 36, 48–49. Also see "Hopewell Holdings Limited, 合和實業有限公司," August 8, 1972, 6–13, https://www.hope wellholdings.com/eng/images/about_us/milestones/HHL_AU_Prospectus _1972.pdf.

78. "Ka Wah Bank Standing Tall in Hong Kong," *Euromoney* (June 1984): S1–S16.

79. For a Chinese-language history of Li & Fung, see Robin Hutcheon (哈特巨), *A Burst of Crackers: The Li & Fung Story* (錦霞滿天: 利豐發展的道路) (Hong Kong: Chinese

University Press, 1992). For the Fungs' business philosophy, see Victor Fung, William Fung, and Yoram (Jerry) Wind, *Competing in a Flat World: Building Enterprises for a Borderless World* (Upper Saddle River, N.J.: Pearson Education, 2008).

80. Victor K. Fung, "Forward," in Feng Bang-yan, *100 Years of Li & Fung: Rise from Family Business to Multinational* (Singapore: Thomson Learning, 2007), xiv–xvi.

81. See Victor Zheng and Wong Siu-lun, "Network Capital and the Li & Fung Group in Hong Kong: Four Generations of Inculcation and Inheritance," in *Rethinking Social Capital and Entrepreneurship in Greater China: Is Guanxi Still Important?*, ed. Jenn-Hwan Wang and Ray-May Hsung (New York: Routledge, 2016), 95–126; author's interview with Jean Li Rogers, March 27, 2018.

82. Feng, *100 Years of Li & Fung*, 5, 7, 8–10, 34–35. For another example, note the creation of a "non-USA" textile group in 1986: 利豐集團 (Li & Fung: Advancing with the Times for 80 Years) (1986), 12–13, HKUSC.

83. Feng, *100 Years of Li & Fung*, 12.

84. Feng, *100 Years of Li & Fung*, 22–24.

85. Hutcheon, *A Burst of Crackers*, 22.

86. Feng, *100 Years of Li & Fung*, 28–30; 利豐: 一九七六年仲冬, 香翰府 (Li & Fung Limited: For 70 Years a Part of Hong Kong's Success) (1976), 7, HKUSC.

87. "HK Newlyweds Back," *SCMP*, August 2, 1969, 6.

88. William Fung, April 9, 2014, http://www.princeton.edu/fungforum/about/william -fung/.

89. Robyn Meredith, "At the Crossroads," *Forbes* 177, no. 8 (April 17, 2006): 45–48.

90. Joan Magretta, "Fast, Global, and Entrepreneurial: Supply Chain Management, Hong Kong Style," *Harvard Business Review* (September–October 1998): 104.

91. Feng, *100 Years of Li & Fung*, 42–44, 45–48, 52, 56–58.

92. Magretta, "Fast, Global, and Entrepreneurial," 104–5.

93. Feng, *100 Years of Li & Fung*, 106, 109.

94. "美徵附稅英將徵稅, 港紡織品勢受影響, 英資聯業紡織團將派員去考察," *Ta Kung Pao* (*TKP*), September 9, 1971, 6.

95. "適應國際生產水準, 聯業紡織精益求精, 去年貿易投資金額六千萬," *KSWP*, May 28, 1973, 6.

96. "紡織業面臨困境盈益仍增3%, 垂直式綜合性企業聯業紡織保持平穩," *KSWP*, September 17, 1973, 6.

97. "Chinese Press Comments," *SCMP*, June 6, 1984, 22; Bosworth Dewey, "Opening Up New Frontiers," *SCMP*, July 10, 1989, 7.

98. "世界貿易困難無解決良策, 紡織業一年內難望好轉, 聯業紡織公司董事會在報告中有此看法," *TKP*, September 3, 1974, 4.

99. Shu-Ching Jean Chen, "Staying Close to Roots, Lees of Hong Kong Restored a Garment Leader," *Forbes Asia*, November 2016, https://www.forbes.com/sites/shuchin gjeanchen/2016/11/21/staying-close-to-roots-lees-of-hong-kong-restored-a -garment-leader/#64beb9e463e6.

100. "聯業紡織公司協議計劃通過," *TKP*, December 7, 1978, 10.

101. Milton Friedman, "A Friedman Doctrine—the Social Responsibility of Business Is to Increase Its Profits," *New York Times*, September 13, 1970.

102. "Women at Work—a Diversity of Talents," *AmCham* 8, no. 5 (May 1977): 18–19.

103. Penny M. Von Eschen, "Globalizing Popular Culture in the 'American Century' and Beyond," *OAH Magazine of Identity* 20, no. 4 (July 2006): 56–63.

104. Carla Lane, "Tang Family Gives $4.7 Million to MIT," *MIT Tech Talk* 37, no. 20 (January 27, 1993), http://newsoffice.mit.edu/1993/tang-0127.

105. "胡應湘百萬美元, 贈普林斯頓每校, 資助聘請中國文化教授," *WKYP*, October 26, 1981, 32; Karen W. Arenson, "Hong Kong Builder, Graduate of Princeton, Gives It $100 Million," *New York Times*, November 10, 1995, B1.

106. Phanindra V. Wunnava and Albert A. Okunade, "Do Business Executives Give More to Their Alma Mater? Longitudinal Evidence from a Large University," *American Journal of Economics and Sociology* 72, no. 3 (July 2013): 765.

107. Aihwa Ong, *Flexible Citizenship: Cultural Logics of Transnationality* (Durham, N.C.: Duke University Press, 1999), 107.

108. On the increasing endowments of elite institutions, see Josh Lerner, Antoinette Schoar, and Jialan Wang, "Secrets of the Academy: The Drivers of University Endowment Success," *Journal of Economic Perspectives* 22, no. 3 (Summer 2008): 207–22.

7. Leading the Way

1. Much of this chapter's content first appeared in *Twentieth-Century China* 43, no. 1 (January 2018): 67–88. Copyright © 2018 Twentieth Century China Journal. Published by Johns Hopkins University Press.

2. Shanghai Textile Import/Export Company was founded in 1957 as 上海市纺织品进出口有限公司 but today is registered as 东方国际集团上海市纺织品进出口有限公司. See China Chamber of Commerce for Import and Export of Textile and Apparel, http://www.ccct.org.cn.

3. Feng Bang-yan, *100 Years of Li & Fung: Rise from Family Business to Multinational* (Singapore: Thomson Learning, 2007), 59–60.

4. Tim Williams, "U.S.-China Trade," *AmCham* 9, no. 10 (October 1978): 12.

5. See Elizabeth Perry and Christine Wong, eds., *The Political Economy of Reform in Post-Mao China* (Cambridge, Mass.: Harvard University, Council on East Asian Studies, 1985), 2; Ezra Vogel, "China and the East Asian Modernization Model," in *Chinese Economy Policy: Economic Reform at Midstream*, ed. Bruce Reynolds (New York: Paragon House, 1988), 10; Stuart Schram, "China After the Thirteenth Congress," *China Quarterly* 114 (June 1988); Nyaw Mee-kau, "Direct Foreign Investment in China: Trends, Performance, Policies and Prospects," *China Review* (1993): 16.2; Yingyi Qian, "The Process of China's Market Transition, 1978–1998: The Evolutionary, Historical, and Comparative Perspectives," in *China's Deep Reform: Politics in Transition*, ed. Lowell Dittmer and Guoli Liu (Lanham, Md.: Rowman & Littlefield, 2006), 231; Yue-man Yeung, "China's Openness and Reform at 30: Retrospect and Prospect," *China Review* 9, no. 2 (Fall 2009): 157–67; Li Lanqing, *Breaking Through: The Birth of China's Opening-Up Policy*, trans. Ling Yuan and Zheng Siying (Oxford: Oxford University Press, 2009), 4.

6. David Harvey, *A Brief History of Neoliberalism* (Oxford: Oxford University Press, 2005), 1.

7. *Resolution on Party History* (Beijing: Foreign Language Press, 1981), 47–73. Also see Julian Gewirtz, *Unlikely Partners: Chinese Reformers, Western Economists, and the Making of Global China* (Cambridge, Mass.: Harvard University Press, 2017), 96–97.

8. 总设计师 or "chief designer." At the opposite extreme, PRC economist Jinglian Wu has argued that Mao's administrative decentralizations in 1956–58 should figure as the starting point of China's "reforms." See Jinglian Wu, *China's Long March Toward a Market Economy* (San Francisco: Long River Press, 2005), 9–23.

9. 中华人民共和国经济史 (Beijing: Zhongguo shidai jingji chubanshe, 2010), 470–72.

10. Mark Selden, "China, Japan and the Regional Political Economy of East Asia, 1945–1995," in *Network Power: Japan and Asia*, ed. Peter J. Katzenstein and Takashi Shiraishi (Ithaca, N.Y.: Cornell University Press, 1997), 306–40.

11. Dali L. Yang, *Calamity and Reform in China: State, Rural Society, and Institutional Change Since the Great Leap Famine* (Stanford, Calif.: Stanford University Press, 1996), 149–79.

12. Wu, *China's Long March*, 23–24; Gewirtz, *Unlikely Partners*, 40.

13. Kazushi Minami, "Re-examining the End of Mao's Revolution: China's Changing Statecraft and Sino-American Relations, 1973–1978," *Cold War History*, September 27, 2016, https://tandfonline.com/doi/full/10.1080/14682745.2016.1218473.

14. Barry Naughton, *Growing Out of the Plan: Chinese Economic Reform, 1978–1993* (Cambridge: Cambridge University Press, 1995), 67–74.

15. Ezra F. Vogel, *Deng Xiaoping and the Transformation of China* (Cambridge, Mass.: Belknap Press of Harvard University Press, 2013), 229.

16. Herbert L. Minich, "American Business in Hong Kong," *AmCham* 6, no. 2 (February 1975): 13–15.

17. "Transition to China's New Era," *AmCham* 8, no. 11 (November 1977): 8.

18. Vogel, *Deng Xiaoping*, 221.

19. Yasheng Huang, *Capitalism with Chinese Characteristics: Entrepreneurship and the State* (Cambridge: Cambridge University Press, 2008).

20. Robert L. Suettinger, *Beyond Tiananmen: The Politics of US-China Relations, 1989–2000* (Washington, D.C.: Brookings Institution, 2003), 18.

21. Gewirtz, *Unlikely Partners*, 194–95.

22. William C. Kirby, "China's Internationalization in the Early People's Republic: Dreams of a Socialist World Economy," *China Quarterly* 188 (December 2006): 872.

23. Chen Jian, *China's Road to the Korean War* (New York: Columbia University Press, 1994).

24. John Parke Wright, "Canton and the China Trade," *AmCham* 9, no. 11 (November 1978): 21–24; John Kamm, "In Guangzhou for Good, Running an Office in Guangzhou Past, Present and Future," *AmCham* 12, no. 10 (October 1981): 6–7.

25. Tareq Y. Ismael, "The People's Republic of China and Africa," *Journal of Modern African Studies* 9, no. 4 (December 1971): 514–15, 522; Kenneth Wang, "Foreign Trade Policy and Apparatus of the People's Republic of China," *Law and Contemporary Problems* 38, no. 2 (Summer–Autumn 1973): 182–200.

26. W. K. Szeto, "Guangzhou Fair Perspective," *AmCham* 11, no. 1 (January 1980): 16.

27. Priscilla Roberts and John M. Carroll, eds., *Hong Kong in the Cold War* (Hong Kong: HKU Press, 2016). Reviewed by this author in "H-Diplo Roundtable Reviews" 18, no. 29 (2017), https://networks.h-net.org/node/28443/discussions/183002/h-diplo -roundtable-xviii-29-hong-kong-cold-war.

28. Yun-wing Sung, "The Role of Hong Kong in China's Export Drive," *Australian Journal of Chinese Affairs* 15 (January 1986): 85; Catherine Schenk, *Hong Kong as an International Financial Centre: Emergence and Development, 1945–1965* (London: Routledge, 2002), 157.

29. Peter E. Hamilton, "Pop Gingle's Cold War," in *Pacific America: Histories of Transoceanic Crossings*, ed. Lon Kurashige (Honolulu: University of Hawai'i Press, 2017).

30. "U.S.-China Trade in Retrospect: Amcham's Role," *AmCham* 6, no. 10 (October 1975): 23–24.

31. See a lively H-Diplo debate from September 2014 among Edwin Moise, Brian Hilton, and Robert Jervis, https://networks.h-net.org/node/28443/discussions/40045/h -diplo-frus-review-us-department-state-foreign-relations-united. Also see U.S. Department of State, *Foreign Relations of the United States, 1977–1980*, vol. 13: *China* (Washington, D.C.: Bureau of Public Affairs, Office of the Historian, 2013).

32. Christopher H. Phillips, "The Next Five Years in Our Trade with the People's Republic of China," *AmCham* 7, no. 6 (June 1976): 29.

33. Robin Hutcheon (哈特巨), *A Burst of Crackers: The Li & Fung Story* (錦霞滿天: 利豐發展的道路) (Hong Kong: Chinese University Press, 1992), 39, University of Hong Kong Library, Special Collections (HKUSC).

34. See Kin-ming Liu, ed., *My First Trip to China: Scholars, Diplomats and Journalists Reflect on their First Encounters with China* (Hong Kong: East Slope Publishing, 2012).

35. Randall E. Stross, *Bulls in the China Shop: And Other Sino-American Business Encounters* (New York: Pantheon Books, 1991), 27–28; Richard D. Lyons, "China Developing Satellite Links," *New York Times*, January 5, 1973, 9.

36. "Expanding PRC Oil Sales in Hong Kong," *AmCham* 7, no. 6 (June 1976): 5–7.

37. "Sales Open Bamboo Curtain," *Mobil World* (November 1973), 7, ExxonMobil Historical Collection (EMHC), Box 2.207/E172, Folder "Asia, China, News Articles," Briscoe Center for American History (BCAH), UT Austin.

38. John Parke Wright, "Canton and the China Trade," *AmCham* 9, no. 11 (November 1978): 24; "HAECO: Hong Kong Excels at Aviation Engineering," *AmCham* 7, no. 2 (February 1976): 10–11.

39. Michael Morrow, "Hong Kong Center for China Oil," *AmCham* 10, no. 10 (October 1979): 29–30.

40. Stross, *Bulls in the China Shop*, 28.

41. Jack Kaikati, "The Reincarnation of Barter Trade as a Marketing Tool," *Journal of Marketing* 40, no. 2 (April 1976): 17–24.

42. Li, *Breaking Through*, 221–25.

43. Alex A. Blum, "China's Textile Trade with America," *AmCham* 10, no. 10 (October 1979): 24.

44. David DeVoss, "A Modern China Trader: In the Steps of Marco Polo, Hong Kong Exporter Alex Blum Swaps California Chardonnay for Chinese Silk," *Los Angeles*

Times, November 10, 1985, https://www.latimes.com/archives/la-xpm-1985-11-10-tm
-3430-story.html.

45. "Alex Blum; Westerner Established Trade Links with Mainland China," *Los Angeles Times*, October 23, 1993, https://www.latimes.com/archives/la-xpm-1993-10-23-mn
-48681-story.html.

46. Anita Li, "Shenzhen Special Economic Zone," *AmCham* 12, no. 10 (October 1981): 21–23.

47. Alan Lau, "Compensation Trade Inside View," *AmCham* 11, no. 1 (January 1980): 19–20.

48. Szeto, "Guangzhou Fair Perspective," 15–17.

49. Stross, *Bulls in the China Shop*, 3–22. Also see Tom Gorman, "In the Shadow of the Canton Trade Fair," *AmCham* 16, no. 3 (March 1985): 63.

50. James A. Brunner and George M. Taoka, "Marketing and Negotiating in the People's Republic of China: Perceptions of American Businessmen Who Attended the 1975 Canton Fair," *Journal of International Business Studies* 8, no. 2 (Autumn–Winter 1977): 70.

51. Melvin Searls, "Two Way Trade," *AmCham* 9, no. 4 (April 1978): 19–21.

52. Jack Chi-Chien Tang, "The Textile Industry and the Development of Hong Kong," oral history conducted by Carolyn Wakeman in 1999, Regional Oral History Office, Bancroft Library, University of California Berkeley, 2003, 71, 105; Rosemary Sayer, *The Man Who Turned the Lights On: Gordon Wu* (Hong Kong: Chameleon Press, 2006), 58–59.

53. "Sales Open Bamboo Curtain," *Mobil World* (November 1973): 7, EMHC, Box 2.207/E172, "Asia, China, News Articles," BCAH.

54. "Amcham Receives Warm Reception at Kwangchow Fair," *AmCham* 6, no. 6 (June 1975): 13–15.

55. "AmCham Delegation Attends Kwangchow Trade Fair: A Round-Up of China-Related Activities," *AmCham* 5, no. 11 (November 1974): 15.

56. "Chinese Trade and Industrialization," *AmCham* 5, no. 11 (November 1974): 18–19; "AmCham's China Seminar Highly Successful," *AmCham* 5, no. 12 (December 1974): 16–19.

57. "AmCham Events: Unanimous Approval," *AmCham* 8, no. 8 (August 1977): 23.

58. Searls, "Two Way Trade," 19.

59. John Kamm, "Reforming Foreign Trade," in *One Step Ahead in China: Guangdong Under Reform*, ed. Ezra Vogel (Cambridge, Mass.: Harvard University Press, 1989), 344–46.

60. Kamm, "In Guangzhou for Good," 9.

61. Thomas D. Gorman, Keynote Address, Global China Connection Conference, Princeton University, February 12, 2011.

62. Li, *Breaking Through*, 211.

63. "Doing Business with China: A View from Peking," *AmCham* 5, no. 12 (December 1974): 25.

64. For some examples, see "AmCham Delegation Attends Kwangchow Trade Fair," 15–17.

65. John Kamm, "My First Trip to China: Shanghaied at the Feather and Down Mini-fair," *Hong Kong Economic Journal*, April 2, 2011, http://forum.hkej.com/node/65488.

66. Author's interview with Thomas D. Gorman, Hong Kong, October 22, 2012.

67. *American Industrial Report* advertisement, *AmCham* 11, no. 4 (April 1980): 16.

68. Gewirtz, *Unlikely Partners*, 28–29.

69. "US Chamber to Have Talks at Consulate," *SCMP*, August 28, 1970, HKRS 70-6-210-1.

70. John Wolf, "The First Five Years of Our Chamber," *AmCham* 5, no. 3 (March 1974): 5–6; "Appreciation Expressed to Henry M. Sperry," *American Chamber of Commerce Newsletter* 4, no. 2 (February 1973): 3, HKUSC.

71. "Membership Target Achieved—Congratulations!" *AmCham* 5, no. 1 (January 1974): 17; "Meet Our New Members," *AmCham* 6, no. 6 (June 1975): 29.

72. "Committee Corner," *AmCham* 8, no. 3 (March 1977): 27.

73. "Chamber Events and Pictures: New Directory," *AmCham* 7, no. 12 (December 1976): 31.

74. "Labor Relations," *AmCham* 11, no. 1 (January 1980): 39.

75. For Cheng, see "Meet Our New Members," *AmCham* 8, no. 4 (April 1977): 35; James W. Sweitzer, "President's Column," *AmCham* 11, no. 2 (February 1980): 2. For Fung, see "Meet 1983 Officers and Board," *AmCham* 14, no. 1 (January 1983): 11.

76. Michael Emmons, "Mutuality of Commercial Interest," *AmCham* 9, no. 1 (January 1978): 5.

77. Kayser Sung, "My Views on MFA III," *AmCham* 11, no. 6 (June 1980): 10–13.

78. "A Tour de Force: The Textile Committee," *AmCham* 9, no. 1 (January 1978): 13.

79. Alex A. Blum, "President's Column," *AmCham* 12, no. 10 (October 1981): 2; "Prevo-cational School Update," *AmCham* 16, no. 11 (November 1985): 11.

80. For another example, see Paulus W. K. Chan, "Letters to Amcham: Promoting Prosperity," *AmCham* 7, no. 12 (December 1976): 35.

81. "How We Help or Hurt Each Other: Taipans View the American Presence," *AmCham* 8, no. 1 (January 1977): 11–15.

82. W. R. A. Wyllie, "How Can a Hong Say No" *AmCham* 11, no. 7 (July 1978): 28.

83. Dorothy Liu Yiu-chu, "International Trade Law and the PRC," *AmCham* 7, no. 9 (September 1976): 19–23.

84. T. C. Chan, "Letters to Amcham: Disagreement," *AmCham* 7, no. 10 (October 1976): 35.

85. Li, *Breaking Through*, 258.

86. Francis G. Martin, "President's Column," *AmCham* 14, no. 9 (September 1983): 9.

87. Tom Gorman, "AmCham's Role in a Changing China Trade Climate," *AmCham* 11, no. 10 (October. 1978): 15.

88. "Transition to China's New Era," *AmCham* 8, no. 11 (November 1977): 8.

89. "The Legal System in the PRC," *AmCham* 7, no. 5 (May 1976): 11–13; "Legal Seminar," *AmCham* 7, no. 5 (May 1976): 35.

90. Brunner and Taoka, "Marketing and Negotiating," 72, 74.

91. "AmCham's China Seminar Highly Successful," *AmCham* 5, no. 12 (December 1974): 16–17.

92. "AmCham's PRC Posture—'Friendship, Patience and Trade,'" *AmCham* 7, no. 6 (June 1976): 19–21.

93. "A Round-Up of Committee Activities," *AmCham* 7, no. 4 (April 1976): 36.

94. "AmCham's PRC Posture," 19.

95. AmCham Events: Foreign Trade," *AmCham* 11, no. 10 (October 1978): 30.

96. Michael L. Emmons, "President's Column: 1978 Fall Canton Trade Fair," *AmCham* 9, no. 10 (October 1978): 2.

97. On NCUST, see Christian Talley, *Forgotten Vanguard: Informal Diplomacy and the Rise of United States-China Trade, 1972–1980* (Notre Dame, Ind.: University of Notre Dame Press, 2018).

98. Melvin W. Searls, Jr., "The Outlook Is Good," *AmCham* 8, no. 2 (February. 1977): 7–10.

99. George H. W. Bush, U.S. Liaison Office Beijing, to Consulate-General, Hong Kong, "Exxon Negotiations with PRC," December 24, 1974, Wikileaks.

100. U.S. Consulate-General, Hong Kong, to Department of State, "Reception for NCUSCT Vice President Searls," October 23, 1975, Wikileaks.

101. "Exit and Enter: AmCham Bids Farewell to Stanley Young and Welcomes Bill Mortson," *AmCham* 8, no. 8 (August 1977): 5.

102. See "Executive Committee, 1991: Lyn W Edinger," *AmCham* 22, no. 2 (February 1991): 47.

103. James W. Sweitzer, "President's Column," *AmCham* 11, no. 5 (May 1980): 2–3; Tim Williams, "CCRC 1981," *AmCham* 13, no. 2 (February 1982): 15; "Melvin Williams Searls Jr.; Commercial Envoy, 59," *New York Times*, January 5, 1995.

104. "Coming Events," *AmCham* 7, no. 10 (October 1976): 44; "Sluggish Growth," *AmCham* 8, no. 12 (December 1977): 36; "AmCham Events: Cautious Prediction," *AmCham* 9, no. 1 (January 1978): 31.

105. Tom Gorman, "Seminar in Canton," *AmCham* 10, no. 10 (October 1979): 36–37; "All About Trade," *AmCham* 10, no. 10 (October 1979): 27; "Hunan Delegation," *AmCham* 10, no. 11 (November 1979): 30.

106. Michael L. Emmons, "President's Column: Washington Trip," *AmCham* 9, no. 6 (June 1978): 3.

107. "AmCham Events: VIP Breakfast," *AmCham* 9, no. 9 (September 1978): 30.

108. Brunner and Taoka, "Marketing and Negotiating," 75.

109. "A Slow Upturn in 1976," *AmCham* 7, no. 2 (February 1976): 5–8.

110. Vogel, *Deng Xiaoping*, 219.

111. Gewirtz, *Unlikely Partners*, 36.

112. Vogel, *Deng Xiaoping*, 224.

113. "招商局昨舉行酒會, 介紹副董事長袁庚," *TKP*, November 2, 1978, 4. On CMSN, see Anne Reinhardt, *Navigating Semi-Colonialism: Shipping, Sovereignty, and Nation-Building in China, 1860–1937* (Cambridge, Mass.: Harvard University Asia Center, 2018).

114. Victor F. S. Sit, "Hong Kong: The China Trade Base," *AmCham* 13, no. 9 (September 1982): 34; also see Li, *Breaking Through*, 186–92.

115. Min Ye, "Policy Learning or Diffusion: How China Opened to Foreign Direct Investment," *Journal of East Asian Studies* 9, no. 3 (September–December 2009): 410.

116. "鄧小平李先念副主席會見, 華僑港澳同胞台胞旅行團," *TKP*, September 30, 1978, 1.

117. Jeffrey S. Muir, "Shenzhen: Guangdong's New Town in the Making," *AmCham* 15, no. 6 (June 1983): 39–41.

118. On Yuan Geng and Shekou, see Mary Ann O'Donnell, "Heroes of the Special Zone: Modeling Reform and Its Limits," in *Learning from Shenzhen: China's Post-Mao Experiment from Special Zone to Model City*, ed. Mary Ann O'Donnell, Winnie Wong, and Jonathan Bach (Chicago: University of Chicago Press, 2017), 46–50.

119. Muir, "Shenzhen," 40.

120. For Fok, see Rosalie L. Tung, *US-China Trade Negotiations: Pergamon Policy Studies on Business and Economics* (Amsterdam: Elsevier, 2014), 93–96. For the others, see Rick Kroos, "Hotel Projects in Beijing, Opening the Doors of Technology to China," *AmCham* 11, no. 8 (August 1980): 35–38; "China's Second Great Wall, America's Role in Building It," *AmCham* 16, no. 10 (October 1985): 20–23.

121. Li, *Breaking Through*, 280–86.

122. George H. Clyde, Jr., "China's New Foreign Investment Law," *AmCham* 10, no. 10 (October 1979): 10–17. For further analysis of the law, see L. Crawford Brickley, "Equity Joint Ventures in the People's Republic of China: The Promised Land Is Not Yet in Sight for Foreign Investors," *University of Pennsylvania Journal of International Law* 10, no. 2 (Spring 1988): 257–303.

123. Timothy A. Gelatt, "Gradualism in Action, Doing Business in China: The Legal Framework," *AmCham* 12, no. 10 (October 1981): 48; "Investment Under China's New Joint Venture Law," *AmCham* 11, no. 1 (January 1980): 21–23.

124. Clyde, Jr., "China's New Foreign Investment Law," 14.

125. Gewirtz, *Unlikely Partners*, 52, 73.

126. Li, "Shenzhen Special Economic Zone," 23–24.

127. Daniel Tretiak, "Investing for the Future: Current Attitudes Toward and Developments in Foreign Investment in Guangdong," *AmCham* 14, no. 6 (June 1983): 44.

128. Li, *Breaking Through*, 275–78.

129. "招商局昨舉行酒會, 介紹副董事長袁庚," *TKP*, November 2, 1978, 4.

130. Succinctly evidenced by the photos for "US-China Relations, an American View from Beijing," *AmCham* 16, no. 4 (April 1984): 9–13.

131. Tom Gorman, "Chamber President Commended," *AmCham* 11, no. 4 (April 1980): 61; "AmCham-PRC Ties Strengthening," *AmCham* (April 1980): 63.

132. "Fall 1979 Guangzhou Trade Fair reviewed," *AmCham* 11, no. 1 (January 1980): 24.

133. "管理民主化經營企業化: 上海申新絲紗廠, 聯合組織新公司," *TKP*, May 15, 1950, 7.

134. 陳穎川, "訪問榮毅仁," *TKP*, June 17, 1978, 2.

135. "前日自北京來港探親訪友, 榮毅仁昨天到本報探訪, 受到本報社長費彝民熱情接待," *TKP*, March 13, 1979, 4; 鐘明, "榮毅仁談香港與內地合作," *TKP*, March 16, 1979, 3; "榮毅仁宴工商人士," *TKP*, March 17, 1979, 4.

136. "榮毅仁昨在京答覆本報詢問, 合資法適用於港澳同胞投資," *TKP*, July 12, 1979, 1.

137. "榮毅仁在港闡釋中外合資問題, 透露投資公司擬在港設分公司," *TKP*, August 31, 1979, 1; "榮毅仁昨離港返京," *TKP*, September 6, 1979, 4.

138. "榮毅仁招待記者介紹公司業務, 首宗協議昨日簽字," *TKP*, October 5, 1979, 1.

139. "應美中貿易委會等團體邀請, 榮毅仁一行赴美與美國政界工商界人士接觸, 謀求促進中美經濟交往加強人民友好," *TKP*, October 7, 1979, 2.

140. "一百多家美公司參加歡迎會，榮毅仁在美談吸收外資，指出我安定局面將持續," *TKP*, October 11, 1979, 2; "榮毅仁在紐約發表談話，希望發展中美經技合作," *TKP*, October 19, 1979, 2.

141. "在華盛頓一次午餐會上，蒙代爾會見榮毅仁，指出美中友好關係應進一步發展，國防部長布朗出席宴會，萬斯當晚會見榮毅仁," *TKP*, October 29, 1979, 1; "中國國際信托投資公司，同芝加哥第一國民銀行簽合作協議，榮毅仁並回答了記者有關中外合資經營法等問題," *TKP*, October 31, 1979, 2.

142. "榮毅仁明天抵港，九日在美總商會午餐會演講," *TKP*, November 7, 1979, 4.

143. "美國商會午餐會榮毅仁演講，外商投資中國，利益可獲保障，中國重視法制促進互惠目的，中外聽眾深感與趣熱鬧罕見," *WKYP*, November 10, 1979, 5; "應邀出席美國總商會午餐會，榮毅仁經港發表演說，談外資在華投資問題," *TKP*, November 10, 1979, 4; "Putting You in the China Trade Picture," *AmCham* 11, no. 1 (January 1980): 12–14.

144. "榮毅仁率考察團，赴美參加研討會，煤炭交通等八部門副部長隨行," *TKP*, May 31, 1980, 2; "應洛克菲勒等邀請考察經濟，榮毅仁率團赴美，中國銀行行長為顧問，石油煤炭等部副部長同行，隨後將率領投資公司代表團訪加拿大," *TKP*, June 1, 1980, 1; "榮毅仁在紐約發表演講，中美經濟交流前景廣闊，兩國都需要發展經濟，互相合作符合共同利益，中國引進外資的方針堅定不移歡迎長短期合作," *TKP*, June 7, 1980, 2; "中國經濟討論會昨結束，榮毅仁在美宣布，與大通銀行合作，兩月內在北京會商具體計劃與時間表," *TKP*, June 8, 1980, 1.

145. Tung, *US-China Trade Negotiations*, 39–41; Stanley J. Marcuss, "United States-China trade relations," *AmCham* 11, no. 8 (August 1980): 51–54; Kenneth S. Chern, "Toward a Sino-American Entente?" *AmCham* 11, no. 11 (November 1980): 53–55.

146. "榮毅仁率考察團，赴美參加研討會，煤炭交通等八部門副部長隨行," *TKP*, May 31, 1980, 2.

147. On Wu Yunchu, see Parks M. Coble, *Chinese Capitalists in Japan's New Order: The Occupied Lower Yangzi, 1937–1945* (Berkeley: University of California, 2003), 175–82.

148. "吳志超應邀在中總午餐會演講，中國國際投資公司，擬發債券籌措資金," *TKP*, December 12, 1979, 5; "常董兼副總經理吳志超透露，中國國際信託投資分公司，預計五月初開始在港營業，他昨在美國商會演講稱中美貿易將迅速增長," *TKP*, February 29, 1980, 4.

149. "Outlook for Sino-US Trade," *AmCham* 11, no. 4 (April 1980): 10–12.

150. Li, "Shenzhen Special Economic Zone," 22–25. For the regulations, see WTO, "Regulations on Special Economic Zones in Guangdong Province (Approved for Implementation at the 15th Meeting of the Standing Committee of the Fifth National People's Congress on August 26, 1980)," https://www.wto.org/english/thewto_e/acc_e/chn_e/WTACCCHN46_LEG_8.pdf.

151. Tim Williams, "Tax and Banking," *AmCham* 11, no. 11 (November 1980): 6–7.

152. Clark T. Randt, Jr., "China's Foreign Exchange and How to Get Your Share," *AmCham* 12, no. 5 (May 1981): 12–14.

153. Li, "Shenzhen Special Economic Zone," 21.

154. Ann Fenwick, "Equity Joint Ventures in the People's Republic of China," *Business Lawyer* 40, no. 3 (May 1985): 839–78. Also see Li, *Breaking Through*, 136–39.

155. Timothy A. Gelatt, "Problems and Prospects, China's Special Economic Zones: The Regulatory Framework, Problems and Prospects," *AmCham* 14, no. 6 (June 1983): 49–50.

156. Li, *Breaking Through*, 143.

157. Li, "Shenzhen Special Economic Zone," 24–25.

158. "Beatrice Foods Co., China Agree to Join in Food Operations," *Chicago Tribune*, November 23, 1981, D11; "Beatrice and China in Joint Venture," *New York Times*, November 24, 1981, D4; Robert M. Knight, "Chinese Make Partial Bow to Chinese-American Food," *Christian Science Monitor*, December 24, 1981, https://www.csmonitor.com/1981/1224/122453.html.

159. Naughton, *Growing Out of the Plan*, 85–88, 119–27; quote on 88.

160. Tim Williams, "Economic Readjustment," *AmCham* 12, no. 5 (May 1981): 6–7; Stross, *Bulls in the China Shop*, 71–75; Li, *Breaking Through*, 290–93.

161. Li, *Breaking Through*, 309; for other JVs, see Frank Hawke, "Joint Ventures in China: A New Phase," *AmCham* 15, no. 6 (June 1984): 21–23; Tung, *US-China Trade Negotiations*, 93.

162. Li, "Shenzhen Special Economic Zone," 22–25; Ruth L. Eliel, "The Special Economic Zones," *AmCham* 13, no. 2 (February 1982): 18–19.

163. Li, *Breaking Through*, 145–47, 114.

164. Xianquan Xu, "Sino-US Economic and Trade Relations," in *China, the United States, and the Global Economy*, ed. Shuxun Chen and Charles Wolf, Jr. (Santa Monica: RAND, 2001), table 11.1, "Trade Statistics for China and the United States," 239; Jin Huang, "Sino-Japanese Relations in a Changing World, 1972–1992: A Chinese Perspective," 81–82, M.A. thesis, Simon Fraser University, 1995.

165. David L. Warner, "A China Joint Venture in Action: CCIC Finance Limited," *AmCham* 13, no. 2 (February 1982): 36.

166. "More Information to Avert Ill-Conceived Decisions, Suggests Wang Guang-ying," *Bulletin: A Hong Kong General Chamber of Commerce Magazine* (November 1984): 20, HKUSC; "Meet Our New Members," *AmCham* 15, no. 7 (July 1984): 81.

167. "American Businessmen Are Bullish About Our Future," *Bulletin* (July 1984): 11, HKUSC.

168. Chu, *Chinese Communists and Hong Kong Capitalists*, 59–63; also see Chalmers Johnson, "The Mousetrapping of Hong Kong: A Game in Which Nobody Wins," *Asian Survey* 24, no. 9 (September 1984): 887–909.

169. "Jardine of Hong Kong Plans Shift to Bermuda," *New York Times*, March 29, 1984.

8. The Gatekeepers

1. Previous delegations met with other senior leaders in 1982 and 1983, but not with Deng and not formally to discuss the handover. See Sze-yuen Chung, *Hong Kong's Journey to Reunification: Memoirs of Sze-yuen Chung* (Hong Kong: Chinese University Press, 2001), 63–67.

2. "Jack Tang ('Mr Textiles') Chairs the Chamber," *Bulletin, A Hong Kong General Chamber of Commerce Magazine* (June 1984), 7–9, HKUSC. Also see "Chairman's Statement/主席報告書," *Hong Kong General Chamber of Commerce Annual Report 1984/香港總商會一九八四年度年報*, 6–20, http://www.chamber.org.hk/FileUpload/20110307 1430269091/1984_Annual%20_Report.pdf.

3. "Humiliation! Deng Turns on Umelco Three," *South China Morning Post* (*SCMP*), June 24, 1984, 1.

4. Cindy Yik-yi Chu, *Chinese Communists and Hong Kong Capitalists: 1937–1997* (New York: Palgrave Macmillan, 2010).

5. Jack Chi-Chien Tang, "The Textile Industry and the Development of Hong Kong, 1949–1999," oral history conducted by Carolyn Wakeman in 1999, Regional Oral History Office, Bancroft Library, University of California Berkeley, 2003, 96–98. Xu also facilitated the UMELCO delegation's visit. See Chung, *Hong Kong's Journey to Reunification*, 95–104.

6. Tang, "The Textile Industry," 99, 100.

7. For "quiet New England accent," see "Jack Tang ('Mr Textiles') Chairs the Chamber," 7. For Tang's Mandarin see Tang, "The Textile Industry," 100. For Xinhua's transcript of this meeting in English, see "What Deng Told Industrialists, NCNA Issues Transcript," *SCMP*, June 29, 1984, 16–17.

8. Tang, "The Textile Industry," 103.

9. Luke S. K. Kwong, "Refurbishing Hong Kong's Image: The 1997 Saga and Chinese Nationalism Under Deng Xiaoping," *European Journal of East Asian Studies* 3, no. 1 (2004), 187; also see Leo Ou-fan Lee, *City Between Worlds: My Hong Kong* (Cambridge, Mass.: Belknap Press of Harvard University Press, 2008), 222.

10. Tang, "The Textile Industry," 100. According to Xinhua's transcript, Deng was referencing his role in mitigating the Cultural Revolution. Also see "Deng Stresses Stability and an Orderly Takeover," *SCMP*, June 29, 1984, 17.

11. Tang, "The Textile Industry," 89, 99.

12. "I254 Tang, Jack Chi Chien," Hong Kong Heritage Project (HKHP), 17.

13. Deng Xiaoping, "We Should Draw on the Experience of Other Countries," June 3, 1988, in *The Selected Works of Deng Xiaoping* (Beijing: Foreign Language Press, 1994), 261–62.

14. Yun-Wing Sung, "The Hong Kong Economy Through the 1997 Barrier," *Asian Survey* 37, no. 8 (August 1997): 709, 711–12.

15. Paul M. F. Cheng, "Don't Forget MFN," *SCMP*, March 15, 1996, 25.

16. Henry Wai-chung Yeung, "The Geography of Hong Kong Transnational Corporations in the ASEAN Region," *Royal Geographical Society* 27, no. 4 (December 1995): 326–27.

17. Michael J. Enright, Edith E. Scott, and David Dodwell, *The Hong Kong Advantage* (Hong Kong: Oxford University Press, 1997), 19–20, 71–72.

18. Yasheng Huang, *Capitalism with Chinese Characteristics: Entrepreneurship and the State* (Cambridge: Cambridge University Press, 2008), 54.

19. "How We Help or Hurt Each Other: Taipans View the American Presence," *AmCham* 8, no. 1 (January 1977): 15. Also see Raymond K. F. Ch'ien and David W. Hamstead, "Showcase for Free Trade, American Investment in Hong Kong," *AmCham* 14, no. 7 (July 1983): 10–11.

20. 利豐 (1976), University of Hong Kong, Special Collections (HKUSC); "The Lingnan Institute: Hong Kong's New Young Managers," *AmCham* 8, no. 8 (August 1977): 27.

21. Tang, "The Textile Industry," 99.

22. U.S. International Trade Commission (USITC), "The Multifiber Arrangement, 1973 to 1980: Report on Investigation No. 332–108 Under Section 332 of the Tariff Act of 1930," 3, 13, https://www.usitc.gov/publications/332/pub1131.pdf, accessed September 23, 2018. On the negotiations, see Stanley J. Marcuss, "United States–China Trade Relations," *AmCham* 11, no. 8 (August 1980): 51–54.

23. USITC, "The Multifiber Arrangement," 15, 18, 25, 35.

24. Irene Brambilla, Amit K. Khandelwal, and Peter K. Scott, "China's Experience Under the Multi-Fiber Arrangement (MFA) and the Agreement on Textiles and Clothing (ATC)," in *China's Growing Role in World Trade*, ed. Robert C. Feenstra and Shang-Jin Wei (Chicago: University of Chicago Press, 2010), 345–87.

25. David Schlesinger, "The Cost of Export Quotas in Hong Kong," *AmCham* 18, no. 11 (November 1987): 10; David Schlesinger, "Hong Kong: Knitting Up the American Rag Trade," *AmCham* 18, no. 11 (November 1987): 9–10.

26. On the MFA negotiations, see Vinod K. Aggarwal, "The Unraveling of the Multi-Fiber Arrangement, 1981: An Examination of International Regime Change," *International Organization* 37, no. 4 (Autumn 1983): 617–45. On Tang's role, see Carmer Robinson, "ATMI Marketing Mission to Hong Kong," *AmCham* 13, no. 7 (July 1982): 26–29; Tang, "The Textile Industry," 108–9; "I254 Tang, Jack Chi Chien," HKHP, 9–10.

27. Nyaw Mee-kau, "Direct Foreign Investment in China: Trends, Performance, Policies and Prospects," *China Review* (1993), 16.19.

28. Ho-fung Hung, *The China Boom: Why China Will Not Rule the World* (New York: Columbia University Press, 2016), 49.

29. Jeffrey S. Muir, "Shenzhen: Guangdong's New Town in the Making," *AmCham* 13, no. 6 (June 1983): 40.

30. On Liang Xiang, see Mary Ann O'Donnell, "Heroes of the Special Zone: Modeling Reform and Its Limits," in *Learning from Shenzhen: China's Post-Mao Experiment from Special Zone to Model City*, ed. Mary Ann O'Donnell, Winnie Wong, and Jonathan Bach (Chicago: University of Chicago Press, 2017), 39–46.

31. D. R. Phillips and A. G. O. Yeh, "China Experiments with Modernisation: The Shenzhen Special Economic Zone," *Geography* 68, no. 4 (October 1983): 289–300.

32. Rosemary Sayer, *The Man Who Turned the Lights On: Gordon Wu* (Hong Kong: Chameleon Press, 2006), 62–63.

33. "深圳特區吸收港商投資，發展福田成為中心市區，面積等於五個舊九龍首次投資廿億，雙方昨簽合同，梁湘胡應湘分別講話," *Ta Kung Pao* (TKP), November 24, 1981, 4.

34. "谷牧在京會見胡應湘何炳章，胡此行討論建廣深高速公路谷牧讚揚港胞支持特區建設," *TKP*, December 9, 1981, 1. Shipping baron Y. K. Pao was also meeting with Deng that day: "鄧小平會見包玉剛," *TKP*, December 9, 1981, 1.

35. "趙紫陽會見胡應湘，對建廣深高速公路計劃表支持," *TKP*, December 10, 1981, 1.

36. Sayer, *The Man Who Turned the Lights On*, 62–63.

37. "廣深高速公路八五年底完成，胡應湘談明年開發深圳福田區新區將建現代化城市合同期限卅年," *TKP*, December 13, 1981, 1.

38. "合和投資廿四億，合約為期三十年，穗深拱240公里高速路，胡應湘謂三年可建成," *TKP*, December 15, 1981, 4.

39. "任仲夷及梁靈光會見港商胡應湘, 對合建中國大酒店表示滿意," *TKP*, March 12, 1981, 4.

40. "由馮景禧及胡應湘陪同, 大衛.洛克菲勒等, 昨參觀蛇口深圳, 受深圳市長梁湘熱情接待," *TKP*, April 10, 1982, 4.

41. "胡應湘陪日商訪深圳, 乘汽車觀察廣深公路, 抵穗後受到梁尚立副市長歡迎," *TKP*, April 22, 1982, 3; "胡應湘陪同日財團代表, 訪問深圳市抵廣州, 考察與建高速公路," *Wah Kiu Yat Po (WKYP)*, April 22, 1982, 2.

42. "聯合委員會昨在穗成立, 廣深珠建高速公路, 正加速可行性研究, 粵交通廳長李牧和胡應湘任聯合委員正副主任," *TKP*, June 30, 1982, 2; "與建廣深珠高速公路, 聯合委員會成立, 胡應湘任副主任," *WKYP*, June 30, 1982, 2.

43. "任仲夷等暗胡應湘, 說特區大原則不變, 某些小調整是為更好前進不要打退堂鼓," *TKP*, August 19, 1982, 1.

44. "合和總經理胡應湘稱, 深穗高速公路, 面臨收地困難, 福田新市計劃亦有問題待解決," *TKP*, November 26, 1982, 6.

45. Sayer, *The Man Who Turned the Lights On*, 61.

46. "趙紫陽谷牧在北京會見胡應湘鄭裕彤," *TKP*, December 10, 1982, 1.

47. "招待首都經濟人士, 胡應湘昨舉行宴會, 表示對合作有信心, 廖承志谷牧胡子昂等出席宴會," *TKP*, December 11, 1982, 2.

48. "胡應湘謂趙紫陽表示, 九七年後收回主權, 港可保留現行制度," *Kong Sheung Yat Po (KSYP)*, December 16, 1982, 8; "胡應湘訪中國歸來講稱, 一九九七年之前, 中國不會收主權," *Wah Kiu Yat Po (WKYP)*, December 16, 1982, 5.

49. "主樓高五十層明年五月落成, 華潤新大廈昨天平頂," *TKP*, December 29, 1982, 4.

50. Chung, *Hong Kong's Journey to Reunification*, 39–43.

51. Sayer, *The Man Who Turned the Lights On*, 88.

52. Sayer, *The Man Who Turned the Lights On*, 64–65.

53. "參與建設的發展商胡應湘透露, 港穗高速公路明春動工," *TKP*, June 29, 1983, 4.

54. "胡應湘與日銀行家, 到北京會谷牧, 談建高速公路," *WKYP*, October 16, 1983, 2; "谷牧會見胡應湘," *TKP*, October 16, 1983, 1.

55. "胡應湘昨對記者表示, 合和實業地產投資, 逐漸轉移內地發展," *TKP*, November 12, 1983, 9.

56. For example: Naughton, *Growing Out of the Plan*, 25, 173–99; Li Lanqing, *Breaking Through: The Birth of China's Opening-Up Policy*, trans. Ling Yuan and Zheng Siying (Oxford: Oxford University Press, 2009), 191.

57. Min Ye, *Diasporas and Foreign Direct Investment in China and India* (Cambridge: Cambridge University Press, 2014), 62–63.

58. "趙紫陽會見胡應湘商談引進外資問題," *TKP*, May 15, 1984, 1.

59. "鄧小平對胡應湘說應請港公務員訪京," *TKP*, June 11, 1984, 4; "[政協] 胡應湘在穗大談九七事, 中共向公務員統戰, 歡迎北上商談出路," *KSYP*, June 11, 1984, 1; "胡應湘在穗表示, 中共歡迎公務員, 被商談出路問題," *Kong Sheung Wan Bo (KSWP)*, June 11, 1984, 8.

60. "合和在廣州週一已簽約建快速公路," *KSWP*, October 9, 1984, 7.

61. Luke S. K. Kwong, "Refurbishing Hong Kong's Image," 187; Jimmy McGregor, "The Chamber in Action: Sino-British Agreement on Hong Kong," *The Bulletin* (February 1985): 2, HKUSC; "香港合和胡應湘, 投資一億美元在桂林建酒店," *WKYP*, December 11, 1984, 2.

62. U.S. consul-general Burton Levin's statement of support appeared in every local newspaper on June 8, 1984, while Secretary of State George Shultz issued his own. See "Continuing Stability and Prosperity," *AmCham* 15, no. 10 (November 1984), 10.

63. Nyaw, "Direct Foreign Investment in China," 16.7.

64. Barry Naughton, "Between China and the World: Hong Kong's Economy Before and After 1997," in *Cosmopolitan Capitalists: Hong Kong and the Chinese Diaspora at the End of the Twentieth Century*, ed. Gary G. Hamilton (Seattle: University of Washington Press, 1999), 84.

65. Olivia Sin, "Textile Makers Shy Away from China Red Tape," *SCMP*, June 26, 1984.

66. For Zhao and the expressway, see Sayer, *The Man Who Turned the Lights On*, 88. Also see "旅國家派員統籌, 沿路縣市參建, 省港澳高速公路將有突破性發展, 胡應湘昨談有關情況期望年底能夠動工," *TKP*, April 19, 1986, 4. On Tianjin-Pukou, see Elisabeth Köll, *Railroads and the Transformation of China* (Cambridge, Mass.: Harvard University Press, 2019), 38–44.

67. Julian Gewirtz, *Unlikely Partners: Chinese Reformers, Western Economists, and the Making of Global China* (Cambridge, Mass.: Harvard University Press, 2017), 178.

68. Yongjin Zhang, *China's Emerging Global Businesses: Political Economy and Institutional Investigations* (Basingstoke, UK: Palgrave Macmillan, 2003), 139–41.

69. "要為外商投資創造更好小氣候, 谷牧在深圳晤港商界, 談共同開拓國際市場," *TKP*, February 10, 1987, 2.

70. "省港合作投資八十億港元, 廣深珠高速公路, 昨簽約後天動工," *TKP*, April 21, 1987, 1.

71. 飛翔編輯部, 女性主宰的世界: 最有权力的中国女人 (Beijing: Feixiang shidai wenhua chuanmei youxian gongsi, 2009), 224. Also see "莫觴清, Moh Song Ching," 上海總商會同人錄 (Shanghai: Shanghai zong shanghui, 1918), 42. Accessed through Modern History Databases (MHDB).

72. "蔡聲白先生," 現代實業家 (Shanghai: Shanghai shang baoshe, 1935), 33–34. Accessed through MHDB.

73. 女性主宰的世界, 225.

74. Antonia Finnane, *Changing Clothes in China: Fashion, History, Nation* (New York: Columbia University Press, 2008), 108–9; "蔡聲白," 現代實業家, 34.

75. Peter Quay Yang, *Recollections at Random* (Hong Kong: Signal Printing, 2013), 59.

76. "鍼後正一抵港, 希望促進港日貿易," *WKYP*, May 31, 1956, 5; "蘇浙同鄉會同人, 宴賀三位鄉彥晉紳, 邱德根楊元龍朱成信," *WKYP*, January 20, 1965, 12; "廠商會新首長選出, 莊重文任會長, 副會長胡永瀚楊元龍洪祥佩," *KSYP*, August 21, 1968, 4; "楊元龍甘銘任, 貿易發展委員," *WKYP*, October 12, 1968, 4.

77. "出席國際棉紡業會議, 港代表團昨飛日內瓦," *WKYP*, January 28, 1962, 8; 賀梅山, "日內瓦棉紡織品會議現狀," *TKP*, February 1, 1962, 2; "楊元龍安子介由歐飛返港," *WKYP*, February 18, 1962, 7; "楊元龍飛歐美, 任港代表顧問," *WKYP*, May 5, 1963, 7; "港府任免令," *WKYP*, July 27, 1963, 12; "談判棉品輸英分類問題, 港棉業團飛英," *TKP*, November 12, 1963, 4; "棉業代表團飛倫敦談判, 研究分類配額問題," *WKYP*, November 12, 1963, 5; "港英棉業談判結果, 港英今日發表," *WKYP*, November 23, 1963, 5.

78. Peter Dunn, "Marjorie Yang '74, Extending a Textile Tradition," *MIT News Magazine*, June 17, 2014, http://www.technologyreview.com/article/528021/marjorie-yang-74/; "Marjorie Yang: Biography," http://www.principalvoices.com/voices/marjorie

-yang-bio.html; Carla Rapoport, "Stitched for Big Time on the Mainland," *SCMP*, September 22, 1997, 14.

79. Harvard Business School: Alumni Stories, "Marjorie M. T. Yang (MBA '76)," January 1, 2002, https://www.alumni.hbs.edu/stories/Pages/story-bulletin.aspx?num=2023.

80. "廖承志副委員長設宴招待, 香港企業家楊元龍車家駛," *TKP*, November 12, 1978, 1.

81. Thomas G. Moore, *China in the World Market: Chinese Industry and International Sources of Reform in the Post-Mao Era* (Cambridge: Cambridge University Press, 2002), 65–66.

82. Yun-wing Sung, "The Role of Hong Kong in China's Export Drive," *Australian Journal of Chinese Affairs* 15 (January 1986): 83–101. Also see "Textile Exports Threat," *AmCham* 15, no. 9 (September 1984), 9–11; Stanley J. Marcuss and Phillip D. Fletcher, "Country of Origin," *AmCham* 15, no. 10 (October 1984): 27–29.

83. Moore, *China in the World Market*, 71–72, 85.

84. On the impact of infrastructure on Esquel's investment, see Tyler Marshall, "Modern Facilities Give China's Competitiveness a New Edge," *Los Angeles Times*, January 16, 2005,http://articles.latimes.com/2005/jan/16/business/fi-quotaside16.

85. Mark L. Clifford, *The Greening of Asia: The Business for Solving Asia's Environmental Emergency* (New York: Columbia University Press, 2015), 161–62.

86. "Hong Kong's Marjorie Yang," *Businessweek* June 28, 1998, https://www.bloomberg .com/news/articles/1998-06-28/hong-kongs-marjorie-yang-intl-edition.

87. Fred S. Armentrout, "Squaring Tiananmen: Blood and Sanctions in the PRC," *AmCham* 20, no. 10 (October 1989): 29.

88. To start, see Louisa Lim, *People's Republic of Amnesia: Tiananmen Revisited* (New York: Oxford University Press, 2014). For a cultural analysis of Tiananmen's origins and legacies, see Wang Hui, Theodore Huters, and Rebecca Karl, eds. *China's New Order: Society, Politics, and Economy in Transition*, trans. Rebecca Karl (Cambridge, Mass.: Harvard University Press, 2006), 43–77.

89. Susan Hill, "American Banks in China: World Sanctions Squeeze PRC Credit," *AmCham* 20, no. 10 (October 1989): 10–12.

90. "The Chinese Economy in 1989 and 1990: Trying to Revive Growth While Maintaining Social Stability," *AmCham* 22, no. 10 (October 1990): 36–43.

91. "Massive Drop in China Visitors," *AmCham* 20, no. 10 (October 1989): 40.

92. On Xu, see 許家屯, 許家屯香港回憶錄 (上下) (Hong Kong: Lianjing chuban gongsi, 1993). On Liang, see Mary Ann O'Donnell, "Heroes of the Special Zone," in O'Donnell, Wong, and Bach, *Learning from Shenzhen*, 58.

93. "4 June 1989: AmCham Takes a Position, Hong Kong Takes to the Streets," *AmCham* 20, no. 7 (July 1989): 10–11.

94. Hill, "American Banks in China," 12.

95. "港日經合委會唐驥千表示, 日對港投資穩定增長, 北京局勢對港經濟構成一定影響," *TKP*, June 7, 1989, 24.

96. "港對美紡品依賴減少, 唐驥千稱北京事件對聯亞無影響," *TKP*, June 30, 1989, 20.

97. Tang, "The Textile Industry," 113, 110.

98. Sayer, *The Man Who Turned the Lights On*, 92–94, 96–107.

99. Jeffrey A. Engel, *The China Diary of George H. W. Bush: The Making of a Global President* (Princeton, N.J.: Princeton University Press, 2011), 461.

100. Robert L. Suettinger, *Beyond Tiananmen: The Politics of US-China Relations, 1989–2000* (Washington, D.C.: Brookings Institution, 2003), 79–93.

101. Fred S. Armentrout, "Squaring Tiananmen: Blood and Sanctions in the PRC," *AmCham* 20, no. 10 (October 1989), 24.

102. Suettinger, *Beyond Tiananmen*, 95.

103. Armentrout, "Squaring Tiananmen," 25.

104. "AmCham's Position on the Escalation of China Sanctions," *AmCham* 20, no. 10 (October 1989), 27; M. C. Jaspersen, "Jensen International Warns Against Further US Trade Sanctions on China," *AmCham* 20, no. 10 (October 1989): 30.

105. Andrew B. Brick, Bryan T. Johnson, and Thomas J. Timmons, "Report: Washington's Agonizing Decision, to Extend or Revoke China's Most-Favored-Nation Trade Status," Heritage Foundation Asian Studies Center, *Backgrounder*, no. 104 (May 8, 1990): 1–12, http://www.heritage.org/research/reports/1990/05/washingtons-agonizing -decision-to-extend-or-revoke-chinas-most-favored-nation-trade-status.

106. Peter Robinson, "Stormy Year Ahead for New Amcham Boss," *SCMP*, January 1, 1987, 3.

107. Robbie Shell, "Alive and Well and Working in . . . Hong Kong," *Wharton Alumni Magazine* (Spring 1997), 15–16, http://whartonmagazine.com/wp-content/uploads/1997 /04/am97spr.pdf, October 4, 2018.

108. Michael Marray, "US Business Build-Up Gathers Pace," *SCMP*, July 13, 1987.

109. Stephanie Jones, *The Headhunting Business* (London: Springer, 1989), 87; Evelyn Cromer, *The Son from the West* (Leicester: Troubador, 2007), 317.

110. "美國商會總裁鄭明訓表示, 美保護主義仍受制衡, 港貨輸美可望再增長," *TKP*, January 3, 1987, 10; "信任美國商會會長鄭明訓指出, 美國保護主義, 仍威脅港出口," *WKYP*, January 7, 1987, 5.

111. Chu, *Chinese Communists and Hong Kong Capitalists*, 69–70.

112. Paul M. F. Cheng, "Presidential Memo," *AmCham* 18, no. 2 (February 1987): 5.

113. "貿易諮詢委會非官委員, 十二人獲延期一年, 美國商會總裁鄭明訓新加入," *WKYP*, June 27, 1987, 5; "Briefs: AmCham President on TAB," *SCMP*, June 27, 1987; Cheng, "Presidential Memo," 5–6.

114. "US Citizen Takes Up His Place in History," *SCMP*, October 12, 1988, 7.

115. Mandie Appleyard, "Sunday Portrait: A Moderate Who Won't Sit on the Fence," *SCMP*, January 15, 1989, 10.

116. Also see "辯論施政報告, 關注人才外流, 議員力主治本, 培訓接班人才," *WKYP*, November 11, 1988, 3; "容許外國律師執業增海外投資者信心, 鄭明訓認為對本港前途有好處," *WKYP*, March 22, 1989, 10.

117. "李嘉誠說學生只是愛國行動, 學運不會帶來危機, 不會改變投資計劃, 對港影響屬暫時性無 意拋售屬下股票, 張鑑泉呼籲勿使遊行變盲潮," *WKYP*, May 26, 1989, 3.

118. "中國學運長遠來看, 鄭明訓說對港有利, 可望促使中國市場更加開放," *WKYP*, May 26, 1989, 3.

119. John Kamm, "Presidential Memo: Sanctions Against China" and letter to President George H. W. Bush, February 5, 1990, *AmCham* 22, no. 3 (March 1990): 56–57.

120. "立法局議員, 前美國商會會長, 鄭明訓盼美顧各方利益勿取消中國最惠國待遇中美貿易關係 若倒退香港難免受沉重打擊," *TKP*, April 20, 1990, 7; "前美國商會主席鄭明訓警告, 若取 消中國最惠國待遇, 港美貿易必受損害," *WKYP*, April 20, 1990, 10.

121. John Kamm, "Presidential Memo: On to Washington!" *AmCham* 22, no. 5 (May 1990): 81.

122. C-SPAN, "China's Most Favored Nation Status, Part 2," May 16, 1990, http://www .c-span.org/video/?14300-1/chinas-favored-nation-status-part-2 (16:00–37:00).

123. Kamm, "Presidential Memo," 81.

124. "Statement by Press Secretary Fitzwater on the Renewal of Most-Favored-Nation Trade Status for China," May 24, 1990, in *Public Papers of the Presidents of the United States: George Bush, 1990, Book I—January 1 to June 30, 1989* (Washington, D.C.: U.S. Government Printing Office, 1991), 715–16.

125. "Bush Says China MFN 'Not A Special Favor,'" *AmCham* 22, no. 8 (August 1990): 40.

126. "AmCham's MFN Maydays in Washington," *AmCham* 22, no. 8 (August 1990): 39.

127. Robert A. Mosbacher, "Hong Kong: America's Business Partner in Asia," *AmCham* 22, no. 9 (September 1990): 93.

128. "羅康瑞當選總商會主席，龐約翰鄭明訓分任副職，麥理覺與羅康瑞就中國問題意見分歧，宣佈不再角逐立局可能由鄭明訓補替," *WKYP*, April 30, 1991, 1.

129. "美中之間最優惠國待遇，浦偉士稱對港經濟重要，王于漸指出若終斷最惠待遇對港打擊大," *TKP*, May 4, 1991, 8.

130. "向華府國會議員游說，總商會廿日派團赴美，促延續對華最惠待遇. 鄭明訓強調美若一意孤行亞洲嚴重受害," *TKP*, May 11, 1991, 8; Sondra WuDunn, "Chamber Takes Smart Tack on MFN Mission," *SCMP Business Post*, May 10, 1991, 12.

131. "鄭明訓率團赴美國，游說予華最惠待遇," *WKYP*, May 18, 1991, 12; "鄭明訓昨率團赴美，促延對華貿易優惠，盼美勿在此問題上附加條件," *TKP*, May 18, 1991, 10.

132. Michael Chugani, "Trade Status a Struggle to the End, Warns Cheng," *SCMP*, May 25, 1991.

133. "鄭明訓強調赴美游說收穫滿意，美續予華最惠國樂觀，港商勿急於撤走資金," *WKYP*, June 7, 1991, 12.

134. "鄭明訓談最惠國地位，稱港商無需過份反應，呼籲去信美國國會進行游說," *TKP*, June 7, 1991, 11.

135. "鄭明訓擬組商界游說團，分訪北京及華盛頓，期望中美談判減少打擊本港," *WKYP*, November 30, 1991, 3.

136. "鄭明訓談最惠國問題，稱港人仍需繼續游說，如中國能加入關貿問題可解決," *TKP*, July 26, 1991, 22.

137. Michael Chugani, "Fung Finds Assurance in Washington," *SCMP*, January 31, 1992.

138. Kevin Murphy, "Lobbyists Seek Key Sino-US Talks Role," *SCMP*, April 30, 1992.

139. Gewirtz, *Unlikely Partners*, 245–54.

140. Enright, Scott, and Dodwell, *The Hong Kong Advantage*, 14.

Conclusion

1. Sheldon H. Lu, "Filming Diaspora and Identity: Hong Kong and 1997," in *The Cinema of Hong Kong: History, Arts, Identity*, ed. Poshek Fu and David Desser (Cambridge: Cambridge University Press, 2000), 273–76.

2. Sze-yuen Chung references three polls conducted in 1982 that favored the status quo by 85 to 93 percent. See Sze-yuen Chung, *Hong Kong's Journey to Reunification: Memoirs of Sze-yuen Chung* (Hong Kong: Chinese University Press, 2001), 50–51. Other opinion polls and outward emigration underscore this conclusion. See Wong Siu-lun, "Deciding to Stay, Deciding to Move, Deciding Note to Decide," in *Cosmopolitan Capitalists: Hong Kong and the Chinese Diaspora at the End of the Twentieth Century*, ed. Gary G. Hamilton (Seattle: University of Washington Press, 1999), 135–36.

3. Wm. Roger Louis, "Hong Kong: The Critical Phase, 1945–1949," *American Historical Review* 102, no. 4 (October 1997): 1055.

4. "東方海外主席董建華認為,航運業今年難好轉," *Kong Sheung Wan Bo*, June 21, 1983, 5.

5. "東方海外主席董建華表示,市場對集團重組後貨櫃運輸服務顯復信心," *Wah Kiu Yat Po* (*WKYP*), July 14, 1987, 18.

6. Jack Chi-Chien Tang, "The Textile Industry and the Development of Hong Kong," oral history conducted by Carolyn Wakeman in 1999, Regional Oral History Office, Bancroft Library, University of California Berkeley, 2003, 141.

7. "董建華航運集團重組,債權人控制主要股權,董建華放棄經濟權益成受薪首席行政員,債權人初步反應良好預料七月底可實施," *Ta Kung Pao* (*TKP*), May 17, 1986, 9.

8. "袁庚董建華昨簽署協議,招商局購入歐亞企業,共斥資一億七千萬元,將把歐亞青衣深水岸線建成多用途碼頭," *TKP*, June 14, 1986, 13.

9. "董氏集團重整重要里程碑,霍英東與董建華簽約,注資一億二千萬美元,霍英東稱注資可加強董氏重整資金實力," *TKP*, September 3, 1986, 9.

10. Tang, "The Textile Industry," 142.

11. Stephen Vines, "Profile: Tung Chee-hwa, China's Secret Weapon," *Independent*, November 24, 1996, https://www.independent.co.uk/voices/profile-tung-chee-hwa-chinas-secret-weapon-1354010.html.

12. Yongjin Zhang, *China's Emerging Global Businesses: Political Economy and Institutional Investigations* (Basingstoke, UK: Palgrave Macmillan, 2003), 138.

13. "利漢釗丁午壽董建華,加入新昌集團董事會," *WKYP*, January 5, 1987, 14.

14. Chung, *Hong Kong's Journey to Reunification*, 235–36.

15. Andy Ho, "Spotlight on Tung," *South China Morning Post* (*SCMP*), February 6, 1996, 17.

16. Simon Beck, "Time to Prove His Mettle," *SCMP*, September 7, 1997, 13.

17. Robbie Shell, "Alive and Well and Working in . . . Hong Kong," *Wharton Magazine* (Spring 1997), http://whartonmagazine.com/issues/spring-1997/alive-and-well-and-working-in-hong-kong/#sthash.ilqeNCzm.dpbs.

18. Hong Kong Government, "Explanations of Some Questions by the Standing Committee of the National People's Congress Concerning the Implementation of the Nationality Law of the People's Republic of China in the Hong Kong Special Administrative Region (Adopted at the 19th Session of the Standing Committee of the 8th National People's Congress on May 15, 1996)," http://www.gov.hk/en/residents/immigration/chinese/law.htm#nat.

19. Most recently, see "百人会中国年会 / C100 China Conference 2018, 2018年12月1日,中国, 北京," 6–7.

20. "The Committee of 100, First Greater China Conference: Bridging the Pacific, January 12–14, 2005, Grand Hyatt Hotel, Hong Kong," University of Hong Kong Libraries, Special Collections.

21. Kathleen and Robert Thurston-Lighty, *The Stars Aligned: Celebrating the 20-Year Anniversary of the MIT-China Management Education Project* (水到渠成: 庆祝麻省理工学院(MIT)中国管理教育项目20周年纪念) (Cambridge, Mass.: MIT Press, 2016), 35, 49, 55, 62.

22. Giovanni Arrighi, *The Long Twentieth Century: Money, Power and the Origins of our Times* (London: Verso, 1994), 118–20.

23. Arrighi, *The Long Twentieth Century*, 152.

Bibliography

Archival Sources

Academia Sinica, Taipei, Taiwan

    Modern History Databases (MHDB)

Columbia University, Rare Book and Library Collections (RBLC), New York, New York

    Kwang Pu Chen Papers, 1936–1958 (KPC)

Dartmouth University, Rauner Special Collections Library (RSCLDC), Hanover, New Hampshire

    Alumni Files
    Tuck Alumni Records

Harvard University, Baker Library, Cambridge, Massachusetts

    Harvard Business School Bulletin

Harvard University, Harvard-Yenching Library (HYL), Cambridge, Massachusetts

    The University Bulletin (UB)

Harvard University, Widener Library, Cambridge, Massachusetts

    Review of Hongkong Chinese Press

Hong Kong Baptist University Library (HKBUL), Special Collections and Archives, Hong Kong

   Carl T. Smith Papers (CTSP)
   Carter Morgan Papers (CMP), Record Group 6
   Papers of the Hong Kong–Macau Baptist Mission (HKMBM), Record Group 3

The Hong Kong Heritage Project (HKHP), Hong Kong
The Hong Kong Public Records Office, Hong Kong

   Hong Kong Record Series (HKRS)

The Hoover Institute, Stanford University (HISU), Stanford, California

   The Asia Foundation Files (AFF)

The HSBC Archive, Hong Kong
The National Archives of the United Kingdom (NAUK), Kew, London
The University of California, Berkeley, The Bancroft Library, Berkeley, California

   Regional Oral History Office
   The Yuen Ren Chao Papers

The University of California, San Francisco, Manuscript Collections, San Francisco, California

   Choh Hao Li Papers (CHLP)

The University of Hong Kong Library, Special Collections (HKUSC), Hong Kong

   AmCham
   The Bulletin

The University of Texas at Austin, Dolph Briscoe Center for American History (BCAH), Austin, Texas

   ExxonMobil Historical Collection (EMHC)

Yale University, Divinity School Library (YUDSL), Special Collections, New Haven, Connecticut

   Archives of the Trustees of Lingnan University (ATLU), Record Group 14
   Archives of the United Board for Christian Higher Education in Asia (UBCHEA),
      Record Groups 11 and 11A
   China Records Project Miscellaneous Personal Papers Collection, Record Group 8
   Chinese Students' Christian Association in North America Archives, Record Group 13
   Merrill and Lucille Ady Papers, Record Group 138
   Papers of Sidney R. Anderson (PSRA), Record Group 200
   Sarah Refo Mason Papers, Record Group 75

Yale University, Manuscripts and Archives (YUMA), New Haven, Connecticut

Yale-China Association Records and Memorabilia (YCA), Record Groups 37, 232, and 233

Primary and Secondary Sources

Abbas, Ackbar. *Hong Kong: Culture and the Politics of Disappearance.* Minneapolis: University of Minnesota Press, 1997.

Abu-Lughod, Janet. *Before European Hegemony: The World System A.D. 1250–1350.* Oxford: Oxford University Press, 1991.

Adams, Walter, ed. *The Brain Drain.* New York: Macmillan, 1968.

Aggarwal, Vinod K. "The Unraveling of the Multi-Fiber Arrangement, 1981: An Examination of International Regime Change." *International Organization* 37, no. 4 (Autumn 1983): 617–45.

Amsden, Alice H. *The Rise of the "The Rest:" Challenges to the West from Late-Industrializing Economies.* New York: Oxford University Press, 2001.

Anderson, Irvine H., Jr. *The Standard-Vacuum Company and United States East Asian Policy, 1933–1941.* Princeton, N.J.: Princeton University Press, 1975.

Anderson, Maurice. *The Survival Strategies of a Complex Organization.* Hong Kong: N.p., 1972.

Andreas, Joel. *Rise of the Red Engineers: The Cultural Revolution and the Origins of China's New Class.* Stanford, Calif.: Stanford University Press, 2009.

Arrighi, Giovanni. *Adam Smith in Beijing: Lineages of the Twenty-First Century.* New York: Verso, 2007.

———. *The Long Twentieth Century: Money, Power and the Origins of Our Times.* 2nd ed. London: Verso, 2010.

Arrow, Kenneth J. "Higher Education as a Filter," *Journal of Public Economics* 2, no. 3 (July 1973): 193–216.

Ayers, William. *Chang Chih-tung and Educational Reform in China.* Cambridge, Mass.: Harvard University Press, 1971.

Babcock, Fenton and Evelyn. *New Lives for Old.* Pittsburgh: RoseDog Books, 2011.

Barclay, Paul D. *Outcasts of Empire: Japan's Rule on Taiwan's "Savage Border," 1874–1945.* Berkeley: University of California Press, 2017.

Barnett, A. Doak. *China on the Eve of Communist Takeover.* New York: Praeger, 1963.

Barrett, Ross. "Aligning India in the Cold War Era: Indian Technological Elites, the Indian Institute of Technology at Kanpur, and Computing in India and the United States." *Technology and Culture* 50, no. 4 (October 2009): 783–810.

Bastid, Marianne. "Servitude or Liberation: The Introduction of Foreign Educational Practices and Systems to China from 1840 to the Present." In *China's Education and the Industrialized World: Studies in Cultural Transfer,* ed. Ruth Hayhoe and Marianne Bastid, 3–20. Armonk, N.Y.: M. E. Sharpe, 1987.

Bays, Daniel H., ed. *Christianity in China: From the Eighteenth Century to the Present.* Stanford, Calif.: Stanford University Press, 1999.

Bays, Daniel H., and Ellen Widmer, eds. *China's Christian Colleges: Cross-Cultural Connections, 1900–1950*. Stanford, Calif.: Stanford University Press, 2009.

Berger, Peter L., and Hsin-Huang Michael Hsiao, eds. *In Search of an East Asian Development Model*. New Brunswick, N.J.: Transaction Books, 1988.

Bergère, Marie-Claire. *The Golden Age of the Chinese Bourgeoisie*, trans. Janet Lloyd. Cambridge: Cambridge University Press, 1989.

——. "The Shanghai Bankers' Association, 1915–1927: Modernization and the Institutionalization of Local Solidarities." In *Shanghai Sojourners*, ed. Frederic Wakeman, Jr., and Wen-hsin Yeh, 15–34. Berkeley: Institute of East Asian Studies, University of California Press, 1992.

Bickers, Robert. *Britain in China: Community, Culture and Colonialism 1900–1949*. Manchester: Manchester University Press, 1999.

Bickers, Robert, and R. G. Tiedemann, eds. *The Boxers, China, and the World*. Lanham, Md.: Rowman & Littlefield, 2007.

Bickers, Robert, and Ray Yep, eds. *May Days in Hong Kong: Riot and Emergency in 1967*. Hong Kong: Hong Kong University Press, 2009.

Boecking, Felix. *No Great Wall: Trade, Tariffs, and Nationalism in Republican China, 1927–1945*. Cambridge, Mass.: Harvard University Press, 2017.

Boorman, Howard L., ed., *Biographical Dictionary of Republican China*. New York: Columbia University Press, 1967.

Borden, William S. *The Pacific Alliance: United States Foreign Economic Policy and Japanese Trade Recovery, 1947–1955*. Madison: University of Wisconsin Press, 1984.

Bourdieu, Pierre. *Distinction: A Social Critique of the Judgment of Taste*. Trans. Richard Nice. 1979. London: Routledge, 1984.

——. "The Forms of Capital." In *Handbook of Theory and Research for the Sociology of Education*, ed. John G. Richardson, 241–58. New York: Greenwood, 1986.

——. *The State Nobility: Elite Schools in the Field of Power*, trans. Lauretta C. Clough. 1989. New York: Polity Press, 1996.

Brambilla, Irene, Amit K. Khandelwal, and Peter K. Scott. "China's Experience Under the Multi-Fiber Arrangement (MFA) and the Agreement on Textiles and Clothing (ATC)." In *China's Growing Role in World Trade*, ed. Robert C. Feenstra and Shang-Jin Wei, 345–87. Chicago: University of Chicago Press, 2010.

Brickley, L. Crawford. "Equity Joint Ventures in the People's Republic of China: The Promised Land Is Not Yet in Sight for Foreign Investors." *University of Pennsylvania Journal of International Law* 10, no. 2 (Spring 1988): 257–303.

Brunner, James A., and George M. Taoka. "Marketing and Negotiating in the People's Republic of China: Perceptions of American Businessmen Who Attended the 1975 Canton Fair." *Journal of International Business Studies* 8, no. 2 (Autumn–Winter 1977): 69–82.

Bu, Liping. *Making the World Like Us: Education, Cultural Expansion, and the American Century*. Westport: Praeger, 2003.

Burt, Ronald S. *Structural Holes: The Social Structure of Competition*. Cambridge, Mass.: Harvard University Press, 1992.

Bush, George H. W. *Public Papers of the Presidents of the United States: George Bush, 1990*. Washington, D.C.: National Archives and Records Administration, 1991.

Buswell, Robert E., Jr., and Timothy S. Lee, eds. *Christianity in Korea*. Honolulu: University of Hawaii Press, 2007.

Carroll, John M. *Edge of Empires: Chinese Elites and British Colonials in Hong Kong*. Cambridge, Mass.: Harvard University Press, 2005.

——. "A Historical Perspective: The 1967 Riots and the Strike Boycott of 1925–1926." In *May Days in Hong Kong: Riot and Emergency in 1967*, ed. Robert Bickers and Ray Yep. Hong Kong: Hong Kong University Press, 2009.

Chan Lau, Kit-ching. "Business and Radicalism: Hong Kong Chinese Merchants and the Chinese Communist Movement, 1921–1934." In *Colonial Hong Kong and Modern China*, ed. Pui-tak Lee, 169–83. Hong Kong: Hong Kong University Press, 2005.

Chang, Chihyun, ed. *The Chinese Journals of L. K. Little, 1943–54: An Eyewitness Account of War and Revolution*. Vols. 1–3. New York: Routledge, 2018.

Chapman, Nancy E., with Jessica C. Plumb. *The Yale-China Association: A Centennial History*. Hong Kong: Chinese University of Hong Kong Press, 2001.

Chen, Janet Y. *Guilty of Indigence: The Urban Poor in China, 1900–1953*. Princeton, N.J.: Princeton University Press, 2012.

Chen, Jian. *China's Road to the Korean War*. New York: Columbia University Press, 1994.

Chen, Kuan-hsing. *Asia as Method: Towards De-Imperialization*. Durham, N.C.: Duke University Press, 2010.

Cheng, Ming Yu, and Ron Mittelhammer. "Globalization and Economic Development: Impact of Social Capital and Institutional Building." *American Journal of Economics and Sociology* 67, no. 5 (November 2008): 859–88.

Cheung Lam, Richard, and Hong-Kin Kwok. "Global Supplier Without a Global Brand Name: A Case Study of Hong Kong's Electronics Industry." *Asian Journal of Social Science* 32, no. 3 (2004): 476–500.

Cheung, Gary Ka-wai. *Hong Kong's Watershed, the 1967 Riots*. Hong Kong: Hong Kong University Press, 2009.

Chin, Angelina Y. "Colonial Charity in Hong Kong: A Case of the Po Leung Kuk in the 1930s." *Journal of Women's History* 25, no. 1 (Spring 2013): 135–57.

Ching, Frank. *The Li Dynasty: Hong Kong Aristocrats*. Oxford: Oxford University Press, 1999.

Chirot, Daniel, and Anthony Reid, eds. *Essential Outsiders: Chinese and Jews in the Modern Transformation of Southeast Asia and Central Europe*. Seattle: University of Washington Press, 1997.

Chiu, Stephen, and Tai-lok Lui. *Hong Kong: Becoming a Chinese Global City*. New York: Routledge, 2009.

Chou, Grace Ai-ling. *Confucianism, Colonialism, and the Cold War: Chinese Cultural Education at Hong Kong's New Asia College, 1949–63*. Leiden: Brill, 2011.

Chu, Cindy Yik-yi. *Chinese Communists and Hong Kong Capitalists: 1937–1997*. New York: Palgrave Macmillan, 2010.

——. *The Maryknoll Sisters in Hong Kong, 1921–1969: In Love with the Chinese*. Basingstoke: Palgrave Macmillan, 2004.

Chung, Sze-yuen. *Hong Kong's Journey to Reunification: Memoirs of Sze-yuen Chung*. Hong Kong: Chinese University Press, 2001.

Clifford, Mark L. *The Greening of Asia: The Business for Solving Asia's Environmental Emergency.* New York: Columbia University Press, 2015.

Coble, Parks M. "Chinese Capitalists and the Japanese: Collaboration and Resistance in the Shanghai Area, 1937–45." In *Wartime Shanghai,* ed. Wen-hsin Yeh, 62–85. London: Routledge, 1998.

——. *Chinese Capitalists in Japan's New Order: The Occupied Lower Yangzi, 1937–1945.* Berkeley: University of California Press, 2003.

Cochran, Sherman. *Big Business in China: Sino-Foreign Rivalry in the Cigarette Industry, 1890–1930.* Cambridge, Mass.: Harvard University Press, 1980.

——, ed. *The Capitalist Dilemma in China's Communist Revolution.* Ithaca, N.Y.: Cornell East Asia Program, 2014.

——. *Encountering Chinese Networks: Western, Japanese, and Chinese Corporations in China, 1880–1937.* Berkeley: University of California Press, 2000.

Cochran, Sherman, and Andrew Hsieh. *The Lius of Shanghai.* Cambridge, Mass.: Harvard University Press, 2013.

Coleman, James S. "Social Capital in the Creation of Human Capital." *American Journal of Sociology* 94 (1988): S95–S120.

Cromer, Evelyn. *The Son from the West.* Leicester, UK: Troubador, 2007.

Cumings, Bruce. "The Origins and Development of the Northeast Asian Political Economy: Industrial Sectors, Product Cycles, and Political Consequences." In *The Political Economy of New Asia Industrialism,* ed. F. C. Deyo, 44–83. Ithaca, N.Y.: Cornell University Press, 1987.

——. *Pacific-Asia and the Future of the World-System.* Westport, Conn.: Greenwood Press, 1993.

de Grazia, Victoria. *Irresistible Empire: America's Advance Through Twentieth-Century Europe.* Cambridge, Mass.: Harvard University Press, 2006.

Deng, Xiaoping. *The Selected Works of Deng Xiaoping.* Beijing: Foreign Language Press, 1994.

Dikötter, Frank. *Things Modern: Material Culture and Everyday Life in China.* London: Hurst, 2007.

Donnithorne, Audrey G. Review of *Economic Development of Communist China* by Choh-Ming Li. *Economica,* New Series, 27, no. 105 (February 1960): 95.

Dore, Ronald. *Taking Japan Seriously: A Confucian Perspective on Leading Economic Issues.* Stanford, Calif.: Stanford University Press, 1987.

Dumbaugh, Kerry. "The U.S. Role During and After Hong Kong's Transition." *Journal of International Law* 18, no. 1 (1997): 343–46.

Dunch, Ryan. *Fuzhou Protestants and the Making of a Modern China, 1857–1927.* New Haven, Conn.: Yale University Press, 2001.

Eckstein, Alexander. "Conditions and Prospects for Economic Growth in Communist China." *World Politics* 7, no. 1 (October 1954): 1–37.

Elman, Benjamin A. *Civil Examinations and Meritocracy in Late Imperial China.* Cambridge, Mass.: Harvard University Press, 2013.

Engel, Jeffrey A. *The China Diary of George H. W. Bush: The Making of a Global President.* Princeton, N.J.: Princeton University Press, 2011.

Engerman, David C. *The Price of Aid: The Economic Cold War in India.* Cambridge, Mass: Harvard University Press, 2018.

Enright, Michael J., Edith E. Scott, and David Dodwell. *The Hong Kong Advantage.* Hong Kong: Oxford University Press, 1997.

Esherick, Joseph W. *Reform and Revolution in China: The 1911 Revolution in Hunan and Hubei.* Michigan Studies on China. Berkeley: University of California Press, 1976.

———, ed. *Remaking the Chinese City: Modernity and National Identity, 1900–1950.* Honolulu: University of Hawai'i Press, 2000.

Evans, Peter. *Embedded Autonomy: States and Industrial Transformation.* Princeton, N.J.: Princeton University Press, 1995.

Fang, Jun. "Lai Jixi and the Development of Chinese Education at the University of Hong Kong." *Journal of the Royal Asiatic Society Hong Kong Branch* 52 (2012): 267–89.

Feenstra, Robert C., and Gary G. Hamilton. *Emergent Economies, Divergent Paths: Economic Organization and International Trade in South Korea and Taiwan.* Cambridge: Cambridge University Press, 2006.

Fei, Xiaotong. *From the Soil: The Foundations of Chinese Society*, trans. Gary G. Hamilton and Wang Zheng. Berkeley: University of California Press, 1992.

Feixiang Editing Department [飞翔编辑部]. 女性主宰的世界: 最有权力的中国女人. Beijing: Feixiang shidai wenhua chuanmei youxian gongsi, 2009.

Feng, Bang-yan. *100 Years of Li & Fung: Rise from Family Business to Multinational.* Singapore: Thomson Learning, 2007.

Finnane, Antonia. *Changing Clothes in China: Fashion, History, Nation.* New York: Columbia University Press, 2008.

———. *Speaking of Yangzhou: A Chinese City, 1550–1850.* Cambridge, Mass.: Harvard University Press, 2004.

Folts, Franklin. *Introduction to Industrial Management.* New York: McGraw-Hill, 1963.

Fong, Eric. "Return Migration from Canada to Hong Kong." *China Review* 12, no. 1 (Spring 2012): 25–43.

Forth, Aidan. *Barbed-Wire Imperialism: Britain's Empire of Camps, 1876–1903.* Berkeley: University of California Press, 2017.

Frank, Andre Gunder. *ReORIENT: Global Economy in the Asian Age.* Berkeley: University of California Press, 1998.

Fredman, Zach. "GIs and 'Jeep Girls': Sex and American Soldiers in Wartime China." *Journal of Modern Chinese History* 13, no. 1 (2019): 76–101.

Friedman, Milton, and Rose D. Friedman. *Free to Choose: A Personal Statement.* 1979. New York: Houghton Mifflin, 1990.

Fu, Poshek, and David Desser, eds. *The Cinema of Hong Kong: History, Arts, Identity.* Cambridge: Cambridge University Press, 2002.

Fung, Pui Wing. "The Development of Higher Education in a Developing City: Hong Kong, 1900–1980." Ph.D. dissertation, University of Hull, September 1988.

Fung, Victor K., William K. Fung, and Yoram (Jerry) Wind. *Competing in a Flat World: Building Enterprises for a Borderless World.* Upper Saddle River, N.J.: Pearson Education, 2008.

Gewirtz, Julian. *Unlikely Partners: Chinese Reformers, Western Economists, and the Making of Global China.* Cambridge, Mass.: Harvard University Press, 2017.

Gilman, Nils. *Mandarins of the Future: Modernization Theory in Cold War America.* Baltimore: Johns Hopkins University Press, 2004.

Gilmartin, Christina Kelley. *Engendering the Chinese Revolution: Radical Women, Communist Politics, and Mass Movements in the 1920s.* Berkeley: University of California Press, 1995.

Gleason, Gene. *Hong Kong.* New York: John Day, 1963.

Goodman, Bryna. *Native Place, City and Nation: Regional Networks and Identities.* Berkeley: University of California Press, 1995.

——. "New Culture, Old Habits: Native-Place Organization and the May Fourth Movement." In *Shanghai Sojourners,* ed. Frederic Wakeman, Jr., and Wen-hsin Yeh, 76–107. Berkeley: Institute of East Asian Studies, University of California Press, 1992.

Grady, Henry F., with John T. McNay. *The Memoirs of Henry F. Grady.* Columbia: University of Missouri Press, 2009.

Granovetter, Mark. "Economic Action and Social Structure: The Problem of Embeddedness." *American Journal of Sociology* 91, no. 3 (November 1985): 481–510.

——. "The Strength of Weak Ties: A Network Theory Revisited." *Sociological Theory* 1 (1983): 201–33.

Guha, Ramachandra. "Pluralism in the Indian University." *Economic and Political Weekly* 42, no. 7 (February 2007): 564–70.

Hahn, Emily. *China To Me.* Garden City, N.Y.: Doubleday, Doran, 1944.

Hamilton, Gary G., ed. *Business Networks and Economic Development in East and Southeast Asia.* Hong Kong: Centre of Asian Studies, University of Hong Kong, 1991.

——. *Commerce and Capitalism in Chinese Societies.* London: Routledge, 2006.

——, ed. *Cosmopolitan Capitalists: Hong Kong and the Chinese Diaspora at the End of the Twentieth Century.* Seattle: University of Washington Press, 1999.

Hamilton, Peter E. " 'A Haven for Tortured Souls': Hong Kong in the Vietnam War." *International History Review* 37, no. 3 (June 2015): 565–81.

——. "An American Family's Mission in East Asia, 1838 to 1936: A Commitment to God, Academia and Empire." *Journal of the Royal Asiatic Society Hong Kong Branch* 49 (August 2009): 229–65.

——. "The Imperial and Transpacific Origins of Chinese Capitalism," special issue of the *Journal of Historical Sociology* 33, no. 1 (March 2020): 134–148.

Hao, Yen-p'ing. *The Comprador in Nineteenth-Century China: Bridge Between East and West.* Cambridge, Mass.: Harvard University Press, 1970.

Harrison, Henrietta. *The Man Awakened from Dreams: One Man's Life in a North China Village, 1857–1942.* Stanford, Calif.: Stanford University Press, 2005.

Hartigan-O'Connor, Ellen. "The Personal Is Political Economy." *Journal of the Early Republic* 36, no. 2 (Summer 2016): 335–41.

Harvey, David. *A Brief History of Neoliberalism.* Oxford: Oxford University Press, 2005.

——. *The Condition of Postmodernity: An Enquiry Into the Origins of Cultural Change.* Oxford: Blackwell, 1990.

Hatch, Walter, and Kozo Yamamura. *Asia in Japan's Embrace: Building a Regional Production Alliance.* Cambridge: Cambridge University Press, 1996.

Heilbroner, Robert L. *Behind the Veil of Economics: Essays in the Worldly Philosophy.* New York: Norton, 1988.

Holdsworth, May, and Christopher Munn, eds. *The Dictionary of Hong Kong Biography.* Hong Kong: Hong Kong University Press, 2012.

Honig, Emily. *Sisters and Strangers: Women in the Shanghai Cotton Mills, 1919–1949.* Stanford, Calif.: Stanford University Press, 1986.

Hsu, Madeline Y. "Aid Refugee Chinese Intellectuals and the Political Uses of Humanitarian Relief, 1952–1962." *Journal of Chinese Overseas* 10, no. 2 (2014): 137–64.

——. "Befriending the Yellow Peril." In *Trans-Pacific Interactions: The United States and China, 1880–1950,* ed. Vanessa Künnemann and Ruth Mayer. New York: Palgrave Macmillan, 2009.

——. "Chinese and American Collaborations Through Educational Exchange During the Era of Exclusion, 1872–1955." *Pacific Historical Review* 83, no. 2 (May 2014): 314–32.

——. *Dreaming of Gold, Dreaming of Home: Transnationalism and Migration Between the United States and South China, 1882–1943.* Stanford, Calif.: Stanford University Press, 2000.

——. *The Good Immigrants: How the Yellow Peril Became the Model Minority.* Princeton, N.J.: Princeton University Press, 2015.

Huang, Jianli, and Hong Lysa. *The Scripting of a National History: Singapore and Its Pasts.* Hong Kong: HKU Press, 2008.

Huang, Jin. "Sino-Japanese Relations in a Changing World, 1972–1992: A Chinese Perspective." M.A. thesis, Simon Fraser University, 1995.

Huang, Yasheng. *Capitalism with Chinese Characteristics: Entrepreneurship and the State.* Cambridge: Cambridge University Press, 2008.

Hung, Ho-fung. *The China Boom: Why China Will Not Rule the World.* New York: Columbia University Press, 2016.

Hunter, Jane. *The Gospel of Gentility: American Women Missionaries in Turn-of-the-Century China.* New Haven, Conn.: Yale University Press, 1984.

Hutcheon, Robin [哈特巨]. *A Burst of Crackers: The Li & Fung Story* [錦霞滿天：利豐發展的道路]. Hong Kong: Chinese University Press, 1992.

Institute of International Education (IIE). *Open Doors, 1948–2004: Report on International Educational Exchange.* New York: IIE, 2005.

Ismael, Tareq Y. "The People's Republic of China and Africa." *Journal of Modern African Studies* 9, no. 4 (December 1971): 507–29.

Ito, Takatoshi, and Anne O. Kreuger, eds. *Deregulation and Interdependence in the Asia-Pacific Region.* Chicago: University of Chicago Press, 2000.

Jao, Y. C. *The Asian Financial Crisis and the Ordeal of Hong Kong.* Westport, Conn.: Greenwood, 2001.

——. *Banking and Currency in Hong Kong: A Study of Postwar Financial Development.* London: Palgrave Macmillan, 1974.

——. "Financing Hong Kong's Early Postwar Industrialization: The Role of the Hongkong and Shanghai Banking Corporation." In *Eastern Banking: Essays in the History of The Hongkong and Shanghai Banking Corporation,* ed. Frank H. H. King, 545–74. London: The Athlone Press, 1983.

Ji, Zhaojin. *A History of Modern Shanghai Banking: The Rise and Decline of China's Finance Capitalism*. New York: Routledge, 2016.

Johnson, Chalmers. *MITI and the Japanese Miracle: The Growth of Industrial Policy, 1925–1975*. Stanford, Calif.: Stanford University Press, 1982.

——. "The Mousetrapping of Hong Kong: A Game in Which Nobody Wins." *Asian Survey* 24, no. 9 (September 1984): 887–909.

Jones, Stephanie. *The Headhunting Business*. London: Springer, 1989.

Jones-Rogers, Stephanie E. *They Were Her Property: White Women as Slave Owners in the American South*. New Haven, Conn.: Yale University Press, 2019.

Kaikati, Jack G. "The Reincarnation of Barter Trade as a Marketing Tool." *Journal of Marketing* 40, no. 2. (April 1976): 17–24.

Karl, Rebecca. *The Magic of Concepts: History and the Economic in Twentieth-Century China*. Durham, N.C.: Duke University Press, 2017.

Kessler, Lawrence D. *The Jiangyin Mission Station: An American Missionary Community in China, 1895–1951*. Chapel Hill: University of North Carolina Press, 1996.

King, Frank H. H., ed. *Eastern Banking: Essays in the History of the Hongkong and Shanghai Banking Corporation*. London: Athlone Press, 1983.

King, Frank H. H., and Catherine King. *The History of the Hongkong and Shanghai Banking Corporation*. Vols. 1–4. Cambridge: Cambridge University Press, 1988–1991.

Kirby, William C. "China's Internationalization in the Early People's Republic: Dreams of a Socialist World Economy." *China Quarterly* 188 (December 2006): 870–90.

——. "Continuity and Change in Modern China: Economic Planning on the Mainland and on Taiwan, 1943–1958." *Australian Journal of Chinese Affairs* 24 (July 1990): 121–41.

Klein, Christian. *Cold War Orientalism: Asia in the Middlebrow Imagination, 1945–1961*. Berkeley: University of California Press, 2003.

Köll, Elisabeth. "Professional Managers at Political Crossroads, Hsia Pin-fang at the Bank of China in New York and London, 1939–1951." In *The Capitalist Dilemma in China's Communist Revolution*, ed. Sherman Cochran, 271–97. Ithaca, N.Y.: Cornell East Asia Program, 2014.

——. *Railroads and the Transformation of China*. Cambridge, Mass.: Harvard University Press, 2019.

Kramer, Paul A. "Power and Connection: Imperial Histories of the United States in the World." *American Historical Review* 116, no. 5 (December 2011): 1348–92.

Kroos, Rick. *Kroos Control: American Roots, Chinese Traditions*. Hong Kong: Inkstone Books, 2012.

Kuhn, Philip. *Chinese Among Others: Emigration in Modern Times*. Lanham, Md.: Rowman & Littlefield, 2009.

Kuo, Huei-Ying. "Chinese Bourgeois Nationalism in Hong Kong and Singapore in the 1930s." *Journal of Contemporary Asia* 36, no. 3 (2006): 385–405.

——. *Networks Beyond Empires: Chinese Business and Nationalism in the Hong Kong-Singapore Corridor, 1914–1941*. Leiden: Brill, 2014.

Kurashige, Lon, ed. *Pacific America: Histories of Transoceanic Crossings*. Honolulu: University of Hawai'i Press, 2017.

Kwan, Man Bun. "Janus-Faced Capitalism: Li Zhuchen and the Jiuda Salt Refinery, 1949–1953." In *The Capitalist Dilemma in China's Communist Revolution*, ed. Sherman Cochran. Ithaca, N.Y.: Cornell East Asia Program, 2014.

Kwok, Jenny Wah Lau. "Besides Fist and Blood: Michael Hui and Cantonese Comedy." In *The Cinema of Hong Kong: History, Arts, Identity*, ed. Poshek Fu and David Desser, 158–75. Cambridge: Cambridge University Press, 2002.

Kwong, Luke S. K. "Refurbishing Hong Kong's Image: The 1997 Saga and Chinese Nationalism Under Deng Xiaoping." *European Journal of East Asian Studies* 3, no. 1 (2004): 171–205.

Kyong-Dong, Kim. "Confucianism and Capitalism in East Asia." In *Capitalism and Development*, ed. Leslie Sklair, 87–106. London: Routledge, 1994.

LaCouture, Elizabeth. "Inventing the 'Foreignized' Chinese Carpets in Treaty-port Tianjin, China." *Journal of Design History* 30, no. 3 (September 2017): 300–314.

LaFargue, Thomas. *China's First Hundred: Educational Mission Students in the United States, 1872–1881*. Pullman: Press of the State College of Washington, 1942.

Lam, Danny Kin-kong, and Ian Lee. "Guerilla Capitalism and the Limits of Statist Theory: Comparing the Chinese NICs." In *The Evolving Pacific Basin in the Global Political Economy: Domestic and International Linkages*, ed. Cal Clark and Steven Chan, 107–24. Boulder, Colo.: Lynne Rienner, 1992.

Lam, Pun-Lee. *The Scheme of Control on Electricity Companies*. Hong Kong: Chinese University Press, 1996.

Lam, Richard Cheung, and Hong-Kin Kwok. "Global Supplier Without a Global Brand Name: A Case Study of Hong Kong's Electronics Industry." *Asian Journal of Social Science* 32, no. 3 (2004): 476–500.

Lamoreaux, Naomi R. *Insider Lending: Banks, Personal Connections, and Economic Development in Industrial New England*. Cambridge: Cambridge University Press, 1996.

Latham, Michael E. *Modernization as Ideology: American Social Science and 'Nation Building' in the Kennedy Era*. Chapel Hill: University of North Carolina Press, 2003.

——. *The Right Kind of Revolution: Modernization, Development, and US Foreign Policy from the Cold War to the Present*. Ithaca, N.Y.: Cornell University Press, 2011.

Laville, Helen, and Hugh Wilford, eds. *The US Government, Citizens Groups and the Cold War: The State-Private Network*. London: Routledge, 2006.

Law, Kar. "The American Connection in Early Hong Kong Cinema." In *The Cinema of Hong Kong: History, Arts, Identity*, ed. Poshek Fu and David Desser, 44–70. Cambridge: Cambridge University Press, 2002.

Leary, William M. *Perilous Missions: Civil Air Transport and CIA Covert Operations in Asia*. Tuscaloosa: University of Alabama Press, 2006.

Lee, James Z. [李中清], Yunzhu Ren [任韵竹], and Chen Liang [梁晨]). 中国知识阶层的来源与形成，1912–1952. Beijing: Social Sciences Academic Press, 2020.

Lee, King Sun, ed. *A Collection of Speeches and Writings of Dr. Lam Chi-Fung*. Hong Kong: Hong Kong Pui Ching Middle School, 1965.

Lee, P. C., ed. *Hongkong Album, Fifth Edition*. Hong Kong: Sin Poh Amalgamated, 1967–1968.

Lee, Leo Ou-fan. *City Between Worlds: My Hong Kong*. Cambridge, Mass.: Belknap Press of Harvard University Press, 2008.

Lee, Sui-ming [李瑞明], and Emily M. Hill, eds. *A Phoenix of South China: The Story of Lingnan (University) College, Sun Yat-sen University* [南國鳳凰: 中山大學嶺南 (大學) 學院]. Hong Kong: Commercial Press, 2005.

Leeming, Frank. "The Earlier Industrialization of Hong Kong." *Modern Asian Studies* 9, no. 3 (1975): 337–42.

Lerner, Josh, Antoinette Schoar, and Jialan Wang. "Secrets of the Academy: The Drivers of University Endowment Success." *Journal of Economic Perspectives* 22, no. 3 (Summer 2008): 207–22.

Lewis, Su Lin. *Cities in Motion: Urban Life and Cosmopolitanism in Southeast Asia, 1920–1940.* Cambridge: Cambridge University Press, 2016.

Li, Bozhong. *Agricultural Development in Jiangnan, 1620–1850.* New York: St. Martin's Press, 1998.

Li, Choh-ming. "China's Industrial Development, 1958–63." *China Quarterly* 17 (January–March 1964): 3–38.

——. "Communist China's Statistical System: 1949–1957." *American Economic Review* 51, no. 2 (May 1961): 499–517.

——. *Economic Development of Communist China: An Appraisal of the First Five Years of Industrialization.* Publications of the Bureau of Business and Economic Research. Berkeley: University of California Press, 1959.

——. "Economic Problems of the Peasant in the Far East." *World Affairs Interpreter* 22, no. 4 (Winter 1952): 431–39.

——. "The Effect of Depreciated Exchange Upon Merchandise Movements." *Quarterly Journal of Economics* 49, no. 3 (May 1935): 495–502.

——. *The Emerging University, 1970–1974: The Vice-Chancellor's Report.* Hong Kong: Chinese University of Hong Kong, 1974.

——. *The First Six Years, 1963–1969.* Hong Kong: Chinese University of Hong Kong, 1969.

——. "Inflation in Wartime China." *Review of Economics and Statistics* 27, no. 1 (February 1945): 23–33.

——. *A New Era Begins, 1975–1978: The Chinese University of Hong Kong.* Hong Kong: Chinese University of Hong Kong, 1978.

——. Review of *The Prospects for Communist China* by W. W. Rostow et al. *American Economic Review* 45, no. 3 (June 1955): 407–9.

——. *The Statistical System of Communist China.* Berkeley: University of California Press, 1962.

——. "Statistics and Planning at the Hsien Level in Communist China." *China Quarterly* 9 (January–March 1962): 112–23.

——. "The Theory of International Trade Under Silver Exchange." *Quarterly Journal of Economics* 53, no. 4 (August 1939): 491–521.

——. "What Happened to the Great Leap Forward?" *Challenge* 11, no. 10 (July 1963): 4–7.

Li, Hongshan. *US-China Educational Exchange: State, Society, and Intercultural Relations, 1905–1950.* New Brunswick, N.J.: Rutgers, 2007.

Li, Huaiyin. *Village China Under Socialism and Reform: A Micro-History, 1948–2008.* Stanford, Calif.: Stanford University Press, 2009.

Li, Lanqing. *Breaking Through: The Birth of China's Opening-Up Policy,* trans. Ling Yuan and Zheng Siying. Oxford: Oxford University Press, 2009.

Li, Zhenjun [李振军]. 送你一座玫瑰园: 香港中文大学. Changsha: Hunan People's Publisher, 2006.

Lim, Louisa. *People's Republic of Amnesia: Tiananmen Revisited*. New York: Oxford University Press, 2014.

Lin, Alfred H. Y. "The Founding of the University of Hong Kong: British Imperial Ideals and Chinese Practical Common Sense." In *An Impossible Dream: Hong Kong University from Foundation to Re-establishment, 1910–1950*, ed. Chan Lau Kit-ching and Peter Cunich, 1–22. Hong Kong: Oxford University Press, 2002.

Lincoln, Toby. *Urbanizing China in War and Peace: The Case of Wuxi County*. Honolulu: University of Hawaiʻi Press, 2015.

Liu, Kin-ming, ed. *My First Trip to China: Scholars, Diplomats and Journalists Reflect on Their First Encounters with China*. Hong Kong: East Slope, 2012.

Lorenzini, Sara. *Global Development: A Cold War History*. Princeton, N.J.: Princeton University Press, 2019.

Louis, Wm. Roger. "Hong Kong: The Critical Phase, 1945–1949." *American Historical Review* 102, no. 4 (October 1997): 1052–84.

Lu, Sheldon H. "Filming Diaspora and Identity: Hong Kong and 1997." In *The Cinema of Hong Kong: History, Arts, Identity*, ed. Poshek Fu and David Desser, 273–88. Cambridge: Cambridge University Press, 2000.

Lundestad, Geir. "Empire by Invitation? The United States and Western Europe, 1945–1952." *Journal of Peace Research* 23, no. 3 (September 1986): 263–77.

——. *The United States and Western Europe Since 1945: From "Empire" by Invitation to Transatlantic Drift*. New York: Oxford University Press, 2003.

Lungu, Gatian F. "Colonial Zambia: The Case of Higher Education for Africans from 1924 to 1964." *Journal of Negro History* 78, no. 4 (Autumn 1993): 207–32.

Lutz, Jessie. *China and the Christian Colleges, 1850–1950*. Ithaca, N.Y.: Cornell University Press, 1971.

Ma, Shu-yun. *Shareholding System Reform in China: Privatizing by Groping for Stones*. Cheltenham, UK: Edward Elgar, 2010.

Macekura, Stephen, and Erez Manela, eds. *The Development Century: A Global History*. Cambridge: Cambridge University Press, 2018.

Madokoro, Laura. "Borders Transformed: Sovereign Concerns, Population Movements and the Making of Territorial Frontiers in Hong Kong, 1949–1967." *Journal of Refugee Studies* 25, no. 3 (2012): 407–27.

——. *Elusive Refuge: Chinese Migrants in the Cold War*. Cambridge, Mass.: Harvard University Press, 2016.

Magretta, Joan. "Fast, Global, and Entrepreneurial: Supply Chain Management, Hong Kong Style." *Harvard Business Review* (September–October 1998): 102–14.

Mark, Chi-kwan. *Hong Kong and the Cold War: Anglo-American Relations, 1949–1957*. Oxford: Oxford University Press, 2004.

——. "The 'Problem of People': British Colonials, Cold War Powers, and the Chinese Refugees in Hong Kong, 1949–62." *Modern Asian Studies* 41, no. 6 (November 2007): 1145–81.

——. "A Reward for Good Behaviour in the Cold War: Bargaining over the Defence of Hong Kong, 1949–1957." *International History Review* 22, no. 4 (December 2000): 837–61.

Matsuda, Takeshi. *Soft Power and Its Perils: US Cultural Policy in Early Postwar Japan and Permanent Dependency.* Stanford, Calif.: Stanford University Press, 2007.

Mazumdar, Sucheta. *Sugar and Society in China: Peasants, Technology, and the World Market.* Cambridge, Mass.: Harvard University Asia Center, 1998.

Mei Foo Investments. "The Story of Mei Foo Sun Chuen." Hong Kong: Mei Foo Investments Ltd., 1974.

Meiksins Wood, Ellen. *The Origin of Capitalism: A Longer View.* New York: Verso, 2017.

Meng, Chih. *Chinese American Understanding: A Sixty-Year Search.* New York: China Institute in America, 1981.

The Methodist Church, Hong Kong. 循道衛理聯合教會北角衛理堂金禧紀念特刊, 1953–2003. Hong Kong: Methodist Church, Hong Kong, 2003.

Meyer, David R. *Hong Kong as a Global Metropolis.* Cambridge: Cambridge University Press, 2000.

Minami, Kazushi. "Re-examining the End of Mao's Revolution: China's Changing Statecraft and Sino-American Relations, 1973–1978." *Cold War History* 16, no. 4 (September 2016): 359–75.

Mitter, Rana. *The Manchurian Myth: Nationalism, Resistance, and Collaboration in Modern China.* Berkeley: University of California Press, 2000.

Mizuoka, Fujio. "Contriving 'Laissez-Faire': Conceptualising the British Colonial Rule of Hong Kong." *City, Culture, and Society* 5, no. 1 (March 2014): 23–32.

Moore, Thomas G. *China in the World Market: Chinese Industry and International Sources of Reform in the Post-Mao Era.* Cambridge: Cambridge University Press, 2002.

Munn, Christopher. *Anglo-China: Chinese People and British Rule in Hong Kong, 1841–1880.* Hong Kong: Hong Kong University Press, 2009.

Naughton, Barry. "Between China and the World: Hong Kong's Economy Before and After 1997." In *Cosmopolitan Capitalists: Hong Kong and the Chinese Diaspora at the End of the Twentieth Century,* ed. Gary G. Hamilton, 80–99. Seattle: University of Washington Press, 1999.

——. *Growing Out of the Plan: Chinese Economic Reform, 1978–1993.* Cambridge: Cambridge University Press, 1995.

Ng, Alice N. H. Lun, ed. *The Quest for Excellence: A History of The Chinese University of Hong Kong from 1963 to 1993.* Hong Kong: Nam Fung Printing, 1994.

Ngai, Mae. *Impossible Subjects: Illegal Aliens and the Making of Modern America.* Princeton, N.J.: Princeton University Press, 2004.

Ngo, Tak-Wing. "Industrial History and the Artifice of *Laissez-Faire* Colonialism." In *Hong Kong's History: State and Society Under Colonial Rule,* ed. Tak-Wing Ngo, 119–40. London: Routledge, 1999.

Nishida, Judith Mary. "Japanese Influence on the Shanghainese Textile Industry and Implications of Hong Kong." Master's thesis, University of Hong Kong, 1990.

Nyaw, Mee-kau. "Direct Foreign Investment in China: Trends, Performance, Policies and Prospects." *China Review* (1993): 16.1–16.38.

O'Donnell, Mary Ann. "Heroes of the Special Zone: Modeling Reform and Its Limits." In *Learning from Shenzhen: China's Post-Mao Experiment from Special Zone to Model City,* ed. Mary Ann O'Donnell, Winnie Wong, and Jonathan Bach, 39–64. Chicago: University of Chicago Press, 2017.

Ogle, Vanessa. "AHR Forum: Archipelago Capitalism: Tax Havens, Offshore Money, and the State, 1950s–1970s." *American Historical Review* 122, no. 5 (December 2017): 1431–58.

Ong, Aihwa. *Flexible Citizenship: The Cultural Logics of Transnationality*. Durham, N.C.: Duke University Press, 1999.

——. *Neoliberalism as Exception: Mutations in Citizenship and Sovereignty*. Durham, N.C.: Duke University Press, 2006.

Oyen, Meredith. *The Diplomacy of Migration: Transnational Lives and the Making of U.S.-Chinese Relations in the Cold War*. Ithaca, N.Y.: Cornell University Press, 2015.

Ozawa, Terutomo. *Institutions, Industrial Upgrading, and Economic Performance in Japan—The "Flying-Geese" Paradigm of Catch-up Growth*. Northampton, Mass.: Edward Elgar, 2005.

——. *Multinationalism, Japanese Style: The Political Economy of Outward Dependency*. Princeton, N.J.: Princeton University Press, 1979.

Padgett, John F., and Christopher K. Ansell. "Robust Action and the Rise of the Medici, 1400–1434." *American Journal of Sociology* 98, no. 6 (May 1993): 1259–1319.

Pan, Lynn. *When True Love Came to China*. Hong Kong: Hong Kong University Press, 2015.

Panitch, Leo, and Sam Gindin. *The Making of Global Capitalism: The Political Economy of American Empire*. London: Verso, 2012.

Patten, Chris. *East and West*. Basingstoke, UK: Macmillan, 1998.

Perry, Elizabeth, and Christine Wong, eds. *The Political Economy of Reform in Post-Mao China*. Cambridge, Mass.: Harvard University, Council on East Asian Studies, 1985.

Peterson, Glen D. "Crisis and Opportunity: The Work of Aid Refugee Chinese Intellectuals (ARCI) in Hong Kong and Beyond." In *Hong Kong in the Cold War*, ed. Priscilla Roberts and John M. Carroll, 141–59. Hong Kong: HKU Press, 2016.

——. "Socialist China and the Huaqiao: The Transition to Socialism in the Overseas Chinese Areas of Rural Guangdong, 1949–1956." *Modern China* 14, no. 3 (July 1988): 309–35.

——. "To Be or Not to Be a Refugee: The International Politics of the Hong Kong Refugee Crisis, 1949–55." *Journal of Imperial and Commonwealth History* 36, no. 2 (June 2008): 171–95.

Phillips, D. R., and A. G. O. Yeh. "China Experiments with Modernisation: The Shenzhen Special Economic Zone." *Geography* 68, no. 4 (October 1983): 289–300.

Piketty, Thomas. *Capital in the Twenty-First Century*. Cambridge, Mass.: Belknap Press of Harvard University Press, 2014.

Polanyi, Karl. *The Great Transformation: The Political and Economic Origins of Our Time*. New York: Rinehart, 1944. Reprint, Boston: Beacon Hill Press, 1964.

Pomeranz, Kenneth. *The Great Divergence: China, Europe, and the Making of the Modern World Economy*. Princeton, N.J.: Princeton University Press, 2000.

——. *The Making of a Hinterland: State, Society, and Economy in Inland North China, 1853–1937*. Berkeley: University of California Press, 1993.

Poy, Vivienne. *Building Bridges: The Life & Times of Richard Charles Lee, Hong Kong 1905–1983*. Scarborough, Ont.: Calyan, 1998.

Putnam, Robert D. *Bowling Alone: The Collapse and Revival of American Community*. New York: Simon & Schuster, 2000.

Qian, Yingyi. "The Process of China's Market Transition, 1978–1998: The Evolutionary, Historical, and Comparative Perspectives." In *China's Deep Reform: Politics in Transition*, ed. Lowell Dittmer and Guoli Liu, 229–50. Lanham, Md.: Rowman & Littlefield, 2006.

Redding, S. Gordon. *The Spirit of Chinese Capitalism*. Berlin: Walter de Gruyter, 1990.

Reed, Christopher A. *Gutenberg in Shanghai: Chinese Print Capitalism, 1876–1937*. Vancouver: UBC Press, 2011.

Reinhardt, Anne. *Navigating Semi-Colonialism: Shipping, Sovereignty, and Nation-Building in China, 1860–1937*. Cambridge, Mass.: Harvard University Asia Center, 2018.

Resolution on CPC History (1949–1981). Beijing: Foreign Language Press, 1981.

Reynolds, Bruce L., ed. *Chinese Economy Policy: Economic Reform at Midstream*. New York: Paragon House, 1988.

Rhoads, Edward J. M. *Manchus & Han: Ethnic Relations and Political Power in Late Qing and Early Republican China, 1861–1928*. Seattle: University of Washington Press, 2000.

——. *Stepping Forth in the World: The Chinese Educational Mission to the United States, 1872–81*. Hong Kong: Hong Kong University Press, 2011.

Richardson, Fred. *Expatriate Adventures*. N.p.: Trafford, 2012.

Roberts, Priscilla, and John M. Carroll, eds. *Hong Kong in the Cold War*. Hong Kong: Hong Kong University Press, 2016.

Robinson, Ronald. "Imperial Theory and the Question of Imperialism after Empire." In *Perspectives on Imperialism and Decolonisation: Essays in honour of A. F. Madden*, ed. R. F. Holland and G. Rizvi, 42–54. London: Frank Cass, 1984.

——. "Non-European Foundations of European Imperialism: Sketch for a Theory of Collaboration." In *Studies in the Theory of Imperialism*, ed. Roger Owen and Bob Sutcliffe, 117–42. London: Longman, 1972.

Rogaski, Ruth. *Hygienic Modernity: Meanings of Health and Disease in Treaty Port China*. Berkeley: University of California Press, 2004.

Rosen, Sherry. *Mei Foo Sun Chuen: Middle-Class Chinese Families in Transition*. Taipei: Chinese Association for Folklore, 1976.

Roy, Reginald H. *David Lam: A Biography*. Vancouver: Douglas & McIntyre, 1996.

Rozman, Gilbert, ed. *The East Asian Region: Confucian Heritage and its Modern Adaptation*. Princeton, N.J.: Princeton University Press, 1991.

Sayer, Rosemary. *The Man Who Turned the Lights On: Gordon Wu*. Hong Kong: Chameleon Press, 2006.

Saxenian, AnnaLee. *The New Argonauts: Regional Advantage in a Global Economy*. Cambridge, Mass.: Harvard University Press, 2006.

Schenk, Catherine R. "Another Asian Financial Crisis: Monetary Links Between Hong Kong and China, 1945–1950." *Modern Asian Studies* 34, no. 3 (July 2000): 739–64.

——. "The Empire Strikes Back: Hong Kong and the Decline of Sterling in the 1960s." *Economic History Review* 57, no 3 (August 2004): 551–80.

——. *Hong Kong as an International Financial Centre, Emergence and Development, 1945–65*. London: Routledge Studies in the Growth Economies of Asia, 2001.

Schram, Stuart. "China After the Thirteenth Congress." *China Quarterly* 114 (June 1988): 177–97.

Schultz, Theodore W. "Investment in Human Capital." *American Economic Review* 51, no. 1 (March 1961): 1–17.

Schwartz, Benjamin. *In Search of Wealth and Power: Yen Fu and the West*. Cambridge, Mass.: Belknap Press of Harvard University Press, 1964.

Selden, Mark. "China, Japan and the Regional Political Economy of East Asia, 1945–1995." In *Network Power: Japan and Asia*, ed. Peter J. Katzenstein and Takashi Shiraishi, 306–40. Ithaca, N.Y.: Cornell University Press, 1997.

Sheehan, Brett. *Industrial Eden: A Chinese Capitalist Vision*. Cambridge, Mass.: Harvard University Press, 2015.

——. *Trust in Troubled Times: Money, Banks, and State-Society Relations in Republican Tianjin*. Cambridge, Mass.: Harvard University Press, 2003.

——. "Urban Identities and Urban Networks in Cosmopolitan Cities: Banks and Bankers in Tianjin, 1900–1937." In *Remaking the Chinese City: Modernity and National Identity, 1900–1950*, ed. Joseph W. Esherick, 47–64. Honolulu: University of Hawai'i Press, 2000.

Shibusawa, Naoko. *America's Geisha Ally: Reimagining the Japanese Enemy*. Cambridge, Mass: Harvard University Press, 2010.

Shiroyama, Tomoko. *China During the Great Depression: Market, State, and the World Economy, 1929–1937*. Cambridge, Mass.: Harvard East Asian Monographs, 2008.

——. "The Hong Kong-South China Financial Nexus: Ma Xuchao and His Remittance Agency." In *The Capitalist Dilemma in China's Communist Revolution*, ed. Sherman Cochran, 203–24. Ithaca, N.Y.: Cornell East Asia Program, 2014.

Skeldon, Ronald. "Emigration and the Future of Hong Kong." *Pacific Affairs* (Winter 1990–1991): 500–23.

——, ed. *Reluctant Exiles?: Migration from Hong Kong and the New Overseas Chinese*. Hong Kong: Hong Kong University Press, 1994.

Sklair, Leslie, ed. *Capitalism and Development*. London: Routledge, 1994.

Sinn, Elizabeth. *Pacific Crossing: California Gold, Chinese Migration, and the Making of Hong Kong*. Hong Kong: Hong Kong University Press, 2013.

——. *Power and Charity: A Chinese Merchant Elite in Colonial Hong Kong*. Hong Kong: Oxford University Press, 1989/2003.

Smart, Alan. *The Shek Kip Mei Myth: Squatters, Fires and Colonial Rule in Hong Kong, 1950–1963*. Hong Kong: Hong Kong University Press, 2006.

Smith, Andrew. "The Winds of Change and the End of the Compradore System in the Hongkong and Shanghai Banking Corporation." *Business History* 58, no. 2 (January 2016): 195–96.

Smith, Carl T. *Chinese Christians: Elites, Middlemen, and the Church in Hong Kong*. Hong Kong: Oxford University Press, 1985.

Snow, Philip. *The Fall of Hong Kong: Britain, China, and the Japanese Occupation*. New Haven, Conn.: Yale University Press, 2004.

Spence, Michael. "Job Market Signaling." *Quarterly Journal of Economics* 87, no. 3 (August 1973): 355–74.

Sperry, Ansie Lee. *Running with the Tiger: A Memoir of an Extraordinary Young Woman's Life in Hong Kong, China, the South Pacific and POW Camp*. N.p.: Sperry Family Trust, 2009.

Stanley, Amy Dru. "Histories of Capitalism and Sex Difference." *Journal of the Early Republic* 36, no. 2 (Summer 2016): 343–50.

Starr, Peter. *Citibank: A Century in Asia*. Singapore: Editions Didier Millet, 2007.

Steinbock-Pratt, Sarah. *Educating the Empire: American Teachers and Contested Colonization in the Philippines*. Cambridge: Cambridge University Press, 2019.

Stewart, Matthew. *The Management Myth: Debunking Modern Business Philosophy*. New York: Norton, 2009.

Stiglitz, Joseph E. "The Theory of 'Screening,' Education, and the Distribution of Income." *American Economic Review* 65, no. 3 (June 1975): 283–300.

Stockwell, A. J. "'The Crucible of the Malayan Nation': The University and the Making of a New Malaya, 1938–62." *Modern Asian Studies* 43, no. 5 (September 2009): 1149–87.

Stross, Randall E. *Bulls in the China Shop: And Other Sino-American Business Encounters*. New York: Pantheon Books, 1991.

Suettinger, Robert L. *Beyond Tiananmen: The Politics of US-China Relations, 1989–2000*. Washington, D.C.: Brookings Institution, 2003.

Sung, Yun-wing. *The China-Hong Kong Connection: The Key to China's Open Door Policy*. Cambridge: Cambridge University Press, 1991.

——. "The Hong Kong Economy Through the 1997 Barrier." *Asian Survey* 37, no. 8 (August 1997): 705–19.

——. "The Role of Hong Kong in China's Export Drive." *Australian Journal of Chinese Affairs* 15 (January 1986): 83–101.

Suryadinata, Leo, ed. *Southeast Asian Personalities of Chinese Descent: A Biographical Dictionary*. Singapore: Institute of Southeast Asian Studies, 2002.

Sussman, Nan. *Return Migration and Identity: A Global Phenomenon, A Hong Kong Case*. Hong Kong: Hong Kong University Press, 2010.

Szczepanik, Edward. *The Economic Growth of Hong Kong*. London: Oxford University Press, 1958.

Tai, Hung-chao, ed. *Confucianism and Economic Development: An Oriental Alternative?* Washington, D.C.: Washington Institute Press, 1989.

Talley, Christian. *Forgotten Vanguard: Informal Diplomacy and the Rise of United States-China Trade, 1972–1980*. Notre Dame, Ind.: University of Notre Dame Press, 2018.

Teng, Emma Jinhua. *Eurasian: Mixed Identities in the United States, China, and Hong Kong, 1842–1943*. Berkeley: University of California Press, 2013.

Tharpe, Gertrude. "The History of Hong Kong Baptist College." M.A. thesis, Furman University, 1965.

Thigpen, Jennifer. *Island Queens and Mission Wives: How Gender and Empire Remade Hawai'i's Pacific World*. Chapel Hill: University of North Carolina Press, 2014.

Thurston-Lighty, Kathleen, and Robert. *The Stars Aligned: Celebrating the 20-Year Anniversary of the MIT-China Management Education Project* [水到渠成: 庆祝麻省理工学院 (MIT) 中国管理教育项目20周年纪念]. Cambridge, Mass: MIT Press, 2016.

Ting, H. C. *Truth and Facts: Recollections of a Hong Kong Industrialist*. Hong Kong: Kader Industrial, 1974.

Tooze, Adam. *The Deluge: The Great War, America and the Remaking of the Global Order, 1916–1931.* New York: Viking Penguin, 2014.

Trescott, Paul B. "H. D. Fong and the Study of Chinese Economic Development." *History of Political Economy* 34, no. 4 (2002): 789–809.

Tsing, Anna Lowenhaupt. *The Mushroom at the End of the World: On the Possibility of Life in Capitalist Ruins.* Princeton, N.J.: Princeton University Press, 2015.

Tu, Wei-ming, ed. *Confucian Traditions in East Asian Modernity: Moral Education and Economic Culture in Japan and the Four Mini-Dragons.* Cambridge, Mass.: Harvard University Press, 1996.

Tuan, Chyau, and Linda F. Y. Ng. "Evolution of Hong Kong's Electronics Industry Under a Passive Industrial Policy." *Managerial and Decision Economics* 16, no. 5 (1995): 509–23.

Tucker, Nancy Bernkopf. *China Confidential: American Diplomats and Sino-American Relations, 1945–1996.* New York: Columbia University Press, 2001.

——, ed. *Uncertain Friendships: Taiwan, Hong Kong, and the United States, 1945–1992.* New York: Twayne of Macmillan, 1994.

Tung, Rosalie L. *US-China Trade Negotiations: Pergamon Policy Studies on Business and Economics.* Amsterdam: Elsevier, 2014.

Ulmer, Melville J. "Multinational Corporations and Third World Capitalism." *Journal of Economics Issues* 14, no. 2 (June 1980): 453–71.

U.S. Department of State. *United States Statutes at Large.* Washington, D.C.: U.S. Government Printing Office, 1953.

Van Dyke, Paul A. *The Canton Trade: Life and Enterprise on the China Coast, 1700–1845.* Hong Kong: Hong Kong University Press, 2012.

Vedres, Balázs, and David Stark. "Structural Folds: Generative Disruption in Overlapping Groups." *American Journal of Sociology* 115, no. 4 (January 2010): 1150–90.

Vogel, Ezra. "China and the East Asian Modernization Model." In *Chinese Economy Policy: Economic Reform at Midstream,* ed. Bruce Reynolds. New York: Paragon House, 1988.

——. *Deng Xiaoping and the Transformation of China.* Cambridge, Mass.: Belknap Press of Harvard University Press, 2013.

——. *The Four Little Dragons: The Spread of Industrialization in East Asia.* Edwin O. Reischauer Lectures, 1990. Cambridge, Mass.: Harvard University Press, 1991.

——. *One Step Ahead in China: Guangdong Under Reform.* Cambridge, Mass.: Harvard University Press, 1989.

Von Eschen, Penny M. "Globalizing Popular Culture in the 'American Century' and Beyond." *OAH Magazine of Identity* 20, no. 4 (July 2006): 56–63.

Vong, Sam. " 'Compassion Gave Us a Special Superpower': Vietnamese Women Leaders, Reeducation Camps, and the Politics of Family Reunification, 1977–1991." *Journal of Women's History* 30, no. 3 (Fall 2018): 107–37.

Wakeman, Frederic, Jr., and Wen-hsin Yeh, eds. *Shanghai Sojourners.* Berkeley: Institute of East Asian Studies, University of California Press, 1992.

Waley-Cohen, Joanna. *The Sextants of Beijing: Global Currents in Chinese History.* New York: Norton, 1999.

Walker, Joseph, ed. *Hong Kong's Who's Who: An Almanac of Personalities and Their Comprehensive Histories, 1970–1973.* Hong Kong: N.p., 1970.

Wang, Andy Chih-ming. *Transpacific Articulations: Student Migration and the Remaking of Asian America*. Honolulu: University of Hawai'i Press, 2013.

Wang, Gungwu. *China and the Chinese Overseas*. Singapore: Times Academic Press, 2003.

Wang, Hui, and Theodore Huters, ed. *China's New Order: Society, Politics, and Economy in Transition*, trans. Rebecca Karl. Cambridge, Mass.: Harvard University Press, 2006.

Wang, Jenn-Hwan, and Ray-May Hsung, eds. *Rethinking Social Capital and Entrepreneurship in Greater China: Is Guanxi Still Important?* New York: Routledge, 2016.

Wang, Kenneth. "Foreign Trade Policy and Apparatus of the People's Republic of China." *Law and Contemporary Problems* 38, no. 2 (Summer–Autumn 1973): 182–200.

Wang, Y. C. *Chinese Intellectuals and the West, 1872–1949*. Chapel Hill: University of North Carolina Press, 1966.

Whitener, Sterling H. *In the Shadow of the Pagoda*. N.p.: CreateSpace, 2013.

Wong, Eleanor. "A History of the Wong Family Textile Business, Part Two: Life in Hong Kong." http://industrialhistoryhk.org/wp-content/uploads/2014/11/A-History-of-the-Wong-Family-Textile-Business-Part-Two-Life-in-Hong-Kong.pdf.

Wong, R. Bin. *China Transformed: Historical Change and the Limits of European Experience*. Ithaca, N.Y.: Cornell University Press, 1997.

Wong, Siu-lun. "Deciding to Stay, Deciding to Move, Deciding Note to Decide." In *Cosmopolitan Capitalists: Hong Kong and the Chinese Diaspora at the End of the Twentieth Century*, ed. Gary G. Hamilton, 135–51. Seattle: University of Washington Press, 1999.

——. *Emigrant Entrepreneurs: Shanghai Industrialists in Hong Kong*. Hong Kong: Oxford University Press, 1988.

Woo, Sing-lim [吳醒濂]. *The Prominent Chinese in Hong Kong* [香港華人名人史略]. Hong Kong: Wuzhou shuju, 1937.

Woo-Cummings, Meredith, ed. *The Developmental State*. Ithaca, N.Y.: Cornell University Press, 1999.

Wu, Ellen D. *The Color of Success: Asian Americans and the Origins of the Model Minority*. Princeton, N.J.: Princeton University Press, 2013.

Wu, Jinglian. *China's Long March Toward a Market Economy*. San Francisco: Long River Press, 2005.

Wu, Li [武力], ed. 中华人民共和国经济史(增订版). Beijing: Zhongguo shidai jingji chubanshe, 2010.

Wunnava, Phanindra V., and Albert A. Okunade. "Do Business Executives Give More to Their Alma Mater? Longitudinal Evidence from a Large University." *American Journal of Economics and Sociology* 72, no. 3 (July 2013): 761–77.

Xi, Lian. *The Conversion of Missionaries: Liberalism in American Protestant Missions in China, 1907–1932*. University Park: Pennsylvania State Press, 1997.

Xu, Dixin, and Wu Chengming, eds. *Chinese Capitalism, 1522–1840*. New York: Palgrave Macmillan, 2000.

Xu, Guoqi. *Chinese and Americans: A Shared History*. Cambridge, Mass.: Harvard University Press, 2014.

Xu, Jiatun [許家屯]. 許家屯香港回憶錄 (上下). Hong Kong: United, 1993.

Xu, Xianquan. "Sino-US Economic and Trade Relations." In *China, the United States, and the Global Economy*, ed. Shuxun Chen and Charles Wolf, Jr., 237–55. Santa Monica: RAND, 2001.

Yang, Dali L. *Calamity and Reform in China: State, Rural Society, and Institutional Change Since the Great Leap Famine*. Stanford, Calif.: Stanford University Press, 1996.

Yang, Mayfair Mei-hui. *Gifts, Favors, and Banquets: The Art of Social Relationships in China*. Ithaca, N.Y.: Cornell University Press, 1994.

Yang, Peter Quay. *Recollections at Random*. Hong Kong: Signal Printing, 2013.

Ye, Min. *Diasporas and Foreign Direct Investment in China and India*. Cambridge: Cambridge University Press, 2014.

——. "Policy Learning or Diffusion: How China Opened to Foreign Direct Investment." *Journal of East Asian Studies* 9, no. 3 (September–December 2009): 399–432.

Yeh, Wen-hsin. *The Alienated Academy: Culture and Politics in Republican China, 1919–1937*. Cambridge, Mass.: Harvard University Asia Center, 1990.

——, ed. *Becoming Chinese: Passages to Modernity and Beyond*. Berkeley: University of California Press, 2000.

——. *Shanghai Splendor: Economic Sentiments and the Making of Modern China*. Berkeley: University of California Press, 2007.

Yeung, Henry Wai-chung. *Chinese Capitalism in a Global Era: Towards Hybrid Capitalism*. London: Routledge, 2004.

——. "The Geography of Hong Kong Transnational Corporations in the ASEAN Region." *Royal Geographical Society* 27, no. 4 (December 1995): 318–34.

Yeung, Yue-man. "China's Openness and Reform at 30: Retrospect and Prospect." *China Review* 9, no. 2 (Fall 2009): 157–67.

Young, Gavin. *Beyond Lion Rock: The Story of Cathay Pacific Airways*. London: Hutchinson, 1988.

Zelin, Madeleine. *The Merchants of Zigong: Industrial Entrepreneurship in Early Modern China*. Studies of the Weatherhead East Asian Institute. New York: Columbia University Press, 2005.

Zhang, Yang. "Cultural Cold War: The American Role in Establishing the Chinese University of Hong Kong (CUHK)." In *The Power of Culture: Encounters between China and the United States*, ed. Priscilla Roberts, 150–61. Newcastle Upon Tyne: Cambridge Scholars, 2016.

Zhang, Yongjin. *China's Emerging Global Businesses: Political Economy and Institutional Investigations*. Basingstoke, UK: Palgrave Macmillan, 2003.

Zhou, Xi. "The Institute of Pacific Relations and the Nankai Institute of Economics." M.A. thesis, University of Hawai'i at Manoa, 1999.

Zia, Helen. *Last Boat Out of Shanghai: The Epic Story of the Chinese Who Fled Mao's Revolution*. New York: Penguin Random House, 2019.

Index

Figures are indicated by an "*f*" after the relevant page number.

American social capital (*continued*)
acquisition through U.S.-backed
Christian projects, 73–74, 89, 97,
120–21, 196; acquisition through
U.S. higher education, 43–47, 49–53,
54–56, 120, 123, 129–30, 131–33, 167,
198–99, 204, 206–7, 209–11, 212–13,
262–63, 271–72; acquisition through
wartime Sino-U.S. alliance, 35,
55–56, 61, 133–36, 168–69, 187–88;
and British decline and informal
decolonization, 14–15, 29, 57–59,
60–63, 68, 73–74, 106–10, 113–14,
125–26, 140–41, 143–45, 155–56; and
donations to U.S. colleges and
universities, 218–19; and exit
strategies, 16–17, 68, 102, 170, 204,
207, 277; and fostering transpacific
circulations, 27, 68, 89–90, 97–98,
102, 114–15, 117, 122–23, 125, 130,
142–45, 156, 195–96, 199–201; and
marketing and production
strategies, 25, 67–68, 165–66, 180–81,
203–4, 206–7, 282; and racial
discrimination, 60–63; relationship
to native-place guanxi, 21–22, 47;
and recruitment of U.S. educational
donations, 101–3, 106–8, 109–13,
114–15, 116–17, 121–22, 125, 139–45,
148–49; and recruitment of U.S.
direct investment, 160, 165–66,
180–81, 184–90, 282; and revival
during reform and opening, 243; and
U.S. Cold War outreach, 79–80,
106–8, 137–39, 156, 169–71, 219; and
U.S. models and post-Fordist
transitions, 195–96, 206, 209–16,
217–18, 256; and U.S. trade
regulations, 29, 67, 173–74, 253,
244–55, 263, 273–78, 283; and women
and patriarchy, 30. *See also* kuashang

strategies; informal decolonization;
networks; Sino-U.S. alliance;
transpacific educational circulations
American Textile Manufacturers
Institute, 255
American University Clubs (China), 44
American Universities Club (Hong
Kong), 99–100, 108
Anderson, Maurice, 121–23
Anderson, Olive L., 76–77, 80, 82, 89–90
Anderson, Sidney, 76–77, 80, 82, 89–90,
109
Andover (Phillips Academy, Andover),
40, 188, 218, 262
Anglican Church: in Hong Kong, 75,
103, 107, 109
Anker Henningsen & Co., 170–71, 173
Ann Tse-kai, 258
anticommunism: in the handover
process, 247, 249; and the Hong
Kong government's educational
agendas, 102–3; in kuashang
strategies, 120–21, 128, 138, 186, 283;
and U.S. Cold War outreach, 71,
99–101, 106–7, 108–9, 115–16
Arrighi, Giovanni, 248; *The Long
Twentieth Century* and comparison
with Genoa, 288–90
Arrow, Kenneth, 19
Asbury Village, 73*f*, 80
Asia Christian Colleges Association
(ACCA), 112–13
Asia Foundation, 101; as Committee for a
Free Asia (CFA), 103, 118, 169–70; and
Francis Pan, 169–70; and Li Choh-
ming, 137–39, 146, 152; and New Asia
College, 116; and United College, 118
Asia Society, 273
Asian Development Bank, 267
Association of Ningbo Sojourners
(Shanghai), 54

Au Bin, 107

Au, David W. K., 14, 102–4, 104f, 106, 117, 125, 196; adolescence and career, 107–8; and comparisons with, 132, 139, 140, 170, 199; development of American social capital and kuashang strategies, 108–9; kuashang strategies and Chung Chi, 109–13, 196; and K. P. Chen, 107; and Song Ziwen, 107; retirement and death, 113–14. *See also* Chung Chi College

Augustine Heard & Co., 39

Australia: Hong Kong students in Australia, 201; migration to Australia from Hong Kong, 16, 199, 262, 280; normalization of relations with the PRC, 231

Aylward, Robert, 91–92

Baerwald, Gustav, 46

Bangkok: trade and investment links with Hong Kong, 7, 65, 120, 262

Bank of America, 210–11

Bank of Canton, 107, 161

Bank of China: and AmCham, 229, 241, 244; and CCIC Finance, Ltd, 246; and Chase Manhattan, 238, 242; and K. P. Chen, 46; and H. J. Shen, 167; in Hong Kong, 161, 246; and Mayar Silk Mills, 262; and the Orient Overseas bailout, 281; and Pei Tsuyee, 79

Bank of East Asia, 39–40, 152, 161, 261

Bank of England, 194

Bank of Guangxi, 168

Bank of Tokyo, 257, 281

Bao'an County. *See* Shenzhen

Baptist World Alliance, 118

Barton, Hugh, 179

Basic Law, The, 235, 267

Baylor University, 122–23; graduates, 120, 124, 210

Beatrice Foods, 244

Bechtel, Harriet, 71–72

Bechtel, John, 71–72

Beijing (city), 60, 187; evacuations during communist transition, 56

Bell, George, 170, 171f, 185–86, 188

Bergère, Marie-Claire, 45

Berkeley Daily Gazette, 137

Besant, Annie, 79

Besant School for Girls (Shanghai), 79

Bian Baimei, 47

bilingualism: as skill, 13, 38, 39, 41, 52, 53, 157, 181, 209, 211, 254; in sources, 17, 25, 40, 77, 94

Black, Robert, 124, 126, 138–139

Blum, Alex, 227–228

Boston University: graduates, 77

Bourdieu, Pierre, 18–19

Boxer Indemnity scholarships, 43, 46; recipients of, 49, 167, 262. *See also* Tsinghua University

Boxer Rising, 74

"brain drain." *See* transpacific educational circulations

Braudel, Fernand, 288

Bray, Dennis, 159

Bretton Woods: conference, 129, 135; end of system, 28, 194–96, 208, 214–16. *See also* GATT; post-Fordism

Brewster, Kingman, 141

Britain: and British National Overseas passport, 284; Hong Kong students in Britain, 201–2, 205, 216, 340n41; migration from empire, 10; migration from Hong Kong, 199, 284; as source of investment, 158–59, 176, 180; and the handover, 247, 279; *See also* British Empire; British social capital; foreign direct investment; Hong Kong colonial government; informal decolonization; handover

the nineteenth-century Pacific, 23,
36–37; the role of higher education
and transpacific circulations, 15–16,
29, 98, 101–2, 129–31, 144–45,
148–49, 155–57, 203–8, 211–14,
216–19, 286–88; U.S.-led systems and
accelerating inequality, 5–6, 29,
191–92, 202, 206–8, 216–19,
286–88

CARE (Cooperative for American
Relief Everywhere), 81, 93

Carroll, John, 37

Carter administration, 242–43

Cathay Pacific, 59

CCIC Finance Ltd., 246

Central Bank of China, 63–64, 169

Central Trust of China, 169

Central Intelligence Agency (CIA), 96,
108, 170

Central Relief Commission, 119

Central School (Hong Kong). See
Queen's College

Cha Cha-ming, 154

Chai Wan, 87

Chan, Anson, 283

Chan, Helen Kar, 231

Chan, Ronnie Chi-chung, 209, 216; and
the C-100, 285; and Harvard's T. C.
Chan School, 218

Chan Chik-ting, 122

Chan Kai-ming, 39

Chan Wing-tsit, 138, 157

Chao Yuen-ren, 141

Chaozhou (Teochew): collaborations
with Britain, 34; elites' U.S.
re-orientations, 102; merchants in
Hong Kong, 11–12, 118; and
native-place networks, 119; See also
Lam Chi-fung

Charbonnages du Tonkin, 119. See also
French Empire

Charities (Land Acquisition) Bill (1958),
86, 88

Chase Manhattan Bank: and David
Rockefeller, 237, 257; and Hong Kong
Carpet Manufacturers, 185; and Ka
Wah Bank, 210–211; operations in
Hong Kong, 39, 238, 242–43

Cheadle, Vernon, 143

Chen, Eric, 174f

Chen, K. P. Guangfu: adolescence and
career, 45–47; and comparisons with,
120; on child labor, 59; and David
Au, 107; and decision to flee, 48,
57–58; and Francis and Cecilia Pan,
168; and John Soong, 188; and Kong
Xiangxi, 46; and Lee Hysan, 60; and
Li Choh-ming, 134, 136; and Sun
Yat-sen, 46; and U.S. aid and
corruption, 55, 64, 168–69; and
Zhang Jia'ao, 46. See also SCSB

Chen, Y. C., 174f

Cheng, Paul M .F., 14; and AmCham,
233, 271; education and kuashang
strategies, 271–73; and HKSAR
Preparatory Committee, 284;
response to Tiananmen Square
Massacre, 273–77

Cheng Yu-tung, 258

Chen Jian, 224

Chen Shih-hsiang, 137

Chen Yun, 245

Cheong, Stephen, 273

Ch'ien, Raymond, 254, 276

Chiang Kai-shek, 7, 55, 58, 60, 134, 136

Chiap Hua Manufactory Company, 120,
190. See also Lam Chi-fung

China Christian Universities
Association, 103

China Council for the Promotion of
International Trade (CCPIT), 225,
229, 230, 236

China Everbright Group, 246

China Institute in America, 43, 44, 132, 167

China International Trust Investment Corporation (CITIC), 241–44, 246, 261; purchase of Ka Wah Bank, 282. *See also* Rong Yiren; Wu Zhichao

China Light and Power (CLP): acquisition by Kadoories, 184; and joint venture with Esso, 160–161, 185–87, 192. *See also* Esso; Lawrence Kadoorie

China Mail, 93–94

China Merchants Steam Navigation Company (CMSN), 239–41; and Orient Overseas bailout, 281

China National Aviation Corporation, 168

China National Chemicals Import and Export Corporation, 226–27

China National Machinery and Equipment Export Corporation, 227, 241

China National Metal and Mineral Import-Export Corporation, 267

China National Native Produce and Animal By-Products Import and Export Corporation, 230

China National Relief and Rehabilitation Administration (CNRRA): and Francis Pan, 168; and Li Choh-ming, 135–36; and Liu Hongsheng, 55; and Y. L. Lee, 103, 114. *See also* Nationalist government; Sino-U.S. alliance

China National Technical Import Corporation, 227

China National Textiles Import and Export Corporation (CHINATEX), 236

China Resources, 228, 246, 258

Chinese Christian and Missionary Alliance, 75, 83

Chinese Christians: elites in Republican era, 47–49, 52, 211; migration to Hong Kong, 71, 75, 96; re-establishment and schools in Hong Kong, 26, 72–74, 76–80, 81–83, 84–89, 96–98; higher educational work, 102–15, 117–18, 119–25. *See also* *individual churches and mission groups*

Chinese civil war, 7, 48, 71, 157, 287; and strategic decisions, 19, 32, 35, 48, 52–53, 56–58, 120, 136, 203. *See also* communist transition; Nationalist government; People's Republic of China

Chinese Colleges Joint Council, 101, 124

Chinese Communist Party (CCP): and Hong Kong elites, 28–29, 238–39, 245, 249, 253, 258, 261, 280; the Politburo, 239, 284; and reform and opening, 222, 227, 238–40, 243–45, 254, 259, 261, 266; views of Hong Kong, 280. *See also* CPPCC; Deng Xiaoping; National People's Congress; People's Republic of China; State Council of the PRC

Chinese diaspora. *See* overseas Chinese

Chinese Educational Mission (CEM), 40, 42; alumni of, 46, 49, 115. *See also* Yung Wing

Chinese Exclusion: defiance of, 212; exemption for Chinese students, 43, 71, 132; repeal and kuashang strategies, 10, 15, 61, 71

Chinese General Chamber of Commerce, 243

Chinese language. *See under individual languages*

Chinese Manufacturers' Association of Hong Kong, 174–75, 248, 263

Chinese Maritime Customs Service, 46, 62, 168

Chinese National Salvation Association, 134

Chinese nationalism: and the handover: 247, 279–80; in the Republican era, 34, 39

Chinese Passengers' Act, 40

Chinese People's Political Consultative Conference (CPPCC), 258; and Hong Kong elites, 283–84. *See also* Chinese Communist Party

Chinese Postal Remittance and Savings Bank, 168

Chinese Students' Christian Association in North America, 47, 99

Chinese Telecommunications Administration, 226

Chinese University of Hong Kong (CUHK), 17, 124, 127–57; and British and Commonwealth universities, 27, 101, 125–26, 129, 142–44; conception, 101; establishment, 27, 98, 126, 139–45; Institute of Chinese Studies, 152; and Japanese universities, 142; Lingnan Institute of Business Administration, 146–51, 254; physical construction, 151–53; and U.S. universities, 129–30, 141–42. *See also* Li Choh-ming; transpacific educational circulations

Chiu, Alfred Kaiming, 143

Chongqing: as wartime capital, 55, 134, 156, 168–69, 187

Chou, Grace Ai-ling, 115–16, 145

Chow, H. C., 236

Chow, Timothy (Y. H.), 77, 83

Chow Shouson, 40

Christianity: in Qing and Republican China, 72, 74–75; the Roman Catholic Church, 75. *See also* Chinese Christians; missionaries; education

Chu, David, 276

Chuang Shih-ping, 245

Chung Chi College, 27, 80, 101, 102–15, 170; and business school, 146–47; comparisons with New Asia, 115–17; comparisons with United College, 118; graduates, 83; and transpacific educational circulations, 199–201. *See also* Au, David W. K.; UBCHEA

Chung Sze-yuen, 250, 258, 283, 359n2

Church of Christ in China (CCC), 71–72, 75, 76, 81–82, 86, 88, 97–98

Church of Jesus Christ of Latter Day Saints, 75

Church World Service (CWS), 72, 75, 80, 81, 92, 93, 139

Chu Yu-kuang, 146–47

Citibank. *See* First National City Bank

City University of Hong Kong, 124

Civil Air Transport (CAT), 56

Clinton administration, 283

"coastal development strategy," 224, 251–53, 264, 266

Coble, Parks, 32

Cochran, Sherman, 53

codevelopment. *See under* U.S. market

Colby College, 204

Cold War, 1–2, 32; and Hong Kong's interstitial position, 4–5, 6–10, 12, 17, 23, 25–26, 29, 34–35, 59, 92–93, 127, 145, 225, 286, 290; and transpacific circulations, 29, 192, 195–98, 199–201, 207, 219, 265; U.S. agendas and collaboration, 10, 26, 29, 63, 68–69, 72–74, 92–98, 99–102, 103, 105–8, 121, 124–25, 128, 137–38, 139, 142–43, 156, 187, 195, 196–98, 199–201, 271, 287. *See* kuashang strategies; networks: U.S. state-private network

Coleman, James, 20
collaboration: between bankers and industrialists, 174–75, 191; and decolonization, 14–15; between the Hong Kong government and U.S.-backed Christian groups, 82–89; between Hong Kong people and the British Empire, 34–39, 108–9, 178–79, 214–15; between Hong Kong people and the U.S. government, 29, 35, 108, 139, 156, 170, 282, 284; between huashang and European empires, 6–7, 10, 107, 118–19; with Japan or Wang Jingwei government, 32, 34–35, 55, 135; and kuashang strategies, 4, 12–14, 34, 107–8, 128, 186–87, 252, 286–87; with the PRC, 251–52, 280–84. *See also* informal decolonization; kuashang strategies
College of Wooster, 79
Columbia University, 118; donations, 218; faculty, 137; students and graduates, 61, 135, 170
Combat Spiritual Pollution campaign, 257
Commercial Press, 167
Committee for a Free Asia (CFA). *See* Asia Foundation
Committee of 100 (C-100), 285
Commonwealth of Nations: educational ties and systems, 27, 100–101, 110, 125–26, 129–31, 142–44, 202–3. *See also* British Empire; informal decolonization
communist transition: definition, 3, 293n6; and flight capital, 57, 158, 161, 170; and evolving strategies, 108, 156, 136–37, 169–70, 190, 282; and prolonged migration, 6, 26, 32, 48–58, 68, 71, 75, 96, 136–37, 169,

203–5, 262, 277, 282. *See also* Chinese civil war; People's Republic of China; refugees
compensation trade: in Bao'an before 1978, 28, 223, 227–28; from 1978, 224, 240–41, 245, 255, 260, 263. *See also* reform and opening; SEZs; Shenzhen
comprador, 37–39; Cantonese compradors in Jiangnan, 41; educational strategies, 41–42; examples, 38, 41, 46, 54, 261
Comprehensive Certificate of Origin system, 67, 158, 165, 287. *See also* U.S.-UN embargoes; U.S. consulate
Corn Products Refining Co., 177
corruption: and the CNRRA, 55, 103, 135; and the Nationalist government, 168–69; and reform and opening, 236, 244, 261
Cotton Goods Exchange (Shanghai), 47
Cotton Textile Association, 174
cotton spinning. *See* textiles
Council for U.S. Aid to China, 169
Crozier, Douglas, 105, 109–11, 116
CUHK. *See* Chinese University of Hong Kong
cultural capital: and social capital, 18–19
Cultural Revolution, 56, 222–23, 225–26, 242, 258; in Hong Kong, 96–97, 145, 183

Dartmouth College: graduates, 167–68, 185; alumni in Hong Kong, 170–71
decolonization. *See under* British Empire; informal decolonization
Dee Ching Chuan, 120
Delano, Warren, Jr., 39
democracy: absence from kuashang strategies, 12, 16, 250, 268–69; lack thereof in Hong Kong, 95, 183, 186, 193, 275, 279; potential

democratization of the PRC, 271, 274–75, 277

Deng Xiaoping, 249f; and cultivating Hong Kong elites, 238–39, 249; mainland reforms, 28, 221–24, 230, 237, 245, 253, 344n8; and Gordon Wu, 239, 256, 258–59; and the handover, 247, 248–52; and meeting with Jack Tang, 248–52, 254, 280, 351n1; and the Resolution on Party History (1981), 221; and the Southern Tour, 267, 278; and the Tiananmen Square Massacre, 268–270, 278

development. *See* economic development

Diocesan Schools (Boys' and Girls'), 75

District Watch Committee, 37

Dolfin, John, 151–52

Donald, W. H., 60

Dongguan County, 227

Duanfang, 46

Duke University: donations, 218; Duke Kunshan University, 2

Dunn, Lydia, 217

Eagleburger, Lawrence, 270

East Sun Textile Mill, 171, 173

economic capital: and conversions of social capital, 19–20, 164–66, 172–73, 192

Economic Cooperation Administration, 168

economic development: and Confucian values, 24, 194; discourse and study of, 22–24; East Asian 'tiger' and 'little dragon' models, 1, 23–24, 160, 193–94, 287; free trade, free market, and laissez-faire mythologies, 1, 6, 8–9, 22, 36, 90–98, 191–92, 194, 217, 287; and global neoliberalism, 8–9, 34, 193, 221, 275, 285–86; and

Jiangnan industrialization, 45–47, 52, 57; through kuashang strategies and transpacific circulations, 3–4, 5–6, 10–11, 13, 18, 27–28, 66–68, 128, 130–31, 140–41, 147–49, 155–57, 158–61, 180–81, 190–92, 193, 195–96, 203–8, 208–14, 216–17, 286–87; postwar interventionism, 8; the PRC's export-driven development, 3, 5, 28–29, 221–24, 235, 246–47, 251–53, 260–65, 277–78; the PRC's socialist development, 137–38; and the U.S. state-private network, 73–74, 90–97. *See also* American social capital; kuashang strategies; "positive non-interventionism"; transpacific educational circulations

education: American versus British/ Commonwealth systems, 27, 100–101, 105, 110, 112–14, 125–26, 129–31, 142–44, 202–3; bilingual education, 38, 101; capitalist education, 27, 131, 145–51; Chinese-language higher education, 27, 99–101, 103, 105, 115, 129; Confucian educations and civil-service examinations, 19, 41–42, 150; education for people with special needs, 95–96; English-language education, 27, 38, 41, 42, 91, 94, 100, 103; Euro-American liberal arts ideals, 145–46; "modern" and missionary educations in Republican era, 11, 34, 41–43, 70–71, 187, 296n31; Neo-Confucian education in Hong Kong, 115–17, 129, 146, 150; U.S.-backed Christian and missionary schools in Hong Kong, 72–75, 77–82, 82–89, 200–201, 271; U.S. educational influence in Republican China, 43–48; vocational education, 73–74, 90–96

Eisenhower, Dwight D., 136
electronics industry: contrast with
    textile industry, 160, 176, 181–82,
    191; in the PRC, 229
embargo. See U.S.-UN embargoes
émigrés. See Jiangnan transplants
energy industry: in Hong Kong,
    182–184. See also China Light and
    Power; Esso; Mobil; Standard-
    Vacuum Oil
Engels, Friedrich, 22
entrepôt: and nineteenth-century Hong
    Kong, 6–7; and postwar shifts, 8, 26,
    35, 289. See also huashang
Epworth Village, 73f, 87
Esso, 27, 195, 236; and joint venture
    with CLP, 160–61, 182–87, 192
Esquel Group, 261–65; and mainland
    investment, 28, 264–65
Eurasians: relationship to British
    colonialism, 34, 39. See also
    interracial sex and marriage
Euromoney, 210
European Economic Community,
    192
European Industrial Report, 230
Eveready Flashlight Co., 176–77
examinations, civil service. See under
    education
Executive Council of Hong Kong, 85,
    102–3, 153
ExxonMobil, 187, 200, 210

Fang Lizhi, 269
Far East Exchange, 208–9
Farrell, Roy, 59
Federation of Hong Kong Industries, 248
Fei Xiaotong, 21
Feng Bang-yan, 211, 213–14
Fenn, William, 106, 108–14. See also
    UBCHEA

First National Bank of Chicago, 210,
    242, 246
First National City Bank (Citibank):
    operations before 1945, 39, 60;
    operations after 1945, 61–64, 160–61;
    as conduit for postwar aid, 63–64;
    and industrial lending in Hong
    Kong, 165, 175, 190–91; and Li &
    Fung, 212–13. See also Sperry, Ansie
    Lee; Sperry, Henry M.
First Opium War, 35–36, 37
First Sino-Japanese War, 42
"First World," 1, 25, 129, 253, 286
First World War, 39, 52, 184; and the
    "golden age," 45
Fitzwater, Marlin, 275
Five Antis Campaign, 56, 293n6
flexible production, 28, 192, 195–96,
    214, 216. See also Bretton Woods;
    outsourcing; post-Fordism
flight capital: in communist transition,
    57, 60, 158, 161, 170; from overseas
    huashang, 158, 161, 170
Florea, Al, 228
Fok, Henry Ying-tung, 224, 239–42, 245,
    261; and Tung Chee-hwa, 281, 283
Folts, Franklin, 147
Fong, Eric, 202
Fong, H. D., 132, 134
Food for Peace, 90
food manufacturing industry, 176–77,
    244
Ford Foundation: and the refugee
    colleges, 101, 116; and Li Choh-
    ming, 137, 142, 152
Ford Motors, 185, 241
foreign direct investment (FDI): British
    investment in Hong Kong industry,
    159, 176, 180; and the diversification
    of textile industry, 160, 175–81, 191;
    Hong Kong investment in the PRC,

Tang family, 186–87. *See also* China Light and Power

Kailuan Mining Administration, 54

Kai Tak Airport, 89

Kamm, John: career and 1970s engagement, 229–30, 237; and the MFN debate, 271, 273–76

kamshanchong (*jinshanzhuang*), 36, 40, 66

Kan Yuet-keung, 258

Kathe, Jacqueline, 64*f*

Ka Wah Bank: origins, 119; evolution, 120, 123, 161, 210–11; sale to CITIC, 282. *See also* Lam Chi-fung

Keio University, 46

Kellogg, 227

Kenya: higher education, 125; trade with Hong Kong, 180

Keswick, John, 105–6

Keswick Committee, 105, 108

Kentucky Fried Chicken, 189

Kerr, Clark, 137, 138, 143

Kirk, Grayson, 118

King, Alice Tung Chee-ping, 206

King, S. T., 174*f*

Kirby, William, 4, 224

Kissinger, Henry, 226, 285

Kong Sheung Wan Pao (*Kong Sheung Evening News*), 149, 215

Kong Sheung Yat Po, 66

Kong Xiangxi (H.H. Kung), 46, 168–69

Korea: and Christianity, 74

Korean War: and trade boom, 9, 26, 35, 65, 165, 173; and U.S.-UN embargoes, 9, 26, 35, 65–68, 158. *See also* U.S.-UN embargoes

Kowloon: acquisition by British, 37; industrial development, 178, 184; and Star Ferry Riots, 145, 183; and U.S.-backed Christian projects, 80, 85, 87, 93

Kowloon-Canton Railway, 226

Kowloon Tsai Park, 73*f*, 97

kuashang strategies: artificial naturalization, 12, 16, 27, 234–35, 282, 286; definition and overview, 3–4, 10–17, 34, 286–88; and end of Cold War, 278, 285–86; evolution after Joint Declaration, 28, 247, 251–53, 260–61, 264–66, 267–78, 282–83; example of Ansie Lee Sperry, 63; example of David Au, 107–13, 124–25; example of Francis Pan and H. J. Shen, 169–73; example of Lam Chi-fung, 118–25; example of Li Choh-ming, 126, 127–57; and exit strategies, 16, 68, 102, 204, 207, 250, 277, 280, 282; and expanding Sino-U.S. trade, 15, 28, 243, 260–61, 263–65, 267–71, 273–78; and transpacific educational circulations, 101–2, 122–23, 141–45, 147–49, 155–57, 192, 195–96, 204–8; and *huashang* strategies, 9–10, 12–13, 15, 107, 118–20, 132, 196; and inherited privilege, 5–6, 191–92, 202, 207–8, 216–19, 286–88; and lack of democratic agendas, 250, 268–69; and the Hong Kong colonial government, 6, 14, 102, 118, 123–24, 146–47, 184, 186; and informal decolonization, 10–17, 60–63, 125–26, 127–31, 139–45, 146–49, 155–56, 184, 186–87, 247; and U.S. imperial expansion, 26, 68–69, 97; overlap and contrasts with guanxi practice, 4–5, 21–22, 108, 120, 264; and post-Fordist shifts, 195–96, 208–16; and PRC citizenship, 284–85; and U.S. citizenship, 12, 14, 15, 53, 63, 67, 68, 128, 137, 165, 187, 205, 213, 272–73, 285; and U.S. direct

opening, 266; U.S. policies, 10, 40, 61–63, 68, 89, 132, 197–98, 273. *See also* Chinese Exclusion; communist transition; Jiangnan transplants; refugees; transpacific educational circulations

Millie's Holdings, 228

Minami, Kazushi, 222

Minich, Herbert, 236

Ministry of Foreign Affairs (PRC), 273

Ministry of Foreign Trade (PRC), 225, 228, 229, 237, 238

Min Ye, 260

missionaries: and devolution, 72, 81–82; and education in Qing and Republican China, 11, 19, 34, 41–47, 49, 52–53, 68, 70–71, 74–75, 98, 131–33, 187, 202–3, 288, 301n50; and higher education in Hong Kong, 27, 103–5, 106–7, 109–14, 121–22; and refugee material relief in Hong Kong, 75–76, 80–81; relocations to Hong Kong, 26, 71–72, 75, 120–21; and transpacific educational circulations, 89–90, 97–98, 195, 197, 200–201; and U.S.-backed schools, 26, 72–74, 77–80, 81–82, 82–89, 96–97; and vocational education, 90–93, 96–97. *See also* Chung Chi College; Hong Kong Baptist College; North Point Methodist

MIT (Massachusetts Institute of Technology), 201, 265; donations, 218; graduates, 20, 49, 53, 55, 117, 154, 206, 212, 263; the MIT-China Management Education Project, 286; the Sloan School of Management, 286

Mitsui & Co., 55, 181

Mobil Oil: and Jack Tang, 53; and Mei Foo Sun Chuen, 160–61, 182–84, 187–90, 189f; Mobil Land Development, 190; and post-Fordism, 27, 190, 192, 195; in the PRC, 226–27, 229. *See also* Soong, John L.; Mei Foo Sun Chuen

Mody, Hormusjee, 38

Mo Huaizhu, 261–62

Mondale, Walter, 242

Moonitz, Maurice, 148

Moore, Thomas, 264

Moore Memorial Church (Shanghai), 76

Morgan, Agnes, 89–90

Morgan, Carter, 89–90

Mosbacher, Robert, 276

Mo Shangqing, 261

Most-Favored Nation status (MFN), 26, 29, 238, 243; and the aftermath of the Tiananmen Square Massacre, 253, 270–71, 273–78. *See also* Hong Kong–U.S. trade; Sino-U.S. trade

Moy, Ernest, 99, 108, 134

mui tsai, 37

Multi-Fibre Arrangement (MFA), 220, 234, 238, 255, 264. *See also* protectionism; textile industry

Munn, Christopher, 36

Mu Xiangyue (Mu Ouchu), 47

Nanjing: as Nationalist capital, 44, 47, 168, 169

Nankai University: faculty, 132–33, 135

Nanking University, 132

Nanyang College (Shanghai). *See* Jiaotong University

National Agricultural Engineering Corporation, 168

National Catholic Welfare Conference (NCWC), 81, 92

National Council on U.S.-China Trade (NCUSCT), 230, 236–37, 242

Nationalist government (Guomindang, GMD): and American-returned students, 44, 52, 129–30, 134–35, 168–69, 173; and anti-PRC activities in Hong Kong, 99; cronyism and instability, 4, 34, 47, 57, 135–36, 168–69; Chinese civil war and relocation to Taiwan, 7, 26, 48, 56–58; economic planning and bureaucracy, 133–36, 156; and elite networks, 107, 119, 129, 134–35, 168–69, 173; and politics in Hong Kong society, 66, 72, 76, 85, 95, 117; Second World War and wartime Chongqing, 31, 55, 168–69; and social welfare, 92; and U.S. aid and alliance, 47–48, 55, 61–62, 63–64, 134–35, 167–69, 187–88. *See also* American-returned students; CNRRA; Sino-U.S. alliance; Taiwan

National Lutheran Council, 81

National People's Congress: Hong Kong delegates, 235; and reform and opening, 240, 243, 284

National Shanghai Business School, 167

National Southwestern Associated University, 133

native-place *guanxi*. *See under* networks

Naughton, Barry, 245

Negros Philippine Lumber Company, 120

Neo-Confucianism, 115–17

neoliberalism, 93, 193, 221; and kuashang strategies, 34, 131, 190, 273–75, 285–86; and China's reforms and Sino-U.S. relationship, 221, 274–75, 285–86

networks: network theory, guanxi, and social capital, 17–22

—American-returned students and transpacific educational networks in Cold War Hong Kong: 2–3, 5, 20–22, 99–100, 202–3. *See also individual examples*; American-returned students; American social capital; transpacific educational circulations

—American-returned students and transpacific educational networks in mainland China: in the Reform era, 243; in the Republican era, 4, 26, 43–48, 52, 54–56, 132–34, 168. *See also individual examples*; American-returned students; American social capital

—British imperial networks, 64–65, 108–9, 159

—Chinese Christian and missionary networks, 71–74, 76–79, 121–24

—native-place guanxi (*tongxiang guanxi*): 4, 21–22, 31–32, 54, 119; in banking and industry, 45–46, 49, 54, 179; in transpacific migration, 40; overlap and/or contrast with American social capital and U.S. educational networks, 4, 21–22, 47, 99–100, 108, 120, 168. *See also* Jiangsu and Zhejiang Residents' Association

—PRC state-private network: 282–84

—transpacific networks in reform and opening: 222–24, 253–55; and AmCham, 231–38; and the Canton Trade Fairs, 228–29; and China Everbright, 246; and CITIC, 241–44; and Gordon Wu and Hopewell, 255–60; and Li & Fung, 220–21; and Tung Chee-hwa and Orient Overseas, 281–82; and the Yang family and Esquel, 261–65

—transpacific networks after Tiananmen: in the handover process,

283–86; in the MFN debate, 270–78; in the neoliberal turn, 285–86
—U.S. state-private network: 9–10, 26; and elementary, secondary, and vocational education in Hong Kong, 72–74, 80–81, 90–98; and higher education in Hong Kong, 99–101, 108, 128, 138, 139, 142; and transpacific educational circulations, 142, 156, 195–97. *See also* Central Intelligence Agency; Cold War; U.S. consulate; U.S. State Department

New Asia College, 27, 101–102, 115–17, 131, 149–51; Qian Mu's conflict with Li Choh-ming, 155; comparisons with Chung Chi College, 115–17; comparisons with United College, 118; and P. Y. Tang, 154; relocation to Shatin, 151. *See also* Qian Mu

New Life Movement, 57

New York City: and Hong Kong people, 53, 61, 135, 164, 166, 167, 170, 180, 186, 199, 205–6, 209, 212, 213, 262–63, 272, 273, 280, 281; as rival center of globalization, 18, 37, 206, 238; and U.S. foundations, 90, 101, 111–13, 146–47, 196; and U.S. corporations, 61, 63, 170, 180, 186, 188, 212, 213, 242, 272, 273

New York Times, 188

New York University (NYU): graduates, 120, 167; NYU Shanghai, 2

New Zealand: and Hong Kong migration, 16; normalization of relations with PRC, 231

Ngai Shiu-kit, 248–49, 249f

Ng Choy (Wu Tingfang), 38

Nieh, Edward Chung-yit, 201

Nigeria, 38; investment from Hong Kong, 179

Ningbo, 41, 53, 67, 205; and native-place networks, 54, 99

Nixon administration: Nixon's visit to China, 223, 226, 228; end of U.S. embargo, 223, 225–26; "Nixon Shock," 192, 195, 209, 215. *See also* Bretton Woods system; Sino-U.S. relations

Noren, Loren, 109

North Point Methodist, 73f, 77–80, 78f, 89–91. *See also* Wei Li Kung Hui

Northeastern University, 276

Northwestern University, 52

Notre Dame University, 187

Oberlin College: graduates, 103, 135, 167–168

Ogle, Vanessa, 9

Oklahoma Baptist University, 122–23

"One Country, Two Systems," 250–51, 273. *See also* handover

Ong, Aihwa, 13, 218–19

opium trade, 34, 35–36, 60. *See also* First Opium War; Second Opium War

Orient Overseas (OOCL): founding and expansion, 205–6; containerization, 206, 208, 280; trouble and bailout, 280–82

outsourcing: by Hong Kong industry, 179–81, 195, 208, 215. *See also* Bretton Woods; flexible production; post-Fordism

overseas Chinese, 71, 107, 127–28, 131; education and identity, 145, 149–51; and flight capital, 158, 161, 170; and kuashang strategies, 15; and 'guerilla capitalism,' 24, 163, 175, 182, 191; and reform and opening, 224, 245, 260, 264. *See also huashang*

Overseas Private Investment Corporation, 270

transpacific educational circulations: and alumni donation feedback loops, 218–19; and "brain drains," 130, 197, 207–8; circulation versus immigration, 196–202; and Hong Kong's 1970s takeoff, 156–57, 192, 195–96, 202–7, 208–17; and Hong Kong's role in reform and opening, 234–35, 253–55, 263–65; and Hong Kong students' rates of self-support and return, 195–98, 202; and kuashang strategies, 15–16, 26–28, 156–57, 192, 195–96, 202–7, 208–18, 286–87; through Li Choh-ming and CUHK, 27, 128–30, 141–46, 155–57; numbers of Hong Kong students in the United States, 3, 16, 28, 89–90, 196–97, 202, 340n41; PRC students in the United States, 2, 270; through U.S.-backed "refugee colleges," 114, 117, 122–23; through U.S.-backed Christian schools, 89–90, 97–98. *See also* American social capital; kuashang strategies; migration; networks: U.S. state-private network

Treaty of Nanjing, 36, 41
Treaty of Tianjin, 41, 74
treaty ports and treaty-port merchants, 7, 12, 13, 41, 252
Trench, David, 151, 190
Tristate Holdings, 180, 268. *See also* Tang, Jack C.
True Light schools, 133
Trump, Donald, 2
Trustees of Lingnan University, 101, 103, 105, 106, 110, 117; and the Lingnan Institute of Business Administration, 146–49. *See also* CUHK; Chung Chi College
Tsang, Donald, 283
Tse, Daniel Chi-wai, 124

Tse Koong-kai, 185
Tseng Sui Primary School (Shanghai), 79
Tseung Fat-im, 118
Tsim Sha Tsui, 267
Tsing, Anna Lowenhaupt, 25, 31
Tsinghua University, 2, 43–44; faculty, 135; graduates, 49, 167, 203, 262, 264; School of Economics and Management (TSEM), 286. *See also* Boxer Indemnity scholarships
Tsing Yi, 187–188
Tsin Mew-ching, 131
Tsuen Wan, 80, 87, 234
Tsun To Kung Wooi, 75–76
Tucker, Nancy Bernkopf, 9
Tuen Mun, 185
Tung, Betty Chiu Hung-ping, 205
Tung, C. Y.: and kuashang strategies, 205–7, 216–17, 260; and Li Choh-ming, 205; and the RMS *Queen Elizabeth*, 205. *See also* Orient Overseas
Tung, John, 154
Tung Chee-chen, 206, 216
Tung Chee-hwa: and the C-100, 285; bailout of Orient Overseas and kuashang strategies, 280–83; and the CPPCC, 283; education and U.S. connections, 205–6, 216, 283; and Jack Tang, 281; selection as Chief Executive, 280, 283–84. *See also* handover
Tung Man College, 118–19
Tung Wah Hospital, 37, 39, 40, 60
Turner Construction, 188
Turnipseed, Robert, 86, 91
Tyson, George, 39

Uganda: trade with Hong Kong, 180
United Board for Christian Colleges in China. *See* UBCHEA

United Board for Christian Higher
Education in Asia (UBCHEA), 101,
147; initial funding for Chung Chi,
103, 105, 106; and loan for Chung
Chi, 110–13; outreach to David Au,
108; and transpacific educational
circulations, 199–201. *See also* Chung
Chi College; Fenn, William
United College, 27, 101–2, 114–15, 124;
founding, 117–18; relocation to
Shatin, 151
United Nations, 61
United Nations Economic Commission
for Asia and the Far East (ECAFE),
136, 152
United Nations Relief and
Rehabilitation Administration
(UNRRA), 55, 135–36, 304n111
United Nations University, 205
United States Agency for International
Development (USAID), 146
United States Information Service
(USIS), 94, 99
University College of Rhodesia and
Nyasaland, 125
University of California, Berkeley:
donations, 218; faculty, 128, 137, 148,
156; students and graduates of, 61,
129, 132–33, 156, 200, 217
University of California, San Francisco:
faculty, 133
University of California, Santa Barbara:
faculty, 143
University of California (system), 130,
143
University of Chicago: graduates, 115,
187, 276
University of Colorado, Boulder, 200
University of Ghana, 125
University of Hong Kong (HKU), 17,
38, 98, 125–26, 143, 205, 235; and

Chinese-language education, 100,
103, 105–6, 129; graduates, 118, 198,
203, 234–35
University of Illinois at Urbana-
Champaign: graduates, 53, 190, 204
University of Leeds, 138
University of Liverpool: graduates,
205–6
University of London, 125; School of
Oriental and African Studies
(SOAS), 143
University of Malaya, 125; faculty 138,
144
University of Michigan: graduates, 79,
243
University of New Mexico, 85
University of Pennsylvania: graduates,
61, 117; and Wharton School
graduates, 46, 55, 208–9, 272
University of the Philippines, 119, 140
University of Pittsburgh: graduates,
124
University of Redlands: graduates, 122
University of Shanghai, 79, 167
University of Strathclyde, 146
University of Washington, 217
University of Western Ontario, 146
Unofficial Members of Executive and
Legislative Council (UMELCO),
248–50
U.S.-China Business Council, 273
U.S. citizenship: examples of
naturalization, 53, 63, 67, 68, 128,
137, 165, 187, 213, 272, 285; and
kuashang strategies, 12, 14, 15, 63, 67,
205, 272–73
U.S. Congress: and Chinese migration,
10; and initial MFN approval, 243;
and the Tiananmen Square Massacre,
269–71, 273–78; and Tung
Chee-hwa's connections, 281

Wan Chai, 210, 258
Wang, Andy Chih-ming, 145
Wang, C. T. (Zhengting), 99–102, 119
Wang, Y. C. (industrialist), 174f
Wang, Y. C. (scholar), 43
Wang Guangmei, 246
Wang Guangying, 246
Wang Gungwu, 15
Wang Jingwei, 55, 135
Wang Tau Hom resettlement estate, 73f, 86
Wang Xizhi, 136
Wang Yanan, 22
Wannamaker, Olin, 106, 108–9
War Brides Act, 62
Ward, Ralph, 77, 80, 85
Ward Memorial Church, 73f, 80, 91
Warner, Rawleigh, 189–90
Washington, Herman, 91–92, 93
Weber, Max, 22, 24
Wei Akwong, 38
Wei Li Kung Hui, 75, 82, 83–84, 87, 91
Wei Yuk, 38–39
Wellesley College: graduates, 52, 170
Wen Bingzhong, (Wan Bing-tsung), 49
Wen Wei Po, 57–58, 58f
Wesley Village, 73f, 80, 82
West Germany: normalization of relations with PRC, 231; trade and investment with Hong Kong, 176, 179; in reform and opening, 246
Wharton School. See under University of Pennsylvania
White, Alan, 286
Whitener, Sterling: and CCC, 70–72, 76, 81–82, 88, 97–98; and Chung Chi College, 109, 114
White Russians, 31
Wing On, 47, 254
Wolff, Lester, 238
Wong, David Yue-kwong (Y. K.), 122

Wong, Peter, 81–82, 97–98
Wong, R. Bin, 23
Wong, Richard Yue-chim, 276
Wong, T. Y., 67, 154
Wong, Y. C., 138
Wong Chi-yue (C. Y.), 67
Wong Chuk Hang, 177
Wong Shing, 38
Wong Siu-lun, 11, 164, 166, 172
Wong Tai Sin (WTS) Community Centre, 73f, 93–95
Wong Tai Sin (WTS) resettlement estate, 73f, 86, 93
Woodwin, Robert, 236
Woo Hon Fai, 234
Woo Sing-lim, 40
World Bank, 24, 193, 260, 267, 271
World Council of Churches (WCC), 81, 94
World Refugee Year, 74, 93
World Rehabilitation Fund (WRF) Day Centre, 73f, 95–96
World Trade Organization, 278
World War I. See First World War
World War II. See Second World War
Wu, Annie Suk-Ching, 241
Wu, Gordon Ying-sheung: American social capital and kuashang strategies, 198–99, 209–10, 216, 231; and Deng Xiaoping, 239, 256, 258–59; and donations to Princeton, 218; first visit to the PRC, 228–29; and founding Hopewell Construction, 199, 208; and founding Hopewell Holdings, 209–10; and Gu Mu, 256, 258, 259, 261; and the Guangshen expressway, 28, 252, 256–59, 260–61, 264; and Hopewell in Shenzhen, 255–56; and the Sino-British Joint Declaration, 260; and Tiananmen, 269; and Zhao Ziyang, 256, 258–59, 269

INDEX [417]

Zhang Jia'ao (Chang Kia-ngau): and Francis Pan, 167; and H. C. Ting, 204; and H. J. Shen, 169; and K. P. Chen, 46, 169; and Cai Shengbai, 262

Zhang Yang, 118

Zhao Chunjun, 286

Zhao Ziyang, 222; and coastal development strategy, 224, 251, 253, 259, 264, 266; and GATT, 261; and Guangshen expressway, 252–53, 256, 258, 260–61; and reorganization of CITIC, 261; and Tiananmen Square Massacre, 253, 266–68. *See also* Deng Xiaoping; Gu Mu; Wu, Gordon

Zhejiang (province), 45; and educational shifts in Republican era, 42–44

Zhejiang Industrial Bank, 46

Zhou Enlai, 56, 222, 225, 230, 236

Zhu Chengzhang (S. C. Chu), 46

Zhuhai, 240

Zhu Rongji, 286

STUDIES OF THE WEATHERHEAD EAST ASIAN INSTITUTE
COLUMBIA UNIVERSITY

Selected Titles
(Complete list at http://weai.columbia.edu/publications/studies-weai/)

The Chinese Revolution on the Tibetan Frontier, by Benno Weiner. Cornell University Press, 2020.

Making It Count: Statistics and Statecraft in the Early People's Republic of China, by Arunabh Ghosh. Princeton University Press, 2020.

Tea War: A History of Capitalism in China and India, by Andrew B. Liu. Yale University Press, 2020.

Revolution Goes East: Imperial Japan and Soviet Communism, by Tatiana Linkhoeva. Cornell University Press, 2020.

Vernacular Industrialism in China: Local Innovation and Translated Technologies in the Making of a Cosmetics Empire, 1900–1940, by Eugenia Lean. Columbia University Press, 2020.

Fighting for Virtue: Justice and Politics in Thailand, by Duncan McCargo. Cornell University Press, 2020.

Beyond the Steppe Frontier: A History of the Sino-Russian Border, by Sören Urbansky. Princeton University Press, 2020.

Pirates and Publishers: A Social History of Copyright in Modern China, by Fei-Hsien Wang. Princeton University Press, 2019.

The Typographic Imagination: Reading and Writing in Japan's Age of Modern Print Media, by Nathan Shockey. Columbia University Press, 2019.

Down and Out in Saigon: Stories of the Poor in a Colonial City, by Haydon Cherry. Yale University Press, 2019.

Beauty in the Age of Empire: Japan, Egypt, and the Global History of Aesthetic Education, by Raja Adal. Columbia University Press, 2019.

Mass Vaccination: Citizens' Bodies and State Power in Modern China, by Mary Augusta Brazelton. Cornell University Press, 2019.

Residual Futures: The Urban Ecologies of Literary and Visual Media of 1960s and 1970s Japan, by Franz Prichard. Columbia University Press, 2019.

The Making of Japanese Settler Colonialism: Malthusianism and Trans-Pacific Migration, 1868–1961, by Sidney Xu Lu. Cambridge University Press, 2019.

The Power of Print in Modern China: Intellectuals and Industrial Publishing from the End of Empire to Maoist State Socialism, by Robert Culp. Columbia University Press, 2019.

Beyond the Asylum: Mental Illness in French Colonial Vietnam, by Claire E. Edington. Cornell University Press, 2019.

Borderland Memories: Searching for Historical Identity in Post-Mao China, by Martin Fromm. Cambridge University Press, 2019.

Arc of Containment: Britain, the United States, and Anticommunism in Southeast Asia, by Wen-Qing Ngoei. Cornell University Press, 2019.

Sovereignty Experiments: Korean Migrants and the Building of Borders in Northeast Asia, 1860–1949, by Alyssa M. Park. Cornell University Press, 2019.

The Greater East Asia Co-Prosperity Sphere: When Total Empire Met Total War, by Jeremy A. Yellen. Cornell University Press, 2019.

Thought Crime: Ideology and State Power in Interwar Japan, by Max Ward. Duke University Press, 2019.

Statebuilding by Imposition: Resistance and Control in Colonial Taiwan and the Philippines, by Reo Matsuzaki. Cornell University Press, 2019.

Nation-Empire: Ideology and Rural Youth Mobilization in Japan and Its Colonies, by Sayaka Chatani. Cornell University Press, 2019.

Fixing Landscape: A Techno-Poetic History of China's Three Gorges, by Corey Byrnes. Columbia University Press, 2019.

The Invention of Madness: State, Society, and the Insane in Modern China, by Emily Baum. University of Chicago Press, 2018.

A Misunderstood Friendship: Mao Zedong, Kim Il-sung, and Sino-North Korean Relations, 1949–1976, by Zhihua Shen and Yafeng Xia. Columbia University Press, 2018.

The Other Milk: Reinventing Soy in Republican China, by Jia-Chen Fu. University of Washington Press, 2018.

Japan's Imperial Underworlds: Intimate Encounters at the Borders of Empire, by David Ambaras. Cambridge University Press, 2018.

Heroes and Toilers: Work as Life in Postwar North Korea, 1953–1961, by Cheehyung Harrison Kim. Columbia University Press, 2018.

Electrified Voices: How the Telephone, Phonograph, and Radio Shaped Modern Japan, 1868–1945, by Kerim Yasar. Columbia University Press, 2018.

Making Two Vietnams: War and Youth Identities, 1965–1975, by Olga Dror. Cambridge University Press, 2018.

Engineering Asia: Technology, Colonial Development, and the Cold War Order, by Hiromi Mizuno, Aaron S. Moore, and John DiMoia. Bloomsbury Press, 2018.

Japan's Occupation of Java in the Second World War: A Transnational History, by Ethan Mark. Bloomsbury Press, 2018.

Navigating Semi-Colonialism: Shipping, Sovereignty, and Nation-Building in China, 1860–1937, by Anne Reinhardt. Harvard University Asia Center, 2018.

Playing by the Informal Rules: Why the Chinese Regime Remains Stable Despite Rising Protests, by Yao Li. Cambridge University Press, 2018.

Raising China's Revolutionaries: Modernizing Childhood for Cosmopolitan Nationalists and Liberated Comrades, by Margaret Mih Tillman. Columbia University Press, 2018.

Buddhas and Ancestors: Religion and Wealth in Fourteenth-Century Korea, by Juhn Y. Ahn. University of Washington Press, 2018.

Idly Scribbling Rhymers: Poetry, Print, and Community in Nineteenth Century Japan, by Robert Tuck. Columbia University Press, 2018.

China's War on Smuggling: Law, Economic Life, and the Making of the Modern State, 1842–1965, by Philip Thai. Columbia University Press, 2018.

Forging the Golden Urn: The Qing Empire and the Politics of Reincarnation in Tibet, by Max Oidtmann. Columbia University Press, 2018.

The Battle for Fortune: State-Led Development, Personhood, and Power Among Tibetans in China, by Charlene Makley. Cornell University Press, 2018.

Aesthetic Life: Beauty and Art in Modern Japan, by Miya Elise Mizuta Lippit. Harvard University Asia Center, 2018.

Where the Party Rules: The Rank and File of China's Communist State, by Daniel Koss. Cambridge University Press, 2018.

Resurrecting Nagasaki: Reconstruction and the Formation of Atomic Narratives, by Chad R. Diehl. Cornell University Press, 2018.

The Army and the Indonesian Genocide: Mechanics of Mass Murder, by Jess Melvin. Routledge, 2018.

China's Philological Turn: Scholars, Textualism, and the Dao in the Eighteenth Century, by Ori Sela. Columbia University Press, 2018.

Making Time: Astronomical Time Measurement in Tokugawa Japan, by Yulia Frumer. University of Chicago Press, 2018.

Mobilizing Without the Masses: Control and Contention in China, by Diana Fu. Cambridge University Press, 2018.

Post-Fascist Japan: Political Culture in Kamakura After the Second World War, by Laura Hein. Bloomsbury, 2018.

China's Conservative Revolution: The Quest for a New Order, 1927–1949, by Brian Tsui. Cambridge University Press, 2018.

Promiscuous Media: Film and Visual Culture in Imperial Japan, 1926–1945, by Hikari Hori. Cornell University Press, 2018.